SUMMIT 1

Teacher's Edition
and Lesson Planner

Joan Saslow ■ Allen Ascher

with Silvia Carolina Tiberio

PEARSON
Longman

Includes
Teacher's Resource Disk
with printable activities

Summit: English for Today's World   1
Teacher's Edition and Lesson Planner

Pearson Education, 10 Bank Street, White Plains, NY 10606

Staff credits: The people who made up the *Summit 1* Teacher's Edition and Lesson Planner team—representing editorial, production, design, and manufacturing—are Rhea Banker, Aerin Csigay, Dave Dickey, Pamela Fishman, Ann France, Charles Green, Aliza Greenblatt, Ray Keating, Mike Kemper, Sasha Kintzler, and Nicole Santos.

Text composition: TSI Graphics

Text font: Palatino 11/12

Cover photograph: "Apex," by Rhea Banker. Copyright © 2006 by Rhea Banker.

ISBN 0-13-110630-9

Illustration credits: Steve Attoe pp. 42, 52, 90, 111; Mark Collins pp. 40, 65, 98; Francois Escalmel pp. 75, 81, 116; Maria LaFrance, p. 10; Marc Mongeau p. 22; Dusan Petricic pp. 30, 101, 105, 118; Craig Spearing p. 68; Eve Steccati p. 104; Jean Wiesenbaugh p. 2

Photo credits: All original photography by David Mager. Page 3 David Zimmerman/Masterfile; p. 8 (top) Denis Scott/Corbis, (left to right) Robert Frerck/Odyssey Productions, Inc., RubberBall/SuperStock, Michael Newman/PhotoEdit, Imageshop-Zefa Visual Media UK Ltd/Alamy, Image100/SuperStock; p. 9 Hulton-Deutsch Collection/Corbis; p. 16 Neal Preston/Corbis; p. 17 Jo Hale/Getty Images; p. 18 (left) Image100/SuperStock, (middle) RubberBall/SuperStock, (right) age fotostock/SuperStock; p. 20 Archivo Iconografico, S.A. /Corbis; p. 21 (left) Lee Celano/Getty Images, (middle) Fox Photos/Getty Images, (right) Bret Thompsett/Alpha/Globe Photos; p. 22 Hemera Technologies/Alamy; p. 26 G. Bliss/Masterfile; p. 27 David Buffington/Getty Images; p. 28 (left to right) Stockbyte, Photomorgana/Corbis, LWA-Dann Tardif/Corbis, BananaStock/Robert Harding; p. 30 Mediacolor's/Alamy; p. 32 Mark E. Gibson/Corbis; p. 33 G. Bliss/Masterfile; p. 34 (left) Camera Press Digital/Retna Ltd., (right) www.newmansown.com; p. 38 (top left) Kaz Mori/Getty Images, (bottom left) Martin Harvey/Alamy, (middle) Reuters/Corbis, (top right) The Art Archive/Musee Carnavalet Paris/Dagli Orti, (top right inset) www.englishcountrydancing.org, (bottom right) Picture Finders Ltd./eStock Photo; p. 39 (left to right) Thinkstock/Alamy, Stadium Studio/Alamy, Royalty-Free/Corbis, Royalty-Free/Corbis; p. 43 (A) Jon Feingersh/Masterfile, (B) Blend Images/Alamy, (C) RubberBall/SuperStock, (D) age fotostock/Medioimages, (E) Pierre Vauthey/Corbis; p. 44 (goatee) Emely/zefa/Corbis, (sideburns) Dennis Galante/Corbis, (buzz) Latin Focus.com, (bald) George Shelley/Corbis, (dyed) Brand X Pictures/Alamy, (long) Mike Powell/Getty Images, (braids) Royalty-Free/Corbis, (highlights) Stockbyte; p. 45 (top left to right) Mauro Fermariello/Photo Researchers, Inc., Apollo/Alamy, Chuck Pefley/Alamy, Getty Images, Cindy Charles/PhotoEdit, (bottom left to right) Gideon Mendel/Corbis, Ariel Skelley/Corbis, Jon Feingersh/Corbis; p. 46 Valentino Maria Chandoha/Corbis Sygma; p. 50 (top) Paul Chesley/National Geographic Image Collection, (bottom) Panoramic Images/Getty Images, (right) Stephanie Maze/Woodfin Camp and Associates; p. 51 (top) Will & Deni McIntyre/Corbis, (bottom) Randy M. Ury/Corbis; p. 52 Christian Zachariasen/Corbis; p. 54 (left to right) Catherine Ledner/Getty Images, Michael Prince/Corbis, age fotostock/Jack Hollingsworth, Roberto Stelzer/Getty Images; p. 56 AP/Wide World Photos; p. 58 (top) Danny Lehman/Corbis, (bottom) age fotostock/SuperStock; p. 62 Private Collection, Archives Charmet/ Bridgeman Art Library; p. 63 Network Photographers/Alamy; p. 66 Ellen Senisi/ The Image Works; p. 67 (parrot) Gerry Ellis/Minden Pictures, (cat) Digital Vision Ltd./SuperStock, (pit bull) Julia Fishkin/Getty Images, (pug) Chris Carlson, (python) Michael & Patricia Fogden/Minden Pictures, (mouse) Chris Collins/Corbis; p. 70 (left) Konrad Wothe/Minden Pictures, (right) age fotostock/SuperStock, (bottom) John Cancalosi/naturepl.com; p. 74 (TV) Jimmy Dorantes/Latin Focus.com, (magazine) Image courtesy of The Advertising Archives, (blimp) Shotfile/Alamy, (billboards) Liu Liqun/Corbis, (radio) Joe Tree/Alamy; p. 75 (left) Imagination Photo Design, (middle) Imagination Photo Design, (right) Frank Siteman/Index Stock Imagery; p. 76 Jon Arnold Images/Alamy; p. 77 (perfumes) Raymond Patrick/Getty Images, (chocolates) C Squared Studios/Getty Images, (watches) allOver photography/Alamy, (sunglasses) Darren Robb/Getty Images, (bags) Samsonite Corporation, (umbrellas) Samsonite Corporation; p. 78 (top left) Stockbyte, (top right) Royalty-Free/Corbis, (bottom left) Robert Fried/ robertfriedphotography.com, (bottom right) Robert Fried/ robertfriedphotography.com; p. 82 Brand X Pictures/Alamy; p. 86 (top) (c)The New Yorker Collection 2004 Lee Lorenz from cartoonbank.com. All rights reserved, (bottom) Marty Bucella http://members.aol.com/mjbtoons/index.html; p. 87 David Young-Wolff/Alamy; p. 88 ER Productions/Corbis; p. 92 (top) Jonathan Smith/Lonely Planet Images, (bottom) Imageshop-Zefa Visual Media UK Ltd/Alamy; p. 94 (top) SCPhotos/Almay, (bottom) View Stock/Alamy; p. 95 (left) Keith Levit Photography/Index Stock Imagery, (middle) age fotostock/Creatas, (right) age fotostock/BananaStock; p. 99 (top) Bettmann/Corbis, (left) Popperfoto/Alamy, (right) WorldAtlas.com/GraphicMaps.com; p. 102 (left) John W. Hoopes, (right) Universtiy of Bologna; p. 103 (left) Richard T. Nowitz/Getty Images, (middle) Yann Arthus-Bertrand/Corbis, (right) David Hardy/Photo Researchers, Inc.; p. 104 Bettmann/Corbis, (inset) Hulton Archive/Getty Images; p. 105 Getty Images; p. 106 (top left) Reuters/Corbis, (top right) AP/Wide World Photos, (left) Popperfoto/Alamy; p. 110 (top left) Image courtesy of The Advertising Archives, (top right) Royalty-Free/Corbis, (middle left) Image courtesy of The Advertising Archives, (middle right) Image courtesy of The Advertising Archives, (bottom left) Peter Cade/Getty Images, (bottom right) Rob Van Petten/Getty Images; p. 112 (go) Royalty-Free/Corbis, (chess) Royalty-Free/Corbis, (video) Michael A. Keller/Corbis, (ping) Agence Images/Alamy, (embroidery) Paul A. Souders/Corbis, (wood) Jim Craigmyle/Masterfile, (crochet) John and Lisa Merrill/Corbis, (karate) Buzz Productions/Alamy, (aerobics) Jose Luis Pelaez, Inc./Corbis, (yoga) Peter Griffith/Masterfile, (antiques) Paul Barton/Corbis, (rabbits) age fotostock/Max Messerli, (coins) Don Farrall/Getty Images; p. 113 (left) John Foxx/Alamy, (middle) Robert Frerck/Odyssey Productions, Inc., (right) Image100/Alamy; p. 115 Dorling Kindersley; p. 118 Chad Slattery/Getty Images; p. 119 (far left) Amy and Chuck Wiley/Wales/Index Stock Imagery, (top left) Rick Doyle/Corbis, (top right) David Madison/Getty Images, (bottom left) Jakob Helbig/Getty Images, (bottom middle) Jess Stock/Getty Images, (bottom right) Joe McBride/Getty Images.

Printed in the United States of America
1 2 3 4 5 6 7 8 9 10–QWD–11 10 09 08 07 06

Contents

Summit unit walk-through

UNIT GOALS. Clearly state the communication goals of the unit.

TOPIC PREVIEW. Previews the content of the unit, builds schema, and develops academic skills.

SOUND BITES. Presents a "snapshot" of authentic conversational language for observation.

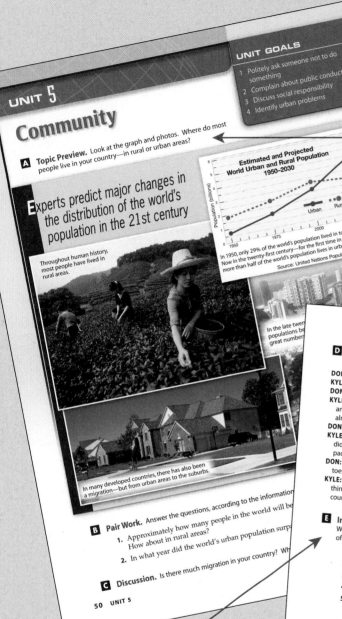

UNIT 5
Community

UNIT GOALS

1 Politely ask someone not to do something
2 Complain about public conduct
3 Discuss social responsibility
4 Identify urban problems

A **Topic Preview.** Look at the graph and photos. Where do most people live in your country—in rural or urban areas?

Experts predict major changes in the distribution of the world's population in the 21st century

Estimated and Projected World Urban and Rural Population 1950–2030

Urban   Rural

In 1950, only 29% of the world's population lived in towns and cities. Now in the twenty-first century—for the first time in human history—more than half of the world's population lives in urban areas.
Source: United Nations Population Division, 2000

Throughout human history, most people have lived in rural areas.

In the late twen[...] populations be[...] great number[...]

In many developed countries, there has also been a migration—but from urban areas to the suburbs.

B **Pair Work.** Answer the questions, according to the information[...]

1. Approximately how many people in the world will be[...] How about in rural areas?
2. In what year did the world's urban population surp[...]

C **Discussion.** Is there much migration in your country? Wh[...]

50 UNIT 5

D 🎧 **Sound Bites.** Read and listen to a conversation about city life.

DON: Hey, Kyle! So how's the big city treating you?
KYLE: Funny you should ask. Not great.
DON: What do you mean?
KYLE: Well, on my way here, I'm crossing the street and this guy in an SUV turns the corner and almost runs me over.
DON: Are you serious?
KYLE: Yeah. The driver was in such a big hurry he didn't even notice. I just can't keep up with the pace here.
DON: Well, you *do* have to learn to stay on your toes in the city.
KYLE: It really gets to me sometimes. I don't think I'll ever get used to it. I guess I'm just a country boy at heart.

"the city"

E **In Other Words.** Read the conversation again. With a partner, explain the meaning of each of the following statements or questions.

1. "So how's the big city treating you?"
2. "I just can't keep up with the pace here."
3. "You *do* have to learn to stay on your toes."
4. "It really gets to me sometimes."
5. "I'm just a country boy at heart."

"the country"

IN OTHER WORDS. Provides practice in inferring meaning of idioms from context.

STARTING POINT

What are some advantages and disadvantages of living in each type of place? Write them in the chart.

	Advantages	Disadvantages
the country		
the city		
the suburbs		

Discussion. Where would you prefer to live—in the country, the city, or the suburbs? Why?

STARTING POINT. Accesses prior knowledge and gets students talking.

COMMUNICATION GOAL. Assures students of what they'll achieve in this two-page lesson.

WORD SKILLS. Increases students' awareness of word features that will help them expand their vocabularies.

CONVERSATION SNAPSHOT. Provides a memorable and practical model of social language and essential conversation strategies.

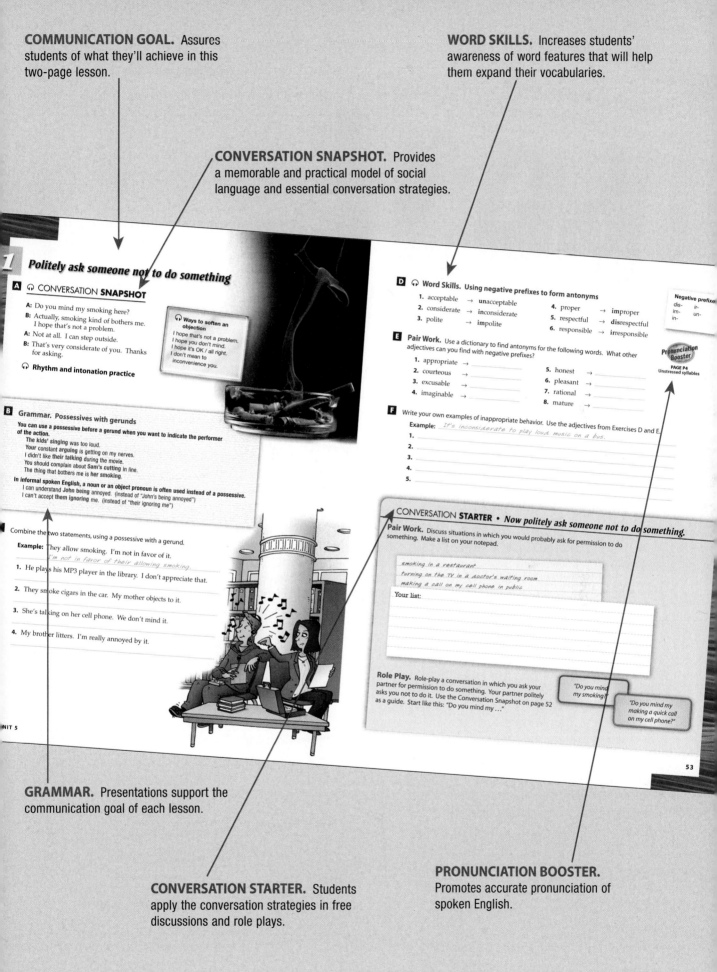

GRAMMAR. Presentations support the communication goal of each lesson.

CONVERSATION STARTER. Students apply the conversation strategies in free discussions and role plays.

PRONUNCIATION BOOSTER. Promotes accurate pronunciation of spoken English.

Unit walk-through **Tv**

GRAMMAR SNAPSHOT. Illustrates grammar in context and provokes interest in the topic of the lesson.

GRAMMAR BOOSTER. Gives additional explanations, charts, and reviews as well as more practice.

GRAMMAR. Clear presentation addresses form, meaning, and use and warns of common learner errors.

GRAMMAR EXCHANGE. Offers students an opportunity to engage in discussion using the target grammar.

2

Complain about public conduct

A · GRAMMAR SNAPSHOT. Read the interview responses and notice the use of paired conjunctions.

What ticks you off?

Wendy Kwon, 23
Chicago, USA

What ticks me off? Well, I can't understand why people litter. Who do they think is going to clean up after them? **Either** they should throw their garbage in a trash can **or** hold on to it till they find one. I think it's great that people have to pay a fine for littering. Maybe they'll think twice before doing it again.

Dana Fraser, 36
Toronto, Canada

You know what gets to me? Smoking. It's such an inconsiderate habit. Secondhand cigarette smoke is **neither** good for you **nor** pleasant to be around. I'd like to see smoking banned from more public places. Don't non-smokers have rights too?

Yuan Yong Jing, 28
Beijing, China

It really bugs me when people spit on the street. **Not only** do I find it disgusting, **but** it's **also** unhygienic. It's important to think about other people's feelings and public health.

Jorge Santos, 31
São Paulo, Brazil

Here's something that gets on my nerves: I hate it when people use their cell phones in public places. They annoy other people, **not only** on trains and buses **but also** in theaters. They should have the courtesy to **either** turn their phones off **or** to leave them at home. It really makes me angry. I guess it's kind of my pet peeve.

Do any of the behaviors described in the interview responses "tick you off"?

B Pair Work. Do any of the behaviors described and rate each of them as follows:
With a partner, discuss and rate each of them as follows:

extremely annoying   somewhat annoying   not annoying at all

PAGE G9
For more ...

C Grammar. Paired conjunctions

You can connect related ideas with paired conjunctions.

either . . . or
Either smoke outside or don't smoke at all.
Cell phones should either be turned off or left at home.

neither . . . nor
I would allow neither spitting nor littering on the street.
Neither eating nor chewing gum is acceptable in class.

not only . . . but (also)
Not only CD players but also cell phones should be banned from trains.

BE CAREFUL! When not only . . . but (also) joins two clauses, notice the subject–verb position in the first clause of the sentence.
Not only **did they forget** to turn off their cell phones, but they also talked loudly during the concert.
Not only **are they** noisy, but they're rude.

Verb agreement with paired conjunctions
When joining two subjects, make sure the verb agrees with the subject closer to the verb.
Either the mayor or local businesspeople need to decide.
Either local businesspeople or the mayor needs to decide.

54   UNIT 5

the sentences with the paired conjunction indicated.

... smoking. My grandparents aren't willing to give up ...

... bothers them. They should just learn to live with ...

... phones in theaters. I don't like it when they use them ...

... smoke bothers me. The danger to my health bothers me. (not only)

GRAMMAR EXCHANGE • Now complain about public conduct.

On your notepad, make a list of some of the things that really get on your nerves in public places. Then write sentences with paired conjunctions to express your opinion. Use some of the adjectives you already know.

In restaurants: talking on cell phones
It's not only annoying, but it's also very impolite.

In restaurants:

In stores:

On buses and trains:

On the street:

In offices:

In movie theaters:

Other:

IDEAS
• cutting in line
• graffiti on walls
• talking in theaters
• strong perfumes
• gossiping

Some adjectives
disrespectful
immature
impolite
inconsiderate
inexcusable
irresponsible
unacceptable
unpleasant

Group Work. One student is an "on-the-street interviewer" and asks the other students about what gets on their nerves. Use the sentences from your notepad in your responses.

What really ticks me off is . . .

I'll tell you what really gets on my nerves. . . .

I can't understand why . . .

You want to know what really bugs me?

Discussion.

1. In your opinion, how should people behave in public places? Do you think it's important to speak up when people behave inconsiderately in public?

2. Do you ever do things that annoy other people? Explain.

Tvi

55

VOCABULARY. Presentation includes words, phrases, and collocations. Opportunities to use the vocabulary always follow.

DISCUSSION BUILDER. Step-by-step discussion activities ensure successful discussion for all learners.

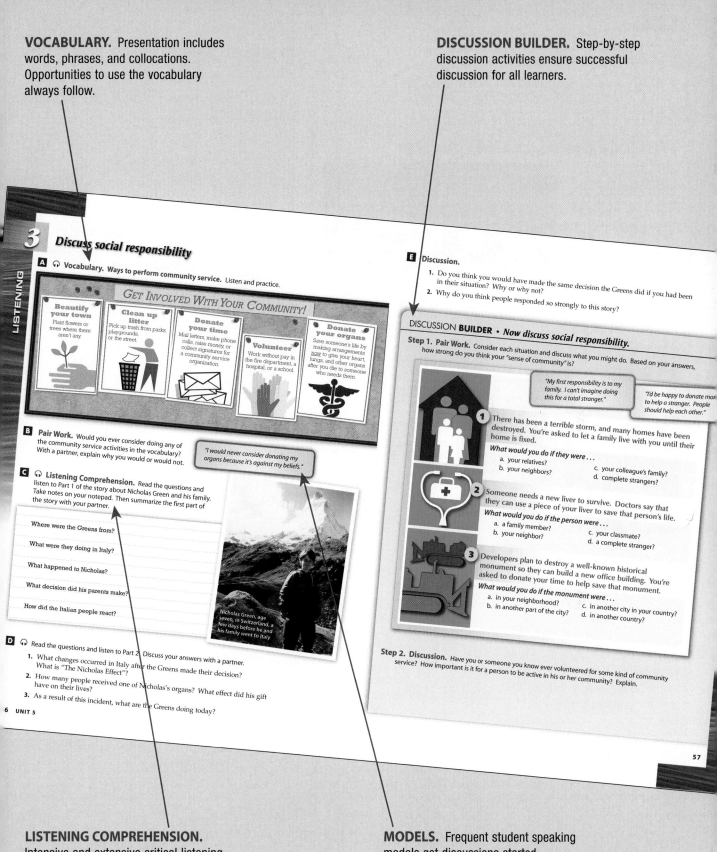

LISTENING

3 Discuss social responsibility

A 🎧 **Vocabulary.** Ways to perform community service. Listen and practice.

GET INVOLVED WITH YOUR COMMUNITY!

Beautify your town
Plant flowers or trees where there aren't any.

Clean up litter
Pick up trash from parks, playgrounds, or the street.

Donate your time
Mail letters, make phone calls, raise money, or collect signatures for a community service organization.

Volunteer
Work without pay in the fire department, a hospital, or a school.

Donate your organs
Save someone's life by making arrangements <u>now</u> to give your heart, lungs, and other organs after you die to someone who needs them.

B **Pair Work.** Would you ever consider doing any of the community service activities in the vocabulary? With a partner, explain why you would or would not.

"I would never consider donating my organs because it's against my beliefs."

C 🎧 **Listening Comprehension.** Read the questions and listen to Part 1 of the story about Nicholas Green and his family. Take notes on your notepad. Then summarize the first part of the story with your partner.

Where were the Greens from?

What were they doing in Italy?

What happened to Nicholas?

What decision did his parents make?

How did the Italian people react?

Nicholas Green, age seven, in Switzerland, a few days before he and his family went to Italy

D 🎧 Read the questions and listen to Part 2. Discuss your answers with a partner.

1. What changes occurred in Italy after the Greens made their decision? What is "The Nicholas Effect"?
2. How many people received one of Nicholas's organs? What effect did his gift have on their lives?
3. As a result of this incident, what are the Greens doing today?

6 UNIT 5

E Discussion.

1. Do you think you would have made the same decision the Greens did if you had been in their situation? Why or why not?
2. Why do you think people responded so strongly to this story?

DISCUSSION **BUILDER** • Now discuss social responsibility.

Step 1. Pair Work. Consider each situation and discuss what you might do. Based on your answers, how strong do you think your "sense of community" is?

"My first responsibility is to my family. I can't imagine doing this for a total stranger."

"I'd be happy to donate more to help a stranger. People should help each other."

1. There has been a terrible storm, and many homes have been destroyed. You're asked to let a family live with you until their home is fixed.
What would you do if they were...
   a. your relatives?
   b. your neighbors?
   c. your colleague's family?
   d. complete strangers?

2. Someone needs a new liver to survive. Doctors say that they can use a piece of your liver to save that person's life.
What would you do if the person were...
   a. a family member?
   b. your neighbor?
   c. your classmate?
   d. a complete stranger?

3. Developers plan to destroy a well-known historical monument so they can build a new office building. You're asked to donate your time to help save that monument.
What would you do if the monument were...
   a. in your neighborhood?
   b. in another part of the city?
   c. in another city in your country?
   d. in another country?

Step 2. Discussion. Have you or someone you know ever volunteered for some kind of community service? How important is it for a person to be active in his or her community? Explain.

57

LISTENING COMPREHENSION. Intensive and extensive critical listening practice provokes lively discussions.

MODELS. Frequent student speaking models get discussions started.

4 Identify urban problems

A **Reading Warm-up.** What problems do you think cities of 10 million or more people might share?

B 🎧 **Reading.** Read the interview. Do you agree with Dr. Perlman's views?

READING WARM-UP. Builds expectations for better reading comprehension.

The Advent of the Megacity

Following is an interview with Dr. Janice Perlman, founder and president of Mega-Cities Project, Inc. Her organization attempts to make cities worldwide more livable places by taking good ideas from one place and trying to make them work in another.

Mexico City
over 18 million (2005)

Q. How do you define "megacity"?

A. We define megacities in our work as cities that have reached populations of 10 million or more. The majority of these are in developing countries. Migration to the city is the route for many people to greater choice, opportunity, and well-being. By coming to settle in the city, they have in effect "voted with their feet."

Q. Why are these places going to be very important in the next hundred years?

A. The 21st century won't be a century of rural areas and small towns but of giant cities that will set the standard of how we live, how our environment is preserved (or not preserved), how our economies work, and what kind of civil society we develop.

Tokyo
over 28 million (2005)

Q. Do megacities in the developed and developing world differ, or are they linked by certain similarities?

A. These large cities have a lot more in common with each other than they do with the small towns and villages in their own countries. For example, every megacity struggles with a widening gap between rich and poor. Every "first-world" city, such as Los Angeles, New York, London, or Tokyo, has within it a "third-world" city of poverty and deprivation. And every third-world city, such as Calcutta, Cairo, or Mexico City, has within it a first-world city of high culture, technology, fashion, and finance.

In addition, all megacities share the problems of providing jobs and economic opportunities, and making housing, education, and health care available. They deal with crime and violence, as well as basic infrastructure such as water, sanitation, and public transportation. This is no easy task. The leaders of these cities recognize that they have similar problems, and they would like to learn more from other cities, particularly about successful solutions.

If we are going to create livable cities for the next century, we will need to be clever enough to do it through collaboration and cooperation. That is why the Mega-Cities Project works to share experiences that work across boundaries of culture and geography.

Q. Is the solution to urban problems strict central planning?

A. Absolutely not. We need decentralized planning that includes local citizens. In my view, attempts to create planned cities or communities—like Brasília or Chandigarh—are too sterile and miss the spontaneity of cities that grew organically, like Rio de Janeiro, Bombay, or even New York City. The best example of urban planning I've seen recently is in Curitiba, Brazil, which set up a brilliant public transportation system in anticipation of population growth. The historic areas of cities like Siena, Paris, or Barcelona all have elements of planning that led to buildings of similar heights and architecture, but they were not centrally planned. There is a lot of diversity within the design, and people love to go to those cities.

Megacities are really very exciting places. The truth is, I've never met a megacity that I didn't like!

The World's Ten Largest Urban Areas	Population (millions) in 1996	in 2015	Rank in 2015
1 Tokyo, Japan	27.2	28.9	1
2 Mexico City, Mexico	16.9	19.2	7
3 São Paulo, Brazil	16.8	20.3	4
4 New York, United States	16.4	17.6	9
5 Mumbai (Bombay), India	15.7	26.2	2
6 Shanghai, China	13.7	18	8
7 Los Angeles, United States	12.6	14.2	15
8 Kolkata (Calcutta), India	12.1	17.3	10
9 Buenos Aires, Argentina	11.9	13.9	1
10 Seoul, Korea	11.8	13	1

Source: U.N. Department of Economic and Social Affairs Population D

Source: http://usinfo.stat

58 UNIT 5

READING. Substantive readings build academic skills and provide information for interesting discussions.

AUTHENTICITY. All readings come from authentic sources and build students' confidence and ability to approach academic content.

COMPREHENSION EXERCISES. Build academic and critical thinking skills and promote discussion.

C Check the types of urban problems Dr. Perlman mentions or suggests in the interview.

☐ poverty
☐ lack of housing
☐ crowding
☐ pollution
☐ disease
☐ crime
☐ unemployment
☐ discrimination
☐ corruption
☐ inadequate public transportation

D **Understanding Meaning from Context.** Read each statement from the interview. Then choose the sentence that is closest to what Dr. Perlman means. Use information from the reading to help explain your answers.

1. "By coming to settle in the city, they have in effect 'voted with their feet.'"
   a. People are making it clear which kind of life they prefer.
   b. People would rather live in the country than live in the city.
   c. People don't have as much opportunity in the city as they do in the country.

2. "Every 'first-world' city . . . has within it a 'third-world' city of poverty and deprivation. And every third-world city . . . has within it a first-world city of high culture, technology, fashion, and finance."
   a. Some megacities have more poverty than others.
   b. All megacities have both poverty and wealth.
   c. Some megacities have more wealth than others.

3. "The Mega-Cities Project works to share experiences that work across boundaries of culture and geography."
   a. The Mega-Cities Project helps megacities communicate their success stories to the people who live in that city.
   b. The Mega-Cities Project helps megacities communicate their success stories to the other cities in that country.
   c. The Mega-Cities Project helps megacities communicate their success stories to megacities in other countries.

E **Discussion.**

1. Why does Dr. Perlman say she prefers cities that are *not* planned over planned cities?
2. Why do you think Dr. Perlman thinks megacities are exciting? Do you agree?
3. Do you live in a megacity, or have you ever visited one? What are the pros and cons of living in a megacity?
4. Do you think life in megacities will improve in the future or get worse? Why?

DISCUSSION BUILDER • Now identify urban problems.

Step 1. Pair Work. Check which urban problems you think exist in your area. Discuss and provide examples.

Step 2. Discussion. Talk about the problems you've identified. As a group, discuss at least five ways to make improvements in your town or city.

Step 3. Writing. Describe the social problems that exist in your town or city. Suggest some possible solutions.

○ poverty
○ crime
○ crowding
○ disease
○ inadequate public transportation
○ pollution
○ corruption
○ lack of housing
○ discrimination
○ unemployment
○ other: _____

Tviii

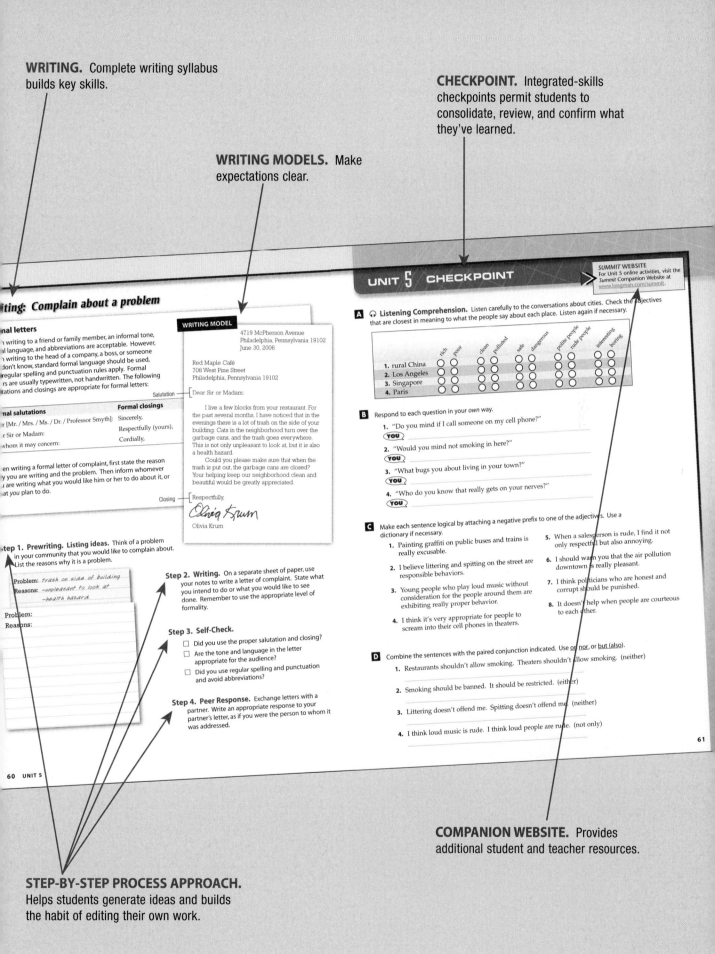

WRITING. Complete writing syllabus builds key skills.

WRITING MODELS. Make expectations clear.

CHECKPOINT. Integrated-skills checkpoints permit students to consolidate, review, and confirm what they've learned.

...iting: *Complain about a problem*

...nal letters

...n writing to a friend or family member, an informal tone, ...al language, and abbreviations are acceptable. However, ...n writing to the head of a company, a boss, or someone ...don't know, standard formal language should be used, ...regular spelling and punctuation rules apply. Formal ...rs are usually typewritten, not handwritten. The following ...ations and closings are appropriate for formal letters:

...nal salutations	**Formal closings**
...r [Mr. / Mrs. / Ms. / Dr. / Professor Smyth]:	Sincerely,
...r Sir or Madam:	Respectfully (yours),
...whom it may concern:	Cordially,

...en writing a formal letter of complaint, first state the reason ...y you are writing and the problem. Then inform whomever ...u are writing what you would like him or her to do about it, or ...at you plan to do.

WRITING MODEL

4719 McPherson Avenue
Philadelphia, Pennsylvania 19102
June 30, 2006

Red Maple Café
708 West Pine Street
Philadelphia, Pennsylvania 19102

Salutation — Dear Sir or Madam:

I live a few blocks from your restaurant. For the past several months, I have noticed that in the evenings there is a lot of trash on the side of your building. Cats in the neighborhood turn over the garbage cans, and the trash goes everywhere. This is not only unpleasant to look at, but it is also a health hazard.

Could you please make sure that when the trash is put out, the garbage cans are closed? Your helping keep our neighborhood clean and beautiful would be greatly appreciated.

Closing — Respectfully,

Olivia Krum

Olivia Krum

...tep 1. Prewriting. Listing ideas. Think of a problem ...in your community that you would like to complain about. ...List the reasons why it is a problem.

Problem: *trash on side of building*
Reasons: *—unpleasant to look at*
—health hazard

Problem:
Reasons:

Step 2. Writing. On a separate sheet of paper, use your notes to write a letter of complaint. State what you intend to do or what you would like to see done. Remember to use the appropriate level of formality.

Step 3. Self-Check.

☐ Did you use the proper salutation and closing?
☐ Are the tone and language in the letter appropriate for the audience?
☐ Did you use regular spelling and punctuation and avoid abbreviations?

Step 4. Peer Response. Exchange letters with a partner. Write an appropriate response to your partner's letter, as if you were the person to whom it was addressed.

60 UNIT 5

UNIT **5** CHECKPOINT

SUMMIT WEBSITE
For Unit 5 online activities, visit the *Summit* Companion Website at www.longman.com/summit.

A 🎧 **Listening Comprehension.** Listen carefully to the conversations about cities. Check the adjectives that are closest in meaning to what the people say about each place. Listen again if necessary.

	rich	poor	clean	polluted	safe	dangerous	polite people	rude people	interesting	boring
1. rural China	○	○	○	○	○	○	○	○	○	○
2. Los Angeles	○	○	○	○	○	○	○	○	○	○
3. Singapore	○	○	○	○	○	○	○	○	○	○
4. Paris	○	○	○	○	○	○	○	○	○	○

B Respond to each question in your *own* way.

1. "Do you mind if I call someone on my cell phone?"
   YOU _____

2. "Would you mind not smoking in here?"
   YOU _____

3. "What bugs you about living in your town?"
   YOU _____

4. "Who do you know that really gets on your nerves?"
   YOU _____

C Make each sentence logical by attaching a negative prefix to one of the adjectives. Use a dictionary if necessary.

1. Painting graffiti on public buses and trains is really excusable.

2. I believe littering and spitting on the street are responsible behaviors.

3. Young people who play loud music without consideration for the people around them are exhibiting really proper behavior.

4. I think it's very appropriate for people to scream into their cell phones in theaters.

5. When a salesperson is rude, I find it not only respectful but also annoying.

6. I should warn you that the air pollution downtown is really pleasant.

7. I think politicians who are honest and corrupt should be punished.

8. It doesn't help when people are courteous to each other.

D Combine the sentences with the paired conjunction indicated. Use *or nor*, or *but (also)*.

1. Restaurants shouldn't allow smoking. Theaters shouldn't allow smoking. (neither)
   _____

2. Smoking should be banned. It should be restricted. (either)
   _____

3. Littering doesn't offend me. Spitting doesn't offend me. (neither)
   _____

4. I think loud music is rude. I think loud people are rude. (not only)
   _____

61

STEP-BY-STEP PROCESS APPROACH. Helps students generate ideas and builds the habit of editing their own work.

COMPANION WEBSITE. Provides additional student and teacher resources.

Other *Summit* Components

WORKBOOK
An illustrated workbook contains exercises that provide additional practice and reinforcement of language concepts and skills from the *Summit* Student's Book and its Grammar Booster.

COMPLETE ASSESSMENT PACKAGE WITH EXAM*VIEW*® SOFTWARE
Ten easy-to-administer and easy-to-score unit achievement tests assess listening, vocabulary, grammar, social language, reading, and writing. Two review tests – one mid-book and one end-of-book – provide additional cumulative assessment. Two speaking tests assess progress in speaking.

In addition to the photocopiable achievement tests, Exam*View*® software enables teachers to customize tests that best meet their own needs.

COMPANION WEBSITE

A companion website at www.longman.com/summit provides numerous additional resources for students and teachers. This no-cost, high-benefit feature includes opportunities for further practice of language and content from the *Summit* Student's Book.

CLASS AUDIO PROGRAM

The audio program contains listening comprehension activities, rhythm and intonation practice, and targeted pronunciation activities that focus on accurate and comprehensible pronunciation.

To prepare students to communicate with a variety of speakers, regional and non-native accents are included.

SUMMIT TV

Real TV news programs and authentic unrehearsed interviews are accompanied by Activity Worksheets and Teaching Notes.

TV documentaries from the ABC Network

On-the-street interviews

The *Summit* Teacher's Resource Disk

A complete menu of free printable activities to personalize YOUR *Summit* classroom.

- **Listening Strategies:** for critical thinking and more effective listening skills
- **Discourse Strategies:** for managing discussion more effectively
- **Vocabulary-Building Strategies:** for application and retention of new vocabulary and word skills
- **Reading Strategies:** for critical thinking and more effective reading skills
- **Grammar Self-Checks:** for reinforcement or for an inductive presentation
- **Conversation Prompts:** for reminding students of language they already know

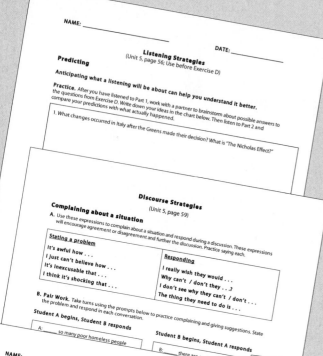

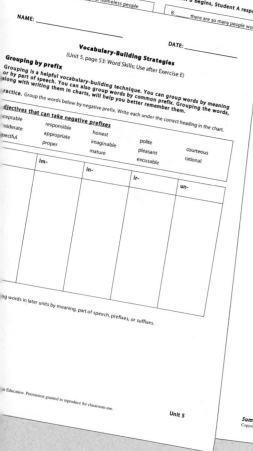

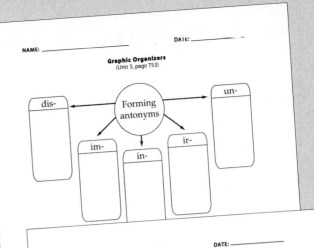

NAME: _____ DATE: _____

Graphic Organizers
(Unit 5, page T53)

dis- Forming antonyms un-

im- in- ir-

NAME: _____ DATE: _____

Pronunciation Activities
(Unit 5)

Unstressed syllables: vowel reduction to /ə/

A. Each of the following words includes one or more vowel sound that may get reduced to the sound /ə/. With a partner, use what you learned about vowel reduction in the Pronunciation Booster to find and circle the syllables that are reduced to the /ə/ sound in conversational English.

1. ru · ral
2. ur · ban
3. de · vel · oped
4. il · lus · tra · tion
5. dis · tri · bu · tion
6. pro · ject · ed

10. ob · jec · tion
11. pes · si · mis · tic
12. beau · ti · fy
13. de · part · ment
14. pol · lu · tion
15. dis · ease

- **Extra Writing Skills Practice:** for additional reinforcement of writing skills

- **Extra Reading Comprehension Activities:** for both traditional comprehension and critical thinking

- **Reading Speed Calculator:** for calculating reading speed for each of the main reading selections

- **Pronunciation Activities:** for additional reinforcement of pronunciation

- **Graphic Organizers:** for better preparation and comprehension

NAME: _____ DATE: _____

Reading Speed Calculator

Keep a record of your reading times for all *Summit 1* readings. Calculate your reading speed (words per minute) in the chart below.

	Total words in reading	286
Unit 1 Maintaining a Positive Perspective	÷ total minutes to read	÷
	= **YOUR READING SPEED**	=
Unit 2 Ludwig van Beethoven: A Passion for Music	Total words in reading	444
	÷ total minutes to read	÷
	= **YOUR READING SPEED**	=
Unit 3 Paul Newman: Actor and	Total words in reading	376
	÷ total minutes to read	÷
	YOUR READING SPEED	
	total words in reading	403
	total minutes to read	÷
	YOUR READING SPEED	
	total words in reading	519
	total minutes to read	÷
	YOUR READING SPEED	=
	total words in reading	550
	total minutes to read	÷
	= **YOUR READING SPEED**	
	total words in reading	351
	total minutes to read	÷
	= **YOUR READING SPEED**	
	Total words in reading	354
	÷ total minutes to read	÷
	= **YOUR READING SPEED**	
	Total words in reading	489
	÷ total minutes to read	÷
	= **YOUR READING SPEED**	
	Total words in reading	468
	÷ total minutes to read	÷
	YOUR READING SPEED	=

...d to reproduce for classroom use.

Unit 5

NAME: _____ DATE: _____

Extra Writing Skills Practice
(Unit 5, page 60)

Formal letters

A. Complete the formal letter by circling the most appropriate langua...

(❶ Dear Sir or Madam: / To whom it may concern: / Dear Mr. Jones:)

It was good to meet you last week, and I very much apprecia...
your plants more carefully. However, since we last talked, I'm (❷ afra...
that water has continued to drip from your balcony onto ours. This is ...
have on our balcony. I'm not sure if (❸ someone else has / your rude...
ignored us and have) been watering the plants carelessly, or whethe...
saucers to catch the water. However, if water continues to drip dow...
you to replace our damaged furniture. I hope we can avoid this.

(❹ Hugs and Kisses, / Sincerely, / See ya,)

Janet Goodman

...tarter)

...age 52 and the language
...on in which you ask your partner
...sks you not to do it.

...essor Smith:)

...mother past your store yester...
...strians on Main Street, this sig...
...rate) to have such a big sign in...
...st knocked over by another p...
...Could you please / I'll destroy...
... place. I'm sure this would ma...

Adjectives

inappropriate   rude
immature   disrespectful
unacceptable   honest
polite   irresponsible
impolite

...eally gets to me.
...n't think I'll ever get used to ___.
...ess I'm just ___.
...a pain in the neck having to ___.
...I known, ___.
...n't you think ___ might be ___?
...aw the line at ___.

...on granted to reproduce for classroo...

NAME: _____ DATE: _____

Extra Reading Comprehension Activities
(Unit 5, page 58)

Comprehension Questions

A. Answer the questions, according to information in the article.

1. Why are the majority of megacities in developing countries?
_____

2. What standard will megacities set in the 21st century?
_____

3. What do "first-world" and "third-world" cities have in common?
_____

4. What basic infrastructure problems do all megacities deal with?
_____

5. What would megacity leaders especially like to learn from other cities?
_____

6. Why does Perlman disagree with strict central planning?
_____

7. Why does Perlman think people love to go to Siena, Paris, or Barcelona?
_____

Critical Thinking Questions

B. Look at the chart in the article to answer the following questions.

1. Which city is predicted to have the same rank in 2015? Why do you think this might be?
_____

2. Which cities are predicted to grow the most in population by 2015? Why do you think this might be?
_____

3. Which city is predicted to grow the least in population by 2015? Why do you think this might be?
_____

Unit 5

Summit: A concise methodology

The *Summit* approach

The following paragraphs describe the major features of the *Summit* approach.

Explicit presentation of language. So that students may use their textbooks both to learn from in class and as a study tool, *Summit* provides explicit presentation of language. The learner-supportive Student's Book depicts or defines all vocabulary taught for productive use; it provides clear grammar presentations with explanations of form, meaning, and use; and it features numerous practical model conversations and models of extended narrative speech and writing.

Daily confirmation of progress. High-intermediate and advanced adult students are often highly motivated, anxious for results, and unwilling to continue if they don't see progress. Moreover, they are often hesitant to reveal their lack of ability and are embarrassed to speak incorrectly. Materials and lessons need to provide observable results and safe opportunities for controlled and free practice. Students should leave each class session with clear knowledge of what they have achieved. Each lesson in *Summit* has a clearly identified communication goal and culminates in an activity to confirm students' progress.

Memorable language models. *Summit* uses short practical language models, including conversation models, that represent the language adult students want and need to learn—for professional, social, and travel situations. Systematic guided practice and free practice help to make language memorable and transferable to students' own lives.

Summit has a social language syllabus that provides adult students with essential language for their real needs. In addition to classic level-appropriate topics, vocabulary, and grammar, *Summit 1* includes highly practical, communicative language such as discussing financial goals, describing one's use of free time, complaining about public behavior, and so on.

Adequate practice. If language is to be acquired, remembered, and accessible to students when they need it, rigorous and ample practice is required. Because the language learner often lacks the opportunity to use English outside of the classroom, *Summit* offers opportunities for both controlled and free practice within the class.

Learner-supportive instruction. The following features provide support to students learning from *Summit*.

    Clear directions. The *Summit* Student's Book contains easy-to-follow directions that students can understand without teacher explanation. Models of hypothetical student responses are often included to help students frame their thoughts and see an example of an acceptable response.

    Preparation. Free-discussion activities are always preceded by activities such as surveys or note-taking so students have a clear and concrete stimulus to get them started and keep them going.

    Reminders. Frequent notes remind students of language they already know to encourage them to use it productively.

Authentic, sourced reading texts. To prepare students for real-world reading, the *Summit* Student's Book contains a variety of texts from authentic sources. Careful attention has been given to comprehensibility of these texts appropriate to the level. Occasional glosses support students with language they are unlikely to know or that they probably can't guess from context.

Real language. Carefully exposing students to authentic, natural English receptively is a necessary component of building understanding. All language models in *Summit* feature the language people really use, not "textbook English" written merely to exemplify grammar. Conversation models also reflect authentic, natural language for effective contemporary expression.

Usage information backed by the Longman Corpus Network. Informed by the Longman Corpus Network— Longman's unique computerized language database of over 328 million words of spoken and written English— *Summit* provides concise and useful information about frequency, collocations, and typical native-speaker usage. Corpus Notes can be found on the Student's Book pages bound into this Teacher's Edition and Lesson Planner. In addition, teachers are alerted to frequent learner errors from the Longman Learners' Corpus so they can target their attention to troublesome vocabulary and structures.

Teacher's Resource Disk. Because teachers have differing ideas of what constitutes the best pedagogy, the Teacher's Resource Disk bound in the inside back cover of this book provides printable, ready-made classroom activities to extend or adapt each section of a *Summit* unit to the teacher's own style or situation.

The following photocopiable sheets can be printed from the Teacher's Resource Disk:

    Vocabulary-Building Strategies. These worksheets help students use and apply new vocabulary and word skills from the unit for more effective learning. They include associating words, personalizing vocabulary, applying words in new contexts, diagramming, and more. The strategies are designed for a variety of learning styles, and students will be able to apply them to other vocabulary they learn as well.

Discourse Strategies. Discourse Strategies for managing discussion more effectively are presented and immediately followed by a pair work activity to practice applying them. Strategies include asking for agreement, showing interest or surprise, paraphrasing an opinion, and more. These can then be applied to the discussion activities in *Summit*.

Listening Strategies. These worksheets are designed to teach specific strategies that support critical thinking and more effective listening. Strategies include inferring point of view, listening for discourse markers, taking notes, predicting, and more.

Reading Strategies. These worksheets are designed to teach specific strategies that support critical thinking and more effective reading. Strategies include classifying information, identifying supporting details, focusing on key causes and effects, and more.

Grammar Self-Checks. These worksheets encourage students to figure out grammar rules based on clear example sentences and provide alternative inductive grammar presentations or cognitive follow-up activities for the Student's Book grammar presentations. They are designed to raise students' grammar awareness and check how well they understand how the grammar works.

Conversation Prompts. The Conversation Prompts remind students of language they have already learned in the unit—and in units from earlier in the course—in order to promote their use in personalizing conversation models from the Student's Book unit. These prompts can be used as a way to get students "out of the book" and communicating.

Extra Writing Skills Practice. These worksheets offer controlled exercises for further reinforcement of the writing skill taught in the unit's writing lesson. They help students build confidence to apply these skills in their own writing.

Pronunciation Activities. Based on the optional Pronunciation Booster activities in the back of the Student's Book, these worksheets further exploit language from each unit for pronunciation practice. In some cases, students can check their work against the Class Audio Program.

Reading Speed Calculator. The Reading Speed Calculator is a single chart that includes total word counts of the main reading selections from every unit and a simple formula for calculating reading speed for each. Students can record and compare their own reading speeds throughout the course.

Extra Reading Comprehension Activities. A set of traditional comprehension questions and critical thinking questions corresponds with each unit's main reading selection for more in-depth work. These questions can be used in addition to or instead of the activities in the Student's Book.

Graphic Organizers. A variety of charts, Venn diagrams, and idea clusters are available to accompany specific grammar, reading, listening, discussion, and writing activities to help students organize their ideas clearly for better preparation or comprehension. These can be completed individually, as a class, or by students in pairs or groups.

Teacher's Edition and Lesson Planner serves as a management tool. In the Lesson Plans beginning on page T2, there are links to all components of *Summit 1*. Icons indicate places where extra and optional activities are available on the Teacher's Resource Disk, in the Complete Assessment Package, or with the *Summit TV* Video Program. The heading *Extras (optional)* precedes references to the Grammar Booster, Pronunciation Booster, and exercises in the Workbook. While the *Summit* Student's Book is a complete course without the necessity of additional components, teachers who have chosen to use one or more of the components will see them integrated at a glance in each lesson plan.

Student's Take-Home Audio CD. Located in the back of each *Summit* Student's Book, the Student's Take-Home Audio CD provides an opportunity for students to listen and practice at their own convenience—on their commute, in the privacy of their homes—any time they choose. The CD provides practice of the Conversation Snapshots and includes all listening exercises from the Pronunciation Booster. Encourage students to listen to the CD on their own time to increase their confidence, to make the language in the models memorable, and to improve their rhythm, stress, and intonation.

The "Pronunciator." To remove any doubts about pronunciation of proper names in English, the *Summit* Companion Website includes a section in which proper names in *Summit* that are not heard on the Class Audio Program can be found transcribed in the International Phonetic Alphabet (IPA). The transcription shows the way a native speaker of English is most likely to pronounce a word. When non-English names or places are included, the pronunciation given is that used in English, which often differs from the one used in the original language. For example, /mɛksɪkoʊ/ NOT /mɛhɪko/ (Mexico). To find the Pronunciator, go to the *Summit 1* Companion Website and click on "Pronunciator."

Methodology for the *Summit* course

The following paragraphs describe suggestions for managing a *Summit* classroom.

The goal of *Summit* is to prepare students to understand spoken and written English and to express themselves confidently, accurately, and fluently in both speaking and writing.

The following general methodology is recommended for *Summit*. Specific suggestions for teaching every exercise of the Student's Book are given in the Lesson Planner beginning on page T2. Note that the extent to which you use these recommendations is up to you. All suggestions may not be appropriate for all groups, and you should tailor the lesson to reflect your own background, personal approach, training, and the specific needs of your students.

Pair work and collaborative activities. On every page of *Summit*, opportunities for pair work, group work, and collaborative activities enable students to take a more active and creative role in learning and allow the maximum number of students to participate. These activities encourage students to use previously learned language, making the lesson more personalized and meaningful. They also ensure that students initiate as well as respond in English. Furthermore, in working together, students get to know each other faster and become more independent, relying less on the teacher for guidance and ultimately taking more responsibility for their own learning. We recommend the following approaches for pair and group work activities:

A student-centered approach. Make sure that group and pair work are a regular part of each lesson. Some students, particularly those accustomed to teacher-centered lessons, may not immediately see the benefits of working in pairs or groups. The first time you do pair and group work, point out to students that working together allows them more time to practice English and allows you to listen to more students individually.

Cooperative learning. Encourage students to help and learn from each other. Whenever possible, try to elicit answers from other students before answering a question yourself. If a student asks a question that was previously asked by another student, direct the question to the student who first asked the question so he or she can answer it. In restating information they have recently obtained, students internalize the language, increasing the likelihood that it will be retained.

Flexible seating arrangement. To ensure that students interact with a variety of partners, have students sit in a different location for each class or work with a different partner for each activity. When dividing the class into pairs or groups, try to match students of different abilities. One method of forming groups is to have students count off according to the number of groups needed. (The 1s work together, the 2s work together, and so on.)

Teacher monitoring. During pair and group work activities, circulate around the room, keeping students on task, listening carefully, and offering help as needed. When dividing the class into pairs, avoid playing a partner role yourself, as this will limit your ability to monitor and offer assistance to the class. If faced with an odd number of students, create a group of three students, with a third role added as a helper to encourage eye contact and to correct mistakes.

Building student confidence. Before asking students to speak in front of the class, build students' confidence by having them rehearse or discuss in pairs or small groups. Students can also collaborate with one or more partners on writing exercises, either by completing the activity together or by comparing what they've written.

Time management. To keep students on task, set time limits for each activity. End activities before most of the class is finished to avoid dead time. For students who finish early, prepare additional activities from any of the *Summit* supplements, or create your own, such as having students who have finished their Conversation Starter activity (see page Txxii) write the conversation that they created.

Correction. Most adult learners like feedback and expect to be corrected when they make a mistake. However, recent research indicates that correcting errors in students' speech and writing is relatively ineffective in promoting correct language use. Studies have shown that it is repeated exposure to correct usage, rather than constant correction, that results in the internalization of new language. In addition, excessive correction in a communicative course can embarrass and discourage students, interfering with communication of ideas, making them reluctant to attempt the experimentation and practice essential to language acquisition. We recommend the following approaches for providing effective positive feedback and striking a balance between the need for correction and maintaining feelings of success:

Self-correction. Students, especially at the upper levels, are often able to correct their own mistakes. First, allow the student to finish the thought, then show by sound or gesture that there has been a mistake. Try to indicate where the mistake was and give the student an opportunity to self-correct. Some techniques for eliciting self-correction include repeating the student sentence and pausing at the mistake, and prompting the student with a missing word. For example, S: *There were much people.* T: *There were . . . ?* S: *There were many people.* A less intrusive method is to correct the student's mistake by reformulating what the student said without stopping the flow of conversation. For example, S: *Many of them has finished.* T: *Oh, many of them have finished?* S: *Yes, many of them have finished.* Note that these techniques often prompt the student to self-correct.

Accuracy. For activities where accuracy is the focus, such as in the Conversation Starter and Grammar Exchange, correct mistakes shortly after they occur. Immediate correction is important for controlled activities where students need guidance in using new language. In writing, focus on clarity of ideas first. Research shows that when teachers focus on accuracy too soon in writing, they often misunderstand what the student is trying to say. It is more effective to address accuracy after students have revised their work. In doing so, students may catch many of their own errors. At that point, try indicating *where* errors have occurred, rather than simply correcting them. Expect students to try to correct their own errors.

Fluency. For the Discussion Builders, refrain from stopping the flow of student discussion with corrections. In these activities, accuracy is less important than the ability to communicate ideas and improvise with known language. Developing these improvisation skills is critical if students are to convert the English they have learned in the classroom into the English they need (or will need) in their own lives. Interrupting students with corrections discourages this experimentation. Instead, focus on the target language only, and take notes on common student mistakes, reviewing those errors as a class at the end of the activity.

Selectivity. Don't discourage or overwhelm students by correcting every mistake. Focus corrections on the skills that are being taught in that particular lesson or mistakes that prevent comprehension.

Support. Above all, avoid making students feel pressured. Give students enough time to think. Be careful not to stigmatize or embarrass students. Be aware that students may be sensitive to criticism in front of their peers and may prefer more private feedback. There is nothing more effective in promoting student practice than their belief that you are "on their side." To that end, it is suggested that you show approval for student experimentation, even if the language is inaccurate. Experimentation is an essential step in language mastery.

Checking answers. For exercises or homework requiring a written response, have students check their answers with a partner. This encourages students to correct their own mistakes and also helps students avoid the possible embarrassment of giving incorrect answers in front of the entire class. When the class has finished comparing answers, review the correct answers as a class, either by eliciting the answers from individual students or by having volunteers write their answers on the board. In classes with time constraints, write answers on the board and have the class self-correct.

Repetition. Even at the upper levels, repetition of the Conversation Snapshots and the Vocabulary (see pages Txx and Txxi) helps students acquire comprehensible

and accurate pronunciation, stress, and intonation. Repetition also helps to make language memorable—an important goal. On the Student's Take-Home Audio CD and in the Class Audio Program, a pause following the speaker's utterance facilitates repetition and permits students to imitate the pronunciation and intonation of the native speaker on the audio. Teacher's notes provide specific suggestions for how to focus students' attention on rhythm, stress, and intonation for each Conversation Snapshot. Here are some general options for using repetition to facilitate learning:

Open or closed books. For activities requiring students to listen and repeat, we recommend having students first listen while looking at the written form in their textbooks. This allows students to link the written form in the book to the sound they hear. In the next step, when students are asked to listen and repeat, have them listen and repeat with their books closed. This serves to reduce distractions and allows students to focus exclusively on listening and repeating rather than reading. It also reduces the confusing effect of English spelling on pronunciation.

Practice drills. Introduce short, fast-paced repetition drills to offer the class more pronunciation practice, reinforce word structures, and provide a fresh change of pace. Practice drills will also help students see how much they can personalize the language they are learning. Start by modeling a sentence from the Conversation Snapshot and having the class repeat after you. For example, T: *She might turn out to be a real sweetheart.* Class: *She might turn out to be a real sweetheart.* Then prompt students to change the sentence. For example, T: *a tyrant.* Class: *She might turn out to be a real tyrant.* Continue in this manner several times. Point to individual students and have them repeat. Modeling the new language before and after each student response helps students build auditory memory while providing them with a correct model for repetition.

Pace. Keeping the pace of repetition drills lively gives the greatest number of students a chance to speak and maximizes exposure to the language. If a student cannot respond or makes a mistake, move on quickly to another student and then return to the student who made the mistake. Maintaining the pace gives weaker students the time that they need to internalize and ultimately acquire new language.

Realia—bringing the outside in. Research has demonstrated that language is easier to comprehend and retain if presented in conjunction with sensory input such as pictures, sounds, props, and authentic documents. In addition, bringing real material into the classroom serves to motivate students and helps them understand the relevance of their language study to their own lives.

The Topic Preview on the first page of the unit and the readings are based on authentic sources. Teaching notes in the Lesson Plans include suggestions for maximizing the value of this material.

Elicitation. Asking questions keeps the class active and involved and helps you to identify what students understand and what they do not. Some effective elicitation techniques to consider include the following:

Warm-up. Direct questions to the entire class before eliciting answers from individual students. This technique reduces the pressure on individual students to produce a response before they are ready and provides the class with a model of a correct response.

One-word answers. It is not always necessary for students to answer in full sentences. Permitting one-word answers is particularly valuable because it clarifies whether students have comprehended both the question and the material it is based on. Moreover, encouraging one-word answers promotes the use of natural language, as one-word responses are very typical of informal spoken English.

Background knowledge. High-intermediate and advanced students have an abundance of receptive language knowledge. Before presenting new material, find out what your students already know.

Teaching multi-level classes. To accommodate diverse levels within the same classroom, we recommend the following approaches:

Modeling. Use more advanced or stronger students to model activities. These students, with their quicker comprehension time, are more likely to respond immediately and correctly. Modeling will allow weaker students, who need longer exposure time to new language, to use the stronger students' responses as a model and respond successfully themselves.

Grouping. In pair and group work activities, vary the approach to grouping students to keep the activities fresh. Partnering more advanced students with weaker students encourages the class to help and learn from each other. Partnering students with similar ability levels also has advantages, as this allows pairs to speak at their own pace and level of production.

Methodology for a *Summit* unit

A *Summit* unit is made up of a series of two-page lessons:

- *Preview and Introduction*
- *Lessons 1 and 2:* Conversation or Grammar focus
- *Lessons 3 and 4:* Free discourse focus with Reading or Listening
- *Writing and Checkpoint*

The icon ⊛ in this section indicates that extension activities can be printed from the Teacher's Resource Disk in the back of this Teacher's Edition and Lesson Planner.

■ *Preview and Introduction*

It is suggested that you open your *Summit* textbook to any unit in order to see each section described below.

The purpose of the Preview is to provide an introduction to the theme. It's important to understand that the Preview includes language at the "+1" level. The reason for this is to give students a motivating glimpse of real language at a comprehensible level, to build their expectations of the topic and language that follow in the unit, to access some prior knowledge, and to build the strategy of determining meaning from context. However, exercises and discussion questions in this Preview are carefully written at the productive level of the student. Great care has been taken to ensure that the language in the Preview is comprehensible. When teaching *Summit* to a group for the first time, make students aware that they will not be expected to "learn" or "produce" all the language in the Preview. However, you may want to encourage them to experiment.

TOPIC PREVIEW. Begin each unit by asking a few questions about the material that is featured in the Topic Preview. The purpose of Exercise A is to focus attention on that material, which usually consists of realia adapted from authentic sources. If necessary, model some answers to the questions in Exercise A yourself. Be sure to answer using language your students already know.

One of the purposes of including a piece of realia with +1 language is to teach students to find meaning in texts that contain some unknown language. Encourage students to use the illustrations and context to determine the meaning of unfamiliar words and phrases—an important learning strategy for understanding material above one's productive level. Help students build their ability to use illustrations and context by asking questions that prompt students to do so. For example, if students don't know the terms *new age* or *world music* on the first page of Unit 2, have them study the kinds of music described under New Age and World on the website. Ask *Which type of music do you think might relax you?* (new age) *How can you describe world music?* (music that comes from a country's traditional music)

Discussion exercises on the left-hand page of the Preview get students to start talking about the unit topic. These activities are designed so that students can use language they already know or that is readily available on the page. When grouping isn't specified, students can discuss in pairs or small groups. After students have finished their discussions, review by asking a few students to share their responses with the whole class.

SOUND BITES. The Sound Bites on the right-hand page of the Preview are not a conversation for student practice, but rather for student observation. These examples of natural conversation will promote comprehension of natural spoken language and build expectation of language students may learn later in the unit or encounter again in authentic sources. An attempt has been made to include highly natural and frequent idiomatic language, language ordinarily not included in textbooks. Because the language is very appealing, many students will pick it up and make it their own. But that should not be your expectation or requirement.

Before students read and listen to the conversation, you can ask questions about the photo(s) or illustration, if appropriate. For variety and to provide listening practice, you may sometimes want to have students listen first with books closed. After students listen to the conversation, ask questions to check comprehension. Use the questions that are provided in each unit or your own questions. (Additional questions are often included in the Lesson Plans in this book.) If students have listened with books closed, ask the comprehension questions, allow students to listen again, and then repeat the questions. Comprehension questions can be asked of the whole class, written on the board for students to answer with a partner, or read aloud for students to write answers to. If appropriate, ask additional questions that relate the content of the conversation to students' own lives.

Important new language in the Sound Bites is highlighted in the exercise(s) that follow. The meaning of almost all new language can be determined from the context of the conversation, but where doubts might occur, notes in the Lesson Plans offer suggestions for conveying meaning. Have students underline in the conversation the word, phrase, or sentence that is asked about in the exercise. Encourage students to reread the lines before and after the underlined portion of the conversation. You can also ask questions about the context that lead students to figure out the meaning of the new language.

STARTING POINT. Each two-page Preview culminates in Starting Point activities that prompt students to relate content from the Preview to their own lives and get them talking about the unit topic. If the Starting Point activity asks partners to compare, ask a couple of students about their responses before pairs discuss. An option for this section is to have students use the third person to tell the class something about their classmate.

UNIT GOALS. Finally, note that each Preview lists in a box four communication goals for the unit. These are the goals for the four core lessons of the unit.

■ *Lessons 1 and 2: Conversation or Grammar focus*

Lessons 1 and 2 offer new language and integrated communication practice with a focus either on conversation or on grammar. Each unit in *Summit* has one Conversation lesson and one Grammar lesson, and each is labeled either Conversation or Grammar. Each of these lessons is also labeled with its communication goal, such as "Discuss your reactions to ads," so students see what they will achieve during the course of the lesson. The lesson ends with a communication activity in which students demonstrate to themselves mastery of the goal.

CONVERSATION SNAPSHOT (in Conversation lessons). Lessons that focus on conversation always begin with a model conversation entitled Conversation Snapshot. To build awareness and facilitate comprehension, begin by asking questions about the photo or illustration, if appropriate. Many questions are provided in the Lesson Plans, but it's not necessary to stop there. When you ask questions, however, be mindful of what students are capable of. Don't elicit language or information that students would not know prior to reading the conversation. Note that one or more examples of the lesson's grammar or vocabulary may be embedded in the Conversation Snapshot to preview that language.

Play the Conversation Snapshot or read it aloud yourself while students read and listen with books open. Then check students' understanding of the conversation by asking comprehension questions. The questions provided in the Lesson Plans help students focus on the essential information in the conversation and determine the meaning of any new language from context. The questions also prepare students to understand any grammar or vocabulary presentation that follows.

An alternative presentation technique, especially in stronger groups, is to have students listen to the conversation with books closed first. When electing this option, have students look at the photo or illustration first to build a holistic awareness of the social situation of the conversation.

RHYTHM AND INTONATION PRACTICE. Following the Conversation Snapshot is a direction line for Rhythm and intonation practice. This second recording of the model directs students to listen and repeat in the pauses. The pause following each line of the model is an opportunity for students to focus on imitating the pronunciation, intonation, rhythm, and stress of the native speaker in the model. The Lesson Plans suggest specific rhythm, stress, and intonation features to call attention to.

Some instructors like to have students look at the text as they repeat. Many prefer to have students do the rhythm and intonation practice with books closed, to avoid the interference of English spelling. We encourage experimentation to see which is more effective. With books closed, students can listen and repeat after each line. Encourage students to imitate the rhythm, stress, and intonation of the conversation as closely as possible. Correct where necessary, helping students to pronounce the language clearly. Encourage students to continue practicing the rhythm and intonation, using the Student's Take-Home Audio CD included in the back of their textbook.

Stress patterns. To help teachers focus on the stress patterns of the Conversation Snapshots, they have been transcribed with a "Morse code-like" feature in the Lesson Plans. These reflect the pattern used in the recording. Note that these patterns may vary in real conversations.

GRAMMAR SNAPSHOT (in Grammar lessons). Lessons that focus on grammar always begin with a Grammar Snapshot, which consists of an article, website, or "interviews," with the target grammar highlighted in boldface text for observation. Each new grammatical structure is previewed in the Grammar Snapshot so students read, hear, and understand the structure in context before they are required to manipulate it.

In the Grammar box, the new structure is presented through authentic examples and clear, concise, easy-to-understand rules. Have students read the information in the Grammar box independently. Then ask them to look again at the Grammar Snapshot and try to apply the rules to the highlighted grammar. The Lesson Plans offer specific suggestions for presenting the grammar from the box and for reinforcing the grammar taught in each unit. Students internalize grammatical structures when they have the opportunity to use them in a meaningful and relevant context. Suggestions prompt students to begin using the new structure in the context of their own lives to express opinions, preferences, and other ideas.

Controlled exercises follow each grammar presentation in the Student's Book. The exercises provide written and/or oral practice with the structure(s) just taught and offer additional examples of its use in context. If necessary, model how to do the first item in each task. Have students complete the exercises independently, in pairs, or in small groups. Review answers as a class or have students check answers with a partner. All answers to the exercises are printed in green type on the Student's Book pages in this book.

You can also use an inductive approach by printing out the Grammar Self-Checks (see below) or by writing the example sentences from the grammar chart on the board for discussion.

GRAMMAR BOOSTER. *Grammar Booster* Following most Grammar boxes is an icon referring students to the Grammar Booster in the back of the Student's Book, where grammar from the unit is extended, review may be included, or additional and related grammar may be presented. The Grammar Booster is an option for teachers who want to go beyond what is normally included in the textbook for this level. If you choose not to use the Grammar Booster for your class, you may wish to selectively assign it to stronger students who are ready for more. Or you may wish to pick and choose those presentations you feel would be most beneficial in certain circumstances. In addition to the presentations, the Grammar Booster contains confirming exercises. Even if you elect not to use the Grammar Booster, students will appreciate having additional material for permanent reference in their textbook.

Grammar Self-Checks. * Grammar Self-Checks can be printed out from the Teacher's Resource Disk. They are designed to check how well students understand the grammar or to help students figure out how the grammar works. If you prefer an inductive presentation of the grammar point, use the Grammar Self-Checks instead of the grammar presentations in the Student's Book. If you prefer a more deductive approach, use the Grammar Self-Checks as follow-up activities after the grammar has been presented.

VOCABULARY. Vocabulary is explicitly presented through context, definitions, and/or pictures. The vocabulary presentations in the Student's Book serve to convey meaning of each new vocabulary item and to provide reference for self-study, which is especially valuable as students prepare for tests. Vocabulary in *Summit* is presented at word, phrase, and sentence levels—including expressions, idioms, and collocations (words that "go together" as phrases).

Begin by focusing students' attention on the illustrations, definitions, or sample sentences. Play the vocabulary or read it aloud as a model. Students can listen and repeat to build awareness of correct pronunciation. If necessary, clarify the meaning of any words or phrases students have difficulty understanding. Convey the meaning physically—through gestures, mime, or reference to people or objects in the room—or through examples or a simple explanation. Specific ideas on how to do this are provided in the Lesson Plans.

When possible, personalize the vocabulary. Use the vocabulary to talk about or ask questions about content familiar to your students. For example, *Use the nouns and adjectives to describe your spending habits or those of a person you know.* (Unit 3, page 32) In open class, or with pairs and small groups, have students talk about their likes/dislikes, preferences, plans, relationships, belongings, habits, etc., in relation to the vocabulary.

WORD SKILLS. As students advance, they not only need new, previously unknown vocabulary, but they also need to build on their existing productive vocabulary. Students can expand their vocabulary by learning word transformation, classification, and association skills. Word Skills presentations increase students' awareness of word features that can be applied to producing or comprehending new vocabulary. For example, an understanding of how prefixes and suffixes, parts of speech, and collocations work can help students more effectively learn new vocabulary by building on existing vocabulary.

One way to present the Word Skills sections is to begin by focusing students' attention on the definitions, explanations, illustrations, or example sentences. Or, when possible or appropriate, another option is to ask students to divide a word such as *self-critical* into its root (*critical*) and its prefix (*self-*) and to define the root. As an example, ask *How would you describe someone who is critical?* (someone who always finds mistakes or problems) Then ask *What do you think self-critical means?* (finding a lot of problems or mistakes with oneself) In this way, students can infer how the prefix *self-* is combined with a number of adjectives and predict similar meaning. Examining words in this way makes it easier to remember them all and expands students' ability to create and understand new words as a group.

Vocabulary-Building Strategies. These worksheets can be printed out from the Teacher's Resource Disk. They are designed to help students use and apply new vocabulary and word skills from the unit for more effective learning. They include associating words, personalizing vocabulary, applying words in new contexts, diagramming, and more. The strategies are designed for a variety of learning styles, and students will be able to apply them to other vocabulary they learn as well.

PRONUNCIATION BOOSTER. *Pronunciation Booster* In addition to the rhythm and intonation practice, each unit offers additional pronunciation practice in the Pronunciation Booster in the back of the Student's Book. The Pronunciation Booster provides presentation of and practice with important features of pronunciation, intonation, or stress. Each concept in the Pronunciation Booster is linked in some way to the content of the unit it accompanies. For example, in Unit 9, the grammar presented in the unit is perfect modals in the passive voice for speculating about the past. Once students have completed the grammar exercise in the unit, an icon

---

*Throughout the Lesson Plans, each time you see this icon there is a printable extension activity on the Teacher's Resource Disk.

refers them to the Pronunciation Booster, where the topic is reduction and linking in perfect modals in the passive voice. The Pronunciation Booster should be considered an option for teachers who want to offer a detailed study of pronunciation in class. If teachers prefer not to use class time for these activities, students can do the Pronunciation Booster activities on their own. The listening exercises are recorded on the Student's Take-Home Audio CD.

Pronunciation Activities. 💿 These activities can be printed out from the Teacher's Resource Disk. Extra activities provide more practice of the pronunciation lesson in the Pronunciation Booster. The activities use language from Grammar Snapshot, Conversation Snapshot, and Vocabulary activities so students have the opportunity to apply what they've learned to familiar language from the Student's Book. A number of activities suggest that students listen to the Class Audio Program in order to check their work.

LISTENING COMPREHENSION. Lessons 1 and 2 often contain exercises labeled Listening Comprehension. These short exercises serve to provide comprehension practice and allow recollection of the vocabulary or grammar. Although short, these tasks require careful listening for sense and critical thinking. The unit's major presentation of Listening Comprehension is included in Lessons 3 and 4 and is more fully described there (see page Txxiv).

CONVERSATION STARTER (in Conversation lessons). The Conversation Starter activity is the culminating activity of the Conversation lessons. In this activity, students demonstrate progress and mastery of the lesson's communication goal. Most activities are facilitated by a "starter"—the first line of the Conversation Snapshot for students to personalize as they like, using names, different vocabulary, or other appropriate social language they have learned. Illustrations, photos, and cues are often provided to help students think of how to develop the conversation. Students are prompted to personalize the conversation model, apply it to another topic, and extend it as much as possible. Many Conversation Starter sections also include related topics to encourage students to extend the topic and target language of the lesson into other, freer discussions.

The most important way to maximize the value of the Conversation Starter practice is to encourage experimentation, showing approval when students create a personal adaptation of the original model and continue it in unscripted ways. Be sure students don't think the purpose of the practice is to test their memory of the original Conversation Snapshot. It is exactly the opposite. As they practice, students should use their own language, as well as the target vocabulary or grammar.

Begin by reading the instructions aloud. Then begin the conversation with a more advanced student to demonstrate that students should use new language from the lesson and draw from other sources. If helpful, point out the language available on the two-page lesson for students to use. Note that the conversations each pair of students creates will vary.

Encourage students to find a new partner for each Conversation Starter activity. As students practice, circulate and offer help as needed. Remind students to make eye contact during conversations to facilitate authentic communication, and encourage them to use natural pronunciation and intonation. An option is to have students do the Conversation Starter a few times with different partners. Also, you can ask a couple of pairs to "perform" or recreate their conversation for the class or have pairs do this for each other. Having different pairs of students perform their Conversation Starter in front of the class reminds all students of how much social language they have learned.

Conversation Prompts. 💿 The Conversation Prompts can be printed out from the Teacher's Resource Disk. They are designed to remind students of language they have already learned in the unit—and in previous units—that they can use in the Conversation Starter activities. They can be used as an alternative approach to the Conversation Starter—with books closed—or simply as additional language support for the Conversation Starter with books open.

GRAMMAR EXCHANGE (in Grammar lessons). Just as the Conversation Starter activity ends Conversation lessons, the Grammar Exchange activity is the culminating activity of the Grammar lessons. In this structured activity, students demonstrate progress and mastery of the lesson's communication goal as well as use the grammar communicatively. Notepads and charts are often provided for students to create a concrete reference to support them as they discuss a topic. Frequent examples of appropriate oral and written responses are included so students know what is expected. In those examples, target grammar from the lesson shows students how the grammar can support their expression.

Begin by reading the instructions and any example sentences aloud. Then ask a more advanced student to demonstrate new language from the lesson, encouraging that student to draw from other sources as well. If helpful, point out the language available on the two-page lesson for students to use. Note that the examples each student creates will vary.

As students practice, circulate and offer help as needed. Keep the lesson's grammar in mind when observing students' discussions. For example, in Unit 8, where students learn double comparatives, encourage them to use that structure as follows:
S: *People are marrying later and later.* T: *And the later people marry? What's a result of that?* S: *The later people marry, the fewer children they have.* Remind students to make eye contact during conversations, and encourage them to use

natural pronunciation and intonation. Vary and change the pairing of students to keep the ideas fresh and interesting.

■ Lessons 3 and 4: Free discourse focus with Reading or Listening

Lessons 3 and 4, labeled either Reading or Listening, begin with a communication goal such as "Describe what makes a person beautiful," and culminate in a Discussion Builder in which students achieve that communication goal.

Lessons 3 and 4 open with either a reading or a listening. These provide authentic, interesting, and stimulating language input and lead students to free communication. Vocabulary or Word Skills are usually included and range from one-word items to collocations and idioms to phrases. Vocabulary meaning is clearly conveyed through illustrations, definitions, and/or contextual sentences. The vocabulary is usually re-entered in the reading or listening and then practiced in the exercises and activities that follow.

READING WARM-UP (in Reading lessons). This exercise consists of a question or series of questions that prompts students to start thinking about the topic of the reading. Before students read, they relate the content of the reading to their own lives. This process generates interest and aids understanding. Read the Reading Warm-up question(s) aloud. Model the activity by answering the questions yourself. Students can answer the questions with a partner or in small groups. To review, ask a few students to share their responses with the class. Specific suggestions can be found in the Lesson Plans.

Before students read, have them look at any photos or illustrations. If appropriate, ask questions about these visuals. Give students a few minutes to look at the selection independently. Encourage them to look at the title and any headings to help give them an idea of what the reading is about.

READING (in Reading lessons). The instructions before the readings also ask a question to help focus students' attention as they read. Ask students to try to answer the question as they read. At the end, the question can be asked of the class to see what conclusions students have come to.

All readings are based on authentic sources. To avoid frustrating students with dense, difficult, lengthy texts, language has often been adapted from the original sources, and most articles have been shortened. However, we have taken great care to maintain the authentic character of the material.

In order to help students grow, readings contain language that students have not yet learned but that they should be able to comprehend through context and similarity to language they know. However, it is important that students understand that it is not necessary for them to know what every word means in order to understand the selection. Encourage students to guess at the meaning of new words as much as possible or to comprehend as much as they can without understanding every word. After students read, ask questions that lead them to figure out the meaning of new language and that help them to identify the essential information from the reading. Such questions and activities are provided in the Lesson Plans.

Comprehension or discussion activities always follow the reading; some exercise types are factual questions, multiple choice activities, and cloze activities that demonstrate understanding of information or of vocabulary from context. Open-ended questions requiring free expression are also frequent. Students are often asked to justify their answers by finding supporting documentation in the text or by providing personal reasoning or examples from their lives or experience.

Some of the exercises that follow the reading also prompt students to use context to figure out the meaning of new language or to identify the most important information from the reading. Read the directions for each exercise aloud or ask for a volunteer to read them. Have students read the exercise items and then reread the selection independently. As students read, they can underline words or information in the reading that will help them to complete the exercise. Allow students a set period of time to refer to the reading as necessary to complete the exercise individually, in pairs, or in small groups. Have students check their work with a partner, have pairs or groups check their work with another pair or group, or review answers as a class. For a challenge, have students practice reading the selection aloud in small groups.

Note that all readings are recorded in the Class Audio Program, and listening to the reading is a recommended optional activity. Listening to a native speaker read aloud gives excellent ear training for the rhythm, stress, and intonation of extended (as opposed to conversational) speech. It also helps students learn collocations. It is recommended that students be given an opportunity to read and listen to each reading. You may treat reading and listening separately, or reading and listening can be done together. We recommend reading first, then listening afterward. However, you may wish to use the reading as a listening activity with closed books.

Reading Strategies. 💿 These worksheets can be printed out from the Teacher's Resource Disk. They are designed to teach specific strategies that support critical thinking and more effective reading. Strategies include classifying information, identifying supporting details, focusing on key causes and effects, and more.

Reading Speed Calculator. 💿 This complete chart can be printed out from the Teacher's Resource Disk. It includes total word counts of the main reading selections from every unit and a simple formula for calculating reading speed for each. If you choose to use this optional worksheet, each student should get a copy at the beginning of the term so he or she can record and compare reading speeds throughout the course.

Extra Reading Comprehension Activities. 💿 If you want more extensive comprehension questions than the ones that appear in the Student's Book or the Lesson Plans, you can print them out from the Teacher's Resource Disk. The Extra Reading Comprehension Activities contain both traditional comprehension and critical thinking questions. You may choose to use either or both with your class.

LISTENING COMPREHENSION (in Listening lessons).
Listening Comprehension activities in Lessons 3 and 4 provide the principle listening comprehension practice of the unit, containing language both at students' productive level as well as at the more challenging receptive (+1) level. All receptive-level language in the listening comprehension text is comprehensible to students through context, intonation, and similarity to language they already know.

Point out to students that a major cause of lack of comprehension is the natural panic that occurs when learners hear unknown words. Explain that it is not necessary to understand every word to understand the selection. To maximize the effectiveness of these activities, avoid providing students with explanations of new language beyond any vocabulary that was taught prior to the Listening. If a student specifically asks about a new word, give the meaning, but do not spend a lot of time on it. Exposure to receptive-level language promotes students' language development and prepares students to communicate in the world outside the classroom, where language is uncontrolled.

In general, it is suggested that students listen to the selection the first time with books closed. (In some cases, the Lesson Plans provide an alternative approach.) In this way, students can focus on the "big picture" without the distraction of completing the exercise. If information about the speakers, the setting, or the situation is included in the directions in the Student's Book, it is helpful to read this information aloud to make sure students focus on it. Alternatively, you might prefer to ask (after the first listening) *Who's talking? Where are the people? What are the people doing?* If students are not forthcoming with answers to those questions, you can restate the question, providing two answers from which to choose. The value of this practice is to convince students that they have, in fact, understood a good deal, even if they have not understood everything. This is an essential listening skill for foreign-language learners.

Before students listen again and complete the exercise, have them look at the exercise first to focus their attention on the specific listening task such as listening for locations or opinions. Play the audio as many times as necessary for students to complete the activity. Do not approach these exercises as "tests." Repeated exposure to each listening sample has substantial instructional value. Increasing students' exposure to challenging language enhances their comprehension and confidence. Review answers as a class, or have students check answers with a partner.

Note that the Listening Comprehension exercises are not on the Student's Take-Home Audio CD. If you do not have the Class Audio Program, read aloud the audioscript located at the back of this book (beginning on page AS1) to your students.

Accented speakers. In order to accustom students to listening to English in the real world, the *Summit* audio program includes a number of non-native speakers of English as well as native speakers with regional variations of both American and British English. The Lesson Plans provide the first language or country of origin of each accented speaker—information that may be interesting or informative to your class.

Note that accented speakers in *Summit* are heard only in receptive listening texts, not in productive models that students repeat.

Listening Strategies. 💿 These worksheets can be printed out from the Teacher's Resource Disk. They are designed to teach specific strategies that support critical thinking and more effective listening. Strategies include inferring point of view, listening for discourse markers, taking notes, predicting, and more.

DISCUSSION BUILDER. Both Lessons 3 and 4 culminate in an activity labeled Discussion Builder. The goal of this activity is to engage students in free and open-ended discussions, role plays, debates, and presentations. The Discussion Builder may also include a writing activity.

Free discussion is the goal of all language learners. But foreign-language students often have difficulty with free expression because the combination of gathering their thoughts and remembering the language they know is very challenging and often leads to silent panic. Students need to move beyond the controlled safety of models and info-gaps to more extensive self-expression. The Discussion Builders are deliberately constructed to provide prepared opportunities for students to experiment and succeed—because each task elicits language that is known.

A series of steps prepares students so they will feel confident. Notepad activities prompt students to make notes that organize their ideas and provide speaking or writing points for the discussions, presentations, or writing activities that follow. Students often compare notes with classmates for additional input. They also fill out surveys, answer questions, and look at visual stimuli such as photos and illustrations. When it is time to actually discuss a topic, they already have the language and the ideas laid out in front of them.

The Discussion Builders have been carefully designed so that students can use language learned from current *and* previous units. Massive opportunities for recycling language occur throughout *Summit*.

Discourse Strategies. 🖭 Discourse Strategies can be printed out from the Teacher's Resource Disk. They are designed to help students manage discussion more effectively. Strategies are presented and immediately followed by a pair work activity to practice them before applying them in the actual Discussion Builder on the Student's Book page. Strategies include asking for agreement, showing interest or surprise, paraphrasing an opinion, and more.

■ *Writing and Checkpoint*

WRITING. Each unit of *Summit* contains a page entirely dedicated to building students' writing skills. The *Summit* writing syllabus includes rigorous practice of important writing skills such as writing topic sentences, providing supporting details, connecting ideas, and organizing the essay. Each writing page begins with a presentation of the writing skill and includes numerous examples. Usually a writing model provides students with a sample of what is expected. When appropriate, there is an error correction exercise. Each assignment is laid out step-by-step, beginning with Prewriting to help students generate ideas. This step usually includes questions to answer, diagrams and charts to complete, or another device to help students organize their thoughts. The next step is Writing, and it has clear instructions on the type and length of writing expected. Because revision is an integral part of writing, each writing page has a Self-Check where students are asked focused questions to help them review their own writing. Sometimes an additional step, Peer Response, is included where students review each other's work and can offer suggestions for revision.

Extra Writing Skills Practice. 🖭 These worksheets can be printed out from the Teacher's Resource Disk. They offer additional reinforcement through controlled practice of the writing skill taught in the unit's writing lesson. They help students build confidence to apply these skills in their own free writing.

Graphic Organizers. 🖭 These charts, Venn diagrams, and idea clusters can be printed out from the Teacher's Resource Disk. They are designed to be used with a variety of *Summit* activities such as grammar, reading, listening, discussion, and writing—whenever the opportunity arises to organize ideas graphically. They can be completed individually, as a class, or by students in pairs or groups. There is usually an example of each graphic organizer on the Lesson Plan page.

CHECKPOINT. The Checkpoint reviews the essential content of the unit and offers students the opportunity to check their progress. It also allows the teacher to identify any areas of particular difficulty that may require additional practice. The Checkpoint page begins with a listening comprehension exercise that focuses on target language from the unit. The Checkpoint page also includes exercises that review vocabulary, grammar, and social language from the unit.

Have students work individually to complete the Checkpoint exercises. Circulate to offer help as needed. Review the correct answers as a class. Note any areas of difficulty and provide additional instruction and practice as necessary.

***Summit* Companion Website.** The website contains resources for teachers and online activities for students to accompany each unit. These activities are appropriate for use at the end of each unit.

We sincerely hope you enjoy *Summit* and that you
and your students find it an effective course.

Joan Saslow and Allen Ascher

SUMMIT

English for Today's World

1

Joan Saslow • Allen Ascher

PEARSON
Longman

Scope and Sequence OF CONTENT AND SKILLS

SCOPE AND SEQUENCE

UNIT	Vocabulary*	Conversation Strategies	Discussion Topics	Gramma
1 **New Perspectives** *Page 2*	• Personality types **Word Skill:** classifying by positive and negative meaning	• Ask a question to buy time • Use *Actually* to soften a negative response • Answer a question and then ask a similar one to show interest • Use *I wonder* to elicit an opinion politely • Use *You know* to indicate that you are about to offer advice or a suggestion	• Finding balance in life • Different personality types • Optimism vs. pessimism • Perspectives on life • Life-changing experiences	• Gerunds and infinitives: changes in meaning
2 **Musical Moods** *Page 14*	• Elements of music • Describing creative personalities **Word Skill:** using participial adjectives	• Use *So* to indicate a desire to begin a conversation • Confirm information with *right?* • Use *You know* to introduce information and be less abrupt • Begin answers with *Well* to introduce an opinion	• Musical tastes • The role of music in your life • Creative personalities • The benefits of music • The uses of music therapy	• The present perfect and the present perfect continuous: finished and unfinished actions • Noun clauses
3 **Money Matters** *Page 26*	• Expressing buyer's remorse • Describing spending habits • Charity and investment	• Use *Hey* to indicate enthusiasm • Use *To tell you the truth* to introduce an unexpected assertion • Ask *What do you mean?* to clarify • Provide an example to back up a statement or opinion	• Your financial IQ • Your short-term and long-term financial goals • Buyer's remorse • Spending habits • Charitable giving	• Future plans and finished future actions • The past unrea conditional: inverted form
4 **Looking Good** *Page 38*	• Describing fashion and style **Word Skill:** using the prefix *self-*	• Use *Can you believe* to indicate disapproval • Use *Don't you think* to promote consensus • Begin a response with *Well* to convey polite disagreement or reservation • Stress the main verb to acknowledge only partial agreement	• Appropriate dress • How clothing affects the way others perceive you • Fashions and hairstyles • How men and women change their appearances • The media's influence on body image • Beauty on the outside vs. beauty on the inside	• Quantifiers
5 **Community** *Page 50*	• Ways to soften an objection • Ways to perform community service **Word Skill:** using negative prefixes to form antonyms	• Use *Do you mind* to express concern that an intended action may offend • Use *Actually* to object politely • Use expressions such as *I hope that's not a problem* to soften an objection • Say *Not at all* to indicate a willingness to comply	• Urban life vs. rural life • Behavior in public places • Social responsibility • Urban problems	• Possessives with gerunds • Paired conjunctions

*Vocabulary presentations in *Summit* include individual words, phrases, and collocations.

iv

Grammar and Pronunciation Boosters	Listening Tasks	Readings	Writing
Grammar Booster • Gerunds and infinitives: summary **Grammar for Writing:** parallelism with gerunds and infinitives **Pronunciation Booster** • Content words and function words	• Rephrase descriptions of people • Identify main ideas • Infer what people mean • Categorize people by personality type	• A magazine article about finding balance in life • A magazine article about optimism vs. pessimism	• Describe personality types **Writing Skill:** the paragraph
Grammar Booster • Finished and unfinished actions: summary • The past perfect continuous **Grammar for Writing:** noun clauses as adjective and noun complements **Pronunciation Booster** • Intonation patterns	• Evaluate three pieces of music • Recognize gist before details • Determine benefits and provide examples • Identify points of view	• Brief CD reviews from a website • Interviews: the role of music in one's life • A biography of Ludwig van Beethoven	• Describe yourself **Writing Skill:** parallel structure
Grammar Booster • The future continuous • The future perfect continuous **Pronunciation Booster** • Sentence rhythm: thought groups	• Infer what people mean • Focus on main ideas • Distinguish advice from other information • Summarize problems	• Financial tips from a newspaper • Interviews: financial goals • A magazine article about Paul Newman's philanthropy	• Explain your financial goals **Writing Skill:** sequencing events
Grammar Booster • Quantifiers: *a few* and *few, a little* and *little* • Quantifiers: using *of* • Quantifiers: used without referents **Grammar for Writing:** subject-verb agreement with quantifiers with *of* **Pronunciation Booster** • Linking sounds	• Identify points of view • Rephrase information • Summarize information • Infer what people mean	• A newspaper article about casual dress at work • A magazine article about how the media affects self-image	• Compare two people's tastes in fashion **Writing Skill:** compare and contrast
Grammar Booster • Conjunctions with *so, too, neither,* or *not either*: usage, form, and short responses **Pronunciation Booster** • Unstressed syllables: vowel reduction to /ə/	• Summarize a detailed story • Collaborate to understand details • Infer what people mean	• A graph depicting world population changes • Interviews: pet peeves about public conduct • An interview with Dr. Janice Perlman about "megacities"	• Complain about a problem **Writing Skill:** formal letters

Scope and Sequence OF CONTENT AND SKILLS

UNIT	Vocabulary	Conversation Strategies	Discussion Topics	Gramma
6 **Animals** *Page 62*	• Ways animals are used or treated • Describing pets • Describing character traits	• Use *I've heard* to introduce a statement of popular opinion • Use *For one thing* to provide one reason among several in supporting an argument • Use *Believe it or not* to introduce surprising information	• The treatment of animals • The advantages and disadvantages of different pets • Animal characters in books, cartoons, TV programs, and movies • The value of animal conservation	• The passive voice with modals
7 **Advertising and Consumers** *Page 74*	• Describing low prices and high prices • Shopping expressions • Ways to persuade	• Soften a wish or a statement of intent with *I think* • Ask questions to narrow scope • Say *Of course* to make an affirmative answer stronger	• Appropriate pricing • Smart shopping • Reactions to ads • Advertising techniques • Compulsive shopping	• Passive forms of gerunds and infinitives
8 **Family Trends** *Page 86*	• Examples of bad behavior • Describing parent and teen behavior **Word Skill:** transforming verbs and adjectives into nouns	• Use *I hate to say it, but* to introduce unwelcome information • Respond with *I suppose* to indicate partial agreement • Use *But* to introduce a dissenting opinion	• Conflicts in relationships • Birthrates and life expectancy • Parent–teen issues • Changing family demographics • Generational issues and concerns • Current family trends • Care for the elderly	• Repeated comparatives and double comparatives
9 **History's Mysteries** *Page 98*	• Ways to say "I don't know." • Ways to express certainty **Word Skill:** using adjectives with the suffix *-able*	• Use *Well* to introduce an encouraging statement • Say *You're probably right* to acknowledge another's encouragement • Ask a question with *Why else* to confirm one's own opinion	• Theories that best explain mysteries • The credibility of stories • Trustworthy news sources	• Indirect speech with modals • Perfect modals in the passive voice for speculating about the past
10 **Your Free Time** *Page 110*	• Ways to express fear and fearlessness **Word Skill:** using collocations for leisure activities **Word Skill:** modifying with adverbs	• Use *kind of* to soften an assertion • Use *I hate to say this, but* to excuse oneself for disagreeing • Use *Well, even so* to acknowledge someone's point but disagree politely	• The benefits of leisure activities • Hobbies and interests • Your use of leisure time • Extreme sports • Risk-taking vs. risk-avoidance	• Order of modifiers

Grammar and Pronunciation Boosters	Listening Tasks	Readings	Writing
• Modals and modal-like expressions: summary • Sound reduction	• Rephrase descriptions • Determine the moral of a story • Identify character traits • Focus on details	• The Chinese Zodiac • A discussion board about the humane treatment of animals • An article about animal conservation	• Express an opinion on animal treatment **Writing Skill:** persuasion
Grammar for Writing: past forms of gerunds and infinitives: active and passive voice • Vowel sounds /i/ and /ɪ/	• Identify points of view • Rephrase what people are doing • Match advertising techniques to ads • Determine people's attitudes	• Interviews: reactions to ads • A presentation of eight advertising techniques • A magazine article about compulsive shopping	• Explain an article you read **Writing Skill:** writing a summary
• Making comparisons: summary • Other uses of comparatives, superlatives, and comparisons with *as . . . as* • Stress placement: prefixes and suffixes	• Summarize demographic information • Rephrase people's points of view • Focus on details • Classify information to compare two generations • Apply logic to information	• A brochure about falling birthrates • A newspaper article about China's elderly population • Case studies: aging parents	• Describe your relationship with a family member **Writing Skill:** avoiding comma splices and run-on sentences
• Reporting verbs *say, ask,* and *tell:* summary **Grammar for Writing:** other reporting verbs • Reduction and linking in perfect modals in the passive voice	• Summarize main ideas • Identify information that supports an argument • Infer what people mean	• "The World's Easiest Quiz" • Descriptions of Bigfoot, the Loch Ness Monster, and the Bermuda Triangle • Encyclopedia entries about well-known mysteries • A magazine article about the world's greatest hoaxes	• Write a news article **Writing Skill:** avoiding sentence fragments
• Intensifiers • Adverbs of manner • Vowel sounds /eɪ/, /ɛ/, /æ/, and /ʌ/	• Classify information to define terms • Match activities with people, according to the information they imply	• Statistics comparing technological promises vs. reality • Case studies: stressful situations • Message-board posts about unusual hobbies • A magazine article about technology and leisure time	• Comment on another's point of view **Writing Skill:** expressing and supporting your opinion

International Advisory Board

Reviewers and Piloters Many thanks also to the reviewers and piloters all over the world who reviewed *Top Notch* and *Summit* in their final forms.

To the Teacher

What is *Summit*?

- *Summit* is a two-level high-intermediate to advanced communicative series for adults and young adults that can follow any intermediate course book.
- *Summit* is designed to follow the *Top Notch* series, forming the top two levels of a six-level course.
- Each *Summit* Student's Book is designed for 60 to 90 instructional hours with options and extensions that enable it to fulfill the needs of longer courses.

Key Elements of the *Summit* Instructional Design

Concise two-page lessons

Each easy-to-teach two-page lesson is designed for one class session and begins with a clearly stated communication goal and ends with free communication practice. Each lesson integrates all four skills with a focus on conversation, grammar, reading, or listening, keeping the pace of a class session lively and varied.

Daily confirmation of progress

Adult students need to observe and confirm their own progress. In *Summit*, students conclude each class session with a culminating productive activity that demonstrates their ability to use new vocabulary, grammar, word skills, and social language in order to perform the communication goal of the lesson. This motivates students and keeps them eager to continue their study of English, and it builds their pride in being able to speak and write accurately, fluently, and authentically.

Real language

Carefully exposing students to authentic, natural, corpus-informed English, both receptively and productively, is a necessary component of building understanding and expression. All Conversation Snapshots and Sound Bites feature the language people *really* use; nowhere to be found is "textbook English" written merely to exemplify grammar.

Memorable model conversations

Even at the advanced levels, learners need models of social language plus strategies they can use conversationally. The full range of social and functional communicative needs as well as a wealth of conversation strategies are presented through practical model conversations that are intensively practiced and applied to the learner's own life experience. Rhythm and intonation practice and an optional Pronunciation Booster provide targeted practice to ensure clear expression.

High-impact vocabulary syllabus

In order to ensure students' solid acquisition of vocabulary essential for communication, *Summit* contains explicit presentation and practice of words, collocations, and expressions appropriate at each level of study. A focus on word skills, such as using prefixes and participial adjectives, builds students' ability to cope with and expand on new vocabulary. Meaning is conveyed in a variety of ways: through captioned photographs and illustrations, within the context of realia and readings, in definitions and contextualized sentences, and in authentic dictionary entries from the *Longman Advanced American Dictionary*. These presentations provide a permanent in-book reference that builds learner independence and helps students prepare for tests.

Learner-supportive grammar

Grammar is approached explicitly and cognitively, through form, meaning, and use, in the following places in *Summit*: in every Student's Book unit, in the bound-in Grammar Booster, in the *Summit* Workbook, in the optional worksheets provided on the Teacher's Resource Disk (found in the Teacher's Edition and Lesson Planner), and on the *Summit* companion website. Grammar charts provide examples and paradigms enhanced by simple usage notes at students' level of comprehension. This takes the guesswork out of meaning, makes lesson preparation easier for teachers, and provides students with comprehensible charts for permanent reference and test preparation. All presentations of grammar, both in the Student's Book and in the Grammar Booster, include exercises to ensure adequate practice.

Detailed writing syllabus

The *Summit* Student's Book contains a writing syllabus that includes rigorous practice and clear models of important rhetorical and mechanical writing skills, such as parallelism, summarizing, and punctuation. Each lesson provides practice in the writing process, from prewriting to revision.

Unique discussion syllabus

All students want and need to participate in real discussions. *Summit* systematically goes beyond conversation model practice through unique step-by-step Discussion Builders that enable students to prepare for successful discourse. This preparation results in increased accuracy, increased fluency, greater complexity of expression, richer use of vocabulary, and much less fossilization. The Teacher's Resource Disk offers further optional practice with Discourse Strategies, to ensure successful communication.

Components of *Summit 1*

Student's Book

The Student's Book contains a bound-in Grammar Booster, a bound-in Pronunciation Booster, and a Student's Take-Home Audio CD that allows students to practice their pronunciation at home or during their commute.

Teacher's Edition and Lesson Planner

The Teacher's Edition and Lesson Planner offers complete lesson plans for each class session. Suggested teaching times are included for each activity to take the guesswork out of planning. Bound into each Teacher's Edition and Lesson Planner is a free Teacher's Resource Disk with the following optional printable activities to personalize your teaching style:

- Vocabulary-Building Strategies
- Discourse Strategies
- Listening Strategies
- Reading Strategies
- Grammar Self-Checks
- Conversation Prompts
- Extra Writing Skills Practice
- Pronunciation Activities
- A Reading Speed Calculator
- Extra Reading Comprehension Activities
- Graphic Organizers

Complete Class Audio Program

The Class Audio Program contains listening comprehension activities, rhythm and intonation practice, and targeted pronunciation activities that focus on accurate and comprehensible pronunciation.

Because *Summit* is a course for international communication, a variety of native *and* non-native speakers are included to prepare students for the world outside the classroom.

Workbook

The tightly linked, illustrated Workbook contains exercises that provide additional practice and reinforcement of language concepts and skills from *Summit* and its Grammar Booster.

Complete Assessment Package with Exam*View*® Software

Ten easy-to-administer and simple-to-score unit achievement tests assess listening, vocabulary, grammar, social language, reading, and writing. Two review tests, one mid-book and one end-of-book, provide additional cumulative assessment. A speaking test and a writing test are included with each review. In addition to the photocopiable achievement tests, Exam*View*® software enables teachers to tailor-make tests to best meet their needs by combining items any way they wish.

Summit TV

An engrossing and informative video offers excerpts from authentic TV documentaries as well as unrehearsed on-the-street interviews with English speakers from around the world. Both the documentaries and the interviews are thematically tied to the *Summit* units in order to initiate and promote classroom discussion.

Summit Companion Website

The *Summit* Companion Website www.longman.com/summit provides numerous additional resources for students and teachers. This no-cost, high-benefit feature includes opportunities for further practice of language and content from the *Summit* Student's Book.

Welcome to Summit!

About the Authors

JOAN SASLOW is author of a number of textbook series for adults and young adults, including *Ready to Go: Language, Lifeskills, and Civics*, a four-level adult ESL series; *Workplace Plus: Living and Working in English*, a vocational English series; *Literacy Plus*, a two-level series that teaches literacy, English, and culture to adult pre-literate students; and *English in Context: Reading Comprehension for Science and Technology*, a three-level series for English for special purposes.

Ms. Saslow is co-author, with Allen Ascher, of *Top Notch: English for Today's World*. She was the Series Director of *True Colors: An EFL Course for Real Communication* and of *True Voices*, a five-level EFL video course. Ms. Saslow's special interest is in distinguishing the needs of the EFL and the ESL learner and creating materials appropriate for each.

Ms. Saslow has taught in Chile and the United States in a variety of programs. In Chile, she taught English and French at the Binational Centers of Valparaíso and Viña del Mar, and at the Catholic University of Valparaíso. In the United States, Ms. Saslow taught English as a Foreign Language to Japanese university students at Marymount College's intensive English program as well as workplace English at the General Motors auto assembly plant, both in Tarrytown, New York. Ms. Saslow is also an editor, a teacher-trainer, a language learner, and a frequent speaker at gatherings of English teachers throughout the world. Ms. Saslow has an M.A. in French from the University of Wisconsin.

ALLEN ASCHER, formerly Director of the International English Institute at Hunter College in New York, has been a teacher, a teacher-trainer, an author, and a publisher. He has taught in language and teacher-training programs in both China and the United States. Mr. Ascher specialized in teaching listening and speaking to students at the Beijing Second Foreign Language Institute, to hotel workers at a major international hotel in China, and to Japanese students from Chubu University studying English at Ohio University in the United States. In New York, Mr. Ascher taught students of all language backgrounds and abilities at the City University of New York, and he trained teachers in the TESOL Certificate Program at the New School. Mr. Ascher has an M.A. in Applied Linguistics from Ohio University.

Mr. Ascher is co-author, with Joan Saslow, of *Top Notch: English for Today's World*. He is author of *Think About Editing: A Grammar Editing Guide for ESL Writers*. As a publisher, Mr. Ascher played a key role in the creation of some of the most widely used materials for adults, including *True Colors, NorthStar, Focus on Grammar, Global Links*, and *Ready to Go*. Mr. Ascher has provided lively workshops for teachers throughout the United States, Asia, Latin America, Europe, and the Middle East.

New Perspectives

UNIT GOALS

1 Suggest ways to enjoy life more
2 Describe people's personalities
3 Compare perspectives on life
4 Share a life-changing experience

A **Topic Preview.** Look at the map of the world. Where do you think the artist is from?

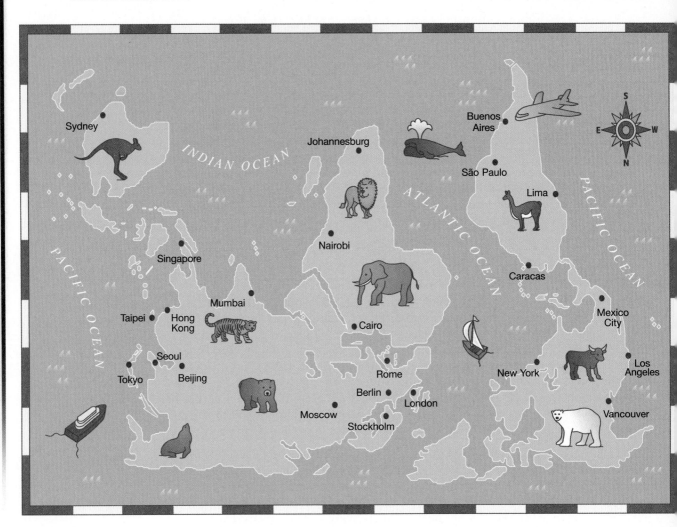

B **Discussion.**

1. What is unusual about the way the map depicts the world?
2. What do you think the artist is trying to say with the illustration? Is the artist being serious or funny?

New Perspectives

How to plan a *Summit* lesson

Suggested teaching times for the activities in each two-page lesson add up to a total of 45–60 minutes. To plan a class of approximately 45 minutes, use the shorter estimated teaching times when a range is shown. To plan a class of 60 or more minutes, use the longer estimated teaching times when a range is shown. Your actual teaching time will vary from the times suggested, according to your schedule and the needs of your class.

Activities labeled Option or Challenge are additional to the 45–60 minutes, and the estimated teaching time for each is noted with the activity. Similarly, any time you spend in class on the Grammar Booster or Pronunciation Booster is additional to the 45–60 minutes.

In addition to the notes, options, and challenges, you will see icons indicating other possible extensions to the material on the Student's Book page. These will also increase the time allotted to the lesson:

An extension activity from the Teacher's Resource Disk in the back of this Teacher's Edition

An episode from the *Summit TV* Video Program

A test from the Complete Assessment Package

At the end of each lesson is an item labeled Extras. These are optional activities that can be assigned as homework or class work. The activities include exercises from the Grammar Booster, exercises from the Pronunciation Booster, and exercises from the Workbook.

The *Summit* authors strongly encourage you to view these teacher's notes and accompanying options, challenges, extensions, and projects as a menu of possibilities in creating the best lesson plan for your class. The amount of class time required for individual projects will vary, as many teachers prefer to spread projects out over a number of lessons or assign them for homework. You may wish to construct your lesson entirely with the options, challenges, extensions, and projects or to extend the lesson, to do all possible activities.

A Topic Preview

Suggested teaching time:	5 minutes
Your actual teaching time:	_____

- To introduce the unit theme of new or unusual perspectives, have students spend a few moments looking closely at the illustration.

- Point to the illustration and ask *What kind of map is this?* (a world map) *Where do you think the artist is from?* Encourage students to explain their answers by asking *Why do you think so?* (Possible response: The artist is from the southern hemisphere because he put that area at the top of the map.)

B Discussion

Suggested teaching time:	5–10 minutes
Your actual teaching time:	_____

- Read the questions out loud. Have students discuss the answers in small groups. Circulate to offer help as needed.

- Review answers as a class. Have a student from each group present his/her response to the class. (Possible responses: 1. It's upside down. The positions of the continents in the southern hemisphere and the northern hemisphere are exchanged. 2. The artist is saying that the southern hemisphere is just as important as the northern hemisphere. The artist is being serious by showing us that our view of the world is affected by who we are and where we live.)

Language note: When you are *being serious,* you are not joking or pretending—you are saying what you really mean. When you are *being funny,* you are trying to amuse others or make them laugh.

Option: Geography review. Have students look at the map. Then walk around the room asking questions about the map, such as *What three cities are in Africa?* (Johannesburg, Nairobi, Cairo) *In which hemisphere is Stockholm?* (the northern hemisphere) Maintain a quick pace. **[+5 minutes]**

C 🎧 Sound Bites
(CD 1, Track 2)

Suggested teaching time:	5–10 minutes
Your actual teaching time:	_____

- Before reading and listening to the conversation, have students look at the photo. Ask *Do you think this photo was taken in this country? Where do you think this city is located? Why do you think so?* (Possible responses: no; France, England, Europe; because of the building styles)

- To provide background for the conversation, tell the class that they will hear a conversation between two colleagues working temporarily in another country. Elicit the meaning of the word *colleague* from the class. (a co-worker, someone you work with at your job)

- After students read and listen, check comprehension by asking *How does Gilbert feel about working in a foreign country?* (He's tired of it/doesn't enjoy it.) *Why?* (He doesn't like the strange food and has difficulty understanding the local language.) *Is Anna also tired of working in a foreign country?* (no) *Why not?* (She enjoys being in a foreign country, eating different food, and trying to figure out how to communicate.) *Do Gilbert and Anna feel the same way about the same experience?* (no)

> **Language note:** *Figure out* is think about something until you find an answer or solution.

D In Other Words

Suggested teaching time:	5–10 minutes
Your actual teaching time:	_____

- To model the activity, write on the board *Am I ready to head home!* Ask *Who said this?* (Gilbert) *What do you think he means?* (He wants to go home.)

- If necessary, help students use the context of the conversation to work out the meaning. For example, write *Oh, man!* before the sentence on the board. Ask *Why does Gilbert say this? How do you think he feels?* (He's unhappy.)

- Have students explain the meaning of each expression with a partner. Circulate to help students work out meaning from context. Students may paraphrase the statements or explain the meanings in indirect speech.

> **Language note:** Inverting the subject and verb can turn a statement into an exclamation. For example, *Am I ready to go home!* is more emphatic than *I am ready to go home.*

E Pair Work

Suggested teaching time:	5 minutes
Your actual teaching time:	_____

- Point to the four statements. To model the activity, read the first statement out loud—*I'm a little uncomfortable with places that are new to me.* Ask *Who do you think said this—Anna or Gilbert? Why do you think*

so? (Possible response: Gilbert, because he didn't like the new experience of working in a foreign country.)

- In pairs, have students read each statement and decide who they think said it. Circulate to offer help as needed.

- Review answers as a class. Have a volunteer read each statement, state who said it, and explain why he/she thinks so. Elicit different opinions or reasons from the class. (Possible response: Gilbert said, "I prefer to stick closer to home" because he prefers home to a foreign country.)

F Discussion

Suggested teaching time:	10 minutes
Your actual teaching time:	_____

- Form small groups and have students discuss the questions.

- Draw a two-column chart on the board with the heads *Anna* and *Gilbert*. Ask *How would you describe Anna's and Gilbert's personalities?* As you get feedback, write students' ideas in the columns. (Possible responses: **Anna:** adventurous; eager to learn more; shows interests in other cultures; **Gilbert:** dislikes different food; misses his home; finds it difficult to adapt to new customs)

- Have volunteers share their responses to item 2. Encourage them to support their choices. (Possible responses: I'm more like Gilbert. I don't like new experiences; I identify with Anna. I enjoy going to places with different customs.)

STARTING POINT

Suggested teaching time:	10 minutes
Your actual teaching time:	_____

- Have a volunteer read the phrases in the box out loud. Clarify any phrases students don't understand. Students may need help with the following: *pretty dull* (not very interesting or exciting); *more trouble than it's worth* (something that takes too much time and effort).

- Have students complete the chart individually. Encourage students to write their own ideas in the last box.

Pair Work

- Have students share their opinions of travel with a partner. Point out that they can use the expressions in Exercises D and E to support their views. (Possible response: In my opinion, travel can be kind of scary. I don't like trying new things or having trouble communicating. I prefer to stick closer to home.)

- Have volunteers share their opinions of travel with the class.

Challenge: If some students in the class have been abroad, ask them to tell the class what they liked / disliked about the experience. Encourage the use of language from Exercises D and E. **[+5 minutes]**

EXTRAS (optional)

Workbook: Exercises 1–2

C 🎧 **Sound Bites.** Read and listen to a conversation between two colleagues working temporarily in another country.

GILBERT: Oh, man! Am I ready to head home!
ANNA: Are you kidding? I can't get enough of this place.
GILBERT: Well, it's been three weeks, and I think I've had about enough. I'm tired of eating strange food. CN
ANNA: Wow! I feel just the opposite. I can't get over how much I enjoy being here. I love how different the food is.
GILBERT: Well, not me. And frankly, it's a pain in the neck having to work so hard to understand what people are saying to me.
ANNA: I actually think it's fun trying to figure out how to communicate. Stop complaining! You'll be home before you know it!
GILBERT: Fine by me. There's no place like home.

D **In Other Words.** Read the conversation again. With a partner, explain the meaning of each of the following statements.
Answers will vary, but may include:
1. "Am I ready to head home!"
   I'm really ready to go back home!
2. "I can't get enough of this place."
   I really like this place.
3. "I think I've had about enough."
   I don't want to be here anymore.
4. "I can't get over how much I enjoy being here."
   I can't believe how much I like it here.
5. "It's a pain in the neck having to work so hard."
   It's difficult to have to work so hard.
6. "There's no place like home."
   I'd rather stay close to home.

E **Pair Work.** Read each statement and decide who you think said it—Anna or Gilbert. Support your opinion with information from the conversation.

"I'm a little uncomfortable with places that are new to me."

"I love trying new things."

"I want some adventure in my life."

"I prefer to stick closer to home."

F **Discussion.**
1. How would you describe Anna's and Gilbert's personalities? How are they different?
2. Who are *you* more like, Gilbert or Anna?

CN **Corpus Notes:** The phrase *have had (about) enough* is frequently followed by the preposition *of* as in *I think I've had enough of being on vacation*. The expression *be tired of* is more frequently followed by a gerund phrase (*be tired of doing [something]*) than a noun (*be tired of [something]*). However, *I'm tired of eating strange food* and *I'm tired of strange food* have essentially the same meaning.

STARTING **POINT**

Pair Work. How do you each feel about travel? Complete the statement to reflect your own opinions. Explain why.

In my opinion, travel can be . . .

☐ a life-changing experience.	☐ pretty dull.	☐ more trouble than it's worth.
☐ kind of scary.	☐ an adventure.	☐ other: _____ .

1 Suggest ways to enjoy life more

A 🎧 GRAMMAR **SNAPSHOT.** Read the article and notice the use of <u>forget</u>, <u>stop</u>, and <u>remember</u>.

Finding Balance

Are you burning the candle at both ends? Do you feel you have no time for yourself? Do you **forget to call** family on birthdays or holidays? Have you **stopped going out** with friends because you're too busy? Do you have trouble relaxing and having fun?

If you recognize yourself, you should **remember to slow down** and **take** more time for everything. Living a balanced life is about integrating the many vital areas of your life, including your health, friends, family, work, and romance.

Here are some tips for restoring a healthy perspective. First, **remember to make** time for the important people in your life. **Stop over-scheduling** and spend quality time with friends and family. Second, learn to eat, talk, walk, and drive more slowly. And **don't forget to turn** your cell phone **off** sometimes. People who really want to talk to you will call back. Third, learn to live in the present and **stop worrying** about the future. And finally, take it easy and begin enjoying the simple things in life. **Stop to smell** the roses.

B **Discussion.**

1. Did you recognize yourself or someone you know in the article? Give examples.
2. Did you find the tips helpful? Why or why not?

1 Suggest ways to enjoy life more

A 🎧 GRAMMAR **SNAPSHOT**
(CD 1, Track 3)

Suggested teaching time:	10–15 minutes
Your actual teaching time:	_____

- Point to the two photos of the woman at her desk. Ask *How are these photos different?* (In the photo on the left, the woman looks stressed and is doing many things at the same time. Her desk is messy. In the photo on the right, she is calm, focused on one task, and her desk is organized.)

- Ask *What do you think is the subject of this article?* Write student guesses on the board. Have students listen to the article with books closed. As a class, decide which of the guesses on the board best summarizes the article.

- Have students listen to the article again as they read along.

- To check comprehension, ask *What does* Finding Balance *mean?* (Possible response: giving enough time to all the important areas of your life such as work, family, friends, health, and romance) *What problems does the article describe?* (not having enough free time, feeling stress, working too much) *What tips are suggested in the article?* (Make time with friends and family; Eat, talk, walk, and drive more slowly; Stop worrying about the future; Enjoy the simple things in life.) Write the tips on the board.

- Encourage students to restate each tip in their own words. Elicit from the class the meaning of expressions such as *make time for something* (find enough time to do something, even though you are busy), *over-scheduling* (schedule too many things), *quality time* (time that you spend giving someone your full attention), and *live in the present* (enjoy the present and not worry about the past or future).

- To preview the concept that verbs can change meaning when followed by a gerund or an infinitive, have students locate the phrases that contain the verbs *forget*, *stop*, and *remember*. As students read these phrases aloud, write them on the board in two columns, with verbs followed by a gerund on the left and verbs followed by an infinitive on the right. Point to the two columns and ask *How are the words on the left different from the words on the right?*

Language note: *Burn the candle at both ends* means be very busy both at work and in your social life. *Stop to smell the roses* means appreciate the beautiful things around you. *Live a balanced life* means find time for all the important aspects of life—work, family, health, and fun.

B Discussion

Suggested teaching time:	10 minutes
Your actual teaching time:	_____

- Have students discuss the questions in small groups.

- Circulate to offer help as needed. To encourage students to use language from the reading, ask questions such as *Do you know anyone who needs to stop over-scheduling? Do you think it's important to stop worrying about the future?*

- To review, have a volunteer from each group share his/her views with the class. Encourage the class to ask questions to get each volunteer to explain his/her answer.

C Grammar

Suggested teaching time:	10–15 minutes
Your actual teaching time:	_____

• To review gerunds and infinitives, write on the board:

SEE

seeing   to see

• Have the class identify the three parts of speech: *see* = base form, *seeing* = gerund, *to see* = infinitive.

• For more practice, make statements with either a gerund or an infinitive, and have students restate them chorally using the form you did not use. For example, say *She can't stand working late* and elicit from the class *She can't stand to work late*. Continue with *I prefer staying home; I started to write the report; He continued to call me Jane; They started to paint their house; She hates taking the train to work.*

• To illustrate that some verbs retain the same meaning when followed by either a gerund or an infinitive, write on the board:

She can't stand to work late.	I prefer to stay home.
She can't stand working late.	I prefer staying home.

Point to and read aloud the two sentences on the left and ask *Do these two sentences have a different meaning?* (no) Repeat for the sentences on the right.

• Have students read the first explanation and study the examples in the Grammar box.

• To illustrate the difference in meaning when a verb is followed by a gerund or an infinitive, write on the board:

Don't worry. I'll remember to pay it.

Yes. I remember paying it.

Ask *Are you going to pay the telephone bill tomorrow?* Point to the two responses on the board and elicit from the class that the correct response is *Don't worry. I'll remember to pay it.* Ask *Did you pay the telephone bill last week?* and elicit that the correct response is *Yes. I remember paying it.*

• Have students read the definitions and study the examples for *remember* + infinitive and *remember* + gerund in the Grammar box.

• On the board, write:

1. John will never forget cooking dinner for his family.
2. John forgot to cook dinner for his family.

Point to the first sentence and ask *Did John cook dinner?* (yes) Point to the second sentence and ask *Did John cook dinner?* (no)

• Have students read the definitions and study the examples for *forget* + infinitive and *forget* + gerund in the Grammar box.

• On the board, write:

Sally has just stopped to talk on the phone.

Sally has just stopped talking on the phone.

Point to the first sentence and ask *Is Sally on the phone?* (yes) Point to the second sentence and ask *Is Sally on the phone?* (no)

• Have students read the definitions and study the examples for *stop* + infinitive and *stop* + gerund in the Grammar box.

• Have a student read the Remember box out loud. Review that verbs can be followed by gerunds, infinitives, and also by objects and infinitives. On the board, write:

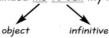

He reminded <u>me</u> <u>to call</u> my mother.

object   infinitive

Grammar Self-Checks

Option: For further practice with verbs followed by gerunds, infinitives, and objects and infinitives, refer students to page A3 in the Appendices. Tell students that you will use a verb incorrectly in a sentence and they will correct it. For example, *I finished to read the book you lent me.* (I finished reading the book you lent me.) *I promise calling you soon.* (I promise to call you soon.) *We decided staying longer.* (We decided to stay longer.) *They suggested to go out to dinner.* (They suggested going out to dinner.) *She offered helping plan the party.* (She offered to help plan the party.) **[+5 minutes]**

D Complete each sentence . . .

Suggested teaching time:	5 minutes
Your actual teaching time:	_____

• To model the exercise, copy item 1 on the board. Elicit from the class that the gerund *traveling* is the correct answer because this person is remembering something that happened in the past.

• Have students compare answers with a partner and review as a class. Have volunteers read the correct sentences and explain their choices.

GRAMMAR EXCHANGE

Suggested teaching time:	10–15 minutes
Your actual teaching time:	_____

Pair Work

• To prepare students for the activity, ask *What can people do to enjoy life more?* Write the example suggestion on the board and point out that the verb *stop* is followed by a gerund. Elicit a few suggestions from the class using *remember* and *forget*. (Possible responses: Remember to spend time with family. Don't forget to slow down.)

• Have students create a list with a partner. Circulate to help students make suggestions with *remember, forget,* and *stop.*

Group Work

• Form small groups. Encourage groups to create a list of at least five suggestions that everyone in the group agrees with.

• Have volunteers from each group share their ideas with the class. Write a list on the board as you get feedback from students.

EXTRAS (optional)

Grammar Booster
Workbook: Exercises 3–5

C Grammar. Gerunds and infinitives: changes in meaning

Some verbs are followed by either a gerund or an infinitive with no change in meaning,
for example: <u>love</u>, <u>hate</u>, <u>can't stand</u>, <u>like</u>, <u>prefer</u>, <u>begin</u>, <u>start</u>, <u>continue</u>.
Begin enjoying the simple things in life. OR **Begin to enjoy** the simple things in life.

Some verbs change meaning, depending on whether they are followed by a gerund or an infinitive.

<u>remember</u> + infinitive = remember to do something
Remember to make time for the important people in your life.
I have to **remember to send** an e-mail to my friend.

<u>remember</u> + gerund = remember something that happened in the past
I **remember having** more time for myself.
Do you **remember going** there when you were a kid?

<u>forget</u> + infinitive = forget to do something
Don't **forget to turn** your cell phone off.
He always **forgets to call** on my birthday.

<u>forget</u> + gerund = forget something that happened in the past
I'll never **forget seeing** the mountains for the first time.
Can you ever **forget going** to the beach?

<u>stop</u> + infinitive = stop in order to do something
Stop to smell the roses.
Can you **stop to pick up** some chocolates for the party?

<u>stop</u> + gerund = stop an ongoing action
Stop over-scheduling and spend quality time with friends and family.
You need to **stop worrying** so much.

> **REMEMBER**
>
> Some verbs are followed by infinitives.
>   Learn to live in the present.
> Some verbs are followed by gerunds.
>   I enjoy spending time with my friends.
> Some verbs are followed by objects and infinitives.
>   He reminded me to call my mother.
> For a complete list of verbs followed by gerunds, infinitives, and objects and infinitives, see page A3 in the Appendices.

PAGE G1
For more …

D Complete each sentence with a gerund or an infinitive.

1. I'll never forget (travel) _traveling_ abroad for the first time.

2. When I feel stressed out, I remember (put) _to put_ things in perspective.

3. You need to stop (try) _trying_ to do everything at once.

4. If I forget (send) _to send_ a card for a friend's birthday, I try to remember (call) _to call_ .

5. We forgot (buy) _to buy_ flowers, so we stopped (pick up) _to pick up_ some on the way to the party.

6. I remember (celebrate) _celebrating_ holidays with my family when I was young.

GRAMMAR **EXCHANGE** • *Now suggest ways to enjoy life more.*

Pair Work. Write a list of suggestions on your notepad for what someone can do to enjoy life more. Use <u>remember</u>, <u>forget</u>, and <u>stop</u>.

Stop worrying about the small things.

Group Work. Share your ideas with your class. Create a list of suggestions that everyone agrees with.

2 Describe people's personalities

A 🎧 CONVERSATION **SNAPSHOT**

A: Have you had a chance to meet the new manager? CN1

B: Liz? Actually, no. Have you?

A: Not yet. I wonder what she's like.

B: Well, everyone says she's bad news.

A: You know, you can't believe CN2 everything you hear. She might turn out to be a real sweetheart.

🎧 **Rhythm and intonation practice**

B 🎧 **Vocabulary. Personality types.** Listen and practice.

Positive	Negative
a sweetheart someone who is likable and easy to get along with	**a tyrant** someone, especially a boss, who makes people work extremely hard
a team player someone who works well with other people so the whole group is successful	**a workaholic** someone who is always working and does not have time for anything else
a brain someone who is intelligent and can solve problems that are difficult for others	**a pain in the neck** someone who complains a lot and often causes problems
a people person someone who likes being with and works well with other people	**a wise guy** someone who says or does annoying things, especially to make himself or herself seem smarter than other people

Pronunciation Booster

PAGE P1
Content words and function words

C 🎧 **Listening Comprehension.** Listen carefully to the conversations about people's personalities. Infer which expression the speaker would use to describe the person.

1. The woman thinks that Shelly is ....
   a. a sweetheart   **b.** a brain   **c.** a pain in the neck

2. The woman thinks that Peter is ....
   a. a workaholic   **b.** a tyrant   **c.** a team player

3. The man thinks that Paul is ....
   a. a team player   **b.** a people person   **c.** a wise guy

CN1 **Corpus Notes:** The expression *have a chance to* is used slightly less frequently in spoken English than *get a chance to*. However, the opposite is true for written English. Note that *get a chance to* is usually used in the past, almost never in the present.

CN2 **Corpus Notes:** *You know* is used very frequently in informal spoken English to begin a sentence, especially to call attention to what the speaker is about to say.

2 Describe people's personalities

A 🎧 CONVERSATION **SNAPSHOT**
(CD 1, Track 4)

Suggested teaching time:	5–10 minutes
Your actual teaching time:	_____

• Have students look at the photo and speculate about the people. Ask *Where are the people? What are they doing? Do you think this is a business or social situation?*

• Have students read and listen to the conversation.

• To check comprehension, ask *What is their relationship?* (They are co-workers.) *Who is Liz?* (the new manager) *Have the man and the woman met Liz yet?* (no) *Do the people in the office think she's nice?* (no) *What are the rumors about her?* (that she's bad news)

> **Language note:** When someone or something *turns out to be* different, it has a result that you did not expect.

🎧 Rhythm and intonation practice
(CD 1, Track 5)

Suggested teaching time:	5 minutes
Your actual teaching time:	_____

• Have students repeat chorally. Make sure they:

  ◦ use rising intonation for *Have you had a chance to meet the new manager?*

  ◦ use rising intonation for *Liz?* and *Have you?*

  ◦ use emphatic stress for you in *Have you had . . .* and *Have you?*

  ◦ use emphatic stress for everyone in *. . . everyone says . . .*

  ◦ stress can't in *. . . you can't believe . . .* and might in *She might turn out to be . . .*

  ◦ use the following stress pattern:

┌─**STRESS PATTERN***─────────────────────┐
│   •   —   •   •   •   •   —   —• •
│ **A:** Have you had a chance to meet the new manager?
│
│   —   —   • •   •   •   —
│ **B:** Liz? Actually, no. Have you?
│
│   •   •   —   •   •   •   —
│ **A:** Not yet. I wonder what she's like.
│
│   —   —   •   •   •   •   •
│ **B:** Well, everyone says she's bad news.
│
│   •   •   •   •   •   —   •   —
│ **A:** You know, you can't believe everything you hear. She
│
│   —   •   •   •   •   —   —
│ might turn out to be a real sweetheart.
└───┘

*The dots [•] and dashes [—] indicate the stress used in the recording. While there may be other correct ways to stress each of these utterances, what you see here is a representation of the stress you'll hear on the audio.

B 🎧 Vocabulary
(CD 1, Track 6)

Suggested teaching time:	5 minutes
Your actual teaching time:	_____

• Have students listen and study the positive and negative personality types and their definitions. Then have students listen and repeat the words chorally.

• Point out that the words are singular count nouns and are preceded by the article *a*.

• To check comprehension, read the following statements out loud and elicit the correct personality type for each: *This person is intelligent.* (a brain); *This person causes problems.* (a pain in the neck); *This person works well in a group.* (a team player); *This person likes working with people.* (a people person); *This person works all day.* (a workaholic); *This person makes people work too hard.* (a tyrant); *This person is very nice.* (a sweetheart); *This person irritates people.* (a wise guy)

Option: In pairs, have students come up with alternative definitions for each word. Join pairs to form groups of four. With books closed, have pairs take turns quizzing each other on the personality types. [+5–10 minutes]

Challenge: Present students with a list of other nouns used to describe personality. In small groups, have students try to guess the meaning of each noun and whether it is positive or negative. Some ideas are: **Positive:** a pussycat (someone who is very nice and gentle); a go-getter (an energetic person who is determined to succeed); a straight shooter (someone who is honest and direct); **Negative:** a know-it-all (someone who behaves as if they know everything); a pushover (someone who is easy to persuade, influence, or defeat); a wet blanket (someone who tries to spoil other people's fun). [+10–15 minutes]

💿 Vocabulary-Building Strategies

C 🎧 Listening Comprehension
(CD 1, Track 7)

Suggested teaching time:	5 minutes
Your actual teaching time:	_____

• Pre-listening: Have students read the items and their choices.

• First listening: Pause after each conversation to allow students time to choose the correct answer. In pairs, have students compare answers.

• Second listening: Have students listen again to check their work. Review answers as a class.

Option: Have students listen again. In pairs, have them listen for and write down a supporting sentence for each correct answer. Review as a class. Have volunteers present their supporting sentences to the class. If necessary, have students listen again to confirm answers. (1. "She's one of the most intelligent people I know!" 2. "He always asks me to work faster!" 3. "He seems to want people to think he's smarter than they are.") [+5 minutes]

AUDIOSCRIPT

For audioscript, see page AS1.

T6

D Word Skills

Suggested teaching time: 5–10 minutes
Your actual teaching time: _____

• Individually, have students classify the words that are familiar to them.

• In pairs, have students take turns asking each other the words they don't know. Have them use a dictionary to look up words that are unknown to both and then classify these words.

• Review as a class.

Challenge: Individually, have students write the names of four famous people and pick two or three adjectives from the box to describe each person. Then have pairs discuss. Student A tells his/her partner about the famous people he/she chose and describes them using adjectives from the box. Student B says whether he/she agrees with the descriptions. Then students change roles. **[+10 minutes]**

E Pair Work

Suggested teaching time: 10 minutes
Your actual teaching time: _____

• To model the activity, write on the board *a sweetheart* and elicit from the class several adjectives that match this personality type. Have students explain their choices. (Possible responses: friendly, helpful, loveable, easygoing)

• In pairs, have students write two to four adjectives for each personality type.

• Review as a class. Have volunteers present their responses and explanations to the class.

Option: Have each pair join another pair. Groups take turns reading the list of adjectives they selected for a personality type as the other pair tries to guess which personality type they are describing. Then pairs compare their lists and discuss why they chose similar or different adjectives. **[+5–10 minutes]**

CONVERSATION **STARTER**

Suggested teaching time: 10–15 minutes
Your actual teaching time: _____

Pair Work

• Have volunteers read the examples out loud. In each example, point out the personality types (*tyrant, people person*) and the supporting sentences describing what the person does or what the person is like.

• Read the words in the Ideas box out loud.

• In pairs, have students choose three people they know and describe them to each other.

• Circulate to encourage students to use adjectives from the Word Skills box and Vocabulary on page 6.

Role Play

• Refer students to the Conversation Snapshot on page 6 to review describing personalities.

• To model the activity, role-play a conversation about a person you haven't met yet with a more confident student.

• In pairs, have students role-play the conversation using language from the Conversation Snapshot and the Vocabulary on page 6.

• Circulate to offer help as needed. Encourage students to use the correct rhythm and intonation. Remind students to use rising intonation for *yes / no* questions and to stress relevant information. For example, *Have you had a chance to meet . . . ? Everyone says she's a pain in the neck.*

 Conversation Prompts

EXTRAS (optional)

Pronunciation Booster
Workbook: Exercises 6–9

D **Word Skills. Classifying by positive and negative meaning.** Fill in the diagram with
the adjectives in the box. Decide which adjectives describe personalities positively, negatively, or
both. Add other adjectives you know.

annoying	funny	lovable	outgoing	silly
easygoing	hardworking	modest	professional	smart
friendly	helpful	nervous	reliable	talkative
fun	impolite	offensive	serious	unfair

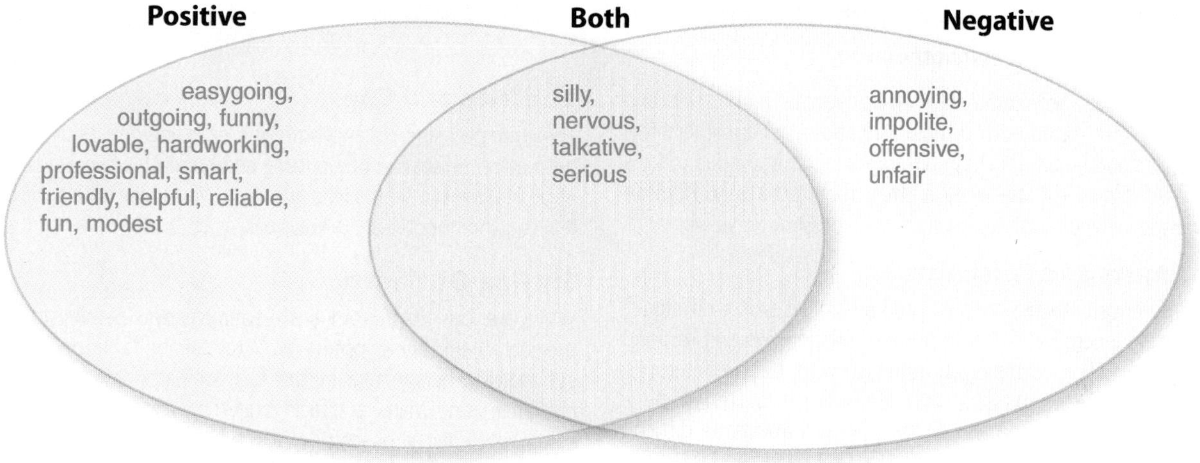

Positive	Both	Negative
easygoing, outgoing, funny, lovable, hardworking, professional, smart, friendly, helpful, reliable, fun, modest	silly, nervous, talkative, serious	annoying, impolite, offensive, unfair

E **Pair Work.** With a partner, write adjectives from the chart you think match each of the
personality types. More than one answer is possible. Explain your choices.
Answers will vary, but may include:
1. a sweetheart lovable, fun, friendly, outgoing
2. a team player helpful, reliable, modest, hardworking
3. a brain smart, serious, hardworking
4. a pain in the neck annoying, offensive
5. a tyrant unfair, annoying
6. a wise guy annoying, offensive, impolite, talkative
7. a people person friendly, talkative, fun, outgoing
8. a workaholic hardworking, serious

CONVERSATION **STARTER** • *Now describe people's personalities.*

Pair Work. Describe the personalities of people you know, using the
vocabulary from page 6 and other adjectives. Give specific examples
to explain.

IDEAS

a boss
a co-worker
a spouse
a classmate

a friend
a neighbor
a teacher
a relative

*"My sister is such a tyrant! She makes
her kids do all the housework!"*

*"My friend Hugo is a real people person.
He's so outgoing and friendly."*

Role Play. Role-play a conversation about a person you
haven't met yet. Use the Conversation Snapshot on page 6 as
a guide. Start like this: "Have you had a chance to meet …?"

3 Compare perspectives on life

A **Reading Warm-up.** Look at the glass of water. Do you see the glass as half full or half empty? What does that say about your perspective on life?

B 🎧 **Reading.** Read the article about optimism. How do optimists and pessimists respond to problems differently?

Maintaining a Positive Perspective

by Kali Munro, M.Ed., Psychotherapist

Have you ever wondered why some people feel down and defeated when faced with difficult situations, while others feel challenged and hopeful? These different reactions are due to how people interpret events—whether they think positively, from an optimistic viewpoint, or negatively, from a pessimistic viewpoint.

Optimists and Pessimists

The difference between optimists and pessimists isn't a difference in life experiences but rather in how people perceive and respond to problems. For example, an optimist who is going through a hard time feels confident that life will get better, while a pessimist is more cynical and believes life will always be difficult and painful. Pessimists tend to expect the worst and see only problems. Optimists, confronted with the same situations, expect the best. While a pessimist may give up, an optimist will look on the bright side and, instead of seeing a problem, will see a solution.

The Pros and Cons

There are pros and cons to both optimism and pessimism. A healthy dose of optimism can be uplifting and hopeful, while a healthy dose of pessimism can be realistic and wise. Achieving a balance of being realistic and hopeful isn't always easy.

Staying Optimistic

While we can learn from both optimists and pessimists, most of us need help being optimistic. Maintaining a hopeful, positive, yet realistic perspective in the face of hard times can be a real challenge—one many are facing right now in the world—but it is essential to living peacefully and happily. Just as it is important to recognize what is unjust and unfair in our lives and the world, it is important to see the beauty, love, generosity, and goodness as well.

Source: www.KaliMunro.com

C **Discussion.**

1. Do you agree with the author that "most of us need help being optimistic"? How do you think people can avoid negative thinking? Describe experiences from your own life.

2. In your opinion, are there times when optimism can be bad, or when pessimism can be good? Explain.

D **Pair Work.** How optimistic or pessimistic do you think these people are? Rate them on a scale of 1 to 5 (1 being very optimistic and 5 being very pessimistic). Circle the number. Explain your answers.

Answers will vary, but may include:

I wouldn't say that I'm cynical, but it's important to be realistic. Let's face it— life is hard.

I think I can keep things in perspective. I try not to think negatively, but I'm realistic about the things I can't change.

I try to look on the bright side. I think it's better to try to see a solution instead of seeing a problem.

I find it difficult when things get tough. I sometimes feel completely hopeless. I just don't expect things to get better.

I've had some bad experiences, but I think they've made me more realistic. It's not always possible to hope for the best, but good things *do* happen.

1 2 3 ④ 5

1 2 ③ 4 5

① 2 3 4 5

1 2 3 4 ⑤

1 ② 3 4 5

3 Compare perspectives on life

A Reading Warm-up

Suggested teaching time:	5 minutes
Your actual teaching time:	_____

- Ask students to look at the glass and write one sentence to describe it. Have a few volunteers read their sentences out loud. You may want to write them on the board. (Possible responses: It's half empty; There is some water.)

- Say *Think about the way you described the glass.* Ask *How does this reflect your outlook on life?*

- Have volunteers share their conclusions with the class. (Possible response: My outlook on life isn't very positive—I saw only a little water in the glass.)

Language note: In English, the analogy of the glass being *half full* or *half empty* is used to describe someone's outlook on life in general or a specific experience.

B ∩ Reading
(CD 1, Track 8)

Suggested teaching time:	10–15 minutes
Your actual teaching time:	_____

- Elicit from the class that an *optimist* is someone who is always hopeful and believes that good things will happen, and that a *pessimist* is someone who expects that bad things will happen.

- Have students underline information in the article that will help them answer the focus question as they read and listen.

- Review as a class. Have volunteers share their answers to the focus question. (Possible response: Optimists see a solution, while pessimists see only the problem and may give up.)

Language note: You may want to share the following definitions if students ask about specific expressions: *defeated* (feeling that you cannot deal with something); *challenged* (feeling that your strength, skills, or abilities are being tested); *perceive* (think of something or someone in a particular way); *cynical* (very sure that things won't be successful or useful); *dose* (amount of something that you experience at one time); *uplifting* (making you feel happy); *wise* (intelligent and sensible, usually because of experience). *To look on the bright side* means see the good aspects and possible benefits of a problem. Clarify the differences between *optimistic / pessimistic, optimist / pessimist, optimism / pessimism*:
  - A person or perspective can be *optimistic* or *pessimistic*. These words are adjectives.
  - A person can be described as *an optimist* or *a pessimist*. These words are nouns.
  - The abstract nouns are *optimism* and *pessimism*. For example, *Some optimism is always good.*

∩ Reading Strategies

∩ Reading Speed Calculator

∩ Extra Reading Comprehension Activities

Option: To use the reading as a listening activity, write the following *yes / no* questions on the board:
  1. Is the difference between an optimist and a pessimist a difference in life experiences?
  2. Do optimists and pessimists react to problems differently?
  3. Does pessimism have any advantages?
  4. Is it good to be both a little optimistic and a little pessimistic?

First listening: With books closed, have students write *yes* or *no* for each question. Review as a class. (1. no, 2. yes, 3. yes, 4. yes)
  Add the following *wh-* questions to the *yes / no* questions already on the board:
  [Add to 1:] What makes the difference?
  [Add to 2:] How do they react?
  [Add to 3:] What are they?
  [Add to 4:] Why?

Second listening: With books closed, have students listen for the answers to the new questions on the board. In pairs, have students compare notes and decide on an answer. Review as a class. Have volunteers present their responses to the class. (1. the way they respond to problems; 2. Optimists see a solution. Pessimists see the problem only and may give up. 3. Some pessimism can help you be realistic and wise. 4. A little of each enables you to be realistic and still be hopeful.) **[+15 minutes]**

C Discussion

Suggested teaching time:	5–10 minutes
Your actual teaching time:	_____

- Read the questions out loud. As students discuss the answers in small groups, circulate to encourage them to use experiences from their own lives to support their views.

- Review as a class. Have a volunteer from each group share the ways people can avoid negative thinking. (Possible responses: by focusing on good things; by replacing bad thoughts with good ones)

D Pair Work

Suggested teaching time:	5–10 minutes
Your actual teaching time:	_____

- Have students rate the people individually.

- Encourage them to use the vocabulary from the reading to discuss the people and support their views.

- Review as a class. Have volunteers share their answers and explain their choices.

DISCUSSION **BUILDER**

Suggested teaching time:	20 minutes
Your actual teaching time:	_____

Step 1.

• Have students complete the survey individually and add up their points to determine whether they are optimists, pessimists, or a little of both.

• Circulate to offer help with unknown words. Students may need help with the following expressions: *It figures* (said when something happens in a way that you expect, but do not like); *warm up* (in this context it means become more friendly with someone); *drop by* (visit someone when you have not arranged to come at a particular time).

Step 2. Pair Work.

• In pairs, have students compare and discuss their answers to each of the items on the survey. Encourage students to support their choices by giving examples of their experiences.

• Ask students if they agree with the results of their surveys.

• Take a poll to find out if most students are optimists, pessimists, or a little of both.

Step 3. Discussion.

• Read the questions out loud. Have students discuss their opinions in small groups.

• Circulate to encourage students to use language from the reading on page 8 and to give examples and ask each other follow-up questions.

• To review item 1, draw the following diagram on the board:

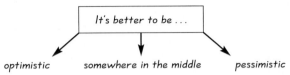

Take a poll to see how many students think it's better to be optimistic, pessimistic, or somewhere in the middle. Have volunteers give reasons to support their responses, and write them on the board.

• To review item 2, have a volunteer from each group present his/her response and explanation to the class.

> **Culture note:** Considered one of the most important political leaders in British and world history, Winston Churchill served as the prime minister of the United Kingdom during World War II and again from 1951 to 1955. He also wrote several books on British history and won the Nobel Prize for Literature in 1953.

Note: The pronunciation of proper nouns can be found on the *Summit 1* Companion Website under "Pronunciator."

EXTRAS (optional)

Workbook: Exercises 10–15

Step 1. Complete the survey.

Do you have a negative or positive perspective?

1. You wake up in the middle of the night with a stomachache. Your first thought is . . .

- **1pt** "I'm sure it's nothing."
- **2pts** "I'll take some medicine."
- **3pts** "I think I should go to the doctor."

2. You apply for your "perfect" job, but you don't get it. You think . . .

- **1pt** "Never mind. I'll find something else."
- **2pts** "That's really unfair."
- **3pts** "It figures. I never get the job I want."

3. When you are introduced to someone new, you . . .

- **1pt** make friends easily with that person.
- **2pts** "warm up" to that person gradually.
- **3pts** make that person prove to you that he or she is likable.

4. News about crime or disasters makes you . . .

- **1pt** want to do something to help.
- **2pts** realize that sometimes bad things happen.
- **3pts** feel unsafe and depressed.

5. When a friend feels down, you . . .

- **1pt** understand and try to offer support.
- **2pts** tell him or her about your problems too.
- **3pts** tell him or her how much worse it could be.

6. Your boss asks you out to lunch. You think . . .

- **1pt** "I must be getting a raise."
- **2pts** "That's really nice."
- **3pts** "Oh, no! I'm getting fired!"

7. If someone unexpectedly knocks on your door, you think . . .

- **1pt** "I wonder which friend is dropping by."
- **2pts** "I wonder who it could be."
- **3pts** "I'm not answering. It must be a salesperson."

> **Add up your points.**
> 7–10 You're an optimist. You always see the glass half full.
> 11–14 You're a bit of an optimist and a pessimist. You're very realistic.
> 15–21 You're a pessimist. You tend to see the glass half empty.

Step 2. Pair Work. Compare and explain your responses to the survey items. Does your score describe you and your perspective on life? Why or why not?

Step 3. Discussion.

1. In your opinion, in order to succeed, how important is your perspective on life? Do you think it's better to be optimistic, pessimistic, or somewhere in the middle? Explain.

2. Read the quotation by Winston Churchill. Do you agree with him? Why or why not?

"The pessimist sees difficulty in every opportunity. The optimist sees the opportunity in every difficulty."

Winston Churchill,
British Prime Minister
(1874–1965)

4 ## *Share a life-changing experience*

LISTENING

A 🎧 **Listening Comprehension.** Listen to each person talking about a life-changing experience. Then choose the best answer to complete each statement.

1. The most significant experience of the first speaker's life was when he ....
   a. became a father
   b. began working
   c. traveled to another country
   d. got married

2. The second speaker's life changed when she ....
   a. got a full-time job
   b. had a baby
   c. got more free time
   d. got married

3. The third speaker's perspective on life changed when he ....
   a. lost his home in a fire
   b. lost his job
   c. got divorced
   d. had a serious illness

B 🎧 **Understanding Meaning from Context.** Read the statements. Then listen again to infer what each speaker means.

1. When the first speaker says, "I was really able to see other people's points of view," he means that ....
   a. he could understand how other people feel about things
   b. he met people of different nationalities

2. When the first speaker says, "It was a real eye-opener for me," he means that ....
   a. the experience was a bit scary
   b. the experience taught him a lot

3. When the second speaker says, "It hit me that I was responsible for her," she means that ....
   a. she realized she had to take care of her baby
   b. she regretted she had to take care of her baby

4. When the second speaker says, "[It] is definitely a life-altering experience," she means that ....
   a. the experience is not rewarding
   b. the experience changes a person

5. When the third speaker says, "That put things in perspective," he means that ....
   a. he realized some things are not so important
   b. he had to work day in and day out

6. When the third speaker says, "You start to see the big picture," he means that ....
   a. he understood what was really important in life
   b. he realized how much he had lost

C **Discussion.** In your own words, summarize each person's life-changing experience from the listening. Which person's experience can you identify with the most? Why?

Share a life-changing experience

A 🎧 Listening Comprehension
(CD 1, Track 9)

Suggested teaching time:	10–15 minutes
Your actual teaching time:	_____

• Pre-listening: Point to the illustration and ask *What do you see?* (Possible responses: images inside a person's head, a bride and groom, a tall building, a house on fire, a man jogging, a man holding a baby, a car, a man graduating from college / high school, a man fishing)

• Ask *What do you think the picture represents?* (Possible responses: important events in life, thoughts, memories, dreams, worries)

• Have students read the incomplete statements and answer choices.

• First listening: As students listen, pause after each speaker to allow students time to choose their answers.

• In pairs, have students compare answers.

• Second listening: Have students listen again to check their answers. Review as a class.

🌀 Listening Strategies

Challenge: Ask *What did each speaker learn from his/her experience?* Have students listen again and take notes. Review as a class. (Possible responses: 1. He learned that different people have different perspectives on life. 2. She realized that she was now responsible for another person because her baby depended on her. 3. He realized that he used to worry about unimportant things.) **[+5 minutes]**

> **AUDIOSCRIPT**
>
> For audioscript, see page AS1.

B 🎧 Understanding Meaning from Context
(CD 1, Track 10)

Suggested teaching time:	5–10 minutes
Your actual teaching time:	_____

• Review the first speaker's experience. Ask *What does the first speaker talk about?* (He talks about a trip to Belgium that was an important experience for him. He was working in Brussels and met people from all over the world.)

• Have students complete items 1 and 2 individually.

• Follow the same procedure with the second speaker for items 3 and 4, and then with the third speaker for items 5 and 6.

• Have students compare answers with a partner and then review as a class.

Option: Write the following expressions on the board:
> an eye-opener
> a life-altering experience
> put things in perspective
> see the big picture
> point of view

In pairs, have students create their own definitions for each expression. To provide practice, have pairs create sentences using the expressions. To review, have volunteers read their sentences out loud. **[+10 minutes]**

C Discussion

Suggested teaching time:	10 minutes
Your actual teaching time:	_____

• In small groups, have students summarize the life-changing experience of each person.

• As students explain which person's experience they most identify with, circulate to encourage them to give specific examples.

• To review, have volunteers share their responses with the class.

DISCUSSION **BUILDER**

Suggested teaching time:	20–25 minutes
Your actual teaching time:	_____

 Discourse Strategies

Step 1. Pair Work.

- Read the list of things that can change one's perspective.

- Have students complete their lists with a partner.

- To review, elicit experiences from the class and write them on the board. (Possible responses: meeting someone, marriage, divorce, a serious illness, the death of a friend or family member, a new job, losing a job, changing schools, school graduation, moving to a different area or country, an accident, being the victim of a crime)

Step 2.

- Have a volunteer read the questions out loud.

- As students take notes about their experiences, circulate to offer help as needed. Encourage students to use the expressions in Exercise B on page 10 to describe how the experiences changed their perspectives.

- Point out that if students can't think of a personal experience—or if they feel more comfortable writing about someone else—they can take notes about a life-changing experience of a famous person or someone they know.

Step 3. Group Work.

- Have volunteers read the examples out loud.

- In small groups, have students use their notes from Step 2 to tell their partners about their experiences.

- Encourage students to ask follow-up questions to find out more as their group members speak and to share similar experiences they have had.

- Review as a class. Have volunteers share their life-changing experiences with the class. After each volunteer describes his/her experience, ask *Has anyone had a similar experience? Did your perspective change in the same way?*

Step 4. Writing.

- Remind students to use their notes from Step 2 to form an organized, thoughtful paragraph.

- You may want to give students starting phrases or sentences such as *The most significant experience of my life was . . . / I will never forget . . . / When. . . . From that moment, everything changed.*

- After correcting your students' work, ask those who would like to share their experiences to put their writings on a bulletin board.

EXTRAS (optional)

Workbook: Exercises 16–17

DISCUSSION **BUILDER** • *Now share a life-changing experience.*

Step 1. Pair Work. What are some experiences that can change a person's perspective on life? Complete the list with your partner.

> **Things that can change one's perspective**
>
> -the birth of a child
> -a disaster
> -travel

Step 2. Think about a life-changing experience *you* have had. Take notes about it on your notepad.

What was the experience? When did it happen? Where?

How did the experience change your perspective? How did you feel at the time?

Step 3. Group Work. Share your life-changing experience with your classmates. Explain how this experience changed your perspective on life.

> "Last year my mother had a serious illness. It really put things in perspective for me. All the disagreements we'd had in the past seemed so unimportant."

> "A few years ago, I went on vacation to Europe. It hit me how useful it was knowing English. It came in handy in a lot of situations."

Step 4. Writing. On a separate sheet of paper, write a paragraph about a life-changing experience you have had.

Writing: Describe personality types

The paragraph

A paragraph consists of sentences about one topic. The most important sentence in a paragraph is the **topic sentence**. It is usually the first sentence, and it introduces the topic of a paragraph. For example:

Workaholics lead unbalanced lives.

In academic writing, all the **supporting sentences** that follow a topic sentence—details, examples, and other facts—must be related to the topic presented in the topic sentence.

The last sentence of the paragraph is often a **concluding sentence**. A concluding sentence restates the topic sentence or summarizes the paragraph. A concluding sentence often includes phrases such as In conclusion or In summary.

WRITING MODEL

Workaholics lead unbalanced lives. They spend all their energy on work. They rarely take time to relax and let their minds rest. I know because my father was a workaholic, and he worked every day of the week. We hardly ever saw him. Even when he was not at work, we knew he was thinking about work. He seemed never to think of anything else. In summary, not knowing how to escape from work makes it difficult for a workaholic to find balance in his or her life.

Step 1. Prewriting. Brainstorming ideas. Write a topic sentence for each personality type.

team players	tyrants	wise guys

Answers will vary, but may include:

1. Team players help make a group successful.
2. Tyrants make the office an unpleasant place to be.
3. Wise guys are not fun to be around.

Now choose one of your topic sentences. On a separate sheet of paper, generate ideas you could use to support the topic.

Workaholics lead unbalanced lives.
–always think about work
–can't relax

Step 2. Writing. On a separate sheet of paper, write a paragraph about the personality type you chose in Step 1. Make sure all the supporting sentences relate to the topic. End with a concluding sentence.

Step 3. Self-Check.

☐ Does your paragraph have a topic sentence?
☐ Do the supporting sentences in your paragraph all relate to the topic?
☐ Do you have a concluding sentence?

Writing Describe personality types

Suggested teaching time: 20 minutes
Your actual teaching time: _____

The paragraph

- Have students read the explanation for *The paragraph* to themselves.

- To check comprehension, ask *What does a paragraph consist of?* As students respond, summarize the information on the board:

  paragraph = topic sentence + supporting sentences + concluding sentence

- Then ask *What does a topic sentence introduce?* (the topic and focus of the paragraph) Point out that the focus gives information about the topic.

- Write a new example topic sentence on the board:

  A people person tends to make friends easily.

  Have students identify the topic (A people person) and the focus (makes friends easily).

- To check comprehension, draw the following diagram on the board. Have students match each item with the type of sentence it is generally located in.

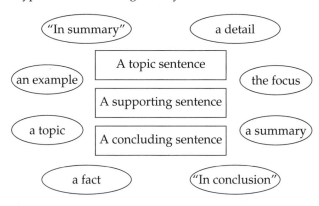

🌀 Graphic Organizers

Have students compare answers with a partner and review as a class. (**A topic sentence:** a topic, the focus; **A supporting sentence:** a fact, a detail, an example; **A concluding sentence:** "In conclusion," "In summary," a summary)

🌀 Extra Writing Skills Practice

Challenge: Pair Work. Refer students to the Reading on page 8, and have students identify the parts of the second paragraph. [+5 minutes]

Step 1. Prewriting.

- Point out that *brainstorming* is the act of trying to develop ideas and think of ways to solve problems, often with a group of people. Point out that when brainstorming, one should express any idea that comes to mind.

- To review the vocabulary for personality types, elicit brief definitions for the three personality types in the box. (Possible responses: Team players work well with other people. They help their group be successful; Tyrants make people work hard. They don't care much about others; Wiseguys play jokes on others. They try to make themselves seem smart.)

- Have students write their topic sentences individually.

- Then have students choose the topic sentence that interests them the most and make a list of ideas to support it. Remind students to list any ideas that come to mind, without judging if they are good or bad ideas.

Step 2. Writing.

- Have students select the best ideas generated in Step 1 and use them to write a paragraph about the personality type they chose.

- As students write, circulate to offer help as needed. Point out that students may want to refer to the definitions for personality types on page 6, as well as the adjectives on page 7.

Step 3. Self-Check.

- Have students complete the Self-Check questions individually.

- Have students make any necessary changes before submitting their paragraphs.

EXTRAS (optional)

     Workbook: Page 9

T12

UNIT | CHECKPOINT

A 🎧 Listening Comprehension
(CD 1, Track 11)

Suggested teaching time:	10 minutes
Your actual teaching time:	_____

- First listening: Have students listen to the three speakers and decide what events in the news each one is talking about. Review as a class. (1. the problems affecting the world—wars, natural disasters, poverty, terrorism; 2. the economic situation; 3. the rising unemployment rate)

- Second listening: Pause after each conversation to allow students time to decide on the speaker's outlook on life.

- Review as a class.

Challenge: Have students listen to the speakers again and write information that supports their answers. (Possible responses: 1. John can't get over what's happening. He believes things are getting worse. 2. Susan has taken action, but she's not stressing out over the problem. She believes things may get better. 3. Matt thinks things will work out in the end. When a door closes, another one always opens.) **[+5 minutes]**

> **AUDIOSCRIPT**
> For audioscript, see page AS1.

B Now read the statements . . .

Suggested teaching time:	5–10 minutes
Your actual teaching time:	_____

- Clarify the task: Tell students that the statements were made by the speakers in Exercise A and that they should decide who could have said them.

- Have students compare answers with a partner. Review as a class and have students support their answers. (Possible responses: This statement must have been said by Susan because she is a realist. Realists are practical people. They see problems and try to deal with them.)

C Complete each conversation . . .

Suggested teaching time:	5–10 minutes
Your actual teaching time:	_____

- To review the personality types, have volunteers call out a personality type and give a brief definition. You may want to start the activity. For example, *A brain is a very intelligent person.*

- Have students compare answers with a partner and then review as a class.

D On a separate sheet of paper . . .

Suggested teaching time:	5–10 minutes
Your actual teaching time:	_____

- Read the first item and example with the class.

- As a class, brainstorm more suggestions for Samantha. (Possible responses: She should stop to take breaks; She should remember to make time for herself; She should stop over-scheduling.)

- As students work, circulate to provide help with the gerunds and infinitives.

- Have students compare answers with a partner.

- Review as a class. As you get feedback from students, you may want to write a list of suggestions for each person on the board.

 Vocabulary-Building Strategies

 You may wish to use the Video Program and activity worksheets for Unit 1 at this point.

Complete Assessment Package
Unit 1 Achievement Test

UNIT 1 CHECKPOINT

SUMMIT WEBSITE
For Unit 1 online activities, visit the
Summit Companion Website at
www.longman.com/summit.

A 🎧 **Listening Comprehension.** Listen to the people talking about their reactions to events in the news. Decide if each speaker is an optimist, a pessimist, or a realist.

1. John __pessimist__   **2.** Susan __realist__   **3.** Matt __optimist__

B Now read the statements. Write the name of the person from the listening who is most likely to have said each statement. Listen again if necessary.

1. "You've got to be practical. There will be some problems in life that you can solve and some that you can't. What's important is realizing when something is beyond your control. Then it's better just to move on." __Susan__

2. "Life is full of hard times. You just have to accept the fact that bad things happen and know that there's very little you can do about it." __John__

3. "It's important to see a problem as both a challenge to be faced and as an opportunity for success. Difficult experiences can make a person stronger." __Matt__

C Complete each conversation with a personality type.

1. A: Looks like I have to work overtime again tonight. My supervisor just gave me three projects to complete by the end of the day.
   B: You're kidding. He sounds like a real __tyrant__!

2. A: You know, without Sarah's help, I would never have completed that presentation in time.
   B: Tell me about it. She really helped me out with my sales campaign last month. She's such a __team player__.

3. A: Tom is really a __workaholic__. I ran into him in the park last weekend, and he was sitting on a bench and working on that report.
   B: Yeah, that's Tom all right. He never stops!

4. A: I don't think Jill had a very good time at the party—she didn't say a word the whole evening.
   B: Well, Jill doesn't feel comfortable in social situations. She's just not a __people person__.

5. A: Have you heard the news? My daughter Audrey got a perfect score on her entrance exam to law school.
   B: Congratulations! I always knew she would do well in school. She's such a __brain__.

6. A: I'm so tired of Ken. The other day I made a mistake at the computer lab at school, and he said something that really made me feel dumb.
   B: Don't let it get to you. Everybody knows he's a __wise guy__. Just try to ignore him.

D On a separate sheet of paper, write advice for each person. Use the verbs <u>stop</u>, <u>remember</u>, and <u>forget</u> with gerunds or infinitives.
Answers will vary, but may include:

   She should stop working so much.

1. Samantha has a demanding job and works long hours. When she finally gets home, she's exhausted. She spends all weekend trying to catch up on housework and shopping.

2. Michael spends most of the day at the computer. Some days he doesn't even get outside except to walk to the bus stop. On the weekends, he just watches a lot of TV.
   He should remember to exercise every day.

3. Philip is a single father with three kids, and he travels a lot for his company. He feels his kids are growing up so fast that he hardly ever sees them.
   He shouldn't forget to make time for his kids.

4. Marisa has been using her credit cards a lot lately, and she can't keep up with the monthly payments. And now she's having a hard time keeping up with *all* her bills.
   She should stop using her credit cards so much.

13

UNIT 2

Musical Moods

UNIT GOALS

1. Describe the music you listen to
2. Explain the role of music in your life
3. Describe a creative person
4. Discuss the benefits of music

A **Topic Preview.** Look at the reviews from the music website. Are you familiar with any of these artists?

TUNE | IN
0 1 2 3 4 5 6 7 8 9 10

| Artist | ⬍ | Go | Search |

Today's Picks

- Home
- New Releases
- Explore by...
  genre
  instrument
  artist
- Editor's Choice
- Top Searches
- Site Guide
- Newsletter
- About Us
- Subscribe

LATIN

PONCE

Carlos Ponce, *Ponce*
Puerto Rican singer / songwriter (and TV star) Carlos Ponce delivers a fun mix of romantic ballads and Caribbean-flavored dance grooves. Even if you don't understand Spanish, you can't help but feel the emotion in Ponce's voice, which ranges from a rough growl to a passionate cry.

JAZZ

marcos ariel
my only passion

Marcos Ariel, *My Only Passion*
Another brilliant set from the richly talented Brazilian keyboardist / composer Marcos Ariel. Check out the unpredictable interplay between the group members in "Bahia Suite," where Meia Noite's exciting percussion sets the tempo, while Ariel's piano races in and around Frank Gambale's surprising guitar lines.

POP

ANDREA BOCELLI SOGNO

Andrea Bocelli, *Sogno*
Sogno finds the classically trained Bocelli moving away from the world of opera with a collection of modern pop ballads. Fans of Bocelli's remarkable voice won't be disappointed. Whether he's singing an Italian pop song or a lovely duet with pop diva Celine Dion, the depth and feeling of his music will touch your soul.

NEW AGE

KITARO

BEST OF SILK ROAD

Kitaro, *Best of Silk Road*
Described as "sound pictures" and "mind music" in his native Japan, Kitaro's electronic music incorporates the sounds of waves, wind, and rain, inspiring listeners to feel and appreciate the natural world. A true masterpiece.

URBAN DANCE

Beyoncé
dangerouslyinlove

Beyoncé, *Dangerously in Love*
Beyoncé kicks off her solo career and keeps the dance floors crowded with her hit singles on this energetic recording. Hear the red-hot "Crazy in Love" (a duet with rap artist Jay-Z) and the playful "Baby Boy" (with dance-hall star Sean Paul) just once and you'll be humming them in your head all day.

WORLD

MUZSIKÁS
THE PRISONER'S SONG

Muzsikás, *The Prisoner's Song*
Singing in Hungarian and playing traditional instruments, Muzsikás arranges ten Eastern European folk songs to tell a haunting story of love, desire, and freedom. Add lead singer Márta Sebestyén's amazing voice, and you've got a sound unlike any you've ever heard.

Source: www.allmusic.com

B **Discussion.**

1. Which reviews did you find the most appealing? Why? Which musical genres in the reviews interest you the most?
2. Can you think of other artists for each genre?

Musical Moods

A Topic Preview

Suggested teaching time:	10–15 minutes
Your actual teaching time:	_____

- To introduce the unit theme of music, have students spend a few moments looking at the website.
- Read the name of the website out loud. Ask *Why is* Tune In *a good name for a website about music?* (because you can *tune in* to a radio station to listen to music) *What kind of information does this website offer?* (music reviews) *What is meant by* Today's Picks? (These are CDs the website recommends.)
- Have students look at the CD covers. Ask if they are familiar with—or if they have ever heard of—any of the artists or bands.
- To draw on students' prior knowledge, have them share general information they might already know about these artists or bands with the class. For example, *Andrea Bocelli is an Italian singer. He can sing operas and has a beautiful voice. He has been blind since the age of 12.*
- On the board, write:

  Find:
  1. the kind of music each CD features
  2. why it is recommended

  Have students scan the text (quickly) to find the information.
- Have volunteers share the information for each review with the class. (Possible response: *The Prisoner's Song* features Eastern European folk songs played with traditional instruments. Muzsikás' lead singer has an amazing voice.)

> **Language note:** *Haunting* means sad but also beautiful; if something is *haunting*, it stays in your thoughts for a long time. *Growl* means make a low noise from your throat with your voice. *Kick off* means begin. *Red-hot* means extremely active, exciting, or interesting.

Option: To expand on embedded vocabulary, use the graphic organizer on the Teacher's Resource Disk. You may want to draw it on the board or print and distribute to the class. Have pairs scan the text to find the words associated with music. Point out that the definitions are given in the order in which the words appear in the reviews. Review as a class. (1. folk song, 2. lead singer, 3. ballad, 4. masterpiece, 5. opera, 6. duet, 7. percussion, 8. tempo, 9. solo, 10. hit, 11. single) **[+10 minutes]**

🔵 **Graphic Organizers**

B Discussion

Suggested teaching time:	10 minutes
Your actual teaching time:	_____

- Have students circle the genres in the reviews that they are interested in. Encourage students to think of reasons for their choices. Ask *Do the genres you chose here reflect the genres you normally listen to?*
- In small groups, have students discuss the questions. Encourage them to give reasons for their choices and ask each other follow-up questions.
- Have students share ideas for other artists from these genres with the class.

Option: Ask students to name different genres. Write a list on the board: *blues, Celtic, country, folk, rap, reggae, rock, hip-hop, heavy metal.* Ask students for the names of some singers or bands from each of the genres on the board. Have a few volunteers tell the class about their favorite genre and give a supporting reason. To finish, take a poll of the class to find out which genre(s) is/are more popular among your students. **[+5 minutes]**

Option: Have students think about which CDs from the website they would choose to give as a gift to a friend or relative. Have pairs discuss which CD they would buy and who they would give it to. Encourage students to explain their choices. **[+5 minutes]**

C 🎧 Sound Bites
(CD 1, Track 12)

Suggested teaching time:	10 minutes
Your actual teaching time:	_____

• Have students look at the photo. Ask *Do you think these people have a social relationship or a business relationship? What do you think they are talking about? Where are they?*

• Have students read and listen to the conversation. To check comprehension, ask:
  Who is giving the party? (Ken)
  What kind of music does Tania like? (jazz)
  What does Ken first suggest listening to? (*Fenix* / Gato Barbieri)
  Does Tania like it? (no)
  What doesn't Tania like about Fenix? (the way Gato Barbieri plays the saxophone and the fact that it's hard to dance to)
  What's Ken's second suggestion? (some later stuff by Gato Barbieri)
  Why does that sound like a good idea to Tania? (because Ken says it's got more of a Latin feel)

Culture note: Gato Barbieri is an Argentinean saxophonist who has won worldwide recognition. His score for the movie *Last Tango in Paris* in 1972 turned him into an international star. His album *Fenix* was released in 1971.

Option: If your students show interest in jazz, ask *Do you like jazz? Are you familiar with Gato Barbieri? Have you ever heard* Fenix? *What other famous jazz musicians do you know?* [+5 minutes]

D In Other Words

Suggested teaching time:	5–10 minutes
Your actual teaching time:	_____

• Have pairs find and underline each statement in Exercise C. Encourage students to use the information in the text to help them figure out the meaning of the sentences. You may want to do the first item with the class.

• In pairs, have students complete the exercise. Then bring the class together and have students share their answers. Write the different ways of saying the statements on the board.

Option: Have two volunteers read the conversation in Exercise C out loud, replacing the selected statements with other ways of saying them. [+5 minutes]

Option: Have pairs create short conversations using the expressions from the exercise. For example, Student A: *I just bought the new U2 CD.* Student B: *Let's give it a listen!* [+5 minutes]

STARTING POINT

Suggested teaching time:	10–15 minutes
Your actual teaching time:	_____

• Have students complete the chart individually. Circulate to help them identify the genre.

• Make sure students complete the three rows.

Pair Work

• Have a volunteer read the models out loud.

• On the board, write:

(+)	(-)
I like *Fenix/*jazz.	I don't like *Fenix/*jazz.
Fenix is fantastic.	I think *Fenix* is terrible.

As a class, brainstorm other ways to say you like / don't like a particular CD or genre and add to the chart on the board. (Possible responses: **(+):** I love *Fenix;* I'm really into *Fenix;* I'm a (big) jazz fan; I listen to *Fenix* all the time; My favorite music is jazz; I find jazz relaxing; **(-):** I hate *Fenix;* I'm just not into *Fenix;* Jazz is not for me; I never listen to jazz; I'm not very big on jazz; Jazz gets on my nerves.)

• Before pairs discuss their charts, point out that they can use some of the expressions in Exercise D to make relevant comments or ask follow-up questions.

• Review as a class. Have volunteers talk about their favorite recordings. Encourage students to support their choices.

EXTRAS (optional)

Workbook: Exercises 1–5

C 🎧 **Sound Bites.** Read and listen to a conversation between two friends comparing musical tastes.

TANIA: Wow! You've got quite a CD collection!
KEN: I guess so. Let's put something on.
TANIA: Got any jazz? **CN**
KEN: How about some Gato Barbieri? I've got *Fenix*.
TANIA: Actually, his saxophone playing kind of gets on my nerves on that one.
KEN: Really? I'm totally into him. *Fenix* is one of my all-time favorites.
TANIA: Yeah, but it's pretty hard to dance to.
KEN: Well, have you heard some of his later stuff?
TANIA: No, what's it like?
KEN: It's got more of a Latin feel. It'll definitely get the party started.
TANIA: Oh yeah? Let's give it a listen.

D **In Other Words.** Read the conversation again. With a partner, explain the meaning of each of the following statements or questions.
Answers will vary, but may include:

1. "You've got quite a CD collection." You have a lot of CDs.

2. "Let's put something on." Let's play some music.

3. "His saxophone playing kind of gets on my nerves on that one." His saxophone playing is a little annoying on that CD.

4. "I'm totally into him." I really like him.

5. "Have you heard some of his later stuff?" Have you listened to some of the music he made later on in his career?

6. "It'll definitely get the party started." It will get people in the mood for a party and dancing.

7. "Let's give it a listen." Let's put that CD on.

CN **Corpus Notes:** The expression *Have you got any…?* is frequently used in spoken American English to mean *Do you have any…?* In spoken English and in written advertising, auxiliaries and subject pronouns are frequently omitted in questions. For example, *Got any ideas?* and *Don't know what to wear?*

STARTING **POINT**

What recordings are your all-time favorites? Complete the chart.

Title of recording	Artist or group	Genre of music

Pair Work. Talk with a partner about the music in your chart. Compare your musical tastes.

"I'm totally into Coldplay. That CD is fantastic!"

"Well, rock usually gets on my nerves, but maybe I'll give it a listen sometime."

15

1 Describe the music you listen to

Youssou N'Dour

A 🎧 CONVERSATION **SNAPSHOT**

A: So what have you been listening to lately? CN

B: Mostly world music. Ever heard of Youssou N'Dour?

A: I think so. He's from Senegal, right?

B: That's right.

A: You know, I've actually never heard his music. What's he like?

B: Well, he's got a terrific voice and a unique sound. I'd be happy to lend you a CD if you'd like.

A: All right, thanks. I'll let you know what I think.

🎧 **Rhythm and intonation practice**

CN **Corpus Notes:** The adverb *lately* comes most frequently at the end of a sentence or clause in spoken English.

B 🎧 **Vocabulary. Elements of music.** Listen and practice.

beat the rhythm of a piece of music
That song has a great beat you can dance to.

lyrics the words of a song
Her catchy lyrics make you want to sing along.

melody the order of notes in a musical piece
His song has an unforgettable melody.

sound the particular style or quality of an artist's or group's music
The band has created a new and exciting sound.

voice the quality of sound produced when one sings
She has a beautiful soprano voice.

C 🎧 **Pair Work.** Listen to the pieces of music. With a partner, use the words from the vocabulary to discuss what you like or don't like about the music.

PAGE P2
Intonation patterns

D Grammar. The present perfect and the present perfect continuous: finished and unfinished actions

Finished actions

Use the present perfect, not the present perfect continuous, when an action is completed at an unspecified time in the past. (Remember that actions completed at a specified time in the past require the simple past tense.)

I**'ve** already **heard** that CD. I heard it yesterday.
How many times **have** you **seen** Youssou N'Dour in concert?
I**'ve seen** him twice. As a matter of fact, I just saw him last week.

Very recently finished actions: an exception

The present perfect continuous is preferred to describe very recently completed actions when results can still be seen.

They**'ve been practicing.** I see them putting their instruments away.

Unfinished or continuing actions

Use the present perfect OR the present perfect continuous to describe actions that began in the past, continue into the present, and may continue into the future.

Have you **listened** to any jazz lately? OR **Have** you **been listening** to any jazz lately?
I**'ve listened** to Beethoven since I was a child. OR I**'ve been listening** to Beethoven since I was a child.

> **Words and phrases used with the present perfect for finished actions**
> already   ever   never   yet
> once, twice, three times
> How many . . . ?

> **Words and expressions often used with unfinished actions**
> for   lately   these days
> since   recently   for a while
> all day   this year   How long . . . ?

PAGE G3
For more . . .

1 *Describe the music you listen to*

A 🎧 CONVERSATION **SNAPSHOT**
(CD 1, Track 13)

Suggested teaching time:	5–10 minutes
Your actual teaching time:	_____

• Have students read and listen to the conversation. To check comprehension, ask *What are the people talking about?* (music they've been listening to; a singer from Senegal—Youssou N'Dour) *Have both speakers heard his music before?* (no, just one of them) *What does this person think about his music?* (that he's great, that he's got a terrific voice and a unique sound)

• Ask students who have heard of Youssou N'Dour to share what they know about him with the class.

> **Culture note:** <u>Youssou N'Dour</u> is an African singer, songwriter, and composer. His music is a mixture of Senegalese traditional music, Cuban samba, hip-hop, dance, and soul.

🎧 Rhythm and intonation practice
(CD 1, Track 14)

Suggested teaching time:	5 minutes
Your actual teaching time:	_____

• Have students repeat chorally. Make sure they:
  ○ use falling intonation for *So what have you been listening to lately?*
  ○ use rising intonation for *Ever hear of Youssou N'Dour?*
  ○ stress <u>think</u> in *I think so.*
  ○ use rising intonation for <u>right</u> in *He's from Senegal, right?*
  ○ use falling intonation but higher pitch for *What's he like?*
  ○ use the contractions <u>I'd</u> and <u>I'll</u> in *I'd be happy to lend you a CD* and *I'll let you know what I think.*
  ○ use the following stress pattern:

STRESS PATTERN

A: So what have you been listening to lately?

B: Mostly world music. Ever heard of Youssou N'Dour?

A: I think so. He's from Senegal, right?

B: That's right.

A: You know, I've actually never heard his music. What's he like?

B: Well, he's got a terrific voice and a unique sound. I'd be happy to lend you a C D if you'd like.

A: All right, thanks. I'll let you know what I think.

B 🎧 Vocabulary
(CD 1, Track 15)

Suggested teaching time:	5 minutes
Your actual teaching time:	_____

• Have students listen to the words and study the definitions and examples. Then have students listen and repeat the words chorally.

💿 **Vocabulary-Building Strategies**

C 🎧 Pair Work
(CD 1, Track 16)

Suggested teaching time:	5 minutes
Your actual teaching time:	_____

• Pause after each piece of music to allow students time to discuss it. Review as a class. Have volunteers give their opinions on each piece of music.

> **AUDIOSCRIPT**
>
> For audioscript, see page AS2.

D Grammar

Suggested teaching time:	10–15 minutes
Your actual teaching time:	_____

• To review the present perfect, ask *How do you form the present perfect?* (form of *have* + past participle)

• To review the present perfect continuous, ask *How do you form the present perfect continuous?* (form of *have* + *been* + present participle)

• Have students read the explanation for *Finished actions* and study the examples. Write the first example on the board:

> *I've already heard that CD.*

Ask *Is the action present or past?* (past) *Is it finished?* (yes) *Do you know when in the past the action occurred?* (no)

• Have a student read the first note. Have volunteers create sentences or questions using the present perfect and the words and phrases in the note. (Possible response: I haven't bought the tickets yet.)

• Have students read the explanation for *Very recently finished actions: an exception* and have a volunteer read the example out loud.

• Ask *What have they been doing?* (practicing) *What is the present result of that recently finished action?* (They are putting their instruments away.)

• Have students read the explanation for *Unfinished or continuing actions* and study the examples. Ask *Is there a difference between* I've listened *and* I've been listening *in the first example?* (no) *When did the action start?* (many years ago) *Is it finished?* (no) *Could it continue into the present or future?* (yes)

• Have a student read the second note out loud. Have pairs create sentences or questions for unfinished or continuing actions with the words and phrases in the note.

💿 **Grammar Self-Checks**

T16

E Read the sentences ...

Suggested teaching time:	5 minutes
Your actual teaching time:	_____

• Model the first item with the class. Make sure students understand that the action is unfinished because the person started playing with the band 10 years ago and he is still playing. Ask *Would the present perfect continuous also be correct in this sentence?* (yes)

• Have students complete the exercise individually.

• In pairs, have students compare answers. Then review as a class.

Culture note: Brazilian <u>Caetano Veloso</u> is an international pop music star. Brazilian <u>Alexandre Pires</u> is a star of Latin music. <u>Ladysmith Black Mambazo</u> is a South African choral group. <u>Carmina Burana</u> is a collection of thirteenth-century songs and poetry that was set to music by Carl Orff in 1937. <u>Johannes Brahms</u> was a nineteenth-century German composer and pianist who combined classical and romantic traditions in his music.

F Complete the biography ...

Suggested teaching time:	5 minutes
Your actual teaching time:	_____

• To review, write on the board:
  1. Finished past action + unspecified past time =
  2. Finished past action + specified past time =
  3. Unfinished action =

Have students say what form they will use for each pattern on the board. (1. the present perfect; 2. the simple past tense; 3. the present perfect continuous)

• Have students complete the biography individually and then compare answers with a partner.

• Review as a class. Encourage students to explain their choices. For example, *For item 1, I chose* has been performing *because she still performs.*

CONVERSATION STARTER

Suggested teaching time:	5–10 minutes
Your actual teaching time:	_____

• Have students look at the examples and then complete the information in note form, individually.

• Remind students to use the language they learned in Exercise B. Make sure students choose three artists or bands.

Pair Work

• Refer students to the Conversation Snapshot on page 16 to review describing the music you listen to.

• Role-play the conversation with a more confident student. Play the role of Student A to show falling intonation for *So what have you been listening to lately?* and rising intonation for *_____ from _____, right?*

• As students interact, circulate to offer help as needed. Encourage them to use the correct rhythm and intonation.

• Have pairs role-play their conversations for the class.

🔊 Conversation Prompts

Challenge: Draw the following diagram on the board and have students complete the blanks with information about themselves. Then have students write one or more sentences for each box. Tell students to use the present perfect or the present perfect continuous. (Possible responses: I like jazz. I've liked it since I was sixteen. I've never liked classical music. I used to listen to Phil Collins, but I haven't been listening to him lately.) Have everyone in the class share a sentence.

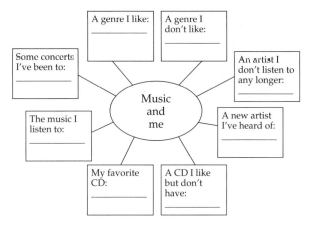

[+10 minutes]

🔊 Graphic Organizers

EXTRAS (optional)

Grammar Booster
Pronunciation Booster
Workbook: Exercises 6–8

E Read the sentences. Write <u>F</u> if the action is finished. Write <u>U</u> if the action is unfinished or continuing.

U **1.** He's played with their band for almost ten years.

F **2.** Caetano Veloso has made dozens of recordings.

F **3.** They've never heard of Alexandre Pires.

U **4.** We've been listening to that CD all day. Let's play something different.

U **5.** Ladysmith Black Mambazo hasn't been playing many concerts lately.

F **6.** Have you ever gone to a classical concert?

F **7.** How many times have you heard Carmina Burana?

F **8.** They've played Brahms's First Symphony twice this year.

F Complete the biography of Vanessa-Mae with the simple past tense, the present perfect, or the present perfect continuous. Use the present perfect continuous if the action is unfinished or continuing.

Vanessa-Mae

Vanessa-Mae <u>has been performing</u> music since she was a little girl.

(1. perform)

Born in Singapore on October 27, 1978, she <u>had</u> her

(2. have)

first piano lesson at the age of three. A year later, she <u>started</u>

(3. start)

taking violin lessons, and when she was just ten years old, she

<u>made</u> her concert debut with the London Philharmonic.

(4. make)

Since then, Vanessa-Mae <u>has made</u> numerous classical

(5. make)

recordings, but it was in 1994 that she <u>entered</u> the field of

(6. enter)

pop music with *The Violin Player*. The album immediately <u>became</u> extremely

(7. become)

popular with pop and classical music fans.

In more recent years, she <u>has played</u> with other pop artists such as Annie Lennox,

(8. play)

Janet Jackson, and Prince. Vanessa-Mae <u>has been entertaining</u> her audiences for over a decade,

(9. entertain)

and she continues to astonish them with her innovative sound.

CONVERSATION **STARTER** • *Now describe the music you listen to.*

Write some of the musical artists or bands you've been listening to lately.

Artist or band	What you like
Étoile de Dakar	great dance beat

Artist or band	What you like

Pair Work. Find out what your partner has been listening to lately. Ask what he or she likes or doesn't like about the music. Use the Conversation Snapshot on page 16 as a guide. Start like this: "So what have you been listening to lately?"

2 *Explain the role of music in your life*

A 🎧 GRAMMAR **SNAPSHOT.** Read the commentaries and notice the use of noun clauses.

Frankly, I can't imagine **what my life would be like without music**. It's **what gets me through the day**. Listening to music is **how I get going in the morning**. Later, at work, it's **how I stay productive**. And in the evening, it's **what helps me unwind**.

Patricia Nichols, 34
Vancouver, Canada

It's my opinion **that music is a kind of international language**—a way for people to communicate with **whomever they meet**. The fact **that enjoyment of music is universal** makes it an ideal way to bring cultures together. Music can open doors for you everywhere you go in the world.

Santigi Matomi, 27
Freetown, Sierra Leone

I'm a performer, and music is a part of who I am. It's a way for me to express **what's in my heart**. The truth is, **whether or not I perform** is not really a choice—I have to do it. **Whatever happens during the day**—good or bad—comes out in my music.

Alison Wu, 19
Shanghai, China

B **Discussion.** Do any of the comments above ring true for you? Why or why not?

C **Grammar. Noun clauses**

A noun clause can be a subject, a direct object, an indirect object, a subject complement, or the object of a preposition.

Whatever happens during the day comes out in my music. [subject]
I don't know **why I'm so crazy about his music**. [direct object]
I'll give **whoever calls first** the tickets. [indirect object]
Music is **what helps me unwind**. [subject complement]
Music is a way for people to communicate with **whomever* they meet**. [object of a preposition]

Indirect speech is expressed using a noun clause.
They asked **whether / if we could recommend some good recordings**.
The violinist explained **that the concerto was quite difficult to play**.

A noun clause can also be introduced by **whoever**, **whomever**, or **whatever**, meaning any person or any thing.
Whoever can combine hip-hop with pop is sure to be a hit.
The audience always loves **whatever they play**.

Noun clauses often follow phrases with impersonal It subjects.
It's my opinion **that music is a kind of international language**.

In writing, subject noun clauses are often preceded by phrases such as **the fact**, **the idea**, etc.
The fact that enjoyment of music is universal is quite interesting.

*very formal **CN** **Corpus Notes:** According to the Longman Learner's Corpus, the learner error of using "question order" in noun clauses occurs quite frequently among intermediate and advanced learners. For example, *I asked them how did they feel* and *They told me how wonderful was your talk last week.*

REMEMBER

A noun clause can begin with <u>that</u>, <u>if</u>, <u>whether (or not)</u>, or a question word.

I believe **that** life would be empty without music.
We asked them **if** they could play the song for us again.
OR We asked them **whether (or not)** they could play the song for us again.
I'm not sure **why** the band decided to break up.
Do you know **which / what** instrument she plays?
They asked her **how** she trained her voice to be so beautiful.

When a noun clause is a direct object, the word <u>that</u> may be omitted.

I believe life would be empty without music.

BE CAREFUL! Use normal, not inverted, word order in noun clauses beginning with question words. **CN**

NOT They asked her how ~~did she~~ ~~train~~ her voice to be so beautiful.

Grammar Booster

PAGE G4
For more …

2 Explain the role of music in your life

A 🎧 GRAMMAR **SNAPSHOT**
(CD 1, Track 17)

Suggested teaching time:	5–10 minutes
Your actual teaching time:	_____

- Have students read and listen to the commentaries.
- Ask *What is the role of music in Patricia's life?* (Patricia listens to music all day—it helps her get going, stay productive, and unwind.) . . . *in Santigi's life?* (It is important because it's a way for people to communicate all over the world.) . . . *in Alison's life?* (Alison performs music, so it's part of her everyday life.)
- Ask students to notice the use of noun clauses. Point out that they are in bold type.

> **Language note:** *Get someone through* means help someone, especially in a difficult situation. *Get going* is an expression that means start doing something or going somewhere. If you *stay productive*, you keep achieving and working hard. *Unwind* means relax and stop feeling anxious. *Open doors* means create opportunities. If you express *what is in your heart*, you express your feelings or emotions. If something *comes out* in your music, work, etc., it can be seen in your music, work, etc.

B Discussion

Suggested teaching time:	5–10 minutes
Your actual teaching time:	_____

- Have students discuss the questions in groups of four.
- Circulate to offer help as students discuss. Remind them to give examples and explain their answers.
- Call on a student from each group to share his/her views with the class.

C Grammar

Suggested teaching time:	10–15 minutes
Your actual teaching time:	_____

- On the board, write:
  > Buy <u>him</u> <u>a CD</u> for <u>his birthday</u>.
  > <u>Classical music</u> is <u>relaxing</u>.

  As a class, identify the subject (classical music), direct object (a CD), indirect object (him), subject complement (relaxing), and object of a preposition (his birthday). You may want to point out that in the first sentence, *you* is implied as the subject.
- Have students read the first explanation and study the examples. On the board, write:
  > 1. *What I like is his voice.*
  > 2. *I recommend this CD to whomever I talk to.*

  3. *I don't know why I find this music so relaxing.*
  4. *Listening to music is how I think more clearly.*
  5. *Give whoever is interested a copy of the lyrics.*

  To check comprehension, have pairs identify the clauses and decide on their grammatical functions. Review as a class. (1. What I like = subject; 2. whomever I talk to = object of a preposition; 3. why I find this music so relaxing = direct object; 4. how I think more clearly = subject complement; 5. whoever is interested = indirect object)
- Have students read the second explanation and study the examples. On the board, write:
  > 6. *He said that he had always been interested in music.*
  > 7. *I told him why I don't like jazz.*
  > 8. *She asked me if I'd like to go to the concert.*

  To check comprehension, have students identify the noun clauses. Review as a class. (6. that he had always been interested in music; 7. why I don't like jazz; 8. if I'd like to go to the concert)
- Have volunteers read the Remember box out loud. To check comprehension, have students look at sentences 6–8 on the board and name the words that are used to introduce the noun clauses. (6. that, 7. why, 8. if) Then have students look at sentence 6 and ask if *that* can be omitted. (yes)
- Have students read the third explanation and study the examples.
- On the board, write:
  > 1. He _____
  > can / whatever / sing / you / want
  > 2. You _____
  > dance / whomever / can / want / you / with
  > 3. Whoever _____
  > beautiful / singing / has / voice / is / a

  To check comprehension, have students put the words in the correct order. Review as a class. (1. He can sing whatever you want. 2. You can dance with whomever you want. 3. Whoever is singing has a beautiful voice.)
- Have students read the last two explanations and study the examples. To check comprehension, call on a few students to share their own examples.
- Have a volunteer read the Be Careful! box out loud. Write the following sentences on the board. To check comprehension, have students correct the sentences.
  > 1. *I wonder where is my favorite CD.*
  > 2. *He wanted to know why did I like reggae so much.*

  Review as a class. (1. . . . where my favorite CD is; 2. . . . why I liked reggae so much)

> **Language note:** Point out that even though *whomever* is formal and correct, *whoever* is typical of modern English usage, particularly spoken English.

 **Grammar Self-Checks**

D Introduce each noun clause . . .

Suggested teaching time: 5 minutes
Your actual teaching time: _____

• Have students complete the noun clauses individually.
• Have students compare answers with a partner and review as a class. Note: In item 3, both *what* and *which* are possible.

Option: For more practice classifying noun clauses, have pairs classify each noun clause from the Grammar Snapshot by its grammatical function within the sentence. Model the first item with the class: Ask students to find the main verb in the sentence (*can't imagine*) and then identify the grammatical function of the noun clause (direct object). Point out that finding the main verb or verb phrase in each sentence will help them determine the grammatical function of the clauses. Review as a class. (*what my life would be like without music* = object; *what gets me through the day, how I get going in the morning, how I stay productive, what helps me unwind* = subject complement; *that music is a kind of international language* = subject complement; *whomever they meet* = object of a preposition; *the fact that enjoyment of music is universal* = subject; *what's in my heart* = object; *whether or not I perform, whatever happens during the day* = subject) **[+10 minutes]**

E Complete each statement . . .

Suggested teaching time: 5 minutes
Your actual teaching time: _____

• Remind students that embedded questions use a period—not a question mark—at the end of each sentence.
• Have students complete the statements individually and then compare answers with a partner.
• Review as a class. Have volunteers present their statements to the class.

GRAMMAR EXCHANGE

Suggested teaching time: 15 minutes
Your actual teaching time: _____

Pair Work

• After identifying the noun clauses as a class, have students identify the grammatical function of each in pairs. Review as a class.
• After pairs discuss the meanings of the quotations and restate them, have several volunteers share with the class. (Possible responses: **Chang's quotation:** People know whether or not the music they are listening to is good. The audience can tell the difference between good music and bad music. **Beethoven's quotation:** I compose because I need to express what I feel. Writing music is how I express my feelings. **Simone's quotation:** Music has always been part of my life. I have musical talent, but I also work hard to produce good music.)

Discussion

• As a class, brainstorm times when you can listen to music and write them on the board. (Possible responses: in the morning/afternoon/evening; before going to bed; while I study/work; on my way to school/work; while I take a bath; while I do my homework/the housework; while I drive)
• Have students read the phrases in the oval on the bottom right corner. Point out that the phrases can all be followed by noun clauses.
• Encourage students to use some of the vocabulary from the commentaries on page 18 to discuss the role of music in their lives.
• Form groups of four and have students discuss the questions.
• To review, have volunteers report to the class on the role of music in one of their group member's life. Point out that students will be using noun clauses as they report what their partners said.

EXTRAS (optional)

Grammar Booster
Workbook: Exercises 9–12

D Introduce each noun clause with <u>that</u>, <u>if</u>, <u>whether (or not)</u>, or a question word.

Question words

who	what
why	which
when	how
where	

1. It's his opinion ......*that*...... classical music is boring.

2. Buying old records is ......*how*...... I spend my Saturday afternoons.

3. I'm having difficulty recalling *which/what* band played at the dance.

4. ......*What*...... I like most is to take a hot bath while I listen to music.

5. Did they tell you ......*when*...... the concert would start? I don't want to be late.

6. I can't really tell you ......*why*...... I like some pieces of music. Maybe it's because they remind me of songs my mother sang to me when I was a child.

7. Robert asked me *whether (or not)* I had bought tickets yet.

8. She can't imagine ......*what*...... she would do without music.

E Complete each statement with a noun clause that represents each question.

1. I don't know *where Mozart lived* .
   (Where did Mozart live?)

2. I have no idea *when George Bizet composed Carmen* .
   (When did Georges Bizet compose *Carmen*?)

3. She told me *where the Black Sheep usually perform* .
   (Where do the Black Sheep usually perform?)

4. I don't know *which genre of music is his favorite* .
   (Which genre of music is his favorite?)

5. I'm not sure *what kind of lyrics she writes* .
   (What kind of lyrics does she write?)

GRAMMAR **EXCHANGE** • *Now explain the role of music in your life.*

Pair Work. Read the following quotations and underline the noun clauses. Classify each noun clause by its grammatical function within the sentence (subject, direct object, etc.). Then discuss the meaning of each quotation. Restate each in your own words.

> direct object
> "The audience knows <u>when they're just listening to notes</u> and <u>when they're truly listening to music</u>." direct object
> **Sarah Chang**, U.S. violinist
> 1980 –

> direct object
> "Music is a gift and a burden I've had since I can remember <u>who I was</u>."
> **Nina Simone**, U.S. singer and pianist
> 1933 – 2003

> subject
> "<u>What I have in my heart</u> must come out. This is why I compose music."
> **Ludwig van Beethoven**, German composer
> 1770 – 1827

Discussion. Explain the role of music in your life. Do you listen to music at specific times during your day? What sorts of music do you listen to? Try to use noun clauses to explain your ideas.

> Listening to music is . . .
> I can't imagine . . .
> It's my opinion . . .

3 Describe a creative person

A 🎧 **Vocabulary. Describing creative personalities.** Listen and practice.

Positive qualities

gifted having a natural ability to do one or more things extremely well
energetic very active, physically and mentally
imaginative able to think of new and interesting ideas
passionate showing a strong liking for something and CN1 being very dedicated to it

Negative qualities

eccentric behaving in an unusual way or appearing different from most people
difficult never satisfied and hard to please CN2
moody quickly and easily becoming annoyed or unhappy
egotistical believing oneself to be better or more important than other people

CN1 Corpus Notes: *Passionate* appears modified by a phrase beginning with the preposition *about* more frequently than it does alone. For example, *He's passionate about Beethoven's symphonies.*

B **Reading Warm-up.** It is often said that gifted people have eccentric or difficult personalities. Do you agree?

CN2 Corpus Notes: Bosses are described as *difficult* more frequently than any other type of person. *Difficult* is also frequently used to describe children and teenagers.

C 🎧 **Reading.** Read the short biography. What effect did Beethoven's personality have on his life?

Ludwig van Beethoven: A Passion for Music

Born in 1770 in Bonn, Germany, Ludwig van Beethoven started playing the piano before he was four years old. By the time he was twelve, this child prodigy had already composed his first piece of music. When Beethoven was just sixteen, he went to study in Vienna, Austria, then the center of European cultural life and home to the most brilliant and passionate musicians and composers of the period. Beethoven proved to be a gifted pianist and an imaginative composer.

Beethoven is remembered for his great genius but also for his strong and difficult personality. In one infamous incident, Beethoven became so upset with a waiter that he emptied a plate of food over the man's head. Despite this type of behavior, many in musical and aristocratic circles admired Beethoven, and music lovers were always Beethoven's greatest supporters. This fact did not prevent him from losing his temper with one or another of them. However, because of his talent, Beethoven's friends always excused his insults and moody temperament.

Beethoven was also notorious for his eccentric behavior. He often walked through the streets of Vienna muttering to himself and stamping his feet. He completely neglected his personal appearance; his clothes would get so dirty that his friends would come and take them away during the night. When they replaced the old clothes with new ones, Beethoven never noticed the difference.

Although Beethoven was respected and admired by his audience, he was not concerned with pleasing them. Beethoven could play the piano so beautifully that some listeners cried; however, when he saw his fans crying, Beethoven only laughed and said they were fools. He was so egotistical that if people talked while he was performing, he would stop and walk away.

Beethoven wrote two famous works, *Moonlight Sonata* and *Für Elise*, for two different women he loved. He was almost always in love, often with a woman who was already married or engaged. Although Beethoven asked several women to marry him, they all rejected him. But the most tragic aspect of Beethoven's life was his gradual loss of hearing, beginning in his late twenties until he was completely deaf. However, even as his hearing grew worse, Beethoven continued to be energetic and productive; his creative activity remained intense, and audiences loved his music. In 1826, Beethoven held his last public performance of his famous Ninth Symphony. By this time, the maestro was completely deaf. When he was turned around so he could see the roaring applause that he could not hear, Beethoven began to cry.

Beethoven died in Vienna in 1827 at age fifty-seven. One out of ten people who lived in Vienna came to his funeral.

Source: www.classicalarchive.com

3 Describe a creative person

A 🎧 Vocabulary
(CD 1, Track 18)

Suggested teaching time:	5–10 minutes
Your actual teaching time:	_____

- Have students listen to the words and study the definitions. Then have students listen and repeat the words chorally.
- To check comprehension, have volunteers use the words in sentences about people they know. Encourage them to give examples of this person's character or actions. For example, *My friend Ted is gifted. He can play the piano, guitar, and drums like a professional musican.*

B Reading Warm-up

Suggested teaching time:	10 minutes
Your actual teaching time:	_____

- As a class, brainstorm names of some people who are considered gifted. (Possible responses: Albert Einstein, Isaac Newton)
- In small groups, have students discuss the Warm-up question. Encourage them to give examples to support their opinions.
- To finish, have volunteers share their opinions with the class.

C 🎧 Reading
(CD 1, Track 19)

Suggested teaching time:	10–15 minutes
Your actual teaching time:	_____

- Read the title of the article out loud.
- Have volunteers share anything they may know about Beethoven. (Possible responses: He was a great composer; Some people consider him the greatest composer of all time; He composed many famous symphonies.)
- Have students read and listen to the biography.
- To check comprehension, ask:
  What are some facts mentioned in the article that show that Beethoven was passionate about music? (Possible responses: He started playing the piano before he was four; Even as his hearing grew worse, he continued to be productive with his music.)
  What are some tragic aspects of Beethoven's life? (Possible responses: His marriage proposal was rejected by several women; He was always in love with women who were married or engaged; He lost his hearing.)
  What are some examples of Beethoven's difficult and eccentric behavior? (Possible responses: He emptied a plate of food over a waiter's head; He talked to himself; He neglected his appearance.)

- In pairs, have students discuss the reading question, *What effect did Beethoven's personality have on his life?* Bring the class together and have a volunteer from each pair share their responses. (Possible response: His strong personality made him an unpleasant person who often lost his temper and behaved selfishly. But it was also his strong personality that enabled him to fight the obstacles and keep working when he lost his hearing.)

> **Language note:** You may want to share the following definitions if students ask about specific expressions: *prodigy* (a young person who is extremely smart or good at doing something); *infamous* (well-known for being bad or morally evil); *notorious* (famous or well-known for something bad); *mutter* (speak quietly or in a low voice); *neglect* (not pay attention to something).

🔄 **Reading Strategies**

🔄 **Reading Speed Calculator**

🔄 **Extra Reading Comprehension Activities**

Option: To use the reading as a listening activity, draw the following event chain on the board:

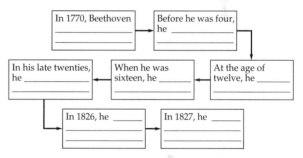

🔄 **Graphic Organizers**

First listening: With books closed, have students listen and complete the event chain about Beethoven's life. Review as a class. (In 1770, Beethoven <u>was born in Germany</u>; Before he was four, he <u>started playing the piano</u>; At the age of twelve, he <u>composed his first piece</u>; When he was sixteen, he <u>went to Vienna to study music</u>; In his late twenties, he <u>started losing his hearing</u>; In 1826, he <u>held his last public performance</u>; In 1827, he <u>died in Vienna</u>.)

On the board, write:
- *Difficult personality*
- *Eccentric behavior*
- *Egotistical behavior*

Second listening: Point out that the biography gives one or two specific examples illustrating each personality trait on the board. Have students listen for the examples and take notes. Review as a class. (**Difficult personality:** He once emptied a plate of food over a waiter's head; **Eccentric behavior:** He walked through the streets muttering to himself and stamping his feet; He neglected his personal appearance and his clothes were often dirty; **Egotistical behavior:** He stopped playing and walked away when people started talking while he was performing.) [+10–15 minutes]

D **Pair Work**

Suggested teaching time:	5–10 minutes
Your actual teaching time:	_____

• Model the first item as a class. (Possible responses: gifted, energetic, passionate) Point out that some items have more than one answer.

• Review as a class. Have volunteers explain their choices.

 **Vocabulary-Building Strategies**

DISCUSSION **BUILDER**

Suggested teaching time:	15 minutes
Your actual teaching time:	_____

Step 1. Pair Work.

• Have students rate their personalities individually on the chart.

• Have a volunteer read the model out loud.

• As students compare their answers, circulate to offer help as needed.

Step 2. Discussion.

• Have volunteers read the quotations out loud.

• Form small groups and have students discuss the questions. Encourage students to use the vocabulary on page 20.

• To review, have students from different groups share their views with the class.

Language note: R & B is rhythm and blues, a type of music.

Step 3. Writing.

• To help students relate the person's creativity to his/her personality, draw the following chart on the board and have students complete. Encourage students to think of specific examples to illustrate this person's personality traits.

Creative person I know: _____	
Achievements	Personality

Project: Form small groups of students with similar musical tastes. Have students choose an artist or band and create a web page for a music website. The web page should include a short biography of the artist or band, a photo of the artist or band with a quotation as caption, and a short review of a CD or piece of music.

EXTRAS (optional)

Workbook: Exercises 13–17

D **Pair Work.** Read each fact about Beethoven. Discuss which adjectives from the vocabulary you think best describe his behavior and actions. Complete the statements.

1. Beethoven was already publishing music and earning a salary at the age of twelve. He was very ⎯⎯ gifted ⎯⎯.

2. Beethoven once told a prince, "There will be thousands of princes. There is only one Beethoven." He could be quite ⎯⎯ egotistical ⎯⎯.

3. Beethoven would work long hours composing and never seemed to tire. He was always ⎯⎯ energetic ⎯⎯ when he performed for his audiences.

4. Beethoven had many close friends who tried to help him with his problems. He continually pushed them away and refused their assistance. He was considered to be a ⎯⎯ difficult ⎯⎯ person.

5. Beethoven became frustrated when he began to lose his hearing. While socializing with his friends, he would often have sudden bursts of anger. He could be rather ⎯⎯ moody ⎯⎯.

6. Beethoven said that his music expressed what was inside of him and that he had no choice but to compose. He was a ⎯⎯ passionate ⎯⎯ composer.

7. Beethoven's attention to feeling in his music began a new "style," different in some ways from Baroque music, which was popular at the time. His compositions were ⎯⎯ imaginative ⎯⎯.

8. Beethoven's friends thought he could be ⎯⎯ eccentric ⎯⎯ at times. For example, when he made coffee, he used to count out exactly sixty beans for each cup.

DISCUSSION **BUILDER** • *Now describe a creative person.*

Step 1. Pair Work. Rate your own personality on a scale of 0 to 3. Compare your answers with a partner's.

> "I'm an extremely passionate person. I think it's really important to love what you do. What about you?"

0 = not at all	1 = a little	2 = somewhat	3 = extremely	
gifted ◯	eccentric ◯	passionate ◯	imaginative ◯	
difficult ◯	energetic ◯	moody ◯	egotistical ◯	creative ◯

Step 2. Discussion. Read the quotations from three famous musicians. Which one do you find the most interesting? After reading the quotations, how would you describe each musician's personality?

"Music is nothing separate from me. It is me. . . . You'd have to remove the music surgically."

Ray Charles, American soul singer, songwriter, and pianist, 1930–2004

"Music will save the world."

Pablo Casals, Spanish cellist and conductor, 1876–1973

"I've outdone anyone you can name—Mozart, Beethoven, Bach, Strauss. Irving Berlin, he wrote 1,001 tunes. I wrote 5,500."

James Brown, American R & B singer and songwriter, 1933–

Step 3. Writing. On a separate sheet of paper, write a brief biography of a creative person you know. Describe his or her personality. Explain how the person's creativity is related to his or her personality and achievements.

4 Discuss the benefits of music

A 🎧 **Listening Comprehension.** Read the questions. Then listen to Part 1 of a talk about an unusual use of music. Discuss the questions with a partner.

1. What does Dr. Schmidt do? She's a music therapist.

2. What sorts of people does she work with? Answers will vary, Explain how she works with these people. but may include: She works with people of various ages who have all sorts of different problems. She designs music sessions based on individual needs.

B 🎧 Read the questions. Then listen to Part 2 of the talk and answer the questions.

1. What are the four benefits Dr. Schmidt talks about?
   a. emotional
   b. social
   c. physical
   d. intellectual

   Answers will vary, but may include:

2. What is one example of each?
   a. clients feel comfortable sharing emotions
   b. clients develop social skills
   c. encourages movement among those in pain
   d. helps young children improve in math

C **Discussion.**

1. Can you think of any other benefits of music therapy?

2. Can you think of anyone who might benefit from music therapy? If so, how?

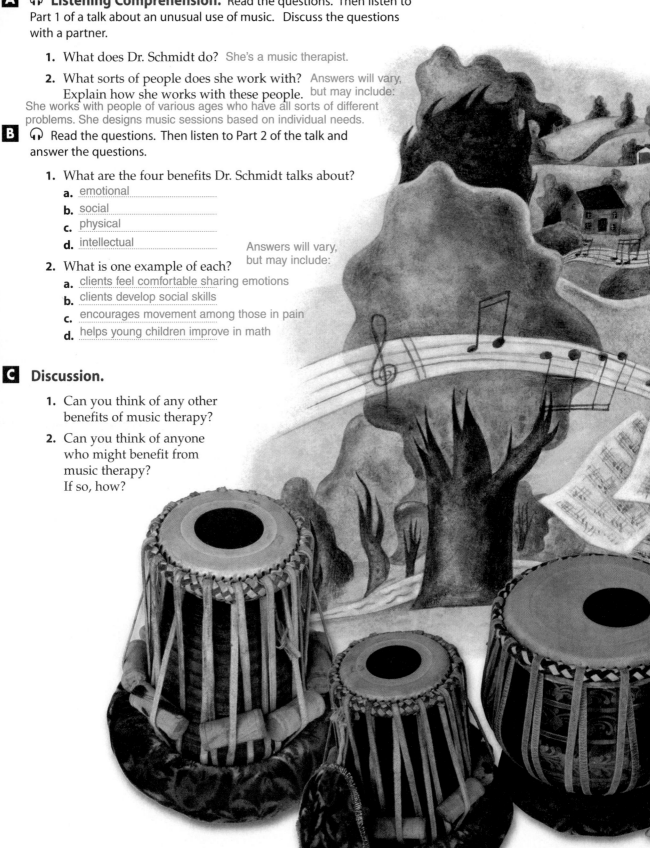

4 *Discuss the benefits of music*

A 🎧 Listening Comprehension
(CD 1, Track 20)

Suggested teaching time:	10 minutes
Your actual teaching time:	_____

- Pre-listening: Have students look at the picture. Ask: *What can you see in the picture?* (Possible responses: drums, trees, small houses, music notes) *How would you describe the atmosphere created by the picture?* (Possible responses: relaxing, peaceful, quiet)
- Have students read the questions and listen to Part 1.
- After students discuss the questions and answers with a partner, review the answers as a class.

AUDIOSCRIPT

For audioscript, see page AS3.

B 🎧 Read the questions ...
(CD 1, Track 21)

Suggested teaching time:	10 minutes
Your actual teaching time:	_____

- First listening: Have students listen and list the four benefits.
- Second listening: Have students listen for specific examples of each benefit.
- To make sure students are on the right track, pause after Dr. Schmidt finishes explaining the emotional benefits. Ask volunteers to share some examples of emotional benefits. (Possible responses: Music can help you express your feelings; Music can help you feel comfortable sharing your emotions.)
- Review as a class. Have volunteers share their responses.

Language note: When Dr. Schmidt refers to her client as *him*, she's not necessarily speaking about a male client—she's referring to any client.

 Listening Strategies

AUDIOSCRIPT

For audioscript, see page AS3.

C Discussion

Suggested teaching time:	5–10 minutes
Your actual teaching time:	_____

- Have a volunteer read the questions out loud.
- Write on the board *Benefits of music therapy*, and have students list as many items as they can think of. (Possible responses: improve memory, control emotions, help you forget worries)
- Draw a two-column chart with the heads *Who?* and *How?* on the board. Ask students to take notes as they discuss item 2.
- Bring the class together to review. Have volunteers share their groups' thoughts on who might benefit from music therapy and how.

T22

D Word Skills

Suggested teaching time:	5–10 minutes
Your actual teaching time:	_____

- Have students read the explanations and study the examples.
- On the board, write:

  a boring song
  a bored audience

  Ask *What's the differencce between* bored *and* boring? Elicit that *a boring song* has an active meaning because the song bores the audience and that *a bored audience* has a passive meaning because the audience is bored by the song.

- To summarize the information, add to the sentences on the board:

  a boring song The song <u>bores</u> the audience.
  (active meaning)

  a bored audience The audience <u>is bored</u> by the song. (passive meaning)

🎧 Present participles, Past participles
(CD 1, Track 22)

- Have students listen to and repeat the participial adjectives in the box.

> **Language note:** If necessary, clarify the meaning of the following adjectives: *touching* (affecting your emotions, especially making you feel pity, sympathy, sadness, etc.); *touched* (having your emotions affected, especially feeling pity or sympathy); *stimulating* (making you feel more active); *stimulated* (feeling active or interested in something); *soothing* (making you feel calmer and less anxious, upset, or angry); *soothed* (feeling calmer and less anxious, upset, or angry).

E Circle the correct adjective ...

Suggested teaching time:	5 minutes
Your actual teaching time:	_____

- Model the first item with the class.
- Have students complete the exercise individually and then compare answers with a partner. Review as a class.

🌐 **Vocabulary-Building Strategies**

🎧 **Option:** Practice using participial adjectives. (Use the audio from Exercise C on page 16 [CD 1, Track 16] for this activity.)

Step 1. In pairs, have students listen to the four pieces of music and choose the genre for each. Then have them think of other songs in that genre. On the board, write:

1. genre: _____   other songs: _____
2. genre: _____   other songs: _____
3. genre: _____   other songs: _____
4. genre: _____   other songs: _____

Step 2. Write these unfinished statements on the board. Have students listen again and choose participial adjectives that best describe each piece. For each piece, complete these two statements:

	Song #1	Song # 2	Song #3	Song #4
This song makes you feel . . .				
This song is . . .				

[+10–15 minutes]

🌐 **Graphic Organizers**

DISCUSSION **BUILDER**

Suggested teaching time:	10–15 minutes
Your actual teaching time:	_____

🌐 **Discourse Strategies**

Step 1. Pair Work.

- Have students take notes on the benefits of music and examples. Encourage students to think of three benefits and examples for each.
- As pairs write their ideas, circulate to offer help as needed. Remind students to use some participial adjectives.

Step 2. Group Work.

- Have each pair join another pair. Have each group choose two benefits to present to the class.
- Review as a class. As groups present their ideas, ask *Do you agree with these benefits?* Have students who agree with the benefits share the examples they wrote. Have students who don't agree explain their reasons.

EXTRAS (optional)

Workbook: Exercises 18–20

D Word Skills. Using participial adjectives CN

The present and past participle forms of many verbs function as adjectives.

The past participle has a passive meaning. Most sentences using past participles can be restated with a **by** phrase.

> The patient is **depressed**. = The patient is depressed [by his life].
> I'm **bored**. = I'm bored [by this movie].

The present participle does not have a passive meaning. Most sentences using present participles can be restated with an active verb.

> That book is **depressing**. = That book depresses [everyone].
> It's so **boring**. = It bores [me].

Present participles	Past participles
amazing	amazed
annoying	annoyed
boring	bored
depressing	depressed
disappointing	disappointed
entertaining	entertained
exciting	excited
interesting	interested
pleasing	pleased
relaxing	relaxed
soothing	soothed
stimulating	stimulated
touching	touched

E Circle the correct adjective to complete the sentence about music therapy.

1. Music can make patients feel ((relaxed) / relaxing).
2. Listening to music makes patients feel less ((depressed) / depressing).
3. Patients find some types of music to be very (soothed / (soothing)).
4. For patients in physical pain, the benefits of music can be (surprised / (surprising)).
5. Studies show that a student's ability to learn is ((stimulated) / stimulating) by music.
6. For patients with emotional problems, music can be very (comforted / (comforting)).
7. Many doctors report they are ((pleased) / pleasing) by the effect music has on their patients.
8. Many patients say that music therapy is (entertained / (entertaining)).

DISCUSSION **BUILDER** • *Now discuss the benefits of music.*

Step 1. Pair Work. What do you think are some benefits music brings to people's lives? Make a list and discuss.

Benefits | Examples
Music can be soothing. | *Playing music at work can relax people so they're more productive.*

Benefits | Examples

Step 2. Group Work. Present your ideas to the class. Comment on your classmates' ideas.

CN **Corpus Notes:** According to the Longman Learner's Corpus, choosing the wrong participle is a common error among intermediate to advanced learners. For example, *We were exciting about the news* and *My life was quite bored at that time.*

23

Writing: Describe yourself

Parallel structure

In a pair or a series, be sure to use parallel structure. All the words, phrases, or clauses should be in the same form.

Incorrect	Correct
He's a composer, singer, and a violinist. (article, no article, article)	He's **a** composer, **a** singer, and **a** violinist. (article, article, article) OR He's **a** composer, singer, and violinist. (one article for all three)
I like dancing, painting, and to sing. (gerund, gerund, infinitive)	I like **dancing, painting,** and **singing.** (gerund, gerund, gerund) OR I like **to dance, to paint,** and **to sing.** (infinitive, infinitive, infinitive) OR I like **to dance, paint,** and **sing.** (one <u>to</u> for all three)
The picture was framed, examined, and they sold it. (passive, passive, active)	The picture was **framed, examined,** and **sold.** (passive, passive, passive)
I like people who have the same interests as I do, make me laugh, or who like outdoor sports. (clause, verb phrase, clause)	I like people **who have the same interests as I do, who make me laugh,** or **who like outdoor sports.** (clause, clause, clause) OR I like people who **have the same interests as I do, make me laugh,** or **like outdoor sports.** (verb phrase, verb phrase, verb phrase)

Step 1. Prewriting. Clustering ideas.

Look at the idea cluster below. On a separate sheet of paper, create your own idea cluster. Draw a circle and write <u>ME</u> inside it. Then write any ideas that come to mind in circles around the main circle. Expand each new idea. Include hobbies, accomplishments, places you have traveled, interests, goals, etc.

ERROR CORRECTION | Correct the three errors.

I have always been a relaxed, passionate, and been a moody person. I love traveling, ~~to meet~~ meeting new people, and learning about new places. I have been to many interesting places; for example, I have been on top of Mount Kilimanjaro, I have gone ice fishing with Eskimos in Alaska, and I ~~rode~~ have ridden on a camel in Morocco. These were some of

Example

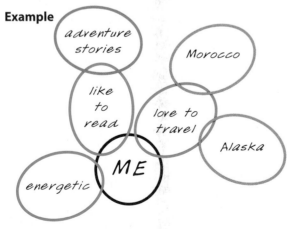

Step 2. Writing.
On a separate sheet of paper, write a paragraph describing yourself, using the information from your cluster. Make sure to use parallel structure.

Step 3. Self-Check.

☐ Did you use parallel structure with pairs or series of nouns, adjectives, and adverbs?

☐ Did you use parallel structure with the clauses, phrases, and tenses?

☐ Does the topic sentence introduce the topic of the paragraph?

Writing *Describe yourself*

Suggested teaching time: 20–25 minutes
Your actual teaching time: _____

Parallel structure

- Have volunteers read the explanation for parallel structure and the correct and incorrect examples.

- To check comprehension, ask *What is parallel structure?* (a pair or series of elements in the same form)

- Write the following sentences on the board, or photocopy and distribute. To check comprehension, have pairs complete the sentences with their own ideas. Review as a class by having several volunteers read their sentences out loud.

  I went sailing, skiing, and _____ .
  I ate biscuits, sandwiches, and _____ .
  He finds the song boring and _____ .
  He asked me what I liked, where I lived, and _____ .
  I learned to sing and _____ .
  My friend Joe is imaginative, eccentric, and _____ .
  I liked the lyrics, the melody, and _____ .

- On the board, write:

  He bought a jacket, a tie, and a sweater.

  To make students aware of punctuation, ask *How many elements does this parallel structure have?* (three) *What are they?* (a jacket, a tie, a sweater) *What are they separated by?* (commas) Point out that the last comma (after *tie*) is optional. Then ask *What word is used before the final element?* (and) Point out that *or* is also possible in a parallel structure, as in the last example on the chart.

- On the board, write:

  I like the beat and lyrics of that song.

  Have students look at the example, and ask *How many elements does this parallel structure have?* (two) *What are they?* (beat, lyrics) *Are they separated by commas?* (no) Point out that if a parallel structure consists of only two elements, no comma is used.

- Have students find the mistakes in the Error Correction paragraph individually and then compare their corrections with a partner. Review as a class.

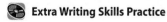 **Extra Writing Skills Practice**

Step 1. Prewriting.

- Have students look at the idea cluster. Ask *What does the cluster reveal about the person who made it?* (Possible responses: The person likes to travel; He or she has been or would like to go to Morocco and Alaska; The person likes to read adventure stories.)

- Point out how the circles containing related ideas overlap each other. For example, *adventure stories* overlaps *like to read*, not *energetic*.

- Have students create their clusters individually. Point out that when drawing their clusters, students should not judge their ideas: they should write everything that comes to their minds.

Step 2. Writing.

- Before students write, point out how circles that overlap the same circle may contain elements to be expressed with parallel structure. For example, *Morocco* and *Alaska* overlap *love to travel*. The sentence *I love to travel to Morocco and Alaska* uses parallel structure.

- As students write, circulate to offer help as needed. Check to see that students are forming parallel structures correctly.

Step 3. Self–Check.

- Read the Self-Check questions with the class.

- Before students submit their paragraphs for correction, have them self-check their work and make any necessary changes.

EXTRAS (optional)

Workbook: Page 20

A 🎧 Listening Comprehension
(CD 1, Track 23)

Suggested teaching time:	10 minutes
Your actual teaching time:	_____

- Pre-listening: You may want to review the words *voice, melody, lyrics, beat,* and *sound* by having volunteers say what they mean.
- First listening: Have students listen to the conversations and decide if the speakers like the artist or group. Point out that they may have to check both boxes for each artist or group.
- Second listening: Have students listen and decide what the people like about the artist or group.
- Have students compare answers with a partner and review as a class.

Option: Have students listen to the speakers again and write information that supports their answers. (1. The woman says he's an amazing singer. 2. The man says he loves the arrangement, and the woman says he knows how to compose music. 3. The man says that they sing without any musical instruments and that they're one of a kind. 4. The man says the dance music was fantastic, and the woman says Beyoncé's music is fabulous. 5. The man says Jobim's songs are beautiful.) **[+5–10 minutes]**

AUDIOSCRIPT

For audioscript, see page AS3.

B Complete the statements . . .

Suggested teaching time:	5–10 minutes
Your actual teaching time:	_____

- You may want to review the adjectives by having volunteers explain their meanings.
- Have students compare answers with a partner. Then review as a class.

C Circle the correct form . . .

Suggested teaching time:	5–10 minutes
Your actual teaching time:	_____

- Have students read the first sentence. Ask *What's the answer to item 1?* (has played) *Why?* (The word *since* implies that the action continues into the present.)
- Have students complete the exercise individually and then compare answers with a partner.
- Review as a class. Ask volunteers to support their choices.

D Underline the noun clause . . .

Suggested teaching time:	5 minutes
Your actual teaching time:	_____

- Model the first item with the class.
- Have students compare answers with a partner. Then review as a class.

Option: Have pairs replace the noun clauses in each sentence to create new sentences. To review, have volunteers read their sentences out loud. **[+5 minutes]**

 You may wish to use the Video Program and activity worksheets for Unit 2 at this point.

 **Complete Assessment Package
Unit 2 Achievement Test**

SUMMIT WEBSITE
For Unit 2 online activities, visit the
Summit Companion Website at
www.longman.com/summit.

A 🎧 **Listening Comprehension.** Listen to the conversations about musical preferences. Determine if each person likes the artist or group. Check the appropriate box or boxes. Then listen again and write what the person likes (voice, melody, lyrics, beat, or sound).

		the man	the woman	what he or she likes
1.	Andrea Bocelli	☑	☐	voice
2.	Gato Barbieri	☑	☑	melody
3.	Ladysmith Black Mambazo	☐	☑	sound
4.	Beyoncé	☑	☑	beat
5.	Antonio Carlos Jobim	☑	☑	lyrics

B Complete the statements with an appropriate adjective from the box.

> eccentric   egotistical   energetic   gifted   moody   passionate

1. Sarah is a very .... gifted .... musician. She started playing the piano when she was three.
2. My neighbor has thirty cats. You could say he's a bit .... eccentric ....
3. Franco is an extremely .... egotistical .... person. He only thinks of himself.
4. Dalia is so .... moody .... lately. She gets angry at the smallest thing.

C Circle the correct form of the verb to complete the paragraph.

Sandile Khemese (**1.** has played / played) the violin since he was a child in Johannesburg, South Africa. In 1989, Sandile (**2.** formed / has formed) the Soweto String Quartet with his brothers, Reuben and Thami, and their friend, Makhosini Mnguni. The group (**3.** played / has played) at President Nelson Mandela's inauguration in 1994. The Soweto String Quartet (**4.** won / has won) many music awards in South Africa, including Best New Artist. They (**5.** have recorded / have been recording) a number of successful CDs. In recent years, the Quartet (**6.** has been giving / gave) concerts all around the world.

D Underline the noun clause in each sentence. Write whether it is a subject, a direct object, a subject complement, or an object of a preposition.

1. I believe that without music life wouldn't be as much fun.   direct object
2. Whatever's playing on the radio is fine with me.   subject
3. That's why Jorge likes only pop music.   subject complement
4. Do you know where some good music is playing?   direct object
5. They'll listen to whatever music is playing.   object of a preposition

Money Matters

A **Topic Preview.** Read these financial tips.
Do you think you have a high financial IQ?

Three Tips for a High Financial IQ

1. Spend less than you earn.

The key to wealth is living below your means. If you make $300,000 a year and spend it all, you're not rich—you just have a lot of stuff. A job loss or serious illness could wipe you out in a few weeks. Your neighbors who make $50,000 and live on $40,000 are much wealthier. Fortunately, with today's technology, keeping a budget has never been easier. Invest in financial planning software that allows you to add up your income and expenses and keep a record of your spending.

2. Have a savings program.

Start saving early. If you invest $50 a week for 40 years and earn 9% interest, you will end up with $1,026,853. People spend because they get a good feeling from spending money. You can get that same good feeling from putting your money away in savings.

3. Pay off your credit cards.

Credit cards can be wonderful things. You can treat yourself to a spa retreat or a gourmet dinner without worrying whether you have the cash to pay for it. The downside, of course, is that credit cards let many people live beyond their means. So use credit cards, but pay the bill in full each month.

Source: *USA TODAY*, December 31, 1999. Reprinted with permission.

B **Discussion.** Which tip do you think is the most important one to follow? Why?
Can you think of any others?

Money Matters

A Topic Preview

Suggested teaching time:	5–10 minutes
Your actual teaching time:	_____

- To introduce the unit theme of money, have students read the title of the article and the numbered tips below. To draw on students' prior knowledge, ask *What do you think a person's financial IQ is?*
- Have students read the financial tips to themselves.
- To check comprehension, write the following exercise on the board or photocopy and distribute it. Have students check the tips that are suggested in the article. (tips that are suggested in article: 2, 3, 5)

  1. _____ Find a job that offers a high salary.

  2. _____ Use a computer program to keep track of your spending.

  3. _____ Save part of your income every week.

  4. _____ Don't use credit cards.

  5. _____ Pay the full balance of your credit card bill every month.

- Bring the class together to review. Have volunteers say whether or not they have a high financial IQ and give a supporting reason.

Language note: Students may need help with the following words or expressions: *live below / beyond your means* (spend less / more money than you have); *wipe someone out* (cause someone to lose all of his/her money); *budget* (a plan of how to spend money); *income* (the money that you earn from working or that you receive from investments); *savings* (all the money that you have saved, especially in a bank); *treat yourself to* (buy something special for yourself that you know you will enjoy); *pay off* (pay someone all the money that you owe them); *IQ* stands for *Intelligence Quotient*, which is a person's level of intelligence based on a standard test.

B Discussion

Suggested teaching time:	10–15 minutes
Your actual teaching time:	_____

- Form small groups. Have students read and discuss the questions. Encourage them to support their views. Circulate to offer help as needed.
- Have groups put the tips in order of importance.
- To draw on students' own experiences, have pairs talk about the tips that they follow/don't follow.
- For each tip, have a volunteer explain why it is the most important. Take a poll to find out which tip the class thinks is the most important.
- To finish, have groups share some other tips they thought of. (Possible tips: Invest your money; Reduce your taxes; Protect yourself with insurance; Use debit cards instead of credit cards; Take financial planning seminars; Don't buy things you don't really need; Plan for the future.)

C 🎧 Sound Bites
(CD 1, Track 24)

Suggested teaching time:	10 minutes
Your actual teaching time:	_____

- Have students look at the picture. Ask *What is it? What do you think it's used for?*
- Then ask *How do children save money in this country?*
- After students read and listen, ask *What did Judy buy?* (an entertainment system) *Did she pay in cash or by credit card?* (in cash) *Is she rich?* (No. She had to save up for it.) *How did she save enough money?* (She cut back on spending; She started living within her means.)
- To draw on students' own experiences, ask *Have you ever put money aside to buy something you wanted, such as an entertainment system, a computer, a bicycle, or a car?* Encourage students to share their experiences. Ask *Was it hard to save the money you needed?*

Language note: Students may need help with the following words or expressions: *strike it rich* (suddenly make a lot of money); *cut back on* (reduce the amount, size, cost, etc., of something); *out of hand* (impossible to control).

Save, save up, put money away, and *put money aside* have the same meaning. (The latter is introduced in Lesson 2.) They can be followed by an infinitive or *for* and a noun. For example, *I want to put money aside to buy a car; I'm saving up for a new car; I'm putting money away for a down payment.*

Kind of is an expression used in spoken English meaning *slightly* or *in some ways*.

Culture note: A *piggy bank* is a container used mainly by children to store coins. Piggy banks are used to encourage good saving and spending habits: the pig must be broken open for the money to be retrieved, forcing the child to justify his or her decision. The name *piggy bank* originated in the twelfth century; *pygg* referred to a type of clay used for making jars people stored their money in. By the eighteenth century, the term *pygg jar* had evolved to *pig bank*.

Option: On the board, write the following expressions:

> *Did you strike it rich?*
> *My bills are totally out of hand.*
> *I need to live within my means.*
> *I cut way back on spending.*

In pairs, have students think of different ways to say each expression. **[+5–10 minutes]**

D Pair Work

Suggested teaching time:	5–10 minutes
Your actual teaching time:	_____

- Have pairs discuss the questions. Review the answers to questions 1–5 as a class. Call on students to share their explanations.
- Have volunteers share whether they are more like Judy or David and give a supporting reason. (Possible responses: I'm more like Judy because I try to live within my means; I identify with David because I spend a lot of money on bills.)

STARTING **POINT**

Suggested teaching time:	15 minutes
Your actual teaching time:	_____

- Have a volunteer read the statements out loud. If necessary, clarify the meaning of *I can't make ends meet.* (The money I earn every month is not enough to cover my expenses.)
- Point out the useful language to talk about managing money: *live within / beyond your means; keep track of your expenses; put money away into savings; pay your bills off / in full; make ends meet.* Have students underline these expressions.
- Have students choose the statements individually.

Pair Work

- As pairs compare their answers, encourage them to give specific examples for each item. For example, *I live beyond my means. When I go shopping, I just can't help buying the things I like.*
- Ask *What habits would you like to change, if any? What can you do to raise your financial IQ?* (Possible response: I only keep track of my most important expenses. I think I should buy some financial planning software to get better organized and keep track of all my expenses.)
- To review, have volunteers talk about their money spending / saving habits with the class.

EXTRAS (optional)
Workbook: Exercises 1–5

C 🎧 **Sound Bites.** Read and listen to a conversation between two friends about saving money.

DAVID: Hey, a new entertainment system! What did you do—strike it rich?
JUDY: I wish! No, I saved up for it.
DAVID: There's no way I could do that. Too many bills. **CN**
JUDY: I know what you mean. My credit card bills used to be totally out of hand.
DAVID: Really? Then how did you manage to save up all that cash?
JUDY: Well, I just decided it was time to start living within my means. I cut way back on my spending.
DAVID: Wasn't that hard?
JUDY: Kind of. But I'm glad I did it.

CN **Corpus Notes:** The most frequent collocations with *too* are *too much, too many,* and *too bad.*

D **Pair Work.** Discuss the questions and explain your answers.

1. Do you think Judy makes a lot of money? No, she does not.
2. Do you think David is good with money? No, he is not.
3. What was Judy's financial situation like in the past? She had a lot of credit card debt.
4. What did Judy do to change her financial situation? She cut back on her spending.
5. How would you describe Judy's financial IQ? She has a high financial IQ.
6. Are you more like Judy or David?

a "piggy bank"

STARTING **POINT**

What's *your* financial IQ? Choose the statements that best apply to you.

1.	☐ I live within my means.	☐ I live beyond my means.
2.	☐ I keep track of my expenses.	☐ I don't know where the money goes.
3.	☐ I regularly put something away into savings.	☐ I spend everything I have and never save.
4.	☐ I always try to pay my credit card bills in full.	☐ I don't worry about paying my credit card bills off every month.
5.	☐ I always have enough money for what I need.	☐ I can't make ends meet!

Pair Work. Compare your answers with a partner's. Who do you think has the higher financial IQ?

1 *Talk about your financial goals*

A ⌒ GRAMMAR **SNAPSHOT.** Read the interview responses and notice how future plans are expressed.

What are your short-term and long-term financial goals?

I find it really helps me to try and picture where I want to be over the next few years. **By next year**, I **hope to have gotten** a good job as a financial consultant. That's my short-term goal. My long-term goal? I **plan to have reached** real financial independence **before I retire**.

Su-jin Lee, 29
Wonju, Korea

I've decided to set a long-term goal for myself—to put aside enough money to buy a new car. **By this time next year**, I'**ll have put away** enough cash for a down payment. My short-term goal is to start living within my means. **Once I've started** sticking to a monthly budget, I think it'll be easy.

David Michaels, 24
Brisbane, Australia

My college expenses are going to get me into a lot of debt. I **don't expect to have begun** making payments **by the time I graduate**, but I do have a plan. After I finish school, my short-term goal is to find a job where I can make some good money and begin a payment plan on my loans. Then, I figure that **by the time I'm thirty**, I **should have paid** back everything I owe.

Robin Kraus, 22
Boston, USA

My long-term goal is **to have saved** enough money to spend a year traveling. **By the time I'm forty**, I'm sure I'**ll have saved** enough. **After I've seen** some of the world, I **plan to settle down** and buy a house.

Andreas Festring, 33
Munich, Germany

B **Discussion.** How similar are you to any of the people in the Grammar Snapshot? Do you share any of the goals they mentioned? If not, what are some of *your* goals?

C **Grammar. Future plans and finished future actions**

Future plans

CN **Express general future plans with <u>expect</u>, <u>hope</u>, <u>intend</u>, or <u>plan</u> and an infinitive.**
    We **hope to start** putting some money away.
    I **don't plan to be** financially dependent for the rest of my life.

Use the perfect form of an infinitive to express that an action will or might take place before a specified time in the future.
    By this time next year, I plan **to have saved up** enough cash to buy a new car.
    Her goal is **to have paid off** all her debt in five years.

Finished future actions

Use the future perfect to indicate an action that will be completed by a specified time in the future.
    By next year, I **will have completed** my studies, but I **won't have gotten** married.
    How much **will** you **have saved** by next month?

Use the present perfect in an adverbial clause to distinguish between a completed future action and one that will follow it.
    Once I'**ve completed** my studies, I'll get married.
    I'm going shopping when I'**ve finished** my report.

BE CAREFUL! Don't use the future perfect in the adverbial clause.
    NOT I'm going shopping when I ~~will have finished~~ my report.

CN **Corpus Notes:**
According to the Longman Learner's Corpus, intermediate and advanced students frequently make errors with the verbs *expect, hope, intend,* and *plan.* For example, *I intend becoming a doctor.*

PAGE G5
For more …

1 Talk about your financial goals

A 🎧 GRAMMAR **SNAPSHOT**
(CD 1, Track 25)

Suggested teaching time:	5–10 minutes
Your actual teaching time:	_____

• After students read and listen, draw the following chart (without the answers) on the board:

	Short-term goal	Long-term goal
David	start living within his means	put aside enough money for a car
Su-jin	get a job as a financial consultant	reach financial independence
Robin	find a job and begin a payment plan	pay off her debt
Andreas		save enough money to spend a year traveling

🔄 Graphic Organizers

To check comprehension, have pairs scan the interview responses and complete the chart in note form. Students should only write the future goals, not the time by which they will be achieved.

• Review as a class. Have volunteers share information from their charts with the class, using complete sentences. (Possible response: David's short-term goal is to live within his means. His long-term goal is to put aside enough money for a car.)

> **Language note:** A *down payment* is a payment you make on something expensive that you will finance or continue to pay for over a long period of time. A *loan* is an amount of money that you borrow from a bank, financial institution, etc.

B Discussion

Suggested teaching time:	5 minutes
Your actual teaching time:	_____

• Form small groups. Read the questions out loud. As students discuss, encourage them to think of other goals they might have.

• Review as a class. Have volunteers share their goals with the class.

C Grammar

Suggested teaching time:	10–15 minutes
Your actual teaching time:	_____

• Have students read the first explanation under *Future plans* and study the examples.

• On the board, write:

  expect / hope / intend / plan

To provide practice, have students find a sentence in the Grammar Snapshot that expresses a general future plan using a verb from the board and an infinitive. Then call on students to express their own general future plans using a verb from the board and an infinitive. (Possible response: I hope to make a good living.)

• Have students read the second explanation and study the examples. To provide practice, have students find a sentence in the Grammar Snapshot that expresses a plan before a specified time in the future. (Possible response: By next year, I hope to have gotten a good job . . .) Then call on students to express their own future plans using the verbs on the board.

• Have students read the first explanation under *Finished future actions* and study the examples. On the board, write:

By 2015, Joe <u>will have paid</u> his debt off.

now   pay off debt   2015

Ask How do you form the future perfect? (will + have + past participle) When will Joe have finished paying off his debt? (by 2015) To provide practice, have students create their own future perfect statements. Have volunteers read their sentences out loud.

• Have students read the second explanation under *Finished future actions* and study the examples. To help clarify, write an example on the board:

  Once Joe <u>has paid</u> off his debt, he <u>will / is going to start</u> saving.

Ask What is Joe going to do first? (pay off his debt) What is he going to do after that? (start saving)

• Draw students' attention to the Be Careful! note.

🔄 Grammar Self-Checks

T28

D Complete the paragraph . . .

Suggested teaching time:	5 minutes
Your actual teaching time:	_____

• Model the first item with the class.
• After students complete the paragraph individually, have them compare with a partner.

Option: Write four situations on the board:
1. Brenda has worked very hard this year.
2. Alison is not pleased with the job she has.
3. Matthew got into huge debt.
4. Stephen is tired of taking the bus to work.

Have pairs imagine a future plan for each person and write down a statement using *expect, hope, intend,* or *plan* and an infinitive. (Possible responses: 1. She hopes to be able to take a vacation soon. 2. She expects to find a new job soon. 3. He plans to repay it in three years. 4. He intends to buy a car.) **[+5 minutes]**

E Complete the paragraph . . .

Suggested teaching time:	5 minutes
Your actual teaching time:	_____

• Model the first item with the class.
• After students complete the paragraph individually, have them compare with a partner.

> **Language note:** When someone is *drowning in debt,* they are heavily in debt, usually to multiple creditors.

Option: Have students add the specified future time to each long-term goal in the chart they completed for the Grammar Snapshot. (David: put aside enough money for a car <u>by this time next year</u>; Su-jin: reach financial independence <u>before she retires</u>; Robin: pay off her debt <u>by the time she's thirty</u>; Andreas: save enough money to spend a year traveling <u>by the time he's forty</u>) With books closed, have pairs use the information to write sentences using *expect, hope, intend,* or *plan* and the perfect form of the infinitive. For example, *By this time next year, David hopes to have put aside enough money for a car.* Review as a class. **[+10 minutes]**

F On a separate sheet of paper . . .

Suggested teaching time:	5 minutes
Your actual teaching time:	_____

• Model the first item with the class.
• After students complete the exercise individually, have them compare answers with a partner.
• Review as a class. Have volunteers read their sentences out loud.

Option: On the board, draw a timeline with information about an imaginary person. For example:

Bob's goals:

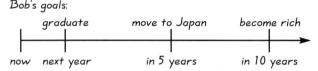

Point to the timeline as you say *By next year, Bob will have graduated. In five years, he will have moved to Japan. In ten years, he will have become rich.* Have students create an imaginary timeline and then write statements using the future perfect. To review, have several volunteers read their sentences out loud. **[+5–10 minutes]**

GRAMMAR **EXCHANGE**

Suggested teaching time:	10–15 minutes
Your actual teaching time:	_____

• Have a volunteer read the Ideas box. Brainstorm some other financial goals as a class. (Possible responses: get a good job; start my own business; make a good investment; get a promotion; get a raise; get a loan for _____)
• Have the class look at the notepad. Point out the short-term and long-term goals and their completion dates.
• Have students write their goals individually. Encourage students to write at least six goals.

Pair Work

• Have a volunteer read the models out loud.
• Have students describe their future financial goals to a partner. Circulate to offer help as needed. Encourage students to use the grammar learned in this lesson.
• To review, have volunteers report their partner's future financial goals to the class.

EXTRAS (optional)

Grammar Booster
Pronunciation Booster
Workbook: Exercises 6–7

D Complete the paragraph about Ms. Kemper's future plans. Use <u>expect</u>, <u>hope</u>, <u>intend</u>, or <u>plan</u> and an infinitive form of the verb.
Answers will vary, but may include:

Jessica Kemper ___expects to complete___ business school this semester, and then she
   (1. complete)

___hopes to find___ a job in the financial industry. However, Ms. Kemper has a lot of debt
   (2. find)

to repay. She's borrowed some money from her parents and some from the bank, but she

___plans to pay___ everyone back as soon as she can. She ___intends to get___ a part-time job to
   (3. pay)   (4. get)

help make ends meet while she's paying off her debt.

E Complete the paragraph about Mr. Randall's future plans. Use <u>expect</u>, <u>hope</u>, <u>intend</u>, or <u>plan</u> and a perfect form of the infinitive.
Answers will vary, but may include:

Paul Randall has been "drowning in debt," so he's decided to make some changes in his

financial habits. By the end of this month, he ___intends to have created___ a realistic budget that he can
                                                        (1. create)

follow. As a matter of fact, he ___hopes to have paid off___ one of his last credit cards by October.
                                       (2. pay off)

In addition, he ___plans to have begun___ putting some money away in savings. If he can stick to his
                        (3. begin)

budget, he ___expects to have paid back___ most of his debt within the year.
                   (4. pay back)

F On a separate sheet of paper, use the cues to write sentences with the future perfect.

1. By the end of this month / I / put 10 percent of my paycheck in the bank.
   By the end of this month, I will have put 10 percent of my paycheck in the bank.
2. By the summer / I / save enough to go to Italy.
   By the summer, I will have saved enough to go to Italy.
3. you / pay off your credit card balance by December?
   Will you have paid off your credit card balance by December?
4. When / they / pay the bill in full?
   When will they have paid the bill in full?

Pronunciation Booster

PAGE P3
Sentence rhythm

GRAMMAR **EXCHANGE** • *Now talk about your financial goals.*

Write your short-term and long-term financial goals on your notepad.

IDEAS

- be financially independent
- save enough to buy ___
- cut back on expenses
- create a budget
- pay my debts in full
- live within my means

short-term goals	completion dates	long-term goals	completion dates
buy a new car	by this time next year	buy a house	by the time I'm thirty

short-term goals	completion dates	long-term goals	completion dates

Pair Work. Describe your future financial goals to your partner.

"Once I've started working, I plan to put a little something into savings every week."

"By the time I graduate, I hope to have saved enough to buy a new car."

29

2 Express buyer's remorse

A ⌒ CONVERSATION **SNAPSHOT**

A: Hey, I heard you got an E-tec MP3 player. Lucky you!

B: Well, to tell you the truth, I could kick myself.

A: What do you mean?

B: I had no idea it would be so hard to operate. It took me hours to figure out how to download a song.

A: What a pain!

B: You're telling me. Had I known, I would have gotten a different brand.

⌒ **Rhythm and intonation practice**

B ⌒ Vocabulary. Expressing buyer's remorse. Listen and practice.

It costs so much to maintain. | It takes up so much room. | It's so hard to operate. | It's so hard to put together. | It just sits around collecting dust.

C ⌒ Listening Comprehension. Listen to the conversations in which people regret having bought something. Complete each statement by inferring the reason for buyer's remorse.

1. He's sorry he bought it because ....
   a. it costs so much to maintain   **b.** it takes up so much room

2. She's sorry she bought it because ....
   a. it's so hard to operate   b. it's so hard to put together

3. She's sorry she bought it because ....
   a. it takes up so much room   **b.** it just sits around collecting dust

4. He's sorry he bought it because ....
   a. it just sits around collecting dust   **b.** it's so hard to put together

5. She's sorry she bought it because ....
   a. it costs so much to maintain   b. it's so hard to operate

2 *Express buyer's remorse*

A 🎧 CONVERSATION **SNAPSHOT**
(CD 1, Track 26)

Suggested teaching time:	5 minutes
Your actual teaching time:	_____

- Have students look at the photo. Ask *What kind of electronic product do you think this is?* (an MP3 player) Elicit from the class that an *MP3 player* is an audio player onto which you can download songs from online music stores or from your own collection of music stored in your computer to listen to.

- Have students read and listen to the conversation. To check comprehension, ask *What did the man buy?* (a new MP3 player) *Is he happy with it?* (no) *Why not?* (because it's very hard to operate) *Did he know this before buying it?* (No. Otherwise, he would have bought a different brand.)

- To draw on students' own experiences, ask them if they have an MP3 player. If some students have one, ask *Are you happy with it? Is it hard to operate? What brand is it? How long does it take to download a song?*

> **Language note:** Students may need help with the following expressions: *Lucky you* (used to say that someone is fortunate); *to tell you the truth* (used to emphasize that you are being very honest); *I could kick myself* (said when you are annoyed with yourself because you have realized that you made a mistake or missed a chance); *What a pain!* (used to say that something is very annoying); *You're telling me* (used to emphasize that you already know and agree with something that someone has just said).

🎧 Rhythm and intonation practice
(CD 1, Track 27)

Suggested teaching time:	5 minutes
Your actual teaching time:	_____

- Have students repeat chorally. Make sure they:
  - use emphatic stress for you in *Lucky you!*
  - pause slightly after truth in *Well, to tell you the truth* . . .
  - use falling intonation but higher pitch for *What do you mean?*
  - use emphatic stress for hours in *It took me hours to figure out* . . .
  - use emphatic stress for me in *You're telling me.*
  - use the contracted form would've in . . . *I would have gotten* . . .

- use the following stress pattern:

┌─ STRESS PATTERN ─────────────────────┐
| **A:** Hey, I heard you got an E-tec M P 3 player. Lucky you!
|
| **B:** Well, to tell you the truth, I could kick myself.
|
| **A:** What do you mean?
|
| **B:** I had no idea it would be so hard to operate. It took me
| hours to figure out how to download a song.
|
| **A:** What a pain!
|
| **B:** You're telling me. Had I known, I would have gotten a
| different brand.
└───────────────────────────────────────┘

B 🎧 Vocabulary
(CD 1, Track 28)

Suggested teaching time:	5–10 minutes
Your actual teaching time:	_____

- Elicit the meaning of *buyer's remorse* from the class. (a strong feeling that it was a mistake to have bought something)

- Have students listen to the statements and look at the illustrations. Then have students listen and repeat chorally.

- To check comprehension, have students look at each picture and ask *What is the woman spending a lot of money on?* (car service) *What is too big for the man's room?* (the TV) *What doesn't the woman know how to use?* (the treadmill) *What is the man trying to figure out?* (how to put the sound system together) *Why is the food processor collecting dust in the closet?* (because nobody uses it)

C 🎧 Listening Comprehension
(CD 1, Track 29)

Suggested teaching time:	5–10 minutes
Your actual teaching time:	_____

- First listening: Have students listen to the five conversations and identify what each person has bought. Review as a class. (1. a juicer, 2. a digital camera, 3. an exercise bike, 4. a sound system, 5. a car)

- Second listening: Have students listen and complete the statements.

- Third listening: In pairs, have students write down phrases from the conversations to support their answers. Review as a class. (1. "It's way too big." 2. "I might like it if I could figure out how to use it." 3. "I just don't use it enough." 4. "There are so many components. And the instructions don't help at all." 5. ". . . it's costing me an arm and a leg!")

AUDIOSCRIPT

For audioscript, see page AS4.

D Grammar

Suggested teaching time:	10 minutes
Your actual teaching time:	_____

• Have students read the explanation in the Grammar box and study the examples. On the board, write:

If she had known it was on sale, she would have
bought it.

Had she known it was on sale, she would have
bought it.

Point out *if* in the first example and the inversion in the second one. Point out that both statements have the same meaning.

• On the board, write:

If she hadn't lent me the money, I wouldn't have
bought it.
Had she not lent me the money, I wouldn't have
bought it.

To help clarify the negative, point out the contraction (*hadn't*) in the condition clause with *if* and the full form (*had she not lent*) in the condition clause with inversion.

• On the board, write:

If I had been warned, I wouldn't have done it.
Had I been warned, I wouldn't have done it.

To help clarify the passive, point out the passive form (*had been warned*) in the first example and its inversion (*had I been warned*) in the second example.

• Have a volunteer read the Remember box out loud. Direct students' attention to the last example. To check comprehension, ask *Was he/she told they wouldn't operate without batteries?* (no) *Did he/she consider getting them?* (yes)

> **Language note:** Remember to use a comma at the end of the condition clause when it comes first in a sentence.

 Grammar Self-Checks

Option: On the board, write:

They didn't study, so they didn't pass. Now they
regret it.
She is sorry that she bought on credit and got into
debt.

To provide practice, have pairs write a statement using the inverted form of the unreal conditional for each situation. Review as a class. Have volunteers read the statements out loud. (Possible responses: 1. Had they studied, they would have passed. 2. Had she not bought on credit, she wouldn't have gotten into debt.) **[+5 minutes]**

Option: To review conditional forms, use the graphic organizer on the Teacher's Resource Disk. You may want to draw it on the board or print and distribute it to the class. Point out that students will write their own examples for each type. **[+10 minutes]**

 **Graphic Organizers**

E On a separate sheet of paper ...

Suggested teaching time:	5 minutes
Your actual teaching time:	_____

• Model the first item with the class.

• After students complete the exercise individually, have them compare answers with a partner. Review as a class.

F Pair Work

Suggested teaching time:	5 minutes
Your actual teaching time:	_____

• Go over the first statement and the model with the class. Point out the two possible positions of *never*: *I would never have gotten it* or *I never would have gotten it*.

• In pairs, have students take turns making statements of buyer's remorse. Remind students to use the Vocabulary on page 30 for expressing buyer's remorse.

• To review, invite five students to share a statement with the class.

CONVERSATION **STARTER**

Suggested teaching time:	5–10 minutes
Your actual teaching time:	_____

Pair Work

• Have a volunteer read the questions on the notepad out loud.

• Have students answer the questions individually. Note: If students can't think of anything they regret buying, have them answer the questions about someone else or create an imaginary situation and invent the answers.

• As students talk with their partners, circulate to remind students to use the language they learned in this lesson.

Role Play

• Refer students to the Conversation Snapshot on page 30 to review expressing buyer's remorse. You may also want to have students listen to the model again.

• Role-play the conversation with a more confident student.

• Make sure each student plays both roles.

• As students interact, circulate to offer help as needed. Encourage students to use the correct rhythm and intonation and to use ideas from their notepads.

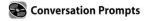 **Conversation Prompts**

EXTRAS (optional)

Workbook: Exercises 8–10

D Grammar. The past unreal conditional: inverted form

Past unreal conditionals can be stated without if. Invert __had__ and the subject.

If I had known it would take up so much room, I wouldn't have bought it.	→	**Had I known** it would take up so much room, I wouldn't have bought it.
I might have gotten another brand **if I had realized** it would be so hard to operate.	→	I might have gotten another brand **had I realized** it would be so hard to operate.
If we hadn't been so busy, we could have shopped around.	→	**Had we not been** so busy, we could have shopped around.
If I'd been told they wouldn't operate without batteries, I would never have considered getting them.	→	**Had I been told** they wouldn't operate without batteries, I would never have considered getting them.

E
On a separate sheet of paper, rewrite the following past unreal conditional sentences, using the inverted form.

1. They would have lent her the money if she had asked.
   They would have lent her the money had she asked.
2. If I had been debt free, I would have considered buying that house.
   Had I been debt free, I would have considered buying that house.
3. If the Carsons hadn't been able to support their son, he would have had to find a part-time job.
   Had the Carsons not been able to support their son, he would have had to find a part-time job.
4. Could you have gotten the car if they hadn't raised the price?
   Could you have gotten the car had they not raised the price?

F
Pair Work. Make statements of buyer's remorse, using the inverted form of the past unreal conditional and the vocabulary.

1. . . . I would never have gotten that espresso maker.
2. . . . we never would have bought such a large sofa.
   Had we known it would take up so much room, . . .
3. . . . I could have gotten an entertainment center with fewer pieces.
   Had I known it would be so hard to put together, . . .
4. . . . we probably would have bought a more economical car.
   Had we known it would cost so much to maintain, . . .
5. . . . I would have gotten a DVD player with simpler directions.
   Had I known it would be so hard to operate, . . .

> *"Had I known it would take up so much room, I would never have gotten that espresso maker."*

CONVERSATION **STARTER** • *Now express buyer's remorse.*

Pair Work. On your notepad, answer the questions about something *you* regret buying. Tell your partner about it.

Role Play. Role-play a conversation about the item on your notepad. Use the Conversation Snapshot on page 30 as a guide. Start like this: "Hey, I heard you got . . . ."

What did you buy?

Why did you buy it?

Do you still have it?

If so, where is it?

If not, what did you do with it?

Would you ever buy a similar item again?

Why or why not?

31

Describe your spending habits

"Money Talks" with *Lara Savino*

A 🎧 **Listening Comprehension.** Read the statements. Then listen to a radio call-in show and check <u>True</u> or <u>False</u>.

	True	False
1. Steve finds it hard to save money.	☑	☐
2. Steve buys a lot on credit.	☑	☐
3. Steve spends less money than he makes.	☐	☑
4. Steve has been on a budget for three months.	☐	☑

B 🎧 Now listen again. What are the three tips Lara Savino gives the caller?

1. <u>Save his change and put it in the bank</u>.
2. <u>Only have two credit cards</u>.
3. <u>Sit down and plan a budget</u>.

C **Discussion.**

1. Why do you think Steve has a problem with money?
2. Which tip do you think is the most useful? Why?

D 🎧 **Vocabulary. Describing spending habits.** Listen and practice.

NOUNS

a big spender someone who likes to spend large amounts of money

a spendthrift someone who spends money carelessly, especially when he or she doesn't have a lot of it

a cheapskate / a tightwad someone who does not like spending money and can be unpleasant about it

ADJECTIVES

generous willing to give more money, time, etc., than is expected

cheap / stingy unwilling to spend or give **CN** money, even when one has a lot of it

thrifty / frugal using money carefully and wisely

CN **Corpus Notes:** *Cheap* occurs much more frequently than *stingy* in spoken English.

E Complete the sentences about people's spending habits.

1. Can you believe what <u>a cheapskate/ a tightwad</u> Martin is! He refused to leave a tip for the waiter!
2. Our grandmother donates to many organizations. She's always been very <u>generous</u> with her money.
3. He's so <u>cheap/stingy</u> that he wouldn't even lend his own son money.
4. George must be wealthy. He's such <u>a big spender</u>. He always insists on treating his friends to dinner.
5. If you try to be more <u>thrifty/frugal</u> with your money, you'll have enough when you really need it.
6. Unless you stop being such <u>a spendthrift</u>, you're going to get deeper in debt.

3 Describe your spending habits

A 🎧 Listening Comprehension
(CD 1, Track 30)

Suggested teaching time:	5–10 minutes
Your actual teaching time:	_____

• Have students look at the photo and read the caption. Ask *What do you think the woman's occupation is?* (a radio host) *Do you ever listen to the radio? What kind of programs do you listen to? What kind of show do you think Lara Savino hosts?*

• Pre-listening: Ask *What's a radio call-in show?* (a radio program in which people call to give their opinions or ask questions)

• Have students read statements 1–4.

• First listening: Have students listen and decide if the statements are true or false.

• Second listening: Have students listen for information to support their answers. Encourage them to take notes.

• Review as a class. Have volunteers share their answers. (Possible answers: 1. True. Steve says he can't make ends meet and never has enough money to save. 2. True. Steve says he's drowning in debt. 3. False. Steve says there's never enough money to put any away in savings. 4. False. Lara suggests that he *try* to keep a budget for three months. He hasn't started yet.)

Language note: When Lara Savino asks Steve if he's *maxing out* on his credit cards, she's asking if he reaches the maximum credit limit on his credit cards each month. *Buying on credit* is an arrangement with a store, bank, credit card company, etc., that allows you to buy something now and pay for it later. *A budget* is a careful plan of how you will spend money.

AUDIOSCRIPT

For audioscript, see page AS4.

B 🎧 Now listen again ...
(CD 1, Track 31)

Suggested teaching time:	5 minutes
Your actual teaching time:	_____

• Have students listen for the three tips Lara gives.

• Have students compare answers with a partner. If necessary, have them listen again for confirmation.

• Review tips as a class. Have volunteers share the tips with the class.

 Listening Strategies

C Discussion

Suggested teaching time:	5 minutes
Your actual teaching time:	_____

• In small groups, have students discuss their answers. Remind them to use the language they learned in discussing a person's financial IQ in the Starting Point on page 27.

• To finish the activity, have a student from each group share which tip they consider the most useful and give a supporting reason.

Option: To personalize the activity, have small groups discuss these questions: *What do you do with your loose change? How many credit cards do you have? Are you on a budget? Why / Why not? Are you planning to follow any of Lara Savino's tips?* **[+5–10 minutes]**

D 🎧 Vocabulary
(CD 1, Track 32)

Suggested teaching time:	5–10 minutes
Your actual teaching time:	_____

• Have students listen to the words and study the definitions. Then have students listen and repeat the words chorally.

• Point out that some of these words have a positive connotation, some have a negative connotation, and one is neutral.

• Have pairs read the definitions carefully and decide the connotation of each word.

• To review, write the column headings *Positive*, *Negative*, and *Neutral* on the board and have students say the vocabulary words for each column. (**Positive:** generous, thrifty, frugal; **Negative:** a spendthrift, a cheapskate, a tightwad, cheap, stingy; **Neutral:** a big spender)

🌐 Vocabulary-Building Strategies

Option: Have students think of someone they know whose spending habits they would describe using one or more of the vocabulary words. In pairs, have students describe that person's habits. To review, have volunteers tell the class about the person their partners described. **[+5 minutes]**

E Complete the sentences ...

Suggested teaching time:	5 minutes
Your actual teaching time:	_____

• Model the first item with the class. Point out that to choose the right words, students should take into account both meaning and grammar. For example, in item 1, *cheap* and *stingy* match the context, but a noun is necessary, so the correct answer is *a cheapskate* or *a tightwad*. Point out that more than one word might be possible.

• Have students compare answers with a partner. Then review as a class.

T32

DISCUSSION **BUILDER**

Suggested teaching time:	20–25 minutes
Your actual teaching time:	_____

Step 1. Pair Work.

• Have students complete the questionnaire individually.

• Explain that students should tally the number of As, Bs, Cs, and Ds that they circled and then find the spending habits description that matches their scores. (Have students who circled three or more Ds decide how they would describe their spending habits.)

• Circulate to encourage students to give their own examples of similar experiences they might have had.

• Have students compare their results with a partner's and say if they agree with their results.

Step 2. Group Work.

• Before students discuss in groups, remind them of the vocabulary they know. Draw the following diagram (without the answers) on the board. As a class, brainstorm positive and negative spending habits.

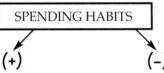

SPENDING HABITS

(+)

live below / within your
    means
pay credit card bills in full
save up
put some money aside
put money away into
    savings
put money in the bank
plan and stick to a budget
keep track of your expenses
cut back on expenses
treat yourself once in a
    while

(–)

live beyond your means
not pay bills in full
have trouble making
    ends meet
get into debt
be drowning in debt
borrow a lot of money
spend as much as /
    more than you earn
have a lot of credit
    cards
buy things that you
    can't afford

• Form groups of three or four. As students talk about their or their partner's spending habits, encourage students who are listening to ask follow-up questions and give advice.

Step 3. Writing.

• Remind students to use the Vocabulary from Exercise D on page 32.

• Tell students they can finish their paragraph by saying:

  ○ which bad habit they are planning to change and give a supporting reason

  OR

  ○ which good habit they hope to be able to maintain and give a supporting reason

Challenge: Write (some of) the following proverbs on the board:

1. I have money, you have money, so we are friends.
                    —Chinese Proverb
2. Money is a good servant but a bad master.
                    —French Proverb
3. When money speaks, the truth is silent.
                    —Russian Proverb
4. In this world generous people have no money and those with money are not generous.
                    —Iranian Proverb
5. Getting money is like digging with a needle. Spending it is like water soaking into the sand.
                    —Japanese Proverb
6. He who would be rich should not collect money, but reduce his needs.
                    —Spanish Proverb
7. A clear conscience is far more valuable than money.
                    —Filipino Proverb

In groups of four or five, have students discuss the meanings of the proverbs and say which ones they agree with. Encourage students to support their views. To review, have several students express their opinions of the same proverb. **[+10–15 minutes]**

EXTRAS (optional)

Workbook: Exercises 11–13

Step 1. Pair Work. First circle the letter that best completes the statement for you. Then compare your answers with a partner's. Find out if your spending habits are the same or different.

Spending Habits Self-Test

1. You hear a great new song on the radio. You . . .

A. buy the CD at the first store you find it in.
B. shop around until you find the CD on sale.
C. borrow it from a friend.
D. other: ....

2. You'd love a state-of-the-art big-screen TV but you just don't have the money right now. You . . .

A. use your credit card and hope you get a raise this year.
B. cut back on other expenses until you've saved enough.
C. wait until big-screen TVs come down in price.
D. other: ....

3. You have lunch with your two best friends. Your meal was cheaper than theirs. When the bill comes, you . . .

A. offer to pay the entire bill.
B. suggest splitting the bill equally.
C. pay only what you owe.
D. other: ....

4. You're invited to a wedding. You . . .

A. spend more on a gift than you can afford.
B. spend as little on a gift as you can.
C. don't go so you don't have to buy a gift.
D. other: ....

5. You discover a hole in your favorite jacket. You . . .

A. go out and buy a new jacket.
B. have the jacket repaired.
C. wear the jacket—it's no big deal.
D. other: ....

Count up your score.

If you circled three or more As:
You can be generous at times, but you're a bit of a spendthrift. Your motto is "Easy come, easy go!"

If you circled three or more Bs:
You're usually very careful with your money—even thrifty. Your motto is "Everything in moderation."

If you circled three or more Cs:
You hate spending money. Some might say you're a tightwad. Your motto is "Money doesn't grow on trees!"

If you circled three or more Ds:
How would *you* describe your spending habits?

Step 2. Group Work. Tell your classmates about your spending habits or your partner's.

Step 3. Writing. On a separate sheet of paper, describe your spending habits.

I make a good living, but I have trouble sticking to a budget and

4 Discuss reasons for charitable giving

A 🎧 **Vocabulary. Charity and investment.** Listen and practice.

char·i·ty /ˈtʃærəti/ *n. plural* **charities 1** [C] an organization that gives money, goods, or help to people who are poor, sick etc. **2** [U] charity organizations in general

con·tri·bu·tion /ˌkɑntrəˈbyuʃən/ *n.* **1** [C] 🅒🅝 something that you give or do in order to help something be successful **2** [C] an amount of money that you give in order to help pay for something
🅒🅝 **Corpus Notes:** The words *contribution, investment,* and *profit* frequently collocate with *make.* For example, *make a contribution, make an investment,* and *make a profit.*

in·vest·ment /ɪnˈvɛstmənt/ *n.* **1** [C,U] the money that people or organizations have put into a company, business, or bank, in order to get a profit or to make a business activity successful **2** [C,U] a large amount of time, energy, emotion etc. that you spend on something

phi·lan·thro·pist /fɪˈlænθrəpɪst/ *n.* [C] a rich person who gives money to help people who are poor or who need money to do useful things

pro·fit /ˈprɑfɪt/ *n.* [C,U] money that you gain by selling things or doing business

Excerpted from *Longman Advanced American Dictionary* © 2005

B **Reading Warm-up.** What are some reasons people donate money? What kinds of people or organizations get contributions? Why?

C 🎧 **Reading.** Read the article. What reasons does Paul Newman give for donating to charity?

Paul Newman: Actor and Philanthropist

Paul Newman has been acting since 1954 and has appeared in more than fifty films. He won an Oscar for best actor in 1986 for *The Color of Money.* In 1993, Newman received a special Oscar for humanitarian service. These two awards reflect his dual success as actor and philanthropist.

In 1982, Newman and a friend, A. E. Hotchner, founded Newman's Own, a not-for-profit food products company. The company's first product was a salad dressing that Newman and Hotchner made at home themselves. Newman was told that the salad dressing would sell only if his face were on the label. Though he didn't want to call attention to himself, Newman agreed because he planned to donate all profits to charity. The salad dressing was a big success: In the first year, Newman contributed approximately US$1,000,000 to charitable organizations.

Newman's Own has expanded, and the company now makes many other food products. Every year, Newman donates 100 percent of the profits from the sale of Newman's Own products to thousands of educational and charitable organizations located in the United States, Japan, France, Brazil, and Australia. Since 1982, Newman has made contributions of more than US$150 million to charities.

One of Newman's special projects is the Hole in the Wall Gang Camps, the world's only network of camps for children with life-threatening illnesses. At these camps, children participate in many outdoor activities where they can temporarily forget their illnesses. Newman and other generous donors have sponsored over 70,000 children to attend these camps free of charge. When asked why he gives so much to children with illnesses, Newman says, "I've had such a string of good fortune in my life.... Those who are most lucky should hold their hands out to those who aren't."

Paul Newman doesn't think that being philanthropic is an exceptional quality. To him, generosity is simply a human trait, a common-sense way of living. "I respect generosity in people. I don't look at it as philanthropy. I see it as an investment in the community. I am not a professional philanthropist," says Newman. "I'm not running for sainthood. I just happen to think that in life we need to be a little like the farmer who puts back into the soil what he takes out."

"I don't look at it as philanthropy.
I see it as an investment in the community."

Source: www.newmansown.com

4 *Discuss reasons for charitable giving*

A 🎧 Vocabulary
(CD 1, Track 33)

Suggested teaching time:	5–10 minutes
Your actual teaching time:	_____

- Have students listen to the words and study the definitions. Then have students listen and repeat the words chorally.
- To check comprehension, photocopy the following exercise and distribute or write on the board:

> charity   contributions   investment
>   Philanthropists   profits
>
> 1. _____ often make _____ to organizations that help people in need.
> 2. Helping people in need does not always require a huge _____ of time and energy.
> 3. All the _____ from the sales will go to a _____.

With books closed, have students complete the sentences with the words in the box. Have students compare answers with a partner and review as a class. (1. Philanthropists, contributions; 2. investment; 3. profits, charity)

Language note: Point out useful synonyms and verb + noun combinations students will need. Write them on the board:
charity = charitable organization
contribution = donation
make a contribution = contribute
make a donation = donate
make an investment = invest
make a profit = profit

Point out the correct prepositions: You make a contribution or donation *of* something *to* a person or organization. Or you contribute / donate something *to* a person or organization.

🔄 Vocabulary-Building Strategies

Option: For further practice, have students discuss the following questions in pairs or small groups: *1. Are there any charities near your home? Which are they? 2. Have you ever made a contribution to a charity? If so, which one?* **[+5–10 minutes]**

B Reading Warm-up

Suggested teaching time:	5 minutes
Your actual teaching time:	_____

- In small groups, have students discuss the questions. Encourage them to write a list of reasons people donate money to others.

- After students have finished discussing, have students from different groups share the reasons they thought of. You may want to write a list on the board as you get feedback from students. (Possible reasons: They want to help people in need; They have more money than they need.)
- To finish, ask students to name people or organizations who get contributions and explain why they get help from others.

C 🎧 Reading
(CD 1, Track 34)

Suggested teaching time:	10–15 minutes
Your actual teaching time:	_____

- Have students read and listen to the article.
- Ask *What reasons does Paul Newman give for donating to charity?* (Those who have good fortune in their lives should help those who don't; Generosity is a human trait; Generosity is an investment in the community; We should be grateful and give back what we receive.)

Language note: You may want to share the following definitions: *camp* (a place where children go and stay for a short time and take part in special activities, often as members of an organization); *life-threatening* (with a potential to result in death); *run for sainthood* (try to do good things).

🔄 Reading Strategies

🔄 Reading Speed Calculator

🔄 Extra Reading Comprehension Activities

Option: To use the reading as a listening activity, draw the following graphic organizer (without the answers) on the board:

> **1954**   Paul Newman started his career as an _____actor_____. With a friend, he invented a __salad dressing__. They founded a __food products company__: Newman's Own. In the first year, they contributed __US $1 million__ to charities. Soon they expanded the business to _____other_____ __food products__. They started contributing to __educational and charitable__ organizations outside the United States. They particularly help children with serious _____illnesses_____. So far, they have
> **NOW**   made contributions of more than __US $150 million__.

🔄 Graphic Organizers

With books closed, have students listen and complete the chronological events. Review as a class. **[+5–10 minutes]**

D Discussion

Suggested teaching time:	10 minutes
Your actual teaching time:	_____

• Have students discuss the questions in small groups. Encourage them to share their opinions.

• Review as a class. Have volunteers from different groups share their responses.

• After volunteers share their responses for item 3, ask *Would your opinion change if **you** were wealthy or famous?* Discuss as a class. Encourage students to support their views.

DISCUSSION **BUILDER**

Suggested teaching time:	15–20 minutes
Your actual teaching time:	_____

 Discourse Strategies

Step 1. Pair Work.

• Have volunteers read the list of reasons out loud.

• Encourage students to write at least one more reason each.

• Remind students to support their views as they discuss in pairs.

Step 2.

• Call on volunteers to read the list of people / organizations out loud.

• Have students write their reasons for giving or not giving on their notepads. Circulate to offer help as needed.

• As students make their choices, encourage them to think of specific examples of people or organizations that they might know about.

Step 3. Discussion.

• Review the model with the class.

• Have students discuss in groups of three. Remind students to use the reasons for giving or not giving from their notepads. Encourage students who are listening to make relevant comments or ask follow-up questions.

• Have volunteers from each group share their views with the class.

Step 4. Writing.

• To help students organize their writing, you may want to write the following chart on the board:

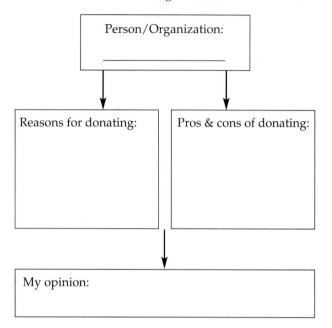

 Graphic Organizers

• Encourage students to use the Vocabulary on page 34.

• Remind students to finish their paragraphs with a concluding sentence stating their personal opinions of whether they are for or against donating to the people or organizations they chose to write about. Refer students to page 12 to remind them about concluding sentences.

Project: In small groups, have students do a search on the Internet for charitable organizations. Ask them to choose an organization that they think is worth helping. Have them write a short report on the organization and present it to the class.

EXTRAS (optional)

Workbook: Exercises 14–16

D Discussion.

1. Why do you think Paul Newman's face has helped to sell his products?
2. Do you think that the work Newman is doing is making a difference?
3. In your opinion, do famous or wealthy people have a responsibility to "give back" or to share what they have with others?

DISCUSSION **BUILDER** • *Now discuss reasons for charitable giving.*

Step 1. Pair Work. Read the list of possible reasons some people donate money. In your opinion, which are good reasons? Explain.

- to change society
- to feel good about themselves
- to get publicity or advertising
- to say "thank you" for past help
- to share what they have with others

- to give new opportunities to people
- to satisfy religious beliefs
- so other people will thank them
- so other people will admire them
- other: ....

Step 2. On your notepad, check the people or organizations to whom you might consider making a contribution. List your reasons for giving or *not* giving.

People / Organizations	Reasons for giving or *not* giving
☐ a homeless person	
☐ a seriously ill person	
☐ a political candidate	
☐ a disaster relief agency	
☐ a hospital	
☐ a school in a poor neighborhood	
☐ a theater or a museum	
☐ a local charity	
☐ an international charity	
☐ a religious institution	
☐ other:	

Step 3. Discussion. Talk about the people and organizations you would or would not give money to. Explain your reasons.

"I would rather give money to a local charity because they'll use it to help people in my community."

Step 4. Writing. Choose one person, charity, or type of organization people donate money to. On a separate sheet of paper, write a paragraph explaining the reasons people have for or against donating.

Writing: *Explain your financial goals*

Sequencing events

When writing a paragraph, the sentences need to be logically organized. **Time order words** are used to clarify the order of events in someone's life, to present the steps in a process, or to give instructions.

Special time order words and expressions help make sequence clear:

- First,
  First of all,
  To begin with,

- Second,
  Third,

- Next,
  Then,

- After,
  Afterwards,
  After that,

- Finally,
  Lastly,
  In the end,

WRITING MODEL

I intend to be financially independent by the time I am sixty. How? **First,** I plan to live within my means. I will cut corners where I can and stick to my budget. **Then,** I hope to open up my own business. **Next,** I intend to start putting some money away. **After that,** I plan to make some smart investments. **Finally,** by the time I am sixty, I will have saved up enough to retire and buy a nice weekend house.

Step 1. Prewriting. Listing ideas. Choose a topic. Then complete the chart.

Topics
- My long-term financial goals
- The steps I need to take in order to buy ....

Topic: ....

	Goal or step	My plan	Completion date
First,			
Then,			
After that,			
Finally,			

Step 2. Writing. Write a paragraph, using your notes. Use time order words and expressions to organize the sequence of goals or steps in your paragraph. Remember to write a topic sentence.

Step 3. Self-Check.

☐ Did you use time order words or expressions in the paragraph?
☐ Does the sequence of events in the paragraph make sense?
☐ Does the topic sentence introduce the topic of the paragraph?

WRITING

36 UNIT 3

Writing **Explain your financial goals**

Suggested teaching time:	25 minutes
Your actual teaching time:	_____

Sequencing events

• Go over the explanation.

• To check comprehension, ask *Why are time words useful?* (because they help to organize ideas; because they help to present events, steps, or instructions in a sequence)

• On the board, write:

   1. *I was very busy yesterday. _____ . I wrote a speech I must give next week. _____ . I had a meeting. _____ . I had an office party.*

   2. *My long-term goal is to open up a restaurant: _____ . I will graduate. _____ . I'll get a job and put away as much money as I can. _____ I'll invest the money I saved in setting up my restaurant.*

To provide practice, have pairs complete the items with time order words. Point out that more than one word might be possible in each blank. Tell students to use each word only once.

• Review as a class. Have several students share their choices for each blank. (Possible answers: 1. First, Next, Then; 2. First of all, After that, Finally)

• Have students read the writing model.

• To make students aware of punctuation, point out that most time words are followed by a comma.

💬 Extra Writing Skills Practice

Option: On the board, write:

   How to . . .
   make an omelet
   start a car and drive off
   plan a party
   other: _____

For further practice, have pairs choose a topic from the board or their own topic and write four or six steps or instructions for that topic. To review, have volunteers give instructions to the class about the topics they chose. **[+10 minutes]**

Step 1. Prewriting.

• Have a volunteer read the topics list.

• Have students choose a topic. Ask students who chose the second topic to decide what they want to buy and write it down.

• Have students complete the chart individually. Encourage them to use as much vocabulary from this unit as they can.

• As students complete the chart, circulate to offer help as needed.

Step 2. Writing.

• Remind students to use the correct punctuation after time words.

• As students write, circulate to offer help as needed.

Step 3. Self–Check.

• Go over the Self-Check questions with the class.

• Before students submit their paragraphs for correction, have them self-check their work and make any necessary changes.

Option: Have students read their paragraphs out loud in small groups or in front of the class. Ask the students who are listening to give useful advice that can help their classmates achieve their goals. **[+10 –15 minutes]**

EXTRAS (optional)

   Workbook: Page 30

T36

UNIT 3 CHECKPOINT

A 🎧 Listening Comprehension
(CD 1, Track 35)

Suggested teaching time:	5–10 minutes
Your actual teaching time:	_____

- Have students read the statements before listening to the conversations.
- Point out that there is a statement that students won't use.
- To review, have students support their choices. (Possible response: Conversation 1: The man bought a new computer table that has too many pieces and he can't figure out how to put it together. He's not going to let it sit around collecting dust. He's going to take it back to the store.)

AUDIOSCRIPT

For audioscript, see page AS5.

B Complete the statements . . .

Suggested teaching time:	5 minutes
Your actual teaching time:	_____

- You may want to model the first item with the class.
- Remind students that apart from meaning, they should evaluate whether the sentence requires a noun or an adjective.
- Have students compare answers with a partner. Then review as a class.

C Write a conditional sentence . . .

Suggested teaching time:	5–10 minutes
Your actual teaching time:	_____

- Model the first item with the class. Elicit sentences from several volunteers.
- Have students share their regrets with a partner.
- To review as a class, have several students share a regret with the class.

D Express your future plans . . .

Suggested teaching time:	5–10 minutes
Your actual teaching time:	_____

- Model the first item with the class. Call on several students to share their plans.
- Have students share their plans and goals with a partner.
- Review as a class. Have several students share a future plan or goal.

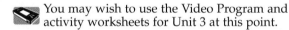 You may wish to use the Video Program and activity worksheets for Unit 3 at this point.

Complete Assessment Package
Unit 3 Achievement Test

SUMMIT **WEBSITE**
for Unit 3 online activities, visit the
Summit Companion Website at
www.longman.com/summit.

A 🎧 **Listening Comprehension.** Listen to the conversations about money matters. Then decide which statement best summarizes each conversation. Listen again if necessary.

Conversation 1. _d_   **Conversation 2.** _c_   **Conversation 3.** _b_

   a. If he'd known it would just sit around collecting dust, he never would have bought it.

   b. He's too much of a spendthrift. He should be more frugal.

   c. He's not a spendthrift. He's just feeling generous.

   d. If he'd known it would be so hard to put together, he never would have bought it.

B Complete the statements with words from the box.

charities
contribution
frugal
generous
investment
philanthropist
profit
stingy
tightwad

   1. Steve Gold, an assistant to a big executive at World Corp, saved his company a lot of money by purchasing airplane tickets online from a discount travel website. His boss appreciated his being so _frugal_.

   2. Bill Gates, founder of the Microsoft Corporation, is not only one of the richest men in the world, but he's also one of the most _generous_. Since 2000, he has donated over US$7.5 billion to improve global health and education.

   3. Dan Fielding expected that his _investment_ in the ComTech Corporation would result in a nice _profit_. However, the business failed and Dan lost all of his money.

   4. One of the richest women in history, Hetty Green was also notoriously _stingy_. She once refused to light the candles on her birthday cake so she could return them to the store for a refund. Hetty is considered to be history's greatest _tightwad_.

   5. Andrew Carnegie was a famous _philanthropist_ who gave away over US$350 million to _charities_. His largest _contribution_ was for US$56 million dollars, which was used to build over 2,500 free public libraries around the world.

C Write a conditional sentence for each regret below. Begin with an inverted form ("Had I ...").
Answers will vary, but may include:

   1. a regret about your financial situation
     Had I been debt free, I would have bought that car.

   2. a regret about something you bought
     Had I known it would shrink, I would never have gotten this sweater.

   3. a regret about a relationship
     Had I known how selfish he was, I would never have dated him.

D Express your future plans and goals. Use the perfect form of an infinitive or the future perfect.

   1. Before the end of today, I plan _____.

   2. By next month, I will _____.

   3. By the end of this English course, I expect _____.

   4. By the end of the year, I intend _____.

   5. Within five years, I hope _____.

UNIT 4

Looking Good

A Topic Preview. These pictures depict concepts of ideal beauty at different times and in different places. Do *you* find any of these fashions attractive?

For centuries in Japan, the geisha defined beauty and grace.

In eighteenth-century Europe, well-to-do men and women wore extravagant wigs and clothing.

Paduang women of Myanmar begin lengthening their necks with gold bands at the age of five or six.

In India, Pakistan, the Middle East, and Africa, women paint their faces and hands with henna for special occasions.

In New Zealand, it is traditional for Maori men to decorate their faces and bodies with tattoos.

B Discussion.

1. What things do people do today to make themselves more attractive? Which techniques do you think are the most successful?

2. In your opinion, why do tastes change over time from culture to culture?

3. What do you think this expression means? Do you agree?

Beauty is in the eye of the beholder.*

*beholder—the person who is looking

Looking Good

A Topic Preview

Suggested teaching time:	10–15 minutes
Your actual teaching time:	_____

- To introduce the theme of appearance, have students spend a few moments looking at the pictures and reading the captions.
- Point to the images and ask *Do you think any of these fashions are attractive?* To encourage students to explain their opinions, ask *Why do you think so?*

Language note: Students may need help with the following: *geisha* (a Japanese woman who is trained in the art of dancing, singing, and providing entertainment, especially for men); *well-to-do* (rich); *extravagant* (very impressive, because something is very expensive, beautiful, etc.); *henna* (a reddish-brown substance used to change the color of hair or to dye the skin).

Culture note: Myanmar is a republic in Southeast Asia. It was known as Burma until 1989. The Paduang are a tribe who live on the border of Myanmar and Thailand. Long-necked women belonging to this tribe have become the most popular tourist attraction in the area. The Maori people are the native inhabitants of New Zealand. They make up about 14 percent of the country's population. Maori men believe their tattoos make them strong warriors and attractive to women.

Option: Have students look at the pictures and read the captions. Ask *What are some adjectives you would use to describe the fashions in these pictures?* (Possible responses: attractive, smart, elegant, unattractive, nice, odd, strange, comfortable, uncomfortable, ridiculous, unhealthy, crazy, practical, impractical) List the adjectives on the board as students respond. Have students make statements about the images using the adjectives on the board. **[+5 minutes]**

B Discussion

Suggested teaching time:	10 minutes
Your actual teaching time:	_____

- Read the questions out loud. Have students discuss the answers in small groups. Circulate to offer help as needed. Students might need help with vocabulary to describe what people do to make themselves more attractive.
- Review answers as a class. Have a student from each group present his/her response to the class. For item 3, call on a student to say what the expression *Beauty is in the eye of the beholder* means. Have other students agree or disagree and support their responses. (The expression means that different people have different opinions about what is beautiful.)

Option: Class poll. Ask *Do you think people spend too much time trying to make themselves look more attractive? Do you think you spend too much time trying to make yourself look more attractive?* On the board, write:

  hair   clothes   makeup

Ask *Do you spend the most time on your hair? Clothes? Makeup?* Keep a tally for each on the board. Ask students to support their opinions. **[+5 minutes]**

C 🎧 Sound Bites
(CD 2, Track 2)

Suggested teaching time:	10 minutes
Your actual teaching time:	_____

- Have students look only at the photos. Ask *What's the man wearing in the first photo?* (a suit and tie) *What's he wearing in the second one?* (jeans and a T-shirt) *Where do you think the people are going?* (Possible responses: to a party, out to dinner, to a friend's house)

- Say *You are going to hear a conversation about dressing up and dressing down.* Ask *What do* dressing up *and* dressing down *mean?* (*dress up*: dress formally, put on formal clothes; *dress down*: dress informally, put on casual clothes)

- Have students read and listen to the conversation.

Language note: Students may need help with the following words or expressions: *overdressed* (dressed in clothes that are too formal for the occasion); *Hello!* (used in spoken English when the other person is not being sensible or is not aware of what is happening); *Oops* (said when you make a small mistake); *make up your mind* (make a decision); *what's with something* (used to ask the reason for something); *baggy* (loose); *slacks* (pants, especially ones made out of good material but that are not part of a suit).

D Pair Work

Suggested teaching time:	5–10 minutes
Your actual teaching time:	_____

- To check comprehension of the words in the box, ask:
  In which photo is Paul wearing formal clothing? (the first)
  In which is he wearing casual clothing? (the second)
  In which photo is Paul overdressed? (the first) *Why?* (because his clothes are too formal for the occasion / because he's wearing a suit)
  Why is he underdressed in the second photo? (because now his clothes are too casual / because he's wearing a T-shirt and jeans)

- In pairs, have students tell the story of what happened in the conversation using the words in the box.

- Circulate to offer help with the new words as needed.

- To review, have a volunteer tell the story to the class. (Possible response: Paul dresses up because he thinks that the party is formal. When Margo tells him he is overdressed for the occasion, he changes into jeans and a T-shirt. Margo thinks jeans are too casual. Paul is now underdressed, so he will have to change clothes again.)

STARTING **POINT**

Suggested teaching time:	10–15 minutes
Your actual teaching time:	_____

Pair Work

- Have students number the photos from left to right.

- Draw the following chart (without the answers) on the board:

	What is the person wearing?	What is the event?	Is he/she dressed appropriately?	If not, what should he/she wear instead?
1	a tuxedo	a company picnic		
2	a cardigan, pants	an outdoor wedding		
3	jeans, a shirt	a dinner party at a friend's home		
4	an evening dress	English class		

🌀 Graphic Organizers

- In pairs, have students complete the chart. Circulate to offer help as needed.

- Review as a class. For each photo, have a volunteer share his/her opinion.

Option: In pairs, have students discuss what occasions the people in the photos are dressed appropriately for. **[+5 minutes]**

Discussion

- Have a volunteer read the questions out loud. In small groups, have students discuss the questions. Circulate to offer help as needed.

- To review, have volunteers share their experiences with the class.

Option: Brainstorm possible reactions to an embarrassing situation such as the one posed in item 2. Write students' ideas on the board. For example:

> feel so embarrassed that you leave
> stay but feel terribly uncomfortable
> stay and see the funny side of it

Encourage students to use the ideas on the board to formulate the best reactions to the embarrassing situation described in item 2. **[+5–10 minutes]**

EXTRAS (optional)
Workbook: Exercises 1–2

C 🎧 **Sound Bites.** Read and listen to a conversation between a couple about dressing up and dressing down.

MARGO: Don't you think you might be a little overdressed?

PAUL: What do you mean?

MARGO: Hello! The invitation said casual.

PAUL: Oops. I thought we were supposed to get dressed up. Be right back.

PAUL: How's this?

MARGO: Now that's a little *too* casual.

PAUL: Margo! I wish you'd make up your mind.

MARGO: And what's with the baggy pants? **CN**

PAUL: OK. If I change into a polo shirt and a pair of slacks, will that work?

MARGO: Perfect.

CN **Corpus Notes:** *What's with [someone or something]?* is very common in informal spoken English but rarely in written English.

D **Pair Work.** Use the following words to tell the story of what happened in the conversation.

underdressed	overdressed	formal	casual

STARTING **POINT**

Pair Work. Look at the pictures. Are the people dressed appropriately for each event? With a partner, use the words from Exercise D to describe how the people are dressed. Then compare your answers with other students'.

Event: a company picnic

Event: an outdoor wedding

Event: a dinner party at a friend's home

Event: English class

Discussion.

1. When was the last time you got dressed up? What did you wear?

2. Have you ever been underdressed or overdressed for an event? What happened? How did you feel?

1 Discuss appropriate dress

A 🎧 GRAMMAR **SNAPSHOT.** Read the article and notice the use of quantifiers.

Dressing Up for Work

Most professionals around the world wear formal business attire to work in company offices. In **many** countries, there is an unwritten dress code making it mandatory for a man to wear a dark suit and tie and for a woman to wear a skirted suit. But in **several** countries, **more** companies are experimenting with casual business dress during working hours.

Formal business attire: a thing of the past?

In Australia, during the hotter summer months, **a number of** companies are allowing employees to leave their suits at home. And in the United States, **a little over half of all** office workers are allowed to dress down on Fridays. **One third of** U.S. companies make the standard business suit optional—allowing casual clothing **every** day. There is **a great deal of** interest in a casual dress code because of its attraction to new employees.

However, **some** critics complain that casual dress in the office causes **a lot of** problems, among them, **less** productivity. **Each** manager needs to decide if "business casual" is right for his or her company. **A few** experts in the fashion industry claim that the trend toward casual office dress is on the way out. But a recent survey found that **a majority of** employees say their company dress code is at least as casual or more casual than it was two years ago.

Some complain that business casual leads to less productivity.

B Discussion.

1. How do professionals dress for work in your country? Do people ever wear "business casual"? What kinds of clothing are mandatory?

2. Do you think the way a person dresses has an effect on how he or she works? In what way?

C Grammar. **Quantifiers**

Some quantifiers can only be used with singular count nouns. 🆑
- **one** person
- **each** manager
- **every** employee

Some quantifiers can only be used with plural count nouns.
- **two** problems
- **a couple of** employees
- **both** companies
- **a few** managers
- **a number of** businesses
- **several** women
- **many** young people
- **a majority of** professionals

Some quantifiers can only be used with non-count nouns.
- **a little** conformity
- **much** choice
- **a great deal of** interest
- **less** productivity
- **not as much** satisfaction

Some quantifiers can be used with *both* count and non-count nouns.

no people	**no** choice
some / any employees	**some / any** conformity
a lot of / lots of companies	**a lot of / lots of** individuality
a third of the companies	**a third of** the money
plenty of businesses	**plenty of** satisfaction
most managers	**most** dissatisfaction
all young people	**all** innovation
more countries	**more** interest

NOTE: The quantifier <u>a majority of</u> can also be used with singular count nouns that include more than one person. Use a third-person singular verb.

- A majority of **the class thinks** business casual is a good idea.
- A majority of **the population prefers** a strict dress code.

🆑 **Corpus Notes:** Some quantifiers can only be used with singular count nouns. It is a common learner error to use *each* and *every* with plural nouns, particularly with irregular plural nouns such as *people* and *children*.

Grammar Booster

PAGE G6
For more ...

1 *Discuss appropriate dress*

A 🎧 GRAMMAR **SNAPSHOT**
(CD 2, Track 3)

Suggested teaching time:	5 minutes
Your actual teaching time:	_____

- Point to the two illustrations. Ask *How are the people dressed in the two pictures?* (casually, formally). *In which illustration are the people dressed up for work?* (the one on the left) Ask *If* dress up *means* dress formally, *what expression means* dress casually? (dress down)

- Ask students to notice the use of quantifiers as they read and listen to the article.

- Draw the following pie charts on the board. Point to the shaded area on the first pie chart and write **55%**. Elicit the percentage the shaded area represents for each chart. (b: 80%, c: 33%, d: 20%)

🌀 Graphic Organizers

Point to the first pie chart and ask *Which of the quantifiers in the article could mean 55%?* (A little over half of all, most, a majority of) Write these quantifiers on the board next to the first pie chart. Repeat in the same way for each pie chart on the board. (b. most, many, a great deal of, a lot of, a majority of; c. a number of, one third of, some; d. some, a few)

Language note: *Attire* is a formal word meaning clothes. Something that is *mandatory* must be done, especially because a law or rule says so. If something is *optional*, you do not have to do it or use it. If something is *on the way out*, it is rapidly becoming less popular. *Clothing* is a non-count noun that refers to clothes in general. *Clothes* is a plural count noun that refers to the particular things that people wear. Since *clothing* is non-count and *clothes* is always plural, use *an item / a piece / an article of clothing* to refer to one thing.

Culture note: The trend to wear casual clothing on Fridays is often referred to as *casual Friday*.

B Discussion

Suggested teaching time:	5–10 minutes
Your actual teaching time:	_____

- Form pairs or small groups. Read the questions out loud and have students discuss the answers. Circulate to offer help as needed.

C Grammar

Suggested teaching time:	10–15 minutes
Your actual teaching time:	_____

- To present the use of quantifiers with singular count nouns, write on the board:

    One manager never wears business casual.
    Every company has a different dress code.

  Point to the noun in each sentence and ask *What do these nouns have in common?* (They are singular count nouns.) Then have students identify the quantifier in each sentence. (one, every) Read the first explanation out loud.

- To present the use of quantifiers with plural count nouns, write on the board:

    Many office workers wear a suit and tie.
    A number of people prefer business casual.

  Point to *office workers* and *people* and ask *What do these nouns have in common?* (They are plural count nouns.) Then have students identify the quantifier in each sentence. (many, a number of) Read the second explanation out loud.

- Have students read the note. On the board, write:

    A majority of the staff _____ casual clothes.

  Have students complete the sentences with the correct form of verbs of their choice. Review as a class. (Possible responses: wears, prefers)

- To present the use of quantifiers with non-count nouns, write on the board:

    A great deal of interest was shown by all employees.
    A little productivity goes a long way.

  Point to the noun in each sentence and ask *What do these nouns have in common?* (They are non-count nouns.) Then have students identify the quantifier in each sentence. (a great deal of, a little) Read the third explanation out loud.

- To present the use of quantifiers that can be used with both count and non-count nouns, write on the board:

    Some employees are in favor of change.
    Some formality is preferred.

  Point to the nouns. Ask *What's the difference?* Elicit from the class that *employees* is a plural count noun, while *formality* is a non-count noun. Read the fourth explanation out loud.

Language note: *A few* and *a little* mean some. *Few* and *little* mean not enough.

🌀 Grammar Self-Checks

Option: To practice the use of quantifiers, use the graphic organizer on the Teacher's Resource Disk. You may want to draw it on the board or print and distribute. Write all of the quantifiers from the Grammar Snapshot and Grammar box on the board. With books closed, have pairs use the diagrams to classify the quantifiers. Then have students use their books to confirm their answers. **[+5–10 minutes]**

🌀 Graphic Organizers

D Circle the correct quantifier.

- Model the first item with the class. Be sure students understand only *most* is possible because *much* can't be used with plural count nouns. (businesspeople)
- Have students compare answers with a partner and review as a class.

E Pair Work

- Point out that there isn't just one possible answer. To review as a class, have several students provide their choices for each sentence.

F 🎧 Listening Comprehension
(CD 2, Track 4)

- First listening: Have students listen for the kind of event that the people are talking about in each conversation. Review as a class. (1. an end-of-year party; 2. a special day at the home of the man's parents; 3. an event that the head of the company is going to attend; 4. a visit to Sid and Jackie's home)
- Second listening: Have students listen and complete the exercise. Tell students that you will ask them to support their answers.
- Review as a class and have students explain their choices. (Possible response: 1. because he doesn't want to wear a suit)

AUDIOSCRIPT

For audioscript, see page AS5.

GRAMMAR **EXCHANGE**

Pair Work
- Have a student read the Events list out loud. If necessary, have students explain each event.

- Have students number the events from 1 to 5. Then draw the following chart on the board:

	Appropriate dress	Inappropriate dress
1.		
2.		
3.		
4.		
5.		

🔄 Graphic Organizers

To model the activity, point to the first row and ask *What clothing would be appropriate for a business meeting?* Write student responses in the second column. (Possible responses: a suit, a skirt, a tie, heels) Then ask *What clothing would be inappropriate for a business meeting?* Write student responses in the third column. (Possible responses: shorts, athletic clothing, sandals) In pairs, have students complete the chart.

Group Work

- Form small groups. Have students compare their opinions of appropriate and inappropriate dress for each event.
- Read the models and point out the use of quantifiers.
- Have each group summarize their ideas with sentences using quantifiers.
- To review, have a volunteer from each group summarize the group's opinion for one of the events.

Discussion

- Read the questions out loud. If necessary, explain that social conventions are opinions and behavior that a majority of people in a culture consider to be correct and normal. In pairs, have students exchange opinions and give reasons to support their views.
- Circulate to offer help as needed.
- After students discuss the questions in pairs, have students who think it is important to dress according to social conventions, share their opinions. Then have students who disagree, share their opinions. You may want to keep a list on the board.
- Have volunteers express their views on how what people wear affect the way others perceive them. Ask *Have you judged someone because of what they were wearing and then found out you were wrong?*

EXTRAS (optional)
Grammar Booster
Workbook: Exercises 3–5

D Circle the correct quantifier.

1. ((Most) / Much) businesspeople today prefer to dress casually.
2. ((A number of) / A great deal of) companies would prefer not to change their dress codes.
3. (All / (Every)) manager has to decide what is best for the company and its employees.
4. ((One) / Several) company in New Zealand decided to try a "casual summer" because the summers are always so hot.
5. Research has shown that a business casual dress code has resulted in ((less) / a few) job dissatisfaction among professionals.
6. (A little / (A few)) companies are returning to a more formal dress code.

E **Pair Work.** Read the Grammar Snapshot again. On a separate sheet of paper, rewrite the article, using different quantifiers with similar meanings.

> **M**ost professionals around the world wear formal business attire to work in company offices.

A majority of professionals around the world wear formal business attire to work in company offices.

Answers will vary, but may include: In **a lot of** countries, . . . ; But in **a number of** countries, **some** companies . . . ; In Australia, during the hotter summer months, **several** companies . . . ; And in the United States, **most** offfice workers . . . , **Some** U.S. companies make the standard business suit optional—allowing casual clothing **each** day. There is **a lot of** interest . . . ; However, **a few** critics complain that casual dress in the office causes **many** problems, among them **not as much** productivity. **Every** manager . . . ; **Some** experts . . . ; But a recent survey found that **most** employees . . .

F 🎧 **Listening Comprehension.** Listen to the conversations about casual and formal dress. Determine how best to complete each statement.

1. He'd prefer to ....   **a.** dress up   **(b.)** dress down
2. She wants to ....   **a.** dress up   **(b.)** dress down
3. He's pretty sure a tie is ....   **a.** optional   **(b.)** mandatory
4. She thinks a dress is ....   **(a.)** optional   **b.** mandatory

---

GRAMMAR **EXCHANGE** • *Now discuss appropriate dress.*

Pair Work. How do you think people in your country would generally suggest dressing for these events? Discuss appropriate and inappropriate dress for each event.

> *"Most people would ...,
> but a few people ...."*

Events
- a business meeting
- dinner at a nice restaurant
- dinner at the home of your friend's parents
- an evening party at a club or restaurant with your classmates
- an in-class party

Group Work. Compare your classmates' opinions. Use quantifiers to summarize your classmates' ideas.

> *"A majority of the class said ...."*

> *"A few students said ...."*

Discussion.

1. Do you think it's important to dress according to social conventions?
2. How does what people wear affect how others perceive them?

2 *Comment on fashion and style*

A 🎧 CONVERSATION **SNAPSHOT**

A: Check out that guy over there. CN1

B: Which guy?

A: The one on the cell phone. Can you believe what he's wearing?

B: What do you mean?

A: Don't you think that shirt's a little flashy?

B: Well, the colors are pretty loud, but that's what's in style.

🎧 **Rhythm and intonation practice**

CN1 **Corpus Notes:** The word *guy* occurs much more frequently than *man* in spoken English. *Man* is used much more frequently, however, in written English.

B 🎧 **Vocabulary. Describing fashion and style.**
Listen and practice.

Attractive

fashionable / stylish
CN2 in style / trendy / hot*
elegant / chic
striking

modern
temporarily popular
in good taste
attention-getting

Unattractive

old-fashioned / out of style
tacky*
flashy*
shocking

no longer popular
in poor taste
attention-getting
offensive

*informal

Pronunciation Booster

PAGE P3
Linking sounds

C 🎧 **Listening Comprehension.** Listen to the conversations about fashion and style. Choose the adjective that best summarizes each speaker's point of view.

1. They think the purses in the magazine are ....
   (a.) hot   **b.** flashy   **c.** elegant

2. He thinks the jacket Carl is wearing is ....
   a. stylish   (b.) flashy   **c.** striking

3. They think the girl's hairstyle is ....
   a. striking   **b.** old-fashioned   (c.) shocking

4. He thinks the dress the salesperson is suggesting is ....
   (a.) elegant   **b.** striking   **c.** trendy

5. She thinks the blouse her friend's holding is ....
   (a.) out of style **b.** tacky   **c.** chic

CN2 **Corpus Notes:** *In style* is used more frequently than *trendy* or *hot* to describe clothing. While *trendy* can be used to describe clothing, it is typically used to describe places, such as neighborhoods and restaurants that are popular places to live, visit, or shop. *Hot* occurs more frequently in spoken English than written.

42   UNIT 4

2 Comment on fashion and style

A 🎧 CONVERSATION **SNAPSHOT**
(CD 2, Track 5)

Suggested teaching time:	5–10 minutes
Your actual teaching time:	_____

- Before students read and listen, have them look at the photo. Ask *What do the man's clothes say about him?* (Possible responses: that he likes fashion; that he wants to attract attention)

- After students read and listen, check comprehension by asking *What does the first woman think about what the man is wearing?* (she's shocked by what he's wearing; his shirt's flashy; she doesn't like his shirt) *What does the second woman think?* (that the man is in style; that his shirt is loud)

Language note: *Check out* is used in spoken English to tell someone to look at someone or something. *Can you believe . . . ?* shows you are surprised or shocked by something.

🎧 **Rhythm and intonation practice**
(CD 2, Track 6)

Suggested teaching time:	5 minutes
Your actual teaching time:	_____

- Have students repeat chorally. Make sure they:
  ○ use falling intonation for *Which guy?* and *What do you mean?*
  ○ use rising intonation for *Can you believe what he's wearing?* and *Don't you think that shirt's a little flashy?*
  ○ pronounce the contraction *'s* in . . . *that's what's in style.*
  ○ use the following stress pattern:

STRESS PATTERN

A: Check out that guy over there.

B: Which guy?

A: The one on the cell phone. Can you believe what he's wearing?

B: What do you mean?

A: Don't you think that shirt's a little flashy?

B: Well, the colors are pretty loud, but that's what's in style.

B 🎧 Vocabulary
(CD 2, Track 7)

Suggested teaching time:	5 minutes
Your actual teaching time:	_____

- Have students listen to the words and study the definitions. Then have students listen and repeat the words chorally.

- Say *Use words that are informal (hot, tacky, flashy) with friends or other people you know well.*

- To provide practice, have pairs use the words or phrases to give their own opinions of the clothes the man in the Conversation Snapshot picture is wearing.

Language note: *Old-fashioned* is always hyphenated. (an old-fashioned jacket; that jacket is old-fashioned) *In style* and *out of style* are only hyphenated before a noun. (an in-style jacket; that jacket is in style) A *style* is a particular fashion. (I prefer a classic style.) If something is *in style*, it is temporarily popular. If something is *stylish*, it is attractive in a fashionable way. If appropriate, you may want to tell students that another meaning of *hot* is sexually attractive.

🔄 Vocabulary-Building Strategies

Challenge: Have students think of items of clothing they own or have seen that can be described with some of the words from the Vocabulary. In small groups, have students talk about these items and make a list of the clothes they come up with. To finish the activity, have a student from each group choose an article of clothing from the list and describe it to the class. **[+10 minutes]**

Project: Bring in photos from a fashion magazine or clothing catalog. Have students describe the different styles and fashions using words from the Vocabulary.

C 🎧 Listening Comprehension
(CD 2, Track 8)

Suggested teaching time:	10 minutes
Your actual teaching time:	_____

- Have students read the statements and choices.
- First listening: Pause after each conversation to allow students time to choose the answer.
- Second listening: Have students listen for information that supports their choices. Ask them to take notes.
- To review as a class, have students explain the answers. (1. Everyone is getting them. She should hurry before they go out of style. 2. It's a "look at me" jacket. It gets attention because it's yellow. 3. She says, "What on earth has she done to her hair?" 4. He says it's very tasteful. 5. She says no one is wearing that anymore.)

AUDIOSCRIPT

For audioscript, see page AS5.

D Discussion

Suggested teaching time:	5–10 minutes
Your actual teaching time:	_____

• Circulate to offer help as needed. Encourage students to ask each other questions as they discuss the fashions and hairstyles in the photos. To prompt students, write on the board:

   Do you like these pants?
   Don't you think these pants are out of style?
   Would you wear this shirt?
   Isn't this jacket chic?

• To review, have volunteers choose a photo and share their opinions with the class.

E Pair Work

Suggested teaching time:	5–10 minutes
Your actual teaching time:	_____

• Have volunteers read the quotes out loud.

• Encourage students to explain their choices using some of the adjectives from Exercise B.

• Have volunteers tell the class which quotes sound the most like them. Encourage them to use specific examples to explain their choices.

Language note: If necessary, explain the following words or expressions: *conform* (behave in the way that most other people in your group or society behave); *stand out* (be very easy to see or notice by looking different from other things or people); *draw the line at something* (set a limit on what you are willing to do, especially because you disapprove of something); *subdued* (calm, not bright); *fad* (something that is fashionable for a short time); *designer labels* (clothes made by a well-known and fashionable designer).

Challenge: Draw the following chart on the board:

A	B
1. I don't like to attract attention to myself.	
2. What you wear should conform to how other people look.	
3. I prefer bright colors.	
4. I wear what's in style, even if it's a fad.	
5. I wear what's in style, even if it's uncomfortable.	
6. I prefer a wild look.	
7. I don't care for brands.	

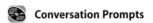 **Graphic Organizers**

Have students scan the quotes for sentences that mean the opposite of the ones in column A. Students should write the opposing quotes in column B. Have students compare answers with a partner and review as a class. (1. I prefer to stand out in a crowd. 2. Clothing should express your individuality. 3. I'm a lot more comfortable in subdued colors. 4. I prefer a look that isn't just a fad that won't be in style for very long. 5. I'd rather be comfortable than fashionable. 6. I draw the line at wild and crazy clothes. 7. I always choose designer labels.) **[+10 minutes]**

CONVERSATION **STARTER**

Suggested teaching time:	10 minutes
Your actual teaching time:	_____

• Have volunteers read the vocabulary in the boxes out loud. Ask *What do the words in each box have in common?* (Possible responses: verbs to do with style; negative adjectives to describe clothes; positive adjectives to describe clothes) Have students label the boxes.

• Have students complete the sentences individually and give specific examples.

Pair Work

• Refer students to the Conversation Snapshot on page 42 to review how to comment on fashion and style.

• Model the activity by discussing your fashion tastes and style.

• If you or your students brought in photos, have students discuss the different photos.

• As students interact, circulate to provide help as needed. Encourage students to use the vocabulary they've learned so far.

Conversation Prompts

EXTRAS (optional)

Pronunciation Booster
Workbook: Exercises 6–9

D **Discussion.** What do you think of these fashions and hairstyles? Use the adjectives from the vocabulary to describe them in your *own* way.

E **Pair Work.** Read and match each quote with a person in the photos in Exercise D. Explain your answers. Which quote sounds the most like *you*?

Answers will vary, but may include:

1. **D** "Clothing should express your individuality. I don't want to conform to how other people look or what they wear—I prefer to stand out in a crowd."

4. **E** "I draw the line at wild and crazy clothes. I just don't like to attract attention to myself. I'm a lot more comfortable in subdued colors and classic styles."

2. **A** "What I wear may not be the most trendy—but I like it that way. I'd rather be comfortable than fashionable."

5. **B** "I prefer a look that isn't just a fad that won't be in style for very long. I prefer clothes that are well made—they may cost a bit more, but they last longer."

3. **C** "The way you dress affects how people perceive you, so it's important to dress well. I always choose designer labels—they're the best."

CONVERSATION **STARTER** • *Now comment on fashion and style.*

Complete each statement about fashions in your *own* way.
Use these words and expressions.

I prefer clothes that . . .
I don't like to . . .
I dislike it when women wear clothes that . . .
I dislike it when men wear clothes that . . .

| conform |
| stand out |
| attract attention |
| express one's |
| individuality |

| old-fashioned |
| out of style |
| tacky |
| flashy |
| shocking |

| well made |
| comfortable |
| wild and crazy |
| classic |
| subdued |
| fashionable |
| stylish |
| elegant |
| striking |
| trendy |

Pair Work. Discuss your *own* fashion tastes and style. Explain why you find some fashions attractive and some unattractive. Refer to the photos on this page or bring in others. Use the Conversation Snapshot on page 42 as a guide.

"Check out . . ."   "Can you believe . . ."

Evaluate ways to change one's appearance

A 🎧 **Listening Comprehension.** Listen to Part 1 of a radio program about men's hairstyles. Then read the statements and listen again. Complete the statements, according to the information in the program.

a goatee

1. In the eighteenth century, wigs were considered ....
   a. chic **b.** tacky **c.** out of style

2. In the nineteenth century, wigs were considered ....
   a. in style **b.** old-fashioned **c.** striking

3. Before the twentieth century, short hair would not have been considered ....
   a. stylish **b.** out of style **c.** shocking

B 🎧 Now listen to Part 2. What generally happened to men's hairstyles in the mid-twentieth century? Men began to wear their hair long, and they grew beards and mustaches.

C 🎧 Read the following statements and listen to Part 2 again. Complete the statements, according to the information in the program.

1. Men changed their hairstyles in the 1960s as a .... statement.
   a. fashion **b.** social and political **c.** religious and moral

2. Twenty years ago, the bald look would have been considered ....
   a. eccentric **b.** stylish **c.** old-fashioned

3. Young people who dye their hair want to ....
   a. be stylish **b.** conform **c.** express their individuality

D **Discussion.** Do you agree with the hair stylist that "anything goes" today for men's hairstyles? Are there any hairstyles that you really don't like on a man? Do you think men's hairstyles have improved or gotten worse in recent times?

sideburns

highlights

long hair

a buzz cut

bald

dyed

braids

3 Evaluate ways to change one's appearance

A 🎧 Listening Comprehension
(CD 2, Track 9)

Suggested teaching time:	10–15 minutes
Your actual teaching time:	_____

- Pre-listening: Have students look at the hairstyles in the pictures. Point to the pictures for a goatee and sideburns. Ask *What are some other styles of facial hair?* (a mustache, a beard)

- First listening: Have students listen and write down the time periods that are talked about. To review as a class, have students name the time periods and list them on the board (17th and 18th centuries; 19th century; early 20th century; 1960s and 1970s)

- Have students read the statements and review the meanings of the words given as choices. If students need help, refer them to the Vocabulary on page 42.

- Second listening: Have students listen and complete the statements. Review as a class and have students support their choices. (Possible responses: 1. Wigs were chic because they were worn by the king of France. 2. Wigs were old-fashioned because the style changed. 3. Short hair would have been considered out of style because long hair was in fashion.)

- Third listening: Erase *1960s and 1970s* from the board and to the right of the time periods on the board, write:

    short hair, almost no beards or mustaches
    wigs
    long hair, beards, and sideburns

    Have students listen again and match the time periods with the fashions. Review as a class. (17th and 18th centuries: wigs; 19th century: long hair, beards, and sideburns; early 20th century: short hair, almost no beards or mustaches)

AUDIOSCRIPT

For audioscript, see page AS6.

B 🎧 Now listen to Part 2 . . .
(CD 2, Track 10)

Suggested teaching time:	5–10 minutes
Your actual teaching time:	_____

- Have students take notes while they listen.
- To review, call on a couple of students to share their answers with the class.

AUDIOSCRIPT

For audioscript, see page AS6.

C 🎧 Read the following statements . . .
(CD 2, Track 11)

Suggested teaching time:	5 minutes
Your actual teaching time:	_____

- Have a volunteer read the statements and answer choices out loud. If necessary, explain the meanings of unfamiliar terms.

- Review answers as a class.

- To have students support their choices, ask (for item 1:) *What were men protesting against when they changed their hairstyles?* (a conservative culture) (for item 2:) *Why would it have been considered eccentric?* (because no one had ever worn it) (for item 3:) *Why do they want to express their individuality?* (to protest strict school dress codes)

💿 Listening Strategies

Option: Form small groups. To personalize the activity, have male students tell their group members which styles they have worn or would like to wear. Encourage group members to ask questions. You may want to ask all students to bring in photos of themselves wearing different hairstyles, for the next class. **[+5 minutes]**

D Discussion

Suggested teaching time:	10 minutes
Your actual teaching time:	_____

- To prepare for the discussion, have students look at the photos depicting hairstyles and decide which they like and which they don't like on a man.

- Have students discuss the questions in small groups.

- To review, take a class poll. With a show of hands, determine which hairstyles depicted in the photos are the least popular on a man. Then have students vote on whether they think hairstyles have improved or gotten worse in recent times. Write the results on the board.

- To finish, have volunteers summarize the results of the poll using quantifiers from page 40. For example, *A majority of the class thinks that long hair is OK on a man.*

DISCUSSION **BUILDER**

Suggested teaching time: 15–20 minutes
Your actual teaching time: _____

STEP 1. Pair Work.

• Have students spend a few moments reading the items in the checklist and looking at the photos. Encourage them to help each other with any unknown language.

• Have volunteers share other ways people spend time and money to make themselves more attractive. (Possible responses: hair extensions, dental surgery, braces)

• After pairs complete the checklist, draw the following chart on the board:

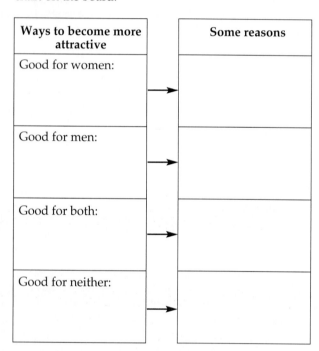

Ways to become more attractive	Some reasons
Good for women:	
Good for men:	
Good for both:	
Good for neither:	

Graphic Organizers

In pairs, have students use the chart to classify the ways people make themselves more attractive and note their opinions.

• As pairs discuss, tell them to think of the possible risks involved with some of these procedures.

STEP 2. Discussion.

• Form small groups to discuss the questions.

• Have groups write a list of examples of things people d that they think is "too much."

• Call on students from different groups to present their ideas to the class. Encourage the class to comment on th ideas. Have students who agree share their own examples and students who disagree explain why.

EXTRAS (optional)

Workbook: Exercises 10–11

DISCUSSION **BUILDER** • *Now evaluate ways to change one's appearance.*

Step 1. Pair Work. Discuss and complete the checklist.

Ways people spend time and money to make themselves more attractive

Which do you think are good ideas for women? How about for men? Which do you think are good for both? Check the appropriate box.

	men	**women**		**men**	**women**
skin lightening	☐	☐	contact lenses	☐	☐
skin tanning	☐	☐	false eyelashes	☐	☐
body piercing	☐	☐	makeup	☐	☐
tattoos	☐	☐	hair coloring	☐	☐
facials	☐	☐	permanents (perms)	☐	☐
manicures	☐	☐	hair transplants	☐	☐
nail extensions	☐	☐	wigs	☐	☐
nail polishing	☐	☐	hair removal	☐	☐
cosmetic surgery	☐	☐	other	☐	☐

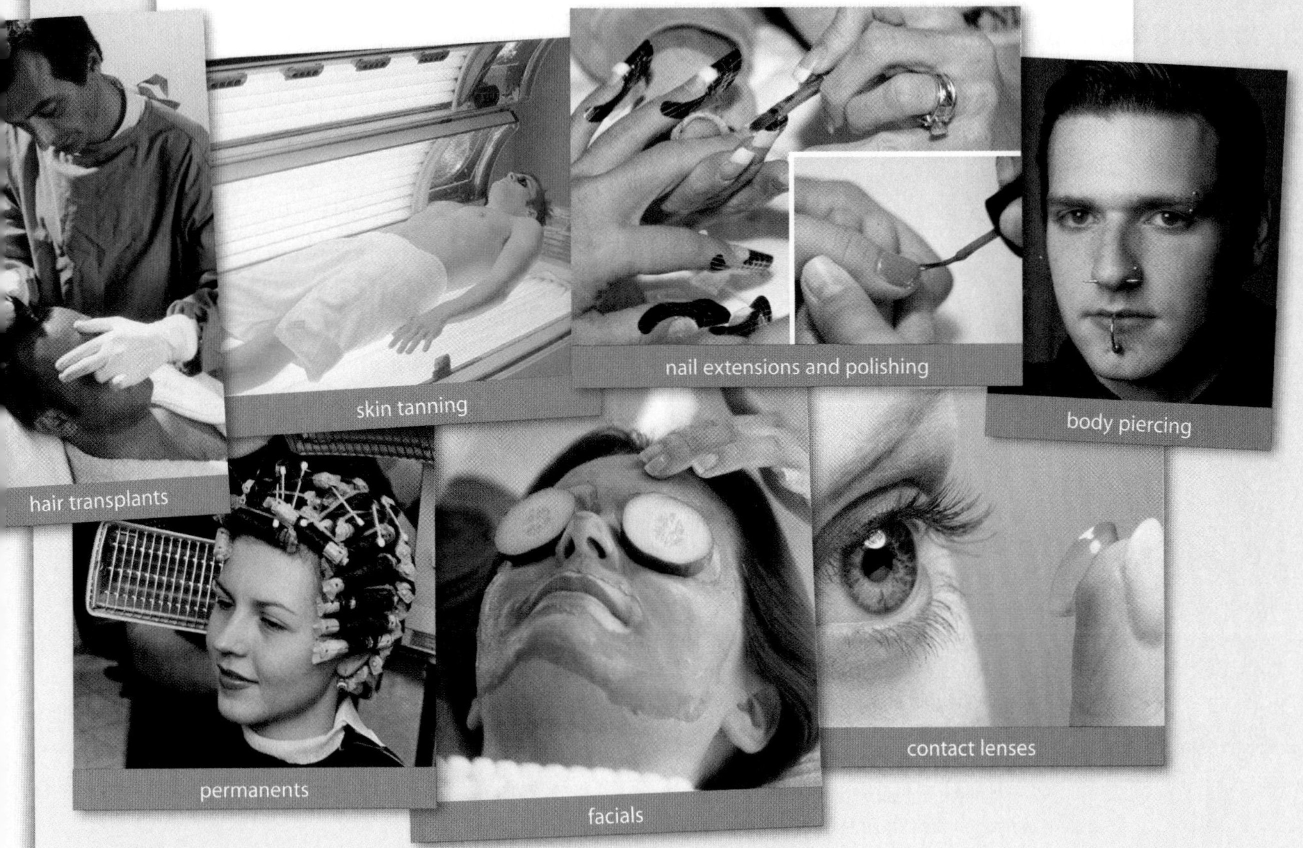

hair transplants
skin tanning
nail extensions and polishing
body piercing
permanents
facials
contact lenses

Step 2. Discussion.

1. Who do you think should spend more time making themselves attractive—men or women? Why?
2. Can people do too much to try to make themselves attractive? If so, what do you think is "too much"?

4 *Describe what makes a person beautiful*

A 🎧 **Word Skills. Using the prefix self-.** Use a dictionary to find other words with the prefix self-.

self-confidence the belief that one has the ability to do things well
Parents can build their children's self-confidence by praising their accomplishments.

self-esteem the attitude of acceptance and approval of oneself
High self-esteem can help a person succeed, and low self-esteem can be damaging.

self-image the opinion one has about one's own abilities, appearance, and character
Mark's self-image improved after he started his new job.

self-pity the feeling of being sorry for oneself
It's easy to indulge in self-pity when you're faced with problems.

self-centered interested only in oneself
Children are naturally self-centered, but they usually learn to be more interested in others as they grow up.

self-confident sure of oneself; not shy or nervous in social situations
Janet is a very self-confident young woman. She'll do well at the university.

self-conscious worried about what one looks like or what other people think of one's appearance
Everyone at the meeting was dressed casually, so I felt self-conscious in my suit.

self-critical tending to find fault with oneself
Paul is too self-critical. He always focuses on his mistakes rather than his accomplishments.

CN Corpus Notes: *Self-conscious* appears modified by a phrase beginning with the preposition *about* more frequently than it does alone. For example, *She's self-conscious about how she looks.*

B **Reading Warm-up.** Do you think most people are self-conscious about how they look?

C 🎧 **Reading.** Read the article about female body image. What do you think is expressed in the song lyrics?

The average fashion model is 5 feet, 11 inches (1.83 meters) tall and weighs 117 pounds (53 kilograms). The average woman is 5 feet, 4 inches (1.65 meters) tall and weighs 140 pounds (63.5 kilograms).

WHO DEFINES BEAUTY?

"Am I not pretty enough?
Is my heart too broken?
Do I cry too much?
Am I too outspoken?
Don't I make you laugh?
Should I try it harder?
Why do you see right through me?"

What makes a girl beautiful? The lines above are from the song "Not Pretty Enough," written and performed by Kasey Chambers, an Australian folk-rock singer and songwriter. The words tell us a lot about what it's like to be female in a society in which media such as television, movies, and magazines define what it means to be beautiful.

In cultures where success and happiness are equated with being thin and attractive "just like models or movie stars," many young women are left feeling either invisible or fat and unaccepted.

It might not surprise you to read that 75 percent of women in the United States think that they are "too fat." But many people do not realize how these ideas about body image have affected teenagers and children. You don't have to look much farther than a billboard sign, magazine advertisement, or popular television show to see how girls and women are being presented and to understand how it affects them.

On average, U.S. children age eight or older spend almost seven hours a day watching television, playing video games, or reading magazines. Studies have revealed these trends:

- If they had just one wish, girls ages eleven to seventeen say they would wish to be thinner.
- Between the ages of ten and fourteen, the percentage of girls who are "happy with the way I am" drops from 60% to 29%.
- 80% of ten-year-old girls are on diets.
- Between 5 and 10 million teenage girls and young women have an eating disorder—extreme dieting—that can be dangerous to their health.
- Teenage cosmetic surgeries more than doubled in the last decade and are growing at an alarming rate.
- 70% of girls say they have wanted to look like an actress. About 30% have actually tried to.

Young people can benefit from realizing how much they are being targeted as a consumer group and how media messages are used to either sell them products or convey messages about body image, self-esteem, social values, and behavior.

Source: www.riverdeep.net

4 Describe what makes a person beautiful

A 🎧 Word Skills
(CD 2, Track 12)

Suggested teaching time:	10 minutes
Your actual teaching time:	_____

- Have students listen to the words and study the definitions. Then have students listen and repeat the words chorally.

- Point out that *self-* is a prefix that is used with many nouns and adjectives and that these nouns and adjectives with *self-* are always hyphenated.

- To show the change in meaning when the prefix *self-* is added to a word, write *image* on the board and define as a class. (the way something is portrayed to the public; what you think someone or something is like or how they look) Add the prefix *self-* and define as a class. (how you see yourself) Note the change in meaning. You may want to do this with several words from the list.

- Ask *Which of the adjectives has a positive connotation?* (self-confident) *Which have a negative connotation?* (self-centered, self-conscious, self-critical)

- Have students find at least three words with the prefix *self-* in the dictionary. Have them share the words and definitions with the class. (Possible responses: self-disciplined, self-educated, self-employed, self-interest, self-opinionated, self-satisfied)

🔧 Vocabulary-Building Strategies

Option: You may want to photocopy and distribute this exercise or write it on the board:
1. "I always make mistakes."
2. "I can do it!"
3. "I'm worried about how I look."
4. "Everyone should feel sad for me."
5. "I'm as important as other people."
6. "I don't care much about what other people need."

In pairs, have students create a sentence using a noun or adjective from Word Skills to describe the person who said each statement. Review as a class. (1. This person is self-critical. 2. This person is self-confident. 3. This person is self-conscious. 4. This person feels self-pity. 5. This person has high self-esteem. 6. This person is self-centered.) [+5–10 minutes]

B Reading Warm-up

Suggested teaching time:	5 minutes
Your actual teaching time:	_____

- In small groups, have students discuss the question.

- To encourage students to explain their answers, ask *What are some things people are self-conscious about?* (Possible responses: hair, clothes) *What are some situations in which people tend to be self-conscious about how they look?* (Possible responses: at parties, at interviews, when they meet someone new)

- Call on some students to share their opinions with the class.

C 🎧 Reading
(CD 2, Track 13)

Suggested teaching time:	10–15 minutes
Your actual teaching time:	_____

- Point to the photo. Ask *Do you think the woman in the photo is beautiful? Why do you think so?*

- After students read the title and song lyrics out loud, have them make predictions. Ask *What issues do you think the article will discuss?* (Possible responses: female body image, beauty, self-confidence, self-esteem)

- Have students think about the meaning of the lyrics as they read and listen to the magazine article.

- Then ask *What do you think is expressed in the song lyrics?* (Possible response: The woman is suffering because she has no "positive" qualities according to the standards in our society.)

- To check comprehension, ask *According to the article, what influences how our society defines beauty?* (television, video games, magazines, movies) *What are some ways that people try to control how they look?* (dieting, cosmetic surgery, buying beauty products, imitating an actress) *What dangers mentioned in the article are associated with a negative body image?* (extreme dieting, eating disorders, low self-esteem)

Language note: Students may need help with the following words: *outspoken* (expressing your opinions honestly, even when it is not popular to do so); *see right through someone* (know what someone is really like, especially what their bad qualities are); *billboard sign* (a large sign used for advertising).

🔧 Reading Strategies
🔧 Reading Speed Calculator
🔧 Extra Reading Comprehension Activities

Project: Choose a period in art such as the Renaissance, and bring in portraits of women of the time. In small groups, encourage students to compare female body image in the past with female body image in modern times. To review, have students from different groups give their opinions of what made a woman beautiful in the past.

D Complete each statement . . .

Suggested teaching time:	5 minutes
Your actual teaching time:	_____

• Model the first item with the class. Have a volunteer complete the statement and explain his/her answer. (Possible response: When young people compare themselves with how the media portrays actors and models, they may become unhappy wth the way they look.)

• As students compare answers with a partner, have them explain their choices.

• Review as a class.

E Discussion

Suggested teaching time:	5–10 minutes
Your actual teaching time:	_____

• Form groups of three and read the items out loud.

• As students discuss item 1, ask *What messages about body image are conveyed in this country?*

• As students discuss item 2, have them write two lists of ideas—one about how to avoid being affected by the media and the other about how to increase self-esteem.

• Have volunteers from different groups share their lists. You may want to write a list on the board. (Possible ideas: **How to avoid being affected by the media:** watch less TV; read fewer fashion magazines; try not to lose perspective—remember that a movie is fiction; don't compare yourself with stars; **How to increase self-esteem:** remember your achievements; eliminate negative thoughts; give yourself a few compliments each day; make a list of the things you're good at; accept the things about yourself that you can't change)

DISCUSSION **BUILDER**

Suggested teaching time:	10–15 minutes
Your actual teaching time:	_____

 Discourse Strategies

Step 1. Pair Work.

• Call on students to read the numbered statements in the survey. Then have students complete the survey individually.

• In pairs, have students explain their choices.

• To review as a class, ask *Are women more or less self-conscious about their bodies than men? Are they more or less self-conscious about their faces than men? Are women or men more likely to want to look like people in the media? Is it more common for women or men to think that beauty is not important?* Have a few volunteers share their opinions with the class.

Step 2.

• Read the examples on the notepad out loud.

• To model the activity, have a volunteer give an example of one thing that makes a person beautiful on the outside. Then have another volunteer give an example of one thing that makes a person beautiful on the inside.

• After students write their ideas individually, have them share their notes with the class. Write a list on the board as you get feedback from students. (Possible responses: **Beauty on the outside:** a warm smile, a happy face, sparkling eyes, a nice hairstyle, clean and tidy clothes, big eyes, a small nose, good posture; **Beauty on the inside:** a friendly attitude, a caring attitude, a sparkling personality, a cheerful disposition, patience, tolerance, sympathy, honesty)

Step 3. Discussion.

• To help students organize their ideas and get ready for discussion, have them make a list of supporting reasons for their answers to questions 1–3.

• Have students discuss their ideas in small groups.

• To finish the activity, have volunteers from different groups express their views on each question.

EXTRAS (optional)

Workbook: Exercises 12–14

D Complete each statement, according to the article. Then explain your answers.

1. The media can be damaging to a young person's _____ .
   a. self-image   **b.** high self-esteem   **c.** self-pity
   (a. circled)

2. If girls had more _____ , they would not want to look like fashion models.
   a. self-pity   **b.** self-confidence   **c.** self-image
   (b. circled)

3. Before the age of ten, most girls are _____ .
   a. self-conscious   **b.** self-confident   **c.** self-critical
   (b. circled)

4. After the age of ten, a lot of teenage girls suffer from _____ .
   a. too much self-confidence   **b.** high self-esteem   **c.** low self-esteem
   (c. circled)

E Discussion.

1. Are girls and women in your country affected by images in the media? Are boys and men also affected? How?

2. What do you think young people can do to avoid being affected by the messages they get from advertising, TV, and the movies? What can they do to be more satisfied with the way they look and to develop their self-esteem?

DISCUSSION **BUILDER** • *Now describe what makes a person beautiful.*

Step 1. Pair Work. Take the survey. Then compare and explain your choices.

How much do you agree with each statement about men and women in your country?

strongly disagree   strongly agree

1. Most women are self-conscious about their bodies.	1	2	3	4	5
2. Most men are self-conscious about their bodies.	1	2	3	4	5
3. Most women are self-conscious about their faces.	1	2	3	4	5
4. Most men are self-conscious about their faces.	1	2	3	4	5
5. Most women want to look more like people in the media.	1	2	3	4	5
6. Most men want to look more like people in the media.	1	2	3	4	5
7. Most women think beauty is not important.	1	2	3	4	5
8. Most men think beauty is not important.	1	2	3	4	5

Step 2. What do you think makes a person beautiful "on the outside"? How about "on the inside"? Take notes on your notepad.

> Beauty on the outside   Beauty on the inside
> *a friendly face*   *a creative mind*

> Beauty on the outside   Beauty on the inside

Step 3. Discussion.

1. What is more important to you—a person's beauty on the outside or on the inside? Explain.

2. Do you think life is easier for people who are attractive? Why or why not?

3. Do you think people should just accept the way they look or try to change their appearances?

Writing: Compare two people's tastes in fashion

Compare and contrast

Connecting words can help a writer examine similarities and differences.

Compare (show similarities)	Contrast (show differences)
like **Like** Sylvia, I wear jeans all the time.	**but** Wendy wears fashionable clothes, **but** her sister does not.
similarly I grew up paying little attention to fashion. **Similarly**, Mel was not very interested in clothes. OR I grew up paying little attention to fashion; **similarly**, Mel was not very interested in clothes.	**however** Lily had to wear a uniform when she was in school. **However**, I was able to wear anything I wanted. OR Lily had to wear a uniform when she was in school; **however**, I was able to wear anything I wanted.
too / also Henry used to wear faded jeans in high school. I did **too**. OR I did **also**. OR I **also** did.	**whereas / while** Sam spends a lot of money on clothes, **whereas** Jeff shops in thrift stores. OR Sam spends a lot of money on clothes, **while** Jeff shops in thrift stores.

Step 1. Prewriting. Organizing ideas.

Choose a topic. Then on a separate sheet of paper, draw a diagram similar to the one on the right. Label the circles with the topics you are comparing and write <u>Both</u> in the middle. List the differences in each circle and the similarities in the middle.

My fashion style
—conservative style
—wear suits, skirts, blouses

Both
—like to wear hats
—buy clothes on sale
—have many pairs of shoes

—kind of eccentric
—likes flashy pants, tacky shoes

My brother's fashion style

Topics
- Compare and contrast your fashion style with that of someone you know.
- Compare and contrast fashion today with fashion five, ten, or twenty years ago.

Step 2. Writing.

On a separate sheet of paper, write two paragraphs comparing and contrasting ideas within the topic you chose, referring to the notes in your diagram. In your first paragraph, write about the differences. In your second paragraph, write about the similarities. Remember to use connecting words and include a topic sentence for each paragraph.

Step 3. Self-Check.

- ☐ Did you correctly use connecting words for comparing?
- ☐ Did you correctly use connecting words for contrasting?
- ☐ Does each paragraph have a topic sentence?

WRITING MODEL

My brother Eric and I have very different tastes in fashion. I wear conservative clothes, **while** he prefers more eccentric outfits. He thinks he looks good in his flashy clothes, **but** I think his style is unattractive.

However, there are some similarities in our styles. Eric likes to wear hats, and I do **too**. **Like** Eric, I am not

Writing Compare two people's tastes in fashion

Suggested teaching time: 15–20 minutes
Your actual teaching time: _____

Compare and contrast

- Call on students to read the explanation and examples out loud.

- To make students aware of the correct punctuation for each connective, ask *Which connectives can be preceded by a comma?* (but, whereas, while) *Which connectives are followed by a comma?* (similarly, however) *What punctuation mark is necessary before* similarly *and* however? (a period or a semicolon)

- Photocopy and distribute this exercise or write it on the board:

A	B
1. Jay likes to dress up.	a. Max loves striking clothes.
2. Jay likes to attract attention to himself.	b. Max is rather old-fashioned.
3. Jay always wears fashionable clothes.	c. Max prefers to dress casually.
	d. Max doesn't like to stand out in a crowd.
	e. Max always wears what is in style.
	f. Max thinks it is important to dress well.

For each statement in column A, have students find a similar and a contrasting statement in column B. (1. f, c; 2. a, d; 3. e, b) Then have pairs join the statements using connectives. (Possible responses: Like Jay, Max likes to dress up; Jay likes to dress up. Similarly, Max thinks it is important to dress well; Max thinks it is important to dress well. Jay does, too; Jay likes to dress up, but Max prefers to dress casually; Jay likes to dress up. However, Max prefers to dress casually; Jay likes to dress up, whereas Max prefers to dress down.) Review as a class by having several students read their sentences out loud.

 Extra Writing Skills Practice

Step 1. Prewriting.

- Read the Topics list out loud. Have students choose one.

- Point to the Venn diagram. Ask *What tastes in fashion do both people have?* (like to wear hats; buy clothes on sale; have many pairs of shoes) *What tastes does the brother have?* (kind of eccentric; likes flashy pants, tacky shoes)

- As students draw their own diagrams, circulate to help students organize their ideas as needed.

Step 2. Writing.

- Before students write, have them read the writing model and identify the topic sentence in each paragraph.

- Point out that the first paragraph is about the differences in tastes and the second is about similarities.

- As students write, circulate to offer help with the use of connecting words.

Step 3. Self-Check.

- Read the Self-Check questions as a class.

- Before students submit their paragraphs for correction, have them self-check their work and make any necessary changes.

Option: Step 4. Peer response. Have students exchange papers with a partner to check if there are any errors with connecting words. If there are, have students suggest corrections. **[+5–10 minutes]**

EXTRAS (optional)

Workbook: Page 38

A 🎧 Listening Comprehension
(CD 2, Track 14)

Suggested teaching time:	10 minutes
Your actual teaching time:	_____

- First listening: With books closed, have students listen for the item of clothing the speakers are talking about in each conversation and decide if the speakers share the same opinion about the items or not. Review as a class. (1. a suit; 2. a dress; 3. a tie; 4. a pair of shoes. In all four conversations the speakers have different opinions of the items discussed.)
- Second listening: Have students listen and choose the adjectives.
- Have students compare answers with a partner and review as a class.

Language note: *To each his own* means that we all have different ideas about how to do things, what we like, etc.

Option: Have students listen to the speakers again and write the statements said by the speakers that support their answers. (1. "Who wears anything like that anymore?" 2. "The colors are way too bright." 3. "Actually I think it's pretty nice." 4. "You know *everyone's* wearing them now.") **[+5 minutes]**

AUDIOSCRIPT
For audioscript, see page AS6.

B Complete each statement ...

Suggested teaching time:	5 minutes
Your actual teaching time:	_____

- Have students review the Grammar Snapshot on page 40 and the Vocabulary on page 42. Call out a word and have students give the definition. Keep the activity fast paced.
- Have students compare answers with a partner and review as a class.

Option: Have pairs write sentences of their own using the Vocabulary from page 42 that wasn't used in Exercise B. **[+5–10 minutes]**

C Cross out the one quantifier ...

Suggested teaching time:	5–10 minutes
Your actual teaching time:	_____

- To clarify the task, point out that two quantifiers are correct and only one is wrong.
- After reviewing answers, have pairs decide how the meaning of the statements change / don't change with each of the correct quantifiers.

Option: Have students use quantifiers to write sentences about what their classmates are wearing today. **[+5 minutes]**

D Writing

Suggested teaching time:	10–15 minutes
Your actual teaching time:	_____

- Call on volunteers to explain the meaning of each expression. (Possible responses: **Beauty is only skin-deep:** The fact that a person is beautiful on the outside does not mean that he/she is also beautiful on the inside. It is what is on the inside that counts; **Beauty is in the eye of the beholder:** Different people have different opinions about what is beautiful.)
- Have students choose an expression to write about.
- Have students take notes before they start writing. Encourage them to think of at least three concrete examples that support their opinions.
- Tell students that they can include the expression in the topic sentence <u>or</u> use it in the concluding sentence.

 You may wish to use the Video Program and activity worksheets for Unit 4 at this point.

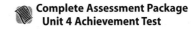 **Complete Assessment Package Unit 4 Achievement Test**

UNIT 4 CHECKPOINT

SUMMIT WEBSITE
For Unit 4 online activities, visit the *Summit* Companion Website at www.longman.com/summit.

A 🎧 **Listening Comprehension.** Listen carefully to the conversations about tastes in fashion. Infer which adjective best describes what each person thinks.

1. The man thinks the suit is ....
   a. stylish   **(b.)** out of style   **c.** tacky

2. The woman thinks the dress is ....
   a. chic   **b.** old-fashioned   **(c.)** flashy

3. The man thinks the tie is ....
   (a.) fashionable   **b.** out of style   **c.** shocking

4. The woman thinks the shoes are ....
   a. out of style   **(b.)** in style   **c.** striking

B Complete each statement with an appropriate word or phrase.

1. A set of rules for how to dress in a particular situation is a dress ____code____ .

2. In the United States and Canada, many companies allow their employees to wear "business ____casual____" on Fridays—they don't have to wear suits, skirts, or ties.

3. Some companies allow employees to dress ____down____ for some business meetings where the focus is on getting to know each other in a more casual setting.

4. When a fashion is ____out of____ style, people no longer wear that fashion. When a fashion is ____in____ style, everyone wants to wear it.

C Cross out the one quantifier that *cannot* be used in each sentence.

1. (~~Every~~ / A few / Most) older people find today's fashions pretty shocking.

2. Our company says that it will allow us to dress down (~~one~~ / a couple of / a few) days a week.

3. (Most / Many / ~~Every~~) young girls aren't worried about the way they look.

4. (~~Much~~ / A majority of / A number of) researchers are concerned about the effect the media has on young boys as well.

5. (Many / Most / ~~Much~~) men wore their hair very short in the 1930s.

6. I'd say your sister could use (some / a little / ~~a few~~) fashion help.

7. There are (several / ~~most~~ / many) reasons why so many people have eating disorders.

8. A new study says that (most / many / ~~every~~) children who watch TV for more than six hours a day may have problems with self-esteem as teenagers.

D **Writing.** Write a paragraph explaining your opinion about one of these expressions. Give concrete examples from your life.

"Beauty is only skin-deep."   "Beauty is in the eye of the beholder."

UNIT 5

Community

UNIT GOALS

1 Politely ask someone not to do something
2 Complain about public conduct
3 Discuss social responsibility
4 Identify urban problems

A **Topic Preview.** Look at the graph and photos. Where do most people live in your country—in rural or urban areas?

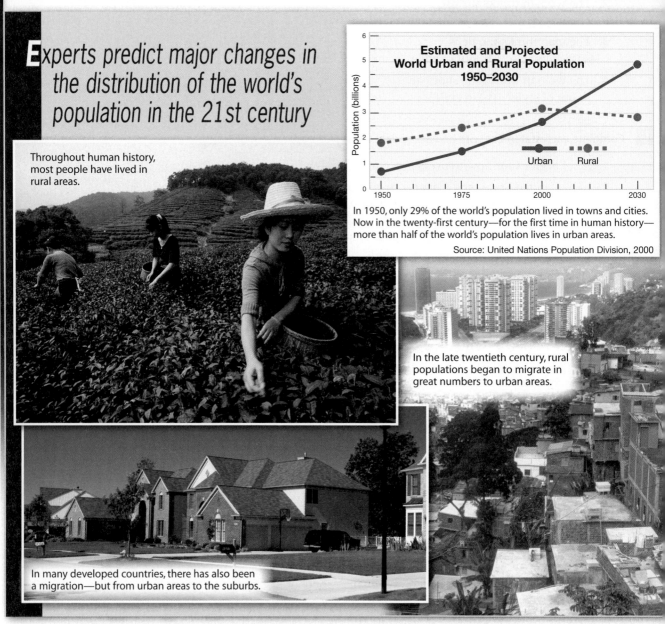

Experts predict major changes in the distribution of the world's population in the 21st century

Throughout human history, most people have lived in rural areas.

Estimated and Projected World Urban and Rural Population 1950–2030

Population (billions)

Urban   Rural

1950   1975   2000   2030

In 1950, only 29% of the world's population lived in towns and cities. Now in the twenty-first century—for the first time in human history—more than half of the world's population lives in urban areas.

Source: United Nations Population Division, 2000

In the late twentieth century, rural populations began to migrate in great numbers to urban areas.

In many developed countries, there has also been a migration—but from urban areas to the suburbs.

B **Pair Work.** Answer the questions, according to the information in the graph.

1. Approximately how many people in the world will be living in urban areas in 2030? 5 billion How about in rural areas? 2.8 billion

2. In what year did the world's urban population surpass the world's rural population? 2005

C **Discussion.** Is there much migration in your country? What are some reasons people migrate?

UNIT 5

Community

A Topic Preview

Suggested teaching time:	10–15 minutes
Your actual teaching time:	_____

- To introduce the theme of community, have students spend a few moments looking at the pictures and chart and reading the captions.
- Have a volunteer read the heading "Experts predict . . ." out loud. Ask *What kind of changes do experts predict for this century?* (that more people will move from the country to cities / from rural areas to urban areas)
- On the board, write *rural*, *urban*, and *suburban*. Have students point to the photo that matches each word (rural: top left; suburban: bottom left; urban: bottom right)
- Have a volunteer summarize the changes in rural / urban population from the chart. (Possible response: In the past, most people lived in rural areas. Then people started migrating to urban areas. Now more people live in urban areas than in rural areas.)
- Then ask *What kind of migration is taking place in developed countries?* (People are moving from urban areas to the suburbs.) *Why do you think this is happening?* (Possible responses: because people seek a better quality of life; because people want to escape hectic city life)
- Ask *Where do most people live in this country—in rural or urban areas?* Have students name some of the most populated areas or cities in this country.

Language note: Students may need help with the following words or expressions: *distribution* (the way in which people are spread out over an area); *migrate* (move to another place or country, usually in order to find somewhere to live or work); *migration* (the movement of a large number of people from one place to another); *suburbs* (a residential area away from the center of a town or city).

B Pair Work

Suggested teaching time:	5 minutes
Your actual teaching time:	_____

- Point to the graph. Explain that the axis on the left side of the graph indicates the population in billions. Ask students how much a billion is. (1,000,000,000)
- After students have finished discussing the questions, review as a class.

C Discussion

Suggested teaching time:	5–10 minutes
Your actual teaching time:	_____

- Have students discuss the questions in small groups.
- As students discuss, encourage them to takes notes of reasons people migrate.
- Have students each share a reason. (Possible responses: to get a job; to have a better quality of life; to get a higher income; to escape political persecution; to escape religious persecution; to escape war; to leave an area affected by a natural disaster)
- Ask *Have you or anyone you know ever moved from the country to the city? If so, why?*

D 🎧 Sound Bites
(CD 2, Track 15)

Suggested teaching time:	10 minutes
Your actual teaching time:	_____

• To set the scene for the conversation, have students look at the photos and brainstorm words to describe them. On the board, write students' ideas:

The city
- people
- crowded   cars
- traffic   buildings
- pollution   noise
- traffic lights
- busy

The country
- trees   hills
- grass   sky
- farmhouses   quiet
- fresh air   peace
- sun

• Have students use the words on the board to compare and contrast the photos. (Possible responses: The city looks crowded and busy whereas the country looks peaceful and quiet; In the city there are buildings and cars while in the country there are trees, hills, and farmhouses.)

• Have students listen with books closed. Ask *What are the men talking about?*

• Have students read the conversation and listen again. To check comprehension, ask *Where does Kyle live now?* (the city) *Has Kyle always lived there?* (no) *What problems is Kyle experiencing?* (He finds it difficult to keep up with the pace in the city; He was almost run over by a car.)

Language note: Kyle uses present tenses (*am crossing, turns, runs over*) to say what happened to him before meeting Don. Present tenses are often used in spoken English to narrate a dramatic anecdote. Use *get used to* to say that you are more comfortable with a situation and that it does not seem strange or difficult anymore. Use *used to* to talk about something that you did regularly in the past and that you do not do anymore. For example, *After two months in London, I finally got used to wet weather. I used to live in the country when I was a kid. Now I live in a big city.* The spoken expressions *country boy / girl* and *city boy / girl* are used to describe someone who has always lived in the country or the city and is used to living there.

E In Other Words

Suggested teaching time:	5 minutes
Your actual teaching time:	_____

• Point out that students should identify the speaker of each phrase and use the context of the conversation to help work out the meaning.

• Have students compare answers with a partner and then review as a class.

STARTING **POINT**

Suggested teaching time:	10–15 minutes
Your actual teaching time:	_____

• Model the activity with the class. Write the following chart on the board (without the answers) and elicit several ideas for each column from the class:

	Advantages	Disadvantages
The country	Clean air, low crime, friendly people, less stress, slower pace	boring, no jobs, too far from good health care

• Have students complete the chart individually in note form.

• Encourage students to write at least three advantages and disadvantages of living in each place.

Discussion

• Group students according to where they prefer to live. If possible, put students with different preferences together.

• Have students discuss their favorite places to live. As students discuss, encourage them to agree or disagree with their group members' views.

• Take a poll of the class to find out how many people would like to live in each place.

EXTRAS (optional)
Workbook: Exercises 1–2

"the city"

D 🎧 **Sound Bites.** Read and listen to a conversation about city life.

DON: Hey, Kyle! So how's the big city treating you?
KYLE: Funny you should ask. Not great.
DON: What do you mean?
KYLE: Well, on my way here, I'm crossing the street and this guy in an SUV turns the corner and almost runs me over.
DON: Are you serious?
KYLE: Yeah. The driver was in such a big hurry he didn't even notice. I just can't keep up with the pace here. **CN**
DON: Well, you *do* have to learn to stay on your toes in the city.
KYLE: It really gets to me sometimes. I don't think I'll ever get used to it. I guess I'm just a country boy at heart.

E **In Other Words.** Read the conversation again. With a partner, explain the meaning of each of the following statements or questions.
Answers will vary, but may include:
   1. "So how's the big city treating you?"
      How do you like living in the city?
   2. "I just can't keep up with the pace here."
      Things move too fast for me here.
   3. "You *do* have to learn to stay on your toes."
      You have to pay attention and be alert all the time.
   4. "It really gets to me sometimes."
      It bothers me sometimes.
   5. "I'm just a country boy at heart."
      I prefer living in the country.

CN **Corpus Notes:** The phrasal verb *keep up* appears modified by a phrase beginning with the preposition *with* more frequently than it does alone.

"the country"

STARTING **POINT**

What are some advantages and disadvantages of living in each type of place? Write them in the chart.

	Advantages	**Disadvantages**
the country		
the city		
the suburbs		

Discussion. Where would you prefer to live—in the country, the city, or the suburbs? Why?

1 *Politely ask someone not to do something*

A 🎧 CONVERSATION **SNAPSHOT**

A: Do you mind my smoking here?

B: Actually, smoking kind of bothers me. I hope that's not a problem.

A: Not at all. I can step outside.

B: That's very considerate of you. Thanks for asking. **CN**

🎧 **Rhythm and intonation practice**

> 🎧 **Ways to soften an objection**
> I hope that's not a problem.
> I hope you don't mind.
> I hope it's OK / all right.
> I don't mean to inconvenience you.

B Grammar. Possessives with gerunds

You can use a possessive before a gerund when you want to indicate the performer of the action.

The kids' singing was too loud.
Your constant **arguing** is getting on my nerves.
I didn't like **their talking** during the movie.
You should complain about **Sam's cutting** in line.
The thing that bothers me is **her smoking**.

In informal spoken English, a noun or an object pronoun is often used instead of a possessive.

I can understand **John being** annoyed. (instead of "John's being annoyed")
I can't accept **them ignoring** me. (instead of "their ignoring me")

C Combine the two statements, using a possessive with a gerund.

Example: They allow smoking. I'm not in favor of it.
_____ *I'm not in favor of their allowing smoking.* _____

1. He plays his MP3 player in the library. I don't appreciate that.
I don't appreciate his playing his MP3 player in the library.

2. They smoke cigars in the car. My mother objects to it.
My mother objects to their smoking cigars in the car.

3. She's talking on her cell phone. We don't mind it.
We don't mind her talking on her cell phone.

4. My brother litters. I'm really annoyed by it.
I'm really annoyed by my brother's littering.

CN **Corpus Notes:** The adjective *considerate* appears as a subject complement (*He is very considerate*) more frequently than as a noun modifier (*He's a considerate man*). *Considerate* appears modified by the preposition *of* more frequently than it does alone.

1 *Politely ask someone not to do something*

A CONVERSATION SNAPSHOT
(CD 2, Tracks 16, 18)

Suggested teaching time:	5–10 minutes
Your actual teaching time:	_____

- After students read and listen, check comprehension by asking *What does the man ask for permission to do?* (smoke) *Does the woman give or refuse permission?* (refuse) *Why?* (because smoke bothers her)

- Point out that both the person who asks permission and the person who refuses it are polite to each other. Ask students to identify and underline polite language in the conversation. (Do you mind my smoking here?; I hope that's not a problem; Not at all; That's very considerate of you; Thanks for asking.)

- Have students read and listen to the ways to soften an objection. Point out that when you refuse permission, it is polite to soften the refusal with a sentence from the box or to offer a reason for refusing.

Language note: Use the question *Do you mind . . .?* when you think what you are asking permission to do might make the other person uncomfortable. Use *That's very considerate of you* to thank a person for being careful not to upset you. To *inconvenience* someone is to cause problems or difficulty for them.

Option: You may want to brainstorm ways of replying to the question *Do you mind . . .?* with the class on the board. (Possible responses: **Ways to say "yes" / refuse permission:** Yes, I do; Yes, actually, I do mind; Actually, smoking kind of bothers me; **Ways to say "no" / give permission:** No, I don't; I don't mind; Not at all; Go right ahead.) Be sure students understand that *Yes* refuses permission and *No* gives permission. **[+5 minutes]**

Rhythm and intonation practice
(CD 2, Track 17)

Suggested teaching time:	5 minutes
Your actual teaching time:	_____

- Have students repeat chorally. Make sure they:
  ○ use rising intonation for *Do you mind my smoking here?*
  ○ pause slightly after *Actually . . .*
  ○ use emphatic stress for <u>hope</u> in *I hope that's not a problem.*

○ use the following stress pattern:

STRESS PATTERN

A: Do you mind my smoking here?

B: Actually, smoking kind of bothers me. I hope that's not a problem.

A: Not at all. I can step outside.

B: That's very considerate of you. Thanks for asking.

B Grammar

Suggested teaching time:	5–10 minutes
Your actual teaching time:	_____

- Have volunteers read the first explanation and examples out loud.

- On the board, write:
  She complained about _____ smoking in the office.

  Have students identify the gerund in the example (smoking). Call on students to complete the sentence on the board with their own examples. Write students' responses on the board. (Possible responses: his, Bill's)

- Have students read the second explanation and study the examples.

- Have students restate the different variations of the sentence on the board, using object pronouns. (Possible responses: She complained about him / Bill smoking in the office.) Point out that the possessive adjective *her* has the same form as the object pronoun *her.*

- Point out that when the possessive gerund is in the object position, a noun or object pronoun can be used, but when the possessive gerund is in the subject position, this is not done. On the board, write:

  1. You constant arguing is getting on my nerves.
  2. I don't like they smoking in here.

  To check comprehension, correct the sentences on the board as a class.

Grammar Self-Checks

C Combine the two statements . . .

Suggested teaching time:	5 minutes
Your actual teaching time:	_____

- Write the example answer on the board. Underline the gerundial phrase (their allowing smoking). Ask students to name its grammatical function within the sentence. (object of the preposition *of*) To quickly review noun clauses, refer students to the Grammar box on page 18.

- Point out that gerundial phrases will have different grammatical functions within the sentence—as subjects, objects, and objects of a preposition.

- Have students compare answers with a partner and review as a class.

T52

D 🎧 Word Skills
(CD 2, Track 19)

Suggested teaching time:	5 minutes
Your actual teaching time:	_____

- Have students listen to and study the words. Clarify the meaning of unknown words.
- Have students listen and repeat the words chorally.
- Point to the negative prefixes in the box. Ask *What is a negative prefix?* (a group of letters added to the beginning of a word to form the word's opposite)
- To check comprehension, write on the board:

  unfriendly   impatient   incomplete   disloyal

  Have students identify the prefixes (un-, im-, in-, dis-) and say the word each negative adjective is derived from. (friendly, patient, complete, loyal)
- Then have pairs think of other words starting with any of the prefixes they identified. (Possible responses: untidy, impossible, incorrect, disagree)

Language note: Many words starting with *m-* and *p-* form their negative with the prefix *im-*. Many words starting with *r-* form their negative with the prefix *ir-*. For example, *immobile, impossible, irregular, immortal, impatient, irreplaceable.* There are exceptions; for example, *displeased, disrespectful.*

Option: Have students study the adjectives for one minute. Then have pairs take turns saying adjectives from the list and naming their opposites. The student who names the opposites should have his/her book closed. Then have students change roles. **[+5 minutes]**

E Pair Work

Suggested teaching time:	5 minutes
Your actual teaching time:	_____

- Have pairs look up the adjectives in a dictionary. Point out that in some dictionaries, antonyms are given at the end of each entry preceded by the word *opposite*. In dictionaries that do not provide antonyms in this way, students should look up the prefix they think is correct and then scan to see if the adjective pairs with it.
- As pairs work with their dictionaries, encourage them to read the definitions of the words they might not know.
- Review as a class.

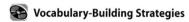 Vocabulary-Building Strategies

F Write your own examples . . .

Suggested teaching time:	5 minutes
Your actual teaching time:	_____

- Have a volunteer read the directions and example out loud.

- After students write their own examples, have them share their sentences with a partner.
- Review as a class. Have students share an example each.

Challenge: Draw the following diagram on the board:

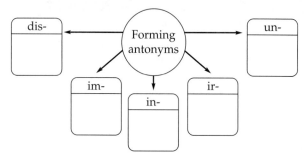

🌐 **Graphic Organizers**

With books closed, say the adjectives from Exercises D and E (without their negative prefixes) in random order and have students write them in the corresponding box according to the prefix they need to form their opposite. Review as a class. **[+5 minutes]**

CONVERSATION **STARTER**

Suggested teaching time:	10–15 minutes
Your actual teaching time:	_____

Pair Work

- Have volunteers read the examples out loud.
- Encourage students to add 3–4 items to their lists.
- Have students share ideas from their lists with the class. You may want to write a list of ideas on the board. (Possible ideas: playing [loud] music; changing the TV channel; leaving work early)

Role Play

- Refer students to the Conversation Snapshot on page 52 to review politely asking someone not to do something. You may also want to have students listen to the conversation again.
- Choose a more confident student and role-play a conversation.
- As students interact, circulate to encourage students to use the correct rhythm and intonation. Remind students to use rising intonation for the question starting with *Do you mind . . . ?* and to pause after *Actually . . .* and then refuse permission. Make sure each student plays both roles.

 Conversation Prompts

EXTRAS (optional)

Pronunciation Booster
Workbook: Exercises 3–5

D 🎧 Word Skills. Using negative prefixes to form antonyms

1. acceptable → **un**acceptable
2. considerate → **in**considerate
3. polite → **im**polite
4. proper → **im**proper
5. respectful → **dis**respectful
6. responsible → **ir**responsible

Pronunciation Booster

PAGE P4
Unstressed syllables

E Pair Work. Use a dictionary to find antonyms for the following words. What other adjectives can you find with negative prefixes?

1. appropriate → inappropriate
2. courteous → discourteous
3. excusable → inexcusable
4. imaginable → unimaginable
5. honest → dishonest
6. pleasant → unpleasant
7. rational → irrational
8. mature → immature

F Write your own examples of inappropriate behavior. Use the adjectives from Exercises D and E.

Answers will vary, but may include:

Example: It's inconsiderate to play loud music on a bus.

1. It's disrespectful to talk back to your parents.
2. It's impolite to be late to class.
3. It's dishonest to cheat on a test.
4. It's inconsiderate to use a cell phone in a restaurant.
5. It's unacceptable to litter on the street.

CONVERSATION **STARTER** • *Now politely ask someone not to do something.*

Pair Work. Discuss situations in which you would probably ask for permission to do something. Make a list on your notepad.

> smoking in a restaurant
> turning on the TV in a doctor's waiting room
> making a call on my cell phone in public

Your list:

Role Play. Role-play a conversation in which you ask your partner for permission to do something. Your partner politely asks you not to do it. Use the Conversation Snapshot on page 52 as a guide. Start like this: "Do you mind my ..."

"Do you mind my smoking?"

"Do you mind my making a quick call on my cell phone?"

53

GRAMMAR

2 *Complain about public conduct*

A 🎧 GRAMMAR **SNAPSHOT.** Read the interview responses and notice the use of paired conjunctions.

What ticks you off?

Wendy Kwon, 23
Chicago, USA

What ticks me off? Well, I can't understand why people litter. Who do they think is going to clean up after them? **Either** they should throw their garbage in a trash can **or** hold on to it till they find one. I think it's great that people have to pay a fine for littering. Maybe they'll think twice before doing it again.

Dana Fraser, 36
Toronto, Canada

You know what gets to me? Smoking. It's such an inconsiderate habit. Secondhand cigarette smoke is **neither** good for you **nor** pleasant to be around. I'd like to see smoking banned from more public places. Don't non-smokers have rights too?

Yuan Yong Jing, 28
Beijing, China

It really bugs me when people spit on the street. **Not only** do I find it disgusting, **but** it's **also** unhygienic. It's important to think about other people's feelings and public health.

Jorge Santos, 31
São Paulo, Brazil

Here's something that gets on my nerves: I hate it when people use their cell phones in public places. They annoy other people, **not only** on trains and buses **but also** in theaters. They should have the courtesy to **either** turn their phones off **or** to leave them at home. It really makes me angry. I guess it's kind of my pet peeve.

B **Pair Work.** Do any of the behaviors described in the interview responses "tick you off"? With a partner, discuss and rate each of them as follows:

extremely annoying   somewhat annoying   not annoying at all

PAGE G9
For more ...

C **Grammar. Paired conjunctions**

You can connect related ideas with paired conjunctions.

either ... or
    Either smoke outside **or** don't smoke at all.
    Cell phones should **either** be turned off **or** left at home.

neither ... nor CN
    I would allow **neither** spitting **nor** littering on the street.
    Neither eating **nor** chewing gum is acceptable in class.

not only ... but (also)
    Not only CD players **but also** cell phones should be banned from trains.

CN **Corpus Notes:** It is common for learners to make the error of using *or* with *neither*. For example, *Television is neither good or bad*.

BE CAREFUL! When not only ... but (also) joins two clauses, notice the subject–verb position in the first clause of the sentence.
    Not only **did they forget** to turn off their cell phones, but they also talked loudly during the concert.
    Not only **are they** noisy, but they're rude.

Verb agreement with paired conjunctions
When joining two subjects, make sure the verb agrees with the subject closer to the verb.
    Either the mayor or **local businesspeople need** to decide.
    Either local businesspeople or **the mayor needs** to decide.

54   UNIT 5

2 Complain about public conduct

A ⟨ GRAMMAR SNAPSHOT
(CD 2, Track 20)

Suggested teaching time: 5–10 minutes
Your actual teaching time: _____

• Point out the title of the lesson. Elicit the meaning of *public conduct* from the class. (how a person behaves around other people)

• Read the interview question out loud. Elicit an alternate way to phrase this question from the class. (Possible response: What annoys you?)

• Draw the following chart (without the answers) on the board:

	Wendy	Dana	Yong Jing	Jorge
What people do that bothers them	litter	smoke	spit on the street	use cell phones in public
What they think people should do	use trashcans or hold on to litter until they find one	not smoke in public places	think about other people and public health	turn cell phones off or leave them at home

🌐 Graphic Organizers

With books closed, have students listen and complete the chart in note form and then compare answers with a partner. Then review as a class. Have students share the information from the chart with the class, using complete sentences.

• Have students read the Grammar Snapshot and notice the use of paired conjunctions.

> **Language note:** Students may need help with the following words: *fine* (money that you have to pay for breaking the law); *ban* (officially say that people must not do something); *secondhand smoke* (smoke that you breathe in from other people who are smoking); *pet peeve* (something that you don't like and that always annoys you).

B Pair Work

Suggested teaching time: 5–10 minutes
Your actual teaching time: _____

• As students discuss, encourage them to support their views by explaining why they find / don't find each behavior annoying.

• Review as a class. Ask various students to share their opinions on each behavior with the class.

C Grammar

Suggested teaching time: 15 minutes
Your actual teaching time: _____

• Point out that a paired conjunction joins two ideas.

• Have students read the first explanation and study the examples with *either . . . or*. Explain that *either . . . or* is used to give two choices. Ask *What are the two choices in the first example?* (smoke outside; don't smoke at all)

• Point out the parallel structure after each part of the paired construction. (*smoke* and *don't smoke*). On the board, write:

> 1. *Either send her an email or* _____.
> 2. *She's not here. She's either having lunch or* _____.

To check comprehension, have a few volunteers complete the sentences with their own ideas. Remind students to use parallel structure. (Possible responses: 1. give her a call; 2. visiting clients)

• Have students read the examples with *neither . . . nor*. Point out that *neither . . . nor* has negative meaning. To help clarify, ask *In the second example, is eating acceptable in class?* (no) *Is chewing gum?* (no)

• Have students read the example with *not only . . . but (also)*. Point out that *also* is optional. To check comprehension, ask *Should CD players be banned from trains?* (yes) *Should cell phones be banned from trains?* (yes)

• Have students read the explanation and examples with Be Careful! out loud.

• Point out that the same word order used in questions is the same used in the first clause of sentences joined by *not only . . . but (also)*.

• Have students read the explanation and examples for *Verb agreement with paired conjunctions.* On the board, write:

> 1. *Either Paul or his friends* _____ *coming.*
> 2. *Either Paul's friends or Paul himself* _____ *coming.*

To check comprehension, have students complete the blanks with the correct form of *be*. Review as a class. (1. are, 2. is)

> **Language note:** Nowadays, it is generally acceptable to split an infinitive. For example, *They should have the courtesy <u>to</u> either <u>turn</u> their phones off or <u>leave</u> them at home.* Notice the different positions of *not only* and *but (also)*:
> Sue bought <u>not only</u> a coat <u>but also</u> a jacket.
>   (*but also* + object)
> Sue <u>not only</u> works here, <u>but</u> she <u>also</u> lives here.
>   (*but* + subject + *also* + verb)
> Sue <u>not only</u> works here, <u>but also</u> lives here.
>   (*but also* + verb; same subject is omitted)

🌐 Grammar Self-Checks

T54

D On a separate sheet of paper ...

Suggested teaching time:	5 minutes
Your actual teaching time:	_____

- Model the first item with the class. Have students underline the information that makes the two sentences different. (My uncle; My grandparents) Then elicit the new sentence with the paired conjunction from the class.

- After students complete the exercise individually, have them compare answers with a partner.

- Review as a class. Elicit alternate placement of *not only* and *but (also)* for items 3 and 4.

Challenge: On the board, write:
1. Someone I like: _____
2. Someone I don't like: _____
3. Something I like: _____
4. Something I don't like: _____

Have students write the information on the board on a slip of paper and complete it with their own information. On a second slip of paper have students write two reasons for liking / not liking each person / thing. Pair work. Student A gives the first slip of paper to Student B. Student B asks Student A why he/she likes / doesn't like each of the items on the list. Student A answers using paired conjunctions. For example, Student A: *Why do you like your sister?* Student B: *Because she's not only kind but also fun to be with.* Then have students switch roles. [+10 minutes]

GRAMMAR EXCHANGE

Suggested teaching time:	15–20 minutes
Your actual teaching time:	_____

- Have a volunteer read the ideas in the box and the example out loud. Point out the paired conjunction. (*not only . . . but also*)

- You may want to share your own idea and example with the class. As a class, brainstorm other things that can get on your nerves. (Possible ideas: loud parties; when people use your parking space)

- Have students write their sentences individually. As students write, circulate to offer help as needed with paired conjunctions.

Group Work

- You may want to write examples of how to finish the ideas on the board:

What really ticks me off is	strong perfumes.
	when people talk in theatres.
I'll tell you what gets on my nerves:	loud parties.
	littering.

- Elicit from the class different ways the interviewer can ask people about what gets on their nerves. For example, *What ticks you off? What really bugs you? What gets on your nerves?*

- Role-play an interview with a more confident student. Have the student play the role of the interviewer. You may respond *I can't understand why people talk in theaters! It's not only annoying, but it's also very rude.*

- Form small groups of three or four. Make sure that each student plays the role of the interviewer.

- Circulate as students interact. Make sure students use paired conjunctions and adjectives to describe inappropriate behavior correctly.

- To finish, have students report to the class on what ticks their partners off. Keep a tally on the board to find out what bothers the class most.

Discussion

- Have a volunteer read the questions out loud. Elicit or explain the meaning of *speak up* (to express your opinion or defend your rights).

- As students discuss the questions in small groups, encourage them to take notes of reasons why it is / isn't important to speak up.

- To review answers to the first question as a class, have volunteers share their ideas for how people should behave in public places. (Possible responses: They should be polite; They should respect others.)

- Write a two-column chart on the board with the heads *Reasons in favor of speaking up* and *Reasons against speaking up*. Have students share reasons for / against speaking up. (Possible reasons: **In favor of speaking up:** People's rights should be respected; If we don't speak up, things will keep getting worse; **Against speaking up:** You might sound rude; It's not nice to complain.)

- To discuss item 2 as a class, have volunteers talk about their own experiences. Ask other students to say whether they would / wouldn't get angry in the situations described by their classmates. Encourage volunteers to say whether or not they intend to change their habits and explain why.

Language note: *Graffiti:* illegal drawings or writings on some public surface (the walls of buildings, trains, etc.) that can state a political opinion, or something funny or rude.

EXTRAS (optional)
Grammar Booster
Workbook: Exercises 6–10

D On a separate sheet of paper, combine the sentences with the paired conjunction indicated. Use or, nor, or but (also).

1. My uncle isn't willing to give up smoking. My grandparents aren't willing to give up smoking. (neither) Neither my uncle nor my grandparents are willing to give up smoking.

2. People should speak up about what bothers them. They should just learn to live with other people's habits. (either) People should either speak up about what bothers them or learn to live with other people's habits.

3. I don't like it when people use cell phones in theaters. I don't like it when they use them on buses. (not only) Not only do I not like it when people use cell phones in theaters but also when they use them on buses.

4. The smell of the smoke bothers me. The danger to my health bothers me. (not only) Not only the smell of smoke but also the danger to my health bothers me.

GRAMMAR **EXCHANGE** • *Now complain about public conduct.*

On your notepad, make a list of some of the things that really get on your nerves in public places. Then write sentences with paired conjunctions to express your opinion. Use some of the adjectives you already know.

IDEAS
- cutting in line
- graffiti on walls
- talking in theaters
- strong perfumes
- gossiping

In restaurants: *talking on cell phones*
It's not only annoying, but it's also very impolite.

In restaurants:

In stores:

On buses and trains:

On the street:

In offices:

In movie theaters:

Other:

Some adjectives
disrespectful
immature
impolite
inconsiderate
inexcusable
irresponsible
unacceptable
unpleasant

Group Work. One student is an "on-the-street interviewer" and asks the other students about what gets on their nerves. Use the sentences from your notepad in your responses.

What really ticks me off is …

I can't understand why …

I'll tell you what really gets on my nerves. …

You want to know what really bugs me?

Discussion.

1. In your opinion, how should people behave in public places? Do you think it's important to speak up when people behave inconsiderately in public?

2. Do *you* ever do things that annoy other people? Explain.

3 *Discuss social responsibility*

A 🎧 **Vocabulary. Ways to perform community service.** Listen and practice.

GET INVOLVED WITH YOUR COMMUNITY!

Beautify your town
Plant flowers or trees where there aren't any.

Clean up litter
Pick up trash from parks, playgrounds, or the street.

Donate your time
Mail letters, make phone calls, raise money, or collect signatures for a community service organization.

Volunteer CN
Work without pay in the fire department, a hospital, or a school.

Donate your organs
Save someone's life by making arrangements <u>now</u> to give your heart, lungs, and other organs after you die to someone who needs them.

B **Pair Work.** Would you ever consider doing any of the community service activities in the vocabulary? With a partner, explain why you would or would not.

"I would never consider donating my organs because it's against my beliefs."

CN Corpus Notes: The verb *volunteer* is most frequently followed by an infinitive (*volunteer to [do something]*) or by a prepositional phrase with *for* (*volunteer for [something]*).

C 🎧 **Listening Comprehension.** Read the questions and listen to Part 1 of the story about Nicholas Green and his family. Take notes on your notepad. Then summarize the first part of the story with your partner.

Where were the Greens from? They were from California in the United States.

What were they doing in Italy? They were on vacation.

What happened to Nicholas? He was shot and died.

What decision did his parents make? They decided to donate his organs to people who were sick.

How did the Italian people react? They were very moved.

Nicholas Green, age seven, in Switzerland, a few days before he and his family went to Italy

D 🎧 Read the questions and listen to Part 2. Discuss your answers with a partner.
Answers will vary, but may include:

1. What changes occurred in Italy after the Greens made their decision? People started to think differently about organ donation.
   What is "The Nicholas Effect"? The number of people who were willing to become organ donors increased by three to four hundred percent.

2. How many people received one of Nicholas's organs? What effect did his gift have on their lives? Seven. One woman was able to see and the rest had their lives saved.

3. As a result of this incident, what are the Greens doing today? They work to support organ donation.

3 *Discuss social responsibility*

A 🎧 Vocabulary
(CD 2, Track 21)

Suggested teaching time:	5–10 minutes
Your actual teaching time:	_____

- Read the title of the lesson out loud. Ask *What is social responsibility?* (the idea that you should do something for the good of your community)
- Point to the art. Ask *What kind of board is this?* (message / bulletin board) *Where would you find a board like this?* (Possible responses: government buildings, libraries, schools)
- Have a volunteer read the directions out loud. Elicit the meaning of *community service* from the class. (work that you do without payment to help the people who live in your town or to make your town a better place to live in)
- Have students listen to the words and study the explanations. Then have students listen and repeat the words chorally.
- To check comprehension of the vocabulary, ask *What can you do to beautify your community?* (plant flowers or trees) *How can you help make your community look cleaner?* (by picking up litter) *How can you help a community service organization?* (by donating your time to mail letters, make phone calls, raise money, or collect signatures) *If you are interested in helping people, where can you volunteer to work?* (in a fire department, hospital, or school) *What can you do to save other people's lives?* (donate your organs)
- As a class, brainstorm other ways to perform community service. (Possible responses: help poor families; visit patients in hospitals)

B Pair Work

Suggested teaching time:	5–10 minutes
Your actual teaching time:	_____

- Have volunteers read the directions and example out loud.
- Allow some time for students to think about what they would / wouldn't consider doing individually. Encourage students to think of supporting reasons.
- Have pairs discuss all five ways to perform community service.
- To finish the activity, bring up ways to perform community service one at a time, and have students express their views.

C 🎧 Listening Comprehension
(CD 2, Track 22)

Suggested teaching time:	10 minutes
Your actual teaching time:	_____

- Pre-listening: Have students look at the photo and read the caption.
- Have students read the questions individually.
- First listening: Have students listen and write the answers to the questions in note form. Then have students compare answers with a partner.
- Second listening: Have students listen again to complete their notes and/or confirm their answers.
- As pairs summarize the story, circulate to offer help as needed.
- To review, have a student summarize the story to the class. Encourage the students who are listening to add any relevant information their classmate did not mention.

💿 Listening Strategies

Challenge: Tell students that they are going to retell the story in the listening as a class. Each student should finish a sentence and provide the beginning of the next. To start retelling the story, say *The Green family was on vacation in Italy. They were driving back to their hotel one night when . . .* Call on a student to continue. Call on a different student to continue after each student has provided his/her input. [**+10 minutes**]

> **AUDIOSCRIPT**
> For audioscript, see page AS7.

D 🎧 Read the questions ...
(CD 2, Track 23)

Suggested teaching time:	10 minutes
Your actual teaching time:	_____

- Have volunteers read the questions out loud.
- Tell students to take notes as they listen to Part 2.
- Have students discuss answers with a partner.
- To review as a class, call on three students to answer the questions.
- Have students listen to Part 2 again to confirm their answers.

Challenge: Writing. Have students write a summary of the story about Nicholas Green and his family, recalling as much information from the listening as possible. [**+10–15 minutes**]

> **AUDIOSCRIPT**
> For audioscript, see page AS7.

E Discussion

Suggested teaching time:	5 minutes
Your actual teaching time:	_____

- Form groups of three. As students discuss the questions, encourage them to support their views.

- To review answers to question 1, have students who would have made the same decision as the Greens raise their hands. Ask these students to explain the reasons for their decision. Then have the rest of the class explain why they wouldn't have done what the Greens did.

- Review answers to question 2. Elicit as many reasons as possible from the class. (Possible reasons: because they were deeply moved; because they valued the fact that the Greens weren't interested in revenge as most people might be in the same situation)

Option: Have students share with the class other stories they might know about people who donated their organs or received an organ from someone else. [+5 minutes]

DISCUSSION **BUILDER**

Suggested teaching time:	10–15 minutes
Your actual teaching time:	_____

Step 1. Pair Work.

- Have volunteers read the three situations and questions out loud.

- If necessary, explain *complete stranger* (someone you don't know), *liver* (an organ in the body that produces bile and cleans the blood), and *monument* (a building or structure built to remind people of an important event or famous person).

- In pairs, have students discuss the questions and take notes.

- On the board, write *How strong is your sense of community?* Elicit the explanation of *sense of community* from the class. (the feeling that you belong to a particular community because people work together to help each other and improve the community)

- In pairs, have students discuss how strong they think their social responsibility is. Circulate to encourage students to support their results with specific examples. (Possible response: I don't seem to have a very strong sense of community because I would neither let neighbors live in my home nor donate a piece of my liver to a neighbor. I would, however, help a relative or a close friend.)

Step 2. Discussion.

- To get students ready for discussion, share any personal history of volunteerism with the class. If you or someone you know has volunteered for community service, tell the class about it.

- As students discuss the questions, encourage them to think of organizations they may have contributed to or programs in which they might have been involved and to list reasons why it is important to get active in the community.

- To finish the activity, have a volunteer from each group share their group's community service experiences with the class. Ask students who think it is important to get active support their view. (Possible reasons: to give back to society; to bring about change)

Project: Have students research community service opportunities in this area. Have them choose a program they would be interested in participating in if they had the time. Ask students to take notes of the program and then share the information with the class.

EXTRAS (optional)
Workbook: Exercises 11–14

E **Discussion.**

1. Do you think you would have made the same decision the Greens did if you had been in their situation? Why or why not?

2. Why do you think people responded so strongly to this story?

DISCUSSION **BUILDER** • *Now discuss social responsibility.*

Step 1. Pair Work. Consider each situation and discuss what you might do. Based on your answers, how strong do you think your "sense of community" is?

> "My first responsibility is to my family. I can't imagine doing this for a total stranger."

> "I'd be happy to donate money to help a stranger. People should help each other."

1 There has been a terrible storm, and many homes have been destroyed. You're asked to let a family live with you until their home is fixed.

What would you do if they were . . .

    a. your relatives?   c. your colleague's family?
    b. your neighbors?   d. complete strangers?

2 Someone needs a new liver to survive. Doctors say that they can use a piece of your liver to save that person's life.

What would you do if the person were . . .

    a. a family member?   c. your classmate?
    b. your neighbor?   d. a complete stranger?

3 Developers plan to destroy a well-known historical monument so they can build a new office building. You're asked to donate your time to help save that monument.

What would you do if the monument were . . .

    a. in your neighborhood?   c. in another city in your country?
    b. in another part of the city?   d. in another country?

Step 2. Discussion. Have you or someone you know ever volunteered for some kind of community service? How important is it for a person to be active in his or her community? Explain.

4 Identify urban problems

A **Reading Warm-up.** What problems do you think cities of 10 million or more people might share?

B 🎧 **Reading.** Read the interview. Do you agree with Dr. Perlman's views?

The Advent of the Megacity

Following is an interview with Dr. Janice Perlman, founder and president of Mega-Cities Project, Inc. Her organization attempts to make cities worldwide more livable places by taking good ideas from one place and trying to make them work in another.

Q. How do you define "megacity"?

A. We define megacities in our work as cities that have reached populations of 10 million or more. The majority of these are in developing countries. Migration to the city is the route for many people to greater choice, opportunity, and well-being. By coming to settle in the city, they have in effect "voted with their feet."

Q. Why are these places going to be very important in the next hundred years?

A. The 21st century won't be a century of rural areas and small towns but of giant cities that will set the standard of how we live, how our environment is preserved (or not preserved), how our economies work, and what kind of civil society we develop.

Mexico City, over 18 million (2005)

Tokyo over 28 million (2005)

Q. Do megacities in the developed and developing world differ, or are they linked by certain similarities?

A. These large cities have a lot more in common with each other than they do with the small towns and villages in their own countries. For example, every megacity struggles with a widening gap between rich and poor. Every "first-world" city, such as Los Angeles, New York, London, or Tokyo, has within it a "third-world" city of poverty and deprivation. And every third-world city, such as Calcutta, Cairo, or Mexico City, has within it a first-world city of high culture, technology, fashion, and finance.

In addition, all megacities share the problems of providing jobs and economic opportunities, and making housing, education, and health care available. They deal with crime and violence, as well as basic infrastructure such as water, sanitation, and public transportation. This is no easy task. The leaders of these cities recognize that they have similar problems, and they would like to learn more from other cities, particularly about successful solutions.

If we are going to create livable cities for the next century, we will need to be clever enough to do it through collaboration and cooperation. That is why the Mega-Cities Project works to share experiences that work across boundaries of culture and geography.

Q. Is the solution to urban problems strict central planning?

A. Absolutely not. We need decentralized planning that includes local citizens. In my view, attempts to create planned cities or communities— like Brasília or Chandigarh—are too sterile and miss the spontaneity of cities that grew organically, like Rio de Janeiro, Bombay, or even New York City. The best example of urban planning I've seen recently is in Curitiba, Brazil, which set up a brilliant public transportation system in anticipation of population growth. The historic areas of cities like Siena, Paris, or Barcelona all have elements of planning that led to buildings of similar heights and architecture, but they were not centrally planned. There is a lot of diversity within the design, and people love to go to those cities.

Megacities are really very exciting places. The truth is, I've never met a megacity that I didn't like!

The World's Ten Largest Urban Areas	Population (millions) in 1996	in 2015	Rank in 2015
1 Tokyo, Japan	27.2	28.9	1
2 Mexico City, Mexico	16.9	19.2	7
3 São Paulo, Brazil	16.8	20.3	4
4 New York, United States	16.4	17.6	9
5 Mumbai (Bombay), India	15.7	26.2	2
6 Shanghai, China	13.7	18	8
7 Los Angeles, United States	12.6	14.2	15
8 Kolkata (Calcutta), India	12.1	17.3	10
9 Buenos Aires, Argentina	11.9	13.9	17
10 Seoul, Korea	11.8	13	19

Source: U.N. Department of Economic and Social Affairs Population Division

Source: http://usinfo.state.gov

Identify urban problems

A Reading Warm-up

Suggested teaching time:	5 minutes
Your actual teaching time:	_____

• With books closed, have students guess the top ten largest cities in the world.

• Ask *What problems do you think these cities might share?* On the board, brainstorm ideas as a class. You may want to refer to this list as students work on Discussion Builder on page 59. (Possible problems: traffic jams; water scarcity; pollution; expensive housing; crime; poverty; unemployment)

B 🎧 Reading
(CD 2, Track 24)

Suggested teaching time:	10–15 minutes
Your actual teaching time:	_____

• Point to the photos. Ask *What do you know about Mexico City and Tokyo?* (Possible responses: Mexico City is the capital of Mexico. It is the largest city in Mexico; There is a lot of pollution. Tokyo is the capital of Japan. It is an important financial and commercial center.)

• Have a volunteer read the title of the interview out loud. Explain that the *advent* of something is the time when it first begins. Ask *What do you think a megacity is?* (a very large city)

• Have students read the introduction. To check comprehension, ask *What organization has Dr. Perlman founded?* (Mega-Cities Project, Inc.) *What is the aim of the organization?* (to get big cities around the world to share their experiences about the ideas that worked in their cities)

• Have students read and listen to the interview.

• To check comprehension, ask:
  Why do people migrate to the city? (to enjoy greater choice, opportunities, and well-being)
  What are some similarities that megacities have? (They struggle with: a gap between the rich and poor; providing jobs; making housing, education, and health care available; crime and violence; basic infrastructure such as water, sanitation, and public transportation.)
  What is Dr. Perlman's opinion on planned cities and communities? (They are sterile and miss the spontaneity of cities that grew naturally.)

• Have students listen again and underline the opinions that Dr. Perlman expresses. Ask volunteers to briefly say if they agree with Dr. Perlman's views. Have different students comment on different views. (Possible responses: I don't think megacities will continue to grow. People will start looking for a better quality of life in small towns or rural areas.)

Language note: Students should be able to complete the exercise without understanding every word. You may want to share the following definitions if students ask about specific expressions: *livable* (nice and pleasant to live in); *well-being* (the state of being healthy and happy, and having enough money to live); *deprivation* (a lack of something that you need to live comfortably); *central planning* (the government plans and designs the buildings, roads, and services of a city); *decentralized planning* (the gradual control of the development of a city by local authorities, as opposed to a central authority); *sterile* (cold, clinical, uninteresting); *spontaneity* (the quality of being done without planning or organization).

🔲 **Reading Strategies**

🔲 **Reading Speed Calculator**

🔲 **Extra Reading Comprehension Activities**

Option: Use this option if you want to do a listening activity. Have students close their books.

First listening: Write the following main ideas on the board or photocopy and distribute:

_____ Identify the common characteristics that large cities share.
_____ Explain why people move to large cities.
_____ Suggest ways that large cities can solve problems.
_____ Explain the term <u>megacity</u>.
_____ Predict the future importance of large cities.

Have volunteers read each line out loud. Have students listen to the interview and put the main ideas in the order that they are discussed. Explain that students should write the numbers 1–5 on the lines. Review as a class.

Second listening: Write the following statements on the board or photocopy and distribute:

_____ 1. Many people in developing countries find a better life by moving from an urban area to a rural area.
_____ 2. Tokyo, Japan has much more in common with São Paulo, Brazil than with smaller cities in Japan.
_____ 3. Every megacity is actually two cities—one for the very rich and one for the very poor.
_____ 4. To create megacities that are good places to live, these cities must share ideas that have been successful.
_____ 5. Cities that are planned are often more interesting and exciting than those that grow without planning.

Have students listen to the interview again and check the statements that express views similar to those expressed by Dr. Perlman. (statements 2–4) Have students check answers with a partner, giving reasons for their choices. Review as a class. Have students rewrite the unchecked statements so that they express a view expressed by Dr. Perlman. (1. Many people in developing countries find a better life by moving from a rural area to an urban area. 5. Cities that grow without planning are often more interesting than cities that are planned.) [+10–15 minutes]

T58

C Check the types ...

Suggested teaching time: 5 minutes
Your actual teaching time: _____

- Have students scan the interview for the problems Dr. Perlman talks about.
- Have pairs compare answers and then find and underline what she says about each of the topics mentioned.
- Review as a class. Have students say what information they found about each of the urban problems. For example, *Dr. Perlman talks about poverty. She says that in megacities there are both very rich and very poor people.*

D Understanding Meaning from Context

Suggested teaching time: 5 minutes
Your actual teaching time: _____

- Have students complete the activity individually and then compare answers with a partner.
- Review as a class. Have students explain their choices.

E Discussion

Suggested teaching time: 5–10 minutes
Your actual teaching time: _____

- Have students read the questions out loud. If necessary, explain *pros* and *cons* (advantages and disadvantages).
- Have students discuss the questions in small groups. Encourage students to take notes of reasons they think life in megacities will get better or worse.
- Have volunteers share their groups' responses to the first two questions with the class.
- On the board, write:
   *We think that there are more <u>advantages</u> /
   <u>disadvantages</u> to living in a megacity.*
   *We believe that in the future megacities will get
   <u>better</u> / <u>worse</u>.*

Have a student from each group summarize his/her group's discussion. Students should start their summaries using the statements on the board and then provide supporting reasons. Encourage students from the same group to add any other relevant information to what their classmates said.

DISCUSSION **BUILDER**

Suggested teaching time: 15–20 minutes
Your actual teaching time: _____

 Discourse Strategies

Step 1. Pair Work.

- Refer students to the list created for problems thought to be shared by the largest cities in the world (Exercise A, page 58). Point out that they may use any of those problems if they are not already included on the list of urban problems.
- On a separate sheet of paper, have students write a list of the problems they selected and note specific examples—or the area where the problem exists—on their lists. (Possible problems: poverty—in the slums surrounding the city; crime—robberies and murders)
- As pairs discuss, circulate to offer help with any vocabulary students might need.

Step 2. Discussion.

- Form small groups. Point out that students should discuss at least five ways to make improvements.
- Draw the following chart (with the example) on the board:

Urban problem	Ways to make improvements
Crime	• *stricter punishments* • *more police on patrol*

 Graphic Organizers

Have students choose at least three problems from their lists to write in the chart. Encourage them to agree on the best ways to approach the problems and write notes in the chart.

- As students discuss, circulate to offer help with any vocabulary they might need.
- Review as a class. Name each problem at a time, and have students who discussed that problem share their ideas for improvements. Ask students who discussed any other urban problems to share their responses.

Step 3. Writing.

- To help students write a coherent paragraph, write on the board:
   Your paragraph:
   *Topic sentence: problems that need attention in your
   town or city*
   Supporting sentences: possible solutions to the problems
   *Concluding sentence: your opinion—are you hopeful
   about change?*
- Remind students to use some of the ideas from their charts from Step 2 as a guide.
- Have students exchange papers with a partner. Have pairs discuss the social problems, and offer additional solutions.

EXTRAS (optional)

Workbook: Exercises 15–18

C Check the types of urban problems Dr. Perlman mentions or suggests in the interview.

☑ poverty   ☑ pollution   ☑ unemployment   ☑ inadequate public
☑ lack of housing   ☐ disease   ☐ discrimination   transportation
☐ crowding   ☑ crime   ☐ corruption

D **Understanding Meaning from Context.** Read each statement from the interview. Then choose the sentence that is closest to what Dr. Perlman means. Use information from the reading to help explain your answers.

1. "By coming to settle in the city, they have in effect 'voted with their feet.'"
   (a.) People are making it clear which kind of life they prefer.
   b. People would rather live in the country than live in the city.
   c. People don't have as much opportunity in the city as they do in the country.

2. "Every 'first-world' city . . . has within it a 'third-world' city of poverty and deprivation. And every third-world city . . . has within it a first-world city of high culture, technology, fashion, and finance."
   a. Some megacities have more poverty than others.
   (b.) All megacities have both poverty and wealth.
   c. Some megacities have more wealth than others.

3. "The Mega-Cities Project works to share experiences that work across boundaries of culture and geography."
   a. The Mega-Cities Project helps megacities communicate their success stories to the people who live in that city.
   b. The Mega-Cities Project helps megacities communicate their success stories to other cities in that country.
   (c.) The Mega-Cities Project helps megacities communicate their success stories to megacities in other countries.

E **Discussion.**

1. Why does Dr. Perlman say she prefers cities that are *not* planned over planned cities?
   They occur spontaneously and are unique.
2. Why do you think Dr. Perlman thinks megacities are exciting? Do you agree?

3. Do you live in a megacity, or have you ever visited one? What are the pros and cons of living in a megacity?

4. Do you think life in megacities will improve in the future or get worse? Why?

DISCUSSION **BUILDER** • *Now identify urban problems.*

Step 1. Pair Work. Check which urban problems you think exist in your area. Discuss and provide examples.

    ◯ poverty   ◯ pollution
    ◯ crime   ◯ corruption
    ◯ crowding   ◯ lack of housing

Step 2. Discussion. Talk about the problems you've identified. As a group, discuss at least five ways to make improvements in your town or city.

    ◯ disease   ◯ discrimination
    ◯ inadequate public   ◯ unemployment
       transportation   ◯ other: ....

Step 3. Writing. Describe the social problems that exist in your town or city. Suggest some possible solutions.

Writing: Complain about a problem

Formal letters

When writing to a friend or family member, an informal tone, casual language, and abbreviations are acceptable. However, when writing to the head of a company, a boss, or someone you don't know, standard formal language should be used, and regular spelling and punctuation rules apply. Formal letters are usually typewritten, not handwritten. The following salutations and closings are appropriate for formal letters:

Formal salutations	Formal closings
Dear [Mr. / Mrs. / Ms. / Dr. / Professor Smyth]:	Sincerely,
Dear Sir or Madam:	Respectfully (yours),
To whom it may concern:	Cordially,

When writing a formal letter of complaint, first state the reason why you are writing and the problem. Then inform whomever you are writing what you would like him or her to do about it, or what *you* plan to do.

4719 McPherson Avenue
Philadelphia, Pennsylvania 191
June 30, 2006

Red Maple Café
708 West Pine Street
Philadelphia, Pennsylvania 19102

Salutation — Dear Sir or Madam:

I live a few blocks from your restaurant. For the past several months, I have noticed that in the evenings there is a lot of trash on the side of your building. Cats in the neighborhood turn over the garbage cans, and the trash goes everywhere. This is not only unpleasant to look at, but it is also a health hazard.

Could you please make sure that when the trash is put out, the garbage cans are closed? Your helping keep our neighborhood clean and beautiful would be greatly appreciated.

Closing — Respectfully,

Olivia Krum

Step 1. Prewriting. Listing ideas. Think of a problem in your community that you would like to complain about. List the reasons why it is a problem.

Problem: *trash on side of building*
Reasons: *—unpleasant to look at*
—health hazard

Problem:
Reasons:

Step 2. Writing. On a separate sheet of paper, use your notes to write a letter of complaint. State what you intend to do or what you would like to see done. Remember to use the appropriate level of formality.

Step 3. Self-Check.

☐ Did you use the proper salutation and closing?
☐ Are the tone and language in the letter appropriate for the audience?
☐ Did you use regular spelling and punctuation and avoid abbreviations?

Step 4. Peer Response. Exchange letters with a partner. Write an appropriate response to your partner's letter, as if you were the person to whom it was addressed.

Writing *Complain about a problem*

Suggested teaching time: 25–30 minutes
Your actual teaching time: _____

Formal letters

- Have a volunteer read the explanation out loud.
- Draw a two-column chart with the heads *Informal letters* and *Formal letters* on the board. To check comprehension, have pairs scan the explanation for information about each type of letter and complete the chart in note form. Review as a class. Complete the chart on the board as you get feedback from students. (**Informal letters:** to friends or family; use casual language; use abbreviations; **Formal letters:** to someone you don't know [head of a company, boss, etc.]; use standard formal language; use regular spelling; respect punctuation rules; use appropriate salutations and closings)
- Have a volunteer read the Formal salutations and Formal closings box out loud.
- To clarify the use of salutations, write the following exercise on the board or photocopy and distribute. Complete as a class. (1. e, 2. b, 3. d, 4. c)

  1. ____ When writing to a woman you don't know
  2. ____ When writing to a man you don't know
  3. ____ When writing to a man named Steven Bale
  4. ____ When you don't know if the person you are writing to is male or female

  a. Dear Mr. Steven
  b. Dear Sir
  c. To whom it may concern
  d. Dear Mr. Bale
  e. Dear Madam

- Have volunteers read the explanation for letters of complaint out loud.
- Have students read the writing model individually. To check comprehension, ask *In which paragraph does Olivia explain why she is writing?* (in the first) *Does she tell the person she is writing to what she would like him/her to do?* (yes—in the second paragraph)
- Then ask *Does Olivia sound polite?* (yes) *What polite language does she use?* (Could you please make sure . . . ; . . . would be greatly appreciated)

 Extra Writing Skills Practice

Step 1. Prewriting.

- Have students look at the model, choose a problem, and list ideas individually.
- You may want to have students who chose the same problem share ideas with each other. After students discuss, encourage them to add new ideas they agree with to their lists.

Step 2. Writing.

- Remind students to include their own address, the date, and the address of the person they are writing to. Refer students to the writing model.
- Remind students to use polite language. You may want to elicit some useful language from the class and write it on the board. (I'm writing to complain about . . . ; I would appreciate it if you could . . . ; I would be most grateful if you could . . . ; . . . would be greatly appreciated; Thank you in advance for . . . ; Could you please . . . ?)
- Encourage students to use paired conjunctions as appropriate. Point out how the reasons *unpleasant to look at* and *a health hazard* are joined with a paired conjunction in the writing model.
- As students write, circulate to offer help as needed.

Step 3. Self-Check.

- Have three students read the Self-Check questions out loud.
- Before students submit their paragraphs for correction, have them self-check their work and make any necessary changes.

Step 4. Peer Response.

- You may want to elicit some useful language from the class and write it on the board. (I'm writing in response to your letter of [date]; With regard to your letter of [date] . . . ; Please accept my apologies for . . . ; Please don't hesitate to contact me again if . . .)
- Point out that the reply is also a formal letter, so students should follow the same rules they used to write the letter of complaint.
- You can tell students to first apologize and give an explanation and then explain what they plan to do about the problem.

EXTRAS (optional)

Workbook: Page 49

A ⌂ Listening Comprehension
(CD 2, Track 25)

Suggested teaching time:	5–10 minutes
Your actual teaching time:	_____

- Give students a moment to look at the adjectives. Explain that students will hear four conversations about cities.
- Point out that students will check more than one adjective for some conversations.
- Have pairs compare answers.
- As students listen again for confirmation, pause after each conversation and have students explain their choices. (Possible response: Conversation 1: The man said he had to live in the countryside in China. There was a lot of poverty, and it was very boring because there was nothing to do but work.)

Challenge: On the board, write the following ideas from the conversations and paired conjunctions:

> The poverty was hard to take. It was really boring.
> I couldn't get used to the pollution. I couldn't get used to the crime.
> There is no graffiti. They banned chewing gum.
> The people were not friendly. The people were not considerate.

not only . . . but (also)	either . . . or	neither . . . nor

Have students join the sentences using the paired conjunctions in box. Then have students listen to the conversations again to check their answers. **[+5–10 minutes]**

AUDIOSCRIPT

For audioscript, see page AS7.

B Respond to each question . . .

Suggested teaching time:	5 minutes
Your actual teaching time:	_____

- Remind students to use polite answers for questions 1 and 2.
- Review answers by having various students share their responses.

Option: Pair work. Have students role-play the conversations in Exercise B. Encourage students to keep the conversation going and make more than 4–6 exchanges for each situation. Make sure each student plays both roles. **[+5–10 minutes]**

C Make each sentence logical . . .

Suggested teaching time:	5–10 minutes
Your actual teaching time:	_____

- Before having students do the exercise individually, refer them to Exercises D and E on page 53 to review using negatives prefixes to form antonyms.
- Have students compare answers with a partner and review as a class.

Option: Have students write their own sentences about what they consider inappropriate behavior. Encourage students to use the sentences they created for Exercise C as a model and replace fragments of their choice. You may want to model the activity for the class. For example, *Littering in parks where there are trashcans is really inexcusable.* **[+5 minutes]**

D Combine the sentences . . .

Suggested teaching time:	5 minutes
Your actual teaching time:	_____

- Model the first item with the class. Point out that students shouldn't use a double negative. (neither . . . should NOT: ~~neither . . . shouldn't~~)
- Have students compare answers with a partner.
- Review as a class. Have volunteers read the new sentences out loud.

 You may wish to use the Video Program and activity worksheets for Unit 5 at this point.

Complete Assessment Package
Unit 5 Achievement Test
Review Test 1
Writing Test 1
Speaking Test 1

UNIT 5 / CHECKPOINT

SUMMIT WEBSITE
For Unit 5 online activities, visit the *Summit* Companion Website at www.longman.com/summit.

A 🎧 **Listening Comprehension.** Listen carefully to the conversations about cities. Check the adjectives that are closest in meaning to what the people say about each place. Listen again if necessary.

	rich	poor	clean	polluted	safe	dangerous	polite people	rude people	interesting	boring
1. rural China	○	⊘	○	○	○	○	○	○	○	⊘
2. Los Angeles	○	○	○	⊘	○	⊘	○	○	○	○
3. Singapore	○	○	⊘	○	○	○	○	○	○	○
4. Paris	○	○	○	○	○	○	○	⊘	⊘	○

B Respond to each question in your *own* way.

1. "Do you mind if I call someone on my cell phone?"
   (YOU) ....

2. "Would you mind not smoking in here?"
   (YOU) ....

3. "What bugs you about living in your town?"
   (YOU) ....

4. "Who do you know that really gets on your nerves?"
   (YOU) ....

C Make each sentence logical by attaching a negative prefix to one of the adjectives. Use a dictionary if necessary.

1. Painting graffiti on public buses and trains is really excusable. (inexcusable)

2. I believe littering and spitting on the street are responsible behaviors. (irresponsible)

3. Young people who play loud music without consideration for the people around them are exhibiting really proper behavior. (improper)

4. I think it's very appropriate for people to scream into their cell phones in theaters. (inappropriate)

5. When a salesperson is rude, I find it not only respectful but also annoying. (disrespectful)

6. I should warn you that the air pollution downtown is really pleasant. (unpleasant)

7. I think politicians who are honest and corrupt should be punished. (dishonest)

8. It doesn't help when people are courteous to each other. (discourteous)

D Combine the sentences with the paired conjunction indicated. Use *or*, *nor*, or *but (also)*.

1. Restaurants shouldn't allow smoking. Theaters shouldn't allow smoking. (neither)
   Neither restaurants nor theaters should allow smoking.

2. Smoking should be banned. It should be restricted. (either)
   Smoking should either be banned or restricted.

3. Littering doesn't offend me. Spitting doesn't offend me. (neither)
   Neither littering nor spitting offends me.

4. I think loud music is rude. I think loud people are rude. (not only)
   Not only do I think loud music is rude but also loud people.

UNIT 6

Animals

A **Topic Preview.** Find your birth year on the Chinese Zodiac.
What's your animal sign?

TIGER
| 1938 | 1950 | 1962 |
| 1974 | 1986 | 1998 |

Self-confident, independent, and emotional. Sometimes you tend to be inconsiderate and selfish.

RABBIT
| 1939 | 1951 | 1963 |
| 1975 | 1987 | 1999 |

Intelligent, kind, and helpful. You are also traditional and somewhat conservative. You tend to tell people what's on your mind.

OX
| 1937 | 1949 | 1961 |
| 1973 | 1985 | 1997 |

Hardworking, serious, and responsible. You can sometimes be a workaholic. It's difficult to get you to change your opinions and beliefs, and you get angry easily.

DRAGON
| 1940 | 1952 | 1964 |
| 1976 | 1988 | 2000 |

Fun loving, artistic, and truthful. You don't always feel confident in yourself or your abilities. You are also a little eccentric at times.

RAT
| 1936 | 1948 | 1960 |
| 1972 | 1984 | 1996 |

Generous, honest, and imaginative. You are usually careful, and sometimes you are a perfectionist.

SNAKE
| 1941 | 1953 | 1965 |
| 1977 | 1989 | 2001 |

Attractive and very calm. You are able to make good decisions and give good advice. Sometimes you can be self-centered.

BOAR
| 1947 | 1959 | 1971 |
| 1983 | 1995 | 2007 |

Generally quiet and honest. You work hard toward your goals. You don't have many friends, but you are very considerate to the friends you have.

HORSE
| 1942 | 1954 | 1966 |
| 1978 | 1990 | 2002 |

Popular, outgoing, and cheerful. You are a real people person. Sometimes you are too talkative.

DOG
| 1946 | 1958 | 1970 |
| 1982 | 1994 | 2006 |

Honest, caring, and modest. You are always there for your friends. You may at times seem cold and unfriendly to people who don't know you.

GOAT
| 1943 | 1955 | 1967 |
| 1979 | 1991 | 2003 |

Passionate, very artistic, and a bit shy. You are good at understanding other people's problems. Sometimes you are too willing to believe what other people say.

MONKEY
| 1944 | 1956 | 1968 |
| 1980 | 1992 | 2004 |

Clever and likable. You have new and interesting ideas, and you learn very quickly. Sometimes you can also be a little egotistical.

ROOSTER
| 1945 | 1957 | 1969 |
| 1981 | 1993 | 2005 |

Attractive and self-confident. You want to be very successful. Sometimes you say things just to make people look up to you.

Source: silverdragonstudio.com

B **Discussion.**

1. How well do the adjectives for your sign describe your personality? How are you different from the description?
2. Do you think the descriptions match the animals in any way? Why or why not?

Animals

A Topic Preview

Suggested teaching time:	10–15 minutes
Your actual teaching time:	_____

- To introduce the theme of animals, have students spend a few moments looking at and reading the Chinese Zodiac.

- As students study the animal signs, encourage them to use the pictures to identify the animals they don't know.

- Ask *What do you know about the Chinese Zodiac?* (Possible responses: Each year has an animal name; According to the Chinese Zodiac, the year when you were born affects your personality.)

- To check comprehension, ask *Which animal sign:*

  is described as having high self-esteem? (tiger, rooster)

  is described as being good-looking? (rooster, snake)

  enjoys meeting new people? (horse)

  tells the truth? (rat, boar, dog, dragon)

  doesn't talk a lot? (boar, goat)

- Before students find their birth years, point out that students who were born before February 4 should use the sign for the previous year. For example, if a person was born on January 15, 1967, he or she should find the sign for 1966. (horse) (Note: The Chinese have a lunar calendar so their new year starts some time before the middle of February. Chinese New Year does not fall on the same day each year, so February 4 is given as an approximate date.)

- Have students read the animal signs that match their birth years. Have students find the adjectives for their signs. Help the class to work out the meaning of any unknown language.

Language note: Students may need help with the following words or expressions: the *zodiac* is an imaginary area through which the sun, moon, and planets appear to travel; if people *look up to* someone, they admire that person.

Culture note: The *zodiac* is related to a *horoscope*, which is a description of your character and your future based on the position of the stars and planets at the time of your birth. It is also related to a *strology*, which is the study of the relationships of the stars and planets and how they influence events and people. The Chinese Zodiac is based on a twelve-year cycle. It represents a cyclical concept of time: every twelve years the cycle is repeated. Each year in the cycle is given an animal name, so every animal reappears every twelve years. There is a popular belief that people who have the same animal sign have similar personality traits.

Option: Discussion. Ask *Have you ever looked up your sign on the Chinese Zodiac? Have you ever read another kind of horoscope? Do you believe in horoscopes?* **[+5 minutes]**

B Discussion

Suggested teaching time:	5–10 minutes
Your actual teaching time:	_____

- Form small groups. Have a volunteer read item 1 out loud. Have students share their signs and explain why they agree / disagree with the descriptions. Encourage students to give concrete examples to support their views. (Possible response: I'm a rat. It's true that I'm generous—I like to help other people—but I'm not too much of a perfectionist. I'm a little impatient, and I sometimes rush to finish my tasks, so I don't think I always try to be perfect in the things I do.)

- Have a volunteer read item 2 out loud. Then have students scan the descriptions to decide if they match the animals. Encourage students to choose a description that matches the animal and one that doesn't (at least partially).

- Then have students share their opinions of the two descriptions with their groups. (Possible responses: The ox is described as hardworking. I agree. In the past, oxen were used to pull carts and carry heavy things; Snakes are described as attractive, but to me, they're disgusting!)

- Review as a class. Have a volunteer from each group present his/her responses to the class.

Option: Say *Astrology is the study of the planets and stars and their influence on us. Some people believe their personalities are influenced by their animal signs (the year in which they were born). Other people believe their personality is influenced by their star sign (the day on which they were born).* In small groups, have students discuss their views on astrology and the Chinese Zodiac and explain why they believe / don't believe it. **[+5–10 minutes]**

C 🎧 Sound Bites
(CD 2, Track 26)

Suggested teaching time:	10 minutes
Your actual teaching time:	_____

- Have students look at the photo. Ask *Where are the people?* (at the zoo) *Have you ever been to a zoo? Did you like it?*

- Have students read and listen to the conversation.

- To check comprehension, ask *Do Alicia and Ben have similar or different views on zoos?* (Different—Ben likes zoos and Alicia doesn't.)

- Write the following statements on the board and have students correct them to make them true. (1. true; 2. false: Ben and Alicia have different views about zoos; 3. false: Alicia likes animals.)
  1. *Ben wanted to go to the zoo more than Alicia.*
  2. *Ben and Alicia have similar views about zoos.*
  3. *Alicia doesn't like animals.*

Language note: If you *talk someone into doing something,* you persuade the person to do it. If an animal is *cooped up,* it is forced to stay in a small place without being able to move around much.

Option: Form small groups for discussion. Ask *Who's opinion do you agree with more, Ben's or Alicia's?* Have students support their opinions. **[+5 minutes]**

D Pair Work

Suggested teaching time:	5–10 minutes
Your actual teaching time:	_____

- Before students read the conversation again, have volunteers read the questions out loud.

- Review answers as a class.

Option: Write the following discussion questions on the board: *Are animals happier in zoos or in the wild? What benefits do wild animals gain from being in zoos? What do wild animals lose by being kept in zoos?* Have students discuss the questions in small groups. **[+5 minutes]**

STARTING POINT

Suggested teaching time:	15 minutes
Your actual teaching time:	_____

Pair Work

- Individually, have students choose five adjectives and an animal that best matches each adjective. In pairs, have students discuss the adjectives and animals they chose.

- As pairs discuss, encourage them to think of reasons to support their choices.

- Draw the following diagram on the board:

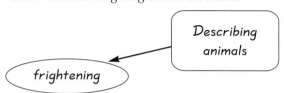

To review as a class, ask *Which animals do you think are frightening? Why?* Elicit answers and supporting reasons from various students. Add the names of animals students mention to *frightening.* Follow the same procedure for a few other adjectives of your choice.

EXTRAS (optional)

Workbook: Exercises 1–4

CN Corpus Notes: The use of *just* for emphasis at the beginning of an imperative statement is very common in spoken English. For example, *Just relax.*

C 🎧 **Sound Bites.** Read and listen to a conversation between two friends at the zoo.

Giraffes in the zoo

ALICIA: I can't believe I let you talk me into coming here. I really have a problem with zoos.

BEN: C'mon. These guys have got it made. They're well-cared for. They're healthy. They've got plenty of food.

ALICIA: You could say the same thing about people in prisons. What about freedom? I hate seeing animals cooped up in cages.

BEN: You think animals are any happier in the wild? Always hungry? Running from some bigger animal that's trying to eat them?

ALICIA: I don't know. Maybe not.

BEN: Just look at that tiger over there. Where else **CN** could you see such a beautiful animal up close?

ALICIA: You're right about that. He *is* magnificent.

D **Pair Work.** Read the conversation again. Discuss the questions and explain your answers.
Answers will vary, but may include:
1. What is Alicia's objection to zoos?
   Animals are kept in cages and are not free.
2. How is Ben's attitude different from Alicia's? He believes animals are well-cared for in zoos.
3. What does Ben mean when he says, "These guys have got it made"? Life is easier for animals in zoos than in the wild.
4. What do Alicia and Ben agree on about zoos? Zoos allow people to see beautiful animals up close.

STARTING **POINT**

Pair Work. What adjectives do you associate with different animals? Choose five adjectives and discuss with a partner an animal you think each adjective describes.

frightening

unusual

fun

friendly

calm

irritating

attractive

loving

unfriendly

independent

shy

disgusting

hardworking

quiet

ADJECTIVE	ANIMAL
1.	
2.	
3.	
4.	
5.	

1 *Exchange opinions about the treatment of animals*

A ∩ GRAMMAR **SNAPSHOT.** Read the posts on a discussion board and notice the use of passive modals.

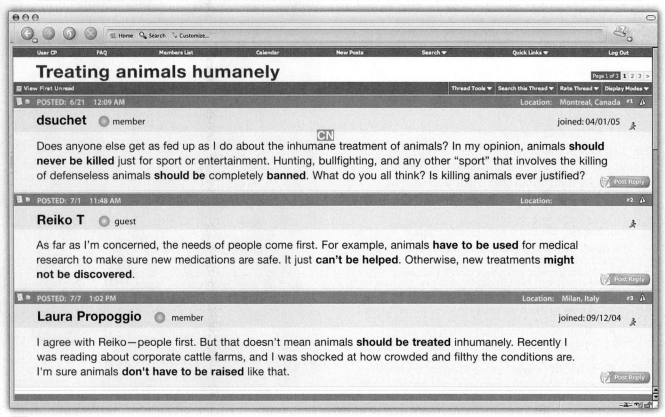

Treating animals humanely

dsuchet ● member   joined: 04/01/05

Does anyone else get as fed up as I do about the inhumane treatment of animals? In my opinion, animals **should never be killed** just for sport or entertainment. Hunting, bullfighting, and any other "sport" that involves the killing of defenseless animals **should be** completely **banned**. What do you all think? Is killing animals ever justified?

Reiko T ● guest

As far as I'm concerned, the needs of people come first. For example, animals **have to be used** for medical research to make sure new medications are safe. It just **can't be helped**. Otherwise, new treatments **might not be discovered**.

Laura Propoggio ● member   joined: 09/12/04

I agree with Reiko—people first. But that doesn't mean animals **should be treated** inhumanely. Recently I was reading about corporate cattle farms, and I was shocked at how crowded and filthy the conditions are. I'm sure animals **don't have to be raised** like that.

CN **Corpus Notes:** In written English, the most frequently used collocation with the adjective *inhumane* is *treatment*.

B **Discussion.** Do you agree with any of the opinions expressed on the discussion board? Why or why not?

C **Grammar. The passive voice with modals**

Can for present possibility or ability
Alternatives **can be found** for medical research on animals.

Might (not) and **could** for present or future possibility
New medicines **might be discovered** through animal testing.
Cattle **might not be mistreated** if people knew about the conditions.
A lot **could be done** to improve conditions.

Couldn't and **can't** for present impossibility
Research **couldn't be done** today without animals.
Sometimes testing on animals **can't be helped**.

Should and **shouldn't** for advisability
Corporate chicken farms **should be shut down**.
People **shouldn't be prohibited** from hunting.

Have to and **must** for necessity
Some animals **have to be killed**.
Traditions like bullfighting **must be preserved**.
NOTE: Must is rarely used in informal English.

Yes / no questions
Can other types of research **be found**?
Should factory farms **be shut down**?
Must animals **be used** for research?
Do animals **have to be used** for research?

Information questions
How **can** animals **be trained** to help humans?
What **could be done** to improve conditions?
Why **must** their lives **be respected**?
Why **do** their lives **have to be respected**?

BE CAREFUL! Don't have to / doesn't have to expresses a lack of necessity, but **must not** expresses prohibition.
Animals **don't have to be killed** for research.
[= it is not necessary]
Animals **must not be killed** for research.
[= it should be prohibited]

PAGE G10
For more …

1 Exchange opinions about the treatment of animals

A 🎧 GRAMMAR **SNAPSHOT**
(CD 2, Track 27)

Suggested teaching time:	5–10 minutes
Your actual teaching time:	_____

• Point to the Grammar Snapshot and ask *What is this?* (an Internet discussion board) Elicit or explain the meaning of *discussion board.* (a site on the Internet where people can post their opinions and get replies from other people)

• With books closed, have students listen and take notes on the different opinions expressed. Review as a class. Write the opinions on the board as students respond.

• Have students read the Grammar Snapshot individually and notice the use of passive modals. To check comprehension, ask *Who thinks that animals should never be killed for sport or entertainment?* (dsuchet) *Who believes that animals have to be used for research?* (Reiko T) *Who agrees with Reiko T?* (Laura Propoggio) *Who thinks animals don't have to be raised in poor conditions?* (Laura Propoggio)

> **Language note:** *Humane* is treating people or animals in a way that is kind. If animals are *raised on corporate farms,* they are grown to be used as food, for cosmetics, for their fur, etc.

B Discussion

Suggested teaching time:	5 minutes
Your actual teaching time:	_____

• Read the question out loud. Have a volunteer explain whether or not he/she agrees with one of the opinions on the discussion board. Ask students with a different opinion to express their views.

• Form small groups. Have students discuss their views on the remaining two opinions. As groups discuss, encourage them to give reasons to support their views.

• To review, have a volunteer from each group report the opinions expressed by the group to the class.

C Grammar

Suggested teaching time:	10 minutes
Your actual teaching time:	_____

• On the board, write:
> *The killing of animals should be banned.*

Point to the sentence on the board and ask *Is this the active or the passive voice?* (the passive voice) *How do you form the passive voice with modals?* (modal + be + the past participle) Label the example on the board:
> *The killing of animals <u>should</u> <u>be</u> <u>banned</u>.*
> modal + <u>be</u> + past participle

• Have students read the five headings in the first column and study the examples.

• Have students read the examples for *yes / no* questions. To point out the difference between *have to* and other modals, write these two examples on the board:
> *Can this be done?   Does this have to be done?*

Have students identify the "modal" in each example. Circle the modals as students respond. (Can, have to) Ask *What is the same in these sentences?* (be done) Underline as students respond. Ask *What's the difference in these two sentences?* (the position of the modals; *does* is used with *have to*, not with *can*) Erase *Can* and *have to* from the board. Ask *Which example on the board do* should *and* must *fit into?* (the first: *Should* this be done? *Must* this be done?)

• Point out that *could* and *might* are not normally used in *yes / no* questions about possibility, but they can be used in answers. Add to the board:
> *Is bullfighting going to be banned? It might be.*
> *Do you think bullfighting will be banned? It could be banned one day.*

• Have students read the examples for information questions. To point out the difference between information questions with *have to* and other modals, write these two examples on the board:
> *Why must they be treated poorly?*
> *Why do they have to be treated poorly?*

Have students identify the "modal" in each example. Circle the modals as students respond. (must, have to) Ask *What is the same in these sentences?* (why; be treated poorly) Underline as students respond. Ask *What's the difference in these two sentences?* (the position of the modals; *do* is used with *have to*, not with *must*) Point out that *do / does* comes before the subject in information questions with *have to* in the passive voice.

• Have a volunteer read the Be Careful! note out loud. Write the following sentences on the board. To check comprehension, have students paraphrase each sentence. (1. It is not necessary to raise animals on crowded farms. 2. Raising animals on crowded farms should be prohibited.)
> *1. Animals don't have to be raised on crowded farms.*
> *2. Animals must not be raised on crowded farms.*

> **Language note:** *Have to* is not a true modal. It has the meaning of a modal and is often referred to as a "modal-like expression." *Must* is often used in speech by people in authority; for example, an employer might tell an employee, "You must come in on time."

 Grammar Self-Checks

D Write sentences ...

Suggested teaching time:	5 minutes
Your actual teaching time:	_____

- Model the first item with the class. As a reminder, elicit from the class how passive modals are formed. (modal + *be* + the past participle)
- Have students compare their sentences with a partner and review as a class.

Option: On the board, rewrite the sentences from items 1–4 in Exercise D, using different modals:

A. *People must be allowed to hunt deer.*
B. *Alternatives to animals research could be discovered.*
C. *Wild animals can't be kept as pets.*
D. *Fox hunting might be banned.*

Have pairs decide if statements 1–4 from Exercise D have the same meaning as statements A–D on the board. If there is a difference in meaning, ask students to take notes of the differences. Review as a class. (1. It is advisable to allow people to hunt deer vs. A. It is necessary to allow people to hunt deer. 2. and B. have the same meaning. 3. It is advisable not to keep wild animals as pets vs. C. It is impossible to keep wild animals as pets. 4. It is advisable to ban fox hunting vs. D. It is possible that fox hunting is/will be banned.) **[+5 minutes]**

E 🎧 Vocabulary
(CD 2, Track 28)

Suggested teaching time:	5–10 minutes
Your actual teaching time:	_____

- Have students listen and study the statements. Then have students listen and repeat chorally.
- Encourage students to use the illustrations to determine the meaning of any unknown words. If necessary, explain that *hide* is the animal's skin that is removed to be used for leather, and *slaughter* means kill.

Language note: *Kill* is a general word, and *slaughter* is a specific word (killing animals for food).

🔄 Vocabulary-Building Strategies

Option: Draw the following diagram (without the answers) on the board.

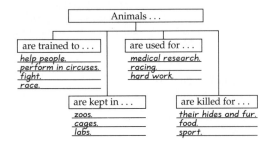

🔄 Graphic Organizers

T65

With books closed, have pairs use the Vocabulary in Exercise E and their own ideas to complete the diagram. To review as a class, complete the diagram on the board as you get feedback from students. **[+10 minutes]**

F On a separate sheet of paper ...

Suggested teaching time:	5 minutes
Your actual teaching time:	_____

- Have a volunteer read the example out loud.
- Have students complete the exercise individually. Encourage them to use as many different modals as possible.
- Then have students compare answers with a partner.
- Review as a class. Have a few volunteers share their opinions with the class. As volunteers respond, encourage students with opposing views to state their opinions.

GRAMMAR **EXCHANGE**

Suggested teaching time:	10–15 minutes
Your actual teaching time:	_____

- Have students read the ways for expressing an opinion, disagreeing, and agreeing, out loud.
- Have two volunteers read the example out loud.
- Ask *What is a different way to respond to the statement in the model?* Elicit other responses from the class. Encourage students to use the phrases from the boxes.
- Have students write down their opinions individually. Encourage students to discuss all the ways animals are used or treated using the Vocabulary in Exercise E.

Pair Work

- In pairs, have students exchange opinions and ask and answers questions using passive modals.
- As students exchange opinions, circulate to offer help as needed. Make sure students use passive modals correctly.

Discussion

- Take a class poll. Ask *Who is in favor of keeping animals in zoos? Who is against it?* Keep a tally on the board. Have a few students give supporting reasons. Follow the same procedure for other ways animals are used or treated from the Vocabulary.
- Have students analyze the chart and say whether or not the majority of the class feels the same way.

EXTRAS (optional)

Grammar Booster
Workbook: Exercises 5–7

D Write sentences using modals and the correct form of the passive voice.

1. People / should / allow to hunt deer.   People should be allowed to hunt deer.
2. Alternatives to animal research / might / discover.   Alternatives to animal research might be discovered.
3. Wild animals / shouldn't / keep as pets.   Wild animals shouldn't be kept as pets.
4. Fox hunting / should / ban.   Fox hunting should be banned.
5. The treatment of animals / could / improve.   The treatment of animals could be improved.

E 🎧 **Vocabulary. Ways animals are used or treated.** Listen and practice.

They're **kept in zoos**.

They're **used for medical research**.

They're **killed for their hides and fur**.

They're **trained to perform in circuses**.

They're **raised for fighting**.

They're **trained to help people with disabilities**.

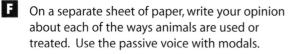

They're **used for racing**.

They're **slaughtered for food**.

F On a separate sheet of paper, write your opinion about each of the ways animals are used or treated. Use the passive voice with modals.

Animals should be kept in zoos so people can enjoy them.

GRAMMAR **EXCHANGE** • *Now exchange opinions about the treatment of animals.*

Pair Work. Exchange opinions about the ways animals are used or treated. Ask and answer questions, using passive modals.

"Animals **have to be used** for medical research. We can't experiment on humans, can we?"

"Actually, I don't think animals **should be treated** that way. I think it's morally wrong."

Expressing an opinion
I think / believe / feel . . .
  it's morally wrong.
  it's OK under some
    circumstances.
  it's wrong no matter what.
I'm in favor of ....
I'm opposed to ....

Disagreeing
I see what you mean, but ....
That's one way to look at it,
  but ....
On the one hand ...., but on
  the other hand ....
I completely disagree.

Agreeing
I couldn't agree with you more.
I completely agree.
You're so right.

Discussion. Compare your classmates' opinions on the treatment of animals. Does the majority of the class feel the same way?

Discuss the benefits of certain pets

CN1 Corpus Notes: Both *consider* and *think* are among the 1,000 most frequently used words in English, but *think about* occurs more frequently than *consider*.

A ◖ CONVERSATION **SNAPSHOT**

A: I've been considering getting an iguana for a pet. **CN1**

B: Are you out of your mind? I've heard they're filthy.

A: Actually, that's a misconception. Iguanas are very clean and make great pets.

B: In what way?

A: Well, for one thing, they're very intelligent. And believe it or not, I find them beautiful.

◖ **Rhythm and intonation practice**

B ◖ Vocabulary. Describing pets. Listen and practice.

Positive traits	
adorable	cute and charming
affectionate	exceptionally friendly and loving
gentle / good-natured	easygoing; good with people and other pets
low maintenance	easy to care for and inexpensive to keep
loyal / devoted	attentive to its owner; reliable

CN2

CN2 Corpus Notes: Both *loyal* and *devoted* are often followed by the prepositional phrase *to [someone]*.

Negative traits	
aggressive	violent; sometimes dangerous
costly	expensive to buy and to take care of
destructive	harmful to furniture and other things
filthy	unclean; makes a mess
high maintenance	time-consuming to take care of

C ◖ Listening Comprehension. Listen to the conversations about pets. Then listen again and complete the chart. Use adjectives you know that best describe the advantages and disadvantages the people talk about. Discuss if you think the people will get the pet.

Answers will vary, but may include:

Pet		Advantages	Disadvantages
Conversation 1	cat	low maintenance, affectionate, loyal, devoted	hair gets everywhere
Conversation 2	rabbit	adorable, gentle, good-natured	destructive
Conversation 3	parrot	beautiful, intelligent, clever	filthy, aggressive, noisy, high maintenance
Conversation 4	tropical fish	beautiful, interesting, fascinating	high maintenance, costly

2 Discuss the benefits of certain pets

A ⌒ CONVERSATION SNAPSHOT
(CD 2, Track 29)

Suggested teaching time:	5 minutes
Your actual teaching time:	_____

- Point to the photo. Ask *What kind of animal is this?* (an iguana) *Would you like to have an iguana as a pet? Why? Why not?* Encourage students to briefly support their opinions.

- After students read and listen, have them summarize what each speaker thinks of iguanas. (One speaker thinks that they are clean, beautiful, and intelligent and that they make great make pets. The other speaker thinks that they are filthy.)

- To check comprehension, ask *Do both speakers agree that iguanas make good pets?* (no) *Why does the man think that iguanas don't make good pets?* (He's heard they're filthy.) *According to the woman, what are some positive qualities of iguanas?* (They're clean, intelligent, and beautiful.)

Language note: *Are you out of your mind?* means *Are you crazy? A misconception* is something that many people believe but is not true. *For one thing* is used to give a reason for something.

⌒ Rhythm and intonation practice
(CD 2, Track 30)

Suggested teaching time:	5 minutes
Your actual teaching time:	_____

- Have students repeat chorally. Make sure they:
  - use statement intonation for *Are you out of your mind?* (This is not a true question.)
  - use falling intonation for *In what way?* with a slight rise in pitch on <u>way</u>.
  - Pause slightly after . . . *for one thing* . . . and . . . *And believe it or not.* . . .
  - use the following stress pattern:

STRESS PATTERN

A: I've been considering getting an iguana for a pet.

B: Are you out of your mind? I've heard they're filthy.

A: Actually, that's a misconception. Iguanas are very clean and make great pets.

B: In what way?

A: Well, for one thing, they're very intelligent. And believe it or not, I find them beautiful.

B ⌒ Vocabulary
(CD 2, Track 31)

Suggested teaching time:	5–10 minutes
Your actual teaching time:	_____

- As a class, brainstorm a list of common and exotic pets and write them on the board. (Possible responses: dog, cat, guinea pig, hamster, tropical fish, turtle, lizard, parrot, ferret, snake)

- Have students listen and study the vocabulary. Then have students listen and repeat chorally.

- In pairs, have students think of a pet that best matches each trait. Students can refer to the list on the board.

- Ask each pair to join another pair and share the pets they thought of. Encourage students to support their choices

Language note: Compound adjectives are hyphenated when they appear before nouns; for example, *a low-maintenance pet*. But *good-natured* is always hyphenated.

⌒ Vocabulary-Building Strategies

Challenge: To draw on students' own experiences, have volunteers briefly talk about any pets they have, pets they've had, or pets they would like to have. Encourage students to use some of the adjectives in Exercise B—and their own ideas—as they talk about the pets. [+5 minutes]

C ⌒ Listening Comprehension
(CD 2, Track 32)

Suggested teaching time:	10–15 minutes
Your actual teaching time:	_____

- Point out that advantages are positive traits and disadvantages are negative traits.

- First listening of Conversation 1: Have students listen for the pet the speakers are talking about and write it in the chart.

- Second listening of Conversation 1: Have students use the adjectives in Exercise B or other adjectives to take notes of the advantages and disadvantages of the pet. Point out that the speakers do not use the Vocabulary words. Students are expected to interpret the information.

- Review answers as a class. Encourage students to support their answers.

- Follow the same procedure for Conversations 2–4.

- As a class, discuss whether or not the people will get the pets.

AUDIOSCRIPT

For audioscript, see page AS8.

D Discussion

Suggested teaching time:	5–10 minutes
Your actual teaching time:	_____

• Read item 1 out loud. On the board, write:
  a family with small children
  a person who works all day
  an elderly person who lives on his/her own
  a person with a disability

Form small groups. Have students discuss if an animal can be a good companion in each of the situations on the board. Encourage them to think of other situations where an animal would / wouldn't be a good companion.

• Have a student read item 2 out loud. If necessary, explain that if people are very *attached to* their pets, they like them a lot. Encourage groups to write a list of reasons people get so close to their animals.

• To review, call on a student from each group to say in what situations an animal can be a good companion. Then call on other students to say why some people get so close to their animals. Encourage students who disagree to express their opinions. Encourage students to ask questions.

CONVERSATION **STARTER**

Suggested teaching time:	15 minutes
Your actual teaching time:	_____

• Have students look at the pictures and read the captions. Then have them share what they know about the animals in the photos.

Pair Work

• In pairs, have students discuss their opinions of good and bad pets and complete the lists. They may use the animals in the photos or other animals.

• Encourage students to use the Vocabulary in Exercise B to take notes of reasons why the animals make good / bad pets. Students can also use their own ideas.

• After pairs discuss and complete their lists, call on a few students to tell the class about an animal they discussed. Have students explain why they think the animal makes a good / bad pet and say if their partner agreed or disagreed with them.

Role Play

• Refer students to the Conversation Snapshot on page 66 to review discussing the benefits of certain pets and the Vocabulary for describing pets. You may also want to have students listen to the conversation again.

• Role-play a conversation with a more confident student. Have the student start the conversation with the prompt given.

• Encourage students to use ideas from their notepads.

• Make sure each student plays both roles.

• As pairs role-play, circulate to offer help as needed. Encourage students to use the correct rhythm and intonation. Remind students to stress words that provide new or important information.

Culture note: <u>Parrots</u> are colorful, tropical birds and can be trained to imitate the human voice. They live longer than other birds, with lifespans ranging from 40–80 years. <u>Siamese cats</u> are originally from Thailand (former Siam). They have short, light hair but their faces, ears, tails, lower legs, and paws are dark. They are good companions and demand attention. <u>Pit bulls</u> are medium-sized, solidly built, short-coated dogs. They are noted for their attachment to their masters as well as for their courage. In the United States, pit bulls are the breed of choice for dog fights due to their incredible strength and dog-aggressive tendencies. Although dog fighting is illegal in the U.S., it is still practiced. <u>Pugs</u> are small dogs with flat, wrinkled faces, compact bodies, and curled tails. They are friendly, alert, and attentive to their owners. They are also compatible with most children and other animals. <u>Pythons</u> are tropical snakes that generally range in size from 5–6 meters (16–20 feet) in length. They are among the longest species of snake in the world. The python feeds on animals and uses its strong body to wind itself around its prey to crush it. Despite their intimidating size and muscular power, they are generally not dangerous to humans. <u>Mice</u> are small pets that are entertaining to watch, are easy to care for, and make very few demands on their owners.

 Conversation Prompts

EXTRAS (optional)

Pronunciation Booster
Workbook: Exercises 8–9

D Discussion.

1. Do you think that an animal can be a good companion? Why or why not?
2. Do you know anyone who is very attached to his or her pet? Why do you think some people get so close to their animals?

Pronunciation Booster

PAGE P5
Sound reduction

CONVERSATION **STARTER** • *Now discuss the benefits of certain pets.*

Pair Work. Which animals do you think make good pets or bad pets? Discuss and make a list on your notepad. Use the pictures or other animals you know. Write complete sentences, using the vocabulary.

Good pets	Why?
Bad pets	Why?

a parrot

Role Play. Role-play a conversation about getting a pet. Use the Conversation Snapshot on page 66 as a guide. Start like this: "I've been considering getting .... for a pet."

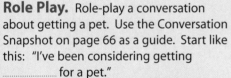

a pit bull

a pug

a Siamese cat

a python

a mouse

3 *Compare animal characters*

A 🎧 **Vocabulary. Describing character traits.** Listen and practice.

> **clever** able to use one's intelligence to do something
> **gullible** too ready to believe what other people say, and therefore easy to trick
> **mean** willing to hurt others, especially with words
> **selfish** caring only about oneself and not likely to share with others
> **sincere** saying what one really feels or believes
> **vain** too proud of one's looks, abilities, or position
> **wise** able to make good decisions and give good advice based on life experiences

B Complete each sentence with an adjective from the vocabulary.

1. Don't be so ___gullible___. When something sounds too good to be true, it usually is!
2. He is so ___vain___ that he won't go out if his hair is a bit messy.
3. Carla is really open and ___sincere___. You can always trust her to say what she means.
4. My parrot is so ___clever___ that he's learned how to say three new words this week.
5. Our neighbor is really ___mean___. When kids play in front of her house, she always yells at them.
6. My grandfather knew how to help me with my problems. He was really ___wise___.
7. It's normal for young children to be ___selfish___. They usually don't want other children to play with their toys.

"The fox saw a crow in a tree."

C 🎧 **Listening Comprehension.** Listen to the fable of "The Fox and the Crow." Choose adjectives to describe each animal. Then listen again and write the moral, or the lesson, of the story in your *own* words.

Answers will vary, but may include:

Adjectives for the fox
clever, selfish, mean

Adjectives for the crow
vain, gullible

The moral of the story
It's not good to be vain.

Don't believe everything other

people say.

3 Compare animal characters

A 🎧 Vocabulary
(CD 2, Track 33)

Suggested teaching time:	5–10 minutes
Your actual teaching time:	_____

- Have a volunteer read the title of the lesson out loud. Elicit the meaning of *character* from the class. (person / animal in a book, play, movie, etc.)
- Point out the Vocabulary heading, *Describing character traits.* Ask *Is the meaning of* character *here the same as in* Compare animal characters? (no) Elicit the meaning of *character traits* from the class. (Possible response: qualities of your personality—like honesty and intelligence—that define what kind of person you are)
- Have students listen to the words and study the definitions. Then have students listen and repeat the words chorally.
- On the board write the Vocabulary words and draw a Venn diagram, as shown below:

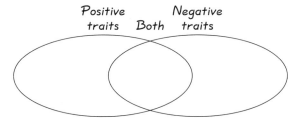

- With books closed, have students classify the Vocabulary words into positive traits, negative traits, and both positive and negative traits individually. Then have students discuss answers with a partner. Review as a class. (**Positive traits:** sincere, wise; **Negative traits:** gullible, mean, selfish, vain; **Both:** clever)

> **Language note:** *Clever* can be negative if someone uses his or her intelligence in a dishonest way to get something.

Challenge: As a class, brainstorm words that are similar to or the opposite of each adjective. (Possible responses: **clever** *[similar]:* smart, tricky, quick-thinking; *[opposite]:* stupid, slow, unintelligent; **gullible** *[similar]:* naïve, trusting, innocent; *[opposite]:* doubtful, wary, skeptical; **mean** *[similar]:* cruel, uncaring, nasty; *[opposite]:* compassionate, warm-hearted, kind; **selfish** *[similar]:* self-centered, egotistical; *[opposite]:* selfless, altruistic, generous; **sincere** *[similar]:* honest, genuine, truthful; *[opposite]:* insincere, deceitful, dishonest; **vain** *[similar]:* egotistical, conceited, narcissistic; *[opposite]:* humble, modest, meek; **wise** *[similar]:* clever, sensible, astute; *[opposite]:* foolish, stupid, thoughtless.) **[+5 minutes]**

B Complete each sentence . . .

Suggested teaching time:	5 minutes
Your actual teaching time:	_____

- Encourage students to cover the Vocabulary box in Exercise A as they complete the sentences.
- Have students uncover the box and confirm their answers.
- Review as a class.

🌐 Vocabulary-Building Strategies

Option: In pairs, have students look at the Topic Preview on page 62 and use the adjectives to further describe the personalities in the Chinese Zodiac. Then have pairs share their descriptions with the class. (Possible responses: The rabbit is sincere; The snake is wise; The goat is gullible; The rooster is vain.) **[+5 minutes]**

C 🎧 Listening Comprehension
(CD 2, Track 34)

Suggested teaching time:	10–15 minutes
Your actual teaching time:	_____

- Before students listen to the fable, have them look at the picture and read the caption. Ask them to identify the animals. (crow, fox)
- Ask *What adjectives would you use to describe a crow? Why? What adjectives would you use to describe a fox? Why?*
- First listening: Have students look at the Vocabulary in Exercise A and decide which adjectives describe each animal. (Possible responses: **fox:** clever, mean, selfish, wise; **crow:** gullible, sincere, vain) Compare these with students' own associations with these animals (as elicited above, before listening to the conversation).
- Second listening: Encourage students to write one or two sentences to explain the moral of the story.
- Form small groups. Have students discuss the adjectives to describe each character and the moral of the story. Tell students to support their choices with information from the story.
- Review as a class. Have a volunteer from each group share the adjectives chosen and the supporting information from the listening. Then have a different volunteer from each group explain the moral of the story.

Option: Form small groups and have students summarize the fable. To guide students, ask:
What was the crow doing when the fox turned up?
What did the fox want?
What did the fox say to get what he wanted?
Why did the crow sing?
[+5 minutes]

> **AUDIOSCRIPT**
>
> For audioscript, see page AS8.

D 🎧 Now listen to the fable . . .
(CD 2, Track 35)

Suggested teaching time:	10–15 minutes
Your actual teaching time:	_____

- Before students listen to the fable, have them look at the picture and read the caption. Ask them to identify the animals. (peacock, sparrow)

- Ask *What adjectives would you use to describe a sparrow? Why? What adjectives would you use to describe a peacock? Why?*

- First listening: Have students look at the Vocabulary in Exercise A and decide which adjectives describe each animal. (Possible responses: **sparrow:** wise, sincere, mean; **peacock:** sincere, vain) Compare these with students' own associations with these animals (as elicited above, before listening to the conversation).

- Second listening: Encourage students to write one or two sentences to explain the moral of the story.

- Form small groups. Have students discuss the adjectives to describe each character and the moral of the story. Tell students to support their choices with information from the story.

- Review as a class. Have a volunteer from each group share the adjectives chosen and the supporting information from the listening. Then have a different volunteer from each group explain the moral of the story.

Language note: "I would pay any price": *pay a (high) price for something* is experience or accept something bad as the result of a decision or mistake.

🎧 **Listening Strategies**

Option: Form small groups and have students summarize the fable. To guide students, ask:
> *What did the peacock wish?*
> *After he got his wish, what did the peacock try to do?*
> *What price did the peacock pay for being beautiful?*
> *Do you think the peacock was happy at the end of the story? Explain.*

[+5 minutes]

┌─ **AUDIOSCRIPT** ─────────────────┐
For audioscript, see page AS8.
└──────────────────────────────────┘

E Discussion

Suggested teaching time:	5 minutes
Your actual teaching time:	_____

- Have a volunteer read the first item out loud.

- Item 1: Individually, have students write down the traits the crow and the peacock share and a sentence explaining each trait. (Possible responses: They are both vain. The crow wants to show its talent and the peacock wants to be beautiful; They are not wise. They both make foolish decisions.)

- Have students discuss the crow's and peacock's trait(s) in small groups. Point out that students can use traits other than those in the Vocabulary.

- Item 2: In small groups, have students write a sentence about the kind of person that each animal represents. Write an example on the board: *The peacock: A person who is willing to pay a high price to improve his/her looks.* (Possible responses: **The crow:** a person who likes to boast about or show his/her talents; **The fox:** a selfish person who tricks other people to get what he/she wants; **The sparrow:** a sincere person who makes people aware of the mistakes they make)

- Have students share concrete examples of people they know who behave like the characters in the fables.

DISCUSSION **BUILDER**

Suggested teaching time:	10 minutes
Your actual teaching time:	_____

Step 1.

- Point out that students can choose three animal characters from the same story or from different stories.

- Remind students to use some of the Vocabulary from Exercise A for the character traits.

Step 2. Pair Work.

- Have pairs take turns telling each other about the animal characters they chose. Encourage students to briefly summarize the story if it is unknown to their partners.

- Then have students discuss the morals or lessons the stories teach.

- After students discuss in pairs, call on volunteers to briefly tell the class about a story they discussed. Elicit the character traits and moral of each volunteer's story from the class.

Step 3. Discussion.

- Have students discuss the questions in small groups. Encourage groups to make a list of reasons for each question.

- To review, ask students from different groups to share some of the reasons they thought of. List the ideas in two columns on the board as you get feedback from students.

Project: Have students use the Internet or a library to find a fable and write a brief report on it. The report should include a summary of the plot, a description of the character traits, a sentence describing the moral of the story, and the student's opinion of why the story is / isn't effective.

EXTRAS (optional)
Workbook: Exercises 10–15

D 🎧 Now listen to the fable of "The Peacock's Tail." Choose adjectives to describe each animal. Then listen again and write the moral of the story in your *own* words.

Answers will vary, but may include:

Adjectives for the peacock
vain

Adjectives for the sparrow
sincere, wise

The moral of the story
Be careful what you wish for—it might come true.

Be happy with who you are.

"*A small brown sparrow sat in a tree watching the peacock.*"

E Discussion.

1. How are the crow and the peacock alike? What trait or traits do they share? They are both vain.

2. Have you ever known anyone who has the same traits as the peacock, the crow, the fox, or the sparrow? Explain.

DISCUSSION **BUILDER** • *Now compare animal characters.*

Step 1. What are your favorite animal stories from books, cartoons, TV programs, or movies? Choose three animal characters and describe the animals' character traits on your notepad.

Animal characters	Character traits
1.	
2.	
3.	

Step 2. Pair Work. Compare and discuss the animal characters you chose. What moral or lesson about life do you think the characters try to teach?

Step 3. Discussion. Why do you think writers often use animals instead of people in stories? Why do you think so many children's stories are about animals?

4 Debate the value of animal conservation

A **Reading Warm-up.** What are some endangered animals you can think of? What are some threats to their survival?

B 🎧 **Reading.** Read the article. Do you agree with the point of view expressed?

Protecting Our Natural Inheritance

The earth is rich in biodiversity with millions of different species of plants and animals. However, many species are disappearing at an alarming rate. Biodiversity is reduced when ecosystems are modified and habitats of plants and animals are destroyed. The one species that is causing this phenomenon is the same one that can stop it—humans.

Many scientists view the current wave of species extinctions as unrivaled since the disappearance of the dinosaurs, more than 65 million years ago. Currently, around 11,000 species of plants and animals are at risk of disappearing forever—this includes over 180 mammals.

There are only about 700 mountain gorillas left in the wild.

Many species cling to survival. Found only in China, the giant panda's habitat has been decimated—the old-growth bamboo forests where the pandas make their home are being destroyed rapidly. It is estimated that as few as 1,600 giant pandas remain in the wild today. In the Arctic, the polar bear's icy habitat is disappearing as a result of global warming, and its survival is at risk. And in Central and East Africa, which have endured decades of civil war, the mountain gorilla population now totals just over 700 individuals.

If present trends continue, humanity stands to lose a large portion of its natural inheritance. Extinction is one environmental problem that is truly irreversible—once gone, these species cannot be brought back.

What can be done? World Wildlife Fund (WWF), the global conservation organization,

The polar bear's habitat is at risk.

has been working since 1961 to conserve the diversity of life on earth. In recent years, WWF has advanced giant panda conservation by training more than 300 panda reserve staff and local government officials, working with the community to help save habitat and guard against illegal hunting. By spreading awareness of the danger of carbon dioxide emissions, and by promoting the use of renewable energy resources such as wind and solar power, WWF is trying to head off the effects of global warming, giving the polar bear a chance to survive. With the help of other organizations in Africa, WWF has established a system to monitor the status of mountain gorillas in order to be able to address potential threats.

Why care about endangered animals? There are many reasons for protecting endangered species, including our own survival. Many of our foods and medicines come from wild species, and each wild species depends on a particular habitat for its food and shelter, and ultimately its survival. If one species in an ecosystem disappears, other species are affected. And when one ecosystem is altered or destroyed, a ripple effect occurs, and the interdependency of all living things becomes clear. Animals not only need protection to ensure their own species' survival, but they also serve as umbrella species; helping them helps numerous other species that live in the same habitat.

Beyond economics and human well-being, however, the rapid extinction of so many creatures on our planet raises profound ethical and moral questions. What sort of world will our children inherit? Do we want the future to be a place where pandas and gorillas only exist in captivity in zoos? If we are unable—or unwilling—to protect the animals we share our planet with, what does that say about humankind's future on earth?

China's giant panda clings to survival.

For more information on WWF and its work, visit www.worldwildlife.org.

4 *Debate the value of animal conservation*

A Reading Warm-up

Suggested teaching time: 5 minutes
Your actual teaching time: _____

- Have a volunteer read the title of the lesson out loud. Ask *What words do you think of when you hear* animal conservation? (Possible responses: endangered, extinct, zoo, panda) Elicit the meaning of *animal conservation* from the class. (protect animals from being destroyed or lost)

- Have a volunteer read the Warm-up questions out loud and elicit the meaning of *endangered* from the class. (at risk of becoming extinct or destroyed forever)

- Draw a two-column chart with the headings *Endangered animals* and *Threats* on the board. As a class, brainstorm endangered animals. Encourage students to say why the animals are in danger of extinction. As students respond, write their ideas in the chart: (Possible responses: elephants—poachers [Elephants are killed for their tusks.]; wolves—farmers [Farmers shoot wolves because they attack their sheep and chickens.])

B 🎧 Reading
(CD 2, Track 36)

Suggested teaching time: 10–15 minutes
Your actual teaching time: _____

- Point to the photos. Ask *Have you ever seen one of these animals at a zoo or nature preserve?*

- Have a volunteer read the title of the article out loud. Elicit the meaning of *inheritance* from the class. (something that is handed down from generation to generation)

- Ask *What do you think the article will discuss?* (Possible response: how to protect endangered animals)

- Have students read and listen to the article.

- To practice scanning for information, photocopy the following exercise and distribute it, or write it on the board. Give students a time limit (4 minutes) to encourage them to locate the information as quickly as possible. (1. 11,000; 2. 1,600, 700; 3. Global warming; 4. WWF; 5. foods, medicines)
    1. *Approximately ___ species of plants and animals are endangered.*
    2. *Only ___ giant pandas and as few as ___ mountain gorillas exist in the wild.*
    3. *____ is putting the polar bears' survival at risk.*
    4. *The ____ has been working since 1961 to help protect endangered animals.*
    5. *One reason humans should value animal conservation is that many important ___ and ___ come from wild plants and animals.*

- Before students discuss whether or not they agree with the point of view expressed, have pairs summarize the point of view in one or two sentences. Then ask them to agree or disagree and briefly state why.

- After pairs discuss whether or not they agree with the point of view expressed in the article, review as a class.

> **Language note:** Students should be able to understand the article without knowing every word. You may want to share the following definitions if students ask about specific expressions: *unrivaled* (more important than any other); *cling to survival* (try hard to survive); *decimate* (destroy a large part of something); *bamboo* (a tall plant with hollow stems); *endure* (suffer through a bad situation for a period of time); *carbon dioxide* (gas that is produced when carbon is burned and when animals and people exhale; it is harmful to the atmosphere and contributes to the greenhouse effect); *head off* (prevent something from happening); *ripple effect* (situation in which one action causes another, which then causes a third, etc.); *umbrella species* (species that protect other species).

💿 **Reading Strategies**

💿 **Reading Speed Calculator**

💿 **Extra Reading Comprehension Activities**

Challenge: Use this option if you want to do a listening activity. Write the following graphic organizer (without the answers) on the board.

Animal	Place where it lives	Current population in the wild	Reasons why it is endangered	Action taken by World Wildlife Fund (WWF)
giant panda	China	1,600	destruction of their home (bamboo forest)	training staff and the community to save the forest and stop illegal hunting
polar bear	the Arctic	not stated	destruction of their home because of global warming	making people aware of the importance of stopping global warming
mountain gorilla	Central and East Africa	700	decades of civil war	monitoring gorillas and getting ready to face threats

💿 **Graphic Organizers**

With books closed, have students listen and complete the chart in note form. Point out that for one of the animals, the current population is not given. If necessary, have students listen again to confirm their answers. Review as a class. **[+10 minutes]**

C Understanding Meaning from Context

Suggested teaching time:	5 minutes
Your actual teaching time:	_____

- To help students use context to figure out meanings, have them scan the article and underline the sentences these words appear in and look at the sentences that come before and after. Model the first item with the class. After students underline the sentence and choose an answer, ask *Which word or phrase helped you to figure out the meaning of* biodiversity? (different species of plants and animals)
- Have students compare answers with a partner and then review as a class.

Challenge: In pairs, have students write a short paragraph about an endangered animal or the extinction of a species, using two to four words from Exercise C. For example, *The panda is in danger of* extinction *because it has lost its* habitat. *The WWF is taking action for the* conservation *of the species. If a species disappears, the* biodiversity *of the area is reduced and the* ecosystem *is affected.* [+5 minutes]

D Discussion

Suggested teaching time:	10–15 minutes
Your actual teaching time:	_____

- Form small groups. Have a volunteer read item 1 out loud. Then have students list the reasons given in the article and then add their own reasons to the list. (Possible responses: **Reasons given in the article:** habitat loss—the bamboo forests are being destroyed, wars in Africa affect the gorilla's habitat; climate change—the ice in the Arctic is melting because of global warming; **Other reasons:** hunting for illegal trade, hunting for sport, pollution, invasion of other species, conflict with man)
- Have a volunteer read item 2 out loud. Encourage groups to find at least three main arguments in the article. (Possible responses: Many of our foods and medicines come from wild species. If one species disappears, other species are affected; An ethical reason—we should learn to protect the animals we share our planet with.)
- Have a volunteer read item 3 out loud. After students think of their own answers to each question individually, bring the groups together again and have students discuss their opinions as a class.

DISCUSSION **BUILDER**

Suggested teaching time:	15–20 minutes
Your actual teaching time:	_____

 Discourse Strategies

Step 1. Pair Work.

- Have volunteers read the pros and cons of animal conservation.

- Have students choose the strongest and weakest arguments individually. You may want to have students circle the bullets that contain the strongest arguments, and cross out the bullets that contain the weakest arguments.
- In pairs, have students discuss which arguments are strongest / weakest. Encourage them to support their arguments.
- Have pairs add to either list with their own ideas.

Step 2. Debate.

- After dividing the class into two groups, have students take notes to support their sides.
- Before students debate, elicit useful language that will help students state their opinions politely; write the useful language on the board. Refer students to the language from the Grammar Exchange on page 65:

Stating your argument "for"	Stating your argument "against"
I'm in favor of ____ because ____.	I'm opposed to ____ because ____.
I think it's right to ____.	I think it's wrong to ____.
I believe it's a good idea to ____.	I'm against____.
I believe ____ is OK under some circumstances.	I feel ____ is morally wrong.

Agreeing	Disagreeing
I completely agree.	That's true, but ____.
I couldn't agree more.	That's one way to look at it, but ____.
That's exactly what I think.	I completely disagree.
You're so right.	On the one hand, ____, but on the
I agree with you on that one.	other hand, ____.

- To promote a friendly debate, encourage students to raise their hands and use polite language.

Step 3. Discussion.

- Have a volunteer read the questions out loud and have students take brief notes of their ideas, individually.
- Form small groups. As students discuss the questions, encourage them to use the Vocabulary from this unit.
- Review as a class. Have a volunteer from each group share the group's ideas.
- Have students name endangered animals. Write a list on the board as students respond. Call on students to explain the reason each animal is endangered, what action is being taken, and why it is / isn't effective. Then have other students express their opinions on why species that are not "popular" are / aren't worth saving.

Challenge: Have students write a response to the article, expressing agreement / disagreement with the point of view expressed. [+5–10 minutes]

EXTRAS (optional)

Workbook: Exercises 16–17

C **Understanding Meaning from Context.** Use the context of the article to determine the meaning of the words and phrases.

1. **biodiversity** (line 1)
   a. endangered animals   (b.) the variety of living things   c. threats to nature

2. **habitat** (lines 4, 24, 28, and 61)
   a. the food animals eat   (b.) the place animals live   c. the extinction of animals

3. **extinction** (lines 12, 36, and 72)
   a. global warming   b. trying to protect animals   (c.) the disappearance of a species

4. **conservation** (lines 40 and 45)
   (a.) trying to protect animals   b. dangers to animals   c. feeding animals

5. **ecosystem** (lines 4, 63, and 64)
   a. trying to protect animals   b. threats to animals   (c.) how plants and animals work together

D **Discussion.**
Answers will vary, but may include:
1. According to the article, what are some reasons animals become extinct? Can you think of any other reasons? Their habitats are destroyed and they are hunted.

2. What arguments are given in the article to support animal conservation? Animal conservation is important because of the interdependecy of all living things and extinction is irreversible.
3. Look again at the last paragraph in the article. How would *you* answer the questions it raises?

DISCUSSION **BUILDER** • *Now debate the value of animal conservation.*

Step 1. Pair Work. Read and discuss the arguments for and against animal conservation. Which arguments are the strongest for each side of the animal conservation debate? Which are the weakest?

Pros	Cons
• Human beings have a responsibility to protect all living things.	• Extinctions are simply part of the natural process—it's the principle of "survival of the fittest."
• Species should be preserved for future generations.	• Environmental protection costs a lot of money. It's "a luxury" for countries that have more serious problems.
• Natural parks and wildlife are big tourist attractions—they generate jobs and income for local economies.	• Millions of species have already become extinct with no significant impact on the environment—it's no big deal.
• Species extinction at the current rate could lead to an ecological disaster.	• Conservation limits land available to farmers, who really need it for their livelihood.
• We miss the chance for new discoveries, such as medicines, with every species we lose.	• Do we really need 2,000 species of mice?
• Your own ideas:	• Your own ideas: ....

Step 2. Debate. Is it important to spend money on animal conservation? Form two groups—one for and one against. Take turns presenting your views.

Step 3. Discussion.

1. Why do you think some animals become endangered? What are some threats to the survival of animals in the wild?

2. In your opinion, are species worth saving even if they aren't "popular" or of any known value to people? Why or why not?

Writing: Express an opinion on animal treatment

Persuasion

To persuade readers to agree with your point of view, provide examples, facts, or experts' opinions that support your argument. Another effective technique is to demonstrate the weakness of opposing arguments. Summarize your main point in your concluding sentence.

Support your point of view	Offer experts' opinions
For example, . . .	[Smith] states that . . .
Another example is . . .	According to [Rivera], . . .
For instance, . . .	

Ways to discuss opposing arguments		Ways to conclude your argument
It can be argued that . . .		In conclusion, . . .
Some people think . . . } However,		In summary, . . .
It is true that . . .		To sum up, . . .

WRITING MODEL

Zoos play an important role in animal conservation. **For instance,** studies suggest that research is more easily conducted in zoos. **It can be argued that** animals should be free and that it is unethical to keep them in zoos. **However,** the survival of these species depends on scientific studies. **In conclusion,** animals should be kept in zoos in order to support conservation efforts.

Step 1. Prewriting. Planning your argument. Choose one of the questions in the following box or write your own question. State your opinion and list your arguments. Then think of possible opposing arguments.

- Is research on animals necessary in order to develop new medicines and procedures?

- Are some traditional forms of entertainment, such as circuses, bullfights, and cockfights, cruel to animals?

- Your own question: ....
  ....

Your opinion: ....

Your arguments:

1. ....

2. ....

3. ....

Possible opposing arguments:

1. ....

2. ....

3. ....

Step 2. Writing. On a separate sheet of paper, write a paragraph arguing your opinion from Step 1. Remember to include a topic sentence at the beginning of the paragraph and a concluding sentence at the end.

Step 3. Self-Check.

☐ Did you state your point of view clearly?

☐ Did you provide examples, facts, or experts' opinions to support your point of view?

☐ Did you discuss opposing arguments?

☐ Did you include a topic sentence and a concluding sentence?

Step 4. Peer Response. Exchange paragraphs with a partner. Do you agree or disagree with your partner's point of view? Write a short response, explaining why. Start like this: I agree / disagree because . . . .

Writing *Express an opinion on animal treatment*

Suggested teaching time: 20–25 minutes
Your actual teaching time: _____

Persuasion

- Call on students to read the explanation and examples out loud.

- To check comprehension, ask *What four things can you do to persuade the reader to agree with you?* As students provide the answers, list them on the board. (give examples; provide facts; offer experts' opinions; demonstrate the weakness of opposing arguments)

- Have students read the writing model. Point out the expressions for supporting your point of view, discussing opposing arguments, and concluding your argument.

- Have volunteers restate each sentence with a different expression from the chart. (For example . . . ; Some people think . . . ; To sum up . . .)

 Extra Writing Skills Practice

Step 1. Prewriting.

- Have a volunteer read the questions out loud. Ask students choose one or write their own.

- As students list their arguments, encourage them to use as much vocabulary from this unit as possible. Remind students to support their arguments by providing examples and facts, and by offering experts' opinions.

- As students take notes, circulate to offer help as needed.

Step 2. Writing.

- Point out that students should state their opinions in the topic sentence and then restate it in the concluding sentence.

- As students write, circulate to offer help as needed.

Step 3. Self-Check.

- After students complete the Self-Check activity, have them correct any mistakes they made.

- Then have volunteers read their paragraphs to the class.

Option: Form small groups of students who wrote about the same question. Have students take turns reading their paragraphs out loud to the other students in their group. Have students discuss the following: *Did you have the same or different opinion on the question you chose? Did you use different or similar arguments to support your point of view? Which was the strongest argument of all?* [+10–15 minutes]

Step 4. Peer Response.

- Have students exchange papers with a partner who wrote about a different topic.

- As students write their responses, encourage them to offer reasons for agreeing / disagreeing.

- Have pairs read their responses to each other and discuss.

- If you think students may be uncomfortable with other students checking their work, you may want to collect papers for correction.

EXTRAS (optional)

Workbook: Page 59

UNIT 6 CHECKPOINT

A 🎧 Listening Comprehension
(CD 2, Track 37)

Suggested teaching time:	5–10 minutes
Your actual teaching time:	_____

- Have students read the statements before listening to the conversations.
- Review answers as a class. After students provide the answer to item 1, ask *What kind of people can these monkeys be particularly helpful to?* (people who can't use their arms or legs) After students provide the answer to item 2, ask *What simple jobs can they do?* (serve food; open and close doors; turn lights on and off; get objects)

AUDIOSCRIPT

For audioscript, see page AS9.

B 🎧 Now listen to Part 2 ...
(CD 2, Track 38)

Suggested teaching time:	5–10 minutes
Your actual teaching time:	_____

- Have students read the statements before listening to the conversations.
- If necessary, explain what an autistic child is. (a child with a mental illness that prevents him or her from communicating well with other people)
- Review answers as a class. Ask volunteers to support their responses with proof from the listening.

AUDIOSCRIPT

For audioscript, see page AS9.

C Change the adjective ...

Suggested teaching time:	5 minutes
Your actual teaching time:	_____

- Have students do the exercise individually.
- In pairs, have students compare answers. If necessary, refer them to page 66.

D Complete each statement ...

Suggested teaching time:	5 minutes
Your actual teaching time:	_____

- Refer students to page 68 to review character traits as a class.
- Have students complete the exercise individually.
- Then have students compare answers with a partner.

E Choose four of the topics ...

Suggested teaching time:	5 minutes
Your actual teaching time:	_____

- Have students share their sentences with a partner.
- Review as a class. Have several students share their opinions with the class.

 You may wish to use the Video Program and activity worksheets for Unit 6 at this point.

 **Complete Assessment Package
Unit 6 Achievement Test**

SUMMIT WEBSITE
For Unit 6 online activities, visit the
Summit Companion Website at
www.longman.com/summit.

A 🎧 **Listening Comprehension.** Listen to Part 1 of a radio program. Choose the phrase that best completes the statements, according to the listening.

1. Capuchin monkeys can be ....
   a. used for medical research   **(b.)** loyal friends to humans   **c.** trained to perform in circuses

2. These monkeys are useful to humans because they ....
   (a.) do simple jobs   **b.** push a wheelchair   **c.** wash dishes

B 🎧 Now listen to Part 2 and choose the phrase that best completes the statements.

1. Dolphin-assisted therapy had a positive effect on children's ....
   a. moral or ethical development   **(b.)** speech development   **c.** physical development

2. Children respond to dolphins because dolphins are ....
   a. good swimmers   **b.** intelligent   **(c.)** playful

3. Many of these children respond better to people after ....
   a. a year of treatment   **(b.)** a few treatments   **c.** a few weeks of treatment

C Change the adjective in each statement so it makes sense.

1. A relaxed pet that never bites is ~~destructive~~.   gentle/good-natured
2. A cat that bites or scratches people is ~~affectionate~~.   aggressive
3. A pet that likes to be with people is ~~aggressive~~.   loyal/devoted
4. A dog that chews on shoes is ~~adorable~~.   destructive
5. A pet that makes a mess is ~~sociable~~.   filthy

D Complete each statement with an appropriate character trait.

1. A person who says or does unkind things to others is .... mean ....
2. People who can't pass a mirror without looking at themselves are .... vain ....
3. If one expresses oneself honestly to others, we say that person is .... sincere ....
4. Someone who is too trusting of others is .... gullible ....
5. People who think mainly about themselves are .... selfish ....
6. People who are skillful at getting what they want are .... clever ....
7. If people have good judgment on matters of importance, we say they are .... wise ....

E Choose four of the topics from the box. Use modals with the passive voice to state your *own* opinion about each topic.

| endangered animals | hunting | pets |
| horseracing | bullfighting | zoos |

Example: *Hunting should be banned because it's inhumane.*

1. ....
2. ....
3. ....
4. ....

UNIT 7

Advertising and Consumers

A **Topic Preview.** Look at the types of advertisements companies use to try to get consumers to buy products. What types of ads do you think you are most exposed to daily?

TV commercials

A BIKE THAT'S EASY TO CARE FOR. AND A BELT TO MATCH.

color perfectamen hermoso

magazine ads

ads on trains, buses, or blimps

AQUAFINA GET SPOTTED

Internet pop-ups

billboards

ContestAlley.com

Platinum Plus $7500

我的网 MyWeb 我的网

www.myweb.com.cn

Be the first to own one!

radio ads

B **Discussion.**

1. Which type of advertising do you find the most effective? Why?

2. Read the information to the right. Are you surprised by these statistics? Do you think they are similar for your country?

Daily Exposure to Advertising
In the United States, the average person is exposed to approximately 254 advertising messages each day—108 from TV, 34 from radio, and 112 from print. If you include brand lab on products and corporate logos on the sides of buildings, th number increases to over 1,000 ads per day.

Advertising Media Inter Center

Advertising and Consumers

A Topic Preview

Suggested teaching time: 10–15 minutes
Your actual teaching time: _____

- To introduce the theme of advertising, have students spend a few moments looking at the ads and reading the captions.

- Point to each ad and ask *What product do you think this ad is for?* (Possible responses: hair dye, shampoo, a motorcycle, a website, a new car, bottled water, a radio)

- To help students decide what the most effective type of advertising is, have them try to remember the last ad that they saw or heard. Ask *What type of ad was it? What product or service was being advertised? How effective was the ad? Did it make you want to buy the product?*

- As the class discusses the most effective types of advertising, encourage students to support their opinions and share examples of effective advertisements they have seen.

- Take a poll to find out which type of advertising the majority of the class thinks is the most effective. Keep a tally on the board. Call on a few volunteers to explain their views and share examples of effective ads they remember. Encourage other students who have seen those ads to share their own views on them.

Language note: *Advertisements* are often referred to as *ads* in informal English. *Advertisement* is a general word. You can find advertisements in newspapers, in magazines, on signs, on billboards, and on blimps. *Commercial* is a specific word for advertisements on TV or on the radio. For example, *a TV commercial, a radio commercial* (*a radio ad* is also possible). Use the preposition *for* after *advertisement* or *commercial*. For example, *an advertisement <u>for</u> orange juice; a TV commercial <u>for</u> orange juice.* It is also possible to say *an orange juice commercial* or *an orange juice ad.*

Option: As a class, brainstorm other types of advertising. Write them on the board. (Possible ideas: direct mail; fliers / handbills; clothing worn by professional athletes; movie theater coming attractions; product give-aways; product placements in movies and TV shows; ads in sports arenas; sponsorships; catalogs) **[+5 minutes]**

B Discussion

Suggested teaching time: 10 minutes
Your actual teaching time: _____

- Have volunteers read the questions and the U.S. statistics on daily exposure to advertising out loud. Elicit the meaning of *corporate logo.* (a small design that represents a company)

- If you haven't done the above option with the class, you may want to do it now.

- Form small groups. As students discuss the questions, circulate to encourage them to explain their answers.

C 🎧 Sound Bites
(CD 3, Track 2)

Suggested teaching time:	10 minutes
Your actual teaching time:	_____

• Point to the ads in the catalog. Ask *What type of ads are these?* (catalog) *Would you buy any of these products? Do you like to browse printed or online catalogs? What kinds of products do catalogs usually offer? Do you sometimes order products from them? Why / Why not?*

• Have students listen to the conversation with books closed. To check comprehension, ask:
  What does Bob want? (an electric massage chair)
  What does Ann think of this idea? (that it's a waste of money and not useful)
  What does Ann want (a self-watering flowerpot)
  What does Bob think of this idea? (He doesn't think she's serious.)

• After students read and listen, have pairs discuss the reasons Bob and Ann give for wanting the electric massage chair and self-watering pot. Ask *Are their reasons good enough? Do you think Bob and Ann should buy them?*

D In Other Words

Suggested teaching time:	5–10 minutes
Your actual teaching time:	_____

• In pairs, have students underline the expressions in the Sound Bites conversation as they find them.

• Review as a class. Have two volunteers read the conversation out loud, replacing the expressions in the conversation with the statements or questions from items 1–5.

Challenge: In pairs, have students talk about a product they would like to buy. [+5 minutes]

STARTING POINT

Suggested teaching time:	10–15 minutes
Your actual teaching time:	_____

• Have volunteers read the ads and models out loud.

• As a class, brainstorm pros and cons for each product on the board. (Possible responses: **Air Pollution Mask:** With a pollution mask, you can breathe safely. / It looks silly; **Porta-Bells:** They help you stay fit while traveling. / They're a waste of money; **Riviera Pool Chair:** It helps you relax at the pool. / It's only useful if you have a pool.)

Discussion

• Form small groups of three or four and have them discuss their opinions for each product and whether or not the product could be useful.

• Review as a class. Call on students to share their groups' opinions and discuss the usefulness of each product. Encourage students to use language from the models and Exercises C and D in their responses.

Option: On the board, draw the following chart (without the answers).

	Noun (person)	Noun (thing)	Verb
I read an underline{advertisement} in the newspaper.		✓	
They used a radio ad to underline{advertise} their product.			✓
underline{Advertisers} persuade people to buy products.	✓		
Companies spend a lot of money on underline{advertising}.		✓	

💿 Graphic Organizers

To familiarize students with vocabulary that will recur in this unit, have students study the examples and decide on the grammatical function of each underlined word. In pairs, have students compare their answers and then discuss the difference in meaning between *advertisement* and *advertising*. Review as a class. Make sure students understand that *advertising* is a general word that refers to the activity of using advertisements to persuade people to use services or buy products. [+5 minutes]

EXTRAS (optional)
Workbook: Exercises 1–3

C 🎧 **Sound Bites.** Read and listen to a couple talking about ads in a catalog.

BOB: I think it's about time I got myself one of these electric massage chairs.
ANN: What on earth for?
BOB: It would just be nice to have one. That's all. **CN1**
ANN: Sounds like a waste of money to me. Don't they have anything useful in there?
BOB: See for yourself.
ANN: Now here's something I'd like to get my hands on—a self-watering flowerpot.
BOB: You've got to be kidding. **CN2**
ANN: No, I'm not. I think one of these could come in really handy.

CN1 **Corpus Notes:** The expression *that's all*, used for emphasis as a separate sentence or at the end of a sentence, occurs most frequently in spoken English and rarely in written English.

D **In Other Words.** Read the conversation again. With a partner, find an expression in the conversation that is similar in meaning to each of the following statements or questions.

1. Why would you do that?
   What on earth for?
2. That's a useless thing to buy.
   Sounds like a waste of money to me.
3. I'd really love to have one.
   Now here's something I'd like to get my hands on.
4. You can't be serious.
   You've got to be kidding.
5. It might be very useful.
   I think one of these could come in really handy.

CN2 **Corpus Notes:** The expressions *Are you kidding?*, *Are you kidding me?*, *You've got to be kidding*, and *You've got to be kidding me* are all commonly used in spoken English. *You've got to be kidding me* occurs more frequently than *You've got to be kidding*, but *Are you kidding?* occurs more frequently than *Are you kidding me?*

Electric Massage Chair

Self-Watering Flowerpot

92

STARTING **POINT**

Discussion. What do you think of these products? Do you think any of them could be useful?

"I'd like to get my hands on one of these. It would really come in handy."

"You've got to be kidding. What a waste of money!"

Air Pollution Mask
Don't let polluted air ruin your health.

PORTA-BELLS
Wherever you are, just fill them with water and start your workout. Perfect for travel!

Riviera **Pool Chair**
Reclining seat and cup holders guarantee a great day at the pool.

1 *Give shopping advice*

A 🎧 CONVERSATION **SNAPSHOT**

A: I think I'd like to pick up a few souvenirs before I go back home. Any suggestions?

B: What do you have in mind?

A: Nothing in particular. Just something to help me remember my trip.

B: Well, the central market would be a good bet if you want to find a bargain.

A: Can you haggle over the prices? **CN**

B: Of course!

🎧 **Rhythm and intonation practice**

CN Corpus Notes: The verb *haggle* is most frequently followed by the preposition *over* (*haggle over the price*). Another frequent collocation is *haggle with [someone]*.

🎧 **Describing low prices**
a good deal	!
a bargain	!!
a great offer	!!!
a steal	!!!!

🎧 **Describing high prices**
no bargain	!
a bit steep	!!
a rip-off	!!!
highway robbery	!!!!

B 🎧 **Vocabulary. Shopping expressions.** Listen and practice.

browse take one's time looking at goods in a shop without necessarily wanting to buy anything
I'm not looking for anything in particular. I'm just browsing.

bargain-hunt look around for goods that one can buy cheaply or for less than their usual price
The best time to go bargain-hunting is at the end of the season when the stores have big sales.

window-shop look at goods in store windows without going inside or intending to buy them
The prices in the shops downtown are a bit steep, but I like to window-shop.

haggle / bargain discuss the amount of money one is willing to pay for something
I hate haggling over prices. / It's a great place if you like to bargain.

shop around / comparison shop go to different stores in order to compare the prices and quality of things so one can decide which to buy
I think I'll shop around first before I make up my mind. / I'd suggest you comparison shop before you buy that new computer.

CN Corpus Notes: The verb *bargain* and phrasal verb *shop around* appear modified by a phrase beginning with the preposition *for* more frequently than they do alone. For example, *You should try bargaining for a lower price* and *We spent the entire day shopping around for school clothes*

C 🎧 **Listening Comprehension.** Listen to the conversations about shopping. Decide whether or not the people think the shop's prices are high. Then listen again and choose the best shopping expression to complete each statement.

Do they think the price is high?

	Yes	No	They don't say.	
1.	◯	✓	◯	They're (bargain-hunting / haggling).
2.	✓	◯	◯	They're going to (window-shop / comparison shop).
3.	◯	◯	✓	They're just (browsing / haggling).
4.	◯	✓	◯	They just want to (bargain-hunt / window-shop).
5.	✓	◯	◯	They're going to (browse / bargain).

1 *Give shopping advice*

A ⌒ CONVERSATION **SNAPSHOT**
(CD 3, Tracks 3, 5, 6)

Suggested teaching time:	5–10 minutes
Your actual teaching time:	_____

- Point to the photo. Ask *What kind of place is this?* (an indoor marketplace) *Have you ever shopped in a marketplace like this? If so, when? Why?*

- After students read and listen, ask *What does the woman want?* (a few souvenirs) *Where does the man suggest she go?* (the central market) *Why?* (because at the market, you can haggle over the prices / find a bargain)

- Have a few volunteers summarize the conversation.

- Have students read and listen to the ways to describe low and high prices. Point out that the language is listed in order of intensity.

Language note: Students may need help with the following expressions: *pick up* something means buy something; if you say something is *a good bet*, you think it will be successful. Point out that *offer* is different from the other words to describe low prices in that it is used to describe a reduction in the price of one or more items for a short time. For example, *There is a special offer on computers at TechnoWorld.* Some expressions for describing prices are commonly preceded by particular words: *a real bargain, a bit steep, a complete rip-off.* All of the expressions can follow *That's*: *That's a good deal, That's highway robbery,* etc. Some expressions are commonly used to describe the product, while others are used to describe the price. For example, *This printer is a real bargain / no bargain / a steal / a complete rip-off at $200; The price on that printer is a real bargain / no bargain / a bit steep / a good deal.* Use *highway robbery* as follows: *Charging so much for that printer is highway robbery.*

Culture note: Haggling over prices is common in markets and street stalls in some countries. It is useful to find out about the local customs regarding bargaining because, though it is expected in some places, it is considered rude in others.

⌒ Rhythm and intonation practice
(CD 3, Track 4)

Suggested teaching time:	5 minutes
Your actual teaching time:	_____

- Have students repeat chorally. Make sure they:
  - use rising intonation for *Any suggestions?* and *Can you haggle over the prices?*
  - use falling intonation for *What do you have in mind?*
  - use emphatic stress for <u>Just</u> in *Just something to help me . . .*

- use the following stress pattern:

STRESS PATTERN

A: I think I'd like to pick up a few souvenirs before I go back home. Any suggestions?

B: What do you have in mind?

A: Nothing in particular. Just something to help me remember my trip.

B: Well, the central market would be a good bet if you want to find a bargain.

A: Can you haggle over the prices?

B: Of course!

B ⌒ Vocabulary
(CD 3, Track 7)

Suggested teaching time:	5–10 minutes
Your actual teaching time:	_____

- Have students listen to the shopping expressions and study the explanations and examples. Then have students listen and repeat chorally.

🔵 **Vocabulary-Building Strategies**

C ⌒ Listening Comprehension
(CD 3, Track 8)

Suggested teaching time:	10 minutes
Your actual teaching time:	_____

- Explain that students will hear five conversations about shopping.

- First listening: Have students listen and decide if the speakers think the prices are high. Encourage students to take notes of the expressions that the people use to describe the prices.

- Review as a class. Have students support their answers with the words or expressions they wrote down. (1. a steal; 2. a bit steep; 3. some great deals; 4. highway robbery; 5. no bargain)

- Second listening: Have volunteers read the statements and answer choices out loud. Then have students listen and choose the correct shopping expressions.

- Review as a class. If necessary, have students listen again to check answers.

AUDIOSCRIPT

For audioscript, see page AS9.

D Pair Work

Suggested teaching time:	5 minutes
Your actual teaching time:	_____

- Have students look at the products and captions in the duty-free catalog. As a class, brainstorm brand names of perfumes and write them on the board.
- In pairs, have students choose a brand name for each of the items.
- To make the activity more varied, ask students to include some very cheap prices and some very high prices.

E Group Work

Suggested teaching time:	5 minutes
Your actual teaching time:	_____

- Have a volunteer read the models out loud.
- Then have each pair join another pair and exchange books. Ask each pair to comment on the other pair's price list. Remind students to use the ways to describe low and high prices from the Conversation Snapshot.
- To finish the activity, call on students to say which items from the Skymarket ad they like. Encourage students to explain whether or not they would buy them, depending on whether they are a good buy or not. Students should explain their decisions using the expressions for describing low and high prices.

CONVERSATION **STARTER**

Suggested teaching time:	10–15 minutes
Your actual teaching time:	_____

- Go over the items in the Ideas box. If necessary, clarify that a clothing / electronics / furniture district is an area in a city or town where clothing / electronics / furniture is sold.
- To model the task, copy the notepad headings on the board. As a class, list several local shopping places and what can be bought there.
- Have students complete the notepad individually.

Role Play

- To get students ready for the activity, have them read the Conversation Snapshot on page 76 again. You may also want to have students listen to the conversation again.
- Choose a more confident student and role-play a conversation.
- Have pairs role-play a conversation. Make sure each student plays both roles.
- As students interact, circulate to offer help as needed. Encourage students to use the correct rhythm and intonation in questions and to place the main stress on important words.

Discussion

- Have volunteers read the questions out loud.
- Before students discuss the questions in groups, have them think about each question individually. Encourage students to think of concrete examples to share with their partners. For example, an occasion when they comparison shopped and got a good deal, an occasion when they bought the first thing they saw and paid too much for it, a good bargain they once spotted, or souvenirs and other things they bought on their travels. Have students take notes of their experiences.
- As students discuss, encourage them to use the expressions for describing prices from the Conversation Snapshot and the shopping expressions in Exercise B.
- After students discuss, review each item at a time. To review item 1, take a poll to find out how many students in the class consider themselves good shoppers. Then call on various students to explain why they are good / bad shoppers and provide concrete examples. To review item 2, have students name things they have bought when traveling. Write a list on the board as students respond. Encourage students to explain why they bought some of the items listed on the board and to explain why they buy / don't buy the same kind of things when they are at home.

 Conversation Prompts

EXTRAS (optional)

Pronunciation Booster
Workbook: Exercises 4–6

D **Pair Work.** With a partner, fill in the duty-free price list with brand-name products you know. Then agree on a price for each product.

E **Group Work.** Compare your items and prices with other classmates'. Discuss whether or not you think the items are a good buy.

"What a steal! I'd buy that in a minute!"

"You've got to be kidding! That's highway robbery!"

Pronunciation Booster

PAGE P6
Vowel sounds

Shop Duty-free at Skymarket *and save!*

Price List

Brand Name	Product	Price

Trendy Tote Bags

Handmade Chocolates

Brand-Name Perfumes

Classic Watches

Designer Sunglasses

Compact Travel Umbrellas

CONVERSATION **STARTER** • *Now give shopping advice.*

Where are the best places to take a visitor shopping in your city or town? On your notepad, make a list.

Name of place or location	What you can buy there

IDEAS
- a shopping mall
- an open-air market
- a clothing district
- an electronics district
- a furniture district
- a boutique
- an art gallery
- a department store

Role Play. Role-play a conversation in which one of you is a visitor and the other gives shopping advice for his or her town or city. Use your notepad and the Conversation Snapshot on page 76 as a guide. Start like this: "I think I'd like to pick up a few souvenirs before I go back home."

Discussion.

1. Are you a smart shopper? Do you comparison shop or buy the first thing you see? Are you good at spotting bargains? Where do you find your best bargains?

2. What kind of shopping do you do when you're traveling? Do you shop differently when you travel from when you're at home?

2 *Discuss your reactions to ads*

A 🎧 GRAMMAR **SNAPSHOT.** Read the interviews and notice the passive forms of gerunds and infinitives.

What's the most touching ad you've ever seen?

Evan Gleason, journalist
Düsseldorf, Germany

There's a billboard for a phone company that I see every day on my way to work. It shows this elderly mother crying as she talks to her son on the phone. I'm not an emotional guy, but that ad chokes me up. It makes me think about my mom back in Los Angeles. Once in a while, we all need **to be reminded** about the important things in life.

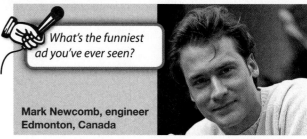

What's the funniest ad you've ever seen?

Mark Newcomb, engineer
Edmonton, Canada

There's this one *really* funny TV commercial for a language school. This cat puts his head into a bowl with a goldfish swimming in it, but the fish barks like a dog and scares the cat away. Then the words "Learn another language" appear on the screen. It always cracks me up when I see it. I enjoy **having** my day **brightened** with a little laughter, even if it's just from an ad.

What's the most annoying ad you've ever seen?

Heather Pullman, lawyer
Sydney, Australia

That would be the soap ad they keep playing on my favorite music station. There's this one line, "Wanna get clean? Get Bream clean!" It absolutely drives me crazy. It gets on my nerves **to be forced** to listen to a dumb ad over and over again when I'm just trying to listen to music.

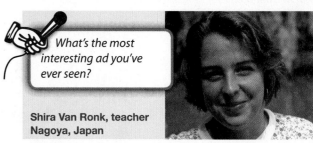

What's the most interesting ad you've ever seen?

Shira Van Ronk, teacher
Nagoya, Japan

Well, I know one that comes pretty close. Suntory—they're a company that produces sports drinks—they had a commercial with these amazing Chinese acrobats. The things they did just blew me away. I don't usually like commercials, but I don't mind **being entertained** by a good one.

B **Pair Work.** Use the context of the interviews to explain the meaning of each expression below.
Answers will vary, but may include:

It blows me away.
It amazes me.

It cracks me up.
It makes me laugh.

It gets on my nerves.
It really annoys me.

It chokes me up.
It makes me very emotional.

C **Discussion.** Do you generally find advertisements annoying or enjoyable? Why?

D **Grammar.** Passive forms of gerunds and infinitives

Use a passive form of a gerund or an infinitive to focus on an action instead of who performed the action.

Use <u>being</u> and a past participle to form a passive gerund.
I enjoy **being entertained** by commercials.
I resent **being forced** to watch ads before movies.
I appreciate **not being treated** like I'm a child.

Use <u>to be</u> and a past participle to form a passive infinitive.
I don't expect **to be told** the truth by advertisers.
Advertisers want their products **to be remembered**.
I was disappointed **not to be asked** to participate in the survey.

REMEMBER

• Some verbs are followed by gerunds, some by infinitives, and some by either.
• Certain adjectives are often followed by infinitives.

See page A3 in the Appendices for a complete list.

PAGE G12
For more ...

2 *Discuss your reactions to ads*

A 🎧 GRAMMAR **SNAPSHOT**
(CD 3, Track 9)

Suggested teaching time:	5–10 minutes
Your actual teaching time:	_____

- On the board, write:
  He/She talks about a/an _____ _____ *for* _____ .

- Tell students that they are going to listen to four interviews in which people describe ads. Explain the task: Students should write what the ad is like—funny, interesting, etc.—in the first blank; the type of advertising—TV commercial, radio ad, etc.—in the second blank; and the product advertised in the third blank.

- Model the first interview with the class. With books closed, have students listen to the first interview. Review the answers as a class. (1. He talks about a <u>touching</u> <u>billboard ad</u> for <u>a phone company</u>.)

- Have students listen to the remaining interviews and complete the sentence on the board for each one. Review as a class. (2. He talks about a <u>funny</u> <u>TV commercial</u> for <u>a language school</u>. 3. She talks about an <u>annoying</u> <u>radio ad</u> for <u>soap</u>. 4. She talks about an <u>interesting</u> <u>(TV) commercial</u> for <u>sports drinks</u>.)

- Then have students read and listen to the interviews and notice the passive forms of gerunds and infinitives.

B Pair Work

Suggested teaching time:	5 minutes
Your actual teaching time:	_____

- Have pairs find and underline the variations of the expressions in the interviews. Remind students to read the sentences before and after each of the phrases in the Grammar Snapshot to get a better understanding of the meaning.

- Review as a class. Have volunteers explain the meanings of the expressions. Encourage alternate sentences for each expression. (Possible response: If something chokes you up, it makes you feel like crying.)

C Discussion

Suggested teaching time:	5 minutes
Your actual teaching time:	_____

- As a class, brainstorm some popular enjoyable and annoying ads. Draw two columns on the board with the headings *Annoying* and *Enjoyable*. Write students' ideas on the board and have students briefly describe the ads.

- After students think of a few ads for each column, have a volunteer read the question out loud.

- Have volunteers share their opinions with the class. Have them give concrete examples of advertisements that they find either annoying or enjoyable. Encourage students with alternate views to share their opinions.

D Grammar

Suggested teaching time:	10–15 minutes
Your actual teaching time:	_____

- Refer students to the last sentence in Evan Gleason's interview: "Once in a while, we all need **to be reminded** about the important things in life." Ask *Do we know who's performing the action?* (no) *Why?* (It's not important.)

- Have students read the explanation for when to use the passive form of a gerund or infinitive.

- Refer students to the passive form of a gerund in the last interview, ". . . I don't mind **being entertained** by a good one." Ask *Who's the performer of the action?* (commercials) *Why is the performer present in this sentence?* (It is necessary for complete understanding.) *Why is this sentence in the passive?* (The action is still more important than the performer of the action.)

- Have a volunteer read the explanation for forming a passive gerund.

- To check comprehension, ask *How do you form a passive gerund?* (*being* + past participle) *How do you form a negative passive gerund?* (*not* + *being* + past participle) Write answers on the board as students respond.

- Remind students that some verbs, like *enjoy*, are always followed by gerunds and some verbs, like *agree*, are always followed by the infinitive.

- Have students read the explanation for forming a passive infinitive. To check comprehension, ask *How do you form a passive infinitive?* (*to be* + past participle) *How do you form a negative passive infinitive?* (*not* + *to be* + past participle)

- Have a volunteer read the Remember box out loud. Draw four columns on the board with the headings: *verb + ger., verb + inf., verb + ger. or inf.,* and *adjective + inf.*

  In pairs, have students write three words for each heading. Then have them refer to pages A3–A4 in the Appendices to confirm their answers.

- To provide practice, have pairs choose one item from each column in the chart and write sentences with a passive gerund or a passive infinitive. Call on students to read their sentences out loud.

Language note: Focus students' attention on the sentence from the Grammar Snapshot, "It gets on my nerves to be forced to listen to a dumb ad . . ." Point out that this is an example of a non-referential *it. To be forced* is the subject of the sentence and can therefore be an infinitive or a gerund (*being forced* is OK).

 Grammar Self-Checks

E Complete each sentence . . .

Suggested teaching time:	5 minutes
Your actual teaching time:	_____

- Model the first item with the class. Read the incomplete statement out loud. Then ask *Is enjoy followed by a gerund or an infinitive?* (a gerund) *What's the passive gerund form of* inform*?* (being informed) Have a volunteer read the complete statement out loud.

- After students complete the exercise individually, have them compare answers with a partner. Review as a class.

F On a separate sheet of paper . . .

Suggested teaching time:	5 minutes
Your actual teaching time:	_____

- Point to the Remember box. Ask *When would we use a* by *phrase?* (when it is important to mention the performer of the action)

- Have a volunteer read the example out loud. Tell students that *by advertisers* is not necessary because it is understood.

- Have pairs compare sentences and review as a class.

Challenge: To provide further guided practice, draw the following chart on the board.

A	B	C
1. I can't stand	being	told _____.
2. I expect	to be	forced _____.
3. I don't mind		treated _____.
		informed _____.

For each item in column A, have pairs choose an item from column B and then an item from column C, which they should complete with their own ideas. Then have pairs write their sentences on a separate sheet of paper. Point out that there isn't only one correct answer. To finish the activity, call on students to read their sentences out loud. (Note: *I can't stand* can be followed by either *being* or *to be*.) **[+10 minutes]**

GRAMMAR **EXCHANGE**

Suggested teaching time:	10–15 minutes
Your actual teaching time:	_____

- Have a volunteer read the directions out loud.
- Point to the list of types of ads. As a class, brainstorm other types of ads. (Possible responses: Internet pop-up ads; on-the-street advertising)
- Have students complete the chart individually.
- Point to the phrases for describing how you feel. Point out that this box contains verbs that can be followed by a gerund, an infinitive, or either a gerund or infinitive. Refer students to pages A3–A4 in the Appendices, if necessary.
- As students write sentences describing how they feel about the ads, circulate to offer help with forming passive gerunds and infinitives.

Pair Work

- Have a volunteer read the model out loud. Point out the preposition *for* after *commercial* (a commercial for shampoo), the expression *gets on my nerves*, and the passive gerund (*being forced*).

- Remind students to use the expressions in the Grammar Snapshot on page 78 (cracks me up, gets on my nerves, etc.) and passive gerunds and infinitives as they discuss the ads in pairs. Remind students to use present tenses to narrate what happens in the ads.

- Students walk around the room and find other students with the ads they've listed in their charts. Have students note how many students had the same / different reactions.

- Review as a class. Call on volunteers to share how they feel about an ad. Encourage students who have seen the same ad to share their views.

Project: On the board, write:

> Find ads that are:
>
> | serious | funny | witty | thought-provoking |
> |---|---|---|---|
> | original | simple | aggressive | short and sweet |

Bring in magazines. Have each pair find an ad that can be described with (some of) the words on the board and discuss the ad. Combine pairs to form groups of four. Have pairs exchange ads and discuss. After each pair has looked at both ads, have pairs share and compare their opinions on the ads.

EXTRAS (optional)

Grammar Booster
Workbook: Exercises 7–9

E Complete each sentence with a passive gerund or infinitive.

1. I think people enjoy (inform) _being informed_ about new products.
2. Companies want their products (advertise) _to be advertised_ on TV during prime time—when the most people are watching.
3. When I read an ad, I would like (tell) _to be told_ the whole truth about the product, not half-truths.
4. My sister was disappointed (not / give) _not to be given_ the chance to appear in that new commercial.

F On a separate sheet of paper, rewrite each sentence. Use a passive form of a gerund or an infinitive to replace the underlined words. Do not use <u>by</u> phrases.

> **REMEMBER**
>
> A <u>by</u> phrase identifies the performer of the action.
>
> The commercial was seen **by millions of people.**

Example: I don't mind <u>when advertisers inform me</u> about new products.

*I don't mind **being informed** about new products.*

1. I can't stand <u>advertisers forcing me</u> to watch commercials over and over again. _being forced_
2. I resent <u>one company's telling me</u> that I shouldn't buy another company's product. _being told_
3. You're lucky <u>the company is giving you</u> an opportunity to work overseas. _to be given_
4. We can't tolerate <u>their calling us</u> while we're eating dinner. _being called_

GRAMMAR **EXCHANGE** • *Now discuss your reactions to ads.*

Complete the chart with ads you are familiar with. Then on a separate sheet of paper, write sentences with passive forms of gerunds or infinitives, describing how you feel about each ad in your chart.

Some types of ads
TV commercials
radio ads
magazine ads
billboards

	Name or type of product	Type of ad
an ad you find interesting		
an ad that cracks you up		
an ad that gets on your nerves		
an ad that blows you away		
an ad that chokes you up		

Describing how you feel

I like . . .	I don't like . . .
I appreciate . . .	I don't appreciate . . .
I love . . .	I can't stand . . .
I enjoy . . .	I dislike . . .
I hate . . .	I resent . . .
I prefer . . .	I miss . . .
I need . . .	I want . . .

Pair Work. Compare the ads you listed in your charts. Describe each ad and how you feel about it.

> *"There's a TV commercial for shampoo that I see almost every night, and it really gets on my nerves. I can't stand **being forced** to watch it every day."*

3 Persuade someone to buy a product

A 🎧 **Vocabulary. Ways to persuade.** Listen and practice.

> **endorse** personally recommend a product in exchange for payment
>
> **promote** make sure people know about a new product in order to persuade them to buy it
>
> **imply** suggest that something is true, without saying or showing it directly
>
> **prove** show that something is definitely true, especially by providing facts, information, etc.

B **Pair Work.** Read about eight advertising techniques. Write the letter of the example that you think each technique uses. Explain your answers.

Eight techniques used by successful advertisers

1. Provide facts and figures `d`
Prove the superiority of a product with statistics and objective, factual information

2. Convince people to "join the bandwagon" `f`
Imply that *everyone* is using a product, and that others should too, in order to be part of the group

3. Play on people's hidden fears `h`
Imply that a product will protect the user from some danger or an uncomfortable situation

4. Play on people's patriotism `g`
Imply that buying a product shows love of one's country

5. Provide "snob appeal" `e`
Imply that use of a product makes the customer part of an elite group

6. Associate positive qualities with a product `c`
Promote a product with words and ideas having positive meanings and associations

7. Provide testimonials `a`
Use a famous person or an "average consumer" to endorse a product so the consumer wants it too

8. Manipulate people's emotions `b`
Use images to appeal to customers' feelings, such as love, anger, or sympathy

Source: www.entrenet.com

Examples

a. A professional soccer player recommends a particular brand of shirts.

b. A hotel chain shows a businesswoman in her room, calling home to talk to her children.

c. A soft drink manufacturer shows young people having a great time drinking its product at the beach.

d. A car manufacturer states how quickly its car can go from 0 to 100 kilometers per hour.

e. A coffee manufacturer shows people dressed in formal attire drinking its brand of coffee at an art exhibition.

f. A credit card company claims that its card is used by more people than any other card.

g. A clothing manufacturer promotes its clothes by saying they are made by and for people in this country.

h. A laundry detergent manufacturer suggests that it will be socially embarrassing if your white clothes are not *really* white.

3 Persuade someone to buy a product

A 🎧 Vocabulary
(CD 3, Track 10)

Suggested teaching time:	5–10 minutes
Your actual teaching time:	_____

• Read the title of the lesson out loud. Ask *What does it mean to persuade someone to buy a product?* (to urge someone to buy something by giving them reasons they should do it)

• Have students listen to the words and study the definitions. Then have students listen and repeat the words chorally.

> **Language note:** Products are usually *endorsed* by famous people or people associated with a certain quality or society. For example, a model might endorse a brand of make-up. The noun form is *endorsement*.

Option: Read the following examples of ways to persuade, out loud. Have students identify the vocabulary word that matches each example:

> *A clothing company shows a man wearing one of their suits being hired for a job.* (imply)
> *A professional baseball player is paid to wear a brand of athletic shoe and to recommend it in a TV ad.* (endorse)
> *A toothpaste company mentions a scientific study that shows that its toothpaste makes teeth 50 percent whiter in two months.* (prove)
> *A soft drink company gives away free cans of their new cola at a sports event.* (promote)

[+5–10 minutes]

B Pair Work

Suggested teaching time:	5–10 minutes
Your actual teaching time:	_____

• Have volunteers read the advertising techniques out loud. If necessary, explain the meaning of *join the bandwagon* (do what most people are doing) and *snob appeal* (supposed to be liked by people who think they are better than others).

• Have students complete the exercise individually and think about why they chose each answer.

• Review as a class. Call on eight students to say what example they chose for each technique. To help students explain their answers, ask:
> 1. *How does the ad prove that the product is good?* (by stating how fast the car can reach 100 kilometers per hour)
> 2. *According to the ad, what are most people using?* (the company's credit card)
> 3. *What does the ad make you worry about?* (an embarrassing situation you might go through if people notice your clothes are not as white as they should be)
> 4. *Why should people buy these clothes if they care about their country?* (because they are made by and for the people in the country)
> 5. *According to the ad, what do rich people do?* (drink a particular brand of coffee)
> 6. *In what way will you be happy if you use the product?* (You'll have a nice time with friends.)
> 7. *What famous person does the ad use?* (a soccer player)
> 8. *What feeling does the ad bring to your mind?* (love)

Project: Collect (or have students collect) ads from magazines and newspapers and bring them to class. Have students decide which techniques are being used in each ad and explain how.

C 🎧 Listening Comprehension
(CD 3, Track 11)

Suggested teaching time:	10 minutes
Your actual teaching time:	_____

- Before students listen, have them say what products and brands the advertisements are for. (**First ad:** product—mouthwash, brand—Nice-Mouth; **Second ad:** product—lemonade, brand—Leon's; **Third ad:** product—cars, brand—Bernard)
- Point out that more than one technique may be used in each ad.
- Model the first item with the class. Have students listen to the first ad and write the advertising technique(s) used. Have students discuss their choices in pairs.
- To review as a class, have a volunteer share and support his/her answer. (Possible response: The ad plays on people's hidden fears by making them worry about losing their jobs or having a bad day because of bad breath. It also provides facts to prove that the product is good.)
- Follow the same procedure for the other two ads.

💿 Listening Strategies

AUDIOSCRIPT

For audioscript, see page AS9.

D Pair Work

Suggested teaching time:	5 minutes
Your actual teaching time:	_____

- Have pairs choose three ads they both know and write the products or services and brands advertised in each. Encourage students to choose different types of advertising.
- Have students take notes for each product / service as they discuss the technique(s) used in its ad.
- Then have each pair join another pair and discuss the ads.

DISCUSSION **BUILDER**

Suggested teaching time:	20–25 minutes
Your actual teaching time:	_____

Step 1. Group Work.
- Have a volunteer read the directions out loud.
- Point to the Ideas box and read the ideas out loud.
- To model the activity as a class, plan an ad on the board from one of the ideas. Decide on a type of product, name, and type of ad. Brainstorm effective techniques for persuading people to buy the product and ideas for an ad using this technique.

- In small groups, have students decide on a product and take notes on their notepads.
- As students create the ads, circulate to offer help as needed.

Step 2. Discussion.
- On the board, draw the following chart (with the examples):

Group	Product	Name	Type of ad	Technique(s)	Comments
1	shampoo	Lavish Locks	radio ad	6 and 8	short and funny

💿 Graphic Organizers

- Tell students that they are going to use the chart to keep a record of the ads as they are presented to the class.
- Before groups present their ads, have students open their books to page 80 to refer to the advertising techniques.
- After each ad is presented, allow the class time to complete their charts.
- After all groups have presented their ads, hand out ballots for students to vote privately. You can photocopy the list below or write it on the board. (Note: To save time, you may want to tally the votes with a show of hands. To maintain privacy, have students close their eyes and vote quietly with a show of hands. Say *Who thinks Group 1 had the funniest ad? Who thinks Group 2 had the funniest ad?* etc.)
  - The funniest ad:
  - The most annoying ad:
  - The most persuasive ad:
  - The most interesting ad:
  - The most touching ad:
- After the votes are tallied and there is a winner for each category, have a volunteer who voted for that ad explain why he/she found it funny.
- Follow the same procedure to assign and discuss the other awards.

EXTRAS (optional)
Workbook: Exercises 10–11

C 🎧 **Listening Comprehension.** Listen to each ad. Then listen again. Decide which technique or techniques the advertiser is using to persuade the consumer to buy the product. Explain your answers.

Technique(s) used
Play on people's
hidden fears

Associate positive
qualities with a
product

Technique(s) used
Associate positive
qualities with a
product

Provide
testimonials

Technique(s) used
Provide snob
appeal

Associate positive
qualities with
a product

D **Pair Work.** Describe some ads you know and explain which techniques you think they use.

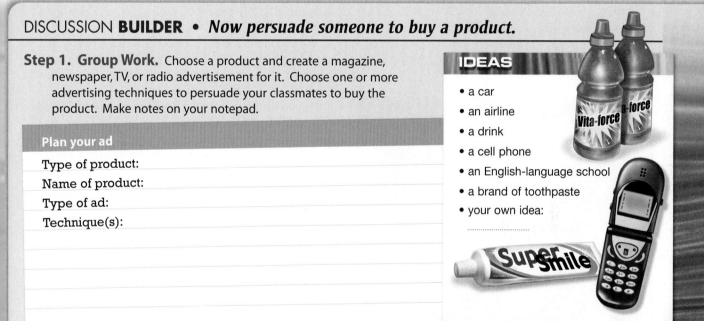

DISCUSSION **BUILDER** • *Now persuade someone to buy a product.*

Step 1. Group Work. Choose a product and create a magazine, newspaper, TV, or radio advertisement for it. Choose one or more advertising techniques to persuade your classmates to buy the product. Make notes on your notepad.

IDEAS

- a car
- an airline
- a drink
- a cell phone
- an English-language school
- a brand of toothpaste
- your own idea:

  ....

Plan your ad

Type of product: ....
Name of product: ....
Type of ad: ....
Technique(s): ....

Step 2. Discussion. Present your ad to your class. Show it, read it, or act it out. Analyze your classmates' ads and discuss which techniques were used. As a class, assign awards for these categories:

The funniest ad

The most annoying ad

The most persuasive ad

The most interesting ad

The most touching ad

4 *Describe consumer shopping habits*

A **Reading Warm-up.** Are you a careful shopper, or do you buy things on impulse?

B 🎧 **Reading.** Read the article. How is compulsive shopping a problem?

Compulsive Shopping: *The Real Cost*

Just in the last century, the way in which we consume material goods has shifted radically. For our grandparents, and some of our parents, shopping meant buying provisions to satisfy physical needs. Today, in addition to buying necessities, we shop to indulge ourselves in luxuries—high-priced gym shoes or the latest, most high-tech entertainment system. And we shop for the sheer fun of it. Most of us acquire continuously—everything from groceries to cars, from clothing to toiletries, from home furnishings to sporting equipment—and through our acquisitions, we express a sense of identity, taste, and lifestyle.

But some people go overboard. Their spending becomes excessive and often carries troubling consequences. Some people cannot resist the temptation, and very often they buy merely to acquire. This type of impulse buying can become so obsessive that people find themselves in considerable financial debt and psychological distress. Recent studies suggest that extreme impulse buying is on the increase, affecting an estimated 5 to 10 percent of the adult population in many countries.

We tend to define ourselves by what we buy and have. This often affects how we feel as well. For many, buying things on impulse is a way of avoiding or hiding feelings of anxiety and loneliness.

However, shopping as a way of dealing with internal distress is seldom effective for long. In fact, research suggests that people who consider shopping to be a priority in their lives tend to experience more anxiety and depression as well as a lower level of well-being than those who don't.

The long and short of it is this—you can't buy happiness.

Tips for Controlling Impulse Buying

- When you're just browsing and get the urge to buy something, ask yourself first if you really need it.
- Avoid sales. Spending any money on something you don't need is overspending.
- Follow the "24-hour rule." Don't buy anything new on the spot. Come back the next day if you think you really need it.
- Stick to a budget. Plan to splurge on the occasional wild purchase, but don't buy if it isn't in your budget.

Source: www.theallengroup.com

C **Understanding Meaning from Context.** Find these expressions in the article. Explain the meaning of each.

Answers will vary, but may include:

1. indulge ourselves
2. go overboard
3. resist the temptation
4. impulse buying
5. get the urge
6. overspending
7. splurge on

1. to let ourselves have or do something we enjoy
2. do too much of something
3. not do something you have a strong wish to do
4. buying something just because you want it on the spur of the moment
5. feel a strong wish to do something
6. spending more than you have
7. buy something indulgent and luxurious

4 Describe consumer shopping habits

A Reading Warm-up

Suggested teaching time:	5 minutes
Your actual teaching time:	_____

- Have a student read the Warm-up question out loud. Clarify the meaning of *buying on impulse*. (buying things without planning or choosing carefully)
- Call on volunteers to share whether they are careful shoppers or if they buy on impulse. Encourage students to support their responses with examples of what they do when they go shopping.

B 🎧 Reading
(CD 3, Track 12)

Suggested teaching time:	10–15 minutes
Your actual teaching time:	_____

- Point out the title of the article. Ask *What is compulsive shopping?* (an uncontrollable or strong desire to buy) *What do you think the subtitle,* The Real Cost, *means?* (Possible response: the consequences of compulsive shopping, not the monetary amount spent)
- Have students try to predict what costs or problems the article will discuss. (Possible responses: debt, anxiety, depression, psychological distress)
- Have students think about the question *How is compulsive shopping a problem?* as they read and listen to the article.
- To check comprehension, ask:
  According to the article, why did our grandparents' generation shop? (to satisfy physical needs)
  Why do we shop? (to buy necessities; to indulge ourselves in luxuries; for the fun of it)
  What do our purchases reflect about ourselves? (our identities, tastes, and lifestyles)
  What sort of emotional problems do compulsive shoppers generally have? (anxiety; depression; a low level of well-being)
- Have students read the tips for controlling impulse buying. Ask *Do you agree with these tips? Do you do these things when shopping?*
- Review the answer to the reading question as a class. (Compulsive shopping causes people to get into debt, feel worried and upset, and feel sad and anxious.)

🔄 Reading Strategies

🔄 Reading Speed Calculator

🔄 Extra Reading Comprehension Activities

Option: To use the reading as a listening activity, have students close their books when listening to the article. Follow the procedure above, making necessary changes to accommodate a listening-only task. **[+10–15 minutes]**

C Understanding Meaning from Context

Suggested teaching time:	5 minutes
Your actual teaching time:	_____

- Have students underline the expressions in the article.
- In pairs, have students discuss the meaning of each. Circulate to provide help as needed. Be sure students look at the sentences before and after the unknown expression to get context clues. For example, for the expression *go overboard*, the sentence *Their spending becomes excessive . . .* helps explain that the behavior is extreme.
- Then have pairs rewrite the sentences that contain these expressions, using their own words. (Possible response: 2. But some people have extreme behavior.)
- Review as a class. Have volunteers share their sentences with the class.

Language note: Students should be able to complete the exercise without understanding every word. You may want to share the following definitions if students ask about specific expressions: *acquire* (buy or obtain); *acquisition* (something that you buy or obtain); *distress* (a feeling of being very worried or upset); *well-being* (a feeling of being healthy and happy).

D Discussion

Suggested teaching time: 5–10 minutes
Your actual teaching time: _____

- Have volunteers read the questions out loud.
- As students discuss the questions in groups, have them take notes. Then bring the class together and have students share their responses.

DISCUSSION **BUILDER**

Suggested teaching time: 20–25 minutes
Your actual teaching time: _____

 Discourse Strategies

Step 1.

- Before students take the self-quiz, point out the title and elicit the meaning of *shopaholic* from the class. (someone who goes shopping too often and buys more things than he/she needs; someone who can't control his/her shopping)
- After students take the quiz, have them work out their scores. Take a poll to find out how many students scored in each category. Keep a tally on the board. Ask *Do you agree with the results?*

Language note: If necessary, clarify the meaning of the expressions *take the bull by the horns* (decide to deal with a difficult situation) and *tighten your purse strings* (control the money you spend—in this case, on shopping). The suffix *-aholic* is used to talk about someone who wants or needs to do or use something all the time.

Option: Have students share the results of their self-quizzes with a partner. Encourage students to say how they feel about the results and support their views with specific examples for some of the statements they checked. Encourage students to give each other advice on how to improve their shopping habits.
[+5–10 minutes]

Step 2. Discussion.

- Have volunteers read the questions out loud.
- Form small groups of students who chose the same topic.
- As students discuss the questions, encourage them to take notes and reach a conclusion as a group.
- To review, have a student from a group that discussed item 1 present the group's opinions to the class. Encourage students to agree or disagree and support their views. Encourage students to use the results of the class poll in their arguments.
- Do the same for items 2 and 3.

Step 3. Writing.

- As a class, brainstorm tips for shopping responsibly. List students' ideas on the board. (Possible tips: Don't buy expensive designer names and labels; Make sure you need something before buying it; Don't buy trendy things that won't be in style for long.)
- Have students choose the ideas from the board that they agree with, and then select the ones that they consider the most useful or important.
- Circulate to offer help as needed. Remind students to include a topic sentence and a concluding statement.

EXTRAS (optional)

Workbook: Exercises 12–17

D Discussion.
Answers will vary, but may include:

1. According to the article, how have shopping habits changed over the last few generations? Do you agree? In the past, people bought just the necessities. Now people shop continuously to indulge themselves.

2. Do you think compulsive shopping is a common problem? Do you know any compulsive shoppers? Give examples.

3. Do you think the tips in the article might be helpful for someone who wants to resist the temptation to overspend? What tips would *you* suggest?

DISCUSSION **BUILDER** • *Now describe consumer shopping habits.*

Step 1. Take the self-quiz. Check the statements that are true for you.

Are you a SHOPaholic?

- ☐ I sometimes feel guilty about how I spend my money shopping.
- ☐ When I'm feeling blue, it cheers me up to go shopping.
- ☐ When I go shopping, I can't resist the temptation to buy something—I just can't come home empty-handed.
- ☐ I feel uncomfortable if I haven't bought anything in a week.
- ☐ When I plan to go shopping for one item I need, I frequently end up coming home with a lot of things I *don't* need.
- ☐ I spend more than I have to in order to get more expensive designer names and labels.
- ☐ I can't pass up a good sale—even if I don't need anything, I just have to indulge myself.
- ☐ I sometimes lie to people about how much my purchases cost.
- ☐ I get more pleasure out of spending money than saving money.
- ☐ My shopping habits have caused problems in my personal relationships in some way.

Total the number of boxes you checked.

If your total is:

0-3 Great!
Keep up the good habits!

4-5 Not too bad!
Congratulations for admitting you're not perfect!

6-8 Uh-oh!
Sounds like trouble may be around the corner! It's time to tighten your purse strings.

9-10 Red alert!
It's time to take the bull by the horns and change some of the ways you shop and spend money.

Step 2. Discussion. Choose one of the following discussion topics and meet in small groups with other classmates who have chosen the same one.

1. Do you think most people tend to go overboard with their shopping? Explain.

2. Do you think people are too influenced by advertising? Explain.

3. Should people only spend money on things they need and never on things they don't need? Is it OK to buy on impulse sometimes? Is it OK to splurge once in a while?

Step 3. Writing. Explain your views on consumer shopping habits. In your opinion, what should people do to shop responsibly?

Writing: Explain an article you read

Writing a summary

A summary is a shortened explanation of the main ideas of an article. When writing a summary, include only the author's main points, not your own reactions or opinions. Be sure to paraphrase what the author says, instead of just copying the author's exact words.

The following guidelines will help you write a good summary:

- As you read an article, underline or highlight important points.
- Read the article again and state the main idea of each paragraph.
- Combine the main ideas to create a summary.

Some common reporting verbs used in summaries are <u>state</u>, <u>argue</u>, <u>report</u>, <u>say</u>, <u>believe</u>, <u>point out</u>, and <u>conclude</u>.

The article states that . . .   The journalist reports that . . .
The writer points out that . . .   The author concludes that . . .

PARAPHRASING

When you paraphrase what a person says, you say it in your *own* words.

The author: "But some people go overboard. Their spending becomes excessive and often carries troubling consequences. Some people cannot resist the temptation, and very often they buy merely to acquire."

You: *The author points out that it is difficult for some people not to buy things on impulse. They just buy anything they want.*

Step 1. Prewriting. Identifying main ideas.
Read the article "Compulsive Shopping: The Real Cost" on page 82 and underline the important parts. Then read the article again and identify the main ideas below.
Answers will vary, but may include:

Main idea of paragraph 1: People now shop for fun and to indulge themselves in addition to getting the necessities.

Main idea of paragraph 2: Many people today are in considerable financial debt because of impulse buying.

Main idea of paragraph 3: Many people shop to avoid anxiety and loneliness.

Main idea of paragraph 4: Compulsive shopping often increases anxiety and depression.

Step 2. Writing.
On a separate sheet of paper, combine the main ideas to write your summary. Be sure to paraphrase what the author says, using your *own* words. Your summary should be no more than four to six sentences long.

Step 3. Self-Check.

- ☐ Is your summary a lot shorter than the original article?
- ☐ Does your summary include only the author's main ideas?
- ☐ Did you paraphrase the author's ideas?
- ☐ Did you include your opinion of the article? If so, rewrite the summary without it.

Writing Explain an article you read

Suggested teaching time:	20–25 minutes
Your actual teaching time:	_____

Writing a summary

- Have a volunteer read the explanation for *Writing a summary* out loud.

- To check comprehension, ask:
  How many times should you read a text before summarizing it? (two)
  What should you do the first time you read it? (underline or highlight important points)
  What should you do the second time? (find the main idea in each paragraph)
  Should you use your own words in a summary? (yes)
  Should you state your opinion in a summary? (no)
  What are some verbs you can use in summaries? (state, argue, etc.)

- Have students read the paraphrasing model.

 Extra Writing Skills Practice

Step 1. Prewriting.

- To help students determine what to underline or highlight, point out that examples and exceptions are not usually the most important parts in a text.

- Model the first paragraph with the class. Have students read the first paragraph to themselves and underline / highlight the important points individually. Then have students read again and write the main idea individually. Compare and discuss the important parts and main idea as a class.

- Have students find the main ideas of the next three paragraphs with a partner. Point out that students must state the main ideas in their own words.

- Review the main ideas as a class.

Step 2. Writing.

- Point out that students can write a first draft and then make a clean copy.

- As students write, circulate to offer help as needed.

Step 3. Self-Check.

- Have students read the Self-Check questions out loud.

- Before students submit their summaries for correction, have them self-check their work and make any necessary changes.

Option: Step 4. Peer review. Exchange summaries with a partner. Read your partner's summary and check if it includes the main points in the article and complies with the Self-Check questions. [+5–10 minutes]

Project: Have students find an interesting article dealing with one of the topics students discussed in this unit, on the Internet. For example, *the power of advertising, advertising techniques,* or *compulsive shopping.* Have students write a brief summary of the article and then read it to the class to share their findings.

EXTRAS (optional)

Workbook: Page 69

A 🎧 Listening Comprehension
(CD 3, Track 13)

Suggested teaching time: 10 minutes
Your actual teaching time: _____

- Have students read the statements for Conversation 1.
- First listening: Have students listen and choose the answers according to what the people think of the prices. Then have them compare answers with a partner.
- Second listening: Have students make notes of key words that helped them choose the answers.
- Review as a class. Have students support their answers with key phrases from the conversation.
- Repeat the procedure for Conversations 2 and 3.

AUDIOSCRIPT

For audioscript, see page AS10.

B Complete each statement ...

Suggested teaching time: 5–10 minutes
Your actual teaching time: _____

- Have a volunteer read the example out loud. Point out the initial gerund (*watching*) and the third-person singular verb (*cracks*).
- You may want to have students look at Exercises A and B on page 78 to remind them of the meanings of the expressions.
- Have students share sentences with a partner.
- Review as a class. Have volunteers read their sentences out loud and explain their answers.

C Complete the statements ...

Suggested teaching time: 5–10 minutes
Your actual teaching time: _____

- Refer students to the Grammar box on page 78 to review passive forms of gerunds and infinitives.
- Model the first item with the class. Ask *Does* recall *need a gerund or an infinitive?* (a gerund) *What's the passive gerund of* send? (being sent) Then call on a student to read the complete sentence out loud. (Note: *having been sent* is also correct in this statement. This is covered in the Grammar Booster for this unit.)
- Have students write their sentences individually and then compare them with a partner.
- To review as a class, have students read the sentences out loud.

D On a separate sheet of paper ...

Suggested teaching time: 5 minutes
Your actual teaching time: _____

- After students answer the questions individually, have them share their answers with a partner. Encourage students to ask follow-up questions to find out a bit more about each of their partner's answers.
- To review as a class, have several volunteers share their answers with the class.

 You may wish to use the Video Program and activity worksheets for Unit 7 at this point.

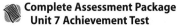 **Complete Assessment Package**
Unit 7 Achievement Test

SUMMIT WEBSITE
For Unit 7 online activities, visit the
Summit Companion Website at
www.longman.com/summit.

A 🎧 **Listening Comprehension.** Listen to the conversations about prices. Then read the statements and listen again. Circle the phrase that best completes each statement, according to what the people say.

1. **a.** The woman thinks the price of the first vase is (a bit steep / (a real bargain)).
      The man thinks it's (a steal / (a rip-off)).
   b. The woman thinks the second vase is (a steal / (a good deal)).
      The man thinks it's (a rip-off / (no bargain)).

2. **a.** The woman thinks the exercise bike from Freeman's was (a great offer / (a rip-off)).
      The man thinks it was (no bargain / (a steal)).
   b. The woman thinks the price of the bike from Mason's is (a bit steep / (a great deal)).
      The man thinks it's ((a better offer) / no deal).

3. **a.** The man thinks the price of the necklace is ((a bit steep) / no deal).
      The woman thinks it's (pretty steep / (a bargain)).
   b. The man thinks the earrings are ((a good deal) / a rip-off).
      The woman thinks they're (a great deal / (no bargain)).

B Complete each statement with your *own* ideas.

Example: *Watching old Charlie Chaplin movies always* cracks me up.

1. _____ cracks me up.
2. _____ blows me away.
3. _____ chokes me up.
4. _____ gets on my nerves.

C Complete the statements with passive forms of gerunds or infinitives.

1. I don't recall _____being sent_____ any information.
      (send)
2. They want _____to be given_____ more time for the project.
      (give)
3. She arranged _____to be taken_____ to the airport.
      (take)
4. I was disappointed _____to be told_____ the news.
      (tell)
5. He risked _____being fired_____ from his job.
      (fire)
6. We were delighted _____to be invited_____ to the wedding.
      (invite)

D On a separate sheet of paper, answer the questions in your *own* way.

1. What kinds of things do you like to splurge on?
2. Have you ever gone a little overboard buying something? Explain.
3. What can't you resist the temptation to do? Why?

UNIT 8

Family Trends

A **Topic Preview.** Look at the two cartoons about families. Then answer the questions with a partner.

"Because this family isn't ready to hold democratic elections—that's why!"

1. Who do you think was speaking before the father spoke? What do you think was said?

2. Is your family a "democracy"? How do decisions get made?

3. What didn't the father have when he was young that the son has now? Do you think the father has a good point, or is he being ridiculous?

4. In your family, is there a "generation gap" between older and younger family members? Explain.

"You have it easy. When I was your age, I had to walk all the way across the room to change the channel."

B **Discussion.** Do you think the cartoons are funny? Do you think they portray typical families? Why or why not?

Family Trends

A Topic Preview

Suggested teaching time:	10–15 minutes
Your actual teaching time:	_____

- Write the unit title on the board. Elicit from the class that a trend is a general tendency in the way a situation is changing or developing.

- To introduce the topic of family trends, have students spend a few moments looking at the cartoons and reading their captions.

- Point to the first cartoon and ask *Who are the people in this cartoon?* (a family: the father, the mother, and their three children)

- Read items 1 and 2 out loud. Before students discuss the questions in pairs, elicit from the class what is meant by a family that is a *democracy*. (Possible responses: a family where everyone can express their opinions; a family where everyone's likes are respected; a family where people are free to choose what to do; a family where decisions are made as a group)

- To review, have various students share their answers. (Possible responses: 1. one of the kids; He might have said "Why do *you* get to make all decisions?" 2. Answers will vary.)

- Point to the second cartoon and ask *Who are the people in this cartoon?* (a father and son)

- Read items 3 and 4 out loud. Before students discuss the questions in pairs, elicit the meaning of *generation gap*. (the difference in opinions and behavior between people of different generations) If necessary, clarify that a generation is a group of people of about the same age.

- Brainstorm ideas for topics that different generations in a family might have conflicting views on. (Possible responses: fashion, music, movies)

- Review as a class. Have volunteers share their responses. (Possible responses: 3. a remote control; The father has a point because modern appliances make life much more comfortable than it was in the past. / The father is being ridiculous because walking to the TV to change the channel isn't very difficult. 4. Answers will vary.)

Language note: If you tell someone "You have it easy," you mean things are so easy for that person.

B Discussion

Suggested teaching time:	5–10 minutes
Your actual teaching time:	_____

- Have a student read the questions out loud. Then have students discuss the answers in small groups.

- Circulate to encourage students to explain their answers.

- Review as a class. Have volunteers share their opinions. If students think the cartoons show typical families, ask them to support their answers by giving examples of decisions that are not usually made *democratically* in a family and examples of problems that are typically caused by generation gaps.

C 🎧 Sound Bites
(CD 3, Track 14)

Suggested teaching time: 5 minutes
Your actual teaching time: _____

- Point to the photo. Ask *What do you think the relationship is between these two people?* (Possible responses: husband and wife; girlfriend and boyfriend; brother and sister) *Why do you think this photo is ripped?* (Possible responses: They broke up; They got divorced; They had a fight.)

- Have students read and listen to the conversation. Note: Bettina has a German accent.

- To check comprehension, ask:
    What happened to Sam and Margaret? (They ended their relationship, but then got back together.)
    What's the problem in Bettina's family? (Her son, Eric, is behaving badly in school.)
    What has Bettina done to try to solve the problem? (She's told Eric he's grounded until his behavior improves.)
    What does Teresa think about this? (It's a good idea.)

Language note: Students may need help with the following words or expressions: *ground a child* (stop a child from doing the things he/she enjoys as a punishment for behaving badly); *a smart move* (a good or wise decision); *be out of touch* (not to have recent information about someone or something).

D In Other Words

Suggested teaching time: 5 minutes
Your actual teaching time: _____

- Have students underline or highlight the related expressions in the conversation.

- Point out that some expressions have similar meanings.

- In pairs, have students figure out the meanings of the expressions. Review as a class.

Language note: You can *split up* and *get back together* with someone with whom you have a romantic relationship. You can *have a falling out* and *patch things up* with someone with whom you have a romantic relationship or a friend, relative, or colleague.

Option: Draw the following diagram (without the answers) on the board:

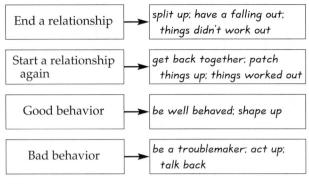

End a relationship	→	*split up; have a falling out; things didn't work out*
Start a relationship again	→	*get back together; patch things up; things worked out*
Good behavior	→	*be well behaved; shape up*
Bad behavior	→	*be a troublemaker; act up; talk back*

🔵 Graphic Organizers

In pairs, have students use the expressions from Exercise D to complete the diagram with words that are related to the themes on the left. Review as a class. **[+5 minutes]**

E Discussion

Suggested teaching time: 10 minutes
Your actual teaching time: _____

- Form small groups. Read the questions out loud. Have students discuss the answers.

- Review answers as a class. Have a student who thinks grounding Eric is a smart move support his/her view. Have students with an opposing view say what they think Eric's mother should do instead. (Possible responses: try to find out what is causing the problem; seek professional help)

STARTING **POINT**

Suggested teaching time: 10–15 minutes
Your actual teaching time: _____

Pair Work

- Read the topics out loud. Elicit or explain that a difference of opinion is a disagreement about something.

- To model the activity, tell the class about one of your own experiences. Encourage students to ask follow-up questions to get more information.

- In pairs, have students tell their partners about their experiences. Circulate to encourage follow-up questions.

- To review, have a few volunteers share their experiences with the class.

EXTRAS (optional)
Workbook: Exercises 1–2

C 🎧 **Sound Bites.** Read and listen to a conversation about relationships.

Sam

Margaret

TERESA: Did you hear that Sam and Margaret got back together?
BETTINA: Wow! I didn't even know they'd split up! It shows you how CN out of touch I am.
TERESA: Well, they had this major falling out about two months ago, and they separated. But it looks like they've patched things up.
BETTINA: Good. They're a nice couple. I hope things work out for them.
TERESA: Me too. So, how's *your* family?
BETTINA: Not bad, but we've been having some trouble with our son.
TERESA: Really? What kind of trouble?
BETTINA: Well, he's been acting up in school. You know, talking back to his teachers, not doing his homework.
TERESA: Eric? I can't believe it! He's always been so well-behaved!
BETTINA: Well, I told him he's grounded until he shapes up. No movies, no games, no trips to the mall.
TERESA: Smart move. Eric's a good kid, but you don't want him to turn into a troublemaker.

CN **Corpus Notes:** *Even* most frequently occurs in negative statements or questions. For example, *I didn't even know…*, and *Did he even know…?*

D **In Other Words.** Read the conversation again. With a partner, use the context of the conversation to figure out what each of the expressions means. (See below.)

1. They **got back together**.
2. They **split up**.
3. They **had a falling out**.
4. They **patched things up**.
5. Things **didn't work out**.

6. My kids have been **acting up**.
7. Don't **talk back**!
8. Your son is so **well-behaved**.
9. He'd better **shape up**!
10. That kid is such **a troublemaker**.

E **Discussion.** Do you think grounding Eric is a smart move? Why or why not? In your opinion, what's the best way to handle or discipline a teenager who has been acting up?

STARTING **POINT**

Pair Work. Choose one of the topics. Tell your partner about a time you …

had a difference of opinion with someone from another generation.

had a falling out with a friend, a family member, or a colleague.

helped patch things up for someone else.

Answers for Exercise D will vary, but may include:
1. reconciled; made up
2. are no longer together
3. had a serious argument
4. fixed their problem(s)
5. weren't able to be fixed
6. behaving badly; causing problems

7. say something disrespectful (to an adult)
8. good-natured; willing to do what he (or she) is told
9. learn to behave
10. person who deliberately causes problems

1 *Describe family trends*

A ⌖ GRAMMAR **SNAPSHOT.** Read the information in the brochure and notice the use of comparatives.

Falling Birthrates

Current trends show the size of families is changing, impacting societies worldwide. Women are marrying later, and couples are waiting longer to have children. And **the longer** couples wait to have children, **the fewer** children they have.

Two key factors that impact family size are the education and the employment of women. Studies show that **the more** education women get, **the smaller** families they have. Moreover, **the longer** women stay in school, **the better** their opportunities for employment. Working women are less likely to marry young and have large families.

In addition to the falling birthrate, there is a rising life expectancy. With people living **longer and longer**, families are going to have to face the challenges posed by an aging population. **The longer** people live, **the more** care they require. Traditionally, children have cared for their elderly parents at home. However, **the more** the birthrate falls, **the harder** the future may be for the elderly. With fewer children, families may find it **more and more** difficult to care for their older members.

Source: United Nations Statistics Division

B **Discussion.** Answers will vary, but may include:

1. According to the brochure, what factors explain why more couples are having fewer children?
   Women are marrying later and couples are waiting longer to have children. Women are working more.
2. Why do you think populations are living longer? What problems does a larger elderly population pose?

C **Grammar. Repeated comparatives and double comparatives**

Repeated comparatives are used to describe actions and things that are increasing or decreasing.
   The birthrate is getting **lower and lower**.
   By the end of the twentieth century, couples were waiting **longer and longer** to marry.
   More and more people are marrying later.
   Fewer and fewer children are leaving school.
   It's becoming **more and more** difficult.

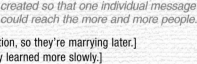

CN **Corpus Notes:** Intermediate and advanced learners frequently make the error of using a definite article with repeated comparatives. For example, *They were created so that one individual message could reach the more and more people.*

Double comparatives are used to describe a cause-and-effect process.
   The more education women get, **the later** they marry. [Women are getting more education, so they're marrying later.]
   The less children studied, **the more slowly** they learned. [Children studied less, so they learned more slowly.]

NOTE: When <u>be</u> is used in double comparatives, it is sometimes omitted.
   The better the quality of health care (is), **the higher** the life expectancy (is).

BE CAREFUL! Don't use continuous verb forms in double comparatives.
   The longer couples **wait** to have children, the fewer children they **have**.
   NOT The longer couples ~~are waiting~~ to have children, the fewer ~~they're having~~.

Grammar Booster

PAGE G13
For more …

1 *Describe family trends*

A 🎧 GRAMMAR **SNAPSHOT**
(CD 3, Track 15)

Suggested teaching time:	5–10 minutes
Your actual teaching time:	_____

- Have a volunteer read the title of the article out loud. Then have students look at the photo. Ask *What does falling birthrates mean?* (Fewer babies are being born.) *What reasons do you think the article will give for the decline in birthrates?*

- Have students read and listen to the brochure and notice the use of comparatives.

- To check comprehension, ask:
  What reasons does the brochure give for falling birthrates? (People are marrying later and waiting longer to have kids.)
  How does education and employment affect family size? (The more schooling women get, the better opportunities they have for employment. Working women marry later and have smaller families.)
  What age group is increasing? (the elderly)
  What challenges does this pose? (With fewer children, there are fewer family members to take care of the elderly.)

Language note: The *birthrate* is the number of people who are born for every 1,000 people in a particular year in a particular place. *Life expectancy* is the length of time that a person is expected to live. *Elderly* is the polite way to refer to people who are old. *Old* is used in talking about the age of someone or something. For example, *How old is your son?*

Culture note: The stork is a type of bird that has traditionally been associated with childbirth in western folk tales. In the tales, the stork delivers newborn babies to their mothers.

B Discussion

Suggested teaching time:	5 minutes
Your actual teaching time:	_____

- Form pairs or small groups. Read the questions out loud and have students discuss the answers. Circulate to offer help as needed.

- Review as a class.

C Grammar

Suggested teaching time:	10–15 minutes
Your actual teaching time:	_____

- On the board, write:
  1. *People are living longer.*
  2. *People are living longer and longer.*

Have pairs discuss the difference in meaning between sentences 1 and 2. Review as a class. (The first sentence indicates that people are living longer than in the past. The second sentence indicates that people are living longer than in the past and that they will continue to live longer.)

- Have volunteers read the explanation for repeated comparatives and the examples out loud.

- To focus on the form of the repeated comparative, write on the board:
  They are offering <u>better and better</u> jobs.
  People are marrying <u>later and later</u>.

Point out that *better* is an adjective in the first example because it modifies the noun *jobs*, and *later* is an adverb in the second example because it modifies the verb *marry*.

- To focus on the form of the double comparative, write on the board:
  <u>The more</u> women work, <u>the fewer</u> children they have.

To reinforce the functions of adjectives and adverbs, clarify that, in the example, *more* is a comparative adverb because it modifies the verb *work*, and *fewer* is a comparative adjective because it modifies the noun *children*.

- Point out that the comma before the second comparative is necessary.

- Have a volunteer read the explanation for double comparatives and the examples out loud.

- To check comprehension of the use of the double comparative, write on the board:
  The longer people live, the more care they need.

- Have pairs identify the cause and the effect in the example. (**Cause:** People live longer. **Effect:** They need more care.)

- Read the Note out loud. On the board, write:
  If your income is higher, your standard of living is also higher.

Have students restate the sentence on the board using a double comparative and omitting *be*. (The higher your income, the higher your standard of living.)

- Read the Be Careful! note out loud. Explain that the present continuous in not used with double comparatives because double comparatives state facts, not ongoing actions. On the board, write:
  Women are getting better jobs because they are staying in school longer.

Have students restate the sentence on the board using a double comparative. (The longer women stay in school, the better jobs they get.)

- Have students locate the comparatives in the Grammar Snapshot brochure.

 Grammar Self-Checks

T88

D Complete each statement . . .

Suggested teaching time:	5 minutes
Your actual teaching time:	_____

• Model the first item with the class. Have a volunteer read the completed statement out loud.

• Tell students to pay attention to meaning to complete each statement logically.

• Have students complete the exercise individually and then compare answers with a partner. Review as a class.

E 🎧 Listening Comprehension
(CD 3, Track 16)

Suggested teaching time:	10 minutes
Your actual teaching time:	_____

• First listening: On the board, write the following topics:

> Education
> Life expectancy
> Marriage age
> Health care
> Dating time

• Have students close their books. Say *Each conversation is about the relationship between two of the topics on the board. Listen and identify the two topics for each conversation.* Point out that one of the topics will be used twice. Review as a class. (1. education and health care; 2. dating time and marriage; 3. education and life expectancy)

• Second listening: Have students listen and complete the exercise.

• Review as a class.

AUDIOSCRIPT

For audioscript, see page AS10.

GRAMMAR **EXCHANGE**

Suggested teaching time:	10–15 minutes
Your actual teaching time:	_____

Pair Work

• Have volunteers read the directions, the items in the Ideas box, and the model out loud.

• Have pairs discuss each topic in the box. Remind them to use repeated comparatives.

• Circulate to offer help as needed with forming repeated comparatives.

Option: In pairs, have students write one sentence using repeated comparatives for each of the topics in the Ideas box. [+5–10 minutes]

Writing

• Review the model and have students identify the repeated comparative and the double comparative.

• Point out how the model relates family size and standard of living.

• Have students write a brief paragraph relating some of the ideas they previously discussed.

Option: Peer review. In pairs, have students review each other's work. Circulate to offer help as needed. [+5–10 minutes]

Discussion

• Form small groups. Read the directions out loud.

• Have students read the model to themselves. Ask *What is the trend?* (People are having fewer children.)

• Have students discuss different trends and their impacts. Refer students to the Ideas box to make sure they discuss different topics. Circulate to offer help as needed.

• To review as a class, call on a student to share a trend that was discussed in his/her group and describe its possible impact. Encourage students who discussed the same trend to say if they think it will have the same impact or a different impact, and support their views. Then call on other students to describe other trends and follow the same procedure.

Project: Have students research a current trend of their choice—for example, how people are getting to work, how people are working from home, the kind of vacations people are taking, the type of car that people prefer, etc. Ask them to write a paragraph explaining the trend using repeated comparatives and double comparatives. Have students share their findings with the class by reading their paragraphs out loud.

EXTRAS (optional)
Grammar Booster
Workbook: Exercises 3–5

D Complete each statement logically, using double comparatives.

1. The older people are when they marry, the fewer children they have.
   (old) (few)
2. The higher the life expectancy, the larger the elderly population is.
   (high) (large)
3. The harder people work, the more successful they are.
   (hard) (successful)
4. The better the quality of health care is, the lower the death rate.
   (good) (low)
5. The less developed the country is, the lower the life expectancy.
   (developed) (low)
6. The younger women are when they have children, the less likely they are to get a higher education.
   (young) (likely)

E 🎧 **Listening Comprehension.** Listen to three people talking about trends in marriage and family life. Then listen again and complete each statement, according to what the speaker implies, using double comparatives.

1. The more education mothers get, the better medical care they receive.
2. The longer couples date, the later they marry.
3. The longer children stay in school, the longer their life expectancy.

GRAMMAR **EXCHANGE** • *Now describe family trends.*

Pair Work. Use repeated comparatives to discuss the ways families are changing in your country.

> "People are getting married later and later."

IDEAS

- birthrate
- life expectancy
- age at marriage
- health
- education
- income
- employment opportunities
- generational differences

Writing. On a separate sheet of paper, write about the impact of the changes you've discussed. Use repeated comparatives and double comparatives.

> In the last few decades, family size has declined. Fewer and fewer people are having big families, so their standard of living is higher. The higher the standard of living is, the healthier the population.

Discussion. In small groups, compare the trends you've identified. How will these changes impact families in the future?

> "It seems like more and more people are having fewer children. This could be a problem later because …."

Discuss parent–teen issues

A 🎧 CONVERSATION **SNAPSHOT**

A: What do you think parents should do if their teenage kids start smoking?

B: Well, I hate to say it, but there's not much they can do.

A: Why's that?

B: Well, teenagers are out of the house most of the day, so parents can't control everything they do.

A: I suppose. But they can ground them if they don't shape up.

🎧 **Examples of bad behavior**
- acting up at school CN1
- staying out late without permission
- being rude and disrespectful
- becoming a troublemaker

🎧 **Rhythm and intonation practice**

CN1 **Corpus Notes:** This meaning of the phrasal verb *act up* is almost exclusively used when talking about a child's behavior, but rarely when talking about an adult.

B 🎧 **Vocabulary. Describing parent and teen behavior.** Listen and practice.

Parents can sometimes be . . . CN2

(too) strict

They set a lot of restrictions and expect kids to obey rules.

(too) lenient

They let their kids have or do anything they want.

overprotective

They worry too much about their kids.

Teenagers can sometimes be . . .

rebellious

They refuse to follow rules and do the opposite of what is expected of them.

spoiled

They expect to have or do whatever they want.

disrespectful

They are rude to adults and think what adults say is not important.

C Correct the adjective in each of the following statements.

1. Parents who always allow their teenage children to stay out late are ~~overprotective~~. *(too) lenient*

2. Teenagers who demand that their parents buy everything they ask for are ~~rebellious~~. *spoiled*

3. When parents never let their children do things because they are afraid that their children will get sick or hurt, they are being ~~strict~~. *overprotective*

4. When a teen gets a tattoo against a parent's wishes, we say that he or she is ~~disrespectful~~. *rebellious*

CN2 **Corpus Notes:** While *strict* and *lenient* are also often used to describe things such as laws, rules, or bosses, *overprotective* is almost always used to describe parents.

2 Discuss parent–teen issues

A ∩ CONVERSATION **SNAPSHOT**
(CD 3, Tracks 17, 19)

Suggested teaching time:	5–10 minutes
Your actual teaching time:	_____

- Read the lesson title out loud. Ask *What does parent–teen issues mean?* (Possible response: conflicts or problems between parents and their teenagers / children)

- As a class, brainstorm some possible conflicts between parents and teens on the board. (Possible responses: curfews, tattoos, grades)

- Point to the photo. Ask *What's happening in the picture? Where are the people? What do you think the women are talking about?*

- After students read and listen, check comprehension. Ask:
    What are the women discussing? (what parents should do if their kids start smoking)
    Do they have similar views? (no)
    What's the first woman's view? (She thinks kids can be grounded if they don't shape up.)
    What's the other woman's view? (There isn't much parents can do.)

- Have students read and listen to the examples of bad behavior. If necessary, clarify the meaning of the expressions. For example, *A boy who acts up at school may not do his homework and may talk back to his teachers.*

- Brainstorm other examples of bad behavior. (Possible responses: dressing inappropriately; getting bad grades; skipping school)

Option: Write the following expressions on the board: *I hate to say it, but . . . ; Why's that?; I suppose; ground (a child); shape up; act up.* Then have students find and underline them in the Conversation Snapshot. In pairs, have students suggest different ways of saying each expression. Encourage students to use context clues to work out the meanings. Have pairs read the conversation out loud, substituting the alternate wording for the underlined expressions. **[+10 minutes]**

∩ Rhythm and intonation practice
(CD 3, Track 18)

Suggested teaching time:	5 minutes
Your actual teaching time:	_____

- Have students repeat chorally. Make sure they:

  ○ use falling intonation for *What do you think parents should do if their teenaged kids start smoking?* and *Why's that?*

  ○ use emphatic stress for <u>can</u> in *. . . there's not much they can do* and *But they can ground them.*

  ○ pause slightly after *I hate to say it* and *I suppose.*

  ○ stress <u>up</u> in *shape up.*

○ use the following stress pattern:

STRESS PATTERN

A: What do you think parents should do if their teenage kids start smoking?

B: Well, I hate to say it, but there's not much they can do.

A: Why's that?

B: Well, teenagers are out of the house most of the day, so parents can't control everything they do.

A: I suppose. But they can ground them if they don't shape up.

B ∩ Vocabulary
(CD 3, Track 20)

Suggested teaching time:	5 minutes
Your actual teaching time:	_____

- Before students listen and practice, have them look at the pictures and read the captions.

- Have students listen to the words and study the explanations. Then have students listen and repeat the words chorally.

Language note: To describe a temporary quality, *spoiled* is often used with the verb *act*. For example, *He's acting spoiled.*

Option: In small groups, have students share specific examples of occasions when they were disrespectful or rebellious or acted spoiled as a child. Have them also use specific examples to explain why their parents were / weren't strict, lenient, or overprotective. To finish the activity, have volunteers share some of their stories with the class. **[+5 minutes]**

C Correct the adjective . . .

Suggested teaching time:	5 minutes
Your actual teaching time:	_____

- Have students complete the exercise individually.

- Then have students compare answers with a partner and review as a class.

 Vocabulary-Building Strategies

D 🎧 **Listening Comprehension**
(CD 3, Track 21)

Suggested teaching time: 10 minutes
Your actual teaching time: _____

• Explain that students will hear six conversations about parent and teen behavior.

• First listening: Have students listen to the conversations.

• Have volunteers read items 1–6 out loud.

• Second listening: With books open, have students listen again and determine which adjective from the vocabulary best completes each statement. Pause after each conversation to allow students time to write.

Option: To check comprehension, ask questions about each conversation. For example:

1. *Why does the woman think the man is strict?* (because he says that when kids break the rules, they should be punished immediately)

2. *Why does the woman think Jason is acting spoiled?* (because he already has a good computer, and he wants his parents to buy him a new one)

3. *Why does the man think the woman is lenient?* (because she says kids should be allowed to make their own decisions, and that it's not necessary to watch over them all the time)

4. *Why does the father think his daughter is being disrespectful?* (because she's talking back to him)

5. *Why does the man think the woman is overprotective?* (because a nineteen-year-old teenager is old enough to learn to drive)

6. *Why does the girl think the boy is being rebellious?* (because he is allowed to stay out until 11:00 but he intends to stay out later)

[+5 minutes]

AUDIOSCRIPT

For audioscript, see page AS10.

E **Discussion**

Suggested teaching time: 5–10 minutes
Your actual teaching time: _____

• Have a volunteer read the questions out loud. Before students discuss, have them identify the people in the conversations.

• In small groups, have students say who they identify with and why, and/or give concrete examples of people they know. Circulate to offer help as needed.

• Review as a class. Have a few volunteers share their responses.

CONVERSATION **STARTER**

Suggested teaching time: 10–15 minutes
Your actual teaching time: _____

Pair Work

• Have students compare and discuss their ratings and additional ideas with a partner and circle their partner's rating for each item. Circulate to remind students to give specific examples to support their opinions.

• Ask pairs if they had similar or different views. Call on students to choose an idea from the survey and express their views on it. Encourage other students in the class to agree or disagree.

Role Play

• Refer students to the Conversation Snapshot on page 90 to review discussing parent–teen issues.

• Choose a more confident student and role-play the conversation.

• Have pairs role-play their own conversations. Encourage students to use the vocabulary they've learned so far.

• Make sure each student plays both roles.

• As students interact, circulate to offer help as needed. Encourage students to use the correct intonation in questions.

Discussion

• Read the questions out loud. Have students discuss the answers in small groups. Encourage students to use the vocabulary they've learned so far. Circulate to offer help as needed.

• On the board, draw a two-column chart with the heads *Advice for parents* and *Advice for teenagers*. Call on volunteers to share their most important pieces of advice for parents and teenagers. (Possible responses: Listen to your kids—step into their shoes and try to understand them; Listen to your parents—they are older and wiser.)

 Conversation Prompts

EXTRAS (optional)

Workbook: Exercises 6–8

5. Parents who make their teenage children clean their rooms every day are ~~lenient~~. *(too) strict*

6. Teens who don't listen to adults and often talk back are ~~spoiled~~. *disrespectful*

D 🎧 **Listening Comprehension.** Listen to the conversations about parent and teen behavior. Then listen again and determine which adjective from the vocabulary best completes each statement.

1. She thinks he's _____(too) strict_____ .

2. She thinks he's acting _____spoiled_____ .

3. He thinks she's _____(too) lenient_____ .

4. He's angry because she's being _____disrespectful_____ .

5. He thinks she's _____overprotective_____ .

6. She criticizes him for being _____rebellious_____ .

E **Discussion.** Can you identify with any of the people in the listening? Are any of the speakers like anyone you know? Explain.

CONVERSATION **STARTER** • *Now discuss parent–teen issues.*

Pair Work. Discuss and complete the survey. Compare your ideas. Give specific examples to support your answers.

Circle the rating that most closely expresses your opinion.				
1 = completely agree **2** = somewhat agree, depending on the circumstances **3** = completely disagree				

		Me	My partner
PARENTS	Parents should let kids make their own mistakes. Being overprotective with children makes kids less responsible.	1 2 3	1 2 3
	It's OK to give in to kids' demands sometimes in order to "keep the peace."	1 2 3	1 2 3
	Parents should include their children in family decision-making. After all, kids' opinions are important, too.	1 2 3	1 2 3
	It's a good idea for parents to use physical punishment to discipline their children. If parents aren't strict, their kids will become troublemakers.	1 2 3	1 2 3
	Your own idea:		1 2 3

		Me	My partner
TEENS	Teenagers don't always have to obey their parents. Sometimes it's OK to say "no."	1 2 3	1 2 3
	Teenagers shouldn't have to help around the house. They already have enough to do with their schoolwork.	1 2 3	1 2 3
	Teenagers are mature enough to make their own decisions. They shouldn't have to ask permission for everything.	1 2 3	1 2 3
	Teenagers have a right to privacy. They shouldn't have to tell their parents about everything they do.	1 2 3	1 2 3
	Your own idea:		1 2 3

Role Play. Role-play a conversation in which you discuss parent or teen behavior. Use the Conversation Snapshot on page 90 as a guide. Start like this:

"What do you think parents should do if their teenage kids …?"   OR   "What do you think kids should do if their parents …?"

Discussion. If you could give parents one piece of advice, what would it be? If you could give teenagers one piece of advice, what would it be?

3 Compare generations

A 🎧 Word Skills. Transforming verbs and adjectives into nouns

common noun endings	nouns		common noun endings	nouns	
-ation **-tion** **-ssion**	expect → explain → frustrate → permit →	expectation explanation frustration permission	**-ness**	fair → rebellious → selfish → strict →	fairness rebelliousness selfishness strictness
-ment	develop → involve →	development involvement	**-ity**	generous → mature → mobile → secure →	generosity maturity mobility security
-y	courteous → difficult →	courtesy difficulty			
-ility	responsible → reliable → capable → dependable →	responsibility reliability capability dependability	**-ance** **-ence**	important → independent → lenient → obedient →	importance independence lenience obedience

NOTE: Sometimes internal spelling changes occur when a noun ending is added to a verb or an adjective.

Pronunciation Booster

PAGE P7
Stress placement

B
Circle all the words that are nouns. Check in a dictionary if you are not sure about the meaning of a word.

1. (dependency)   depend   (dependence)   (dependent)
2. impatient   (impatience)   impatiently
3. (confidence)   confident   confide   confidently
4. unfair   (unfairness)   unfairly
5. consider   (consideration)   considerate   considerately
6. (closeness)   close   closely
7. different   (difference)   differentiate   (differentiation)
8. happily   happy   (happiness)
9. (attraction)   attract   attractive   (attractiveness)

Vilnius, the capital of Lithuania

C 🎧 Listening Comprehension.
Listen to Part 1 of a man's description of the generation gap in his family. Then answer the questions.

1. In terms of family size, how did Rimas grow up differently from his parents? Rimas lived with his immediate, not extended, family.

2. Why does Rimas's father think teenagers nowadays have more problems than when he was growing up? There's not as much parental involvement in teenagers' lives.

D 🎧 Listen to Part 1 again. Then complete each statement.

1. Rimas grew up in _____Vilnius_____, but his parents grew up in _a small village in the east of Lithuania_.

2. Rimas's extended family includes _____seven_____ aunts and uncles on his mother's side.

3. When Rimas's mother was growing up, every evening she ate dinner _(See below.)_. However, when Rimas and his sister were kids, they sometimes had to eat _by themselves_.
with her brothers and sisters, parents, and grandparents

Rimas Vilkas

3 *Compare generations*

A 🎧 Word Skills
(CD 3, Track 22)

Suggested teaching time:	10 minutes
Your actual teaching time:	_____

- Have students close their books. To show that spelling changes are sometimes necessary, write *responsible* on the board. Elicit the part of speech from the class. (adjective) Ask *What is the noun form of* responsible? Erase *-le*, and add the ending *-ility*. You may want to do this with other words such as *generous, mature,* and *important.*

- Have students listen to the words and study the transformations. Then have students listen and repeat the words chorally.

- Point out that the charts contain examples of both verbs and adjectives that can be transformed into nouns. Have students identify the verbs and the adjectives. (There are verbs in the first two rows of the first chart. The remaining rows contain adjectives.)

- In pairs, have students find and underline all the words that underwent spelling changes when they were transformed into nouns. Review as a class. (explanation, frustration, permission, courtesy, responsibility, reliability, capability, dependability, generosity, maturity, mobility, security, importance, independence, lenience, obedience)

- Have students look up words they do not know in the dictionary. Then have students share the words and definitions with the class.

Language note: Point out that most words do not follow rules for the formation of nouns; they just have to be learned.

B Circle all the words . . .

Suggested teaching time:	5 minutes
Your actual teaching time:	_____

- Point out that there can be more than one noun for each item.
- Model the first item with the class. Have a volunteer explain the answer. (The nouns *dependency* and *dependence* end in common endings for nouns: *-y* and *-ence. Dependent* is both a noun and an adjective.)
- Have students compare answers with a partner and use a dictionary to confirm their answers and check meanings. Circulate to provide help as needed.

🌐 Vocabulary-Building Strategies

C 🎧 Listening Comprehension
(CD 3, Track 23)

Suggested teaching time:	5–10 minutes
Your actual teaching time:	_____

- Pre-listening: Direct students' attention to the photo of Vilnius, the capital of Lithuania. Elicit from the class what they know about Lithuania. (Lithuania is in Eastern Europe, near Poland. It was occupied by the Soviet Union for many years.) If there is a world map in the classroom, have a volunteer point out the country and its capital.

- Have a volunteer read the questions out loud.

- Then have students listen and take notes of the answers to the questions. Review as a class.

Language note: Your immediate family consists of your parents, children, brothers, and sisters. Your extended family includes your grandparents, aunts, uncles and cousins.

AUDIOSCRIPT

For audioscript, see page AS11.

D 🎧 Listen to Part 1 again . . .
(CD 3, Track 24)

Suggested teaching time:	5 minutes
Your actual teaching time:	_____

- Have students read the statements to themselves.
- Then have students listen and complete the statements individually.
- Review as a class. Call on students to read the completed statements out loud.

🌐 Listening Strategies

Option: Photocopy and distribute this exercise, or write on the board:

rebellious	involve	expect	close	disobedient

When Rimas's parents were young . . .

1. it was the common _____ that three generations would live together.
2. there was more parental _____ in teenagers' lives.
3. there was more _____ between parents and teenagers.
4. _____ and _____ were highly unusual behaviors in teenagers.

Have students transform the words in the box into nouns to complete the statements. To confirm their answers, have students listen to Part 1 again. Have students use Exercises A and B to check spelling. (1. expectation, 2. involvement, 3. closeness, 4. rebelliousness / disobedience) [+5–10 minutes]

E 🎧 Now listen to Part 2 ...
(CD 3, Track 25)

Suggested teaching time: 5–10 minutes
Your actual teaching time: _____

- First listening: Have students listen and complete the chart in note form.
- Then have students compare and discuss answers with a partner.
- Second listening: Have students listen to confirm their answers.
- Review as a class. Have students use their notes to describe the differences in each field. (Possible response: Rimas's parents' generation didn't have many career choices. Rimas's generation had more opportunities because the country was not part of the Soviet Union anymore.)

AUDIOSCRIPT

For audioscript, see page AS11.

F Discussion

Suggested teaching time: 5 minutes
Your actual teaching time: _____

- To prepare for discussion, have students spend a few moments reading the questions and thinking about their answers.
- Form small groups and have students discuss the questions.
- Review as a class. Have volunteers share their responses. Encourage students to ask questions or add to the discussion.

DISCUSSION **BUILDER**

Suggested teaching time: 10–15 minutes
Your actual teaching time: _____

Step 1. Pair Work.
- Have students write their ideas on their notepads individually.
- In pairs, have students discuss the differences between their generation and their parents' generation.

Step 2. Discussion.
- Have students read the discussion questions out loud.
- Form small groups to discuss the questions. Have groups write a list of ideas describing the next generation.
- Review as a class. Have volunteers share their responses with the class. Encourage the class to comment on the responses and share their own ideas about it.

EXTRAS (optional)

Pronunciation Booster
Workbook: Exercises 9–11

E 🎧 Now listen to Part 2. Then listen again and complete the chart by describing the differences between the two generations. Compare your chart with a partner's.

How are they different?		
	Rimas's parents' generation	Rimas's generation
career choices	weren't many choices	several choices
mobility	no mobility	a lot of mobility
influences from other cultures	there wasn't much	there's a lot
age at marriage and childbearing	young	older
work experience	one job for entire life	several jobs
closeness of family	families were very close	families not as close

F **Discussion.**
Answers will vary, but may include:
1. Why do Rimas's parents worry about him and the future? Why do you think parents always worry about their children? They worry about his security and his ability to take care of them when they get older.

2. In what ways is the Vilkas's family story similar to or different from yours?

DISCUSSION **BUILDER** • *Now compare generations.*

Step 1. Pair Work. Compare your parents' generation with your generation. Write your ideas on your notepad. Discuss them with a partner.

	My parents' generation	**My generation**
music		
style of clothes		
hairstyles / facial hair		
attitude toward elders		
family responsibility		
language (idioms, slang)		
marriage and childbearing		
values and beliefs		
other:		

Step 2. Discussion.

1. In what ways is your generation most different from your parents' generation? What do you like best or respect most about your parents' generation?

2. What contributions do you think your generation will make to the next generation? How do you think the next generation will differ from yours?

4 *Describe care for the elderly*

A **Reading Warm-up.** In previous generations, how have older family members traditionally been cared for in your country?

B 🎧 **Reading.** Read the article. What impact has China's one-child policy had on care for the elderly?
Answers will vary, but may include: There are fewer young people to care for the elderly.

Uncertain Future for China's Elderly

Due to a sharp increase in its aging population, China faces new social problems in the future, according to a recent report from the Chinese Academy of Sciences. In China today, the elderly—people aged 60 or older—make up about 11 percent of the population. However, according to United Nations statistics, by 2050 the number of elderly will increase to more than 31 percent. If this trend continues, the elderly could eventually outnumber young people—a dramatic change for China.

While lower birthrates and higher life expectancies are causing similar population shifts in many countries, this transformation is happening faster in China due to the strict one-child policy introduced in 1979. Under this policy, couples can have only one child. The policy's purpose was to stop China's burgeoning population from growing too fast. It created a generation of "only children" growing up without brothers or sisters who can share the burden of caring for elderly family members.

According to Chinese tradition, the elderly have always been honored and respected by the young; for generations, parents and grandparents have relied on their children to care for them in old age. But today an increasing number of single young adults face the difficult situation of caring for both their parents and their grandparents. This phenomenon is known as a 4-2-1 family: For every *one* child, there are *two* parents and *four* grandparents to look after. Breaking with tradition, many young adults who can afford it are beginning to transfer the responsibility of looking after their elderly relatives to private nursing homes. This change in attitude is causing some conflict and anger between generations.

The aging of China's population will have a big impact on the country's future. The less the old can depend on the young, the more they may have to depend on the government. In one attempt to deal with this problem, the government has started a national lottery to raise money for elder care. However, it may still need to create more resources to care for its graying population.

China's one-child families have had an unexpected effect on care for the elderly.

Source: Adapted from the *Beijing Times* (August 21, 2002)

C **Discussion.**
Answers will vary, but may include:
1. Describe how China's population is changing. What is causing those changes?
   As a whole, the population is getting older. This is because of China's one-child policy and higher life expectancies.
2. According to the article, what challenges are China's young people facing today?
   Each young person is responsible for caring for two parents and four grandparents.
3. How may elder care in China differ in the future from the traditions of the past?
   Nursing homes may become much more common.

94 UNIT 8

4 *Describe care for the elderly*

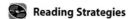

🔄 **Reading Strategies**

🔄 **Reading Speed Calculator**

🔄 **Extra Reading Comprehension Activities**

A Reading Warm-up

Suggested teaching time:	10 minutes
Your actual teaching time:	_____

• On the board, write:
> *where the elderly have lived*
> *who they have lived with*
> *who pays for their care / living expenses*
> *the advantages / disadvantages of how they have been cared for*

• Form small groups and have students discuss the Warm-up question using the prompts on the board to help them generate ideas. Then have students share their responses with the class.

B 🎧 Reading
(CD 3, Track 26)

Suggested teaching time:	10–15 minutes
Your actual teaching time:	_____

• Have students look at the two photos and read the caption. Encourage students to say as much as they can about the photos.

• Have students read the title of the newspaper article and make predictions. Ask *Why could the future of the elderly be uncertain in China?* (Possible response: because there are too many elderly people in the country)

• To check comprehension, ask:
> *What was the intent of China's one-child policy?* (to keep China's population from growing too fast)
> *What is the result of the trend of putting the elderly in nursing homes?* (There is anger and conflict between generations.)
> *What impact has the one-child policy had on the elderly?* (Because of the one-child policy, in each extended family there is only one adult to look after the elderly.)

• Draw the following chart (without the answers) on the board. To check comprehension, have students complete the chart in pairs.

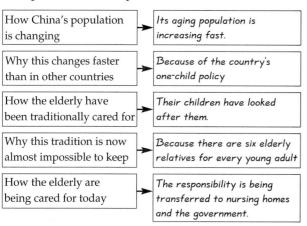

How China's population is changing	Its aging population is increasing fast.
Why this changes faster than in other countries	Because of the country's one-child policy
How the elderly have been traditionally cared for	Their children have looked after them.
Why this tradition is now almost impossible to keep	Because there are six elderly relatives for every young adult
How the elderly are being cared for today	The responsibility is being transferred to nursing homes and the government.

🔄 **Graphic Organizers**

Language note: To refer to a person aged 60 or older, say *an elderly person.* (This is more polite than *an old person.*) To refer to old people in general, say *the elderly.* Students may need help with the following words: *outnumber* (If a group outnumbers another, it is bigger in number.); *burgeoning* (A burgeoning population is increasing quickly.); *burden* (something difficult that you are responsible for).

Culture note: China was a country often hit by floods and famine. In 1979, the Chinese government introduced the one-child policy to ensure that the country would have enough food to feed its people. According to this policy, couples living in the city are allowed by law to have only one child and those living in the country are allowed up to two children.

Option: To use the reading as a listening-only activity, have students listen to the article with books closed and take notes. Follow the procedure above, making necessary changes to accommodate a listening-only task. Review as a class. **[+10–15 minutes]**

C Discussion

Suggested teaching time:	10–15 minutes
Your actual teaching time:	_____

• Form small groups, and have students discuss the questions. Encourage students to scan the article for the answers, if necessary.

• Review as a class. Call on students from different groups to answer the questions.

Option: On the board, write:
> *What do you think about China's one-child policy?*
> *What are the advantages / disadvantages of a generation of "only children"?*
> *Do you think China should reverse the one-child policy? Why / Why not?*

Form small groups, and have students use the questions on the board as a guide to express their views on the situation in China. **[+5–10 minutes]**

DISCUSSION **BUILDER**

Suggested teaching time: 15–20 minutes
Your actual teaching time: _____

 Discourse Strategies

Step 1. Pair Work.

• Have volunteers read the statements out loud.

• In pairs, have students discuss the statements and check those they think are true. Encourage students to provide a reason for their answers, for example, why the elderly are/aren't adequately cared for, how elder care has been changing, etc.

• Review as a class. Have volunteers share other statements they added to the list. Then take a poll to find out if the elderly are adequately cared for in this country.

Step 2. Pair Work.

• Have students read the case studies individually and underline the main challenges each person is facing.

• Have students think of a solution for each case study. Encourage students to think of solutions their family or friends may have found to similar problems.

• Have students discuss the challenges and possible solutions in pairs. Encourage each pair to come to a conclusion as to what the best solution for each case would be.

• Then have pairs report their solutions to the class. Encourage students to say whether or not they agree with the solutions and support their views.

Step 3. Discussion.

• Draw a two-column chart with the heads *Likely future elder care* and *Ideal future elder care* on the board. To prepare for discussion, have students add notes to the chart individually. Explain that under *Likely . . .* they should note how they think the elderly will be cared for in the future, and under *Ideal . . .* they should note how they think the elderly *should* be cared for in the future. Encourage students to use their own ideas and language from the checklist in Step 1.

• Then have students discuss their ideas in small groups.

• Have volunteers from different groups express their predictions and describe the ideal situation for elder care. Ask *Do you think you will be cared for the way you would like to be cared for?*

Step 4. Writing.

• Have students write a paragraph describing elder care.

• Encourage students to use the language from the checklist in Step 1 and their own ideas. Circulate to offer help as needed.

EXTRAS (optional)

Workbook: Exercises 12–15

Step 1. Pair Work. Discuss the statements and check those you think are true about care for the elderly in your country.

- ☐ Most elderly people are adequately cared for.
- ☐ The way the elderly are cared for has been changing.
- ☐ The elderly usually live with younger family members.
- ☐ The elderly usually live in their own homes or apartments.
- ☐ The elderly usually live in special nursing homes.
- ☐ The government makes sure the elderly have affordable care.
- ☐ Younger people accept care for elderly relatives as their responsibility.
- ☐ Older people generally prefer not to socialize with younger people.
- ☐ Other: ....

Step 2. Pair Work. Read each case study. Discuss the challenges each person is facing and recommend solutions.

Robert's parents, who live in another city, are in their eighties. They continue to have a full social life, and they still enjoy traveling with organized tours. But they are not as strong as they used to be and need help with cooking and cleaning.

Ingrid is divorced and has three young daughters. Her mother died years ago, and her seventy-five-year-old father can no longer take care of himself. He often forgets things. She worries that he might get hurt.

Nick is married and has two teenage children. His mother just turned seventy-nine and lives alone. Nick and his family live in a very small apartment with two bedrooms. He and his wife both work overtime, putting in long hours in order to make ends meet. Nick is concerned about his mother's health and well-being.

Step 3. Discussion. How do you think the elderly will be cared for by the time you are old? How would *you* like to be cared for? Describe the ideal situation for elder care. Use language from the checklist in Step 1.

Step 4. Writing. Write a description for a visitor to your country of how the elderly are cared for.

Writing: *Describe your relationship with a family member*

Avoiding comma splices and run-on sentences

Note two common errors that writers often make when joining two sentences.

Comma splice (connecting two sentences with a comma and no conjunction)
INCORRECT: My grandmother taught me how to bake, now I know how to make great cookies.

Run-on sentence (connecting sentences without using punctuation)
INCORRECT: My grandmother taught me how to bake however I never do.

To correct a comma splice or a run-on sentence, choose one of the following:

- Use a period and capitalize the following word.

  My grandmother taught me how to bake. Now I know how to make great cookies.
  My grandmother taught me how to bake. However, I never do.

- Use a semicolon.

  My grandmother taught me how to bake; now I know how to make great cookies.
  My grandmother taught me how to bake; however, I never do.

- Use a comma and a coordinating conjunction.

  My grandmother taught me how to bake, and now I know how to make great cookies.
  My grandmother taught me how to bake, but I never do.

Coordinating conjunctions			
and	for	or	yet
but	nor	so	

Answers will vary, but may include:
Everyone tells me I am a great cook; however, everything I know about baking I learned from my grandmother. I always helped my grandmother when she baked. We made cookies, cakes, pies, and breads together. I even had more fun baking than eating the food! At first I wondered how she was able to put various ingredients together without measuring cups and written recipes, but with time, I also learned the tricks. When my grandmother died, she left me all her baking and cooking equipment and many years of wonderful memories.

Step 1. Prewriting. "Freewriting" to generate ideas.

Writing quickly without stopping is one way to generate ideas. First, choose a family relationship you would like to write about. Then, write anything that comes to mind for five minutes. Write quickly and do not worry about spelling, punctuation, etc. Finally, read what you wrote. Select some of the ideas from your freewriting and organize them logically.

My grandparents
—in their seventies
—always help me
—grandfather likes to fish
—grandmother loves when I visit

Step 2. Writing. On a separate sheet of paper, write a paragraph about the relationship you chose. Include a topic sentence that expresses your main idea. Avoid comma splices and run-on sentences.

Step 3. Self-Check.

☐ Did you write any run-on sentences? Comma splices? If so, correct them.
☐ Do all the sentences support the topic sentence?
☐ Is the paragraph interesting? What could you add to make it more interesting?

Writing *Describe your relationship with a family member*

Suggested teaching time: 20–25 minutes
Your actual teaching time: _____

Avoiding comma splices and run-on sentences

• Call on students to read the explanations and examples of comma splices and run-on sentences out loud.

• Give students a few moments to study the ways to correct comma splices and run-on sentences. For the third bullet, point out the coordinating conjunctions in the box.

• On the board, write:

> His grandparents live in the country, he doesn't see
> them very often.

In pairs, have students identify the type of mistake in the sentence (comma splice) and think of ways to correct it.

• Have three volunteers explain how to correct the sentence, each in a different way. Erase the incorrect portion of the sentence (, he) and correct it on the board as students provide the answers:

> . . . live in the country. He doesn't . . .
> . . . live in the country; he doesn't . . .
> . . . live in the country, so he doesn't . . .

Error Correction

• Have students correct the paragraph individually. Remind students that there is more than one way to correct comma splices and run-on sentences.

• Then have students compare answers with a partner.

• Review as a class. Call on different students to provide different ways to correct each error.

> **Language note:** The comma is sometimes omitted when a coordinating conjunction joins two short independent clauses. For example, *I live in Bristol and my brother lives in Oxford.* The comma is often omitted when the subject is the same in both clauses. For example, *I like coffee and I like tea.*

 Extra Writing Skills Practice

Step 1. Prewriting.

• Read the explanation for freewriting and the model out loud.

• Have students choose a family relationship to write about.

• Give students five minutes to write what comes to their minds.

• When time is up, tell students to highlight or underline the ideas they like best and to number the ideas they selected to organize them logically.

• As students select and number their ideas, circulate to offer help as needed.

Step 2. Writing.

• Before students write their paragraphs, remind them that the supporting sentences should support the idea expressed in the topic sentence.

• As students write, circulate to offer help with avoiding comma splices and run-on sentences.

Step 3. Self-Check.

• Read the Self-Check questions as a class.

• Brainstorm ideas for making the paragraphs more interesting. (Possible ideas: anecdotes; happy moments together; description of what is special about the person)

• Have students circle their topic sentences and underline their supporting sentences.

• Before students submit their paragraphs for correction, have them self-check their work and make any necessary changes.

EXTRAS (optional)

Workbook: Page 81

UNIT 8 CHECKPOINT

A 🎧 Listening Comprehension
(CD 3, Track 27)

Suggested teaching time:	10–15 minutes
Your actual teaching time:	_____

• First listening: With books closed, have students listen and decide the relationship between the speakers and who / what they are talking about. Review as a class. (1. husband and wife; their son, who's been acting up in school; 2. friends; the first woman's daughter, who never comes home early; 3. friends; the girl's father, who won't let her wear makeup to school; 4. two sisters; their parents' behavior when they were young)

• Second listening: Have students listen and complete the statements.

• Then have students compare answers with a partner.

• Review as a class. After students provide the answer for each question, ask: After 1: *What is Philip spending a lot of time on?* (the Internet) After 2: *Why is Sandi staying out so late?* (because she has a driver's license) After 3: *Why is Jill becoming more rebellious?* (because she said she might get a tattoo) After 4: *Why do they appreciate their parents more?* (because they realized how smart their parents were)

AUDIOSCRIPT

For audioscript, see page AS12.

B Write the adjective . . .

Suggested teaching time:	10 minutes
Your actual teaching time:	_____

• Have students review the adjectives on page 90. Call out an adjective and have students give the definition. Keep the activity fast-paced.

• Have students compare answers with a partner and review as a class.

C Correct the part of speech . . .

Suggested teaching time:	5–10 minutes
Your actual teaching time:	_____

• To clarify the task, point out that some underlined words are correct.

• Have students compare answers with a partner and use the chart on page 92 to confirm their answers.

Option: Have pairs replace the underlined word in each sentence above with a different one of their choice. They may use the words from Exercises A and B on page 92. Review as a class. **[+10 minutes]**

 You may wish to use the Video Program and activity worksheets for Unit 8 at this point.

 Complete Assessment Package
Unit 8 Achievement Test

SUMMIT WEBSITE
For Unit 8 online activities, visit the *Summit* Companion Website at www.longman.com/summit.

A 🎧 **Listening Comprehension.** Listen to the conversations about generational issues. Then listen to each conversation again and complete each statement with the correct comparative.

1. Philip is spending _____ time on his homework.
   a. more and more   **b.** less and less

2. _____, the more her mother worries.
   a. The later Sandi stays out   **b.** The older Sandi gets

3. The stricter Jill's father gets, _____ she becomes.
   a. the more rebellious   **b.** the more spoiled

4. The older the sisters get, _____.
   a. the smarter they become   **b.** the more they appreciate their parents

B Write the adjective that best describes the behavior in each statement.

1. Mark's parents don't allow him to watch more than two hours of TV a day, but most of his friends can watch as much as they want. He feels that his parents are __(too) strict__.

2. Karen has a closet full of expensive clothes, yet she always complains about not having anything to wear. Her parents usually buy her whatever she wants. A lot of people think Karen is __spoiled__.

3. Even though she has had her driver's license for a year and a half, Marissa's parents worry about her driving at night. They say that it's too dangerous, but Marissa thinks they're just being __overprotective__.

4. When Clyde's grandfather asked him to turn down the volume on his CD player, he ignored him and continued to listen to his music. Clyde's grandfather thought this was very __disrespectful__.

5. Rodney and Carolyn believe parents don't need to be so concerned about their children. They rarely set rules for their kids. Carolyn's sister thinks this is a bad idea. She feels they're __(too) lenient__.

6. Deanna wears clothing that her parents find shocking. She also has friends that her parents don't approve of. Her mother wishes she weren't so __rebellious__.

C Correct the part of speech of any of the incorrect underlined words.

1. Teenagers were given a lot more <u>responsibility</u> when I was young.
2. I think teenagers today lack the ~~mature~~ maturity to make decisions for themselves.
3. The main reason young people are rebellious today is <u>selfishness</u>.
4. If kids today were taught about ~~courteous~~ courtesy, they would be better behaved.
5. There's no question that teenagers today demand more ~~independent~~ independence than they did fifty years ago.
6. It's important to be involved in your child's <u>development</u>.
7. Young people have a lot more ~~mobile~~ mobility than they did several generations ago.
8. It seems like there's a lot more ~~rebellious~~ rebelliousness among teenagers today.

UNIT 9

History's Mysteries

UNIT GOALS

1 Speculate about the out-of-the-ordi
2 Present a theory about a past event
3 Discuss how believable a story is
4 Evaluate the trustworthiness of news sources

A **Topic Preview.** Take the quiz with a partner and discuss your answers.

The World's Easiest Quiz . . .

or is it?

How long did the Hundred Years' War last? The answer *has* to be a hundred years, right? Well, the answer may not be what you think. Take a stab at this quiz and see how many answers you can guess correctly. Then check your answers below.

1. How long did the Hundred Years' War in Western Europe last?
a. 100 years   c. 50 years
b. 116 years   d. 200 years

2. Which country makes Panama hats?
a. Panama
b. the Philippines
c. Ecuador
d. Italy

3. From which animals do we get catgut for violin strings?
a. cats   c. sharks
b. sheep   d. dogs

4. The former U.S.S.R. used to celebrate the October Revolution in which month?
a. October   c. December
b. November   d. June

5. What is a camel hair paintbrush made of?
a. camel hair   c. cat hair
b. squirrel hair   d. human hair

6. The Canary Islands in the Atlantic Ocean are named after what animal?
a. the canary   c. the dog
b. the cat   d. the camel

7. What was King George VI of England's first name?
a. George   c. Jose
b. Charles   d. Albert

8. What color is a male purple finch?
a. dark purple   c. sky blue
b. crimson red   d. white

9. What country do Chinese gooseberries come from?
a. China   c. Sweden
b. Japan   d. New Zealand

10. How long did the Thirty Years' War in Central Europe last?
a. 30 years   c. 20 years
b. 40 years   d. 100 years

SCORING

1–2 correct	Hmm . . . Maybe you need to work on your guessing skills!
3–5 correct	Not a bad job at guessing! Or did you already know a few of the answers?
6–10 correct	Either you're a great guesser, or you're a real scholar!

ANSWERS: 1. b. 116 years (The war ran from 1337 to 1453, but with interruptions.) **2. c.** Ecuador (In the 16th century, the hats were shipped through the Panama Canal.) **3. b.** sheep (Catgut comes from the German *kitgut*, a type of violin.) **4. b.** November (Russians used to use the Julian calendar, which was different from the Gregorian calendar by 13 days.) **5. b.** squirrel hair (The brush was named after its inventor, whose surname was Camel.) **6. c.** the dog (The word *canary* comes from the Latin *Insularia Canaria*—Island of the Dogs.) **7. d.** Albert (British kings usually take new names.) **8. b.** crimson red (This is the only "red finch" with purple on its chest.) **9. d.** New Zealand (New Zealanders renamed them kiwi fruit to avoid confusion.) **10. a.** 30 years, of course! (The war lasted from 1618 to 1648.)

B **Discussion.** Did you have a particular reason for each of the answers you chose? Did you just take "wild guesses," or did you use "the process of elimination"? Which method do you think works better? Why?

History's Mysteries

A Topic Preview

Suggested teaching time:	10 minutes
Your actual teaching time:	_____

- Have pairs take turns reading the questions, helping each other with any unknown language and using the pictures to help them work out meaning.
- Have students choose answers individually and then discuss them in pairs.
- After students take the quiz, have them use the key to check their answers, count the number of correct answers, and read the information. If necessary, explain that a *scholar* is a person who knows a lot about a subject.
- Call on students to share their results with the class. Encourage students to explain whether or not they agree with their scoring descriptions.

Language note: *Or is it?* is used to express that what you said before may not be true. If you *take a stab at something*, you try to do something, especially something you have never done before. Students may need help with the following: *catgut* (a strong string for musical instruments that is made from the intestines of animals); *finch* (a small wild bird that has a short, thick beak); *Chinese gooseberry* or *kiwi fruit* (a small round green fruit with a thin brown skin covered in short hairs).

B Discussion

Suggested teaching time:	5–10 minutes
Your actual teaching time:	_____

- Read the questions out loud. Elicit or explain that if you take *a wild guess* to choose an answer, you choose it without much thought or background knowledge; and that if you choose an answer by a *process of elimination*, you decide which answers are not possible and then choose from the answers that are left.
- To prepare for discussion, have students list the questions they guessed correctly. Ask them to note how they chose each of the answers.
- Then have students count how many of their correct answers they knew, how many they guessed, and how many they chose by eliminating the others.
- Point out that students should use their lists to discuss which method worked better for them.
- To finish, take a poll to find out which method worked better for the majority of the class.

C 🎧 Sound Bites
(CD 4, Track 2)

Suggested teaching time:	10 minutes
Your actual teaching time:	_____

- Have students look at the image and read the caption. Ask:
  Who's Bigfoot? (a hairy human-like creature)
  Where was he seen? (in the United States)
  Is this image proof that Bigfoot existed? (no)
  Why? (because the creature in the image is a man dressed in a costume)
  Do you think it was ever believed to be proof of Bigfoot's existence? (Probably. It was taken in 1967, and Bob Heironimus didn't tell the truth until 2004.)

- Have students read and listen to the conversation.

- To check comprehension, ask:
  What led Victor to believe that Bigfoot exists? (a TV program)
  What would Patty need to believe Bigfoot exists? (to see it herself)

Language note: *Could've been* is the short form used in spoken English of *It could have been. There's no such thing as . . .* is an expression that means that something does not exist.

Culture note: The image is a still from a sixty-second film by Roger Patterson. It was one of the most important pieces of evidence that Bigfoot existed until Bob Heironimus confessed in 2004 that he dressed in a costume for the picture. People have claimed to have seen Bigfoot in the U.S. and Canada for hundreds of years. The creature was originally named Sasquatch, which means *hairy giant*, by Native Americans and then nicknamed Bigfoot because of large footprints that have been found and are thought to be from this creature.

D In Other Words

Suggested teaching time:	5–10 minutes
Your actual teaching time:	_____

- Have students find and underline the statements in the conversation and note who said them. Encourage students to consider Victor's and Patty's views on the Bigfoot mystery to help them work out the meaning of the expressions.

- In pairs, have students write a sentence explaining the meaning of each statement or question.

- Review as a class. Call on different students to explain the meanings of the statements.

Option: If they haven't already done so, have students underline the statements from Exercise D in the Sound Bites conversation. Using their explanations of the meanings of the statements, have pairs think of different ways to say each of the statements. Call on pairs to read the Sound Bites conversation again, substituting the new statements for the underlined ones. **[+5–10 minutes]**

Option: In pairs, have students describe Victor's and Patty's personalities. If necessary, prompt students by asking *Who would you describe as gullible? Who would you describe as skeptical?* Have students support their answers with information from the conversation. Encourage students to discuss who they identify with and why. **[+5 minutes]**

STARTING POINT

Suggested teaching time:	15–20 minutes
Your actual teaching time:	_____

Pair Work

- Have students spend a few moments looking at the pictures and reading the captions.

- Have students share additional information they might know about the mysteries with the class.

- Individually, have students rate the possibility that each mystery is true and decide whether they think the Bigfoot claim could be true. (You can ask students to draw a scale for this mystery and rate it in the same way.)

- Encourage students who believe the mysteries are true to think of reasons why they believe in them. (Possible reasons: Many people have seen the Loch Ness Monster over the years; So many ships and planes have disappeared in the Bermuda Triangle.) Encourage students who believe the mysteries are not true to think of logical explanations to account for the stories. (Possible explanations: The Loch Ness Monster was created to attract tourists; The ships disappeared because there are many violent storms in the area.)

- Have pairs compare and discuss their ratings and opinions.

- Review results as a class. Take a poll to find out what most students think of the mysteries. Then have a few students with opposing views about each mystery share their opinions with the class.

EXTRAS (optional)

Workbook: Exercises 1–3

C 🎧 **Sound Bites.** Read and listen to a conversation about a well-known mystery.

VICTOR: I saw the most fascinating TV program about Bigfoot last night.
PATTY: Bigfoot? Don't tell me you buy that story! CN
VICTOR: You're such a skeptic! Who's to say those things don't exist? How else would you explain all those sightings over the years?
PATTY: Could've been gorillas.
VICTOR: In the U.S.? I don't think so. There's no question—Bigfoot is real.
PATTY: Get out of here! There's no such thing as Bigfoot. You have such a wild imagination!
VICTOR: You'd change your mind if you'd seen that program.
PATTY: The only way I'd change my mind is if I saw one of them with my own two eyes. Seeing is believing, as far as I'm concerned.

Bigfoot
Many people claim to have seen a hairy, human-like creature—called "Bigfoot"—in the western mountains of the United States. In 2004, Bob Heironimus admitted that he dressed in a costume for this famous 1967 image.

D **In Other Words.** Read the conversation again. With a partner, explain the meaning of each of the following statements.
Answers will vary, but may include:

1. "Don't tell me you buy that story!"
   I can't believe you think that story is true!
2. "You're such a skeptic!"
   You always doubt everything!
3. "There's no question—Bigfoot is real."
   Bigfoot is definitely real.
4. "Get out of here!" You've got to be kidding!
5. "You have such a wild imagination!"
   You think up some crazy things!
6. "Seeing is believing."
   I have to see something with my own eyes to believe it's true.

CN **Corpus Notes:** The expression *buy [that] story* is used almost exclusively in informal spoken English.

STARTING **POINT**

Pair Work. Read about these two mysteries. How possible is it that each is true? Discuss your opinions with a partner.

The Loch Ness Monster
For centuries, people have reported sightings of a very large, unfamiliar animal living in the deepest lake in the United Kingdom — Scotland's Loch Ness.

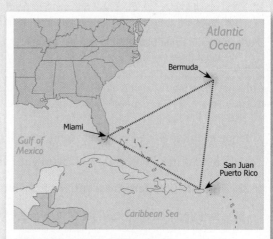

The Bermuda Triangle
Over several centuries, in a triangular area of the Caribbean Sea, numerous ships have mysteriously disappeared—never to be seen again. Many believe that there is something about that area that causes ships simply to disappear into thin air.

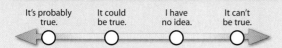

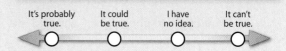

1 Speculate about the out-of-the-ordinary

A 🎧 CONVERSATION **SNAPSHOT**

A: I wonder where Stacey is. She said she'd be here by ten.

B: Do you think something happened?

A: Beats me.

B: Well, I'm sure it's nothing. I'll bet she's stuck in traffic.

A: You're probably right.

B: Why else would she be late?

A: I can't imagine.

🎧 **Rhythm and intonation practice**

> 🎧 **Ways to say "I don't know."**
>
> Beats me.
> I can't imagine.
> I don't have a clue.
> I have no idea.
> Your guess is as good as mine.
> You got me.
> Who knows?

B Grammar. Indirect speech with modals

REMEMBER: When a reporting verb is in a past form, the verb in the indirect speech statement usually changes or "backshifts."

"I **went** to the store." → She said [that] she **had gone** to the store.

Some modals also backshift in indirect speech.

"I**'ll** be there by six." → I said [that] I **would** be there by six.

"You **must** come on time." → She said [that] they **had to** come on time.

"You **have to*** pay in cash." → They told me [that] I **had to** pay in cash.

Some modals don't backshift in indirect speech.

"You **should** hurry." → She told him [that] he **should** hurry.

"He **might** call tonight." → He said [that] he **might** call tonight.

Perfect modals never backshift in indirect speech.

"We **must have** forgotten." → He said [that] they **must have** forgotten.

Grammar Booster

PAGE G14
For more ...

Modals that backshift		Modals that don't backsh
will → would		would → would
can → could		could → could
may → might		might → might
must → had to		should → should
have to → had to		ought to → ought to

REMEMBER

In indirect speech, pronouns and possessives change in order to preserve the speaker's meaning.

"**My** brother got **me** a gift." → She said [that] **her** brother had gotten **her** a gift.

* <u>Have to</u> is not a true modal, but it is often referred to as a "modal-like expression."

 **Corpus Notes:** Indirect speech occurs much more frequently without *that* than with.

C Change each sentence from direct to indirect speech.

1. He told me, "You shouldn't worry if I arrive a little late." He told me [that] I shouldn't worry if I arrive a little lat

2. He said, "Students must arrive fifteen minutes early." He said [that] students had to arrive fifteen minutes ea

3. "Jack may have gotten lost," he said. He said [that] Jack might have gotten lost.

4. "They might have forgotten their luggage," she said. She said [that] they might have forgotten their luggage.

5. She told me, "I'll call you as soon as I get there." She told me [that] she'd call me as soon as she got there.

6. She told us, "I may have to cancel the meeting." She told us [that] she might have to cancel the meeting.

7. He told me, "I'll come early." He told me [that] he would come early.

8. "You ought to phone first," she told me. She told me [that] I ought to phone first.

1 Speculate about the out-of-the-ordinary

A ⌂ CONVERSATION SNAPSHOT
(CD 4, Tracks 3, 5)

Suggested teaching time:	5–10 minutes
Your actual teaching time:	_____

- Before students read and listen, have them look at the photo and predict what the women are talking about. To prompt students, ask *What is the woman on the left looking at?* (her watch) *How many plates are there on the table?* (three) *What do you think they are talking about?* (Possible response: the person they are waiting for)

- After students read and listen, check comprehension by asking *Who are the women waiting for?* (Stacey) *Do they know why she's late?* (no) *What might have caused her delay?* (the traffic)

- Have students read and listen to the ways to say "I don't know." Point out that they are all informal ways to say that you don't know something. *Beats me* is very informal, but it is not offensive.

> **Language note:** The *out-of-the-ordinary* is something that is different from what is usual or expected. *I'll bet* means that you're almost sure something is true.

⌂ Rhythm and intonation practice
(CD 4, Track 4)

Suggested teaching time:	5 minutes
Your actual teaching time:	_____

- Have students repeat chorally. Make sure they:
  - pronounce the contraction *'d* in *She said she'd . . .*
  - use rising intonation for *Do you think something happened?*
  - use falling intonation for *Why else would she be late?*
  - use emphatic stress for <u>sure</u> in *I'm sure it's nothing,* for <u>I'll</u> in *I'll bet she's . . . ,* for <u>else</u> in *Why else . . . ,* and for <u>can't</u> in *I can't imagine.*
  - use the following stress pattern:

---STRESS PATTERN---------------------

```
      •  __   •   •    __  •  __  •  •   __
A:  I wonder where Stacey is. She said she'd be here by ten.

      •  •   __   •   •  __
B:  Do you think something happened?

      •   __
A:  Beats me.

    __   •  __   •  __  •  •   __   •  __  •  •  __
B:  Well, I'm sure it's nothing. I'll bet she's stuck in traffic.

      •   __  •  __  •
A:  You're probably right.

      •  __   •  •  •   __
B:  Why else would she be late?

    •  __   •  __  •
A:  I can't imagine.
```

B Grammar

Suggested teaching time:	10–15 minutes
Your actual teaching time:	_____

- Have a volunteer read the Remember note and the example out loud. Write the example on the board:
  > "*I went to the store.*" → *She said [that] she had gone to the store.*

  Point to the reporting verb in the indirect speech statement (*said*) and ask *Is this verb in a present or past form?* (past) *Did the verb in the reported speech change?* (yes) *How did it change?* (*went* changed to *had gone*)

- Remind students that when the verb in the reported speech changes or "backshifts," present becomes past and past becomes past perfect.

- Have students read the second and third explanations and study the backshifts in the examples.

- Point out that both *must* and *have to* change to *had to* in indirect speech.

- Point to the box of modals that backshift and modals that don't backshift.

- Read the Remember box and the example out loud. Remind students to change pronouns and possessives when they change direct speech to indirect speech.

- To check comprehension, write on the board:
  > *John told Irene, "I may work late because I have to finish a report."*

  Ask *What words in these sentences will change when we put them into indirect speech?* Circle the words as students respond. (I, may, I, have) Then elicit the correct indirect speech from the class. (John told Irene [that] he might work late because he had to finish a report.)

- Have a student read the last explanation out loud. To check comprehension, write the following on the board. Elicit the indirect speech from the class:
  > "*They should have known.*" → *He said _____.*

 Grammar Self-Checks

C Change each sentence . . .

Suggested teaching time:	5–10 minutes
Your actual teaching time:	_____

- To review the difference in use between *say* and *tell,* ask *When do we use* say *and* tell? (We use *say* when we don't mention the listener. We use *tell* when we mention the listener.) Elicit contrasting examples from students. (Possible responses: He said that he would be late; He told me that he would be late.) If necessary, write an example with each verb on the board.

- Model the first item with the class. Ask *What is going to change in indirect speech?* (You → I; I → he; arrive → arrived)

- Have students compare answers with a partner and review as a class.

T100

D Vocabulary
(CD 4, Track 6)

Suggested teaching time:	5 minutes
Your actual teaching time:	_____

- Have students read and listen to the ways to express certainty. Then have students listen and repeat chorally.
- Point out that the ways to express certainty in each box express the same degree of certainty.

Language note: Point out that *It's obvious, There's no question, I'll bet, I guess, I imagine, I suppose, It's possible,* and *It could be* can be followed by *that,* but it's optional. For example, *There's no question the train is delayed* or *There's no question that the train is delayed.*

Option: Draw the following on the board:

It could be	I suppose	Most likely	It's obvious
I guess	Maybe	I'll bet	It's possible
There's no question	Probably	Clearly	I imagine

(+ +) → very certain | almost certain | somewhat certain | not certain → (+)

Graphic Organizers

Give students a few moments to study the ways to express certainty and the degree of certainty they express. With books closed, have pairs classify the ways to express certainty by writing them under the correct boxes. Have students use their books to confirm their answers. **[+5–10 minutes]**

Option: On the board, write:
I wonder why / who / what / where / when . . .
Individually, have students write three imaginary sentences starting with *I wonder* and a question word. In pairs, have students take turns saying their sentences and replying with a way to express certainty from Exercise D. For example, Student A: *I wonder why Ben didn't take that job.* Student B: *Maybe he wasn't pleased with the pay.* **[+5–10 minutes]**

CONVERSATION **STARTER**

Suggested teaching time:	15 minutes
Your actual teaching time:	_____

Pair Work

- Read the four situations and review the model as a class.
- In pairs, have students discuss and speculate about what might have happened in one of the out-of-the-ordinary situations of their choice. Point out that students should use the ways to express certainty from Exercise D.
- Individually, have students write four sentences about the situation they discussed. Each sentence should express a different degree of certainty. Then have students compare their sentences with their partners.
- Review as a class. Have a volunteer share his/her speculation about one of the situations with the class. Encourage students with different speculations about the same picture to share their ideas. Repeat this procedure with the remaining situations. You may want to write some on the board.

Option: Have each pair join another pair who chose the same situation and compare and discuss their speculations. **[+5 minutes]**

Role Play

- Refer students to the Conversation Snapshot on page 100 to review how to speculate about the out-of-the-ordinary.
- Choose a more confident student and role-play the conversation.
- Have pairs role-play their own conversations. Encourage students to use the ways to say "I don't know" and the vocabulary they've learned so far.
- Make sure each student plays both roles.
- As students interact, circulate to offer help as needed. Encourage students to stress main words and to use the correct intonation in questions.

Conversation Prompts

EXTRAS (optional)
Grammar Booster
Workbook: Exercises 4–6

very certain	
Clearly ⎫ It's obvious ⎬ he's not coming. There's no question ⎭	

almost certain	
Most likely ⎫ Probably ⎬ someone found it. I'll bet ⎭	

somewhat certain	
I guess ⎫ I imagine ⎬ she's lost. I suppose ⎭	

not certain	
Maybe ⎫ It's possible ⎬ he forgot. It could be ⎭	

CONVERSATION **STARTER** • *Now speculate about the out-of-the-ordinary.*

Pair Work. Choose one of the out-of-the-ordinary situations below or create your own. Discuss and speculate about the situation. On a separate sheet of paper, use the vocabulary to write four sentences about the situation in which you are very certain, almost certain, somewhat certain, and not certain.

I'll bet the elevator isn't working.

You're trying to take the elevator downstairs to get some lunch. You've been waiting for the elevator for over ten minutes.

It's 9:30, and your teacher hasn't arrived yet for your 9:00 class.

CLASS BEGINS 9:00

Role Play. Role-play the situation you chose or choose another one, speculating about what you think happened. Use the Conversation Snapshot on page 100 as a guide. Start like this: "I wonder …."

You expected a package to arrive on Monday. It's Friday, and it still hasn't come.

CAFÉ OPEN

You go to your favorite restaurant. The lights are on, but the doors are locked, and there's no one inside.

2 Present a theory about a past event

A ⌒ GRAMMAR **SNAPSHOT.** Read the articles and notice the use of perfect modals in the passive voice.

THE STONE BALLS OF COSTA RICA

One of the strangest mysteries in archaeology was discovered in the Diquis Delta of Costa Rica. Since the 1930s, hundreds of stone balls have been found, ranging in size from a few centimeters to over two meters in diameter. Some weigh as much as 16 tons. Almost all of them are made of hard stone and are clearly made by human hands. Nobody knows for sure, but it's believed that the balls **could have been made** by the ancestors of native peoples who lived in the region at the time of the Spanish conquest. But what they **might have been used** for is a total mystery.

Source: www.world-mysteries.com

B **Discussion.** Are you familiar with either of these stories? Have you heard about any other similar mysteries? Describe them.

An Explosion in Tunguska

At 7:17 A.M. on June 30, 1908, an explosion of catastrophic proportions occurred in the forests of Tunguska in northern Siberia, 3,540 kilometers east of Moscow. All over Europe there were reports of strange colors in the sky. It was impossible to investigate the incident because it was so far from where people lived at the time. Most scientists assume that the area **must have been struck** by a huge meteorite. But there are some researchers who claim that the area **couldn't have been hit** by a meteorite because there was no evidence of a crater—the type of hole a meteorite would have caused.

Source: en.wikipedia.org

C **Grammar. Perfect modals in the passive voice for speculating about the past**

You can use <u>may</u>, <u>might</u>, <u>could</u>, <u>must</u>, or <u>had to</u> to speculate with different degrees of certainty about the past. Use the passive voice if the performer of the action is unknown or if you want to focus on the receiver of the action.

not certain	The dinosaurs **might (or may) have been killed** by a meteor. The trees **could have been destroyed** by a fire. The gold figures **might not (or may not) have been lost**.
almost certain	The stone balls **must have been moved** using animals. The drawings **must not have been discovered** until later.
very certain	The crater **had to have been caused** by a meteorite. The trees **couldn't (or can't) have been burned** in a fire.

CN Corpus Notes: *Might have been* occurs more frequently in spoken English; *may have been* occurs more frequently in written English.

Short responses with perfect modals in the passive voice

Is it possible they were killed by a meteorite?	They **may have been**.
Do you think they were made by hand?	They **had to have been**.
I wonder if they could have just been lost.	They **couldn't have been**.
Could they have been stolen?	They **might have been**.

2 Present a theory about a past event

A ⌓ GRAMMAR SNAPSHOT
(CD 4, Track 7)

Suggested teaching time:	10 minutes
Your actual teaching time:	_____

• Have students close their books. On the board, write:
  1. *What's the article about?*
  2. *Where? / When?*
  3. *What's the mystery?*

• Tell students that they are going to listen to two articles for information that will answer the questions on the board. Encourage students to take notes as they listen.

• Have students answer the questions on the board as they listen and then discuss the answers with a partner.

• Have students listen again to correct or confirm their answers. (**First article:** 1. stone balls; 2. in Costa Rica; 3. No one knows what they were used for; **Second article:** 1. an explosion; 2. in the forests of Tunguska, in Siberia, near Moscow / June 30, 1908; 3. No one knows what caused the explosion.)

• Have students read the Grammar Snapshot and notice the perfect modals in the passive voice.

• Review as a class. Call on students to use their notes to summarize each article.

> **Language note:** Students may need help with the following words: *archaeology* (the study of ancient societies by examining their buildings, graves, tools, etc.); *catastrophic* (causing a lot of damage); *meteorite* (a piece of rock or metal from space that lands on Earth); *crater* (a large round hole in the ground caused by a meteorite or an explosion).

B Discussion

Suggested teaching time:	5–10 minutes
Your actual teaching time:	_____

• Have a volunteer read the questions out loud.

• Form pairs or small groups and have students discuss.

• To describe other mysteries, encourage students to provide information that will answer the questions *What? Where? When? What makes it a mystery?* Encourage other students in the group to ask questions to find out more. Circulate to offer help as needed.

• Review as a class. Call on students from different groups to share additional information about the stone balls of Costa Rica or the explosion in Tunguska and other mysteries they talked about.

C Grammar

Suggested teaching time:	10–15 minutes
Your actual teaching time:	_____

• Read the first explanation out loud.

• Write two examples on the board:
  1. *The explosion could have destroyed millions of trees.*
  2. *The trees could have been blown down by an explosion.*

Have the class identify the modal and past participle in each sentence. Label the sentences as students respond. (1. could, destroyed; 2. could, blown) To focus on form, point to the first example and ask *How do you form a perfect modal?* (modal + *have* + past participle) Point to the second example and ask *How do you form a perfect modal in the passive voice?* (modal + *have been* + past participle)

• To focus on the meaning of perfect modals, ask *Do perfect modals have present or past meaning?* (past meaning)

• To focus on the meaning of active and passive sentences, ask *Does the first example focus on the performer or the receiver of the action?* (on the performer—the explosion) *And the second example?* (on the receiver—the trees)

• Have a volunteer read the examples for *not certain* out loud. (Note that *may have*, *might have*, and *could have* have the same meaning. They express possibility that something happened. To express possibility that something did not happen, use *may not have* or *might not have*.) Point out that *could not have* has a different meaning—it expresses certainty (see examples for *very certain*).

• Have a volunteer read the examples for *almost certain* out loud.

• Have a volunteer read the examples for *very certain* out loud. (Note that to express that you are very certain something is impossible, use *can't have* or *couldn't have*.) Point out that *had to have* is not normally used in negative statements.

• Refer students to the phrase from the article *Most scientists assume that the area* **must have been struck** *by a huge meteorite*. Ask *How certain are scientists that the area was struck by a meteorite?* (almost certain) Repeat this procedure with the other perfect modals in the passive voice in the articles.

• Have a volunteer read the explanation for short responses and the examples out loud.

• Have students identify the modal in the questions. (could) Point out *may have*, *had to have*, *couldn't have*, *might have* in the short responses. Tell students that not all modals of speculation can be used in questions, but all of them can be used in short responses. (Note that *been* in the short answers indicates an answer in the passive voice.)

Option: In pairs, have students write two questions about the extinction of dinosaurs, the beginning of the Earth, or any other mystery. Then have each pair join another pair and take turns asking and answering the questions they wrote. [+5–10 minutes]

 Grammar Self-Checks

D Complete each conversation . . .

Suggested teaching time:	5–10 minutes
Your actual teaching time:	_____

- Call on a student to read the headlines. Then say *These are all sensational headlines. What do you think a sensational headline is?* (Possible response: a headline that makes stories seem as exciting or shocking as possible)

- Model the first item with the class. Point out that there isn't only one correct answer. Write the conversation on the board and complete it with students' ideas. Include all logical perfect modals in the passive voice.

- Have students complete the other three conversations individually.

- Have students compare answers with a partner. Then review as a class. Call on pairs to read each conversation out loud.

Project: Have students bring in sensational headlines from printed or online newspapers and make speculations about them in small groups. On the board, have volunteers from different groups write a headline they discussed and share their speculations with the class.

GRAMMAR EXCHANGE

Suggested teaching time:	15 minutes
Your actual teaching time:	_____

Pair Work

- Have students read about each mystery individually and circle the letter that expresses the theory that they think is most possible.

- To prepare students for pair work, have them decide if they are not certain, almost certain, or very certain about each theory.

- In pairs, have students speculate about each theory using phrases with perfect modals in the passive voice.

- Circulate as students discuss to make sure they use perfect modals in the passive voice, correctly.

Option: Have students discuss other aspects of each mystery and speculate using perfect modals in the passive voice; for example, how the stones could have been carried, what the Nazca lines could have been carved for, or where Atlantis could have been located. **[+5 minutes]**

Presentation

- Read the model out loud and tell students to notice the perfect modal in the passive voice. Point out that students should use perfect modals in the passive voice in their presentations.

- Give students a few moments to choose a mystery and draft their presentations.

- Bring up each mystery one at a time and have students who chose that mystery express their views. Keep a tally on the board to find out which theory for each mystery is supported by the majority of students.

EXTRAS (optional)

Pronunciation Booster
Workbook: Exercises 7–9

D Complete each conversation about these sensational headlines, using perfect modals in the passive voice. Make sure each conversation makes sense.

Harvard Professor Claims Egyptian Pyramids Built by Aliens from Outer Space

1. **A:** Do you think the pyramids <u>may / might / could have been built</u> by aliens from outer space?
   B: No way! They <u>couldn't / can't have been</u> I just don't believe that!

New Zealand Scientist Argues Dinosaurs Killed by Giant Tsunami

2. **A:** Do you believe the dinosaurs <u>may / might / could have been killed</u> by a giant tsunami?
   B: They <u>may / might / could have been</u>. It might explain how they all disappeared so quickly.

SHOCKING NEW REVELATION:
Artist van Gogh was actually murdered by brother

3. **A:** Do you think van Gogh <u>may / might / could have been killed</u> by his brother?
   B: Oh, come on! He <u>couldn't / can't have been</u> Everyone knows he killed himself.

Woman Attacked by Tiger While Shopping in London

4. **A:** Do you think someone <u>may / might / could have been attacked</u> by a tiger in London?
   B: Get out of here! That story <u>must / had to have been</u> made up!
   A: I guess you're right. It <u>must / had to have been</u>.

PAGE P9
Reduction and linking

GRAMMAR **EXCHANGE** • *Now present a theory about a past event.*

Pair Work. Read about each mystery and the theories explaining it. Which theory do you think is the most possible? Speculate with perfect modals in the passive voice when possible.

Stonehenge

This formation in southern England was built over 3,000 years ago. The stones were brought from mountains far away, but no one knows for sure how the stones were carried or put into place. The purpose for the stone formation is unknown.

Theories:
a. It was used as a type of calendar.
b. It was used for religious ceremonies.
c. It wasn't made or used by people at all—it was formed naturally.

The Nazca Lines

These shapes were carved into the earth in Peru more than 1,500 years ago. However, the people who made them could not have seen what they were carving—the figures can only be seen from an airplane. No one knows how they were made.

Theories:
a. They were carved by ancient people, who used small drawings to design them.
b. With the help of airplanes, they were carved in 1927, right before they were supposedly "discovered."
c. They were created by aliens, who were able to see them from their spaceships.

Atlantis

Around 350 B.C.E., the Greek philosopher Plato wrote about a lost continent called "Atlantis." He describes this advanced civilization in great detail. Researchers argue whether the story is true or comes from Plato's imagination.

Theories:
a. It was a real community established by the Greeks that was destroyed by an earthquake and sank into the ocean.
b. It was a real place discovered by ancient explorers. We know it today as Iceland.
c. Plato was tricked into believing the story by one of his students.

Presentation. Choose one of the mysteries. Present the theory that you think best explains the mystery and tell the class why you believe it.

> "I believe the stones **may have been used** for religious purposes. That's what makes the most sense to me."

3 Discuss how believable a story is

A 🎧 Word Skills. Using adjectives with the suffix -able

believable can be accepted as true because it seems possible
The story he told seems believable. He backed it up with a lot of details.

debatable not easy to prove because more than one explanation is possible
The cause of the explosion is debatable; experts still disagree.

provable can be shown to be definitely true
I don't think your theory will be provable, unless clear evidence can be found.

questionable uncertain, but more likely to **CN** be untrue
Her convincing account of the events makes his version highly questionable.

unsolvable impossible to prove
This mystery may be unsolvable. Everyone who saw what happened is no longer alive.

B Complete each statement, using an adjective with the suffix -able. Use each adjective only once.

1. His story is really <u>questionable</u>. I doubt that those things could have really happened.

2. I think she's telling the truth. Her description of the events sounds very <u>believable</u> to me.

3. It is highly <u>debatable</u> whether "lie-detector" testing should be used as evidence. Experts continue to argue about what the test results really mean.

4. What happened to the dinosaurs is not really <u>provable</u>. There is nothing that can show with certainty what really happened.

5. The mystery of what happened to the famous U.S. pilot Amelia Earhart is most likely <u>unsolvable</u> since her body and the plane have never been found.

CN Corpus Notes: The collocation *highly questionable* occurs much more frequently than *very questionable*.

C 🎧 Listening Comprehension. Listen to Part 1 of a historical mystery. What happened to the Russian royal family? What's mysterious about this event? The entire family was murdered. It's mysterious because until 1991, the bodies had not been found. Also, there was a woman who claimed to be one of the daughters.

Russia's Royal Family: An Enduring Mystery

St. Petersburg

Ural Mountains

Yekaterinburg

RUSSIA

Anna Anderson, who claimed to have been Anastasia

Russia's last royal family: Czar Nicholas II and Empress Alexandra with their children, Olga, Maria, Anastasia, Alexei, and Tatiana.

D 🎧 Now listen to Part 2. What happened in 1991, and what facts did it seem to prove? Why is it still a mystery? Researchers found nine bodies in the Ural Mountains. Medical testing showed that five of them were members of the royal family. But the bodies of the son and one of the daughters were still missing.

3 Discuss how believable a story is

A 🎧 Word Skills
(CD 4, Track 8)

Suggested teaching time:	5–10 minutes
Your actual teaching time:	_____

- Have students listen to the words and study the definitions. Then have students listen and repeat the words chorally.

- Point out that words ending in the suffix *–able* are adjectives. Ask students what verb each adjective comes from. (believe, debate, prove, question, solve)

- To check comprehension, draw a continuum (without the answers) and word box on the board. With books closed, have students choose the correct words from the box to complete the continuum with:

believable	debatable	provable	questionable

+ true ◄─────────────────────────► untrue
provable   believable   debatable   questionable

🔵 **Graphic Organizers**

Language note: Be sure students don't confuse *provable* ['pruvəbəl] with *probable* ['prabəbəl], which means *possible*. *Questionable* also means *possibly not honest or morally wrong*; for example, *His behavior is highly questionable.* While *believable* implies that something is possibly true, *unbelievable* implies that something is almost certainly not true.

B Complete each statement . . .

Suggested teaching time:	5 minutes
Your actual teaching time:	_____

- Have students compare answers with a partner and review as a class.

🔵 **Vocabulary-Building Strategies**

C 🎧 Listening Comprehension
(CD 4, Track 9)

Suggested teaching time:	10 minutes
Your actual teaching time:	_____

- Pre-listening: Ask *Who are these people?* (the Russian royal family) Elicit from the class any information that they know about the Russian royal family.

- Have students read the title, look at the map and photos, and read the captions.

- First listening: Have students listen for information about what happened to the royal family and why it is a mystery. Then have students discuss in pairs.

- Second listening: Have students listen to confirm or correct their answers. (Possible response: They were murdered. It is a mystery because the bodies weren't found until 1991, and Alexei and Anastasia were said to have escaped. Several women have claimed to be Anastasia.)

- To review, have volunteers share their answers with the class.

Language note: If necessary, explain the following: *enduring* (lasting for a long time); *czar* (ruler of Russia before 1917).

Culture note: The October Revolution of 1917 put an end to the absolute monarchies that ruled Russia for centuries. After the revolution, the country was named Union of Soviet Socialist Republics (USSR) under the leadership of Vladimir Lenin, the first dictator of the USSR. Yekaterinburg (on the map) is where the family is believed to have been moved and then killed.

AUDIOSCRIPT

For audioscript, see page AS12.

D 🎧 Now listen to Part 2 . . .
(CD 4, Track 10)

Suggested teaching time:	5 minutes
Your actual teaching time:	_____

- Have students listen for the answers to the questions. Ask them to take notes while they listen.

- To review, call on volunteers to share their answers with the class.

🔵 **Listening Strategies**

Option: On the board, write:
1. *The results of the medical testing in 1991 are* _____ *because* _____.
2. *Anna Anderson's story could have been* _____ *through medical testing if* _____.
3. *Professor Morgan says the mystery might be* _____ *because* _____.

Have students complete the first blank with an adjective from Exercise A and the second blank with their own ideas to make a logical sentence. Review as a class. (Possible statements: 1. questionable, a lot of errors were made; 2. provable, it had been properly done; 3. unsolvable, proof of what actually happened may never be found) **[+10 minutes]**

AUDIOSCRIPT

For audioscript, see page AS12.

E Complete each statement . . .

Suggested teaching time:	5–10 minutes
Your actual teaching time:	_____

- Have students complete the statements individually and compare answers with a partner.
- If necessary, have students listen again to confirm or correct their answers.
- In pairs, have students support their answers with information from the listening.
- Review as a class. Have students support their answers. For example, 1. *The correct answer is* **a** *because Alexei's body has never been found, so there is no proof that he was executed.*

Option: To give students a chance to express their personal opinions, have them speculate about the mystery of Russia's last royal family in small groups. Ask students to support their views. Encourage the use of perfect modals in the passive voice for speculating about the past on page 102. To finish, call on a few volunteers to share their speculations with the class. **[+5–10 minutes]**

DISCUSSION **BUILDER**

Suggested teaching time:	15–20 minutes
Your actual teaching time:	_____

Step 1. Group Work.

- Have a volunteer read the directions and the first speech balloon out loud.
- Give students a few moments to think of one or two things they have done that might surprise their classmates.
- Form groups of three. As students share their experiences with their groups, encourage them to ask follow-up questions to find out more about their partners' experiences. Tell them to look at the ideas for questions in the box. Point out that the more questions they ask, the better prepared they will be to play the game in Step 2.
- Circulate as students share their experiences to provide help as needed.

Step 2. Game.

- Have each group choose one experience.
- Go over the box for possible questions the class can ask.
- Have a group come to the front and say their experience chorally to the rest of the class. Have other students raise their hands to ask one of the group members a question. Remind students that the purpose of asking questions is to find out who is lying and who is telling the truth.
- After each student from the front has answered a couple of questions, take a vote on who the class thinks is telling the truth.
- Call on the remaining groups to come to the front one at a time and follow the same procedure.

Step 3. Discussion.

- Review the models as a class. Point out that students should share what they thought as each group was being asked questions. Have students focus on why they found the stories *believable* or *questionable*.
- Form small groups and have students share their views.
- Call on various students to share their ideas with the class. Encourage the class to comment on the ideas. Have students who agree share their views and students who disagree explain why.

EXTRAS (optional)

Workbook: Exercises 10–12

E Complete each statement, according to the listening. Listen to Part 2 again if necessary.

1. The czar's son, Alexei, ...
   a. might have been executed with the rest of the family
   b. must have been executed with the rest of the family

2. Researchers believed that five of the nine bodies discovered in 1991 ....
   a. couldn't have been the royal family
   b. had to have been the royal family

3. Anna Anderson, who claimed to be Anastasia, ...
   a. couldn't have been Anastasia
   b. might have been Anastasia

4. More recently, some scientists believed that the bodies ....
   a. might not have been the czar's family
   b. had to have been the czar's family

DISCUSSION **BUILDER** • *Now discuss how believable a story is.*

Step 1. Group Work. Think of things you have done that might surprise your classmates. In groups of three, tell each other about one such experience.

Step 2. Game: To tell the truth. In your group, choose one experience that all three of you will claim as your own. The rest of the class asks members of your group questions in order to determine which of you is telling the truth. Make your stories believable to your classmates.

Finally, after all questions have been asked, the class takes a vote on who they think is telling the truth.

I studied to be an opera singer.

I studied to be an opera singer.

Some ideas for questions

How old were you when you did this?
Where exactly were you?
Were you alone or were other people with you?
What did you learn from the experience?
Your own question: ....

Step 3. Discussion. After each group plays the game, explain why you think some students' stories were more believable than others'.

"I thought your story was questionable because ...."

"It was obvious that you were telling the truth because ...."

4 *Evaluate the trustworthiness of news sources*

A **Reading Warm-up.** Look at the photos and headings in the magazine article. Are you familiar with either of these stories? What do you know about them?

B 🎧 **Reading.** Read the article. Why do you think so many people believed these stories?

Gerd Heidemann

Konrad Kujau

SPECIAL EDITION

The W♺RLD'S Greatest Hoaxes

Although they occurred fifty years apart, both of these spectacular hoaxes took the world by storm.

The Loch Ness Monster Story

Snapshot of the "Loch Ness Monster," published by the *Daily Mail*

It was quite a surprise when London's *Daily Mail* printed a photo in 1933 of a creature in Scotland's Loch Ness, the largest and deepest freshwater lake in the United Kingdom. People had been telling stories about such a creature for over a thousand years. But when a respected London surgeon, Colonel Robert Kenneth Wilson, took this photo, the stories suddenly seemed believable. He claimed that while driving by Loch Ness, he saw something strange in the water and quickly grabbed his camera. The photo he took was seen worldwide and began an increased public interest in the "Loch Ness Monster."

Sixty years later, in November 1993, Christian Spurling told a different story. His stepfather, filmmaker and actor Duke Wetherell, had been hired by the *Daily Mail* to look for evidence of the Loch Ness Monster. But instead, he asked his stepson, Spurling, to make a "monster" with his own hands—from a toy boat. His other son, Ian, took the photo. Then, in order to make the story believable, Wetherell asked the surgeon, Colonel Wilson, to say that he had taken the photo.

The story created so much publicity in 1933 that they decided not to admit the hoax. The true story remained a secret for over sixty years. In the meantime, those who believe there is a creature in the lake, continue to do so.

The "Hitler Diaries" Hoax

In 1983, the German magazine *Der Stern* announced that reporter Gerd Heidemann had made an incredible discovery: diaries written by Adolf Hitler. The magazine explained that the diaries had been found by farmers after a Nazi plane crashed in a field in April 1945. *Der Stern* paid almost 10 million marks to a Dr. Fischer, who claimed to have retrieved them.

The discovery caused a lot of excitement. Magazines and newspapers in London and New York rushed to print excerpts from the diaries, and scholars and researchers couldn't wait to get their hands on the material to learn more about the century's most infamous dictator. But some skeptics argued that the story couldn't be true—it was well-known that Hitler didn't like to take notes. Nonetheless, *Der Stern* insisted that the authenticity of the diaries was unquestionable.

However, when experts began to examine them, it became clear that the diaries were fake. It turned out that "Dr. Fischer" was actually Konrad Kujau, an art forger who had written the diaries himself, imitating Hitler's own handwriting. And both he and Heidemann had been putting the money from *Der Stern* into their own bank accounts. Both were sent to prison for fraud.

Interestingly, Kujau made a living selling copies of paintings by the world's greatest artists after he was released from prison.

Source: en.wikipedia.org

GLOSSARY	
admit =	tell the truth
claim =	say that something is true without proof
evidence =	information that proves that something is true
fake =	not real
a forger =	a person who makes things that aren't authentic, such as copies of famous paintings or money
fraud =	the crime of telling a lie to gain money
a hoax =	a story designed to make people believe something that isn't true
infamous =	well-known for having done something bad or morally evil
a skeptic =	a person who doesn't believe claims easily

4 Evaluate the trustworthiness of news sources

A Reading Warm-up

Suggested teaching time:	5–10 minutes
Your actual teaching time:	_____

- Give students a few moments to look at the photos and read the headings.
- Write *hoax* on the board, and either elicit its meaning from the class or have students read the definition in the Glossary at the bottom of the page.
- Have students share what they know about the stories.

> **Language note:** If something *takes [a place] by storm,* it is very successful.

B 🎧 Reading
(CD 4, Track 11)

Suggested teaching time:	15 minutes
Your actual teaching time:	_____

- Have students read and listen to the article about the Loch Ness Monster. Remind students that knowing every word is not necessary in order to understand the main ideas in the text.
- To check comprehension, ask:
  What did London's Daily Mail *publish?* (a photo of the Loch Ness Monster)
  What did this photo seem to prove? (that the monster was real)
  Was the photo of a real monster? (no)
- Have students read and listen to the article about the "Hitler Diaries" Hoax.
- To check comprehension, ask:
  What did the German magazine Der Stern *announce?* (that it had discovered diaries written by Hitler)
  Why did this cause so much excitement? (because everyone wanted to learn more about Hitler—one of the cruelest dictators)
  Were the diaries real? (no)
- Have students read the articles a second time and use the Glossary to look up unknown words.
- Then ask *What impact did each of these stories have on the world when they happened?* (Possible responses: **The Loch Ness Monster Hoax:** The photo was published worldwide; There was increased public interest in the Loch Ness Monster; It created so much publicity that the hoax wasn't admitted until sixty years later; **The "Hitler Diaries" Hoax:** Excerpts from the diaries were published in London and New York; Scholars and researchers wanted to study them; Some argued that they couldn't be real.)

- Call on students to answer the reading question *Why do you think so many people believed these stories?* (Possible responses: because they sounded real, because the people who claimed they were true seemed trustworthy enough)

> **Language note:** Students may need help with the following: *surgeon* (doctor who performs operations); *retrieve* (find something and bring it back); *excerpt* (short piece of writing taken from a book, poem, etc.). To say "a [person's name]" means "a person named [person's name]." Use of this expression usually implies a certain amount of "suspicion" about the person (*a Dr. Fischer* in the text).

🔊 **Reading Strategies**
🔊 **Reading Speed Calculator**
🔊 **Extra Reading Comprehension Activities**

Option: For a listening-only activity, draw the diagram below (without the answers) on the board. Have students listen to the article with books closed and answer the questions for each story in note form. For question 4, have students write what the people did for a living—not their names. To review answers, have students discuss in pairs and then use their books to confirm their answers. Review as a class. **[+10–15 minutes]**

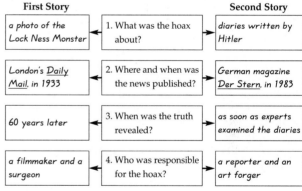

First Story		Second Story
a photo of the Lock Ness Monster	1. What was the hoax about?	diaries written by Hitler
London's Daily Mail, in 1933	2. Where and when was the news published?	German magazine Der Stern, in 1983
60 years later	3. When was the truth revealed?	as soon as experts examined the diaries
a filmmaker and a surgeon	4. Who was responsible for the hoax?	a reporter and an art forger

🔊 **Graphic Organizers**

Challenge: With books closed, have students use the information in the diagram to write a brief summary of each story. **[+10 minutes]**

Project: In pairs or small groups, have students use the Internet to do a search on famous hoaxes and then choose one. Have them use the questions in the diagram above as a guide to take notes about the hoaxes they chose, and add any other relevant information. Then have students share their findings with the class.

C Pair Work

Suggested teaching time: 5–10 minutes
Your actual teaching time: _____

- Have students scan the text for the names of the people involved in each hoax. Ask students to underline them.
- On the board, draw a two-column chart with the heads *The Loch Ness Monster Story* and *The "Hitler Diaries" Hoax*. As students say the names, write them in the appropriate column. Then ask students what other information is given about each person. As you get feedback from students, add the information next to each person's name. (**The Loch Ness Monster Story:** Robert K. Wilson—a respected surgeon; Duke Wetherel—a filmmaker and actor; Christian Spurling—Wetherell's stepson; Ian—Wetherell's son; **The "Hitler Diaries" Hoax:** Gerd Heidemann—a reporter; Konrad Kujau—an art forger who claimed to be Dr. Fischer)
- Have students complete the exercise in pairs and review as a class.

D Discussion

Suggested teaching time: 5–10 minutes
Your actual teaching time: _____

- As students discuss item 1, encourage them to write a list of reasons the media get fooled by hoaxes and publish them so quickly. (Possible responses: because they want to break the news and don't check the accuracy of the information; because they want credit for being the first to inform)
- As students discuss Item 2, ask them to think of the Loch Ness Monster, "Hitler Diaries," and Bigfoot hoaxes. Encourage them to takes notes about why they think each hoax is a crime or harmless.
- To review, have volunteers from different groups share their ideas with the class.

DISCUSSION **BUILDER**

Suggested teaching time: 15 minutes
Your actual teaching time: _____

 Discourse Strategies

Step 1. Pair Work.

- Have students complete the survey individually.
- Encourage students to think of reasons why the people / sources in the survey tend to give accurate / inaccurate information.
- Then have students discuss their answers in pairs and discuss which of the pair is more skeptical.
- Take a poll of the class. Ask *Who thinks he or she is a skeptic? Who thinks he or she is rather gullible?* Then have a few students who consider themselves gullible and a few students who consider themselves skeptical share with the class why they tend to believe or not believe what they read or hear.

Step 2.

- As a class, brainstorm a list of news sources and write them on the board. (Possible ideas: newspapers, magazines, TV news programs)
- Encourage students to write the names of two sources they trust and two they don't trust, and write the reasons.

Step 3. Discussion.

- Read the questions out loud. Form small groups and have students discuss.
- Ask students to say news sources they trust and news sources they don't trust. Keep a list on the board. Call on volunteers to explain why they trust / don't trust the sources in each list. Encourage students who disagree to explain why.

EXTRAS (optional)

Workbook: Exercises 13–15

C **Pair Work.** Discuss how best to complete each statement with names from the article.

The Loch Ness Monster Story

1. Christian Spurling
   _____ admitted that the Loch Ness Monster photo was a hoax.

2. The fake Loch Ness Monster was made by Christian Spurling

3. Colonel Wilson
   _____ didn't really take the photo of the Loch Ness Monster; the photo was actually taken by Duke Wetherell's son, Ian

4. The Loch Ness Monster hoax was created by Duke Wetherell

The "Hitler Diaries" Hoax

1. Gerd Heidemann
   _____ claimed to have discovered the Hitler Diaries.

2. *Der Stern*'s claim that Adolf Hitler had written the diary was questionable.

3. Konrad Kujau was claiming to be Dr. Fischer

4. The evidence showed that the Hitler Diaries were actually written by Konrad Kujau

5. *Der Stern* paid almost 10 million marks to Kujau and Heidemann, not to Dr. Fischer.

D **Discussion.**

1. Why do you think the media get fooled by sensational hoaxes? Why do they seem to publish these stories so quickly?

2. Do you think hoaxes should be considered a crime, or are they harmless? Why?

DISCUSSION **BUILDER** • *Now evaluate the trustworthiness of news sources.*

Step 1. Pair Work. Complete the survey. Which of you do you think is more skeptical? Explain your answers.

Are you a skeptic?

	100%	90%	70%	50%	30%	10%	0%
What percentage of the news you read in the newspaper do you think is true?	○	○	○	○	○	○	○
What percentage of the news you hear on TV or radio do you think is true?	○	○	○	○	○	○	○
What percentage of what politicians say do you think is true?	○	○	○	○	○	○	○
What percentage of what you read on the Internet do you think is true?	○	○	○	○	○	○	○
What percentage of what advertisers say do you think is true?	○	○	○	○	○	○	○
What percentage of what your family says do you think is true?	○	○	○	○	○	○	○

Step 2. On your notepad, list media news sources from print, radio, TV, or the Internet that you trust and ones that you don't. Give reasons for your choices.

The news sources I trust the most	Some news sources I don't trust
Why?	Why not?

Step 3. Discussion. Why do you trust some news sources and not others? Do you and your classmates agree on any? How can you determine if the information you read or hear is true or not?

Writing: Write a news article

Avoiding sentence fragments

A sentence fragment is a group of words that does not express a complete thought.

Two common fragments are:

- **a dependent clause:** a group of words that contains a subject and a verb but begins with a subordinating conjunction, making it an incomplete thought.

    FRAGMENT: Because the banker admitted to fraud.

- **a phrase:** a group of words that does not contain a subject and a verb.

    FRAGMENT: With his help.
    FRAGMENT: At the end of the year.
    FRAGMENT: The man giving the speech.

To correct a sentence fragment, do one of the following:

- Attach the fragment to an independent clause to complete the thought.

    Because the banker admitted to fraud, **the bank was closed down.**

    We found the hospital with his help.

- Add a subject and / or a verb to make the fragment into a sentence.

    She graduated at the end of the year.
    The man giving the speech **needs a microphone.**

An independent clause:
- contains a subject and a verb
- expresses a complete thought

A complete sentence:
- starts with a capital letter
- ends with a period
- expresses a complete thought
- needs at least one independent clause

Subordinating conjunctions

after	since
as soon as	unless
because	until
before	when
even though	whenever
if	while

ERROR CORRECTION | Correct the three errors.

Benefit to Save Library

Last Wednesday, our town hosted a benefit concert. To help save the old building that used to be the library. Developers announced a plan to tear the building down. Two months ago. Because many people feel a connection to the library. The town decided to raise money to restore the building. The benefit concert was a success. Many local musicians performed, and we raised a lot of money.

Step 1. Prewriting. Generating ideas with information questions.

A news article usually answers information questions about an event. Think of a recent news event. This will be the topic of your article. On your notepad, write information questions about the topic to help generate ideas.

Topic:

Who?

What?

When?

Where?

Why?

How?

Step 2. Writing. On a separate sheet of paper, write an article about the event, answering your questions from Step 1. Try to include as much information as you can. Choose a title that reflects the main idea of your article.

Step 3. Self-Check.

- ☐ Did you write any sentence fragments? If so, correct them.
- ☐ Do you have a clear topic sentence?
- ☐ Is the article interesting? Could you add any more details?

Writing Write a news article

Suggested teaching time:	25–30 minutes
Your actual teaching time:	_____

Avoiding sentence fragments

- Have a volunteer read the definition of a sentence fragment out loud. Point out that while a sentence expresses a complete thought, a sentence fragment expresses an incomplete thought.

- Have a volunteer read the explanation and the example for *a dependent clause*. As a class, label the parts of the dependent clause in the example—the subordinating conjunction, the subject, and the verb. Label the example on the board as students identify the parts:

      Because the banker admitted to fraud.
      sub. conj.   subject   verb

- Have a volunteer read the explanation and the examples for *a phrase*. Emphasize that a phrase does not have a subject or a conjugated verb. Point out that *giving* in the last example (The man giving the speech) is not a conjugated verb. You may want to write two contrasting examples on the board:

      The man giving the speech. The man is giving the speech.
          present participle   conjugated verb

- Have students study the information in the boxes about independent clauses, complete sentences, and subordinating conjunctions. Remind students that subordinating conjunctions introduce dependent clauses and join two independent clauses.

- To check comprehension, write on the board:

      The man took a picture of the monster as soon as he
        saw it.
      When the man saw the monster.
      The man took a picture from the car.

  In pairs, have students identify the following in the three sentences on the board: 1. a complete sentence with one independent clause; 2. a complete sentence with two independent clauses; 3. a fragment; and 4. a subordinating conjunction. Review as a class. Label the examples on the board as students respond. (1. The man took a picture from the car; 2. The man took a picture of the monster as soon as he saw it; 3. When the man saw the monster; 4. as soon as, when)

- Have a volunteer read the explanation for how to correct a sentence fragment.

- Point out that when the fragment is a dependent clause, it can be attached to an independent clause. To illustrate further, write on the board:

      When the man saw the monster, he ran away.

  To provide practice, erase *he ran away* and have pairs attach their own independent clauses to the fragment. To review, have various students read their sentences out loud. (Possible responses: he got into his car; he hid behind a tree)

- Point out that when the fragment is a phrase, it can be corrected by adding a subject and/or a verb. Write a phrase on the board:

      in the mountains

  To provide practice, have pairs add a subject and verb to the fragment. To review, have various students read their sentences out loud. (Possible responses: The monster was seen; They got lost)

Error Correction

- Have students correct the article individually. Point out that the fragments can be corrected by attaching them to existing information in the article.

- Have students compare answers with a partner.

- Review as a class. Call on students to say how they corrected the fragments.

 Extra Writing Skills Practice

Step 1. Prewriting.

- Point out that students can choose to write a news article about any theme. Encourage students to think of an interesting article they have recently read.

- Model the activity as a class. Tell students that the topic is the Bigfoot sighting. Generate information questions from the class. (Possible questions: Who saw Bigfoot? When did this person see Bigfoot?) Write them on the board.

- Encourage students to write one question for each question word. As students write questions, circulate to help students frame the questions as needed.

Step 2. Writing.

- Tell students to base their articles on the answers to the questions they wrote.

- Encourage students to choose a title that is short and clear. Remind students to write a topic sentence.

- As students write, circulate to offer help as needed.

Step 3. Self-Check.

- Read the Self-Check questions as a class.

- Before students submit their paragraphs for correction, have them self-check their work and make any necessary changes.

Option: Step 4. Peer Review. Have students exchange papers with a partner and read their partner's article to check if there are any fragments. If there are, encourage them to suggest corrections. Circulate as students correct their partner's work to provide help as needed. [+5–10 minutes]

EXTRAS (optional)

   Workbook: Page 90

A 🎧 Listening Comprehension
(CD 4, Track 12)

Suggested teaching time:	10–15 minutes
Your actual teaching time:	_____

- First listening: With books closed, have students listen and note what the people are talking about. Review as a class. (1. Bill, who should have been with them; 2. a wallet that someone left behind; 3. a bank scandal; 4. a story about a hairy creature)

- Second listening: Have students listen and choose the best statement for each conversation.

- Have students compare answers with a partner and review as a class.

Option: Have students listen to the conversations again and take notes of phrases from the listening that support their answers. (1. "He might've overslept." 2. "You're that certain?" "You bet." 3. "How much more evidence do you need? It's in the paper!" 4. "The guy must have been drinking." "And I can't understand how someone so smart could possibly fall for a story like that!") **[+5 minutes]**

AUDIOSCRIPT

For audioscript, see page AS13.

B Change each sentence ...

Suggested teaching time:	5 minutes
Your actual teaching time:	_____

- Refer students to the Grammar box on page 100.
- Model the first item with the class.
- Remind students that there are modals that backshift and modals that don't backshift.
- Have students compare answers with a partner and review as a class.

C On a separate sheet of paper ...

Suggested teaching time:	5–10 minutes
Your actual teaching time:	_____

- Read the model out loud. If necessary, refer students to Exercise D on page 101 to review ways to express certainty.

- Encourage students to explain their theories.

- Have students compare and discuss answers with a partner.

- Review as a class. Call on students to share their responses to each question.

 You may wish to use the Video Program and activity worksheets for Unit 9 at this point.

Complete Assessment Package
Unit 9 Achievement Test

SUMMIT WEBSITE
For Unit 9 online activities, visit the *Summit* Companion Website at
www.longman.com/summit.

A 🎧 **Listening Comprehension.** Listen to the conversations. Then listen to each conversation again and choose the statement that is closer in meaning to what each person said.

1. The woman said she thought ....
   a. it was possible Bill had overslept *(circled)*
   b. most likely Bill had overslept

2. The woman said she thought ....
   a. it was possible the wallet could be Gina's
   b. it was obvious the wallet was Gina's *(circled)*

3. The man said he thought ....
   a. the president may have been involved in the scandal
   b. the president had clearly been involved in the scandal *(circled)*

4. The man said he thought ....
   a. the story could possibly be a hoax
   b. the story couldn't possibly be true *(circled)*

B Change each sentence from direct to indirect speech.

1. She said, "The job will be completed by Monday."
   She said [that] the job would be completed by Monday.

2. He told me, "Your parents should take the early flight."
   He told me [that] my parents should take the early flight.

3. My boss said, "Rita may be interested in visiting the art museum."
   My boss said [that] Rita might be interested in visiting the art museum.

4. The school director told us, "Your children must come to class on time."
   The school director told us [that] our children had to come to class on time.

5. The clerk said to him, "Your package can be picked up anytime before 5:00 P.M."
   The clerk said [that] my package could be picked up anytime before 5:00 P.M.

6. The agent told them, "Your passports have to be renewed by tomorrow."
   The agent told them [that] their passports had to be renewed by tomorrow.

C On a separate sheet of paper, write your *own* response to each question, using varying degrees of certainty. Explain your theory.

1. Do you think Bigfoot is real?

   I suppose it's possible, but I really don't believe it . . .

2. We know that the photograph of the Loch Ness Monster was a hoax, but do you think the Loch Ness Monster exists?

3. Do you believe there's something mysterious about the Bermuda Triangle that causes ships to disappear?

4. Do you think the damage to the forests in Tunguska was caused by a meteorite?

PREVIEW

Your Free Time

UNIT GOALS

1 Explain the benefits of leisure activi
2 Describe hobbies and other interest
3 Compare your use of leisure time
4 Discuss the risk-taking personality

A **Topic Preview.** Read about these technological advances. Do you know of any other inventions that didn't achieve their promises?

Does technology always live up to its promises?

The promise
Cars were supposed to make it easy to get away from it all.

The reality
Drivers today spend an average of 101 minutes a day driving. And they spend over 40 hours a year stuck in traffic.

The promise
Television was supposed to bring families closer for quality time together.

The reality
Families spend an average of 170 minutes a day watching TV—a lot more time than they spend talking to each other.

The promise
New household appliances were supposed to increase free time and cut back on time spent doing chores.

The reality
Despite increased spending on "laborsaving" devices, people still spend an average of 23.5 hours a week on housework—the same as people living at the beginning of the 20th century.

Information based on U.S. and Canadian government statistics

B **Discussion.**

1. In your opinion, what technological advances *do* save us time?
2. With all the laborsaving and timesaving inventions available to us today, why is it that everybody complains about not having enough free time?

Your Free Time

A Topic Preview

Suggested teaching time:	10–15 minutes
Your actual teaching time:	_____

- Have a student read the direction line out loud. Elicit from the class that a technological advance is a discovery that brings progress. Have students scan the photos and illustrations for the three technological advances presented. (cars, television, household appliances)

- Read the heading *Does technology always live up to its promises?* out loud. Ask *What does it mean to* live up to your promises? (to succeed in doing what you have said you would do)

- Point to the illustration of the car at the top left and ask the class to describe the picture. List the responses on the board. (Possible response: People are enjoying driving along a beach in a car.) Ask *How do the people feel?* (They are having a good time.) *Does this picture show the past or the present?* (the past)

- Have a volunteer read *The promise* caption out loud. Elicit from the class that *get away from it all* means take a vacation away from work and stress. Ask *How do you think a car could make it easier to get away from it all?* (Possible response: Cars make it easier for people to drive to vacation areas like beaches that are far from their homes.)

- Point to the photo of a highway at the top right and ask the class to describe the picture. List the responses on the board. (Possible response: There is a traffic jam.) Ask *What's the problem?* (There are too many cars on the highway.) *How often do you get stuck in traffic? How do you feel when this happens?*

- Have a volunteer read *The reality* caption out loud. Point out that the statistics are from the United States and Canada. Ask *According to these statistics, has the car achieved its promise? Do you think these statistics are similar in this country? Why or why not?*

- Have students compare and contrast the two car images. Ask *Do you agree that the car has not lived up to its promise?* (Possible responses: I agree because there are too many cars on the road and driving is no longer easy or a pleasure; I disagree because without a car I would have to stay home all day.)

- Continue in the same manner for the television and household appliances images and captions.

- As a class, brainstorm other inventions that have not achieved their promises. Have students describe the advantage that each invention promised and the reality of how that promise was not achieved. (Possible response: The computer promised to make office workers more productive, but it is more often used for games and instant messaging than for work.)

> **Language note:** A *laborsaving device* is something that makes tasks easier to do.

B Discussion

Suggested teaching time:	5–10 minutes
Your actual teaching time:	_____

- Have a volunteer read the discussion questions out loud. Elicit from the class that a laborsaving or timesaving invention is one that reduces the amount of work that people must do or the time people must spend doing that work.

- In small groups, have students make a list of timesaving inventions. Circulate to encourage students to explain why they think these technological advances save time.

- For item 2, have students discuss reasons inventions have not increased the amount of free time people have.

- To review, have volunteers share their groups' opinions with the class.

C 🎧 Sound Bites
(CD 4, Track 13)

Suggested teaching time:	10 minutes
Your actual teaching time:	_____

- Before students read and listen to the conversation, have them look at the photo. Ask:
    Where are these people? (Possible responses: in an office, at home)
    What is their relationship? (Possible responses: co-workers, friends)
    What are they talking about? (Possible responses: a long report; The man is complaining about having too much work to do.)

- Have students read and listen to the conversation.

- To check comprehension, ask:
    What's wrong with Ed? (He has a lot of work to do.)
    What does Kim suggest? (taking a break)
    Do you think Ed will find it easy to take his mind off of work? (Possible response: No. He said he could use his laptop to catch up on his work when he takes some time off.)

- Have volunteers retell the situation in their own words. (Possible response: Ed complains about having a lot of work. Kim tells him to relax and take a break.)

Language note: The phrase *come to think of it* is used when you've only just remembered or realized something. The split infinitive in *You need **to just take** it easy* sounds more natural than the grammatically preferred no-split infinitive, *You need just **to take** it easy.*

Option: To draw on students' own experiences, ask *Have you ever been in Ed's situation? What did you do?* Have students share their experiences in small groups. **[+5 minutes]**

D In Other Words

Suggested teaching time:	10 minutes
Your actual teaching time:	_____

- Have students underline or highlight the expressions in the conversation and note who said them.

- In pairs, have students try to determine the meaning of each expression from the context of the conversation.

- Have pairs write a sentence explaining the meaning of each expression.

- To review, call on various pairs to explain the meaning of each expression.

Option: Have pairs identify language in the conversation to complain about work and to give advice to someone who has too much work. Review as a class. (**Complaining about work:** This job is really getting to me; I'm up to my ears in paperwork; **Giving advice to someone who has too much work:** Sounds like you could use a break; Take some time off; A little R and R would do you some good; You need to just take it easy for a while.) **[+5 minutes]**

Option: For items 1–6, have pairs create alternative phrases with similar meanings. Then call on pairs to read the Sound Bites conversation out loud, substituting their new statements for the underlined ones. **[+5 minutes]**

STARTING **POINT**

Suggested teaching time:	10–15 minutes
Your actual teaching time:	_____

- Point to the illustrations. Ask *What are the people doing?* (sitting in the park; using a computer; snowboarding; learning a language)

- Read the directions out loud. Elicit from the class that free time is time you are able to spend as you like when you have no work or anything else you must do.

- Have volunteers read the bulleted list of free-time activities out loud. If necessary, work out the meaning of any unfamiliar words as a class.

- Individually, have students check the statements that apply to them. Encourage them to also write their own ideas for the last item.

Pair Work

- Have pairs compare how they spend their free time. Circulate to encourage students to give specific examples and provide help as needed.

- Review as a class. Call on pairs to say how similar they are and to support their conclusions with examples.

Language note: If necessary, explain the meaning of *hang out with other people* (spend time with people) and *catch up on work / chores* (do things that need to be done that you haven't had time to do yet).

EXTRAS (optional)
Workbook: Exercises 1–3

C 🎧 **Sound Bites.** Read and listen to a conversation between two close friends at the office.

ED: I can't take it anymore. This job is really **CN** getting to me.

KIM: Hey, sounds like you could use a break.

ED: Are you kidding? I'm up to my ears in paperwork.

KIM: When was the last time you took some time off?

ED: Come to think of it, it's been over a year. I was supposed to take off a few weeks in January, but it just got too busy around here.

KIM: Then it sounds like a little R and R* would do you some good.

ED: You're right. And anyway, I can always bring my laptop along and catch up on my work.

KIM: Listen, leave the laptop at home! You need to just take it easy for a while.

* R and R = rest and relaxation

D **In Other Words.** Read the conversation again. With a partner, explain the meaning of the following statements.
Answers will vary, but may include:

CN **Corpus Notes:** The expression *can take [something]*, meaning be able to handle or tolerate something, occurs most frequently in the negative. For example, *He left because he couldn't take the pressure*.

1. "This job is really getting to me."
   This job is creating a lot of stress for me.
2. "Are you kidding?"
   You can't be serious.
3. "I'm up to my ears in paperwork."
   I have too much work to do.
4. "A little R and R would do you some good."
   You would benefit from taking some time off.
5. "I can catch up on my work."
   I can get ahead with my work.
6. "You need to just take it easy."
   You need to take a break and relax.

STARTING **POINT**

How do you usually spend your free time? Check all that apply.

☐ I hang out with other people.
☐ I spend my time alone.
☐ I take it easy.
☐ I find something exciting to do.
☐ I catch up on the chores I never have time for.
☐ I catch up on work.
☐ I use my time to learn something new.
☐ I sit around and worry about what I need to do.
☐ Other: ....

Pair Work. Compare how you spend your free time. How similar are you and your partner?

Explain the benefits of leisure activities

A 🎧 CONVERSATION **SNAPSHOT**

A: I've taken up Go recently. Do you play?

B: No. I've never even heard of it. What's Go?

A: It's a great Japanese game. Kind of like chess. **CN**

B: I hate to say this, but I find chess a little boring.

A: Well, even so, you should give it a try. I think it's intellectually stimulating. I'm sure you'd like it.

the board game Go (Japan)

🎧 **Rhythm and intonation practice**

CN **Corpus Notes:** The expressions *kind of like* and *sort of like* have the same meaning, but *kind of like* occurs more frequently. Both occur most frequently in spoken English.

B 🎧 **Word Skills. Using collocations for leisure activities.** Add your own game, fitness activity, hobby, or handicraft.

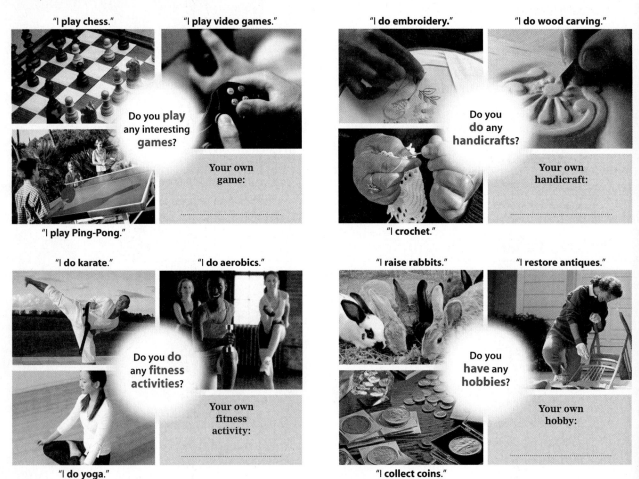

"I **play** chess."
"I **play** video games."
Do you **play** any interesting games?
Your own game:
....
"I **play** Ping-Pong."

"I **do** embroidery."
"I **do** wood carving."
Do you **do** any handicrafts?
Your own handicraft:
....
"I **crochet**."

"I **do** karate."
"I **do** aerobics."
Do you **do** any fitness activities?
Your own fitness activity:
....
"I **do** yoga."

"I **raise** rabbits."
"I **restore** antiques."
Do you **have** any hobbies?
Your own hobby:
....
"I **collect** coins."

C **Discussion.** Which, if any, leisure activities do you do? Which would you like to take up someday? Which activities are the most popular in your class?

1 Explain the benefits of leisure activities

A 🎧 CONVERSATION **SNAPSHOT**
(CD 4, Track 14)

Suggested teaching time:	5 minutes
Your actual teaching time:	_____

- Before students read and listen to the conversation, have them look at the photo. Ask *Have you ever heard of this game?* If they have, ask *What do you know about it?*
- Have students read and listen to the conversation.
- To check comprehension, ask:
  What has the woman started doing recently? (playing a game called Go)
  Why doesn't the man think he'd like Go? (because it's like chess and he finds chess boring)
  What does the woman recommend? (that the man try the game)
  Does she think the man will like Go? (yes)
  Why? (because she thinks it's intellectually stimulating)

Language note: If you *take up* an activity, you become interested in it and start doing it regularly. *Kind of like [chess]* is an informal way to say *It's similar to [chess]*. If an activity is *intellectually stimulating*, it makes you think. *Even so* means *nonetheless* or *despite that*.

Culture note: Go is played by placing black and white stones on the intersections of lines on a square board. The aim is to win more territory than the opponent by capturing opposing stones and protecting one's stones from being captured. Although the rules are simple, Go is considered one of the most intellectually challenging games.

🎧 Rhythm and intonation practice
(CD 4, Track 15)

Suggested teaching time:	5 minutes
Your actual teaching time:	_____

- Have students repeat chorally. Make sure they:
  ○ use rising intonation for *Do you play?*
  ○ use falling intonation for *What's Go?*
  ○ pause slightly after *I hate to say this, . . .* and *Well, even so, . . .*
  ○ use emphatic stress for I in . . . *I find chess a little boring* and *I think it's intellectually stimulating.*
  ○ use emphatic stress for <u>heard</u> in *I've never even heard of it*, for <u>you</u> in . . . *you should give it a try*, and for <u>sure</u> in *I'm sure you'd like it.*

○ use the following stress pattern:

```
STRESS PATTERN
A: I've taken up Go recently. Do you play?
B: No. I've never even heard of it. What's Go?
A: It's a great Japanese game. Kind of like chess.
B: I hate to say this, but I find chess a little boring.
A: Well, even so, you should give it a try. I think it's
   intellectually stimulating. I'm sure you'd like it.
```

B 🎧 Word Skills
(CD 4, Track 16)

Suggested teaching time:	5–10 minutes
Your actual teaching time:	_____

- Before students listen and practice, have them look at the photos and read the captions. Ask *What's a leisure activity?* (something you do for fun when you are not working or studying)
- Have students listen and repeat the statements chorally.
- Point out that a collocation is the way in which some words are often used together. Point to the games and ask *How are these statements the same?* (They all use the verb *play.*) Point to the fitness activities and ask *How are these all the same?* (They all use the verb *do.*)
- Point to the three games photos. Point out that games often use the verb *play.* As a class, brainstorm other games that people play. (Possible responses: cards, soccer) Have students write a game that they enjoy in the fourth box.
- Do the same for the fitness activities, handicrafts, and hobbies.

Language note: *I embroider* is used equally as often as *I do embroidery.*

C Discussion

Suggested teaching time:	5 minutes
Your actual teaching time:	_____

- Have a volunteer read the questions out loud.
- To model the discussion, tell the class about any leisure activities that you do and any that you would like to take up. Encourage students to ask follow-up questions about your interests.
- In small groups, have students discuss the leisure activities they enjoy and those they would like to take up. Circulate to encourage student to ask follow-up questions.
- Review as a class. Keep a tally on the board as students state their favorite leisure activities.

D Word Skills

Suggested teaching time:	5–10 minutes
Your actual teaching time:	_____

- Have volunteers read the directions and example sentences out loud.
- On the board, write the following sentences:
    1. *Yoga is physically relaxing.*
    2. *Doing handicrafts can help you emotionally.*
    3. *I find origami creatively stimulating.*

To check comprehension, ask pairs to identify the adverbs in the examples and to indicate the verbs or adjectives they modify with arrows. (1. *physically* modifies *relaxing*; 2. *emotionally* modifies *help*; 3. *creatively* modifies *stimulating*) Label the examples on the board as students identify the items.

∩ Adjectives, Adverbs
(CD 4, Track 17)

- Have students read and listen to the adjectives and adverbs in the box. Then have students listen and repeat the adverbs chorally.

Language note: These adverbs usually follow the verbs they modify and precede the adjectives they modify. For example, *Putting some money aside will help you <u>recover financially</u>; If you open up your own business, you will become <u>financially independent</u>.*

E Complete the statements ...

Suggested teaching time:	5 minutes
Your actual teaching time:	_____

- To model the activity as a class, identify the adjective that the adverb modifies in the first statement. (satisfying) Then have a volunteer choose an appropriate adverb and read the statement out loud.
- Have students complete the statements individually with an adverb from Exercise D. Encourage students to pay attention to meaning to make logical statements.
- Have students compare answers with a partner and review as a class.

F Pair Work

Suggested teaching time:	5–10 minutes
Your actual teaching time:	_____

- Have a volunteer read the first situation out loud. Then read the sample recommendation.
- Model the first item with the class. Ask *What is Suzy's problem?* (Possible response: She doesn't have a lot of time and needs to do something creative.) *Why would some kind of handicraft do her good?* (because she might find it relaxing and creatively stimulating)

- Elicit other recommendations for Suzy from the class. Have students give reasons for their choices.
- Encourage students to use the vocabulary from Exercise B to make recommendations and the adverbs from Exercise D to explain their choices.
- In pairs, have students recommend a leisure activity for Lionel and Solange and explain why they made those choices. Circulate to offer help as needed.
- Review as a class. Call on a pair to share their recommendations for Lionel with the class. Encourage other pairs to share their recommendations. Follow the same procedure for Solange.

CONVERSATION **STARTER**

Suggested teaching time:	10 minutes
Your actual teaching time:	_____

Pair Work

- As students discuss the leisure activities, encourage them to describe the adjectives they chose. For example, *Jogging is physically challenging. It will keep you in shape.*
- Refer students to the Conversation Snapshot on page 112 to review how to explain the benefits of leisure activities.
- Choose a more confident student and role-play the conversation.
- Have pairs role-play their own conversations. Encourage students to use the vocabulary they've learned so far.
- Make sure each student plays both roles.
- As students interact, circulate to offer help as needed. Encourage students to stress the right words for emphasis and to use the correct intonation in questions.

Vocabulary-Building Strategies

Conversation Prompts

Project: At a library or on the Internet, have students research a leisure activity that they are interested in taking up. Have students write a description of the activity, explain why it interests them, and describe the benefits. Then have students make a short presentation to the class about their chosen leisure activity. If possible, have students bring in visual aids such as photographs, handicraft items, collectible items, etc.

EXTRAS (optional)

Grammar Booster
Workbook: Exercises 4–6

D **Word Skills. Modifying with adverbs.** Use an adverb to modify a verb or an adjective. Many adverbs are formed by adding -<u>ly</u> to an adjective.

> Karate challenges you **physically**. You have to work your body really hard if you want to be good at it. [modifies verb]

> I find chess **intellectually** stimulating. You have to use your head to play it well. [modifies adjective]

Adjectives	Adverbs
creative	→ **creatively**
emotional	→ **emotionally**
financial	→ **financially**
intellectual	→ **intellectually**
physical	→ **physically**
social	→ **socially**
spiritual	→ **spiritually**

Grammar Booster

PAGE G16 for more...

E Complete the statements with an appropriate adverb. Compare your choices with a partner.

1. Building one-of-a-kind furniture is what makes woodworking so ....*creatively*........ satisfying.

2. While it doesn't feature the punching and kicking found in karate or kung fu, a serious yoga workout can be as ....*physically*........ difficult as any martial art.

3. Even though there are computer programs that can defeat the greatest chess players, there has never been a program "smart" enough to win the ....*intellectually*........ challenging game of Go.

4. They say raising tropical fish can really set you back ....*financially*......... They're very expensive.

F **Pair Work.** Recommend a leisure activity for each of the people below. Explain why you made that choice.

I've just opened up my own graphic design business. I'm also a full-time mom. Balancing work and family is really challenging. When I do get some free time, I need to do something creative.

Suzy Tanaka

"I think Suzy should take up some kind of handicraft. She might find it relaxing, and it might stimulate her creatively."

I'm a businessperson, and my job is very demanding. Sometimes the stress really gets to me. I have to travel a lot for work—I'm on the go from morning to night. I often get headaches and backaches from all the tension. I really need to get some R and R into my life.

Solange Teixeira

Being a computer programmer, I have to sit at a desk all day long. I work long hours, and by the time I get home at night, I'm pretty exhausted. The only free time I have is on the weekends. But even then, I can't always let go of the job. I've got to find a way to take my mind off of work.

Lionel Espinoza

CONVERSATION **STARTER** • *Now explain the benefits of leisure activities.*

Pair Work. Discuss and list leisure activities you think fit in each category.

physically challenging	emotionally satisfying	intellectually stimulating	just plain fun!

Talk to your partner about a leisure activity you have taken up or that you would like to try. Explain why you like it. Use the Conversation Snapshot on page 112 as a guide. Start like this: "I've taken up .... recently."

2 Describe hobbies and other interests

GRAMMAR

A GRAMMAR **SNAPSHOT.** Read the message-board posts and notice the use of noun modifiers.

Home | Search | Customize...

User CP | FAQ | Members List | Calendar | New Posts | Search | Quick Links | Log Out

inter.boards

Go

Does anyone out there have any weird or unusual hobbies or interests?

Back to: INTER Homepage > Message Boards > Hobbies > **A weird hobby?**

1 2 3 4 of **4** Pages Next > Last >>

Post New Message

Started: Sep 12
Last Post: Nov 16

A weird hobby? Posted Sep 12 4:17AM

Sameer
1 Posts (View)

I have **a weird ten-year-old** hobby that I know no one will ever understand. I like to walk up and down the beach with one of **those silly metal** detectors looking for lost coins and watches. Hey, it keeps me out of trouble.

23 replies, view all | Reply

Hobbies can be obsessive. Posted Sep 17 11:45AM

Eric B.
5 Posts (View)

Too much time on your hands, Sameer? LOL*! Actually, I'm **an obsessive comic book** collector. It's just this thing I've been into since I was a teenager. CN

1 reply, view all | Reply

My hobby takes all my time! Posted Sep 18 2:12PM

Susieq
1 Posts (View)

Speaking of obsessions, mine is knitting. Really, I can't stop! **Six-foot-long** scarves, **thick multicolored** sweaters, **cute little teapot** warmers. . . . I keep churning them out whether my friends and family want them or not!

1 reply, view all | Reply

*LOL = laughing out loud

CN **Corpus Notes:** The expression *be into [something]*, meaning be interested or involved in something, occurs frequently in informal spoken English.

B **Grammar. Order of modifiers**

When a noun is modified by more than one word, modifiers usually appear in the following order.

1. **determiners**: a, an, the, this, my, Judy's
2. **ordinals**: first, one thousandth
3. **quantifiers**: one, a few, some, many
4. **adjectives** (in the following order):
   - **size**: small, huge, tall, wide
   - **an opinion or quality**: beautiful, clear, weird, obsessive
   - **age or temperature**: young, middle-aged, antique, freezing
   - **shape**: round, triangular
   - **color**: black, greenish
   - **origin**: British, handmade
   - **material**: glass, silk, metal
5. **nouns**: student, childhood, book, teapot

my (1) first (2) few (3) beautiful antique Czech crystal (4) sugar (5) bowls

BE CAREFUL! When the modifier is a noun, never use a plural form.
a delicious **vegetable** soup
NOT a delicious ~~vegetables~~ soup

BE CAREFUL! Hyphenate compound modifiers when they precede CN **the noun. Don't use a plural form.**
a **two-year-old** house
NOT a two-~~years~~-old house
BUT The house is two years old.

Grammar Booster PAGE G16 for more...

CN **Corpus Notes:** According to the Longman Learner's Corpus, learners often make the error of using plural forms in hyphenated compound modifiers. For example, *She was a thirty-years-old lady* and *I taught 14-years-old students.*

2 Describe hobbies and other interests

A 🎧 GRAMMAR **SNAPSHOT**
(CD 4, Track 18)

Suggested teaching time:	5–10 minutes
Your actual teaching time:	_____

- Point to the message-board screen. Ask *What kind of Internet site is this?* (a message board) Elicit from the class that a message board is a web page that allows people to post or leave messages for other people to read and reply to. Ask *Have you ever posted on a message board? If so, what was the discussion topic? Do you think message boards are a good place to meet people with similar hobbies or interests?*

- Have students quickly scan the message-board posts to find each person's hobby. (Sameer looks for objects with a metal detector; Eric B. collects comic books; Susieq knits.)

- Have students read and listen to the message-board posts and notice the use of noun modifiers.

- Then have volunteers retell each person's hobby in their own words. (Possible response: Sameer has had this hobby for ten years. He looks for coins on the beach with a metal detector.)

Option: Have pairs share their opinions of each person's hobby. Ask *Do you find the hobbies weird or unusual? Why? / Why not? Do you have any weird or unusual hobbies?* **[+5 minutes]**

B Grammar

Suggested teaching time:	10–15 minutes
Your actual teaching time:	_____

- Have volunteers read the explanation and examples of modifiers out loud.

- Direct students' attention to the example at the bottom of the Grammar box (my first few beautiful antique Czech crystal sugar bowls). Point out that this phrase includes an example of each type of modifier. Also point out that this many modifiers preceding a noun is not common.

- Have a volunteer read the Be Careful! note out loud.

- To help clarify, say *Nouns can be modified by other nouns.* On the board, write:

a <u>teapot warmer</u> (= a warmer for teapots)
    noun   noun

Point out that nouns acting as modifiers are never plural. Contrast *a teapot warmer* with *a warmer for teapots* in the example on the board.

- To check comprehension, write on the board:
  a book of comics
  a room for meetings

Have pairs use the cues to write phrases using nouns as modifiers. Then review as a class. (a comic book, a meeting room)

- Have a volunteer read the second Be Careful! note out loud.

- Point out that nouns that are part of a hyphenated phrase are never plural. Elicit other compound modifiers from the class. (Possible responses: a hand-painted vase, a tailor-made gown)

- On the board, copy the statements in bold text from the Grammar Snapshot. Have students identify each modifier, using the numbers in the Grammar box. For example:

a weird ten-year-old
1 4   4
determiner / opinion or quality / age

🌐 **Grammar Self-Checks**

Language note: An adjective indicating opinion or quality can come before or after the one indicating size, depending on the combination of words. For example, *a beautiful miniature vase, a small fragile cup.* Compound nouns are two words commonly used together to describe one thing and are different from noun modifiers. In compound nouns, the words can take the plural form. For example, *a sports car.*

Option: To provide practice with order of noun modifiers, bring in photographs (your own or clippings from magazines) of different objects. Have students first brainstorm three to five adjectives for each item. Then have students make a statement describing the object, putting the adjectives in the correct order. **[+5–10 minutes]**

Challenge: In pairs, have students write two more modifiers that fit into categories 1–4. To review as a class, call on students to say the words they wrote and list them on the board. (Possible responses: 1 **determiners:** that, his; 2 **ordinals:** third, tenth; 3 **quantifiers:** a lot of, a little; 4 **adjectives: size:** short, narrow; **an opinion or quality:** interesting, wonderful; **age or temperature:** new, hot; **shape:** square, oval; **color:** white, golden; **origin:** historic, artificial; **material:** cotton, paper) **[+10 minutes]**

C On a separate sheet of paper ...

Suggested teaching time: 10 minutes
Your actual teaching time: _____

- Model item 1 with the class. Write the following on the board:

  that green ugly cotton

  Label the phrase on the board as students identify each modifier by number and category. (**that:** 1, determiner; **green:** 4, color; **ugly:** 4, opinion; **cotton:** 4, material) Then decide on the correct order.

- Review as a class. Have volunteers read the corrected sentences out loud.

D Complete the sentences ...

Suggested teaching time: 5 minutes
Your actual teaching time: _____

- Model the first item with the class. As students provide the answer, write it on the board. Point out the hyphen and the singular form of *ten* and *speed*.

- Have students compare the compound modifiers they wrote with those of a partner and review as a class.

Option: In pairs, have students take turns describing some of the objects in their homes. Encourage students to use at least three modifiers for each object. Review as a class. Call on students to choose one of the items their partners described and share it with the class. **[+5–10 minutes]**

GRAMMAR **EXCHANGE**

Suggested teaching time: 15–20 minutes
Your actual teaching time: _____

- Have volunteers read the directions and examples on the notepad. Ask *What kinds of adjectives are used in the first example?* (opinion, age, origin, material) *What kinds of adjectives are used in the second example?* (age, color, origin)

- Encourage students to write about three or four interests or hobbies they or people they know have. Circulate to offer help as needed. To help students think of noun modifiers, ask questions about the hobby or interest. For example, if the student makes or collects an object, ask *What size / shape / color is it? What's it made of? Where does it come from?*

- After students write the sentences, have them use the Grammar on page 114 to confirm that they used the modifiers in the correct order.

- Circulate as students write to offer help as needed with modifiers.

Group Work

- Read the directions out loud. Have students interview four or five classmates.

- Encourage students who are being interviewed to use modifiers as they describe their hobbies or interests. Encourage students who are conducting the interview to takes notes about their classmates' hobbies or interests and ask questions to find out more.

- To finish, call on a student to share a hobby or interest he/she heard about from one of his/her classmates. Encourage other students who interviewed the same classmate to share more information they found out about that classmate's hobby. Then call on other students to describe other hobbies or interests, and follow the same procedure.

Option: Guessing game. Call on a student to share a hobby or interest he/she heard about from one of his/her classmates, withholding his/her classmate's name. The students who didn't interview that classmate guess whose hobby it is. Then call on other students to describe other hobbies or interests, and follow the same procedure. **[+5 minutes]**

EXTRAS (optional)

Grammar Booster
Workbook: Exercises 7–9

C On a separate sheet of paper, rewrite each sentence, correcting the order of the noun modifiers.

1. Are you going to wear that green ugly cotton shirt?
   Are you going to wear that ugly green cotton shirt?
2. That was the most interesting French old film I've ever seen.
   That was the most interesting old French film I've ever seen.
3. I gave her a wooden beautiful round box that I picked up during my trip.
   I gave her a beautiful round wooden box that I picked up during my trip.
4. She bought an Italian hundred-year-old expensive violin.
   She bought an expensive hundred-year-old Italian violin.
5. Isn't this the third mystery historical novel you've read this month?
   Isn't this the third historical mystery novel you've read this month?
6. He bought her a silk white gorgeous handkerchief.
   He bought her a gorgeous white silk handkerchief.

D Complete the sentences with compound modifiers, using the descriptions in parentheses.

1. She bought a new _____ ten-speed _____ bike.
   (It has ten speeds.)

2. They offer a _____ three-month _____ introductory class at the new yoga school.
   (It runs for three months.)

3. We gave her a small _____ hand-embroidered _____ pillow.
   (It was embroidered by hand.)

4. The company sent him a _____ praise-filled _____ letter.
   (It was filled with praise.)

5. The government announced a _____ five-point _____ plan for protecting
   (It has five points.)
   the environment.

GRAMMAR **EXCHANGE** • *Now describe hobbies and other interests.*

Think of some things you and people you know like to do or make. On your notepad, write sentences about these hobbies or interests, using at least three noun modifiers to describe each.

I've been collecting *beautiful antique handmade paper* dolls for years.

My sister has always liked to watch *old black-and-white Hollywood* movies.

Group Work. Walk around the classroom and interview your classmates about the hobbies and interests they wrote about on their notepads. Then tell your class about the most interesting hobbies or interests you heard about, using noun modifiers.

3 Compare your use of leisure time

A **Reading Warm-up.** Are you satisfied with the amount of leisure time you have in your life?

B 🎧 **Reading.** Read the article. What's the author's main point about technology today?

IS TECHNOLOGY KILLING LEISURE TIME?
by Jon Katz

New surveys suggest that the technological tools we use to make our lives easier are killing our leisure time. We are working longer hours, taking fewer and shorter vacations (and when we do go away, we take our cell phones, PDAs, and laptops along). And we are more stressed than ever as increased use of e-mail, voice mail, cell phones, and the Internet are destroying any idea of privacy and leisure.

Since the Industrial Revolution, people have assumed that new laborsaving devices would free them from the burdens of the workplace and give them more time to grow intellectually, creatively, and socially— exploring the arts, keeping up with current events, spending more time with friends and family, and even just "goofing off."

But here we are at the start of the 21st century, enjoying one of the greatest technological boom times in human history, and nothing could be further from the truth. The very tools that were supposed to liberate us have bound us to our work and study in ways that were inconceivable just a few years ago. It would seem that technology almost never does what we expect.

In "the old days," the lines between work and leisure time were markedly clearer. People left their offices at a predictable time, were often completely disconnected from and out of touch with their jobs as they traveled to and from work, and were off-duty once they were home. That's no longer true. In today's highly competitive job market, employers demand increased productivity, expecting workers to put in longer hours and to keep in touch almost constantly via fax, cell phones, e-mail, or other communications devices. As a result, employees feel the need to check in on what's going on at the office, even on days off. They feel pressured to work after hours just to catch up on everything they have to do. Workers work harder and longer, change their work tasks more frequently, and have more and more reasons to worry about job security.

Bosses, colleagues, and family members—lovers, friends, and spouses too—expect instant responses to voice mail and e-mail messages. Even college students have become bound to their desks by an environment in which faculty, friends, and other members of the college community increasingly do their work online. Studies of time spent on instant messaging services would probably show staggering use.

This isn't what technology was supposed to be doing for us. New technologies, from genetic research to the Internet, offer all sorts of benefits and opportunities. But when new tools make life more difficult and stressful rather than easier and more meaningful—and we are, as a society, barely conscious of it—then something has gone seriously awry, both with our expectations for technology and our understanding of how it should benefit us.

Reprinted from slashdot.org; written by Jon Katz

3 Compare your use of leisure time

A Reading Warm-up

Suggested teaching time:	10 minutes
Your actual teaching time:	_____

• Read the Warm-up question out loud.

• On the board, write:

> How many hours a day do you spend on leisure activities?
> How much leisure time would you like to have each day?

• Form small groups and have students discuss the Warm-up question, using the questions on the board as prompts.

• Have a few students share their experiences and opinions with the class.

B 🎧 Reading
(CD 4, Track 19)

Suggested teaching time:	10–15 minutes
Your actual teaching time:	_____

• Have students look at the photos. Ask *What technology products are these?* (cell phone, PDA, laptop) *Do you have any of these products? What are the advantages of having them? Can you think of any disadvantages?*

• Have a volunteer read the title of the article out loud and then make predictions. Ask *How do you think technology such as laptops, PDAs, and cell phones could be killing leisure time?* (Possible responses: Technology makes it harder to get away from the office or school; Technology makes it harder to have private time.)

• Read the focus question out loud. Have students read and listen to the article, listening for the author's main point about technology today.

• As a class, compare ideas generated by students' predictions with the content of the article.

• In pairs, have students discuss the answer to the reading question. (Possible response: Instead of giving us more time to spend with friends and family or do the things we like, technology is consuming our time and making our lives more difficult by forcing us to constantly be in touch.)

• To check comprehension, draw a two-column chart with the heads *The promise* and *The reality* on the board. Have students read and listen to the article again and take notes in the chart. Have students compare answers with a partner and review as a class. (**The promise:** It would help people with their responsibilities at work; It would give people more time to do things that stimulate them intellectually and creatively; It would give people more time to spend with family and friends; It would help people have more free time; **The reality:** It binds people to work and study; People are never off-duty; People work longer and harder; People are forced to reply to messages at any time; It makes life more stressful.)

Language note: *Goof off* means waste time and not work. If something goes *awry*, it does not happen in the way that was planned.

Culture note: The Industrial Revolution started in England in the last half of the 18th century when machines began to replace manual labor in factories. It soon spread to other countries in Western Europe and North America and, eventually, to the rest of the world. It led to an important change in population distribution, since people who had traditionally worked in homes and workshops producing all kinds of goods had to move to urban areas—where factories were located—in search of work.

💿 **Reading Strategies**

💿 **Reading Speed Calculator**

💿 **Extra Reading Comprehension Activities**

Challenge: To use the reading as a listening-only activity, have students listen to the article with books closed and take notes. Follow the procedure above, making necessary changes to accommodate a listening-only task. Review as a class. **[+10–15 minutes]**

C Discussion

Suggested teaching time:	10–15 minutes
Your actual teaching time:	_____

- Have volunteers read the questions out loud.
- Give students a few moments to make notes about their ideas for each question.
- Form small groups and have students discuss the questions.
- Review as a class. To review item 2, call on students to name some new technologies and list them on the board. Then have volunteers choose a technology from the list and explain the expectations people have for it. Encourage students to explain why they think the technologies will / won't live up to their promises.
- To review item 3, have students who agree with the author's point of view raise their hands. Tally the results. Do the same for students who don't agree. Have various students share reasons why they agree / don't agree with the author.

Option: According to the author, the lines between work and leisure time are not as clear as they were in the past. Form small groups and have students discuss whether or not they agree with that opinion. Encourage them to support their views with specific examples of their own work / school day or the work / school day of people they know. **[+5–10 minutes]**

Option: The article deals with the drawbacks of communication technologies. In small groups, have students list some advantages of communication technologies. Then have students draw a conclusion as to whether or not the disadvantages outweigh the advantages. **[+5–10 minutes]**

DISCUSSION **BUILDER**

Suggested teaching time:	15–20 minutes
Your actual teaching time:	_____

Step 1.

- Have a volunteer read the list of activities out loud. Clarify any unfamiliar terms.
- Have students complete the survey on their own and add an activity in the last row. If necessary, explain that *run an errand* is go out for a short time to buy something, pick up something, deliver something, etc.
- Have students circle the activities they consider to be true leisure activities.

Step 2. Pair Work.

- To get students ready for pair work, have them list the activities they would like to spend more time on and the ones they spend too much time on.

- Have pairs take turns sharing the activities on their lists. Encourage them to explain why they would like to spend more time on some of them and less time on others. You may want to model this for the class. For example, *I wish I could exercise more often. Exercising helps me feel refreshed, but I can only find time to go to the gym once a week.*

Step 3. Discussion.

- Read the questions and the model out loud.
- On the board, draw the following chart (with the example):

What is a technology that is part of your everyday life?	Does it add to or interfere with your leisure time? Why?	What are some ideas to stop it from interfering with your leisure time?
my cell phone	Interferes—because it keeps ringing and interrupting me	turn it off when I go out and only turn it on if I need to make a call

🔄 Graphic Organizers

To prepare students for discussion, have them list two or three technologies that are part of their everyday lives in the first column and complete the chart for each technology.

- Form small groups and have students share the technologies they use and discuss the questions.
- Review as a class. Have volunteers from different groups share the best ideas they came up with for balancing leisure time and work / study with the class. List them on the board. Then have volunteers say if they are planning to put any of the ideas into practice.

Option: Divide the class into two groups and debate both sides of the technology issue *Is technology killing leisure time?* **[+10–15 minutes]**

Option: Writing. Have students write a response to Jon Katz, giving their own opinions about technology and leisure time. Tell them to begin with *In my opinion, technology is / is not killing leisure time.* **[+5–10 minutes]**

Project: Have students keep a daily record of their leisure time for one week, recording every leisure activity they enjoy and the amount of time spent on that activity. Have students write a paragraph about their results, using the following questions as a guide:

What was your total leisure time spent this week?
Were you surprised by this number?
Were you satisfied by the amount of leisure time you had?
Did anything interfere with your leisure time?
Is there anything you could do to add to your leisure time?

EXTRAS (optional)

Workbook: Exercises 10–15

C Discussion.

1. The author states that advances in technology such as e-mail, voice mail, cell phones, and the Internet are "destroying any idea of privacy and leisure." How do you think each of these technologies do that in his view? Give specific examples.

2. The author states that "technology almost never does what we expect." What expectations do people have each time a new technology appears? Give examples with specific technologies.

3. Do you agree with the author's point of view in the article? Why or why not?

DISCUSSION **BUILDER** • *Now compare your use of leisure time.*

Step 1. Complete the survey. Then circle the activities you truly consider to be "leisure activities."

Check how frequently you do each of the following activities.

	Very often	Frequently	Sometimes	Rarely	Never
running errands	◯	◯	◯	◯	◯
doing housework	◯	◯	◯	◯	◯
surfing the Web	◯	◯	◯	◯	◯
catching up on personal e-mail	◯	◯	◯	◯	◯
keeping in touch with friends by telephone	◯	◯	◯	◯	◯
spending time with family	◯	◯	◯	◯	◯
attending cultural events	◯	◯	◯	◯	◯
working on a hobby or interest	◯	◯	◯	◯	◯
playing games (video, board games, sports)	◯	◯	◯	◯	◯
reading for pleasure	◯	◯	◯	◯	◯
listening to music	◯	◯	◯	◯	◯
watching TV	◯	◯	◯	◯	◯
exercising	◯	◯	◯	◯	◯
taking naps	◯	◯	◯	◯	◯
eating out	◯	◯	◯	◯	◯
other:	◯	◯	◯	◯	◯

Source: www.questionpro.com

Step 2. Pair Work. Compare how you spend your time. Which activities do you wish you spent more time on? Are there any you think you spend too much time on?

Step 3. Discussion. In what ways does technology add to or interfere with your leisure time? What can you do to keep work or study balanced with leisure time in your life?

> "E-mail keeps me in touch with more of my friends. I don't think it interferes with my leisure time at all."

4 *Discuss the risk-taking personality*

Do people who ride roller coasters have a "big T" or "small t" personality?

LISTENING

A 🎧 **Listening Comprehension.** Listen to the interview with a psychologist. Then listen again and write a description for each of the two personality types the psychologist describes.

Answers will vary, but may include:

What is a "big T" personality?	What is a "small t" personality?
Someone who likes risks, likes doing new things, is not afraid of danger, and looks for excitement. This type of person can be described as a "risk-taker."	Someone who prefers certainty and routine, does not like taking risks, hates thrills and prefers to avoid them. This type of person can be described as a "risk-avoider."

B **Discussion.** Where do you fit on the risk-taking continuum? Do you have a "big T" or a "small t" personality? Give examples to support your opinion.

◄ **RISK-TAKER**   **RISK-AVOIDER** ►

Pronunciation Booster

C 🎧 **Vocabulary. Ways to express fear and fearlessness.** Listen and practice.

PAGE P10
Vowel sounds

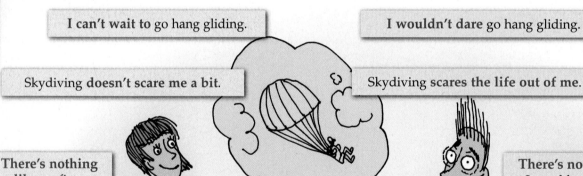

I **can't wait** to go hang gliding.

I **wouldn't dare** go hang gliding.

Skydiving **doesn't scare me a bit.**

Skydiving **scares the life out of me**.

There's nothing like surfing.

There's not a chance I would go surfing.

I **can't get enough of** white-water rafting.

You wouldn't catch me white-water rafting.

You'd have to be out of your mind to go bungee jumping.

Bungee jumping **is no sweat.**

4 Discuss the risk-taking personality

A 🎧 Listening Comprehension
(CD 4, Track 20)

Suggested teaching time:	10 minutes
Your actual teaching time:	_____

- Pre-listening: Point to the photo and ask *What are these people doing?* (riding a roller coaster) *How do you think they feel? If you were riding this roller coaster, how would you feel? Do you enjoy roller coasters? Why or why not?*
- Elicit from the class that a risk is the possibility that something bad or dangerous might happen and that someone with a risk-taking personality is willing to, or enjoys, taking risks.
- First listening: Have students listen to the interview and answer the question *Do people who ride roller coasters have a "big T" or "small t" personality?*
- Second listening: Have students listen and take notes on each personality type on a sheet of paper.
- Then have students write descriptions of each of the two personality types.
- Review as a class. Call on different students to read their descriptions out loud.

💿 Listening Strategies

Option: Have students listen again and take notes of the positive and negative sides of people with a "big T" personality. Have students compare their notes with a partner. To review as a class, have volunteers describe the positive and negative sides. Write notes on the board as students respond. You may want to refer to this list for Step 3, item 2, in the Discussion Builder on page 119. (Possible responses: **Positive side:** They play an important role, socially; They are responsible for achievements in creative fields; **Negative side:** They put themselves in danger; They have more accidents.) **[+5–10 minutes]**

> **AUDIOSCRIPT**
> For audioscript, see page AS13.

B Discussion

Suggested teaching time:	5–10 minutes
Your actual teaching time:	_____

- Point out that the continuum is a scale for identifying how much risk you take. Elicit from the class that a risk-taker has a "big T" personality and a risk-avoider has a "small t" personality.

- Draw a two-column chart with the heads *big T* and *small t* on the board. Individually, have students complete the chart by writing examples of ways they have a "big T" personality or a "small t" personality.
- Ask students to mark where they think they fit on the risk-taking continuum.
- Form small groups and have students share their opinions of their personality type and give examples.
- Review as a class. Take a poll to find out whether most students in the class consider themselves risk-takers or risk-avoiders. Write some examples in the chart on the board as students respond.

C 🎧 Vocabulary
(CD 4, Track 21)

Suggested teaching time:	10 minutes
Your actual teaching time:	_____

- Point to the images. Ask *What sports are shown?* (Possible responses: skydiving, parachuting, bungee jumping) *Which of the two people do you think would enjoy these sports? Why do you think so?*
- On the board, write:
  hang gliding
  skydiving
  surfing
  white-water rafting
  bungee jumping
- To make sure students know the extreme sports used in the vocabulary presentation, have volunteers describe the sports on the board. For example, *Skydivers jump from a plane and fall freely for a while before opening their parachutes.* Explain any sports students don't know.
- Have students listen and study the statements. Elicit from the class that the statements on the right express fear and those on the left express fearlessness.
- Have students listen again and repeat chorally.
- In pairs, have students write each of the statements in another way. Review as a class. (Possible responses: Hang gliding is a crazy thing to do; I'm eager to go hang gliding.)

D Pair Work

Suggested teaching time:	5–10 minutes
Your actual teaching time:	_____

- Model the activity with a more advanced student. Have the student use one of the expressions from Exercise C to express how he/she feels about one of the extreme sports. To encourage the student to explain his/her statement, ask follow-up questions such as *Why do you think so? Have you ever tried it? Why or why not? How does it make you feel?*
- In pairs, have students look at the photos and express how they feel about the sports.
- Circulate to encourage students to ask their partners questions.
- Call on pairs to say if they felt similarly or differently about some of the sports and give examples.

 Vocabulary-Building Strategies

DISCUSSION **BUILDER**

Suggested teaching time:	15–20 minutes
Your actual teaching time:	_____

 Discourse Strategies

Step 1. Pair Work.

- To model the activity, tell the class about a risky activity that you have done. Write *What? Where? When? How?* on the board and elicit follow-up questions from the class. Have students place you on the continuum on page 118.
- Have students use the question words on the notepad to frame questions to find out about their partner's riskiest activities.
- After students interview their partners, have them decide where their partners belong on the risk-taking continuum on page 118. Encourage students to think of reasons to support their decisions.
- Then have students take turns saying where they placed each other on the continuum and why. Encourage them to say whether or not they agree with their partner's description of them and why.

Step 2. Group Work.

- Form small groups. Have students share their experiences with their groups. Encourage students who are listening to ask relevant questions to find out more.
- Have students in each group vote for the student they think is the most fearless.
- Call on a member from each group to describe what the most fearless member of their group did. Write each group's most fearless member's experience on the board.
- Then have the class vote for the most fearless person.

Step 3. Discussion.

- Have a volunteer read the questions out loud.
- You may want to refer to the list you created for the option on page 118.
- Give students a few moments to think of their answers to the questions individually.
- Form small groups and have students discuss the questions.
- To review item 1, call on students from different groups to say what can cause a person to develop into a risk-taker or a risk-avoider. (Possible responses: the way the person was brought up; the person's level of self-esteem)
- To review item 2, have students who think risk-taking is a healthy type of behavior raise their hands. Keep a tally. Do the same for people with an opposing view. Then have students who support both views express their reasons. (Possible responses: To me, it's better to have a "big T" personality. A "small t" takes fewer chances, so he/she finds it more difficult to achieve dreams; I think it's safer to have a "small t" personality. The fewer risks you take, the fewer problems you have.)

EXTRAS (optional)

Pronunciation Booster
Workbook: Exercises 16–17

D **Pair Work.** Use the expressions from the vocabulary to discuss which extreme sports you would or would not be willing to do.

"Rock climbing scares the life out of me."

surfing

rock climbing

mountain biking

extreme skiing

skydiving

waterfall jumping

DISCUSSION **BUILDER** • *Now discuss the risk-taking personality.*

Step 1. Pair Work. What's the riskiest thing your partner has ever done? Interview him or her and take notes on your notepad. Where would *you* place your partner on the risk-taking continuum?

What?	Other details:
Where?	
When?	
How?	

Step 2. Group Work. In small groups, compare your partners' experiences. Then decide who is the most fearless.

Step 3. Discussion.

1. In your opinion, why does one person develop into a risk-taker and another into a risk-avoider?
2. Do you think risk-taking is a healthy type of behavior? Where do you think the best place to be on the risk-taking continuum is? Why?

Writing: *Comment on another's point of view*

Expressing and supporting your opinion

When you write to critique or comment on another's spoken or written ideas, present your reasons logically, using connecting words to give reasons and to sequence your ideas.

Giving reasons

I disagree **because** I think people actually have lots of free time today.

This is why I think the author is wrong.

We definitely have more free time **since** we are able to work from home.

On account of people using laptops, they get work done faster.

Sequencing ideas

First of all, I agree with Jon Katz's main point.

I **also** think he makes a good point about modern technology.

In addition, I think he's right about technology in the workplace.

Finally, we need to decide what we want technology to do for us.

WRITING MODEL

I disagree with almost all of Jon Katz's ideas in his article "Is Technology Killing Leisure Time?" **since** most new inventions actually help us increase the time we have for leisure activities. **First of all,** when Katz says, "Technology almost never does what we expect," he is ignoring the popularity of most new technologies. If a technology did not achieve its promise, it would not be so popular. **In addition,** I

Step 1. Prewriting. Developing arguments.

Read the article "Is Technology Killing Leisure Time?" on page 116 and underline sentences that you agree with or do not agree with. On a separate sheet of paper, do the following:

- paraphrase each sentence you underlined
- provide the reasons why you agree or disagree

Quoting the author

You can write short statements in direct speech using quotes, as shown in the Writing Model. Paraphrase longer statements in indirect speech.

The author says that technology almost never does what we expect.

I disagree because it isn't true for most new inventions. The popularity of most new technologies proves that people are happy with them.

Step 2. Writing. On a separate sheet of paper, write a critique of the article. State your own opinion at the beginning. Use the sentences you underlined and the comments you wrote to support your opinion.

Step 3. Self-Check.

☐ Is your opinion clearly stated?

☐ Did you use connecting words to support your reasons and sequence your ideas?

☐ Did you use quotation marks when using the author's own words?

☐ Did you paraphrase the author's words when you didn't use direct speech?

Writing Comment on another's point of view

Suggested teaching time: 20–25 minutes
Your actual teaching time: _____

Expressing and supporting your opinion

- Have a volunteer read the explanation out loud. If necessary, explain that if you *critique* a piece of writing, you give your opinion about it.

- Have a volunteer read the examples for *Giving reasons*. Point out the connecting words and the grammatical differences: use a subject and a verb after *because*, *this is why*, and *since*; use a noun or noun clause after *on account of*.

- Have a volunteer read the examples for *Sequencing ideas*. Point out the sequencing phrases and the punctuation: use a comma after *first of all*, *in addition*, and *finally*.

- Have a volunteer read the Writing Model out loud.

Language note: Use a comma after a clause / phrase starting with *because*, *since*, or *on account of* if it comes first in a sentence. For example:
People never turn their cell phones off <u>because</u> they want to be in touch.
<u>Because</u> people want to be in touch, they never turn their cell phones off.
I couldn't send you an e-mail <u>on account of</u> the power outage.
<u>On account of</u> the power outage, I couldn't send you an e-mail.
Because and *since* are subordinating conjunctions that introduce dependent clauses. A dependent clause with *because* or *since* must be attached to an independent clause to make a complete thought.

 Extra Writing Skills Practice

Option: To check comprehension, have students complete each blank in the paragraph below with a connecting word from the box. You may write this exercise on the board or photocopy and distribute it.

> *I completely disagree with the author ___1___.*
> *I think technology does not make our lives more difficult but much easier. ___2___. technology saves us time. If we didn't have computers, we would take much longer to do each task. ___3___ . it simplifies our tasks. ___4___ computers, we can edit our work without having to type it all over again.*

Review as a class. (1. because; 2. First of all; 3. In addition; 4. On account of) **[+5–10 minutes]**

Option: Elicit other sequencing words that students may know. (Possible responses: moreover, furthermore, additionally, likewise) **[+5 minutes]**

Step 1. Prewriting.

- Have volunteers read the directions, the note for quoting the author, and the model out loud.

- Have students find and underline the direct quote in the Writing Model.

- Have students underline four to six sentences in the article on page 116 that give important information.

- As students write the reasons they agree / disagree with the ideas they underlined, circulate to offer help as needed.

Step 2. Writing.

- Have a volunteer read the directions out loud.

- Using all or some of the ideas they underlined in their critique of the article, have students express their opinions on whether they agree / disagree with the author in the topic sentence. Then have them support their opinions in the supporting sentences that follow.

- As students write, circulate to help them clearly state their opinions and use connecting words. Be sure students paraphrase or use quotation marks when referring to the author's opinion.

Step 3. Self-Check.

- Read the Self-Check questions as a class.

- Before students submit their paragraphs for correction, have them self-check their work and make any necessary changes.

Option: Step 4. Peer Review. On the board, write:
> 1. *Does your partner agree with the article?*
> 2. *What is the opinion he or she expresses?*
> 3. *Does your partner give good reasons to support his or her point of view? What are they?*
> 4. *Do you agree with your partner? Why or why not?*

Have students exchange critiques with a partner and answer the questions. Then have pairs share their answers to the questions. **[+10 minutes]**

EXTRAS (optional)

Workbook: Page 100

A 🎧 Listening Comprehension
(CD 4, Track 22)

Suggested teaching time:	10 minutes
Your actual teaching time:	_____

- First listening: Have students listen and write the leisure activity being discussed. Review as a class. (1. collecting soda cans; 2. an Indian form of fighting; 3. a board game from West Africa; 4. quilting)

- Second listening: Have students listen and check the kind of leisure activity that the people are talking about.

- Have students compare notes with a partner and review as a class.

Option: Have students listen to Conversations 2 and 3 again and take notes of the advantages of each activity. Then have students compare answers with a partner and review as a class. (2. It helps you develop spiritually. It is physically and mentally challenging. 3. It is mentally stimulating.) **[+5 minutes]**

> **AUDIOSCRIPT**
>
> For audioscript, see page AS13.

B Categorize the leisure activities . . .

Suggested teaching time:	5–10 minutes
Your actual teaching time:	_____

- Have pairs first help each other with any unknown words and then use a dictionary to look up the words they don't know.

- Have students categorize the activities individually. Encourage them to add two more activities to each category.

- Have students compare answers and share their additional activities with a partner.

- Review as a class. Have volunteers share the new activities they thought of. You may want to write a list on the board.

Option: Have pairs use adjectives or verbs of their choice and the adverbs in Exercise D on page 113 to describe five activities from the chart. For example, *Lifting weights challenges you physically; Growing roses can be emotionally rewarding.* Then have each pair join another pair and share their descriptions. **[+5–10 minutes]**

C Use the words in the box . . .

Suggested teaching time:	5–10 minutes
Your actual teaching time:	_____

- Point out that there are many possible correct answers. Model the first item with the class and write students' ideas on the board. Make any necessary corrections. (Possible responses: his large green handmade sweater; many new cotton sweaters)

- Point out that even though item 1 was done as a class, students should write their own ideas for this item.

- Point out that if students use the quantifiers *some* and *many*, they should make the noun plural.

- Tell students to use each modifier only once.

- After students write their descriptions, have them look at the Grammar box on page 114 to confirm that they used the modifiers in the correct order.

- Then have students share their descriptions with a partner.

- Review as a class. Call on various students to read their descriptions out loud. Correct any mistakes as a class.

D Complete the statements . . .

Suggested teaching time:	5 minutes
Your actual teaching time:	_____

- Point out that students can write about extreme sports or any other kind of activity.

- Point out that the expressions *You wouldn't catch me* and *There's nothing like* are followed by gerunds.

- Have students share their sentences with a partner.

- Review as a class. Call on various students to read their sentences out loud.

 You may wish to use the Video Program and activity worksheets for Unit 10 at this point.

 Complete Assessment Package
Unit 10 Achievement Test
Review Test 2
Writing Test 2
Speaking Test 2

SUMMIT WEBSITE
For Unit 10 online activities, visit the *Summit* Companion Website at www.longman.com/summit.

A 🎧 **Listening Comprehension.** Listen to the conversations about free time. Infer the kind of leisure activity the people are discussing.

1. ☐ a game   ☐ a fitness activity   ☑ a hobby   ☐ a handicraft
2. ☐ a game   ☑ a fitness activity   ☐ a hobby   ☐ a handicraft
3. ☑ a game   ☐ a fitness activity   ☐ a hobby   ☐ a handicraft
4. ☐ a game   ☐ a fitness activity   ☐ a hobby   ☑ a handicraft

B Categorize the leisure activities in the box. Use a dictionary for words you don't know. Add other activities.

hobbies	games	handicrafts	fitness activities
collecting stamps growing roses restoring old cars raising iguanas	playing checkers doing puzzles playing cards	making jewelry sewing knitting	lifting weights doing tae kwon do

collecting stamps   lifting weights
making jewelry   sewing
playing checkers   doing puzzles
doing tae kwon do   knitting
playing cards   restoring old cars
growing roses   raising iguanas

C Use the words in the box to modify the nouns. Use at least three modifiers for each noun.

a / an	this / that	his / her	new	intelligent	English
some	many	green	stylish	black	handmade
adorable	destructive	sincere	clever	antique	South American
flashy	young	small	cotton	friendly	law

Answers will vary, but may include:

1. A stylish black cotton .... sweater
2. Her new destructive green .... parrot
3. That young intelligent South American .... student
4. An antique handmade English .... teacup

D Complete the statements in your *own* way.

1. .... scares the life out of me.
2. You'd have to be out of your mind to ....
3. You wouldn't catch me ....
4. .... doesn't scare me a bit.
5. I can't wait to ....
6. There's nothing like ....

Pronunciation table

These are the pronunciation symbols used in *Summit 1*.

Vowels

Symbol	Key Word	Symbol	Key Word
i	beat, feed	ə	banana, among
ɪ	bit, did	ɚ	shirt, murder
eɪ	date, paid	aɪ	bite, cry, buy, eye
ɛ	bet, bed	aʊ	about, how
æ	bat, bad	ɔɪ	voice, boy
ɑ	box, odd, father	ɪr	beer
ɔ	bought, dog	ɛr	bare
oʊ	boat, road	ɑr	bar
ʊ	book, good	ɔr	door
u	boot, food, student	ʊr	tour
ʌ	but, mud, mother		

Consonants

Symbol	Key Word	Symbol	Key Word
p	pack, happy	z	zip, please, goes
b	back, rubber	ʃ	ship, machine, station, special, discussion
t	tie		
d	die		
k	came, key, quick	ʒ	measure, vision
g	game, guest	h	hot, who
ʧ	church, nature, watch	m	men, some
		n	sun, know, pneumonia
ʤ	judge, general, major	ŋ	sung, ringing
f	fan, photograph	w	wet, white
v	van	l	light, long
θ	thing, breath	r	right, wrong
ð	then, breathe	y	yes, use, music
s	sip, city, psychology	ţ	butter, bottle
		t˺	button

Irregular verbs

base form	simple past	past participle	base form	simple past	past participle
be	was / were	been	forget	forgot	forgotten
beat	beat	beaten	forgive	forgave	forgiven
become	became	become	freeze	froze	frozen
begin	began	begun	get	got	gotten
bend	bent	bent	give	gave	given
bet	bet	bet	go	went	gone
bite	bit	bitten	grow	grew	grown
bleed	bled	bled	hang	hung	hung
blow	blew	blown	have	had	had
break	broke	broken	hear	heard	heard
breed	bred	bred	hide	hid	hidden
bring	brought	brought	hit	hit	hit
build	built	built	hold	held	held
burn	burned / burnt	burned / burnt	hurt	hurt	hurt
burst	burst	burst	keep	kept	kept
buy	bought	bought	know	knew	known
catch	caught	caught	lay	laid	laid
choose	chose	chosen	lead	led	led
come	came	come	leap	leaped / leapt	leaped / leapt
cost	cost	cost	learn	learned / learnt	learned / learnt
creep	crept	crept	leave	left	left
cut	cut	cut	lend	lent	lent
deal	dealt	dealt	let	let	let
dig	dug	dug	lie	lay	lain
do	did	done	light	lit	lit
draw	drew	drawn	lose	lost	lost
dream	dreamed / dreamt	dreamed / dreamt	make	made	made
drink	drank	drunk	mean	meant	meant
drive	drove	driven	meet	met	met
eat	ate	eaten	mistake	mistook	mistaken
fall	fell	fallen	pay	paid	paid
feed	fed	fed	put	put	put
feel	felt	felt	quit	quit	quit
fight	fought	fought	read /rid/	read /rɛd/	read /rɛd/
find	found	found	ride	rode	ridden
fit	fit	fit	ring	rang	rung
fly	flew	flown	rise	rose	risen
forbid	forbade	forbidden	run	ran	run

base form	simple past	past participle		base form	simple past	past participle
say	said	said		spring	sprang / sprung	sprang / sprung
see	saw	seen		stand	stood	stood
sell	sold	sold		steal	stole	stolen
send	sent	sent		stick	stuck	stuck
set	set	set		sting	stung	stung
shake	shook	shaken		stink	stank / stunk	stunk
shed	shed	shed		strike	struck	struck / stricken
shine	shone	shone		string	strung	strung
shoot	shot	shot		swear	swore	sworn
show	showed	shown		sweep	swept	swept
shrink	shrank	shrunk		swim	swam	swum
shut	shut	shut		swing	swung	swung
sing	sang	sung		take	took	taken
sink	sank	sunk		teach	taught	taught
sit	sat	sat		tear	tore	torn
sleep	slept	slept		tell	told	told
slide	slid	slid		think	thought	thought
smell	smelled / smelt	smelled / smelt		throw	threw	thrown
speak	spoke	spoken		understand	understood	understood
speed	sped / speeded	sped / speeded		upset	upset	upset
spell	spelled / spelt	spelled / spelt		wake	woke / waked	woken / waked
spend	spent	spent		wear	wore	worn
spill	spilled / spilt	spilled / spilt		weave	wove	woven
spin	spun	spun		weep	wept	wept
spit	spit / spat	spit / spat		win	won	won
spoil	spoiled / spoilt	spoiled / spoilt		wind	wound	wound
spread	spread	spread		write	wrote	written

Stative verbs

amaze	desire	hear	need	seem
appear*	dislike	imagine	owe	smell*
appreciate	doubt	include*	own	sound
astonish	envy	know	please	suppose
be*	equal	like	possess	surprise
believe	exist	look like	prefer	taste*
belong	fear	look*	realize	think*
care	feel*	love	recognize	understand
consist of	forget	matter	remember*	want *
contain	hate	mean	resemble	weigh*
cost	have*	mind	see*	

*These verbs also have action meanings. Example: I see a tree. (non-action) I'm seeing her tomorrow. (action)

Verbs that can be followed by a gerund

admit	dislike	miss	resist
appreciate	don't mind	postpone	risk
avoid	enjoy	practice	suggest
can't help	finish	quit	tolerate
complete	keep (as in *continue*)	recall	understand
consider	mention	recommend	
discuss	mind (as in *object to*)	resent	

Expressions that can be followed by a gerund

be excited about	be opposed to	believe in	blame [someone or something] for
be worried about	be used to	participate in	forgive [someone or something] for
be responsible for	complain about	succeed in	thank [someone or something] for
be interested in	dream about / of	take advantage of	keep [someone or something] from
be accused of	talk about / of	take care of	prevent [someone or something] from
be capable of	think about / of	insist on	stop [someone or something] from
be tired of	apologize for	look forward to	
be accustomed to	make an excuse for		
be committed to	have a reason for		

Verbs that can be followed directly by an infinitive

afford	deserve	offer	swear
agree	expect	plan	threaten
appear	fail	prepare	volunteer
arrange	hesitate	pretend	wait
ask	hope	promise	want
care	intend	refuse	wish
claim	learn	regret	would like
decide	mean	seem	
demand	need	struggle	

Verbs that must be followed by an object before an infinitive

advise	encourage	invite	require
allow	expect	need	teach
ask	forbid	order	tell
beg	force	permit	urge
cause	help	persuade	want
challenge	hire	promise	warn
convince	instruct	remind	would like

Adjectives that can be followed by an infinitive

anxious	depressed	lucky	relieved
ashamed	disappointed	pleased	sad
certain	fortunate	prepared	sorry
content	glad	proud	upset
delighted	happy	ready	

Verbs that can be followed by a gerund or an infinitive

with a change in meaning

forget (+ gerund)	=	forget something that happened
(+ infinitive)	=	forget something that needs to be done
regret (+ gerund)	=	regret a past action
(+ infinitive)	=	regret having to inform someone about an action
remember (+ gerund)	=	remember something that happened
(+ infinitive)	=	remember something that needs to be done
stop (+ gerund)	=	stop a continuous action
(+ infinitive)	=	stop in order to do something

without a change in meaning

begin	love
can't stand	prefer
continue	start
hate	try
like	

Participial adjectives

alarming	–	alarmed	disturbing	–	disturbed
amazing	–	amazed	embarrassing	–	embarrassed
amusing	–	amused	entertaining	–	entertained
annoying	–	annoyed	exciting	–	excited
astonishing	–	astonished	exhausting	–	exhausted
boring	–	bored	fascinating	–	fascinated
comforting	–	comforted	frightening	–	frightened
confusing	–	confused	horrifying	–	horrified
depressing	–	depressed	inspiring	–	inspired
disappointing	–	disappointed	interesting	–	interested
disgusting	–	disgusted	irritating	–	irritated
distressing	–	distressed	moving	–	moved

paralyzing	–	paralyzed
pleasing	–	pleased
relaxing	–	relaxed
satisfying	–	satisfied
shocking	–	shocked
soothing	–	soothed
startling	–	startled
stimulating	–	stimulated
surprising	–	surprised
terrifying	–	terrified
tiring	–	tired
touching	–	touched

and

Grammar Booster

Unit 1

Gerunds and infinitives: summary

Gerunds

- Have volunteers read the explanation and examples out loud.
- To check comprehension, have pairs create three sentences using gerunds as different grammatical functions and write them on a slip of paper. Circulate as students write to offer help as needed. Then have each pair join another pair, exchange slips of paper, and identify the grammatical functions of the gerunds in their classmates' sentences.

Infinitives

- Have volunteers read the first explanation and examples out loud.
- Emphasize that although infinitives can be used as subjects, impersonal *It* and gerund phrases are more common.
- On the board, write:

  To spend time with friends is important.

  To check comprehension, have students rephrase the sentence twice, using *It* and a gerund as the subject. Review as a class. (It is important to spend time with friends. Spending time with friends is important.)
- Have a volunteer read the second explanation and examples out loud.
- Point out that infinitives can never be the object of a preposition.
- On the board, write:

  I plan . . .

  To check comprehension, call on students to complete the sentence with their own ideas.

- Have a volunteer read the last explanation and examples out loud.
- On the board, write:

  I got up early . . .
  She called me . . .

  To check comprehension, have pairs complete the sentences with an infinitive or an infinitive phrase. To review, call on volunteers to share their sentences with the class.
- Have volunteers read the Remember box out loud.
- On the board, write:

  1. He advised us not to swim in the river.
  2. They just started playing / to play the second half.
  3. I was shocked to hear the news.
  4. She plans to go on vacation soon.
  5. They don't mind working late.

  To check comprehension, have students identify verbs and adjectives followed by gerunds, infinitives, or objects and infinitives. To review as a class, label the examples on the board as students provide the answers. (1. verb + object + inf.; 2. verb + ger./inf.; 3. adj. + inf.; 4. verb + inf.; 5. verb + ger.) In pairs, have students match each sentence with the category it falls under in the Remember box. (1. 4th, 2. 3rd, 3. 5th, 4. 2nd, 5. 1st)
- To provide practice, have pairs write five sentences of their own, using verbs or adjectives from pages A3–A4 in the Appendices. To review, call on various students to share their sentences with the class.

A Complete each sentence . . .

- Have students complete the sentences and then refer to page A3 in the Appendices to confirm their answers.
- Review as a class.

B On a separate sheet of paper . . .

- Model the first item with the class.
- Have students compare sentences with a partner and review as a class.

Grammar Booster

The *Grammar Booster* is optional. It provides more explanation and practice as well as additional grammar concepts.

Unit 1

Gerunds and infinitives: summary

Gerunds

A gerund functions as a noun. A gerund or gerund phrase can be the subject of a sentence, a direct or indirect object, a subject complement, or the object of a preposition.

> **Living a balanced life** is about integrating all parts of it. [subject]
> I love **spending time with my family**. [direct object]
> The best part of life is **learning new things**. [subject complement]
> Here are some tips for **getting a healthy perspective on life**. [object of a preposition]

Infinitives

An infinitive also functions as a noun. An infinitive or infinitive phrase can be the subject of a sentence, but infinitives as subjects are often considered awkward. It is more common to use an impersonal **It** as the subject.

> **To be honest** isn't always easy. [subject]
> OR **It** isn't always easy **to be honest**.

An infinitive or infinitive phrase can be a direct object or a subject complement.

> I want **to feel less stressed**. [direct object]
> My favorite thing is **to spend time with friends**. [subject complement]

An infinitive or infinitive phrase can express a purpose.

> Make time **to relax**.
> We stopped **to buy some gas**.

A Complete each sentence with a gerund or infinitive form of the verb. Refer to page A3 in the Appendices if necessary.

1. We were delighted ___to find___ out that we had won the contest.
   (find)

2. Be sure to thank your father for ___helping___ me get that interview.
   (help)

3. She goes to the gym five times a week ___to stay___ in shape.
   (stay)

4. Don't be surprised if he refuses ___to cooperate___ with them.
   (cooperate)

5. ___Asking___ other people for help is sometimes hard to do.
   (ask)

6. They definitely won't permit you ___to carry___ that on board.
   (carry)

B On a separate sheet of paper, rewrite the following sentences, using an impersonal <u>It</u> as the subject of the sentence.

1. To pass the examination is not the easiest thing in the world.
   It is not the easiest thing in the world to pass the examination.
2. To speak English fluently is my greatest wish.
   It is my greatest wish to speak English fluently.
3. To live in an English-speaking country might be an exciting experience.
   It might be an exciting experience to live in an English-speaking country.
4. To know when to use an infinitive and when to use a gerund is pretty confusing.
   It is pretty confusing to know when to use an infinitive and when to use a gerund.

Grammar for Writing: parallelism with gerunds and infinitives

A common error in formal written English is mixing gerunds and infinitives when listing items in a series. A list of items should either be all gerunds or all infinitives.

When I take time off from work, I prefer **relaxing** at home, **spending** time with my family, and **getting** things done around the house.

NOT I prefer relaxing at home, spending time with my family, and ~~to get~~ things done around the house.

I can't stand **getting up** late and **missing** the bus.

NOT I can't stand getting up late and ~~to miss~~ the bus.

In a series, either use _to_ with all the infinitives or only with the first one.

When I take time off from work, I prefer **to relax** at home, **spend** time with my family, and **get** things done around the house.

NOT When I take time off from work, I prefer to relax at home, spend time with my family, and ~~to~~ get things done around the house.

C On a separate sheet of paper, correct the errors in parallelism in the following sentences.

1. After she arrived in London, she began to write long letters home and ~~calling~~ her parents at all hours of the night.
   (call)

2. There are two things I really can't stand doing: speaking in front of large audiences and ~~chat~~ with people I don't know at parties.
   (chatting)

3. Right before midnight, everyone began to sing, dance, and ~~to~~ welcome in the new year.

4. There's no question I prefer using all my vacation time and ~~take~~ a long vacation.
   (taking)

D Complete the following sentences, using appropriate gerund or infinitive forms. Refer to page A3 in the Appendices if necessary.

1. I would suggest ___filling___ out the form immediately and ___making___ a copy for
   (fill) _(make)_
   your records.

2. Did you remember ___to turn___ off the stove, ___close___ the windows, and
   (turn) _(close)_
   ___lock___ the door before you left?
   (lock)

3. It's obvious from her e-mails that she really loves ___experiencing___ the culture, ___meeting___
   (experience) _(meet)_
   new people, and just ___being___ there.
   _(be)_

4. I don't think they permit ___taking___ photographs or ___using___ a recorder.
   (take) _(use)_

5. I really wouldn't mind ___taking___ them out to dinner or ___showing___ them
   (take) _(show)_
   around if you'd like me to.

6. He promised ___to take___ the report home, ___read___ it carefully, and ___respond___
   (take) _(read)_ _(respond)_
   to any questions by the next day.

Grammar for Writing: parallelism with gerunds and infinitives

- Have a volunteer read the first explanation and correct and incorrect examples out loud.
- Point out that in the first example, *prefer* refers to the three activities: relaxing at home, spending time with family, and getting things done around the house.
- Have a volunteer read the second explanation and correct and incorrect examples out loud.
- You may want to write two correct, contrasting examples on the board:
  I managed to catch the train, to get there on time, and to buy the tickets.
  I managed to catch the train, get there on time, and buy the tickets.

C On a separate sheet of paper . . .

- Model the first item with the class. Call on a student to identify the items in a series. (to write long letters; calling her parents)
- Encourage students to first identify the items listed in a series in each sentence as they complete the exercise.
- Have students compare answers with a partner and review as a class.

D Complete the following sentences . . .

- Remind students that when the infinitive and gerund are both grammatically possible, they should pay attention to the meaning of the sentence. You may want to refer them to the Grammar box on page 5.
- Have students review answers in pairs, using page A3 in the Appendices to confirm or correct their answers. Then review as a class.

Option: On the board, write:

A	B
On weekends, I enjoy . . .	Next year I'm planning to . . .
Right now I feel like . . .	Last year I managed to . . .
Sometimes I can't help . . .	I can't wait to . . .

To provide more practice with parallelism with gerunds and infinitives, have pairs choose two phrases from each column and take turns completing them. Encourage them to respond with two or more ideas for each phrase. (Possible responses: On the weekends I enjoy getting up late, doing sports, and eating out with friends; Next year I'm planning to take up a sport and get a new job.)

Unit 2

Finished and unfinished actions: summary

Finished actions

- To review verb tenses, ask
    How do you form the simple past of regular verbs?
    (verb + -ed)
    What are some examples of irregular verbs in the simple past? (Possible answers: ate, sold)
    How do you form the present perfect? (have / has + past participle)
    How do you form the present perfect continuous?
    (have / has + been + present participle)
    How do you form the past perfect? (had + past participle)

- Have volunteers read the explanations and examples out loud. Then have students close their books.

- On the board, write:

finished action
1. *that happened at an unspecified past time*
2. *that happened at a specified past time*
3. *that happened before another action in the past*
4. *that was in progress and finished very recently*

To check comprehension, have pairs decide what form is used for each situation. Then have students use their books to confirm their answers. Review as a class. (1. present perfect; 2. simple past; 3. past perfect; 4. present perfect continuous)

Unfinished actions

- Have a volunteer read the explanation and examples out loud.

Option: On the board, write:

1. *I _____, but I'm done now.*
2. *I _____ several times.*
3. *When I got here, _____.*
4. *I _____ last week.*
5. *I _____ for / since _____.*

To provide practice, have students complete the sentences with their own ideas. Point out that they should first identify the correct verb tense required and then complete the sentences with their own ideas. (1. present perfect continuous; 2. present perfect; 3. past perfect; 4. simple past; 5. present perfect continuous) Encourage them to write true information about themselves. Circulate as students write to offer help as needed. Then have them share their sentences with a partner.

A Complete the article . . .

- Point out that students should decide whether each of the actions happened at a specified or unspecified time in the past.

- Have students compare answers with a partner and review as a class.

B Read each statement . . .

- Encourage students to read the first statement and decide the order in which the events occurred before choosing statement **a** or **b.**

- Have students compare answers with a partner and review as a class.

Unit 2

Finished and unfinished actions: summary

Finished actions

Use the simple past tense or the past of **be** for an action finished at a specified time in the past.
   They **watched** that DVD yesterday.

Use the present perfect for an action finished at an unspecified time in the past.
   They**'ve watched** that DVD three times.

Use the past perfect for an action that was finished before another action in the past.
   When I arrived, they **had** already **watched** the DVD.

NOTE: Although the continuous aspect is used for actions in progress, the present perfect continuous is sometimes used for very recently completed actions, especially to emphasize duration.
   They**'ve been watching** that DVD all afternoon, but they're done now.

Unfinished actions

Use the present perfect OR the present perfect continuous for unfinished actions that began in the past and may continue into the future. Use the present perfect continuous to further emphasize that the action is continuous.
   She**'s listened** to Ray Charles for years. [And she may continue.]
   OR She**'s been listening** to Ray Charles for years. [And she may continue.]

A Complete the article, using the simple past tense, the past of **be**, or the present perfect.

World Music is not really a true genre of music—it is a combination of musical genres from around the world. For a number of years, recording companies ___have used___ the term to describe the music of artists who
(1. use)
they feel could appeal to new audiences across cultures. The concept of World Music ___was___ first created
(2. be)
after U.S. singer / songwriter Paul Simon ___recorded___ his hugely successful *Graceland* album in 1986. At that
(3. record)
time, he ___invited___ South Africa's male choir Ladysmith Black Mambazo and rock group Savuka to accompany
(4. invite)
him on the recording. Both groups later ___toured___ with him around the world. This exciting collaboration
(5. tour)
immediately ___appealed___ to European and North American audiences, who were attracted to this different sound.
(6. appeal)

Since that time, as more artists ___have tried___ to reach new audiences, there ___has been___ an increased amount
(7. try)   (8. be)
of "crossover"—that is, musicians influencing each other across cultures. Enthusiasm for music from other cultures
___has risen___ steadily. Artists such as Angélique Kidjo and Carlos Vives, who were well-known within specific
(9. rise)
regions such as Africa or Latin America, ___have become___ international stars, and mainstream music ___has incorporated___
(10. become)   (11. incorporate)
many of the features of these artists.

B Read each statement. Then decide which description is closer in meaning.

1. By the time I heard about it, the concert had sold out.
   a. First I heard about the concert. Then it sold out.
   (b.) First the concert sold out. Then I heard about it.

2. After he'd won the award, he got a big recording contract.
   a. First he got the recording contract. Then he won the award.
   (b.) First he won the award. Then he got the recording contract.

3. We wanted to go to his performance because we'd heard his new CD.
   (a.) First we heard his CD. Then we wanted to go to his performance.
   b. First we wanted to go to his performance. Then we heard his CD.

4. He'd played at a lot of different halls before he performed at Carnegie Hall.
   a. First he performed at Carnegie Hall. Then he played at a lot of different halls.
   (b.) First he played at a lot of different halls. Then he performed at Carnegie Hall.

The past perfect continuous

Use the past perfect continuous for a continuous action that occurred and finished before an earlier time or event.

By 1998, he **had been studying** French for about five years.

When the test began, the students **had been waiting** for over an hour.

NOTE: This structure tends to occur more in formal writing than in speaking.

C Use the present perfect continuous or the past perfect continuous to complete each statement.

1. Stella is such a big fan of Bob Marley that she has been collecting nothing but his recordings for years.
   (collect)

2. Jill Morsberger had been performing at clubs for ten years before Greenwood Entertainment invited her
   (perform)
   to sign a recording contract.

3. Jeff had been waiting at the airport for his girlfriend when he saw the lead singer for U2.
   (wait)

4. She must be extremely popular. The audience has been standing in line to buy tickets for over two
   (stand)
   hours.

5. The lead guitarist for the band has been rehearsing the new songs for weeks. That's why they sound
   (rehearse)
   so good tonight.

6. Shakira had been recording songs only in Spanish before she decided to branch out and try recording
   (record)
   songs in English for the U.S. market.

Grammar for Writing: noun clauses as adjective and noun complements

Noun clauses as subjects are awkward and generally avoided. Two ways to rewrite such sentences follow.

Use a noun clause as an adjective complement.

AVOIDED **That Frankel is quite critical of modern art** is obvious.

PREFERRED It is obvious **(that)** Frankel is quite critical of modern art.

Use a noun clause as a noun complement.

AVOIDED **That her job was so difficult** was why she quit.

PREFERRED The fact **that her job was so difficult** was why she quit.

Impersonal expressions that introduce noun clauses

It is **important** (that)
It appears **obvious** (that)
It seems **clear** (that)
It becomes **essential** (that)
It is **possible** (that)
It looks **likely** (that)

Noun phrases that can precede a noun clause

the announcement that	**the news** that
the argument that	**the possibility** that
the belief that	**the proposal** that
the chance that	**the reason** that
the claim that	**the recommendation** that
the demand that	**the report** that
the fact that	**the suggestion** that
the idea that	

The reason that she refuses to appear in films is a mystery to everyone.

The argument that classical music is dead makes no sense.

The news that the new CEO is retiring surprised a lot of people.

D On a separate sheet of paper, rewrite each sentence, using the impersonal It.

1. That developing countries address the problems caused by global warming is extremely important.
   It is extremely important (that) developing countries address the problems caused by global warming.

2. That the president plans on resigning appears obvious to everyone.
   It appears obvious to everyone (that) the president plans on resigning.

3. That not providing disaster relief will only worsen the situation seems quite clear.
   It seems quite clear (that) not providing disaster relief will only worsen the situation.

4. That a cure for cancer will be discovered in the next twenty years is certainly possible.
   It is certainly possible (that) a cure for cancer will be discovered in the next twenty years.

5. That the governments of Argentina and Chile will reach an agreement looks very likely.
   It looks very likely (that) the governments of Argentina and Chile will reach an agreement.

6. That Max Bianchi won't be participating in the Olympics next year is not important.
   It is not important (that) Max Bianchi won't be participating in the Olympics next year.

The past perfect continuous

- Have a volunteer read the explanation, examples, and Note out loud.
- Direct students' attention to *By* and *When* in the examples in the Grammar box. Point out that phrases with words like *by* and *when* often show the "earlier time (1998) or event (the test began)" in sentences with the past perfect continuous.
- To clarify, write a new example and draw a timeline on the board:

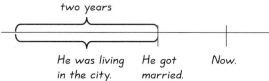

By the time he got married, he had been living in the city for two years.

Point out that the action (living in the city) was in progress for some time before a past time or event (He got married).

- To provide practice, have students choose a past moment or event and write a true statement about themselves using the past perfect continuous. (Possible response: By the time I got my first promotion, I had been working in the company for two years.) To review as a class, call on students to read their sentences out loud.

C Use the present perfect continuous ...

- Point out that students should first decide if the action is unfinished (and may continue into the future) or finished (and happened before another past time or event).
- Have students compare answers with a partner and review as a class.
- You may want to point out the use of *before* in items 2 and 6 to show the "earlier time or event."

Option: To provide practice with the past perfect continuous, have pairs create three true or imaginary sentences using the past perfect continuous with *by*, *when*, and *before*. (Possible responses: By the time my brother turned ten, he had been taking piano lessons for four years; When she arrived, I had been waiting for two hours; I had been talking for two minutes before I realized that the phone was disconnected.) To review, call on students to share some of their sentences with the class.

Grammar for Writing: noun clauses as adjective and noun complements

- Before students study the Grammar box, review with them that noun clauses often follow phrases with impersonal *It* subjects. You may want to refer them to the Grammar box on page 18. Write an example on the board:

    It is my opinion that classical music is relaxing.

- Have volunteers read the explanations and examples out loud.
- On the board, write:
    1. That he will win first prize is possible.
    2. That his project was the best was why he won first prize.

To check comprehension, have students identify the noun clause in each example. Underline the clauses as students identify them. (1. That he will win first prize; 2. That his project was the best) Ask *What is the grammatical function of the noun clauses in these sentences?* (They are subjects.)

- Point out that noun clauses as subjects are generally avoided not only in writing but also in spoken English.
- Add to the board:
    3. It is possible that he will win first prize.

    4. The fact that his project was the best was why he won first prize.

Ask *What is the grammatical function of the noun clause in sentence 3?* (adjective complement) *Why?* (because it gives information about an adjective—*possible*) *What is the grammatical function of the noun clause in sentence 4?* (noun complement) *Why?* (because it gives information about a noun—*fact*)

- Point out that *that* can usually be omitted after adjectives.
- Erase the clauses from sentences 3 and 4. To provide practice, have pairs complete the sentences with their own ideas, using noun clauses. To review, call on volunteers to share their sentences with the class.
- Have a volunteer read the list of impersonal expressions that introduce noun clauses and the list of noun phrases that can precede a noun clause and the examples out loud.

Option: On the board, write:
    pollution   population   education   poverty

To provide practice, have pairs take turns using impersonal expressions that introduce noun clauses to express their opinions on some of the world issues on the board. Model the activity for the students. For example, *It is essential that all children get a good education.* To review, call on volunteers to share their views with the class.

D On a separate sheet of paper ...

- Model the first item with the class. Call on a student to identify the expression that will be used to introduce the noun clause. (is extremely important) Have a volunteer read the correct sentence out loud.
- Have students compare answers with a partner and review as a class.

E Read each quote ...

- Point out that the two sentences should be combined into one sentence.
- Have a volunteer read the example out loud. As a class, identify the noun phrase and noun clause. (The announcement; that Volkswagen would unveil a new car design early next year)
- Have students compare answers with a partner and review as a class.

Answers to Grammar Booster, Unit 2—Exercise E

1. The announcement that the Health Ministry will begin vaccinating all infants for measles was greeted with criticism from the opposition party.
2. The possibility that the president would resign by the end of this year has taken everyone by surprise, including the news media.
3. The report that Dr. Regina Blair of the Glasgow Medical Center has discovered a new protein is attracting much interest in the world of science.
4. The claim that a 95-year-old New Zealand man had broken the world record for growing the longest beard has triggered similar claims across three continents.

Unit 3

The future continuous

- Have a volunteer read the first explanation and examples out loud.
- Write a new example on the board:

> Next year, I ⎰'ll be living   ⎱ in London.
> ⎱'m going to be living⎰

Point out that both forms of the future continuous ('ll be living, 'm going to be living) have the same meaning.

- To provide practice, address different students and ask questions eliciting the future continuous. For example, *Where will you be living in three years? What will you be studying next week? Where are you going to be spending your next vacation? What will you be doing tomorrow at this time?* Encourage students to answer in complete sentences.
- Have a volunteer read the second explanation and examples out loud.

- Have students study the Remember box. Point out that the simple future should be used with stative verbs. You may want to refer student to page A3 in the Appendices for a list of stative verbs.
- Have students read the examples under *Questions and short answers.*
- Have a volunteer read the last explanation and examples out loud.
- On the board, write:

> *I'll be preparing the decorations while she makes the cake.*

As a class, identify the time clause and the future continuous. (while she makes the cake; 'll be preparing)

Option: Have students think about what they and the people in their family will be doing this weekend and write two sentences using the future continuous with a time clause. (Possible response: My brother will be riding his bike while I repair my car.) To review, have a few students share their sentences with the class.

A On a separate sheet of paper ...

- Model the first item with the class. Have students identify the time clause. (when she's going to be attending the meeting) Ask *What tense do we use with the time clause?* (a present tense) Point out that either the present simple tense or the present continuous are possible in the time clause.
- Have students compare answers with a partner and review as a class.

E Read each quote from a radio news program. Then, on a separate sheet of paper, complete each statement, using the noun clause as a noun complement.

Example: "Volkswagen announced that they would unveil a new car design early next year. This is causing a lot of excitement in the auto industry." [The announcement . . .]

> *The announcement that Volkswagen would unveil a new car design early next year is causing a lot of excitement in the auto industry.*

1. "The Health Ministry announced that they will begin vaccinating all infants for measles. This was greeted with criticism from the opposition party." [The announcement . . .]
2. "The president said it was possible that he would resign by the end of this year. This has taken everyone by surprise, including the news media." [The possibility . . .]
3. "The *London Sun* reported that Dr. Regina Blair of the Glasgow Medical Center has discovered a new protein. This is attracting much interest in the world of science." [The report . . .]
4. "The *Auckland Times* claimed that a 95-year-old New Zealand man had broken the world record for growing the longest beard. This has triggered similar claims across three continents." [The claim . . .]

Unit 3

The future continuous

Use the future continuous for actions that will be in progress at a specific time or over a period of time in the future.
To form the future continuous, use <u>will</u> + <u>be</u> + a present participle OR <u>be going to</u> + <u>be</u> + a present participle.

At this time next week, I { 'll be lying / 'm going to be lying } on a beach in Hawaii. [specific time]

I { 'll be studying / 'm going to be studying } English in the United States for about two years. [period of time]

REMEMBER

Stative verbs are "non-action" verbs such as <u>be</u>, <u>have</u>, <u>know</u>, <u>remember</u>, <u>like</u>, <u>seem</u>, <u>appreciate</u>, etc.

Do not use the continuous with stative verbs.
DON'T SAY By next month, I'll be having a new car.

For a complete list of stative verbs, see page A3 in the Appendices.

Sometimes sentences in the simple future and the future continuous have almost the same meaning. Choose the future continuous to emphasize a continuous or uninterrupted activity.
Next year, I'll study English in the United States.
Next year, I'll be studying English in the United States.

Questions and short answers
Will you be working at home? Yes, I will. / No, I won't.
Are you going to be working at home? Yes, I am. / No, I'm not.

Use the future continuous and a time clause with <u>while</u> or <u>when</u> to describe a continuous activity that will occur at the same time as another activity. Do not use a future form in the time clause.
I'll be looking for a job while my wife continues her studies.
NOT I'll be looking for a job while my wife will be continuing her studies.

When the mayor is speaking, we'll be listening carefully.
NOT When the mayor will be speaking, we'll be listening carefully.

A On a separate sheet of paper, correct the errors in the following sentences.

1. She'll be staying at the Newton Hotel when ~~she's going to be attending~~ [she attends] the meeting.
2. We won't be spending much time sightseeing while ~~we'll be visiting~~ [we visit] London.
3. When ~~he's going to stay~~ [he stays] in town, he's going to be meeting with some friends.
4. She'll be correcting homework while the students ~~will be~~ [are] taking the test.
5. While Michelle ~~will be~~ [is] serving dessert, Randy will already be washing the dishes.
6. Won't they be going to sleep in New York when ~~you'll be~~ [you're] getting up in Taipei?

B Complete the following sentences, using the future continuous with <u>will</u> when possible. If the future continuous is not possible, use the simple future with <u>will</u>.

1. After I've completed my studies, I _will be looking_ for a job.
   (look)
2. She _will be photographing_ historic sites while she's in Turkey.
   (photograph)
3. In a few years, they _won't remember_ all the problems they had.
   (not / remember)
4. _Will_ he _be waiting_ between flights for very long?
   (wait)
5. I'm sure she _won't be sleeping_ when you call.
   (not / sleep)

The future perfect continuous

Use the future perfect continuous to emphasize the continuous quality of an action that began before a specific time in the future. To form the future perfect continuous, use <u>will</u> + <u>have</u> + <u>been</u> and a present participle.
   By next year, I'**ll have been studying** English for five years. [Describes an action that began before "next year" and may still continue.]

Combine a statement using the future perfect continuous with a time clause to show the relationship between two future actions. Use the simple present tense in the time clause.
   By the time I **arrive** in New York, I'**ll have been sitting** in a plane for over ten hours.
   NOT   By the time I'll arrive in New York, I'll have been sitting in a plane for over ten hours.

C Complete the notecard, using the future continuous or the future perfect continuous.

Dear Ida,

Venice was great, but finally on to Paris! By tomorrow afternoon, I _will be strolling_ down
   (1. stroll)
the Champs Elysées and _will be taking_ in
   (2. take)
the beautiful sights of that great city. In the evening, I _will be enjoying_ an opera by Bizet
   (3. enjoy)
in the city where he was born. Just think, by Saturday, I _will have been eating_ delicious French
   (4. eat)
food for a whole week! Plus, I _will have been practicing_
   (5. practice)
my French with real native speakers.

Then, after Paris, it's off to the Riviera, where I _will be lounging_ around on the beaches of
   (6. lounge)
Nice and Saint-Tropez for a week. By that time, I _will have been traveling_ for three weeks, and it will
   (7. travel)
almost be time to come home—a long trip for a homebody like me!

See you soon!

Pavel

Unit 4

A **Review.** Check *all* the quantifiers that can complete each sentence correctly.

1. If a child watches .... television, he or she may develop a self-image problem.
   ☑ a lot of   ☐ several   ☐ a number of   ☑ a great deal of
2. I don't think you can say that .... young people are self-conscious about their bodies.
   ☑ most   ☐ a great deal of   ☐ every   ☑ a majority of
3. It's clear that .... company needs to make its own decision about it.
   ☐ some   ☑ each   ☑ every   ☐ most
4. There are .... beauty treatments available to our customers.
   ☑ a number of   ☑ a few   ☑ plenty of   ☐ a little
5. I was surprised to read that .... men are considering cosmetic surgery.
   ☑ a lot of   ☑ some   ☐ every   ☐ less

B Complete the following sentences . . .

- Remind students not to use the future continuous with stative verbs. You may want to refer them to the Remember box on page G5.
- Have students compare answers with a partner and review as a class.

The future perfect continuous

- Have a volunteer read the first explanation and example out loud.
- To clarify the use of the future perfect continuous, write on the board:

  Use the future perfect continuous for an action that:
  - *starts before a future time*
  - *will be in progress for some time*
  - *may continue after the stated future time*

- To illustrate the explanation, write an example on the board:

  By June next year, Joan will have been running her own business for ten months.

  Addressing each of the bullets above, point out that:
  - Joan will start running her own business before June next year.
  - By June, the action will have been in progress for ten months.
  - Joan may continue running her own business after June.

- Have a volunteer read the second explanation and examples out loud.
- Ask *What are the two actions taking place?* (arriving in New York, sitting on a plane) *Which action happens first?* (sitting in a plane) Point out that the action in the future perfect continuous begins first.
- On the board, write:

  By the time he _____ , he _____ abroad for six years.
  (graduate)   (live)

  To check comprehension, ask *What is the time clause?* (By the time he . . .) *What tense do we use with the time clause?* (the simple present tense) Elicit the correct tenses to complete the sentence on the board.

- Point out that the time clause usually starts with *By the time.*

Option: On the board, write:

  Where I live: _____
  A course I'm taking: _____
  A sport I do: _____
  A hobby I have: _____

Have students complete the ideas on the board. Then add to the board:

  By _____ , I _____ for _____?

Have students write future perfect continuous statements about themselves, using the ideas on the board. Have students write at least three sentences. Circulate to offer help as needed. Have volunteers share a sentence with the class. Encourage all students to respond.

C Complete the notecard . . .

- You may want to refer students to the Grammar box on page G5 to quickly review the future continuous.
- Have students complete the exercise in pairs, and then review as a class.

Challenge: Have pairs imagine they are going on their ideal vacation next week. Ask them to write a notecard similar to the one in Exercise C explaining what they will be doing and will have already done on different days and at different times.

Unit 4

A Review

- Point out that more than one quantifier may be correct in each sentence.
- Review with students that some quantifiers can only be used with singular count nouns (for example, *one, each, every*), some quantifiers can only be used with plural count nouns (for example, *a few, many, a number of*), some quantifiers can only be used with non-count nouns (for example, *a little, much, a great deal of*), and other quantifiers can be used with both count and non-count nouns (for example, *some, any, a lot of*). You may want to refer students to the Grammar box on page 40 to quickly review quantifiers.
- Model the first item with the class. Point out that *television* is a non-count noun.
- Have students compare answers with a partner and review as a class.

Quantifiers: <u>a few</u> and <u>few</u>, <u>a little</u> and <u>little</u>

- Have a volunteer read the explanation and examples out loud.
- To summarize, draw a chart on the board (without the answers) and complete as a class:

	Plural count nouns	Non-count nouns
some	a few	a little
not many / much	few	little

- Photocopy and distribute this exercise or write it on the board:
    1. I have very _____ time. We can't discuss that today.
    2. I have _____ time. Let's discuss the project now.
    3. There were _____ interesting places. She liked the city.
    4. There were _____ interesting places. She didn't quite like the city.

To check comprehension, have students complete the blanks with the most suitable quantifier from the chart. Review as a class. (1. little, 2. a little, 3. a few, 4. few)

B   Change the underlined quantifiers …

- Ask *What two quantifiers mean* some? (a few, a little)
- Have a volunteer read item 1 out loud. *Why can't we use* a few *in item 1?* (because music is a non-count noun) As students work on the exercise, have them identify the type of noun the quantifier refers to. Point out that in item 5, the infinitive *to do* acts as the noun. If students have trouble, explain that infinitives and gerunds as nouns are non-count.
- Have students compare answers with a partner and review as a class.

Quantifiers: using <u>of</u>

- Have volunteers read the first explanation, examples, and Be Careful! note out loud.
- Have a volunteer read the second explanation, examples, and Be Careful! note out loud.
- Have students study the explanation and examples for *one* and *each*.
- Emphasize that both forms (*one* and *one of* / *each* and *each of*) have the same meaning.
- Have students study the last explanation and list of quantifiers that must include *of*.
- Write contrasting examples on the board:
    I have <u>a lot of</u> fashion magazines. (general noun)
    She likes fashion magazines. She has <u>a lot</u>! (no noun)
- To check comprehension, ask a few volunteers to use one of these quantifiers in a sentence. Point out that these sentences must have a noun or a noun phrase. (Possible response: Plenty of people prefer dressing up for work.)

Option: Photocopy and distribute this exercise or write it on the board:
    1. I have <u>a few</u> / <u>a few of</u> designer clothes.
    2. Just <u>a few</u> / <u>a few of</u> my clothes are formal.
    3. <u>Most of</u> / <u>Most</u> employees dress down on Fridays.
    4. <u>Most of</u> / <u>Most</u> our employees dress down on Fridays.
    5. Please take <u>both of</u> / <u>both</u> dresses to the dry-cleaner's.
    6. <u>Both</u> / <u>Both of</u> these dresses are expensive.
    7. <u>Each</u> / <u>Each of</u> school has its own rules.

To check comprehension, have pairs choose the correct quantifiers. Point out that both choices are correct in one sentence. Review as a class and have students explain their choices. (1. a few; 2. a few of; 3. Most; 4. Most of; 5. both; 6. Both / Both of; 7. Each)

Quantifiers: <u>a few</u> and <u>few</u>, <u>a little</u> and <u>little</u>

Use <u>a few</u> with plural count nouns and <u>a little</u> with non-count nouns to mean "some." Use <u>few</u> with plural count nouns and <u>little</u> with non-count nouns to mean "not many" or "not much."

A few companies are allowing their employees to dress casually on Fridays. [some companies]
Few companies are allowing their employees to dress casually on Fridays. [not many companies]
Employees are showing **a little interest** in this new dress code. [some interest]
Employees are showing **little interest** in this new dress code. [not much interest]

B Change the underlined quantifiers to <u>a few</u>, <u>few</u>, <u>a little</u>, or <u>little</u>.

a little
Example: Would you like to listen to ~~some~~ music?

little
1. We actually eat <u>almost no</u> meat.

a little
2. The newspaper had <u>a bit of</u> information about the concert tonight.

a few
3. There were <u>several</u> new students in my class today.

few
4. To tell the truth, I've seen <u>hardly any</u> movies in the last month.

little
5. I enjoy visiting my hometown, but there's <u>not much</u> to do there.

a few
6. If you look in the refrigerator, there should be <u>some</u> eggs.

Quantifiers: using <u>of</u>

Use <u>of</u> (to refer to something specific) when a noun is preceded by a possessive adjective, a possessive noun, a demonstrative pronoun, or the article <u>the</u>.

most of Jack's co-workers	–	**most** co-workers in Italy
several of these companies	–	**several** companies
a few of the choices	–	**a few** choices
a little of the cake	–	**a little** cake
many of those books	–	**many** books
any of her friends	–	**any** friends
much of the coffee	–	**much** coffee
some of his students	–	**some** students
each of the classes	–	**each** class
one of my cats	–	**one** cat
all of our employees	–	**all** employees

possessive adjectives my, her, their, etc.
possessive nouns John's, the doctor's
demonstrative pronouns this, that, these, those

BE CAREFUL! In the superlative, do not use <u>of</u> with <u>most</u>.
DON'T SAY Tokyo is the city with the most ~~of~~ people in Japan.

Using <u>of</u> after <u>all</u> or <u>both</u> is optional, with no change in meaning.
all of our employees   OR   **all** our employees   NOT   **all** ~~of~~ employees
both of those choices   OR   **both** those choices   NOT   **both** ~~of~~ choices

BE CAREFUL! <u>Of</u> must be included when using an object pronoun.
both of them   NOT   ~~both them~~

<u>One</u> and <u>each</u> are used with singular nouns only. But <u>one of</u> and <u>each of</u> are used with plural nouns only. However, the meaning of both expressions is still singular.
One student   –   **One of** the students
Each class   –   **Each of** the classes

Some quantifiers must include <u>of</u> when they modify a noun or noun phrase.

a lot of	a majority of
lots of	plenty of
a couple of	a bit of
a number of	a great deal of

C   Only one of each pair of sentences is correct. Check the correct sentence and correct the mistake in the other one.

Example: a. ____✔____ She went with several of her classmates.

        b. _____ Several ~~of~~ classmates went out for coffee.

1. a. _____ Most ~~of~~ companies in the world are fairly formal.

      b. ____✔____ Most of the companies in the United States have dress-down days.

2. a. _____ All ~~of~~ hot appetizers were delicious.

      b. ____✔____ Everyone tried all of the cold appetizers.

3. a. ____✔____ A lot of my friends have traveled to exotic places.

      b. _____ There are a lot _^ places I'd like to see. *(of)*

4. a. ____✔____ I read a few of Steinbeck's novels last year.

      b. _____ A few ~~of~~ novels by Steinbeck take place in Mexico.

5. a. _____ Several managers were interviewed, and many _^ them liked the new policy. *(of)*

      b. ____✔____ Many of the employees we spoke with liked the new policy.

Quantifiers: used without referents

Most quantifiers can be used without the noun they describe as long as the context has been made clear earlier.

A number of people believe there is life on other planets. But **many** don't. [many people]

Grammar for Writing: subject-verb agreement with quantifiers with _of_

In quantifiers with _of_, the verb must agree with the noun that comes after _of_.

Some of **the movie is** in English.   –   Some of **the movies are** in English.

A lot of **the music was** jazz.   –   A lot of **the musicians were** young.

In formal English, _none of_ is followed by a singular verb. However, in everyday spoken English, it is common to use it with a plural verb.

Formal: **None of** the students **was** late for class.

Informal: **None of** the students **were** late for class.

> **BE CAREFUL!** The quantifiers <u>one of</u>, <u>each of</u>, and <u>every one of</u> are always followed by a plural noun, but they always take a singular verb.
>
> **One of** the students **likes** rap music.

D   Choose the verb that agrees with each subject.

1. Every one of these choices (sound / (sounds)) terrific!
2. One of the teachers ((was) / were) going to stay after class.
3. A lot of the problem ((is) / are) that no one wants to work so hard.
4. Each of the employees (want / (wants)) to work overtime.
5. Half of the city ((was) / were) flooded in the storm.
6. None of the players ((is coming) / are coming) to the game.
7. Only 8 percent of their workers prefer shorter work weeks, while at least 90 percent ((don't) / doesn't).

C Only one of each pair of sentences . . .

- Go over the example with the class. Call on a student to explain the correct answer. (*Of* is not correct in **b** because *classmates* isn't preceded by a possessive adjective, a possessive noun, *this, that, these,* or *those.*) Ask *How else could we correct* **b**? (Several of **her** classmates went out for coffee.)
- Have students compare answers with a partner and review as a class.

Challenge: Fashion survey. In pairs, have students write four questions about clothes, dress codes, and/or fashion. For example, *Are you interested in fashion? What kind of clothes do you usually wear?* Have students interview their classmates and take notes of their answers. Then have them report their findings to the class using quantifiers. (Possible responses: All the students are interested in fashion; None of the men we interviewed likes formal clothes.)

Quantifiers: used without referents

- Have a volunteer read the explanation and examples out loud.
- On the board, write:
    Most of the exercises are easy. But some _____.
    Most of the homework is easy. But some _____.

Have students identify what *some* refers to in each sentence. Underline the nouns (exercises, homework). Point to the first example and ask *Is* exercises *count or non-count?* (count) *Plural or singular?* (plural) Elicit the answer from the class. (aren't) Point to the second example and ask *Is* homework *count or non-count?* (non-count) Elicit the correct answer from the class. (isn't)

- On the board, write:
    1. *Twenty percent of the class was late. Eighty percent* _____.
    2. *Twenty percent of the students were late. Eighty percent* _____.

To check comprehension, have students complete the sentences. Review as a class. (1. wasn't, 2. weren't)

Grammar for Writing: subject-verb agreement with quantifiers with <u>of</u>

- Have a volunteer read the first explanation and examples out loud.
- If necessary, clarify that *some of the movie* means a part of the movie.
- Have a volunteer read the Be Careful! note out loud.
- Write two examples on the board:
    One child _____ leaving early.
    All of the children _____ leaving early.
    Each of the children _____ leaving early.

To check comprehension, have students complete the sentences with the correct tense of the verb *be* and review as a class. (is, are, is) To clarify, point to the first example and ask *How many children are leaving early?* (one) Point to the second example and ask *How many children are leaving early?* (all of them) Point to the third example and ask *How many children are leaving early?* (all of them)

- Explain that in the last example, even though we are talking about all of the children, we are referring to each individually.
- Have students study the last explanation.
- Point out that even though *none of* plus a plural verb is acceptable in spoken English, we shouldn't use it in writing.

D Choose the verb . . .

- Model the first item. Elicit from the class the noun that the quantifier modifies. (choices) Ask *Which verb is correct?* (sounds) *Why?* (because the quantifier *every one* always takes a singular verb)
- Have students compare answers with a partner and review as a class. For item 6, point out that *are coming* is only possible in everyday spoken English.

Challenge: Guessing game. In pairs, have students write six to eight sentences describing a movie, using quantifiers. Then have each pair join another pair and take turns reading the descriptions and guessing the movie. You may want to model some questions for the class. For example, *One of the scenes takes place in the jungle. A lot of the movie takes place in Rome. Some of the movie was filmed on location. Three of the actors were nominated for an Oscar.*

Unit 5

Conjunctions with <u>so</u>, <u>too</u>, <u>neither</u>, or <u>not either</u>

- Have a volunteer read the first explanation and examples, and the second Be Careful! note out loud.
- On the board, write:

Gossiping is impolite. Shouting is impolite.

Gossiping is impolite, and ⟨ _____.
_____.

To check comprehension, elicit the two ways to finish the sentence from the class, and add to the board. (so is shouting; shouting is too)

- Point out the comma after the first statement.
- To check comprehension, ask *Are additions with so and too used for affirmative or negative statements?* (affirmative statements) *Do so and too have the same meaning?* (yes) *Do they have the same form?* (No. *So* needs subject-verb inversion.)
- Have a volunteer read the second explanation and examples out loud.
- On the board, write:

Smoking is not considerate. Using cell phones is not considerate.

Smoking is not considerate, and ⟨ _____.
_____.

To check comprehension, elicit the two ways to finish the sentence from the class, and add to the board. (using cell phones isn't either; neither is using cell phones)

- Point out the comma after the first statement.
- To check comprehension, ask *Are additions with* neither *and* not either *used for affirmative or negative statements?* (negative statements) *Do* neither *and* not either *have the same meaning?* (yes) *Do they have the same form?* (No. *Neither* needs subject-verb inversion.)
- Have a volunteer read the first Be Careful! note out loud.
- Point out that *neither* has negative meaning, so it needs an affirmative verb. *Either* has positive meaning so it needs a negative verb. To help clarify, you may want to add to the board:

<u>neither</u> <u>is</u> using cell phones = using cell phones <u>isn't</u> <u>either</u>
  (-) (+)   (-) (+)

Option: On the board, write:

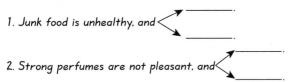
1. Junk food is unhealthy, and ⟨ _____.
_____.

2. Strong perfumes are not pleasant, and ⟨ _____.
_____.

To provide practice, have pairs complete the statements with their own ideas. They should express each idea twice using *so* and *too*, and *neither* and *not either*. To review, call on volunteers to read their statements out loud. (Possible responses: 1. smoking is too; so is smoking; 2. neither are cigars; cigars aren't either)

- Have a volunteer read the third explanation and examples out loud.

- Have students number the examples from 1 to 4. To check comprehension, have pairs identify the example(s) that use the verb *be*, an auxiliary verb, and a modal. (be: 1; an auxiliary verb: 2 [does], 3 [has]; a modal: 4 [can])
- Have a volunteer read the fourth explanation and example out loud.
- On the board, write:

Wendy wears strong perfumes, and so _____ *Katie.*
Wendy wears strong perfumes, and so _____ *Katie and Christine.*

Point out that the verb in the second statement must agree with the subject: *Katie* is singular, so it needs a singular verb; *Katie and Christine* is plural, so it needs a plural verb. Elicit the correct verbs from the class and complete the sentences on the board. (does, do)

- Have a volunteer read the third Be Careful! note out loud.
- Review with students the subject-verb inversion they studied in the previous box.

A Find and underline the nine errors ...

- Model the first error correction with the class. Call on a student to read the first sentence. As a class, identify the verbs. (is, does) Ask *What's wrong with this sentence?* (Since the first clause uses the verb *be*, the second clause has to use the same structure.)
- Have students compare answers with a partner and review as a class.

B On a separate sheet of paper ...

- Call on a student to read the example out loud. Point out the change in the verb (*have* changed to *has*) and the comma after the first statement. Also point out *does*, which is needed because the verb in the first statement isn't *be*, an auxiliary verb, or a modal.
- Have students complete the exercise individually, and then compare answers in pairs. Review as a class.

Challenge: On the board, write:
Things people do that are
  considerate:
  rude:
  irresponsible:
  unacceptable:

Have pairs write a few ideas for each adjective. Then have students express their ideas in statements using *too, so, neither* or *not either*. Circulate as students write to provide help as needed. To review, have pairs share some of their sentences with the class.

Unit 5

Conjunctions with <u>so</u>, <u>too</u>, <u>neither</u>, or <u>not either</u>

Use <u>and so</u> or <u>and . . . too</u> to join affirmative statements that are similar.
Spitting on the street is offensive, **and so** is littering.
OR Spitting on the street is offensive, **and** littering is **too**.

Use <u>neither</u> or <u>not either</u> to join negative statements that are similar.
Spitting on the street doesn't bother me, **and neither** does littering.
Spitting on the street doesn't bother me, **and** littering doesn't **either**.

If the first clause uses the verb <u>be</u>, an auxiliary verb, or a modal, use the same structure in the second clause.
Tokyo **is** a huge city, and so **is** São Paulo.
New York **doesn't** have a lot of industry, and neither **does** London.
Mexico City **has** grown a lot, and so **has** Los Angeles.
Nancy **can't** tolerate loud radios, and neither **can** Tom.

If the first clause does not include the verb <u>be</u>, an auxiliary verb, or a modal, use a form of <u>do</u>.
John **thinks** graffiti is a big problem, and so **does** Helen.

> **BE CAREFUL!** Use a negative with <u>either</u> and an affirmative with <u>neither</u>.
> . . . and neither does littering.
> NOT . . . and ~~neither doesn't~~ littering.
> . . . and littering doesn't either.
> NOT . . . and littering ~~does either~~.

> **BE CAREFUL!** Notice the subject-verb order.
> . . . and so is littering.
> . . . and littering is too.
> . . . and neither does littering.
> . . . and littering doesn't either.

> **BE CAREFUL!** With <u>so</u> and <u>neither</u>, the verb (or auxiliary verb) goes before the subject.
> Nancy can't stand loud boom boxes, and neither **can** Tom.
> NOT . . . neither ~~Tom can~~.
> Tokyo is a huge city, and so is São Paulo.
> NOT . . . and so ~~São Paulo is~~.

A Find and underline the nine errors. On a separate sheet of paper, write each sentence correctly.

New York is one of the most famous cities in the world, and so ~~does~~ [is] London. While these two cities differ in many ways, they also share a number of characteristics. Here's a quick comparison:

- If you're looking for peace and quiet, New York is not the place to be, and neither [London is]. They are both exciting and noisy places. If you're not used to it, New York's traffic can be deafening at times, and so ~~does~~ [can] London's.
- The best way to get around in both cities is the subway (or the Tube in London). New York's subway system is quite old and elaborate, and [is London's] too.

- If you're looking for first-rate entertainment, New York is filled with theaters, and so [is] London ~~does~~.
- Hungry? London's restaurants feature exciting dishes from around the world, and New York's ~~are~~ [do] too.
- Both cities offer a huge choice of museums to visit. The museums in New York can't possibly be seen in a day, and [either] [London's can't].
- New York offers some of the world's most famous tourist sites—for example, the Statue of Liberty and the Empire State Building—and so ~~is~~ [does] London, with Buckingham Palace and the Millennium Wheel.

It's clear that New York shouldn't be missed, and <u>neither</u> [should] London ~~shouldn't~~!

B On a separate sheet of paper, rewrite each statement, using the word in parentheses. Make any necessary changes in verbs or possessive adjectives.

Example: Both Vilnius and Riga have large historic districts. (so)

> *Vilnius has a large historic district, and so does Riga.*

1. Both Bangkok and São Paulo face many problems caused by too much traffic. (so)
   Bangkok faces many problems caused by too much traffic, and so does São Paulo.
2. Both Athens and Barcelona have hosted the Olympic Games in the past. (too)
   Athens has hosted the Olympic Games in the past, and Barcelona has too.
3. Vancouver and Taipei don't ever get very cold. (neither)
   Vancouver doesn't ever get very cold, and neither does Taipei.
4. Mexico City and Tokyo won't experience a decrease in their populations any time soon. (not either)
   Mexico City won't experience a decrease in its population any time soon, and Tokyo won't either.
5. Both Hong Kong and Rio de Janeiro are famous for their physical beauty. (so)
   Hong Kong is famous for its physical beauty, and so is Rio de Janeiro.
6. Prague and Krakow attract people who like great architecture. (too)
   Prague attracts people who like great architecture and Krakow does too.
7. The Prado Museum in Madrid and the Louvre in Paris shouldn't be missed. (neither)
   The Prado Museum in Madrid shouldn't be missed, and neither should the Louvre in Paris.
8. Tokyo and Mexico City haven't lost their places among the world's largest cities yet. (not either)
   Tokyo hasn't lost its place among the world's largest cities yet, and Mexico City hasn't either.

So, too, neither, or not either: short responses

Use **so**, **too**, **neither**, or **not either** in short responses to express agreement.

A: I hate littering. B: **So** do I. / I do **too**. NOT So do I ~~hate~~. / I do ~~hate~~ too.
A: I can't stand smoking. B: I can't **either**. / **Neither** can I. NOT I can't ~~stand~~ either. / Neither can I ~~stand~~.

In English, it is common to express agreement with <u>me too</u> or <u>me neither</u>.

A: I hate littering. B: **Me too.**
A: I can't stand smoking. B: **Me neither.**

C Agree with each statement. Use short responses with <u>so</u>, <u>too</u>, <u>neither</u>, or <u>not either</u>.

1. **A:** I've never been to Ulan Bator. **B:** I haven't either. / Neither have I. / Me neither.
2. **A:** I can't figure this out. **B:** I can't either. / Neither can I. / Me neither.
3. **A:** I loved going there! **B:** So did I. / I did too. / Me too.
4. **A:** I have to get some cash. **B:** So do I. / I do too. / Me too.
5. **A:** I'm getting really tired. **B:** So am I. / I am too. / Me too.
6. **A:** I used to travel more. **B:** So did I. / I did too. / Me too.
7. **A:** I'll call her tomorrow. **B:** So will I. / I will too. / Me too.
8. **A:** I'm not going to tell her she's late. **B:** I'm not either. / Neither am I. / Me neither.

Unit 6

Modals and modal-like expressions: summary

Make polite requests
Could I get your phone number?
Can my son have just one more cookie?
Would you please hold this for a second? (with <u>you</u> only)
May I have a cup of coffee? (with <u>I</u> or <u>we</u> only, formal)

Express preferences
I **would like to** see that movie.
Would you **like to** go running?
I'**d rather not** see a movie.
I **would rather** have left earlier.

Give or ask for permission
You **can** open the window if you want.
Can I leave this here?
You **may** leave early if you need to.
May I leave my coat here? (with <u>I</u> or <u>we</u> only, formal)

Express ability or lack of ability
He **can** complete the job for you in an hour.
Can you write well in English?
We **couldn't** finish the report yesterday.
Couldn't you find the restaurant?
My grandmother **isn't able to** walk any more.
Is she **able to** take care of herself?
She **was able to** do a lot more when she was younger.

Express possibility
It **may** rain this afternoon.
He **may not** be able to come this morning.
She **may** have forgotten to lock the door.
She **may not** have remembered.
It **might** be noisy at that restaurant.
She **might not** want to eat anything.
He **might** have gone home already.
He **might not** have paid yet.

Draw conclusions
Your father **must** be very smart.
She **must not** think it's important.
They **must** have been exhausted when they got home.
He **must not** have sent it.

Suggest alternatives
You **could** take the next train.
She **could** have bought it for less.

Give suggestions
They really **should** think about
  staying longer.
He **shouldn't** have waited to
  make a reservation.
They **should** have called first.
You **shouldn't** stay at that hotel.
They really **ought to** think about staying longer.
They **ought to** have called first.
Should we have called first?

> **NOTE:** <u>Ought to</u> is not usually used in negative statements or questions. Use <u>shouldn't</u> or <u>should</u> instead.

So, too, neither, or not either: short responses

- Have a volunteer read the first explanation and examples out loud.
- Point out the subject-verb inversion with *so* (So do I) and *neither* (Neither can I) in the examples.
- Also point out that main verbs that are not *be* (for example, *hate, like*) are not used in short responses, and the verb *be*, auxiliary verbs, and modals are used. For example, A: *I'm tired.* B: *So am I.*
- To provide practice, address different students and have them agree with the statements you say. For example, *I can speak two languages.* (So can I; I can too.) *I got up late this morning.* (So did I; I did too.) *I'm giving a party this Friday.* (So am I; I am too.) *I don't like horror films.* (Neither do I; I don't either.) *I've never been to Sweden.* (Neither have I; I haven't either.)
- Have a volunteer read the second explanation and examples out loud.
- To provide practice, address different students, and have them agree with the statements you say. You can use the same statements as above or your own.

C Agree with each statement . . .

- Model the first item with the class. Elicit all possible answers for item 1. (I haven't either; Neither have I; Me neither.)
- Point out that students should agree with each of the statements, even if the information is not true for them.
- Point out that there are three correct answers for each statement. You may want to have students write all three possible responses.
- Review as a class. Read each statement out loud and call on students to agree with you.

Challenge: On the board write:
> IDEAS
> - *Activities you do on the weekends*
> - *Things you like / dislike*
> - *Things you are good at*
> - *Things you could do when you were small*
> - *Things you were never able to do*
> - *Things you would like to do*

In pairs, have students find things they have in common. They can use the ideas on the board or their own ideas. As students talk, encourage them to use *so, too, neither,* or *not either* in short responses. Model the activity with a more confident student. For example, *I clean my room on the weekends.* Student: *I do too. / So do I. / Me too. / I don't.* Then have students share some of the things they have in common with their partners, with the class.

Unit 6

Modals and modal-like expressions: summary

- Have volunteers read the uses of modals/modal-like expressions and examples out loud.
- After the group of examples for each use, have a volunteer give his/her own example.
- To review modals, ask students the following questions and write answers on the board as students respond:
  > *How do we form negative modals?* (modal + *not* + verb)
  > *How do we form* yes / no *questions with modals?* (modal + subject + verb)
  > *How do we form information questions with modals?* (question word + modal + subject + verb)

Remind students that in information and *yes / no* questions with *have to*, we have to add *do / does* before the subject. You may want to refer students to the Grammar box on page 64.

- Have pairs find an example for each item on the board, in the Grammar box.

Modals and modal-like expressions: summary (continued)

- Have volunteers read the uses of modals/modal-like expressions and examples out loud.
- After the group of examples for each use, have a volunteer give his/her own example.
- In pairs, have students think of possible situations in which they would use these modals/modal-like expressions and write an example for each use. You may want to model the first one for the class. For example, (for *Give a warning*) *A mother warning her child: "You'd better do your homework!"*

Option: On the board, write the twelve categories in the Grammar box (Make polite requests, Express preferences, etc.). In pairs, have students take turns reading sentences from the Grammar box and saying what category they fall under. Have one student read a sentence from the Grammar box while the other student (with his/her book closed) names the category.

Challenge: In pairs, have students choose four sentences from the Grammar box and put them in context in short conversations. Students can make any necessary variations. Model a conversation for the class. For example, A: *My father is the CEO of a big company.* B: *He must be very smart!* Circulate to offer help as needed. To finish, call on pairs to share one of their conversations with the class.

A Cross out the one modal ...

- Model the first item with the class. Have a volunteer name the category from the Grammar box that it falls under (Make polite requests) and explain why *may* is not possible. (Because *may* can only be used with *I* or *we* in polite requests.)
- Have students first choose the category each item falls under and then cross out the incorrect modal. Point out that some items might fall under more than one category.
- Have students discuss their choices with a partner. Review as a class and have students explain their choices.

B Circle the one modal ...

- Model the first item with the class. Have a volunteer explain why *had to* is correct. (because the statement is about what happened last night, so a modal with past meaning is necessary)
- Have students discuss their choices with a partner. Review as a class and have students explain their choices.

Give a warning

Your mother **had better** see a doctor right away.
You **had better not** forget about your appointment.
He **had better** have called this morning.
They **had better not** have hurt any animals when they
made that movie.

> NOTE: Had better is generally not used in questions. In spoken English, the contraction 'd better is almost always used.

Express necessity

All students **have to** take the test.
All students **must** take the test. [formal]
All students **have got to** take the test. [spoken only]

Express lack of necessity

You **don't have to** have a passport.
She **didn't have to** pay a late fee.

Express prohibition or deny permission

New employees **shouldn't** park their cars in the garage.
New employees **cannot** park their cars in the garage.
New employees **must not** park their cars in the garage. [formal]
New employees **may not** park their cars in the garage. [formal]

> NOTE: In questions, have to is generally used. Questions with must are very formal and not very common. Past necessity is expressed with had to.
> Does everyone have to take the test?
> Must everyone take the test?
> All students had to take the test.

A Cross out the one modal that *cannot* be used in each sentence or question.

1. (~~May~~ / Can / Could) your mother please call me tonight?
2. I (wasn't able to / couldn't / ~~shouldn't~~) get there on time because the traffic was so bad.
3. She (may / had better / ~~can~~) be able to complete the job by tomorrow.
4. (Can / Should / ~~Ought to~~) my students listen in while you practice?
5. Shoppers (may / ~~have to~~ / must) not load their cars in front of the main entrance.
6. Thank goodness she (doesn't have to / ~~must not~~ / was able to) renew her passport for another five years.
8. You (~~could~~ / had better / should) let his assistant know you won't be able to make it on time, or you may not get the job.
9. This restaurant is so good we (ought to / might / ~~would rather~~) come here more often.

B Circle the one modal that best completes each conversation.

1. **A:** Why didn't you come to the party last night?
   B: I (had to / have to / must / have got to) study for a test.
2. **A:** You really (can't / should / mustn't / are able to) call more often.
   B: You're right. I'm sorry.
3. **A:** She ('d better not have / should have / had to have / must have) forgotten the tickets!
   B: Uh-oh. I hate to tell you this, but I think she did.
4. **A:** Do you think I ('m able to / must / would / could) get your phone number?
   B: Sure.
5. **A:** Did you get to go to the movies?
   B: Yeah. But I (must have / 'd rather have / should not have / would have) stayed at home.
6. **A:** Unfortunately, the doctor (shouldn't / has to / won't be able to / had better) see you until tomorrow.
   B: That's OK. No problem.
7. **A:** What do you think happened to Judy?
   B: She (must not have / shouldn't have / isn't able to / didn't have to) known we were starting so early.

Unit 7

Grammar for Writing: past forms of gerunds and infinitives

Gerunds and infinitives have past forms to express actions that occurred in the past.
I appreciate **having had** the opportunity to meet our overseas colleagues.
They were disappointed **not to have met** everyone from the Jakarta office.
We didn't mind **having been delayed** so long in Paris.
He's surprised **to have heard** about your resignation.

If the main verb is in the simple past tense or the past of <u>be</u>, the gerund or infinitive can be in either the present or past form, with no change in meaning. It is more common to use the present form of a gerund or an infinitive in everyday spoken English.
They were disappointed **not to meet** everyone from the Jakarta office.
We didn't mind **being delayed** so long in Paris.

Past forms	
Active voice	
gerund	<u>having</u> + past participle
infinitive	<u>to have</u> + past participle
Passive voice	
gerund	<u>having been</u> + past participle
infinitive	<u>to have been</u> + past participle

A Use a past gerund or infinitive form of each verb to complete the statements. Use the passive voice where necessary. Refer to page A3 in the Appendices if necessary.

1. It was clear that many passengers were shocked about _having been bumped_ from the flight without
   (bump)
   warning.

2. The ministers were found guilty of _having accepted_ personal gifts from foreign companies.
   (accept)

3. At the news conference, the president mentioned _having spoken_ with his advisers about the
   (speak)
   problem.

4. The mayor apologized today for _not having responded_ immediately to the disaster.
   (not / respond)

5. Most of the seniors expressed their happiness at _having been chosen_ as participants in the event.
   (choose)

6. They were accused of _having taken_ money from the cash register.
   (take)

7. The newspaper reporter appeared _to have been contacted_ by a government worker who claimed she knew
   (contact)
   what had really happened.

8. We want you to know how much we regret _having made_ such a serious mistake.
   (make)

Unit 7

Grammar for Writing: past forms of gerunds and infinitives

- To review present forms of gerunds and infinitives, draw the following chart (without the answers) on the board. Have volunteers complete each example with the correct form of the verb *interview*.

Present form		
Active voice	gerund	I enjoy *interviewing* people.
	infinitive	I prefer *to interview* people.
Passive voice	gerund	I enjoy *being interviewed*.
	infinitive	I prefer *to be interviewed*.

- Have a volunteer read the first explanation and first example out loud.
- Point out that the first example uses the past gerund because of the verb *appreciate*. You may want to refer students to pages A3–A4 in the Appendices for lists of words followed by a gerund, an infinitive, or both.
- Have a volunteer read the remaining examples out loud.
- Have students study the Past forms note.
- Draw a new chart on the board:

Past form		
Active voice	gerund	I regret _____ . (lie)
	infinitive	I was lucky not _____ a ticket. (get)
Passive voice	gerund	I appreciated _____ . (interviewed)
	infinitive	I was happy _____ . (invited)

To check comprehension of the past forms of gerunds and infinitives, have pairs complete the statements in the chart with the correct form of the verbs in parentheses. Review as a class. Complete the statements on the board as students provide the answers. (I regret <u>having lied</u>; I was lucky not <u>to have gotten</u> a ticket; I appreciated <u>having been interviewed</u>; I was happy <u>to have been invited</u>.)

- On the board, write:

  I dislike being bothered. → *I disliked having been bothered.*

  Ask *What tense is the first sentence in?* (present) *Is the second sentence in a past or present form?* (past form) Underline *dislike* and *disliked* in the two sentences. Ask *How did* being bothered *change?* (It changed to *having been bothered.*) Tell students that when the main verb is in a past form in formal written English, the gerunds and infinitives should backshift.

- Backshifting occurs from a present form to a past form. Point out that in the first example for the first explanation, *I appreciate having had the opportunity to meet our overseas colleagues, having had* is already in the past form, so it wouldn't backshift further if we changed the sentence to *I appreciated . . .*

- Erase *having been* from the second sentence on the board and replace it with *being*. Point out that in everyday spoken English, we don't usually backshift.

A Use a past gerund or infinitive form . . .

- Model the first item with the class. You may want to refer students to pages A3–A4 in the Appendices.
- Remind students that prepositional phrases can be followed by a gerund.
- Have students compare answers with a partner and review as a class.

Challenge: On the board, write:

A present regret about a past action:
Something you appreciate now that happened in the past:
Something that happened that surprised you:
Something that happened that you didn't expect to happen:

For further practice, have students complete the items on the board with their own ideas and then write sentences using past gerunds and infinitives in the active or passive voice. Students can write true or imaginary sentences. You may want to give your own example for one of the items. (Possible responses: I regret not having been at the office when the president made a surprise visit; I appreciate having been told the truth when my son crashed my car; I was surprised to have been invited to my colleague's house; I didn't expect to have been given a prize for that project.) Circulate as students write to offer help as needed. To finish, call on students to share their sentences with the class.

Unit 8

Making comparisons: summary

- Have a volunteer read the explanation and examples for comparative forms of adjectives and adverbs out loud.

- Have students number the examples from 1 to 4 and identify what or who are being compared. (1. John and Rob; 2. this movie and the last one; 3. my sister's typing and my typing; 4. corruption now and corruption before)

- To review how comparatives are formed, ask *How do you form the comparative of short adjectives or adverbs such as* fast? (adjective or adverb + *-er*) *How do you form the comparative of long adjectives or adverbs such as* interesting? (*more* or *less* + adjective or adverb)

- To review irregular comparative forms, have students look at the Irregular forms note.

- To provide practice, have volunteers share sentences comparing the people in their families. Give your own example. (Possible responses: My brother drives faster than I do; My uncle's house is much bigger than mine.)

- Have a volunteer read the explanation and examples for superlative forms of adjectives and adverbs out loud.

- Have students number the examples from 1 to 5 and identify the examples of superlative adjectives and the examples of superlative adverbs. (superlative adjectives: 1, 2, 4; superlative adverbs: 3, 5)

- To review how superlatives are formed, ask *How do you form the superlative of short adjectives and adverbs such as* fast? (*the* + adjective or adverb + *-est*) *How do you form the superlative of long adjectives or adverbs such as* beautiful? (*the most / the least* + adjective or adverb)

- To review irregular superlative forms, have students look at the Irregular forms note.

- To provide practice, have volunteers share sentences with superlatives. Give your own example. (Possible responses: My friend Brad is the funniest person I've ever met; Of all my friends, Sam is the most responsible.)

- Have a volunteer read the Be Careful! note out loud.

- On the board, write:
  1. Which is best?
  2. Which is best brand?
  3. Which is the best brand?
  4. Which brand is best?

To check comprehension, have students identify the examples that are correct. (1, 3, 4) Elicit from the class why 2 is incorrect. (You can't omit *the* if the superlative is followed by a noun.)

- Have a volunteer read the explanation and examples for comparisons with *as . . . as*.

- Point out that *just* emphasizes that the things being compared are equal.

- Point out that *not as . . . as* shows how two things are different. For example, *Tom is not as tall as George*.

- Have volunteers read the last two explanations and examples out loud.

- On the board, write:
  1. The new bridge is as wide as the old one.
  2. The new bridge is almost as wide as the old one.
  3. The new bridge is three times as wide as the old one.

To check comprehension, make a statement and have students identify which sentence on the board has the same meaning. Say *The old bridge was wider than the new one.* (2) *The new bridge is wider than the old one.* (3) *Both bridges have the same width.* (1)

Option: To provide practice with *as . . . as*, have students write a statement about themselves for each of the three explanations for *as . . . as*. Have students discuss and correct their sentences in pairs. To review, have a few volunteers read their sentences out loud. You may want to write a few examples on the board.

A Read each quoted statement . . .

- Model the first item with the class. Ask *Is one textbook better than the other?* (no) Elicit the correct answer from the class.

- Have students compare answers with a partner and review as a class.

Challenge: Have pairs choose two cities they both know and write six to eight sentences comparing the cities using comparatives, superlatives, and *as . . . as*. Encourage students to use *almost, about, not quite, twice,* or *(X) times* with *as . . . as* in some of their sentences. To review, have volunteers share their sentences with the class.

Unit 8

Making comparisons: summary

Comparative forms of adjectives and adverbs show how two things are different.

John is **taller than** Rob (is).
This movie was **less interesting than** the last one (was).
My sister types **a lot faster than** I (do).
There is **less corruption** in the government **than** there used to be.

Superlative forms of adjectives and adverbs show how one thing is different from everything else.

She was **the nicest person** I ever met!
That was **the least entertaining** movie I ever saw.
Of all the actors, she sang **the most beautifully**.
Among my friends, Ned and Stacey definitely have **the most money**.
Of all the cars we looked at, the Linkus **costs the most**.

> **BE CAREFUL!** Use <u>the</u> with a superlative form. However, you can omit <u>the</u> if the superlative is not followed by a noun.
> Which student is **the tallest** OR **tallest**?
> NOT ~~Which is tallest student?~~

Comparisons with <u>as</u> . . . <u>as</u> show how two things are alike.

Tom is just **as tall as** George (is).
She still sings **as beautifully as** she did when she was young.
My nephew now **weighs as much as** I do.
I have **as much money** in the bank **as** I did last year.

Use <u>as</u> . . . <u>as</u> with <u>almost</u>, <u>about</u>, and <u>not quite</u> to show how two things are similar, but not equal.

My nephew weighs **almost as** much as I do.
   [I weigh a bit more.]
The movie is **about as** long as his last one.
   [But it's a bit shorter.]
This coat isn't **quite as** expensive as it looks.
   [It's actually cheaper.]

Irregular forms

adjective	adverb	comparative	superlative
good	well	better (than)	the best
bad	badly	worse (than)	the worst
far	far	farther / further (than)	the farthest / furthest
a little	a little	less (than)	the least
a few	a few	fewer (than)	the fewest
many / a lot of	—	more (than)	the most
much / a lot of	—	much / a lot more (than)	the most

Use <u>as</u> . . . <u>as</u> with <u>twice</u>, <u>three times</u>, etc., to show that things are not equal at all.

A Linkus sedan is about **twice as** expensive **as** a Matsu.
My new computer is **ten times as** fast **as** my old one.

NOTE: In informal spoken English, it is more common to say ". . . as tall as me" instead of the more formal ". . . as tall as I."

A Read each quoted statement. Then complete each sentence using a comparative, superlative, or comparison with <u>as</u> . . . <u>as</u>.

1. "The textbook we are using now is very good. The textbook we were using last year was also very good."

   The textbook we're using now is ___as good as___ the one we were using last year.

2. "Star shampoo costs about $6.00. Ravel shampoo costs about $7.00. Sanabel shampoo costs about $5.00."

   Among the three shampoos, Sanabel is ___the cheapest___.

3. "We paid four hundred euros each for our tickets. They paid three hundred euros."

   We paid ___more than___ they did.

4. "Hank has only a little experience working with children. Nancy has a lot of experience."

   Hank has ___less experience than___ Nancy.

5. "John's laptop weighs 4 kilos. Gerry's laptop weighs 4.1 kilos."

   John's laptop isn't ___as heavy as___ Gerry's is.

6. "Mark knows only a little Japanese. Jonah knows a lot."

   Mark knows ___less Japanese than___ Jonah does.

7. "Bart ate a lot for lunch. Susan ate a lot for lunch too."

   Susan ate ___as much as___ Bart did for lunch.

Other uses of comparatives, superlatives, and comparisons with <u>as</u> . . . <u>as</u>

For emphasis
The Nile River is **more than** 5,500 kilometers long. [emphasizes that the river is very long]
The Dickens School now has **fewer than** 900 students. [emphasizes that this is a relatively small number]
A newborn Asian elephant can weigh **as much as** 150 kilos. [emphasizes that this is fairly heavy]
As many as 200 of these animals are killed every year. [emphasizes that this is a high number]
That was **the worst** movie **ever**. [emphasizes that this was a bad movie]
This meal was **the best ever**! [emphasizes that this was a great meal]

To show progression
My son is getting **taller** every day. [He's growing.]
The economy is **stronger** now. [It's improving.]

To show tendencies or preferences
We eat out **more than** in. [We tend to eat out.]
Sara likes being alone **more than** socializing. [She prefers to spend time alone.]

To clarify
He's a lot **friendlier than** you would think. [You may think he's not friendly, but in fact he is.]
She's **more of a singer than** a dancer. [People may think she's mainly a dancer, but in fact she's mainly a singer.]
The movie's **more annoying than** scary. [You may think this movie will be scary, but in fact it's just annoying.]
It looks **more like** snow **than** rain. [You may think it's going to rain, but in fact it looks like it's going to snow.]

B Use a comparative, a superlative, or a comparison with <u>as</u> . . . <u>as</u> to complete each statement so it has a similar meaning to the information in quotes.

1. "Our meal last night was really inexpensive. It only cost 48 euros for the two of us."
   Our meal last night cost ____less than____ 50 euros.

2. "Our reading club meetings are getting pretty big. On some nights there are thirty students."
   Our reading club meetings sometimes have __as many as thirty__ students.

3. "I think our teacher is really great!"
   Our teacher is ____the greatest____ ever!

4. "The garden you planted last month has become so beautiful!"
   Your garden is getting ____more beautiful____ every day!

5. "You may think snails might taste strange, but they actually taste quite good."
   Snails taste ____better than____ you may think.

6. "You may think Kate is shy, but she's actually very talkative."
   Kate is __more talkative / less shy__ than you might think.

Unit 9

<u>Say, ask,</u> and <u>tell</u>: summary

<u>Say</u> and <u>ask</u> are the most common reporting verbs in direct speech. Use <u>say</u> for statements and <u>ask</u> for questions.
"I completely disagree with the president on this issue," **said** the education minister.
"Who do they think is in control of this government?" **asked** the president.

Note the use of <u>say</u>, <u>ask</u>, and <u>tell</u> in indirect speech.
She **said (to the press)** that she completely disagreed with the president.
She **asked (the press)** if they disagreed with the president.
She **told the press** that she completely disagreed with the president.

BE CAREFUL!
DON'T SAY She ~~said the press~~ that she completely disagreed with the president.
DON'T SAY She ~~told~~ that she completely disagreed with the president.
DON'T SAY She ~~told to the press~~ that she completely disagreed with the president.

Other uses of comparatives, superlatives, and comparisons with <u>as . . . as</u>

- Have volunteers read the examples under *For emphasis*.
- On the board, write:
  1. It costs $90.
  2. It was a bad concert.
  3. The album can hold 200 photos.

  To provide practice, have students add emphasis to the statements on the board. Point out that in some cases there may be more than one way to add emphasis. Review as a class. (Possible responses: 1. It can cost as much as $90. 2. It was the worst concert ever. 3. The album can hold as many as 200 photos.)
- Have students study the examples under *To show progression*.
- Point out that the second part of the comparison (than) is not used.
- On the board, write:
  1. Prices are getting _____.
  2. The book is becoming _____.

  To provide practice, have students complete the statements with their own ideas. To review as a class, have volunteers read their sentences out loud. (Possible responses: 1. Prices are getting higher. 2. The book is becoming more interesting.)
- Have students study the examples under *To show tendencies or preferences*.
- On the board, write:
  1. In class, we _____ more than _____.
  2. At home / work, I spend more time than _____.
  3. Your idea: _____

  To provide practice, have pairs complete the statements with their own ideas. Review as a class. Have volunteers read their sentences out loud. (Possible responses: 1. In class, we <u>speak</u> more than <u>write</u>. 2. At home, I spend more time <u>in the garden</u> than <u>inside</u>.)
- Have students study the examples under *To clarify*.
- On the board, write the following prompts:
  1. ice skating–not difficult but easy
  2. vacation–not relaxing but tiring

  To provide practice, have pairs form sentences with the prompts on the board, using the comparative form to clarify. To review as a class, have volunteers read their sentences out loud. (Possible responses: 1. Ice skating is a lot easier than you would think. 2. My vacation was more tiring than relaxing.)

B Use a comparative, a superlative . . .

- Model the first item with the class. Point out that students should pay attention to the meaning of the sentence in quotes and choose the best use from the Grammar box above. Call on one student to say the use and another to complete the statement out loud.
- Have students complete the exercise individually and then compare answers with a partner. Review as a class.

Option: Photocopy and distribute this exercise or write it on the board:

I'm getting _____ every day.
On the weekends, I _____ more than _____.
I read _____ than _____ a year.
I'm a lot _____ than people think.

For further practice, have students complete the sentences with true information about themselves. In pairs, have students exchange sentences and decide on the use of the comparative, superlative, or comparison with *as . . . as* in their partners' sentences. Have a few volunteers read their sentences out loud and say the use. Then encourage students to create other sentences about themselves using comparatives, superlatives, and comparisons with *as . . . as* to show emphasis, progression, tendencies or preferences, and to clarify. Circulate as students write to provide help as needed. To finish, have students share their sentences with a partner.

Unit 9

<u>Say, ask,</u> and <u>tell</u>: summary

- With books closed, ask *Does direct speech or indirect speech use the exact words the speaker said?* (direct speech) *What's the function of indirect speech?* (to report the words the speaker said without using the exact words)
- Write three examples of indirect speech on the board:

  He said (<u>to me</u>) that he would go to the party.
  He asked (<u>me</u>) if I was going to the party.
  He told <u>me</u> that he was going to the party.

  Point to the first example. Ask *Is* to me *a direct or indirect object?* (indirect) Point to the second example. Ask *Is* me *a direct or indirect object?* (direct) Point to the third example. Ask *Is* me *a direct or indirect object?* (direct)
- Tell students that in indirect speech, *say* is followed by an indirect object (*to* + listener) or no object, *ask* is followed by a direct object (listener) or no object, and *tell* is followed by a direct object (listener).
- Point out *that* in the first and third examples. Remind students that *that* is not usually dropped after nouns.
- Have volunteers read the explanations, examples, and Be Careful! note out loud.

A Complete the sentences . . .

- Model the first item with the class. Tell students to first identify if the sentence has a direct or indirect object in order to decide between *say*, *ask*, or *tell*.

- Have students compare answers with a partner and review as a class.

Grammar for Writing: other reporting verbs

- With books closed, brainstorm ideas for reporting verbs other than *say* and *ask* as a class. Write a list on the board.

- Have volunteers read the explanation and examples out loud.

- Have students study the list of reporting verbs and look up the verbs they don't know in a dictionary.

Option: In pairs, have students choose another verb from the list of reporting verbs for each example in the Grammar box. Review as a class. Have volunteers read their sentences out loud.

B On a separate sheet of paper . . .

- Model the first item with the class. Identify the reporting verb (says) and brainstorm other possible replacements as a class. (Possible responses: reports, states)

- Have students compare answers with a partner and review as a class.

Challenge: Bring in newspapers and distribute. In pairs, have students choose an article that uses indirect speech, underline the sentences in indirect speech, and circle the reporting verbs. Then have each pair join another pair. Have pairs take turns reporting the articles they read, using different reporting verbs. Encourage students to include information about what people said.

A Complete the sentences with a form of say, ask, or tell.

1. She ___asked___ the waiter if she could pay with a credit card.
2. We ___said___ that we would come back later when they were less busy.
3. He ___told___ his friends that he would be a few minutes late.
4. She ___said___ to her teacher that she needed a bit more time.
5. I ___asked___ my kids whether they would mind if we stopped at the store on the way home.
6. They ___told___ the reporter that they were ready to provide information about the case.
7. He ___said___ to the clerk that it was the longest he'd ever had to wait on line.
8. I ___asked___ them if they enjoyed the movie.

Grammar for Writing: other reporting verbs

Writers use a variety of reporting verbs to describe actions more specifically and accurately.

argue
"Things are definitely getting worse," **argues** Charles Wilder, a leading economic advisor to the president.
Charles Wilder, a leading economic advisor to the president, **argues** that things are getting worse.

claim
"Baylor was taking bribes," **claims** the *Daily Sun*.
The *Daily Sun* **claims** that Baylor was taking bribes.

declare
"The mayor has been doing a brilliant job!" **declared** the governor on Tuesday.
On Tuesday, the governor **declared** that the mayor had been doing a brilliant job.

explain
"You should always discuss dieting with your doctor," Dr. Fish **explained**.
Dr. Fish **explained** that people should always discuss dieting with their doctors.

report
The New York Times **reports**, "Obesity is a growing problem in Asia."
Last year, *The New York Times* **reported** that obesity was a growing problem in Asia.

state
The new CEO **stated**, "Things are going to change around here."
The new CEO **stated** that things were going to change at the company.

More reporting verbs	
add	maintain
announce	mention
answer	promise
comment	remark
complain	reply
exclaim	reveal
imply	write

B On a separate sheet of paper, restate each sentence with a different reporting verb. Use a dictionary if necessary.
Answers will vary, but may include:

1. The *Bangkok Post* ~~says~~ _reports_ that the president of Chile will be visiting Thailand next month.
2. The minister of education ~~said~~ _declared_ yesterday that major improvements have been made in schools across the country.
3. The secretary of the United Nations ~~says~~ _maintains_ that more should be done to alleviate world hunger.
4. The scientists who conducted the study ~~said~~ _stated_ that more research would have to be conducted.
5. The children who wrote on the walls ~~said~~ _promised_ that they wouldn't do it again.
6. The BBC ~~said~~ _announced_ that it would increase its coverage of the news in the Middle East.

Unit 10

Intensifiers

Adverbs of degree, also called "intensifiers," modify adjectives and add emphasis.

An intensifier goes before a modifying adjective or series of modifying adjectives.

    a **really** interesting book

    a **considerably** large round orange

Intensifiers	
really	somewhat
very	fairly
pretty*	slightly
extremely	wonderfully
rather	considerably

*informal spoken

A   Complete the restaurant review with appropriate intensifiers.

Answers will vary, but may include:

> **Chez Pierre: Fine dining at its best!**
>
>   Upon arriving at this ....**really**.... lovely restaurant, guests are greeted by Chef Pierre, who proudly explains the ....**extremely**.... impressive new menu. There are some ....**rather**.... inexpensive dinner choices that are sure to satisfy even the most demanding diners. The elegant European-style décor at Chez Pierre only adds to the experience. However, the ....**slightly**.... subdued lighting makes it hard to read the menu and is ..**somewhat**.. disappointing. Be sure to ask about their **considerably** extensive dessert choices, which don't require good lighting for you to enjoy them thoroughly!

Adverbs of manner

Adverbs of manner show how something is done or happens. They usually go at the end of a clause when the adverb provides important information in the sentence.

    He ate his dinner **slowly**.   She sings really **well**.

Adverbs of manner ending in –**ly** can go before the verb or verb phrase when they are not the main focus of the sentence.

    I **slowly** opened the door. [focus is on opening the door]

    I opened the door **slowly**. [focus is on how the door was opened]

    He **angrily** hung up the phone. [focus is on hanging up the phone]

    He hung up the phone **angrily**. [focus is on how the phone was hung up]

Adverbs of manner can go before the past participle in the passive voice.

    His report was very **poorly** written.

BE CAREFUL! Do not place an adverb of manner between a verb and a direct object.

    He drank his coffee **quickly**. NOT He drank ~~quickly~~ his coffee.

Adverbs of manner	
angrily	poorly
badly	quietly
fast	sadly
happily	slowly
hard	softly
nicely	suddenly
noisily	well

B   Check if the adverb is correctly used. If not, make corrections.

☐ **1.** When the game was over, he left quickly the court. OR . . . he left quickly the court.

☑ **2.** As she drove into town, she sang to herself softly.

☑ **3.** The meeting was suddenly postponed after the CEO arrived.

☐ **4.** They pretended noisily to wash the dinner dishes as they listened in on the conversation.

☑ **5.** He congratulated her for her nicely presented report.

☐ **6.** They entered quietly the room and sat in the corner. OR They entered quietly the room . . .

Unit 10

Intensifiers

- Have volunteers read the explanation, examples, and list of intensifiers out loud. Encourage them to use a dictionary to look up any unknown intensifiers.
- On the board, write:
  1. cheap / jacket / incredibly / leather
  2. small / fairly / bowl / hand-carved

To check comprehension, have students put the words in order. To remind students about the order of modifiers, refer them to the Grammar box on page 114. To review as a class, call on a student to rewrite the descriptions on the board. (1. an incredibly cheap leather jacket; 2 a fairly small hand-carved bowl)

- To provide practice, have pairs write their own examples using some of the intensifiers from the list.

A Complete the restaurant review ...

- Have students (quickly) read the paragraph to find out what it is about. Then have them read it again and insert appropriate intensifiers. You may want to point out that there is more than one appropriate intensifier for each item.
- Have students compare answers with a partner and review as a class.

Adverbs of manner

- Have volunteers read the first two explanations and examples out loud.
- On the board, write:
  1. They entered the room noisily.
  2. They noisily entered the room.
  3. They entered noisily the room.

With books closed, check comprehension by having students decide which statements are correct. (1, 2) Point out that an adverb of manner can never separate a verb (entered) from its object (the room). Cross out the third example. Then ask *What is the focus in sentence 1?* (the way they entered the room—noisily) *What is the focus in sentence 2?* (the action—entering the room)

- Point out that adverbs that do not end in -*ly* must go after the verb phrase.
- Have a volunteer read the last explanation and example, the Be Careful! note, and the Adverbs of manner list out loud.

Option: To provide practice, have pairs use three adverbs from the list in sentences of their own. To review, call on volunteers to share their sentences with the class. You may want to write a few sentences on the board.

B Check if the adverb ...

- The have students circle the adverb of manner in each sentence.
- Then have students compare answers with a partner. To review as a class, have students explain what was wrong in each incorrect sentence.

Pronunciation Booster

Note about the Pronunciation Booster

Many will elect to do the Pronunciation Booster as self-study. If you choose to use the Pronunciation Booster as a classroom activity instead, included in these pages are teaching notes for the pronunciation presentations and exercises.

Unit 1

Content words and function words

- Have a volunteer read the explanation and examples out loud. Point out that stressed content words are set in capital letters.

- Direct students' attention to the lists of content words and function words. As a class, brainstorm more words for each category in the Content words box. (Possible responses: **nouns:** window, frustration; **verbs:** walk, have; **adjectives:** friendly, wide; **adverbs:** beautifully, painfully; **possessive pronouns:** ours, theirs; **demonstrative pronouns:** these; **reflexive pronouns:** myself, himself; **interrogative pronouns:** when, why)

- On the board, write:
  1. *She left her keys on that desk.*
  2. *He wants to sell his bicycle.*

  To check comprehension, have pairs decide which words receive the stress. To review, underline the content words in the examples as students say them. (1. left, keys, that, desk; 2. wants, sell, his bicycle)

- Explain that the existence of stressed and unstressed syllables creates the rhythm of English. (This makes English sound different from those languages in which *all* the syllables are stressed.)

Stress in compound nouns

- Have a volunteer read the explanation and examples of compound nouns and adjective + noun combinations out loud.

- On the board, write:
  1. *a library book*   3. *a fast car*   5. *a movie star*
  2. *a good book*   4. *a sports car*   6. *a bright star*

  To check comprehension, have students identify compound nouns and adjective + noun combinations. (**compound nouns:** 1, 4, 5; **adjective + noun combinations:** 2, 3, 6) Call on students to read items 1–6 out loud and stress the appropriate words. Underline the stressed words as students identify them. (1. library; 2. good book; 3. fast car; 4. sports; 5. movie; 6. bright star)

- Direct students' attention to the Be Careful! note. Make sure students understand that although auxiliary verbs are function words, they are stressed in short answers because they carry meaning—they represent the main verb in the question.

Language note: In English, words are often stressed for emphasis. This can often include function words that are not normally stressed. For example, in the sentence "He's such a wise guy," *such* is stressed to show emphasis.

A ⌒ Listen and practice.
(CD 5, Track 2)

- First listening: Have students listen and study the examples.

- Second listening: Have students listen and repeat individually or chorally.

- **Note:** This procedure for first and second listening is repeated in each unit.

B Circle the content words.

- In pairs, have students take turns reading the sentences. Then have them highlight or circle the stressed words.

⌒ Now practice ...
(CD 5, Track 3)

- Have students read each sentence out loud and listen for how their choices compare with the speakers' on the audio. If necessary, have them listen again and repeat chorally.

Note: To build students' confidence, make sure they have ample practice before reading. Students will say the item out loud when they hear the item number and then will hear the speaker say the same item immediately after.

C ⌒ Listen and practice.
(CD 5, Track 4)

- Refer to the procedure for Exercise A.

D ⌒ Practice reading ...
(CD 5, Track 5)

- Have students highlight or circle the stressed words. In pairs, have them take turns saying the compound nouns.

- Then have students listen for confirmation. If necessary, have them listen again and repeat chorally.

⌒ **Option:** To provide more practice, have pairs choose a paragraph from the Grammar Snapshot on page 4 and take turns reading it out loud, focusing on content words. Then have them listen to compare (CD 1, Track 3).

Pronunciation Activities

Pronunciation Booster

The *Pronunciation Booster* is optional. It provides more information about pronunciation as well as additional practice. The exercises can be found on both the Class Audio Program and the Student's Take-Home Audio CD.

Unit 1

Content words and function words

In English, content words are generally stressed.
Function words are generally unstressed.

My **BOSS** is a **PAIN** in the **NECK**!
He's **REALLY** a **TERRIFIC BOSS**.
MARK is such a **SMART GUY**.
I'm **SURE** she'll be a **GREAT MANAGER**.

Content words	
nouns	boss, Julie, happiness
verbs	find, meet, call
adjectives	talkative, small, green
adverbs	quietly, again, slowly
possessive pronouns	mine, yours, his
demonstrative pronouns	this, those, that
reflexive pronouns	ourselves, herself
interrogative pronouns	what, who, where

Stress in compound nouns

A compound noun is a noun that is made up of two or more words.
Stress generally falls on the first word in compound nouns.

compound noun		adjective + noun
He's a **WISE** guy.	BUT	He's a **WISE LEADER**.
She's a **PEOPLE** person.	BUT	She's a **NICE PERSON**.
It's an **APARTMENT** building.	BUT	It's a **TALL BUILDING**.
They're **EXERCISE** machines.	BUT	They're **NEW MACHINES**.

Function words	
prepositions	of, from, at
conjunctions	and, but, or
determiners	a, the, some
personal pronouns	he, she, they
possessive adjectives	my, her, their
auxiliary verbs	have + [past participle]
	be + [present participle]

BE CAREFUL! When an auxiliary verb is negative or used in short answers, it is generally stressed.
I **CAN'T GO**.   He **WON'T LIKE** it.
No, they **DON'T**.   Yes, I **HAVE**.

A 🎧 Listen and practice.

1. My **BOSS** is a **PAIN** in the **NECK**!
2. He's **REALLY** a **TERRIFIC BOSS**.
3. **MARK** is such a **SMART GUY**.
4. I'm **SURE** she'll be a **GREAT MANAGER**.

B Circle the content words.

1. (Learn) to (live) in the (present).
2. He (reminded) me to (call) (my) (mother).
3. He (asked) me to (work) (faster).
4. I (prefer) to (stick) (closer) to (home).

🎧 Now practice reading each sentence aloud and listen to compare.* (Note that your choices may differ from what you hear on the audio.)

C 🎧 Listen and practice.

1. He's a **WISE** guy.   He's a **WISE LEADER**.
2. She's a **PEOPLE** person.   She's a **NICE PERSON**.
3. It's an **APARTMENT** building.   It's a **TALL BUILDING**.
4. They're **EXERCISE** machines.   They're **NEW MACHINES**.

D 🎧 Practice reading each compound noun aloud and listen to check.*

1. a swimming pool
2. tennis courts
3. an answering machine
4. a telephone directory
5. office managers
6. the bullet train

*NOTE: Whenever you see a listening activity with an asterisk (*), say each word, phrase, or sentence in the pause *after* each number. Then listen for confirmation.

Unit 2

Intonation patterns

In statements, commands, and information questions, lower pitch after the stressed syllable in the last stressed word. If the last syllable in the sentence is stressed, lower pitch on the vowel by lengthening it.

I haven't been to many concerts lately.   Don't forget to watch them on TV tonight.

What do you like about that song?

Raise pitch after the stressed syllable in the last stressed word in <u>yes</u> / <u>no</u> questions and requests. If the last syllable in the sentence is stressed, raise pitch on the vowel by lengthening it.

Have you ever heard of Annie Lennox?   Could you pick up their new CD for me?

Do you think she has a nice voice?

A ⌒ Listen and practice.

1. I haven't been to many concerts lately.
2. Don't forget to watch them on TV tonight.
3. What do you like about that song?
4. Have you ever heard of Annie Lennox?
5. Could you pick up their new CD for me?
6. Do you think she has a nice voice?

B Circle the last stressed content word in each of the following sentences. If that word has more than one syllable, underline the stressed syllable.

1. That song has a great beat you can (dance) to.
2. Her catchy lyrics make you want to sing (along).
3. Didn't you like that song's (melody)?
4. What time do you think the concert will be (finished)?

⌒ Now practice reading each sentence aloud, using the intonation patterns you have learned. Listen to check.*

Unit 2

Intonation patterns

- Tell students that intonation patterns are important because they affect meaning.

- Explain that *pitch* refers to how high or how low a sound is.

- Have a volunteer read the first explanation out loud and have students study the examples. You may want to model the examples for students.

- To clarify, point out that a rising line indicates rising intonation. A falling line indicates falling intonation.

- Point out that the last stressed word is usually the last content word in a sentence.

- Have students identify the last stressed word in each example under the first explanation. (concerts, TV, song) Then ask *In which example is the last syllable stressed?* (in the third: *song*) Point out that in this sentence, the vowel in *song* is lengthened to lower pitch.

- Summarize on the board:

  statements
  commands   } pitch falls after last stressed syllable
  information
  questions

- Have a volunteer read the second explanation out loud and have students study the examples. You may want to model the examples for students.

- Have students identify the last stressed word in each example. (Lennox, CD, voice) Then ask *In which example will the vowel be lengthened?* (in the third: *voice*) Why? (because *voice* is the last syllable in the sentence and is stressed)

- Summarize on the board:

  yes / no
    questions   } pitch rises after last stressed syllable
  requests

Option: On the board, write:

1. I like the Beatles.   command
2. Change the channel.   yes / no question
3. Is he a good singer?   request
4. What's on TV?   statement
5. Can you play it louder?   information question

To check comprehension, have students match the examples on the left with the types of sentences and questions on the right, and decide the intonation pattern for each. Review as a class. (1. statement—falling intonation; 2. command—falling intonation; 3. *yes / no* question—rising intonation; 4. information question—falling intonation; 5. request—rising intonation)

A ⌒ Listen and practice.
(CD 5, Track 6)

- Refer to the procedure for Exercise A on page TP1.

B Circle the last stressed content word ...

- Have students circle the words individually. You may want to have students compare their choices with a partner.

- In pairs, have students practice reading each line aloud.

⌒ Now practice ...
(CD 5, Track 7)

- Have students listen to confirm their choices or make corrections.

⌒ **Option:** Have students identify *yes / no* questions and information questions in the Sound Bites conversation on page 15. Then have pairs practice the conversation using the intonation patterns they learned. To finish, have students listen to the conversation to compare the intonation they chose with the intonation used by the speakers on the audio (CD 1, Track 12).

 **Pronunciation Activities**

Unit 3

Sentence rhythm: thought groups

- Have a volunteer read the explanation and examples out loud.
- To help convey meaning, point out that the speaker says the words in each thought group together and pauses slightly between thought groups.
- Have students study the examples of thought groups in the box. As a class, brainstorm additional examples for each thought group. (Possible responses: **subject + verb:** she will be going; **noun phrases:** his spending habits; **prepositional phrases:** at the end of this year; **predicates:** are gradually getting out of debt; **noun clauses:** where I parked my car; **adjective clauses:** that they bought last week; **adverbial clauses:** when I've paid off my credit cards)
- On the board, write:
   1. *She will go on vacation as soon as she graduates.*
   2. *I don't know where I put the money that you lent me.*

To check comprehension, have students divide the sentences into thought groups. To review as a class, identify the variations of possible thought groups on the board. (Possible response: 1. She will go / on vacation / as soon as she graduates. 2. I don't know / where I put / the money / that you lent me.)

Pitch in longer sentences

- Have a volunteer read the explanation and examples out loud. As students study the examples, remind them that a falling line indicates falling intonation, and a rising line indicates rising intonation.
- To clarify, tell students that in longer sentences pitch can sometimes rise or fall within thought groups randomly.

A ⌒ Listen and practice.
(CD 5, Track 8)

- Refer to the procedure for Exercise A on page TP1.

B Read the following sentences . . .

- Have students break the sentences into thought groups individually and then compare their choices with a partner. Review as a class.

⌒ Now practice . . .
(CD 5, Track 9)

- Have students listen to compare. Point out that students' choices may vary. The recorded sentences are only one example of what is correct.

Challenge: On the board, write the following sentences from the Grammar box on page 28:
   1. *I don't plan to be financially dependent for the rest of my life.*
   2. *By this time next year, I plan to have saved up enough cash to buy a new car.*
   3. *Once I've completed my studies, I'll get married.*

In pairs, have students break down the sentences into thought groups. (Possible responses: 1. I don't plan to be / financially dependent / for the rest of my life.
2. By this time next year, / I plan to have saved up / enough cash / to buy a new car. 3. Once I've completed my studies, / I'll get married.) Review the variations of possible thought groups as a class. Individually, have students replace one or more thought groups in each sentence with their own ideas to create true sentences about themselves. For example, *By this time next year, I plan to have saved up enough cash to travel abroad.* Then have students share their sentences with a partner. To finish, call on volunteers to share a sentence with the class.

 Pronunciation Activities

Unit 4

Linking sounds

Linking with vowels

- Have a volunteer read the explanation and examples out loud.
- Point out that a final consonant sound and an initial vowel sound are needed.
- Emphasize that sound—not spelling—is what counts. To help clarify, write two examples on the board:

   Leave it here.   In an hour.
       ⌣   ⌣ ⌣

Point out the final consonant sound in *leave* (which is spelled with a final -*e*) and the initial vowel sound in *hour* (which is spelled with an initial *h*-).

Linking identical consonants

- Have a volunteer read the explanation and examples out loud.
- Once again, point out that sound—not spelling—is what counts. To help clarify, write an example on the board:

   Write to me.
        ⌣

Point out the final consonant sound in *write* (which is spelled with a final -*e*).

> **Language note:** Note that some similar sounds also link. For example, on page P4, Exercise B, item 6: "I think Kyle has stylish taste." The final /z/ sound in *has* links with the initial /s/ sound in *stylish*. Other examples of similar sounds that link include /t/ and /tʃ/ as in *that church*, /d/ and /dʒ/ as in *old judge*, and /s/ and /ʃ/ as in *this shirt*. Note, however, that the linking occurs only when the sounds occur in a particular order. For example, the final /s/ sound links with the initial /ʃ/ sound, as in *this shirt*, but the final /ʃ/ sound does not link with the initial /s/ sound, as in *fresh soup*.

Option: On the board, write:
   1. *Is it open?*   3. *I like cookies.*
   2. *Have a seat.*   4. *He's a good dog.*

To check comprehension, have pairs decide which words are linked in the examples. Review as a class. (1. is⌢it⌢open; 2. have⌢a; 3. like⌢cookies; 4. he's⌢a; good⌢dog)

Unit 3

Sentence rhythm: thought groups

Longer sentences are usually divided by rhythm into smaller "thought groups" —groups of words that naturally or logically go together. Exactly how statements may be divided into thought groups will vary among speakers.

Examples of thought groups	
subject + verb	I don't know
noun phrases	my short-term goal
prepositional phrases	by the end of the month
predicates	is drowning in debt
noun clauses	where the money goes
adjective clauses	that I paid off last year
adverbial clauses	when I've finished my report

My short-term goal / is to start living / within my means.
NOT ~~My short-term / goal is to / start living within my / means.~~
I don't plan / to be financially dependent / for the rest of my life.
By next year / I hope to have gotten / a good job / as a financial consultant.

Pitch in longer sentences

In longer sentences, pitch may fall—or rise—after the last stressed syllable in each thought group, with no change in meaning.

Once he tries keeping / a realistic budget / he'll find it easy / to save money. OR

Once he tries keeping / a realistic budget / he'll find it easy / to save money.

A 🎧 Listen and practice.

1. My short-term goal is to start living within my means.
2. I don't plan to be financially dependent for the rest of my life.
3. By next year, I hope to have gotten a good job as a financial consultant.
4a. Once he tries keeping a realistic budget, he'll find it easy to save money.
4b. Once he tries keeping a realistic budget, he'll find it easy to save money.

B Read the following sentences. Decide how you might break each sentence into thought groups.
Answers will vary, but may include:
1. By the end of this month/I hope to have finished/paying off my student loans.
2. In two months/when we've finally paid off our house,/we're going to have a big party/to celebrate.
3. To be perfectly honest,/I couldn't tell you/where the money goes.
4. By next year,/I will have completed my studies/but I don't think I/will have gotten married.

🎧 Now practice reading each sentence aloud, paying attention to pitch. Listen to compare.*
(Note that your choices may differ from what you hear on the audio.)

Unit 4

Linking sounds

Linking with vowels

When the final consonant sound of a word is followed by a vowel sound, link the sounds together.

It's in style now.

She bought him an elegant tie.

I've already bought a new suit.

Linking identical consonants

When the final consonant sound of a word is followed by the same sound, link the sounds together as one sound.

She thinks the blouse is striking.

They preferred dark suits.

What an attractive vest!

A 🎧 Listen and practice.

1. It's in style now.
2. She bought him an elegant tie.
3. I've already bought a new suit.
4. She thinks the blouse is striking.
5. They preferred dark suits.
6. What an attractive vest!

B Underline all the places where you think the sounds should be linked.

1. She wants Susan to dress up next time.
2. It's fashionable and elegant.
3. It's out of style.
4. I wish she preferred dressing down.
5. That blouse isn't trendy enough for my taste.
6. I think Kyle has stylish taste.

🎧 Now practice reading each sentence aloud and listen to check.*

Unit 5

Unstressed syllables: vowel reduction to /ə/

In conversation, the vowels in unstressed syllables are often reduced to the sound /ə/. The vowel sound /ə/ occurs more often in English than any other vowel sound and contributes to maintaining the rhythm of English.

ac cept a ble → /əkˈsɛptəbəl/	re spect ful → /rəˈspɛktfəl/	
con sid er ate → /kənˈsɪdərət/	ir re spon si ble → /ˌɪrəˈspɑnsəbəl/	
po lite → /pəˈlaɪt/	in ex cus a ble → /ˌɪnəkˈskyuzəbəl/	

A 🎧 Listen and practice.

1. acceptable
2. considerate
3. polite
4. respectful
5. irresponsible
6. inexcusable

B 🎧 Listen to each word and circle the unstressed syllables that have the sound /ə/.

1. un ac cept a ble
2. in con si de rate
3. im po lite
4. un pleas ant
5. ir ra tion al
6. im ma ture
7. un i mag i na ble
8. dis re spect ful
9. in ap pro pri ate

🎧 Now practice reading each word aloud and listen again to check.*

A 🎧 **Listen and practice.**
   (CD 5, Track 10)

• Refer to the procedure for Exercise A on page TP1.

B **Underline all the places ...**

• Have students mark the linking sounds individually. Remind students that sound—not spelling—is important.

🎧 **Now practice ...**
   (CD 5, Track 11)

• Have students listen to confirm their answers or make corrections.

Challenge: On the board, draw a two-column chart with the heads *Linking with vowels* and *Linking identical consonants*. Have pairs look at the Grammar Snapshot on page 40 for examples of linking sounds and write them in the chart. Ask students to highlight or circle the sounds that are linked. Then call on volunteers to share some of the examples they found, with the class. Complete the chart on the board as students respond. (Possible responses: dressing⌢up; business⌢attire; business⌢suit)

 Pronunciation Activities

Unit 5

Unstressed syllables: vowel reduction to /ə/

• Explain that symbols are used to represent and clarify sounds across languages.

• Write /ə/ on the board. Explain that this is a pronunciation symbol for the sound *uh*.

• Have volunteers read the explanation and examples out loud. Point out that dots indicate unstressed syllables and lines indicate stressed syllables. Explain that when a vowel is reduced, it is made weaker and shorter.

• To help clarify, point out that:
   1. English has stressed and unstressed syllables.
   2. Stressed syllables are longer than unstressed syllables.
   3. The vowel in a stressed syllable is never reduced.

• On the board, write:
   1. *about*   3. *edible*
   2. *grateful*   4. *literate*

To check comprehension, have pairs identify the unstressed syllable in each word. Review as a class.

(1. about, 2. grateful, 3. edible, 4. literate)

A 🎧 **Listen and practice.**
   (CD 5, Track 12)

• Refer to the procedure for Exercise A on page TP1.

B 🎧 **Listen to each word ...**
   (CD 5, Track 13)

• Have students listen and circle the syllables individually.

🎧 **Now practice ...**
   (CD 5, Track 13)

• Have students read each word out loud and listen for confirmation.

• Then have students compare answers with a partner and review as a class.

Option: Have pairs identify vowels reduced to the sound /ə/ in Exercise E on page 53. Then have them look up the words in a dictionary to compare. Have students practice saying the words out loud.

 Pronunciation Activities

Unit 6

Sound reduction

Vowel reduction

- Have volunteers read the explanations and examples for reductions of /u/, /æ/, and /ɑr/ and /ɔr/ out loud.

- Review the pronunciation of /ə/: *uh*.

- Emphasize that reduction often occurs in function words. Remind students that function words are generally unstressed.

- To illustrate further, write on the board:

  Give two to Sandra.   *I bought four for Sarah.*

  Point to the first example and ask *What is the function word?* (to) Point to *two* and ask *Is two a function word or a content word?* (content word) Point to the second example and ask *What is the function word?* (for) Point to *four* and ask *Is four a function word or a content word?* (content word) Label the examples on the board as students answer. Say *Two and four are content words, so they are not reduced in spoken English. To and for are function words, so they are reduced.*

- Draw students' attention to the Be Careful! box.

- Point out that function words at the end of sentences are stressed, so they are not reduced.

- Have a volunteer read the explanation and examples for the reduction of *and* out loud.

- Emphasize that the weaker form of *and* is used when *and* occurs between two items in a series.

- Have a volunteer read the Be Careful! note out loud. Call on a few students to give their own examples. (Possible response: Stan is buying an iguana, and Shelly is buying a snake.)

- Have students study the explanation and examples for the reduction of /h/.

- On the board, write:

  What if he's happier now?

  To check comprehension, have students identify the word in which the /h/ sound is dropped. (he's)

Language note: The phonetic transcription of the words presented may differ from what appears in the dictionary. In cases where they differ, the reduced sound /ə/ occurs in conversation.

Option: Photocopy and distribute this exercise or write it on the board:

1. She's pretty <u>and</u> smart.
2. She's pretty. <u>And</u> she's so smart!
3. Take this <u>to</u> the dry cleaners.
4. Who's she shouting <u>to</u>?
5. Who are you waiting <u>for</u>?
6. I'm waiting <u>for</u> Brian.

To check comprehension, have pairs decide in which examples the underlined words are reduced. (1, 3, 6) Review as a class.

A 🎧 Listen and practice.
(CD 5, Track 14)

- Refer to the procedure for Exercise A on page TP1.

B Circle the words …

- Have students circle the words individually. Circulate to offer help as needed.

- In pairs, have students compare answers and take turns reading the sentences out loud.

🎧 Now practice …
(CD 5, Track 15)

- Have students read each sentence out loud and listen for confirmation.

Option: Have students identify words that would be reduced in spoken English in Exercise E on page 65. Then have students practice reading the sentences, focusing on reduced sounds.

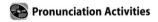 **Pronunciation Activities**

Unit 6

Sound reduction

In everyday speech, sounds in unstressed words are often "reduced"; that is, vowels change to /ə/ or /ɚ/ or consonants are dropped.

Vowel reduction

The /u/ sound in the function word <u>to</u> is often reduced to /ə/.
> I'll be going to the airport after dinner. /tə/
> It's ten to two. /tə/

The /æ/ sound in many one-syllable function words is often reduced to /ə/.
> Look at that. /ət/
> I got an iguana. /ən/
> That's more than I need. /ðən/

The /ɑr/ and /ɔr/ sounds in function words are often reduced to /ɚ/.
> Pets are no trouble. /ɚ/
> Is it black or white? /ɚ/
> Where's your farm? /yɚ/
> He's been gone for days. /fɚ/

> **BE CAREFUL!** Function words that occur at the end of a sentence are never reduced.
> What a beautiful bird you are! /ɑr/
> What are you looking at? /æt/
> What are you waiting for? /fɔr/
> Who's she talking to? /tu/

The function word <u>and</u> /ænd/ is often reduced to /ən/ when it occurs between two subjects, objects, modifiers, verbs, or phrases.
> They have long arms and legs. /ən/
> She laughed and cried when she heard the news. /ən/
> We stayed out late and went dancing. /ən/

BE CAREFUL! The vowel sound /æ/ in <u>and</u> is generally not reduced when it occurs at the beginning of a clause, but the consonant sound /d/ may still be dropped.
> He wore a black suit, and she wore a green dress. /æn/

The initial /h/ sound is usually dropped in function words.
> What does he mean? /dʌzi/
> It's in his bag. /ɪnɪz/

A 🎧 Listen and practice.

1. I'll be going to the airport after dinner.
2. It's ten to two.
3. Look at that.
4. I got an iguana.
5. That's more than I need.
6. Pets are no trouble.
7. Is it black or white?
8. Where's your farm?
9. He's been gone for days.
10. They have long arms and legs.
11. She laughed and cried when she heard the news.
12. We stayed out late and went dancing.
13. He wore a black suit, and she wore a green dress.
14. What does he mean?
15. It's in his bag.

B Circle the words in the following sentences you think will be reduced.

1. Alternatives (can) be found (for) medical research on animals.
2. A lot (can) be done (to) improve conditions on those farms.
3. Animals (are) trained (to) perform in circuses.
4. Do animals have (to) be killed (for) their hides (and) fur?

🎧 Now practice reading each sentence aloud and listen to check.*

Unit 7

Vowel sounds /i/ and /ɪ/

The sound /i/ is longer and is formed by tensing the tongue.
The sound /ɪ/ is shorter and formed with the tongue relaxed.

/i/	/ɪ/
leave	live
team	Tim
feel	fill
steal	still
feet	fit

The vowel sound /ɪ/ also appears frequently in unstressed syllables.

— •   — •   — • •   — •   — •
places   market   artisan   minute   women

The vowel sounds /i/ and /ɪ/ are represented in spelling in a number of ways.

/i/	/ɪ/
steal	blimp
steep	syllable
people	busy
handy	building
believe	women
receive	pretty
boutique	been
key	give

A 🎧 Listen and practice.

1. leave   live
2. team   Tim
3. feel   fill
4. steal   still
5. feet   fit

B 🎧 Listen and practice.

1. places   2. market   3. artisan   4. minute   5. women

C 🎧 Listen to each pair of words. Circle if they are the <u>same</u> or <u>different</u>.

1. (same)   different   5. same   (different)
2. same   (different)   6. same   (different)
3. (same)   different   7. (same)   different
4. same   (different)   8. (same)   different

D 🎧 Listen and check which sound you hear.

	/i/	/ɪ/			/i/	/ɪ/			/i/	/ɪ/
1.	☑	☐		6.	☑	☐		11.	☑	☐
2.	☐	☑		7.	☐	☑		12.	☑	☐
3.	☐	☑		8.	☐	☑		13.	☐	☑
4.	☑	☐		9.	☑	☐		14.	☑	☐
5.	☑	☑		10.	☑	☑		15.	☑	☑

🎧 Now listen again and practice.

Unit 7

Vowel sounds /i/ and /ɪ/

- Point out that producing the correct sound is important because it affects meaning. This is particularly important in words like *sheep* and *ship* where the only difference between the words is the vowel sound.
- On the board, write:

  /i/ ⟶ tense and long (sheep)
  /ɪ/ ⟶ relaxed and short (ship)

- Have a volunteer read the first explanation and examples out loud.
- On the board, write:

  1. slip   2. sleep   3. heat   4. hit   5. seat   6. sit

  To check comprehension, say the words on the board in random order, and have students say the number of the word they hear.
- Have students study the possible spellings for each sound.
- In pairs, have students think of another example for some of the spellings of /i/ and /ɪ/ and then share them with the class. Point out that students may want to look through their books for examples. (Possible responses: **/i/**: scream, sleep, fancy, relieve, deceive, unique, monkey; **/ɪ/**: flip, bicycle, business, live)
- Have a volunteer read the second explanation and examples out loud.
- Point out that although many unstressed vowels are reduced to /ə/, some are not.
- On the board, write:

  magic   incredible   dolphin   united

  To check comprehension, have students identify the /ɪ/ sound in the unstressed syllables. (mag**i**c, **i**ncred**i**ble, dolph**i**n, unit**e**d) Review as a class.

A 🎧 Listen and practice.
(CD 5, Track 16)

- Refer to the procedure for Exercise A on page TP1.

B 🎧 Listen and practice.
(CD 5, Track 17)

- Have students listen and circle the unstressed /ɪ/ sound in each word.
- Then have students listen and repeat chorally.

C 🎧 Listen to each pair of words ...
(CD 5, Track 18)

- Have students listen and circle the answers.
- Then have students listen again to confirm or correct their choices. (1. live, 2. steal, still, 3. fit, 4. feel, fill, 5. team, Tim, 6. wheel, will, 7. been, 8. seat)

D 🎧 Listen and check ...
(CD 5, Track 19)

- Have students listen and complete the exercise.
- Then have students compare answers with a partner and listen again to confirm or correct their answers. Note that some words may have both sounds. (1. steal, 2. syllable, 3. blimp, 4. believe, 5. busy, 6. boutique, 7. women, 8. building, 9. handy, 10. pretty, 11. people, 12. steep, 13. give, 14. key, 15. receive)

🎧 Now practice ...
(CD 5, Track 19)

- To finish, you may want to have students listen, write the words, and practice saying them in pairs.

🎧 **Option:** For further practice, have students identify words with /i/ and /ɪ/ sounds in the Conversation Snapshot on page 76. Have students focus on the conversation and the ways to describe prices in the boxes. Then have students listen to confirm or correct their choices (CD 3, Tracks 3, 5, 6). (**/i/**: before, any, me, remember, be, deal, steal, steep, robbery; **/ɪ/**: think, pick, suggestion, in, nothing, particular, something, trip, if, bargain, prices, bit, rip-off)

 **Pronunciation Activities**

Unit 8

Stress placement: prefixes and suffixes

- On the board, write:

  understand   misunderstand   misunderstanding

  Point out how the three words are stressed on the same syllable.

- Have a volunteer read the first explanation and examples out loud.

- On the board, write:

  technology   technological

- Point out how the words are stressed on different syllables.

- Have a volunteer read the second explanation and examples out loud.

- On the board, write:

  1. library   librarian
  2. communicate   communication
  3. mobile   mobility
  4. tolerate   tolerance

  To check comprehension, have pairs decide which syllable is stressed in each word and whether the stress changes when the suffixes are added.

- Ask *In which sets of words will stress change?* (1, 2, 3) *Why?* (because the suffixes *-ian, -ion,* and *-ity* were added)

- Have volunteers read the last explanation and examples out loud.

- To check comprehension, have various students read the words in the box out loud, first as nouns and then as verbs. Make sure students use the correct intonation.

A 🎧 Listen and practice.
(CD 5, Track 20)

- Refer to the procedure for Exercise A on page TP1.

B 🎧 Listen and practice.
(CD 5, Track 21)

- Refer to the procedure for Exercise A on page TP1.

Unit 8

Stress placement: prefixes and suffixes

Stress placement does not change when most prefixes and suffixes are added to a word.

important   unimportant   importance   importantly

obedient   obedience   disobedience   obediently

happy   unhappy   happiness   happily

However, adding the suffixes -ion, -ic, -ity, -ical, and -ian generally shifts stress to the syllable before the suffix.

educate   →   education

photograph   →   photographic

dependable   →   dependability

politics   →   political

music   →   musician

Some nouns and verbs have the same spelling. When the word is a noun, the stress is on the first syllable. When the word is a verb the stress is on the second syllable.

nouns	verbs
rebel	rebel
protest	protest
present	present
object	object
progress	progress

Other words in this category
conduct
conflict
contrast
convert
permit
record
survey
suspect

A 🎧 Listen and practice.

1. important   unimportant   importance   importantly
2. obedient   obedience   disobedience   obediently
3. happy   unhappy   happiness   happily

B 🎧 Listen and practice.

1. educate   education
2. photograph   photographic
3. dependable   dependability
4. politics   political
5. music   musician

C Look at the stressed syllable of each word in Column A. According to the rules given in the chart on page P7, mark the stressed syllable of each word in Column B.

A	B
1. fa mil iar	fa mil iar i ty
2. e mo tion al	e mo tion al ly
3. reg u late	reg u la tion
4. ap pre ci a tive	ap pre cia tive ly
5. sym pa thy	sym pa thet ic
6. hy poth e size	hy po thet i cal
7. beau ty	beau ti fy
8. his to ry	his tor i cal
9. ma te ri al ist	ma te ri al is tic
10. pol i tics	pol i ti cian

🎧 Now practice reading each word aloud and listen to check.*

D 🎧 Listen and practice.

nouns	verbs
1. rebel	rebel
2. protest	protest
3. present	present
4. object	object
5. progress	progress

E Circle the syllable you think will be stressed in each blue word.

1. A summer fishing **permit permits** you to fish all you want.
2. The **protest** was organized to **protest** government spending.
3. All the employees were **surveyed** so the results of the **survey** would be useful.
4. The **contrast** between them now is not great compared to how much they **contrast** at other times of the year.
5. We strongly **object** to the decision to sell art **objects** outside the museum.

🎧 Now practice reading each sentence aloud, paying attention to words that are both nouns and verbs. Listen to check.*

C **Look at the stressed syllable ...**

• Have students circle the stressed syllables of the words in Column B individually. Then have students compare choices with a partner.

🎧 **Now practice ...**
(CD 5, Track 22)

• Have students listen and confirm answers or make corrections.

• You may want to have students listen again and repeat chorally.

D 🎧 **Listen and practice.**
(CD 5, Track 23)

• Refer to the procedure for Exercise A on page TP1.

E **Circle the syllable ...**

• Have students decide if each word is a noun or a verb and compare their choices with a partner.

🎧 **Now practice ...**
(CD 5, Track 24)

• Have students read each sentence out loud and listen for confirmation.

🎧 **Option:** Have students circle the stressed syllables in the words in Exercise A on page 92. Then have students listen to check their answers (CD 3, Track 22).

💿 **Pronunciation Activities**

Unit 9

Reduction and linking in perfect modals in the passive voice

- Have volunteers read the first two explanations and examples out loud.
- To help clarify, summarize on the board:

  Perfect modals in the passive voice
  affirmative: <u>MODAL + have been</u> + MAIN VERB

  linked

- Have a volunteer read the last explanation and examples out loud.
- To help clarify, add to the summary on the board:

  negative: MODAL + <u>NOT + have been</u> + MAIN VERB
  linked

- To check comprehension, have students read the sentences with perfect modals in the passive voice from the Grammar Snapshot on page 102, out loud. Make sure students use the proper intonation and link words correctly.

A 🎧 Listen and practice.
(CD 5, Track 25)

- Refer to the procedure for Exercise A on page TP1.

B Underline ...

- Have students underline the words that are linked and compare their choices with a partner.
- In pairs, have students practice reading the sentences out loud.

🎧 Now practice ...
(CD 5, Track 26)

- Have students read the sentences out loud and listen for confirmation.

Challenge: Individually, have students underline the words that are stressed and indicate the words that are linked in the examples from the Grammar box on page 102. Have students confirm or correct with a partner. In pairs, have students take turns reading the examples out loud. Encourage partners to correct each other when necessary.

🔄 **Pronunciation Activities**

Unit 9

Reduction and linking in perfect modals in the passive voice

In perfect modals in the passive voice, the modal and the auxiliary verbs <u>have been</u> are said together as one unit. Note that stress falls on the modal and the main verb. In everyday speech, the /h/ sound in the auxilliary <u>have</u> is dropped and /æ/ is reduced to /ə/.

/'kʊdəvbɪn/
They **COULD have been KILLED**.

/'maitəvbɪn/
They **MIGHT have been LOST**.

/'məstəvbɪn/
They **MUST have been MOVED**.

/'meiyəvbɪn/
They **MAY have been DISCOVERED**.

With <u>had to</u>, stress <u>had</u> and the main verb. Say <u>had to</u> and <u>have been</u> as one unit.

/'hætuəvbɪn/
They **HAD to have been STOLEN**.

In negative perfect modals, stress falls on the modal, the word <u>not</u>, and the main verb. In everyday speech, <u>not</u> and the auxiliary verbs <u>have been</u> are generally said as one unit.

/'natəvbɪn/
They **MIGHT NOT have been LOST**.
They **MUST NOT have been MOVED**.

A 🎧 Listen and practice.

1. They could have been killed.
2. They might have been lost.
3. They must have been moved.
4. They may have been discovered.
5. They had to have been stolen.
6. They might not have been lost.
7. They must not have been moved.

B Underline where you think the words should be linked and which sounds should be reduced.

1. The dinosaurs <u>may have been</u> killed by a meteor.
2. The trees <u>could have been</u> destroyed by a fire.
3. The gold figures may <u>not have been</u> lost.
4. The stone balls <u>must have been</u> moved using animals.
5. The drawings must <u>not have been</u> discovered until later.
6. The crater <u>had to have been</u> caused by a meteorite.
7. The trees <u>couldn't have been</u> burned in a fire.

🎧 Now practice reading each sentence aloud, paying attention to reductions. Listen to check.*

Unit 10

Vowel sounds /eɪ/, /ɛ/, /æ/, and /ʌ/

The sound /eɪ/ is longer and is formed by tensing the tongue with the lips spread.
The sounds /ɛ/, /æ/, and /ʌ/ are shorter and are formed with the tongue relaxed.
Say /eɪ/ and /ɛ/ with the lips spread wide. Say /æ/ with the lips spread slightly and the
mouth slightly open. Say /ʌ/ with the tongue and jaw completely relaxed.

Mouth positions for vowels	
tongue tensed (long)	/eɪ/
tongue relaxed (short)	/ɛ/, /æ/, /ʌ/
lips spread	/eɪ/, /ɛ/, /æ/
jaw relaxed	/ʌ/

/eɪ/	/ɛ/	/æ/	/ʌ/
pain	pen	pan	pun
Dane	den	Dan	done
mate	met	mat	mutt
bait	bet	bat	but

The vowel sounds /eɪ/, /ɛ/, /æ/, and /ʌ/ may be represented by these spellings.

/eɪ/	/ɛ/	/æ/	/ʌ/
pay	get	catch	jumping
weigh	sweat	have	nothing
shape	says	laugh	touch
wait	said	half	does
table	friend	guarantee	blood
great	guest	relax	what

A 🎧 Listen and practice.

1.	pain	pen	pan	pun
2.	Dane	den	Dan	done
3.	mate	met	mat	mutt
4.	bait	bet	bat	but

B 🎧 Listen to each word and place it in the correct column.

edge games enough can't bungee rafting nothing chance sweat wait scare

/eɪ/	/ɛ/	/æ/	/ʌ/
games	edge	can't	enough
wait	sweat	rafting	bungee
	scare	chance	nothing

🎧 Now practice reading each word aloud and listen again to check.*

C 🎧 Listen to each sentence and circle the word you hear.

1. Give the money to the (men / (man)).
2. I think it's ((Dan) / done).
3. What is that (rag / (rug)) made of?
4. Do you need this ((pen) / pan)?
5. He's a perfect (mutt / (mate)).
6. My (date / (debt)) is causing me trouble.
7. Could you take that (bug / (bag)) off the counter?
8. Please put a bandage on the ((cut) / cat).

Now practice reading the sentences both ways.

Unit 10

Vowel sounds /eɪ/, /ɛ/, /æ/, and /ʌ/

- Have students study the explanation for each sound, the examples, and the Mouth positions for vowels box.
- On the board, draw the following chart (without the answers):

A	B	C
tongue tensed, lips spread	/eɪ/	rain, date
tongue relaxed, lips spread slightly, mouth open slightly	/æ/	math, cat
tongue relaxed, lips spread wide	/ɛ/	wet, send
tongue and jaw relaxed	/ʌ/	lump, cut

To check comprehension, have students write the sounds in the correct row in Column B. Review as a class.

- Add to the board:

  lump   rain   wet   date   cut   math   send   cat

To check comprehension, have students classify the words in Column C. Review as a class.

> **Language note:** /ə/ and /ʌ/ are the same sound, but /ʌ/ is used for stressed syllables.

Option: Have students add their own examples to the chart. You may want to encourage students to add two examples for each vowel sound. Then have volunteers share their examples with the class. (Possible responses: **/eɪ/:** stain, face; **/æ/:** ran, last; **/ɛ/:** best, lend; **/ʌ/:** stuck, come)

A 🎧 Listen and practice.
(CD 5, Track 27)

- Refer to the procedure for Exercise A on page TP1.

B 🎧 Listen to each word . . .
(CD 5, Track 28)

- Have students listen and write the words in each column.
- Then have students compare with a partner.

🎧 Now practice . . .
(CD 5, Track 28)

- Have students read the words out loud and listen to confirm their answers or make corrections.
- You may want to have students practice reading the words aloud in pairs.

C 🎧 Listen to each sentence . . .
(CD 5, Track 29)

- Have students listen and circle the words.
- Then have students listen again to confirm their answers or make corrections.
- As students practice saying the sentences, circulate to offer help as needed. If necessary, remind students how to produce each sound correctly.

🔄 **Pronunciation Activities**

AUDIOSCRIPT

UNIT 1

Page 6. Exercise C.

Conversation 1 [M = Korean][1]
M[2]: Hey, I just met that new student, Shelly.
F: Really? So, what'd you think?
M: Well, she seems really serious—and smart!
F: Smart? She's one of the most intelligent people I know!

Conversation 2 [F = Spanish]
M: Adrianna, how's the project going?
F: Don't ask. I'll never finish all this work! Peter never lets up!
M: Yeah, he's not exactly an easygoing boss!
F: You can say that again. He always asks me to work faster! I'm going as fast as I can!

Conversation 3
M: Hey, have you met Val's new boyfriend, Paul?
F: Yeah, I have. Very outgoing. Seems like a good guy.
M: That's not the impression I got!
F: What do you mean?
M: Well, he jokes around a lot.
F: What's wrong with that? Sounds like a real people person.
M: Well … his jokes just aren't that funny. He seems to want people to think he's smarter than they are. It's really annoying.

Page 10. Exercises A and B.

Speaker 1 [U.S., African American]
M: What's changed my perspective on life? Hmm … getting married sure changed things.… But the *most* significant experience of my life? Without a doubt, I'd have to say going abroad. Well, one of my most memorable trips was my first—it was the summer I worked in Brussels, in Belgium. It was amazing! So many people from all over the world living and working together in this one city! There's *so* much diversity there, you know! People come to Brussels from all these different countries, and they bring all their own cultures. Seems like everyone has his own unique perspective on life. I was really able to see other people's points of view. Getting to know people who've had such different experiences from mine—it was a real eye-opener for me. Travel has really broadened my horizons.

Speaker 2 [Russian]
F: Definitely, my daughter. When she was born, everything changed. I had to stay home to take care of her full-time, so I had to leave my job. My whole perspective on life changed. It hit me that I was responsible for her—for this other person, and that she needed me for everything.

Having a child is definitely a life-altering experience. It's not just that you don't have as much time for yourself, or that you don't have as much freedom; you're simply never the same. It's not always easy, but being a parent has been the most enriching and rewarding experience of my life.

Speaker 3
M: I'll never forget coming home and seeing those flames.… No one was hurt, but a number of apartments were completely destroyed. Ours was one of them. Our life totally changed. Everything we'd worked for was gone. You can be sure, *that* put things in perspective. You know, you go to work day in and day out, you worry about things that seem so important. And all of a sudden, all that seems so insignificant when you think about your life, your family's safety. You start to see the big picture, and what had seemed so important before doesn't really matter after that kind of experience.

Page 13. Exercise A.

Speaker 1 [J = John, England]
J: Last night I turned on the news … I wish I hadn't. I can't get over everything that's happening in the world right now. Seems like every time you turn around you hear about another war, natural disaster, poverty, terrorism … it's really depressing, and it's just getting worse. In fact, it makes me want to just give up watching the news altogether—I mean, who needs more reasons to get depressed?

Speaker 2 [S = Susan]
S: On my way into work this morning, I heard this report on the radio. They said the economy is not doing very well. And you can't help noticing that everything just keeps getting more expensive—food, gas, housing. Of course, all this bad news makes me a little nervous. I've cut down on a lot on my spending—I've stopped buying lunch every day at the office, and I've put off buying a new car until next year. But, to be honest, I'm not stressing out over it. I mean, things may get better, and if not, well, I'll get by.

Speaker 3 [M = Matt, U.S., Southern]
M: I read in the paper today that the unemployment rate is rising. A lot of people I know have lost their jobs over the last couple of years. In fact, both of my sons lost their jobs in the same week. But I think it'll work out in the end. My younger son will have time to go back to school and finish his degree—something he's always wanted to do. And my older son—well, I'm sure opportunity will come his way. When one door closes, another one always opens.

---

[1]All recorded speakers are standard U.S., unless designated otherwise. These include U.S. regional, varieties of British English, and non-native speakers of English. First language or country of origin is indicated for your information.

[2]M refers to a male speaker, and F refers to a female speaker.

UNIT 2

Page 16. Exercise C.

Song 1: Endless Holiday
Day after day,
all my thoughts drift away
before they've begun.
I sit in my room
in the darkness and gloom
just waiting for someone
to take me to a tourist town,
with parties in the street and people dancing to a joyful sound.
(CHORUS)
It's a song that people sing.
It's the laughter that you bring
on an endless holiday.
It's the happiness inside.
It's a roller coaster ride
on an endless holiday.
I try and I try
to work hard, but I
get lost in a daze,
and I think about
how sad life is without
a few good holidays.
I close my eyes, pull down the shade,
and in my imagination I am dancing in a big parade,
and the music is loud.
I get lost in the crowd
on an endless holiday.
It's a picnic at noon.
It's a trip to the moon
on an endless holiday,
with flags and confetti,
wild costumes and a great big marching band,
as we wish each other well
in a language we all understand.
The sky above fills with the light
of fireworks exploding, as we dance along the street tonight.
(CHORUS)

Song 2: Lucky To Be Alive
(CHORUS)
Thank you for helping me to survive.
I'm really lucky to be alive.
When I was caught in a freezing snowstorm,
you taught me how to stay warm.
When I was running from a landslide
with no place to hide,
you protected me from injury.
Even the world's biggest tsunami
has got nothing on me,
because you can go faster.
You keep me safe from disaster.
You're like some kind of hero—
you're the best friend that I know.
(CHORUS)
When the big flood came with the pouring rain,
they were saying that a natural disaster loomed.
You just opened your umbrella.
You were the only fellow who kept calm and prepared.
You found us shelter.
I never felt like anybody cared
the way that you did when you said,

"I will always be there—
you can bet your life on it."
And when the cyclone turned the day into night,
you held a flashlight and showed me the safe way home.
You called for help on your cell phone.
You said you'd never leave me.
You said, "Believe me,
in times of trouble you will never be alone."
They said it wasn't such a bad situation.
It was beyond imagination.
I'm just glad to be alive—
and that is no exaggeration.
(CHORUS)

Song 3: Reinvent the Wheel
You've got your digi camera with the Powershot,
four mega pixels and a memory slot.
You've got your e-mail and your Internet.
You send me pictures of your digi pet.
I got the digi dog and the digi cat,
the digi this and the digi that.
I hate to be the one to break the news,
but you're giving me the digi blues,
(CHORUS)
And you don't know
the way I really feel.
Why'd you have to go and
reinvent the wheel?
You've got your cordless phone and your microwave,
and your Reflex Plus for the perfect shave.
It's super special, top of the line,
with the latest new, cutting-edge design.
You've got your SLR and your LCD,
your PS2 and your USB.
I've seen the future and it's pretty grim:
they've used up all the acronyms.
(CHORUS)
I keep waiting for a breakthrough innovation:
something to help our poor communication.
Hey, where'd you get all of that high tech taste?
Your faith in progress is such a waste.
Your life may be state of the art,
but you don't understand the human heart.
(CHORUS)

Song 4: It's a Great Day for Love
Wherever you go,
there are things you should know,
so be aware
of the customs and views—
all the do's and taboos—
of people there.
You were just a stranger in a sea of new faces.
Now we're making small talk on a first-name basis.
(CHORUS)
It's a great day for love, isn't it?
Aren't you the one I was hoping to find?
It's a great day for love, isn't it?
By the time you said hello,
I had already made up my mind.
Wherever you stay
be sure to obey
the golden rules,
and before you relax,
brush up on the facts

you learned in school.
Try to be polite and always be sure to get
some friendly advice on proper etiquette.
(CHORUS)
And when you smiled at me
and I fell in love,
the sun had just appeared
in the sky above.
You know how much I care, don't you?
And you'll always be there, won't you?
(CHORUS)

Page 22. Exercise A.

Part 1 [A = Andre; B = Dr. Bettina Schmidt, German]

A: Welcome to tonight's talk. We have with us tonight Dr. Bettina Schmidt from the Schubert Institute. Dr. Schmidt is going to tell us about … well, an unusual use of music. Dr. Schmidt, welcome. Why don't you tell us what you do?

B: Good evening, Andre. Well, I'm a music therapist. I've been doing that for, oh, I'd say about twelve years now.

A: And just what does a music therapist do?

B: Essentially, we try to help people with their problems by using music.

A: And who exactly would benefit from music therapy?

B: We work with all sorts of people—children, teenagers, adults. These are people who have a wide range of problems—sometimes physical, sometimes emotional.

A: And how does music help?

B: Well, often just listening to music can be beneficial. So, in a typical music therapy session, I'll play, maybe, some gentle classical music. This helps my client to relax and feel more comfortable.

A: That's it? Basically it's about using music to relax people?

B: Um, not exactly. Music therapy is much more than that. Music therapists design music sessions for individuals and for groups based on their specific needs.

A: So, what kinds of activities do you do?

B: Well, we often do structured activities—like singing, or listening, playing instruments, composing music, moving to music.

A: And this is in a doctor's office?

B: Not necessarily. We work in all kinds of settings—hospitals, schools, senior centers—all around the community.

A: So, how exactly does music help your clients?

B: Well, there are four main benefits of music therapy: emotional, social, physical, and intellectual.

A: Can you give us some examples?

B: Of course.

Page 22. Exercise B.

Part 2

B: Let's start with the emotional benefits. People who are depressed, for example, have difficulty expressing their feelings. Music creates a safe setting where we can express the feelings inside of us.

A: I see.

B: In a typical session, I'll begin by asking my client to talk about how the music makes him feel. That opens him up. The idea is to help my client feel comfortable sharing his emotions.

A: And what about the other benefits?

B: Well, another benefit of music therapy is tied to the social context music provides. Listening to music in groups—with other people—builds an environment for communication—both verbal and *non*-verbal.

A: But isn't listening to music basically a solitary activity?

B: It can be, but it can also be a social activity—involving sharing. That means that my clients can develop their social skills and will have more confidence in their ability to form relationships.

A: Now you also mentioned physical benefits.

B: Yes. Music can be stimulating and encourage physical movement. Some of my clients are in hospitals, and many are in serious pain because of an illness or an accident. Moving around is often difficult for them. Listening to music helps them forget their pain for a little while, and at the same time it stimulates them to move.

A: OK. That's three benefits. Didn't you say there were four?

B: That's right. The fourth benefit is intellectual. Some parents come to me because their kids aren't doing well in school. Research has shown that listening to music can help young children improve in math. Other research suggests that among university students, listening to music while studying can improve reading comprehension. We don't know exactly how music improves learning, but perhaps it helps students concentrate, so they can think better. We just know that music improves our ability to learn.

A: Simply amazing! Thank you so much, Dr. Schmidt.

Page 25. Exercise A.

Conversation 1 [M = Chinese]

F: So what have you been listening to?

M: Well, lately I've been listening to a lot of opera.

F: Really? I can't get into opera. It's too intense.

M: What about Andrea Bocelli? He's got more of a pop sound. I think he's an amazing singer.

F: You know, I'm not really into him either—he's just too loud and overpowering for me.

Conversation 2

M: Have you heard this Gato Barbieri piece before?

F: No, I haven't. Let's give it a listen … wow! I *love* the arrangement!

M: Yeah, me too. He's a great composer.

F: You can say that again.

Conversation 3 [F = U.S., Southern]

F: What do you think of Ladysmith Black Mambazo?

M: I don't think I've heard of her.

F: It's not a *her*—it's a group. They're a vocal group from South Africa.

M: Well, I'm not very big on world music.

F: Well, you should definitely check these guys out. They sing *a cappella*—without any musical instruments. They're one of a kind.

M: I don't know. I'm just not into that kind of music.

Conversation 4 [F = French]

F: Wasn't that a great party last night?

M: Yeah, it was really cool—especially that fantastic dance music.

F: Yeah, Beyoncé's music is fabulous. I could have danced to it all night.

M: Well, actually you almost did.

F: Yeah, well, once I started dancing, I couldn't stop!

Conversation 5

M: I can't believe you like Antonio Carlos Jobim so much. Isn't he kind of old-fashioned?

F: Are you kidding? I think his songs are just as beautiful now as they were forty years ago.

M: Well, many of his songs *do* have beautiful words.

F: Absolutely. There aren't many people who can put words to music like Jobim can. I never get tired of listening to his songs.

UNIT 3

Page 30. Exercise C.

Conversation 1

F: Wow, what a great juicer! That's even big enough for *my* family!

M: Actually, I hardly ever use it. It's way too big. I have such a small kitchen.

F: So, why'd you buy it?

M: I got it on sale—at a great price.

Conversation 2

M: I see you bought a digital camera. How do you like it?

F: Well, I might like it if I could figure out how to use it. Truth is, it's a pain in the neck.

M: What do you mean?

F: It has way too many features. Believe me, if I had known you couldn't just point and shoot, I never would have gotten it.

Conversation 3

F1: Hey, I love your new exercise bike! It must be great having one of those.

F2: Well, yes and no.

F1: What does *that* mean?

F2: I like it, but I guess I'm just a couch potato. I just don't use it enough.

Conversation 4

M1: What a cool sound system! You just get it?

M2: Yeah.

M1: Look at all those pieces. When are you going to put it all together?

M2: Well … that's a problem actually. There are so many components. And the instructions don't help *at all*. Look.

M1: Whoa! That looks pretty complicated.

M2: Had I known how complicated it was going to be, I would have gotten a different model.

Conversation 5

M: Love your new car! You must be on cloud nine driving that thing!

F: Oh, it's fun to drive, but I'm not so sure it's worth it.

M: Really? Why?

F: You wouldn't believe it. Between the premium gas and visits to the mechanic … it's costing me an arm and a leg!

M: Ouch!

F: I can't afford to drive it! I probably wouldn't have bought it had I given it more thought.

Page 32. Exercises A and B.

[L = Lara Savino, U.S., New York; S = Steve]

L: Welcome back to *Money Talks*. I'm still your host, Lara Savino. We've got some listeners on the line with financial questions. Let's go to our first caller … Steve, you're on the air. Talk to me.

S: Hi, Lara. I'm afraid I'm really having problems making ends meet.

L: Tell me about it.

S: I earn a good living, but it seems like no matter how much money I make, I can't seem to catch up.

L: Believe me, you're not alone, Steve.

S: Sometimes it feels that way.

L: Let me ask you something. Do you put anything away for a rainy day?

S: You mean savings? No way. There's never enough for that.

L: Well, here's a tip for you, Steve. From now on when you spend money throughout the day …?

S: Uh-hmm.

L: Don't spend any of your change. When you get home every evening, put your loose change in a jar. You'll be surprised how much you'll have saved up in even a few weeks.

S: Wow! I never thought of doing that.

L: And put that change you've saved up in the bank—say, once a month, OK?

S: OK. I'll try that.

L: Steve, what about debt? Are you maxing out on your credit cards?

S: Well, yes, I do use credit cards, if that's what you mean.

L: Do you pay your bills on time?

S: I try to.

L: Do you pay the minimum, or do you pay off the whole thing each time?

S: Well, it kind of depends on how much it is.

L: Well, are you drowning in credit card bills, or have they been fairly reasonable so far?

S: Well … I guess I'd have to say I've been drowning in debt.

L: OK, Steve. Here's what I want you to do. How many credit cards do you have?

S: Maybe ten or twelve.

L: Steve, that's a lot of cards. Decide which two you want to use regularly, OK?

S: OK.

L: Take all the other cards and cut them up.

S: Cut them up?

L: You heard me. Cut them up. You can get along just fine with two credit cards. If you're using ten or twelve credit cards, Steve, that tells me there's something wrong with this picture. You see what I mean?

S: Well, I'm not sure.

L: Steve, if you want to keep your head above water, you've got to live within your means. That means spending less than you're making, not more.

S: Oh.

L: OK, Steve. Here's one other thing I'd like you to do.

S: Yeah?

L: Sit down and plan a budget for yourself.

S: A budget?

L: That's right. If you feel like your finances are out of control, then you need to take the bull by the horns and take control of your finances. You follow me?

S: I think so.

L: Sit down and make a list of all your regular expenses. Keep track of how much you're spending on everything—and I mean *everything*, OK? Try that for three months and see if it doesn't help you out.
S: OK, I'll give it a try.
L: And Steve.
S: Yeah?
L: When you plan that budget, make sure you treat yourself to something nice once in a while, OK?
S: Really?
L: You bet. If your budget is nothing but don't spend, don't spend, it isn't going to work. Know what I mean?
S: I hear you.
L: Good luck, Steve. Next caller. You're on the air! Talk to me!

Page 37. Exercise A.

Conversation 1
F: Didn't you tell me you bought a new computer table?
M: Uh … yeah, I did.
F: So, where is it?
M: Well, I hate to admit it, but I just can't figure out how to assemble it. You wouldn't believe how many pieces there are!
F: So you're just going to let it sit around in a box collecting dust?
M: No, no. I'm going to take it back to the store and get my money back. I shouldn't have bought it in the first place.

Conversation 2
M: Hey, you want to go out to dinner?
F: Uh, I don't think so. I'm trying to save money.
M: I just got a big raise! C'mon! Let's celebrate!
F: I'm sorry, but I just don't have the cash right now.
M: Don't worry about it—it's on me.
F: No, I couldn't let you pay for dinner.
M: Forget about it! It's my pleasure.
F: Thanks! That's really nice of you.

Conversation 3
M: Hey! A new flat-screen TV! It's fabulous!
F: Thanks. I'm really happy with it.
M: That must've been pretty expensive. How'd you manage?
F: Well, I saved up for it. I put away a little bit every month.
M: Wish I could do that. Everything's gone by the end of the month. I never can seem to save any money.
F: Yeah, it can be tough.

UNIT 4

Page 41. Exercise F.

Conversation 1 [M = French]
M: Are you going to the end-of-year party this weekend?
F: Yeah, I was planning on it. Why?
M: Do you know if you're supposed to wear a suit?
F: Oh, I really don't think it matters. A lot of people will probably dress casually, but if you *want* to wear a suit …
M: Actually, I'd rather not.
F: Well, I'm sure that'll be fine. As long as you aren't *too* casual.

Conversation 2
F: Honey, I'm ready to go.
M: You're not going to wear that, are you?

F: Uh. What do you mean?
M: Well, look what I'm wearing.
F: We're just going to your parents' house. I don't want to be overdressed.
M: Yeah, but it's a special occasion. We should look nice.

Conversation 3
M: I wish I didn't have to wear a tie tonight. I've been wearing it all day at work.
F: Who says you have to wear a tie?
M: The head of the company is going to be there.
F: I thought you said it was a casual event.
M: They *say* casual, but you know what that means. Everyone shows up dressed to the nines.
F: *Now* you tell me. OK, I'm going to have to go change. Just give me a few minutes.

Conversation 4
F: What time's the party again?
M: I'm pretty sure Jackie said to come after nine.
F: Well, I'm going to put on my new slacks and a nice sweater. What are you going to wear?
M: Well, I'm not sure…. Aren't you going to wear a dress? I thought we were supposed to get dressed up.
F: I never said that. I mean I *could* wear a dress. But I don't think Sid and Jackie would ever expect people to dress formally.
M: Oh. OK. I'll go put on something casual.

Page 42. Exercise C.

Conversation 1
F1: What magazine are you reading?
F2: *Metropolitan*. Want to have a look?
F1: Do you mind?
F2: Not at all.
F1: These purses are fantastic!
F2: Which ones? Oh yeah. Everybody's getting those now.
F1: I've got to have one.
F2: Better hurry before they go out of style!

Conversation 2
M1: Hey, Jim.
M2: Hey, Carl. Whoa! That's some jacket you've got on.
M1: Oh, yeah. It's my "Look at me" jacket.
M2: It's very … yellow.
M1: Hey, yellow gets attention.
M2: OK, if you say so.

Conversation 3
F1: Oh, look at that. I don't believe it.
F2: Where?
F1: That kid over there. What on earth has she done to her hair? What is she, thirteen?
F2: Sounds about right. Oh, that hair!
F1: I just can't believe it.
F2: Me neither.

Conversation 4 [M2 = U.S., New York]
M1: Mr. Spano! How can I help you today?
M2: I want to get my wife something nice, you know, for her birthday.
M1: Of course! What did you have in mind?
M2: Well, actually I was thinking about—I don't know—a nice dress.

M1: Oh, I see! Are you thinking about a party dress?

M2: Sounds good.

M1: May I suggest this simple black silk dress?

M2: Hmm, nice. Very tasteful.

M1: Very nice. I think your wife will find it very attractive.

M2: Yeah, I like it very much. But I want to look around and see what else you've got.

Conversation 5 [F2 = U.S., Midwest]

F1: Stacy, thanks so much for coming over to help. You're a real friend.

F2: Hey, I understand. It's hard to clean out your closet alone.

F1: OK. Let's start with this blouse.

F2: All righty then. Hold it up so I can see it…. Whoa! When did you get that?

F1: Must have been about … oh, maybe eight years ago.

F2: Uh, I think that one can go.

F1: Toss it?

F2: Yup. No one's wearing that anymore.

Page 44. Exercise A.

Part 1 [C = Chuck Sims, host; S = Susan Yigal, Australia]

C: Chuck Sims here, and you're listening to *In Style*. Today we welcome Susan Yigal, a hairstylist who does a lot of work for the film industry. Susan has won *numerous* awards for her *beautiful* work.

S: Oh, thanks.

C: Susan, I love your work. So many movies. So many gorgeous actors.

S: Thank you, Chuck. Great to be here.

C: Susan is an expert on the history of hairstyles, and today we're going to focus on men's hairstyles. Susan, tell us something about how men's hairstyles changed in the twentieth century.

S: Absolutely. But before I do, let's not forget some of the styles that were in fashion *before* the twentieth century. Remember that back in the seventeenth and eighteenth centuries, among the European upper classes, the wig was a fashion must. Everyone wore one.

C: Think wigs will ever come back?

S: These days, you never know. Do you know why they became so fashionable?

C: Not really.

S: Well, you see, in the seventeenth century, King Louis XIV of France was going bald—so he had a staff of about forty wig makers working on long curly wigs for him to wear.

C: Forty wig makers!

S: Yes. And of course it then became the rage for all men to wear long curly wigs—until the nineteenth century. At that time, the style changed, and men stopped wearing wigs by the beginning of the nineteenth century. After that, they generally wore their own hair fairly long, and most men wore very long beards or sideburns.

C: Which we see in some of the very early photos from that time.

S: Right. But by the early twentieth century, that had changed. The norm for men was to wear their hair cut very, very short. And beards were something only grandfathers wore. If a man wore a mustache at all, it was cut very short.

C: Until the 1960s and '70s, of course.

S: Of course.

Page 44. Exercises B and C.

Part 2

S: By the 1960s, in Europe and throughout the Americas, men began to wear their hair long, and they grew beards and mustaches—pretty much as a protest against decades of what they saw as a very conservative culture.

C: I remember that.

S: At that time there had been an unwritten fashion code that said any man who didn't wear his hair very short—or who had a beard—was a radical.

C: That's hard to believe today.

S: But that's how it was. In the UK and the U.S., rock musicians led the way with hair, beards, and mustaches seeming to get longer each year.

C: Men today don't always realize what an incredible change that was. Isn't that true?

S: Absolutely. How a man wore his hair was a social and political statement. But today, men's hair fashions are all over the place—which was certainly not true back then. Men can wear their hair either long *or* short. Anything goes.

C: Ponytails. Braids.

S: Yup. A short beard or moustache.

C: The goatee has been the beard of choice for a number of years now.

S: *And,* of course, the bald look has become very popular now. Who would have thought twenty years ago that men would actually *choose* to shave off all their hair! No way!

C: Any other trends worth looking at?

S: Well, we haven't said anything yet about men dyeing their hair. Over the last decade some men have chosen to dye their hair bright blond, red, yellow—even green or purple.

C: Yeah, as a matter of fact, I saw that last time I was in Tokyo.

S: That's right. I've heard that in Japan this is a kind of social statement in response to strict school dress codes.

C: Well, thank you, Susan, for … ahem … letting your hair down about a very interesting subject.

S: Good one, Chuck. Thanks for having me.

Page 49. Exercise A.

Conversation 1 [F and M = U.S., Southern]

F: What do you think of that suit?

M: Whoa! You've got to be kidding.

F: What do you mean? You think it's tacky?

M: It's not that it's tacky. It's just … who wears anything like that anymore?

F: Well, I guess that's true.

Conversation 2 [M = Italian]

M: Wow! Look at that dress!

F: Don't you find it a little strange?

M: Strange? Not at all. I think it's fantastic!

F: You've got to be kidding. The colors are way too bright.

M: I think it's beautiful.

F: I guess it's just not my style.

Conversation 3

M: Hey, what do you think of this tie?

F: It's kind of wild.

M: Really? Actually I think it's pretty nice.

F: Well, to each his own.

M: I think I'm going to get it.

Conversation 4

F: Whoa! Check out those shoes!
M: Yeah. So?
F: They're incredible.
M: Yeah?
F: Yeah. You know *everyone's* wearing them now.
M: Hmm.
F: I don't care what you think. I'm getting them.

UNIT 5

Page 56. Exercise C.

Part 1

M: Reg and Maggie Green were on vacation with their children on the island of Sicily in southern Italy. It was a long way from their home in California in the United States. They had just spent the day sightseeing and were driving on a highway back to their hotel. It was evening, and their seven-year-old son, Nicholas, and four-year-old daughter, Eleanor, were fast asleep in the back seat.

Suddenly, another car with two men pulled up beside them. The man on the passenger side had a gun, and he was screaming at them through the window. As Reg Green stepped on the accelerator and drove away quickly, he could hear gunshots. He drove as fast as he could to the nearest town. Maggie was relieved to see that the children were still sleeping. But when they stopped, they both realized that Nicholas had been shot, and they rushed him to a hospital. Sadly, after two days in the hospital, Nicholas died.

One can only imagine the grief and sadness Reg and Maggie Green must have felt at that moment. But they made a decision that touched the lives of many people and the hearts of millions around the world. They decided to donate Nicholas's organs to Italians who were very sick and needed them. By giving them Nicholas's organs, Reg and Maggie felt that they could help others. Nicholas's future had been taken away, so the Greens wanted to give a future to someone else.

Their gift turned a senseless tragedy into a lesson in giving. Italians were very moved. They could not believe that visitors from another country—who had suffered such a terrible loss—could be so giving at such a terrible moment.

Page 56. Exercise D.

Part 2

M: Within days the Green family's personal experience erupted into a worldwide story. In Italy, strangers walked up to them on the street, with tears in their eyes, to say thank you. People started naming streets, schools, and hospitals for Nicholas Green.

When the Greens returned home, they received letters from thousands of people around the world. The letters told how the Greens' decision changed their attitudes about donating organs. In Italy, the number of people who were willing to become organ donors increased by three to four hundred percent—they called it "The Nicholas Effect."

The Green family returned to Italy more than a dozen times after Nicholas's death. And they met all of the people who received Nicholas's organs—seven people in all.

A fifteen-year-old boy got Nicholas's heart. During his illness, he had weighed only 27 kilograms and had spent half his life in hospitals. After the surgery, he was healthy and full of energy.

One girl was two days from death—the doctors had given up on her. But with one of Nicholas's organs, she got better. She later got married, and she gave birth to two babies—one a boy, whom she named Nicholas.

A woman who had never seen her own child's face now can see—thanks to the corneas from Nicholas's eyes.

An eight-year-old boy was arriving at the hospital for his surgery to get one of Nicholas's organs. He was asked to think about something nice. He said, "I'm thinking of Nicholas."

The Greens say that the love of life these people have shown—and the looks on their families' faces—is a wonderful reward. They often talk about how comforting it has been to know that people who would have died by now are leading normal lives, and that another who would have been blind can now see.

Maggie and Reg Green have become very busy doing work to support organ donation. While it doesn't take away the pain of Nicholas's senseless death, it helps the Greens to believe that something good has come out of the tragedy.

Page 61. Exercise A.

Conversation 1 [M = Chinese]

M: Have I ever told you that when I was growing up in China I was sent to live in the countryside?
F: No, you never have. How was that?
M: Oh, it was terrible. Not only was the poverty hard to take, but it was also really boring. There was nothing to do but work.
F: Didn't you have a choice?
M: Actually, no. Everybody pretty much had to go.
F: It must have been very hard.
M: For this city boy? You have no idea.

Conversation 2 [F = Spanish]

M: So by the time we got back, we were pretty tired.
F: Wow. Your telling me about your trip reminds me of the time I lived in Los Angeles.
M: Really? You never told me about that.
F: Didn't I? I guess I didn't really have many positive things to say.
M: You didn't like it?
F: Well, I couldn't get used to either the pollution or the crime. Maybe it was just the neighborhood I lived in. I've heard it's pretty nice in other places.
M: Too bad you didn't have a good experience.

Conversation 3

F: Hey! You never told me you were in Singapore!
M: Yeah, I was. I lived there for about a year.
F: Was it great?
M: Yeah, it was fascinating. It's unbelievably clean. Not only is there no graffiti, but at that time they actually banned chewing gum. It was against the law!

F: They banned chewing gum? Sounds a little extreme.

M: Well, I guess it's a trade-off.

Conversation 4 [F = Australia]
M: Didn't you live in Paris for a few years?

F: That's right. That was back in '03. I mean, I came back that year.

M: What was it like?

F: Paris is a wonderful city—so much to do and see. But I'll tell you, the people were neither friendly nor considerate. But I guess I just got used to it.

M: Hmm. I've heard that about a number of big cities, actually.

F: It's true. They're all the same.

UNIT 6

Page 66. Exercise C.

Conversation 1
M: What do you think about getting a nice pet?

F: A pet? Depends. What kind of a pet are we talking about?

M: Well, you remember Frank—the guy who works in the mailroom at my office?

F: Tall guy? Mustache?

M: That's him. Well, he wants to find a good home for his cat. So I was thinking—what about us?

F: Oh … gee, I don't know. I've heard their hair gets everywhere—on the furniture … clothing …

M: OK, hair can be a problem. But generally they're pretty clean. Carl tells me they're really easy to take care of.

F: Well, my grandmother used to have one. I have to admit he could be sweet, and he was very loving with her. He would sit in her lap for hours.

M: So, are you convinced?

F: Let's sleep on it, OK? We can decide tomorrow.

Conversation 2 [F = Australia]
F: Just look at her. She's a real cutie.

M: I guess.

F: They're really easygoing.

M: Are you sure?

F: Look at her! Those long ears! Aren't you a cute, fuzzy wittle wabbit?

M: Look. I really don't know if I want to keep a rabbit in the house.

F: C'mon! The kids would love her.

M: Yeah, but rabbits chew things. I don't want to have to worry about what it's going to do to the furniture, OK?

F: But you keep it in a cage. She'd be no trouble at all. She won't chew or destroy anything. You know the kids have always wanted one.

M: Well, I've heard they *are* good with children.

F: And the kids having a pet to take care of would teach them a little responsibility. Don't you think?

M: I suppose so.

Conversation 3
F: I'm thinking about getting us a pet.

M: You are? Like what?

F: Well, I was thinking about a parrot. I think they're really gorgeous.

M: Well, they *can* be beautiful. But aren't they pretty dirty? And don't they bite? That's all I need. Some noisy, dirty animal around the house who's always trying to bite me.

F: Oh, please. They're really intelligent. As a matter of fact, *you* could teach it to talk.

M: Me? Well … I've heard that you have to spend a lot of time with them or they get really, really noisy.

F: It's true, they need a lot of attention, but they make great pets. They love being around people.

M: The noise would drive me crazy, you know.

F: Let's just go to the pet store and check them out. OK?

M: OK. I'll look. But that's it.

Conversation 4 [M = U.S., New England]
M: Look at these pictures. Red betas, electric yellows, silver angelfish. The colors are incredible, aren't they?

F: Yeah, nice. But you can't play with them. What good are they?

M: If you wanna play, get a dog. But if you want something interesting to watch, you can't beat tropical fish.

F: But they don't *do* anything.

M: What do you mean? They swim around and look great. It's fun watching them swim. Very relaxing.

F: You know, you'll have to keep the aquarium very clean. You can't get lazy about that … or they might die. It's a lot of work.

M: I can do that.

F: And they're expensive.

M: Well, if they're as fascinating as I think they'll be, it'll be worth it.

Page 68. Exercise C.

[F = England]

F: The Fox and the Crow

One morning, a hungry fox was walking in the forest. The fox saw a crow in a tree. The crow had a piece of cheese in his mouth. "I'd love to eat that cheese for breakfast," thought the fox. He sat under the tree and looked up at the crow.

"What a beautiful bird you are!" the fox said. "Your feathers are as black as night. Your eyes are as yellow as the sun. But I've heard that you can't sing. That's too bad. If only you could sing, you would be the most beautiful bird of all!"

The crow listened and thought, "The fox is right. I *am* beautiful! But what does he *mean* I can't sing? I can sing as well as other birds." Then the crow opened its mouth and went "Caw, caw!"

The cheese fell to the ground, and the fox ate it. "Thank you for breakfast!" the fox called. "I see you have a voice, but where is your brain?"

Page 69. Exercise D.

M: The Peacock's Tail

A long time ago, the peacock used to fly higher than any other bird. And his feathers were short and brown—not like they are today. One day after flying around, the peacock rested next to a lake. The peacock saw his reflection in the water. He was disappointed. "I wish I were beautiful," the peacock thought. "If only I could be beautiful, I would pay any price." The peacock fell asleep, feeling sad.

When the peacock woke up the next day, he had beautiful feathers of blue and green. He had a long tail that he could open like a fan. The peacock walked through the forest, showing his beautiful feathers to all the other birds.

Then the peacock thought, "Everyone must see me! I'll fly high above the trees and show my beautiful feathers to everyone." He tried to fly, but his long tail was too heavy. He couldn't do it.

A small brown sparrow sat in a tree watching the peacock. "You are very beautiful," the sparrow said. "But is being beautiful worth such a high price?" Before the peacock could answer, the little sparrow flew away.

Page 73. Exercise A.

Part 1 [A = male annnouncer; T = Tina Rotenburg]

A: As part of our four-part series on animal-assisted therapy, today's report by Tina Rotenburg focuses on some special human and animal relationships.

T: When people become quadriplegics, they lose more than control of their arms and legs; they lose control of their lives. Each day is a challenge to regain more control and become more independent. Many quadriplegics use an electric wheelchair to move around, but family or friends cannot always be there to assist them.

In recent years, Capuchin monkeys have been trained to help improve their lives. These intelligent and dexterous monkeys have hands similar to human hands. They assist quadriplegics by performing practical tasks such as serving food, opening and closing doors, turning lights on and off, and retrieving objects. Capuchins are dependable and devoted helpmates, giving their partners independence, dignity, and companionship.

Page 73. Exercise B.

Part 2

T: Children who have autism, Down's syndrome, and other mental or physical conditions are often not responsive and have difficulty interacting with people and learning to talk. But in Miami, Florida, children like these are swimming with dolphins in a special program that is showing some promising results.

Dolphins are extremely intelligent and gentle animals and they show a special fondness for children. When the children swim with them, the dolphins are playful and they make noises that sound like singing. Scientists theorize that, because children have a natural capacity for joy and playfulness, this time spent together helps the children relax and open up. After swimming with dolphins just two or three times, some children can speak their first words. Many of these children have also become more interactive and have responded better to people after therapy.

UNIT 7

Page 76. Exercise C.

Conversation 1

M: What a terrific deal on this sweater!

F: Let me see.... Wow! That's a steal!

M: I'll bet it would cost a lot more at one of those stores downtown.

F: I would imagine. You should get it. It's definitely you.

M: You were right about this place. Why pay more than you have to?

F: You know me—I can't pass up a good deal!

Conversation 2 [F = England]

F: Look what I found. A Casanti watch!

M: Haven't you been looking for one of those?

F: I sure have. But you know, the price is a bit steep.

M: Well, why don't we check online and see if we can find a better deal?

F: Good idea.

Conversation 3

F1: Look at those funky mirrors! Aren't they great? This shop is a real find, isn't it?

F2: Very nice.... But you know something, I don't want to buy anything on our first day here. I think I'll just look around and see what's nice.

F1: Me, too.

M: Can I help you with anything?

F1: No thanks.

F2: Just looking.

Conversation 4

F: Look at those sunglasses.

M: Which ones?

F: The ones in the back with the round frames.

M: Oh, yeah. They're nice.

F: Hard to see from here, but it looks like they're 30 percent off.

M: That's a good deal. Feel like going in and trying them on?

F: No, I don't think so. I'm in the mood for looking—not buying. Let's just keep walking and see what other shops they've got down the street.

Conversation 5 [F2 = Mexico]

F1: I like this rug, but the price is a little high.

F2: Why don't you ask the clerk for a discount?

F1: Do you think he can drop the price?

F2: I don't know. Let's try. The worst he can do is say no.

F1: You're right. I'll ask. Excuse me …

Page 81. Exercise C.

Ad number 1

F: Honey, you're going to be late for the meeting!

M1: Bye-bye, sweetie.

F: Bye-bye.... Hey, wait a minute. Oh, phew! Your breath! I hate to ask you this, but did you remember to brush your teeth this morning?

M1: Sure I did. What's wrong?

F: You can't go to the meeting like that. You'll lose your job!

M1: Maybe it was something I ate.

M2: Morning mouth. And he didn't even know. Don't let bad breath get in your way—don't let bad breath spoil your day. Nice-Mouth Mouthwash, five times a day, will make your breath smell fresh!

F: Honey, you're going to be late for the meeting!

M1: Take care, sweetie.

F: Mmm. Much better.

M1: Thank you, Nice-Mouth.

M2: Nice-Mouth Mouthwash. Ninety percent of dentists surveyed worldwide say that regular use of Nice-Mouth freshens breath better—and longer—than other brands. So, what are you waiting for?

Ad number 2

F: Picture this. You're at the beach. The sun is shining, and there's a cool breeze blowing through your hair. The palm trees are swaying, and they're playing your favorite song.

And you're drinking a tall glass of Leon's Lemonade. Mmm-mm. Talk about paradise!

M: Hello.

F: Aren't you …?

M: Sean Connery. Or maybe you know me better as Bond. James Bond.

F: You're my favorite actor!

M: Is that a Leon's Lemonade you're drinking?

F: Uh, yes.

M: I *always* drink Leon's Lemonade. May I have one too?

F: Of course.

M: Ah! Nice. Very nice.

F: As I was saying. Talk about paradise …

Ad number 3

M: You've been working very hard.

F: Yes, it's true.

M: And you're ready for something new.

F: How true.

M: And you're tired of driving what *everyone else* is driving.

F: Very true.

M: You want to live the good life now.

F: It's so true.

M: And you're ready to make your move.

F: Yes, yes! It's true!

M: Then isn't it time you drove a Bernard?

F: A Bernard?

M: Refined elegance. Classic looks. Beauty and grace. Not *everyone* drives a Bernard. But why shouldn't *you*? Are you ready?

F: Yes, I am.

Page 85. Exercise A.

Conversation 1

F: Hey, look at this vase!

M: That's gorgeous. I wonder how much it is.… You've got to be kidding!

F: It's not *that* much. In fact, I think it's pretty cheap.

M: You call that cheap?! Let's keep looking.

F: You're impossible.

M: Don't worry. We'll find something.

F: What about this one?

M: Nice. How much?

F: See for yourself.

M: Well, that's a *bit* better. But still not great.

F: Look, it's beautiful, and it's a fair price.

M: OK. I guess I can live with that.

Conversation 2

M: Ta-dah!

F: Where did that come from?

M: I just bought it at Freeman's … it's the X-30 exercise bike we've been talking about. You're going to love it.

F: Uh-oh. I'm afraid to ask how much it cost.

M: Aha! That's why you're going to be surprised. Not as expensive as you might think! Here's the receipt.

F: *What!* I can't believe you paid this much! Don't you remember the ad I showed you from Mason's? They have the exact same bike for a lot less!

M: A lot less? That's impossible.

F: Yes, a *lot* less. Let's face it—you got taken.

M: Where's that ad from Mason's?

F: Look.

M: Wow! That *is* cheap.

Conversation 3 [M2 = Italian]

F: Let's go inside. I love their jewelry.

M1: I thought we were just window shopping.

F: We're just browsing. Come on. Maybe they'll have some good deals.

M1: Hey, that's not browsing.

F: Look at that necklace. Isn't it stunning?

M1: And look at that price! *That's* stunning too.

F: For *this* necklace? This is an amazing price.

M1: No way! Hey, those earrings are really nice.

F: They are. You've got great taste.

M1: Probably means they're pretty expensive. I'll find out. Excuse me.

M2: How can I help you?

M1: These earrings don't seem to have a price on them.

M2: Let me get them out for you. Here you are. The price is on the back.

M1: That's all?

F: That's *all*? The price seems a little high to me.

M1: We'll take them.

F: You're getting them for me?

M1: You bet. Enough with the browsing. I'm ready to buy.

UNIT 8

Page 89. Exercise E.

Speaker 1 [F = India]

F: There is a strong relationship between the education women get and the quality of medical care they receive. Research shows that mothers with more education are likely to receive better medical care when they have children. In Egypt, for example, about 75 percent of women with a secondary education receive medical care before having children. By contrast, only about 33 percent of women without an education receive medical care.

Speaker 2

F: In Japan, the average age that men get married is twenty-eight, and for women, it's around twenty-six. Compared to other countries in the world, Japanese men and women seem to be getting married at a later age. According to a government study, the main reason Japanese marry at an older age is that they date each other longer. The study shows that, over the past fifteen years, the gap between a couple's first date and the time they get married has increased from two to three years.

Speaker 3 [M = Brazil]

M: New studies show a direct relationship between the number of years one stays in school and life expectancy. Worldwide, for every year beyond the age of sixteen that students stay in school, they live an average of two additional years. According to a new United Nations report, this is compelling evidence for compulsory education past middle school.

Page 91. Exercise D.

Conversation 1

M: I believe in setting limits. When kids break the rules, you punish them immediately—no excuses. No ifs, ands, or buts about it.

F: I think that's a little harsh, Stan. Sometimes there are reasons for breaking the rules. I think you have to take this on a case-by-case basis.

Conversation 2

M: I think it's only fair that my parents buy me a new computer. I mean, my friends' parents love their kids enough to get them whatever they want, so why shouldn't mine?

F: Jason! You already *have* a pretty decent computer. Don't be so selfish.

Conversation 3

F: I'm not overly concerned about my kids. I think they can be trusted to behave without my watching over them all the time like a mother hen. Kids should be allowed to make their own decisions—what's the point in worrying? They'll figure it out as they go along.

M: Well, that's not how I see it. You need to be watching your kids all the time or they'll just get themselves into trouble.

Conversation 4

M: That boyfriend of yours is a troublemaker.

F: Why don't you have any respect for my friends? What do you know, anyway? Just because you're an adult doesn't mean you know everything.

M: Young lady, I don't like that tone of voice. You're grounded!

Conversation 5 [F = Arabic]

F: I'm so worried about my daughter.

M: Uh-oh. What's going on?

F: Well, she wants to learn how to drive.

M: Oh, yeah? How old is she?

F: Nineteen.

M: Then what's the problem?

F: Oh, I don't know. What does she need to drive for? I mean—what if she gets in an accident?

M: But she's nineteen. Don't you think she's old enough to start learning how to take care of herself? Like driving herself to work or going shopping?

F: I'm just not comfortable with it. I could drive her anywhere she needs to go.

M: You know, you have to let your kids be adults at some point.

Conversation 6

M: Wanna go to the late show? There's a cool movie tonight.

F: Uh, Ryan, don't you have to be home by 11:00 on school nights?

M: Yeah. But I'm sick and tired of being told what to do. I'm not a kid anymore. I'm almost sixteen. I'll go home when I feel like it!

F: Well, I have an eleven o'clock curfew too—and *I'm* going home. What are you trying to prove? Your parents aren't so strict.

Page 92. Exercises C and D.

Part 1 [M = Lithuanian]

M: My name's Rimas Vilkas and I come from Vilnius, the capital city of Lithuania. I live in Chicago now, but I grew up in Vilnius in the '80s and '90s in a house with my immediate family—my sister, my mother, and my father, and of course, me!

My parents, however, didn't grow up in Vilnius. They grew up in a small village in the east. Both my parents came from very large families. And they both lived with their extended families when they were growing up. At that time it was the common expectation that three generations would live together in a house: children, parents, and grandparents.

My mother said that everyone—her seven brothers and sisters, her parents, and her grandparents—all ate dinner together every night of the week. This kind of togetherness was pretty different from the way my family grew up. When I was growing up, my sister and I usually ate with our parents. But sometimes, when they had to work, we didn't. We'd have to eat by ourselves.

This may be why my father says that families were closer back then—he says there was more parental involvement in teenagers' lives. My dad thinks that closeness is the reason why teenagers had fewer problems. He says it was rare for a teenager to be a troublemaker at school—he thinks rebelliousness and disrespect are more modern teen problems. In his day, he says, that kind of disobedience would have been highly unusual.

Page 93. Exercise E.

Part 2

M: A lot of other things were different when my parents were growing up. Lithuania was still a part of the Soviet Union, and life was very limited in some ways. My parents dealt with a lot of difficulties. Back then, they didn't have as many choices—you know, for things like what direction your career would take, or traveling abroad—not so many opportunities. And it was very rare that someone would move away and live somewhere else. Because of that, when my parents were teenagers, they really didn't know much about life outside the Soviet Union—at least firsthand. Most people got married at about the same age and had children shortly afterward. And they usually had one job for their whole life. For all those reasons, I would say there was a difference in the world view that teenagers had then—different from the one I had when I was growing up, which was, of course, during the breakup of the Soviet Union.

By the time I was in my teens, a generation gap had pretty much opened up. Teenagers began to develop different tastes in music … the way they dressed. It's not surprising when you think about it—a lot of the food Lithuanians eat now, a lot of the movies they watch, even some of the fashions, come from Western Europe or the U.S. Before, in my parents' generation, it used to be a big deal if somebody left their small village and moved to Vilnius! But today a lot of my friends have moved away from Lithuania altogether. I have friends living all over Europe, some in the States, and even a friend in New Zealand. That was almost unheard of for my parents' generation. My parents can't understand that kind of independence— why anyone would want to move so far away. So, mobility is a huge difference.

So, some of the changes I'm describing shouldn't be too surprising: Young people are leaving home earlier; they're more likely to move far away, marry later, and choose a career instead of having children right away.

I still consider myself close to my parents, but I can't deny that there is a generation gap. My parents find it hard to understand why I live far away from them, why my wife and I don't have children yet…. And they can't figure out how it is that I've had so many different jobs over the years. It's hard for me to explain to them. Sometimes it's so frustrating! They worry about me, about my security—like parents have always worried about their kids. And I think they worry a lot about whether I'll be able to handle the responsibility of taking care of them in their old age the way they took care of their own parents.

Page 97. Exercise A.

Conversation 1 [F and M = U.S., Southern]
F: Just look at this e-mail from Philip's English teacher! It says Philip's missing his last two book reports.
M: No way. Every time I see him in front of the computer, he tells me he's doing homework.
F: He's probably spending hours on the Internet. That's it. No more Internet until he shapes up at school.

Conversation 2 [F2 = U.S., African American]
F1: I'm really getting worried about Sandi. I don't know what to do.
F2: Sandi? She's such a good kid. What's up?
F1: Well, ever since she got her driver's license last month, she's been staying out later and later. Last night she didn't come home until after eleven. She's no baby, but I worry about her. I'm losing sleep!
F2: Well, you need your sleep. Why don't you give her a curfew? Tell her if she gets in one minute late, she's grounded.

Conversation 3
M: Hey, Jill, what's up?
F: I'm grounded. I can't go to the concert.
M: What did you do?
F: Absolutely nothing. My dad told me to take off all my makeup before I went to school, and I told him he was being ridiculous.
M: You told him that?
F: Yeah. He's just so annoying. Next time he tells me I can't wear makeup, I think I'll get a tattoo. That'll show him!

Conversation 4
F1: You know, Jen, Mom and Dad aren't that bad. Now that I think back on how much trouble we gave them, I appreciate them more.
F2: Me, too. I used to think they were so dumb. But it turns out they were pretty smart. You know, I hope when I have kids, I'll be as smart about kids as Mom and Dad.

UNIT 9

Page 104. Exercise C.

Part 1 [H = male host; J = Professor John Morgan, England]
H: Our guest tonight is John Morgan, professor of Russian history at Cambridge University. Professor Morgan, the murder of Czar Nicholas II and the royal family of Russia in 1918 is one of the great mysteries of the twentieth century. Tell us the basic story of what happened.

J: Well, in 1917, during the Russian Revolution—with the end of the Russian monarchy—the czar's family was moved from St. Petersburg east to the Ural Mountains, supposedly for their protection. There was, of course, the czar … his wife Alexandra … and their children—four daughters and a son, Alexei, who would have been the next czar—and also the family doctor and several servants. According to the story, late one evening, they were all brought into a room and told that they were going to have their photograph taken. But to their surprise, soldiers suddenly came into the room firing guns and the entire family was murdered.
H: And what makes this story such an enduring mystery?
J: Well to begin with, until 1991 at least, no one had ever found the bodies. Stories spread about how the son, Alexei, and maybe also Anastasia, the youngest daughter, had escaped the execution and were still alive. Several women claimed to have been Anastasia—the most famous person who claimed to have been Anastasia was an Anna Anderson, in Berlin in 1920. Many people found her story very believable, including other members of the Russian royal family. Anna Anderson—or Anastasia, if you believed her—died in the United States in 1984.

Page 104. Exercise D.

Part 2
H: Professor Morgan, you mentioned no one had a clue where the bodies were until 1991. Tell us about that.
J: Well, people assumed that the bodies must have been lost forever, until 1991, when researchers found nine bodies in the Ural Mountains. Through medical testing they were able to confirm that five of the bodies had to have been Czar Nicholas, his wife, and three of their four daughters.
H: That must've been pretty exciting news for a lot of people.
J: No doubt about it. And they were able to conclude that the other four bodies were definitely *not* members of the czar's family. Instead, it was believed that they were most likely the bodies of the doctor and three of the servants. But the bodies of the son, Alexei, and one daughter were still missing.
H: Well, what about Anna Anderson, who claimed to be their daughter, Anastasia? Wouldn't her story have been provable through medical testing too?
J: Yes—and it was. After they found the bodies of the royal family in 1991, medical testing on Anna Anderson's body proved that she was *not* a member of the royal family. As a matter of fact, it proved that she wasn't even Russian!
H: How do you like that! Well, that's *one* mystery solved.
J: Right. But just when we thought the mystery of what happened to their bodies was solved, a team of scientists have recently argued that the results of the medical testing done on the nine bodies in the 1990s was highly questionable—poorly done and full of errors, and it might not have proved without a doubt that the bodies were the royal family after all.
H: Well, I guess some mysteries just never die, do they?
J: Not this one. It might just be an unsolvable case.
H: Well, thank you Professor Morgan. That was very interesting.
J: Thank you for having me.

Page 109. Exercise A.

Conversation 1 [F = Korean]
M: Where's Bill?
F: I don't know. I haven't seen him.
M: He was supposed to be here an hour ago.
F: He might've overslept. I heard he stayed out pretty late last night.
M: That's what you heard?
F: Yeah. But who knows. Maybe something else happened to him.

Conversation 2 [F and M = U.S., Upper Midwest]
F: Whose wallet is this?
M: Beats me.
F: Well, you were sitting here. Didn't you see anyone come by?
M: Yeah. But I was too busy to notice.
F: I'll bet Gina forgot it.
M: Why would you think that?
F: Well, it's a red wallet, and she *always* wears red.
M: Hmm. You're that certain?
F: You bet.

Conversation 3
M: Did you read the newspaper today?
F: Uh-huh. Why?
M: Did you read about the latest bank scandal? Sounds like the president is in big trouble now.
F: Yeah, I read about it. But don't you think it's a little premature to claim that the president himself was involved?
M: What? You can't be serious.
F: Where's the evidence?
M: How much more evidence do you need? It's in the paper!
F: C'mon. You can't believe everything you read in the paper.

Conversation 4
F: Did you watch the *News Hour* last night?
M: No. Was there something interesting I missed?
F: Oh, yeah. Some guy in Italy says he saw a large, hairy animal that looked kind of like a human eating pasta in the Roman Coliseum.
M: Get out of here!
F: No, for real!
M: The guy must have been drinking.
F: Don't be such a skeptic! There are a lot of things out there we just can't understand.
M: Right. And I can't understand how someone so smart could possibly fall for a story like that!

UNIT 10

Page 118. Exercise A.

[I = male interviewer; S = Sue Franklin]
I: When you stop to think about it, people do a lot of strange stuff. We actually *pay money* for the thrill of watching scary movies. We enjoy going to amusement parks to ride roller coasters and other crazy rides for the thrill of going at high speeds and getting turned upside down. And the list of wacky extreme sports, where the adventurous face their fears—bungee jumping, skydiving, extreme skiing—seems to get longer every year. And then of course, there are those of us—the faint of heart—who wouldn't *dare* do any of these things. Well, Sue Franklin is an expert on this topic, and she's here to tell us about two personality types—the person who loves thrills and can't get enough of them—known as the "big T" personality—and the person who hates thrills and prefers to avoid them—the "small t" personality. Welcome Sue Franklin.
S: Thank you.
I: You call this the type-T analysis. What is that, and what does it tell us about human nature?
S: Well, it's based on the work of psychologist Frank Farley, and it's a way of studying a person's risk-taking behavior. It indicates how comfortable a person is with taking chances—living on the edge. What Farley calls a big T personality is a person who likes risk. A big T likes thrills, whereas a small t does not. In fact, it's more like a continuum—from risk-taking to risk-avoidance. Most of us are willing to take *some* risks from time to time—but we may still tend to avoid risk in general. So *generally* speaking, if you like to take risks, do new things, then you're a big T. If you prefer certainty and routine, then you're a small t.
I: What's the motivation for seeking thrills?
S: Much of it is for the adrenaline rush that comes with going right up to the edge. Actually, big Ts may physically need a higher level of stimulation than other people do—and they need to take risks in order to get that stimulation.
I: So do big T types have an important role to play socially?
S: Absolutely. Farley believes that human progress depends on big T–type behavior. These are people who are not afraid of danger or pushing the limits.
I: Is there another side to big T behavior?
S: Definitely. There are both positive and negative sides. There's the healthy, constructive risk-taking that you see in most creative fields—like science, for example. But there's a negative side as well—crime, drinking and driving … crazy risk-taking in general. As a matter of fact, big Ts have twice as many highway accidents as small ts because they take more chances and put themselves in danger more often.
I: I love riding on roller coasters at the amusement park. Does that make me a big T?
S: Not necessarily. One of the great things about roller coasters is that they allow people who are afraid of taking risks to feel like they're really taking a big risk by riding one—because they're so scary. But everyone also knows that roller coasters are pretty safe. But if you told me you'd *never* ride on them, I'd tell you you were a small t for sure. The big T personality is the one standing up in the front seat.

Page 121. Exercise A.

Conversation 1 [F2 = Russian]
F1: So what do you do to relax?
F2: Me? Well this might sound a little strange, but I collect soda cans from around the world. I keep my eye out for nice ones when I'm traveling.
F1: That doesn't sound strange. I think it could be pretty interesting.
F2: Well, *I* think it is.

Conversation 2 [F = Puerto Rico]

F: I've been thinking about taking up something called kalaripayattu.

M: Kalaripa-what?

F: It's a form of fighting—from India— and it's supposed to help you develop spiritually.

M: Oh. So it's a kind of martial art then?

F: Right. They say it's really challenging both physically *and* mentally.

M: Well, you can't beat that.

Conversation 3 [M = Pakistan]

M: Have you ever played awari?

F: No. Where's it from?

M: West Africa. It's a lot of fun.

F: Oh, yeah? How do you play?

M: Well, you have to move small stones across the board from hole to hole. It involves a lot of counting. You win when you've captured twenty-five of the other player's stones.

F: Well, let's play sometime.

M: OK. Sounds good.

Conversation 4

M: Wow! That's beautiful! Who made it?

F: My mom, believe it or not. She's been working on it for years.

M: She cut up all those pieces of cloth?

F: Uh-hum. And she sewed all the pieces together by hand.

M: Wow. She's something else. Very creative.

Workbook Answer Key

Note: In communicative exercises where several answers are possible, this answer key contains some examples of correct answers, not all possible answers. Any valid answer in this type of exercise should be considered acceptable.

UNIT 1

Exercise 1   Answers will vary.

Exercise 2
1. I can't get over how much I enjoy it. / I can't get enough of it.   **2.** It's a pain in the neck. / I've had about enough of it.
3. It's more trouble than it's worth.   **4.** It's a pain in the neck. / I've had about enough of it. / It's more trouble than it's worth.
5. I can't get over how much I enjoy it. / I can't get enough of it.

Exercise 3
a. to call   **b.** eating   **c.** to make   **d.** meeting   **e.** to tell
1. b   **2.** e   **3.** a   **4.** d   **5.** c

Exercise 4   Answers will vary.

Exercise 5
1. Remember to buy coffee. / Don't forget to buy coffee.
2. Remember to wish your wife happy anniversary. / Don't forget to wish your wife happy anniversary.   **3.** Stop working so much.   **4.** Remember to turn off your cell phone. / Don't forget to turn off your cell phone.

Exercise 6   **1.** c   **2.** a   **3.** d   **4.** b

Exercise 7   Answers will vary.

Exercise 8   Answers will vary.

Exercise 9
Answers will vary. Following are examples of appropriate responses:
A: Have you had a chance to meet _the new employee_?
B: No, I haven't. I wonder what _she's_ like.
A: Well, everyone says _she's a pain in the neck_.
B: Yeah, but you can't believe everything you hear. _She could just be shy_.

Exercise 10
1. P   **2.** P   **3.** O   **4.** O   **5.** P   **6.** P
1. O   **2.** P   **3.** O   **4.** P   **5.** P   **6.** O

Exercise 11
1. to look   **2.** expecting   **3.** to see   **4.** believing   **5.** to avoid   **6.** to try

Exercise 12   Answers will vary.

Exercise 13
Answers will vary but may include the following: **1.** He was diagnosed with cancer.   **2.** He was optimistic. He found treatments, and he trained. He prepared for his future.
3. Yes. He survived cancer and won the Tour de France seven times.   **4.** Answers will vary.

Exercise 14   Answers will vary.

Exercise 15   **1.** b   **2.** a   **3.** c

Exercise 16   Answers will vary.

Exercise 17   Answers will vary.

GRAMMAR BOOSTER
Exercise A
1. to come   **2.** to spend   **3.** to try, slowing
4. to disappoint, advancing   **5.** to live, working, bringing
6. to take, doing

Exercise B
Answers will vary. Following are examples of appropriate responses: **1.** going on vacation next week   **2.** living in the city   **3.** to have a wonderful family   **4.** to meet my deadlines   **5.** getting spam   **6.** to pursue my interests
7. listening to music   **8.** to learn to fly a plane
9. watching ads on TV   **10.** to get a better job

Exercise C   Answers will vary.

UNIT 2

Exercise 1   Answers will vary.

Exercise 2   Answers will vary.

Exercise 3
Answers will vary. Following are examples of appropriate responses:
A: So, what's in your CD collection?
B: _Lots of rock, some blues..._
A: Let's put something on.
B: How about _Steel Dragon_?
A: What's it like?
B: _Unusual. You might like it._

Exercise 4   Answers will vary.

Exercise 5   Answers will vary.

Exercise 6   Answers will vary.

Exercise 7
1. have, been listening   **2.** have, been humming   **3.** did, listen   **4.** did, buy   **5.** have, been listening
Answers to the questions will vary.

Exercise 8
Items 2, 3, and 5 should be checked.
1. I've already listened to Shakira's new CD. / I already listened to Shakira's new CD.   **4.** She has gone to five concerts this month. / She went to five concerts this month.
6. How many times have you listened to that song? / How many times did you listen to that song?   **7.** Have you played my favorite song yet? / Did you play my favorite song yet?

Exercise 9   Answers will vary.

Exercise 10
Answers will vary. Following are examples of appropriate responses: **1.** wrote that song   **2.** the concert was canceled   **3.** I started listening to music   **4.** we're going to eat tonight   **5.** type of music he likes   **6.** bus we should take   **7.** they do that

Exercise 11

Answers will vary. Following are examples of appropriate responses:
2. what he's interested in.   **3.** what helps you relax.
4. what they talked about.

Exercise 12

The following clauses should be underlined:
when I started really listening to music; I was about 14; what I would do without music; how I spend my free time; what helps me focus and get things done; how I relax; how I have fun with my friends; that life would be dull and empty without music

Exercise 13   Answers will vary.

Exercise 14

Adjectives that describe Ray Charles's music: original; groundbreaking; unique; emotional; intense; exciting; spiritual; churchy; religious; passionate; intelligent
Adjectives that describe Ray Charles's personality: energetic; gifted; imaginative; passionate; humble

Exercise 15   **1.** c **2.** e **3.** b **4.** g **5.** a **6.** f **7.** d

Exercise 16   Answers will vary.

Exercise 17

Answers will vary but may include the following:
Beethoven: difficult personality; rejected by women; classical music; deaf
Both: played the piano; interested in music at a young age; imaginative; energetic; geniuses
Ray Charles: not difficult; a ladies' man; soul music; blind; humble

Exercise 18

1. a. soothing **b.** soothed **2. a.** interesting
b. interested **3. a.** amazed **b.** amazing **4. a.** touched
b. touching **5. a.** bored **b.** boring **6. a.** exciting
b. excited

Exercise 19

1. soothed **2.** entertaining **3.** depressing
4. disappointed **5.** relaxing **6.** pleased
Sentences will be completed in various ways.

Exercise 20

Answers will vary but should include some of the following:
1. The CDs soothe babies. They help parents relax. They promote intellectual development. They can improve reading and math, abstract thinking skills, and spatial intelligence. They stimulate creativity and imagination.
2. Answers will vary.

GRAMMAR BOOSTER
Exercise A

1. listened **2.** have played / have been playing
3. had already performed **4.** saw **5.** worked / has worked / has been working

Exercise B

1. What have you listened to lately? / What have you been listening to lately? **2.** Sarah Cho played that CD for me yesterday. **3.** I've watched that video four times already.
4. I bought that DVD yesterday. **5.** How many concerts have you gone to? How many concerts did you go to? **6.** The performance had already begun by the time we arrived.
7. When we got to the ticket window, the concert had already sold out. **8.** Many people downloaded world music last year.

Exercise C

Answers will vary. Following are examples of appropriate responses:

1. been studying English for three years **2.** Slovakia, eaten halusky **3.** mountains, I traveled to Switzerland **4.** Richard Thompson, I had heard him in concert **5.** my children had already gone to bed

Exercise D

Wording of answers will vary but verb tenses should remain the same as the following: **2.** She had been sleeping for only four hours when her alarm clock went off.   **3.** They had been driving their car for ten years when it broke down.
4. I had been waiting for 45 minutes when the train arrived.
5. We had been living in London for five years when we decided to move to Dublin.

Exercise E   Answers will vary.

 UNIT 3

Exercise 1

Answers will vary but may include suggestions such as:
Buy things on sale. Use financial planning software. Take the subway / metro instead of taxis. Don't buy prepared food. Find a bank with no fees.

Exercise 2   Items 1, 3, 4, 7 and 9 should be checked.

Exercise 3   Answers will vary.

Exercise 4

Wording of answers will vary but should reflect the following:
1. You see where your money actually goes and can plan where to cut back on spending.   **2.** If you're not paying your bills in full, you may be spending more money than you're earning.   **3.** It requires you to put some money away in savings. You can use that money in an emergency.
4. Answers will vary.

Exercise 5

Answers will vary but may include suggestions such as:
Keep a budget, see where you can cut back on spending, pay off credit card bills, set a goal for when you plan to buy a new TV, calculate how much a new TV would cost and how much you need to save.

Exercise 6   Answers will vary.

Exercise 7   Answers will vary.

Exercise 8

1. just sits around collecting dust **2.** is so hard to operate
3. is so hard to put together **4.** takes up so much room
5. costs so much to maintain

Exercise 9

Wording of answers will vary but should use the inverted form of the past unreal conditional correctly.   **2.** Had he known it would be hard to operate, he wouldn't have bought the PDA.
3. Had they known it would be so hard to put together, they wouldn't have bought the crib.   **4.** Had she known it would take up so much room on her desk, she wouldn't have bought the computer.   **5.** Had he known it would cost so much to maintain, he wouldn't have bought the boat.

Exercise 10   Answers will vary.

Exercise 11   **1.** b **2.** e **3.** c **4.** a **5.** d **6.** g **7.** f

Exercise 12   **1.** c **2.** a **3.** c **4.** a **5.** b

Exercise 13   Answers will vary.

Exercise 14   Answers will vary.

Exercise 15
Wording of answers will vary but should include some of the following:
World Wildlife Fund; animals (especially endangered species), plants, and natural areas; protect the habitats of endangered species and other wild animals, address threats to the natural environment
Doctors Without Borders; people who need medical assistance, especially people in remote areas and victims of war, epidemics, natural disasters; provide health care, get hospitals up and running, perform surgery, vaccinate children, operate feeding centers, and offer psychological care
The United Nations Children's Fund; children; provide education, vaccinations, protective environments, HIV/AIDS prevention and treatment, and other health and education services to give children a good start in life

Exercise 16   Answers will vary.

GRAMMAR BOOSTER
Exercise A   Answers will vary.

Exercise B   Answers will vary.

Exercise C
2. While Tom Lee is working, Tina Lee is going to / will be lying on the beach.   **3.** While Tom Lee is cleaning the house, Tina Lee is going to / will be going horseback riding. **4.** While Tom Lee is doing laundry, Tina Lee is going to / will be playing tennis.

Exercise D   Answers will vary.

UNIT 4

Exercise 1   Answers will vary.

Exercise 2   Answers will vary.

Exercise 3   Answers will vary.

Exercise 4
1. Each / Every   **2.** Some / Several / Three / A few / A number of   **3.** Four / Most / A majority of / A few / Some **4.** Two / A couple of   **5.** One

Exercise 5
Answers will vary. See answers to Exercise 4 for alternate quantifiers.

Exercise 6
Answers will vary. Following are examples of appropriate answers: **2.** These pants are sloppy.   **3.** This dress is fashionable and striking.   **4.** This tie is old-fashioned and eccentric.   **5.** These shoes are flashy and trendy.   **6.** This jacket is in style and striking.   **7.** This hat is out of style. **8.** This coat is elegant.

Exercise 7   **1.** e   **2.** c   **3.** a   **4.** b   **5.** g   **6.** f   **7.** d

Exercise 8   Answers will vary.

Exercise 9
Answers will vary. Answers to item 1 may be similar to: People should dress the way they like and not worry about what others think.

Exercise 10   Answers will vary.

Exercise 11   Answers will vary.

Exercise 12   Answers will vary.

Exercise 13
1. muscular   **2.** unrealistic   **3.** self-conscious **4.** self-esteem   **5.** dangerous

A K 3

Exercise 14
1. In the media (television, movies, and magazines)   **2.** It has made them more self-conscious and self-critical and has contributed to negative body image and low physical self-esteem.   **3.** Eating disorders, smoking for weight loss, obsessive exercising and weight lifting, muscle dysmorphia, steroid abuse   **4.** That character and intellect are more important than physical appearance

GRAMMAR BOOSTER
Exercise A
1. Not many   **2.** Some   **3.** Some   **4.** Not much   **5.** Not many   **6.** Some

Exercise B
3. A few of my friends …   **5.** A majority of people … **7.** Each of the employees …

Exercise C
Answers will vary. Following are examples of appropriate answers: **1.** are self-confident   **2.** is quite good   **3.** dress casually   **4.** wears contact lenses   **5.** has tattoos

UNIT 5

Exercise 1   Answers will vary.

Exercise 2
Answers will vary. Following is an example of an appropriate response: I think a move to the city is a good idea. You might love the city. There are great cultural opportunities, like theaters, concerts, and museums. There's always something to do. Disadvantages include crowding and noise. You should try to find an apartment above street level. And make sure you live within walking distance of public transportation. Good luck!

Exercise 3
2. Julie can't stand her husband's checking his PDA constantly.   **3.** Patricia resents her co-workers' calling her Patty.   **4.** I'm so tired of their complaining all the time. **5.** Our father objects to our taking calls during dinner. **6.** Do you mind my humming while I work?   **7.** Mr. Yu objects to your being late so often.

Exercise 4
Answers will vary. Following are examples of appropriate answers: **1.** Smoking at work.   **2.** Making fun of co-workers, having loud personal phone conversations.   **3.** I don't appreciate Dan's playing with objects on my desk. **4.** Do you mind my whistling?   **5.** Your smoking bothers me. Do you mind stepping outside?

Exercise 5
Answers will vary. Following are examples of appropriate answers: **2.** It's impolite to take a call in a movie theater. **3.** It's considerate to turn your cell phone off in class.   **4.** It's inconsiderate to have a loud, personal conversation on the train.   **5.** It's acceptable to talk on the phone while shopping. **6.** It's courteous to turn your phone to silent mode in a restaurant.   **7.** It's unacceptable to leave your phone on during a flight.

Exercise 6
Answers will vary. Following are examples of appropriate answers: **2.** People should either wait until after the movie to talk or go outside to talk.   **3.** People should either wear headphones or play their music quietly.   **4.** People should either say nice things about others or not say anything at all. **5.** People should either eat before class or after class.

Exercise 7

2. Neither leaving a cell phone on nor putting your feet up on the seat in front of you is courteous in a movie theater. **3.** Neither talking on a cell phone nor smoking while driving is responsible. **4.** Neither talking nor laughing while the teacher is talking is respectful. **5.** Neither touching the art nor taking flash photography in a museum is appropriate.

Exercise 8 Answers will vary.

Exercise 9

2. Waiters and waitress should either wait until they leave the table to cough or cover their mouths. **3.** Dog owners should either clean up after their dogs or not have a pet. **4.** Ignoring customers is not only rude but also bad for business. **5.** Drivers who neither use their turn signals nor look behind them before they open their car doors create a real danger for cyclists.

Exercise 10 Answers will vary.

Exercise 11

Answers will vary. Following are examples of appropriate sentences: **1.** Not only have I raised money, but I've also volunteered. **2.** I've neither picked up trash nor collected signatures. **3.** I'd like to either make phone calls or donate money.

Exercise 12 Answers will vary.

Exercise 13

1. to a rural village in Guatemala **2.** They helped raise money for an irrigation system. **3.** They wanted to help people. **4.** They wanted to plan a similar trip. **5.** They founded a service organization called Global Volunteers.

Exercise 14 Answers will vary.

Exercise 15

They're too sterile and miss the spontaneity of cities that grew organically.

Exercise 16

1. False: Canberra has beautiful galleries and museums, as well as excellent restaurants, bars, and cafes. **2.** False: Canberra offers the shortest average commute times in Australia. **3.** False: Canberra has clean air and water. **4.** True: Canberra has affordable housing. **5.** False: Canberra has low unemployment. **6.** True: Canberra is a safe city, with no murders reported in 1999/2000.

Exercise 17 Answers will vary.

Exercise 18 Answers will vary.

GRAMMAR BOOSTER
Exercise A

2. The restaurant doesn't allow smoking, and the bar doesn't either. **3.** Her company has adopted a casual dress code on Fridays, and so has his. **4.** Shorts aren't appropriate in the office, and jeans aren't either. **5.** She was annoyed by his behavior, and so were we. **6.** We've decided to volunteer, and they have too. **7.** Dave Clark doesn't like the city, and neither do we. **8.** We're not going on vacation this summer, and neither are they.

Exercise B Answers will vary.

Exercise C

1. I don't either. / Neither do I. (Informal: Me neither.) **2.** So am I. / I am too. (Informal: Me too.) **3.** So do I. / I do too. (Informal: Me too.) **4.** I can't either. / Neither can I. (Informal: Me neither.) **5.** So do I. / I do too. (Informal: Me too.) **6.** I don't either. / Neither do I. (Informal: Me neither.) **7.** So would I. / I would too. (Informal: Me too.)

UNIT 6

Exercise 1 Answers will vary.

Exercise 2

1. e **2.** a **3.** b **4.** h **5.** c **6.** g **7.** d **8.** f

Exercise 3

2. as strong as an ox **3.** as quiet as a mouse **4.** as playful as a kitten **5.** as brave as a lion **6.** as fat as a pig **7.** as hairy as a gorilla **8.** as slow as a snail

Exercise 4 Answers will vary.

Exercise 5

1. should be treated **2.** should be provided **3.** should be provided **4.** should be allowed **5.** should be given **6.** should be protected **7.** should be treated **8.** should be kept

Exercise 6

1. can't be raised **2.** shouldn't be harmed **3.** don't have to be killed **4.** can be eliminated **5.** might not be mistreated **6.** might be developed

Exercise 7

Answers will vary. Following are examples of appropriate responses: Laws can be passed to protect animals. Alternatives can be found for medical research on animals. Conditions in zoos and on corporate farms can be improved.

Exercise 8

Answers will vary but should include some of the following:
Dogs: eager to please, affectionate, loyal; need lots of time, attention, and exercise—daily walks, frequent baths, and feeding; range in price from free to quite expensive
Rabbits: sociable, intelligent; require daily attention and care—exercise, a dry spot to live, and time out of the cage; not costly
Hamsters: amusing, affable; easy to care for—a dry living space with gnawing log and hiding place; cheap
Birds: intelligent, independent; not difficult—need a comfortable temperature, interaction, and time out of their cages; can be costly to buy
Snakes: range from placid and docile to aggressive; require careful attention, owners with special knowledge—eat live animals, need appropriate temperature and lighting; costly
Fish: quiet, peaceful; relatively simple—monitoring the food and water; not expensive

Exercise 9

1. cats, hamsters, fish, (birds) **2.** dogs, rabbits, snakes, (birds) **3.** purebred dogs, birds, snakes **4.** cats, dogs that aren't purebreds, rabbits, hamsters, fish **5.** Answers will vary.

Exercise 10

Positive: **1.** clever **2.** sincere **3.** wise
Negative: **1.** gullible **2.** mean **3.** selfish **4.** vain

Exercise 11 Answers will vary.

Exercise 12 Answers will vary.

Exercise 13
Adjectives for the stag's antlers: beautiful, elegant
Adjectives for the stag's legs: skinny, spindly, bony
The moral of the story: What is truly valuable is often unappreciated. (Answers will vary.)

Exercise 14
1. dinosaur 2. fish 3. eagle 4. owl 5. lion

Exercise 15
Answers will vary. Following are examples of appropriate responses: 1. Night owls shouldn't take early classes. 2. I bought a new computer because my old one was a dinosaur. 3. My eagle-eyed sister found three mistakes on my resumé.

Exercise 16
Answers will vary but should include some of the following:
Giant pandas; China; destruction of old-growth bamboo forests; training panda reserve staff and local government officials, working with the community to help save habitat and guard against illegal hunting
Polar bears; the Arctic; global warming; spreading awareness of the danger of carbon dioxide emissions, promoting the use of renewable energy sources
Mountain gorillas; Central and East Africa; civil war; has established a system to monitor the status of mountain gorillas

Exercise 17   Answers will vary.

GRAMMAR BOOSTER
Exercise A
1. b 2. c 3. d 4. b 5. a 6. d 7. c 8. c

Exercise B
1. can / may 2. may / might (not) / could 3. Could / Can / May 4. may / might (not) / could 5. should / ought to / had better / must / have to 6. could 7. would 8. must 9. can't / had better not / must not / may not / shouldn't / cannot 10. couldn't / wasn't able to

Exercise C
Answers will vary. Following are examples of appropriate responses: 2. You can turn on the air-conditioning if you want. 3. We could go out. 4. You should consider going to Turkey. 5. The teacher must have been sick. 6. You ought to see a doctor. 7. We could try the new restaurant on Avenue B. 8. He had better not get a snake!

UNIT 7

Exercise 1   Answers will vary.

Exercise 2   Answers will vary.

Exercise 3
1. positive 2. negative 3. positive 4. negative 5. negative

Exercise 4
Answers will vary. Following are examples of appropriate responses: 2. You ought to window-shop in Rittenhouse Square. The bookstore on the corner of 17th and Walnut has great coffee. 3. The electronics stores on Commerce Street are good places to comparison shop. 4. The mall would be a good bet. It's perfect for browsing.

Exercise 5   Answers will vary.

Exercise 6
1. 100-yen shops 2. the Akihabara district 3. Oriental Bazaar 4. the Ginza 5. Nakamise Shopping Arcade 6. Answers will vary. 7. Answers will vary.

Exercise 7   Answers will vary.

Exercise 8
1. to be informed 2. being called / to be called 3. being entertained 4. being forced / to be forced 5. being asked 6. being ignored / to be ignored 7. being treated

Exercise 9
Answers will vary. Following are examples of appropriate responses: 2. I resent being forced to watch ads before a movie that I have paid to see. 3. I dislike being interrupted by pop-up ads when I'm using the internet. 4. I can't stand being forced to look through so many ads to find my mail. 5. I don't like to be called by telemarketers, especially at dinner time. 6. I like to be shown new fashions and beauty products in magazine ads. 7. I love being given free product samples. 8. I prefer to be exposed to advertising through product placement in movies, rather than being forced to sit through ads before movies.

Exercise 10   1. endorse 2. prove 3. promote 4. imply

Exercise 11   Answers will vary.

Exercise 12   Answers will vary.

Exercise 13
1. Answers will vary but should include some of the following: Men enjoy shopping more, are more likely to shop for themselves, are more willing to shop alone, and shop more often. 2. Answers will vary. 3. Answers will vary.

Exercise 14   Answers will vary.

Exercise 15   Answers will vary.

Exercise 16
Answers will vary. Following are examples of appropriate responses: Advantages: You can buy at any time of the day or night; you save time because you don't have to travel to the store; you can read other consumers' reviews of a product you're planning to buy.
Disadvantages: You can't try on clothes or see other products in person; there's no sales person to assist you; you can't haggle; you may worry about security and privacy.

Exercise 17   Answers will vary.

Exercise 18   Answers will vary.

GRAMMAR BOOSTER
Exercise A
1. having met 2. to have been given 3. having been fooled 4. having stolen 5. to have had 6. to have sold

Exercise B
2. He mentioned having gone to a conference last week. 3. I resent not having been told about the meeting. 4. She made an excuse for having missed the appointment. 5. The manager apologized for having given the client the wrong information. 6. I didn't expect her to have finished her degree already. 7. He was proud to have received a promotion. 8. We had a good reason for having missed the train. 9. She was ashamed to have used her corporate credit card for personal expenses. 10. I pretended not to have been offended by her remarks.

UNIT 8

Exercise 1
1. Jack talked back to his mother. 2. Eva and Lana had a falling out. 3. Tomas and Rachel patched things up. 4. Jason has shaped up. 5. Things worked out for Anna and Mike Gunn.

Exercise 2

Answers will vary. Following are examples of appropriate responses:

Should: Kids should be grounded when they don't follow the rules; kids should be praised when they're well-behaved; kids should be expected to do chores.

Shouldn't: Kids shouldn't be allowed to talk back; kids shouldn't be given too much freedom; kids shouldn't be ignored.

Exercise 3

Sentences can be rewritten more than one way. Following are sample correct responses.   **3.** Men are getting more and more involved in caring for their children.   **4.** People are spending less and less time with their extended families.   **5.** Fewer and fewer mothers are staying home to take care of their children.   **6.** More and more couples are choosing to remain childless.   **7.** Young adults are moving out of their parents' homes later and later.   **8.** Adolescents are receiving less and less adult supervision.

Exercise 4

1. The more, the less [Note: This item is also correct in the reverse order: *The less people work, the more time ...*]   **2.** The more developed, the better   **3.** The lower, the fewer   **4.** The more, the higher   **5.** The better, the longer   **6.** The older, the fewer

Exercise 5

Answers will vary. Following are examples of appropriate responses: **1.** the more time I can spend with the people I love.   **2.** the more goals you achieve.   **3.** the smarter you become.   **4.** the stronger our friendships.   **5.** the more exciting life is. Students' choice of quote and interpretations will vary.

Exercise 6   Answers will vary.

Exercise 7

1. too lenient   **2.** Nolife's parents are overprotective.   **3.** Norules's parents are too lenient.

Exercise 8   Answers will vary.

Exercise 9   **1.** d   **2.** c   **3.** e   **4.** b   **5.** a

Exercise 10   **1.** c   **2.** a   **3.** b   **4.** d

Exercise 11

1. differences in values, attitudes, and goals between one generation and another, especially between young people and their parents   **2.** Answers will vary.   **3.** Answers will vary.

Exercise 12   Answers will vary.

Exercise 13

(Wording of answers will vary.)   **1.** People who are caring for their children and their aging parents at the same time.   **2.** The caregivers are caught in the middle; their children and their parents are like slices of bread, one on each side.   **3.** People are having children later in life. People are living longer. More adult children are living at home.   **4.** depression, sleeplessness, headaches, other health problems, guilt   **5.** Because it's usually women who are caring for their children and parents, and more and more women are also working.

Exercise 14

1. responsibility   **2.** participation   **3.** obligations   **4.** depression   **5.** sleeplessness   **6.** patience   **7.** guidance   **8.** interaction   **9.** inclusion   **10.** relaxation

Exercise 15
Answers will vary.

GRAMMAR BOOSTER
Exercise A

2. as fast as a cheetah   **3.** the oldest   **4.** farther from here than Park City   **5.** not as strict as / less strict than his   **6.** fewer children than Mr. Lane   **7.** better now than I did ten years ago   **8.** as many people in my family as in Irene Lee's   **9.** the shortest commute   **10.** as old as my grandmother

Exercise B   Answers will vary.

Exercise C   Answers will vary.

Exercise D

(Wording of answers will vary.)   **2.** The population of Greenland is less than 60,000.   **3.** The movie we watched last night was the most depressing ever!   **4.** Alexis McCarthy is becoming a better violin player every day.   **5.** He reads more than watches TV.   **6.** The new French restaurant on City Avenue is less expensive than it looks.

UNIT 9

Exercise 1   Answers will vary.

Exercise 2   5, 2, 8, 1, 6, 9, 3, 7, 4
Challenge: Answers will vary.

Exercise 4

Answers will vary. To say that they don't know, students can use *Beats me, I can't imagine, I don't have a clue, I have no idea, Your guess is as good as mine, You got me,* or *Who knows.*

Exercise 5

2. Melanie said (that) she had another meeting and (that) she might be late.   **3.** Allison said (that) she couldn't come in today because her son wasn't feeling well.   **4.** Alex said (that) he had to make some copies and (that) he would be there by 9:15.

Exercise 6

Answers will vary. Following are examples of appropriate responses: **1.** She could be looking for the right exit.   **2.** I guess her train is late.   **3.** I'll bet she wasn't on the train.   **4.** Clearly she missed the train.

Exercise 7

2. not certain; The dinosaurs may / might / could have been killed by climate changes.   **3.** almost certain; The giant stone statues on Easter Island must have been carved by the ancestors of the Polynesian people who live there today.   **4.** almost certain; Amelia Earhart must have been killed when her plane ran out of fuel and went down in the Pacific Ocean.   **5.** very certain; The fire had to have been started intentionally.   **6.** very certain; The ship had to have been sunk by a collision with an iceberg.

Exercise 8   Answers will vary.

Exercise 9

Answers will vary. Following are examples of appropriate responses: **1.** The captain could have been killed by the crew, but that doesn't really make sense. The captain was an honest and fair man, and nothing was stolen from the ship.   **2.** The crew must have been forced by alcohol fumes to leave the ship. This theory seems more likely than the other two.   **3.** The crew couldn't have been snatched from the ship by a giant octopus. That's a ridiculous theory!

Exercise 10

unsolvable, questionable, debatable, believable, provable

Exercise 11

1. questionable   **2.** debatable   **3.** believable   **4.** unsolvable   **5.** provable

Exercise 12   Answers will vary.

Exercise 13   Answers will vary.

Exercise 14
Answers will vary but should include some of the following:
1. that he was dying   **2.** I'll bet the newspapers rushed to print the poem.   **3.** No, because he didn't claim that the poem had been written by García Márquez.   **4.** Answers will vary.

Exercise 15
Answers will vary. Following is an example of an appropriate response: The Internet has allowed questionable claims and stories to spread more quickly and to more people all over the world.

GRAMMAR BOOSTER
Exercise A
2. The salesperson told Neil (that) the video cameras might go on sale tomorrow.   **3.** Stephen said (that) he had to work tonight.   **4.** Caroline asked if / whether she could turn on the TV.   **5.** Allen told the kids (that) they had to clean up their toys.   **6.** Professor Johnson asked the class whether / if they had completed the assignment.

Exercise B
Answers will vary. Following are examples of appropriate responses: **2.** The attorney maintained that his client couldn't be guilty of the charges.   **3.** Smith Pharmaceuticals explained that there was no scientific evidence of negative side effects.   **4.** *The Daily Journal* reported that the earthquake had left one million people homeless.
5. Strauss-Lyon, Inc. announced that they might have to lay off some employees.   **6.** Coach Moore exclaimed that his team would make the championships this year.   **7.** Anna Graham, director of City Kids, complained that there weren't enough services for poor families.

UNIT 10

Exercise 1
Answers will vary. Following are examples of appropriate responses: **1.** People can shop, bank, and do research on the Internet. This saves trips to stores, the bank, and the library.   **2.** People can check work e-mail at home. They can spend too much time surfing the Web.   **3.** Answers will vary.

Exercise 2   Answers will vary.

Exercise 3
2. The more time people spend on the Internet, the more time they spend working at the office.   **3.** The more time people spend on the Internet, the less time they spend talking to friends and family on the phone.   **4.** The more time people spend on the Internet, the less time they spend with family and friends.   **5.** The more time people spend on the Internet, the less time they spend attending events outside of the home.

Exercise 4
Answers will vary. Following are examples of appropriate responses: **2.** I'd like to give Karate a try. It sounds challenging.   **3.** Chess is difficult, but it's a great game.
4. I find aerobics stimulating.   **5.** I'd like to take up yoga. I've heard it's very relaxing.   **6.** I think ping-pong is fun.
7. I find embroidery a little boring.   **8.** Wood carving sounds interesting.

Exercise 5
Answers will vary. Following are examples of appropriate responses:

yoga; It sounds relaxing. Is it difficult?
crocheting; I hate to say this, but I find crocheting a little dull.

Exercise 6
1. do; circle *emotionally*, underline *soothing* (A)
2. play; circle *intellectually*, underline *stimulating* (A)
3. do; circle *socially* and *financially*, underline *interact* (V) and *pays off* (V)
4. restore; circle *physically*, underline *demanding* (A)

Exercise 7   Answers will vary.

Exercise 8
2. Megan Bloom has a large antique English porcelain teapot.
3. Sam Dentel has a rare 1987 Chinese gold giant-panda coin.

Exercise 9
1. three-hundred-year-old   **2.** one-and-a-half-hour
3. two-carat   **4.** nine-hundred-page   **5.** twentieth-century
6. thousand-dollar

Exercise 10
Answers will vary. Following are examples of appropriate responses:
cellphones: don't have to be home to make and receive calls; leisure activities and time with friends may be interrupted
PDAs: can check e-mail anywhere; might be expected to respond to work messages at night or on the weekend
laptops: don't have to be at your desk to use your computer; work doesn't end when you leave the office—can work at home, on vacation
e-mail: can make fewer phone calls; friends and family might not talk as much
voice mail: don't miss any calls; have to return lots of calls

Exercise 11
Answers may vary but should include some of the following: the longer hours we work; the fewer and shorter vacations we take; the more stressed we are

Exercise 12   Answers will vary.

Exercise 13   Answers will vary.

Exercise 14
1. blurry   **2.** invades   **3.** virtually   **4.** plugging away
5. 24/7

Exercise 15
Answers may vary but should include some of the following:
1. checking e-mail, taking business calls, checking PDAs, working on a laptop   **2.** checking sports scores, shopping, reading the news, ordering tickets, planning vacations, chatting with friends, browsing the Web   **3.** A more definite separation of work and home life would be better not only for employees but also for employers.   **4.** Answers will vary.

Exercise 16   Answers will vary.

Exercise 17   Answers will vary.

GRAMMAR BOOSTER
Exercise A
Answers will vary. Following are examples of appropriate intensifiers: **1.** rather   **2.** slightly   **3.** really   **4.** very
5. wonderfully   **6.** considerably   **7.** extremely   **8.** fairly

Exercise B
1. quickly   **2.** softly   **3.** angrily   **4.** beautifully   **5.** fairly
6. hard

Exercise C   Answers will vary.